An unusual photograph of Maxim Gorky, taken by the Soviet photograper Moisei Nappelbaum (1928).

FROM FURMANOV TO SHOLOKHOV

An Anthology of the Classics of Socialist Realism

Edited by Nicholas Luker

Ardis, Ann Arbor

Copyright © 1988 by Ardis Publishers
All rights reserved under International and
Pan-American Copyright Conventions.
Printed in the United States of America

Translated from the original Russian

Ardis Publishers
2901 Heatherway
Ann Arbor, Michigan 48104

Library of Congress Cataloging-in-Publication Data

From Furmanov to Sholokhov.

Translation from Russian.
1. Russian prose literature—20th century—Translations into English. 2. English prose literature—Translations from Russian. 3. Socialist realism in literature. I. Luker, Nicholas J. L. II. Title.
PG3266.F76 1988   891.78'42'08012   88-16635
ISBN 0-87501-036-9 (alk. paper)
ISBN 0-87501-037-7 (pbk.)

CONTENTS

Preface 9

Introduction 11

Dmitri Furmanov CHAPAEV 39

Alexander Serafimovich THE IRON FLOOD 129

Fyodor Gladkov CEMENT 199

Alexander Fadeev THE ROUT 315

Nikolai Ostrovsky HOW THE STEEL WAS TEMPERED 381

Mikhail Sholokhov THE FATE OF A MAN 479

For my son,
Nathaniel,
Who has brought more than I can ever say

And
To the memory of
Max Hayward

FROM FURMANOV
TO
SHOLOKHOV

The front cover of the first edition of "Chapaev," published in Moscow and Petrograd by the State Publishing House (1923).

Preface

This anthology arose from the need often felt by both students and teachers of Soviet Russian literature to have conveniently available in one volume the classic prose works of Socialist Realism. It was in order to satisfy this need that in 1978 the late Carl Proffer asked me to embark on an anthology for Ardis Publishers. This book is, therefore, his brainchild, and I am proud to have been responsible for bringing it into being. I hope that it might be what he would have wished.

For reasons of space, of course, it has been necessary to abridge the works contained in this collection. I trust, though, that by exercising care in the process, I have not caused undue damage to the Russian text. At the same time, so as not to mislead the reader, the numbering of chapters and sections in the originals has been retained.

I wish to record my gratitude to many people, both friends and colleagues, for their kind assistance at various stages in the preparation of this work. My special thanks must go to Professor Marcus Wheeler of The Queen's University of Belfast, Northern Ireland, who painstakingly read all the translations in typescript, commented most encouragingly on my renderings, and made many valuable suggestions and corrections. In addition, I am greatly indebted to Dr. David Denton, my former student at the University of Nottingham and now of the RAF, who not only gave unsparingly of his time to read the versions in draft, but also checked the biographical sections and Introduction with scrupulous care. I also wish to thank my colleague Brian Lee, Head of the Department of American Studies at the University of Nottingham, for reading Fadeev's *The Rout* in typescript and for commenting on various points in the Introduction. Needless to say, the responsibility for any inelegancies and errors which remain in the anthology is not theirs but wholly mine.

My thanks must also go to Garth Terry, Slavonic Librarian at the University of Nottingham, for his help in obtaining Russian material from abroad and for providing bibliographical information; to the staff of the University Library's Photographic Unit who produced the plates; to Dr. Derek Spring of the Department of History at the University of Nottingham for supplying historical information for several footnotes; to Dr. Jane Grayson, once my fellow-undergraduate at the University of Oxford and now at the School of Slavonic and East European Studies in the University of London, who clarified historical points in Furmanov's *Chapaev;* to my former student at Nottingham, Peter Hellyer, of the British Library, London, who traced a number of highly obscure place names; and to my Russian-born former colleague, Lisa Lacy, for her kind help with several problems of translation.

I also wish to express my profound thanks to Dorothy Honniball of Nottingham University Library and to Heather Phoenix of the Department of Slavonic Studies, who between them typed my shamefully untidy manuscript with exemplary accuracy and care. Without their sterling efforts, my drafts would never have seen the light of day.

To my young son, Nathaniel Max, I owe an inestimable debt of gratitude. During the preparation of this book he has displayed a patience, understanding and kindness beyond his years towards a father who is all too often preoccupied with his work at the expense of infinitely more pleasurable pursuits such as football, cricket, swimming or table-tennis. Moreover, he has shown remarkable tolerance and adaptability in living in a house—and particularly its kitchen—that is frequently littered with books and manuscripts. Above all, I cannot thank him enough for his cheerfulness, energy and unfailingly impish sense of humour, all of which have proved a source of immense and abiding encouragement and inspiration.

Nicholas Luker

Grassington,
Skipton,
North Yorkshire,
England

May 1985

Introduction

The Bolshevik Revolution of October 1917 not only destroyed the autocratic Tsarist regime but also initiated fundamental changes in Russian culture. With the ascendancy of Stalin after Lenin's death in 1924, those changes were to involve a frontal assault upon literature and the arts which would inflict severe and permanent damage on them. Most of this damage was to be caused by the regime's increasing demands that art should become the handmaiden of the state, and by its insistence that all spheres of Soviet cultural activity should faithfully reflect the proletarian ethic and actively promote the policies of the Communist Party. By the time Stalin died in 1953, literature and the arts in Russia had suffered traumas from a degree of regimentation and coercion that is without parallel in the history of the world. Indeed, it is arguable whether they will ever fully recover.

This anthology of Soviet Russian literature presents six well-known prose works which are officially regarded as exemplifying the doctrine of Socialist Realism. While five of the works belong to the early Soviet period and reflect the triumphs of the Civil War and the industrial reconstruction which followed it, the piece by Sholokhov, published in 1956, shows the heroism of the ordinary Russian soldier during the victorious national struggle against Nazi Germany. Despite their differences in theme and technique, all are classic illustrations of the Communist politicalization of art, and as such take pride of place in what has aptly been called the "gold fund of Soviet letters."[1]

This introductory essay will attempt briefly to outline the political and literary circumstances in which the doctrine of Socialist Realism came into being, to clarify the meaning of the term, and to examine the effects it has had as an artistic "method" on Soviet writers.

I

> "The socialist proletariat must put forward the principle of *party literature*, must develop this principle and put it into practice as fully and completely as possible."
>
> *Vladimir Lenin*[2]

The first decade after the Revolution brought a level of freedom and variety to the Soviet literary scene which in retrospect seems well-nigh unbelievable. With the end of the Civil War and the introduction of the New Economic Policy (NEP) in March 1921, private publishing houses appeared alongside the State-owned ones, and there was vigorous competition between them, fuelled by the intellectual fervor generated by the Revolution. Writers were free to write virtually how and what they wished, and some even went so far as to criticize Communist doctrine. There was censorship, it is true, exercised by a new body called *Glavlit* (the Chief Directorate for Literary Affairs), but its control was little more than nominal and was only designed to prevent the publication of works which were openly "counter-revolutionary."

In this creative atmosphere of free competition and experimentation, various independent writers' groupings came into being with very different artistic and ideological attitudes. Foremost among them were the Serapion Brothers, who asserted the artist's right to be free of political controls, the Proletkult, a movement which championed proletarian art produced by artists of proletarian origin, and the Formalist group, which evaluated literary work in a purely technical, formal way.

Writing by members of these and other groups, both Communist and non-Communist, was often published in the monthly *Red Virgin Soil (Krasnaya nov')*, the first and best-known Soviet literary periodical which was founded by the Party on Lenin's initiative in 1921.[3] Its editor, Alexander Voronsky, was a prominent Marxist literary critic and the guiding spirit of a group called "The Pass" *(Pereval)*, formed in late 1923, which was associated with the journal. Like Trotsky, Voronsky believed that there could be no specifically proletarian art in Russia until material and cultural circumstances favorable to it had emerged. Stressing the primacy of the intuitive and subconscious in art, Voronsky maintained that good literature was more important than ideology and that art should not be narrowly propagandist or devoted solely to serving the proletarian cause.

Most of the best writers of these years belonged to the category known as "fellow travellers" *(poputchiki)*, a term first used by Trotsky in his book *Literature and Revolution (Literatura i revoliutsia,* 1923), so as to distinguish them from writers who had given their unqualified support to the Communists. (Less flatteringly, he also described them as "manure for proletarian culture."[4]) Chiefly intellectuals in origin, the fellow travellers varied greatly both in their literary attitudes and in their degree of loyalty to the new regime. Their extreme left wing, for example, was represented by Vladimir Mayakovsky, famous for his revolutionary agitational (or *agit*) poetry, while their extreme right was associated with Evgeny Zamyatin, well-known for his anti-Utopian novel *We (My,* 1921). The fellow travellers had no common program and did not consider themselves a school, but because—like "bourgeois specialists" in other fields—their special abilities and skills made them indispensable to the regime, they were at first protected from undue interference at the hands of proletarian writers. Although throughout the 1920s the latter attempted to force the fellow travellers to subscribe to their view of art as political propaganda, they were to receive little official backing until 1929.

Under Anatoly Lunacharsky, the Soviet Commissar for Enlightenment (Education) and himself a talented and cultured writer, there was an uneasy truce between the two camps—the fellow travellers grouped mainly in the All-Russian Union of Writers, and the proletarian writers concentrated chiefly in the Association of Proletarian Writers (known as RAPP), formed in January 1925 with Fadeev as its most notable member. Lunacharsky, who was on record as saying that a revolutionary government should safeguard the right of individual creation, maintained that "all individual artists and all groups of artists should be allowed to develop freely"[5] and that no single trend should be allowed to dominate another. Though his handling of cultural affairs was both tactful and careful, there was considerable friction between the rival camps, the left demanding Party support for the promotion of proletarian literature, and the right insisting on complete creative freedom. Far from backing one side at the expense of the other, however, as was to be the case later, the Party mediated between them. But whereas prominent Party officials publicly sided with both factions in acrimonious disputes in the press, Trotsky came down firmly on the side of the fellow travellers when he wrote: "The domain of art is not one in which the Party is called upon to command. It can and must protect and help it, but it can only lead it indirectly."[6]

During 1924 and early 1925 the Central Committee of the Party moved towards a statement of policy designed to settle the dispute between the two camps. The deliberations of a special commission resulted in the famous Central Committee Resolution "On the Party's Policy in the Field of Literature,"[7] issued in June 1925. While it reaffirmed the fundamental principle of Party interference in art—point 4 of the document stated that "in a class society there is and can be no neutral art"[8]—the Resolution rejected the proletarian writers' demands for superiority in literary circles and at the same time recommended that fellow travellers, those potential converts to the Communist faith, be treated with tolerance and care. No one group, the Party asserted, should be allowed a monopoly in Soviet literature. Though the ambivalence of the official stance was seen as a triumph for Voronsky and the fellow travellers, it meant that *Red Virgin Soil* could not hope for a privileged position in Soviet letters. Essentially, as Robert Maguire has shown, the significance of the 1925 Resolution lay not so much in the Party's avowed liberalism and neutrality in literary matters as in its clear assumption that it could intervene in the dispute if it saw fit.[9] Needless to say, this liberal state of affairs was not to last, for within the next decade the Party would achieve total control over literature and the arts. For the time being, however, it made no attempt to regiment literature and went on encouraging free competition between various groups without favoring any of them. Indeed, the cultural atmosphere still remained so free that several proletarian writers were even able publicly to criticise the Party's 1925 Resolution.

Already by 1927, though, the political tide was clearly turning against artistic freedom. In that year Voronsky was dismissed from his post as editor of *Red Virgin Soil* and in the following year was expelled from the Party. (He was arrested as a Trotskyite in 1937 and is thought to have died in a labor camp in 1943.) His journal went swiftly into decline, and though it survived until 1942, it never regained the leading role it had played in the 1920s. The end of the NEP in 1928 meant that no private publishing firms were left to rival the State publishers, and so heralded the end of free competition in literature. With Stalin's triumph over Trotsky and his other opponents, and the inauguration of the First Five-Year Plan of industrialization and collectivization in 1928, the Party felt confident of its right to intervene further in the arts and to impose stricter ideological controls on literature.

The summer of 1928 saw the first decisive move in that direction, when the Central Committee convened a conference on questions of agitation and propaganda. One of the resolutions passed instructed that literature, drama and film should be designed to reach the whole population in order to foster new cultural attitudes which would better reflect the requirements and successes of the Five-Year Plan. Following this conference, in December 1928 the Central Committee issued a formal directive to publishing houses which stipulated the kind of work they were to publish and the topics their writers were to employ. In stark contrast to the liberal decree of 1925, the directive was openly political, representing the regime's first positive attempt to lay hold on literature and subordinate it to its ideological purpose. But the move was more radical still because it marked the end of the Party's policy not to back any of the competing literary groups. It now declared its open support for the most powerful organization, the Russian Association of Proletarian Writers, maintaining that RAPP was best able to mold Soviet writing into convenient propaganda in support of the Five-Year Plan. The rise of RAPP thus signalled the end of artistic independence in the Soviet Union.[10]

With heavy backing from the Party and under the chairmanship of the belligerent critic Leopold Averbakh, RAPP set about asserting the hegemony of proletarian literature and soon assumed powers that were virtually dictatorial. In a short time the organization had gained control of many publishing houses and journals, and so could refuse any writer publication if he failed to toe the ideological line. In keeping with the doctrine of "social command" *(sotsial'nyi zakaz)*, literature was harnessed to the Five-Year Plan, and writers were expected to reflect and applaud the Plan's achievements in their work. Literature of fact was proclaimed supreme. Writers were encouraged to become literary "shock-workers" *(udarniki)* and "worker-correspondents," to form small artistic groups or "brigades," and to take part in collective writing schemes such as the ambitious *History of Factories and Plants* devised by Maxim Gorky. Mass visits to construction sites, collective farms and military exercises, often in remote areas, were organized so as to enable writers to describe them at first-hand in informative factual sketches *(ocherki)*. The leaders of RAPP genuinely believed that Soviet literature had become too apolitical, and were convinced that only the proletariat could produce an art that would reflect the new socialist reality. So they resolved to redress the balance by waging class warfare on "neo-bourgeois" elements in cultural circles, by bringing the fellow travellers to heel, and by forcing them to make a positive commitment to Communist ideology. In addition, as Max Hayward has shown, by their insistence that Soviet writers must learn from the classics and put the literary techniques of nineteenth-century Russian realism (especially of Tolstoy) at the service of the proletariat, the RAPP leaders were advancing what was to be the main esthetic requirement of Socialist Realism.[11]

Needless to say, the domination of RAPP not only severely limited the writer's choice of themes but also greatly restricted his creative independence. In December 1929 an editorial in *Pravda* stated that RAPP was pursuing a line in literature "closest to the line of the Party," and therefore recommended that all proletarian literary forces should be consolidated around RAPP. This was a far cry from the neutral Resolution of 1925, and plainly, the Party was moving towards organizational uniformity and centralization in the literary community. As a result, 1930 saw the absorption by RAPP of many formerly independent groups and individuals, a process which made the organization more powerful still. If in political and social terms 1929—which brought the "revolution from above"—was the "year of the great turning point" (Stalin's words), 1930 was momentous in the cultural sense for the mass adherence and individual capitulations to RAPP which it witnessed. Not for nothing has that year been described as the "year of acquiescence."[12]

Just two years later the domination of RAPP was suddenly brought to an end. On April 23, 1932 the Central Committee of the Party unexpectedly issued a decree entitled "On the Reformation of Literary-Artistic Organizations," which dissolved RAPP and other groups, and resolved to set up in their place a single Union of Soviet Writers containing a Communist fraction.[13] A special Organizational Committee under the chairmanship of Ivan Gronsky, the editor of *Izvestiya,* was established to implement this resolution. (It should be said that during preceding months there had been signs that the Party was growing dissatisfied with RAPP; a *Pravda* editorial in April 1931, for example, had criticized the RAPP leadership for its "overbearing administrative methods" and its "insufficient self-criticism".[14]) The Party's decisive step had been brought about, the decree stated, by the "achievements of socialist reconstruction" during the successful Five-Year Plan (1928–32). It was considered that, given the tremendous progress made towards socialism, all literature in the country must now be essentially socialist, so there was no longer any need for specifically "proletarian" writing. The existence of separate proletarian and other literary groupings such as RAPP was therefore superfluous. Moreover, it was thought that the framework of the existing proletarian literary organizations was too narrow and hindered the proper development of artistic work. An editorial published in *Pravda* on the day the decree was announced accused the RAPP leadership of abusing their position for factional advantage and of causing by their intolerance and regimentation a serious decline in literary standards.

The by now all-powerful hand of Stalin himself was clearly to be seen in the Party's *volte-face*. By liquidating the over-zealous RAPP—which had served its purpose of cowing the fellow travellers—and by establishing a single and homogeneous Writers' Union which would combine various groupings into one, he made it far easier both to direct literary activity and to impose ideological controls upon it. At the time, however, most writers saw the 1932 reform as a gesture of reconciliation made by the Party and failed to perceive its sinister implications because of the enormous relief which they felt at the disbanding of RAPP. Though the new Union of Writers was not to be formally established until 1934, after two years of detailed administrative preparation, the Soviet literary stage was now irrevocably set for total Party control over the creative artist.

In the organizational sense, the most significant element of the 1932 resolution was the decision to establish a single Union of Soviet Writers. Though many authors, including former members of RAPP, opposed the move, they succumbed to considerable Party pressure applied during the two years before the new Union was inaugurated in 1934. It was made clear to them that if they wished to make a living by writing, membership in the new organization, though technically voluntary, was essential. The new Union was to "unite all writers supporting the platform of Soviet power and aspiring to participate in the building of socialism."[15] In becoming members of the Union, most former fellow travellers—who were just as important in it as proletarian writers—were officially upgraded to become allies of the cause. (At the same time, while writing of the Five-Year Plan years was not actually devalued, Averbakh and his RAPP colleagues were denounced and their policies rejected. Averbakh himself later disappeared and probably perished in the purges.) In addition, membership in the Union was made extremely attractive by offering writers a wide variety of material blandishments and social privileges beyond the average Soviet citizen's wildest dreams.[16]

As Gleb Struve has pointed out, by joining the Union a Soviet writer consciously limited the scope of his creative work, and agreed to serve the state and support its policies in his writing.[17] It is clear, therefore, that the Union was the direct offspring of the totalitarian Stalinist regime and served formally to institutionalize "proletarian" artistic trends supportive of Party policy which had been developing throughout the 1920s.[18] It was not a professional body in the Western sense, because its members were not only required to advocate a specific political program but also, as we shall see, were restricted to the application in their work of a specific literary method—Socialist Realism.

II

> "Socialist Realism is the art of the truth of life, comprehended and interpreted by the artist from the point of view of devotion to Leninist Party principles."
>
> **Mikhail Sholokhov**[19]

The formulation of the doctrine of Socialist Realism and the elaboration of its central principles took place between the liquidation of RAPP in April 1932 and the First Congress of Soviet Writers held to inaugurate the new Union in August 1934. During those two years, both writers and critics engaged in wide discussion of the new method. At the same time, encouraged by Stalin's unprecedented triumph at the Seventeenth Party Conference, the "Congress of Victors," in early 1934, the Party became more involved still in literary matters, and appointed several prominent officials charged with imposing ideological controls on the artistic community.

As far as is known, the term Socialist Realism was first used by Gronsky in an address given to leading writers in Moscow on May 20, 1932, when he said: "The basic demand that we make on the writer is: write the truth, portray truthfully our reality that is in itself dialectic. Therefore the basic method of Soviet literature is the method of socialist realism."[20] His statement was quoted in *The Literary Gazette (Literaturnaya Gazeta)* three days later, and consequently May 23, 1932 is taken as marking the term's first appearance in print. Whether Gronsky himself or another high Party functionary invented the formula is not known, but at a meeting of writers in Gorky's apartment three months later, Stalin used the term and was later credited with its formulation. Some commentators believe that it was in fact devised by Gorky in consultation with Stalin.

The doctrine of Socialist Realism was promulgated at the First Writers' Congress by the Party's spokesman Andrei Zhdanov (1888–1948), a secretary of the Central Committee and Stalin's satrap in cultural affairs. He began his lengthy inaugural address, entitled "Soviet Literature—the Richest in Ideas, the Most Progressive Literature in the World," by reminding the delegates that the Congress was convening at a time "when under the leadership of the Communist Party, under the guiding genius of our great leader and teacher, Comrade Stalin,"[21] the socialist system had finally triumphed in the Soviet Union. Soviet culture, he went on, was developing in "exuberant splendor,"[22] and the key to the successes of Soviet literature, the youngest of all literatures, lay in the successes of socialist construction. That literature, he declared, had as its heroes the "active builders of a new life—working men and women, collective farmers, Party members, business managers, engineers, members of the Komsomol, Pioneers."[23] Reminding his audience of the demands made on them by the Second Five-Year Plan (1933–37), he declared that Soviet literature was "impregnated with enthusiasm and the spirit of heroic deeds," and that it was essentially optimistic because it was the literature of the "rising class of the proletariat, the only progressive and advanced class."[24]

What Zhdanov said next was more important still, because it amounted to a definition of Socialist Realism:

> Comrade Stalin has called our writers engineers of human souls. What does this mean? What duties does the title impose upon you?
>
> In the first place, it means knowing life so as to be able to depict it truthfully in works of art, not to depict it in a dead, scholastic way, not simply as "objective reality," but to depict reality in its revolutionary development.
>
> In addition to this, the truthfulness and historical concreteness of the artistic portrayal should be combined with the ideological remolding and education of the working people in the spirit of socialism. This method in literature and in literary criticism is what we call the method of socialist realism.[25]

He went on to declare that Soviet literature was not afraid of being accused of tendentiousness, for in an age of class struggle, non-tendentious and apolitical writing does not and cannot exist. Soviet writers, he said, could say to "any thick-headed bourgeois, to any philistine, to any bourgeois writer"[26] who might complain of the tendentiousness of Soviet writing, that Soviet literature *is* tendentious and that "we are proud of it, because the aim of our tendency is to liberate the workers, to free the whole of mankind from the yoke of capitalist slavery."[27]

Before concluding his address, Zhdanov turned once more to Stalin's (or, properly speaking, his own) now notorious description of the writer:

> To be an engineer of human souls means standing with both feet firmly planted on the basis of real life. And this in its turn denotes a rupture with romanticism of the old type, which depicted a non-existent life and non-existent heroes, leading the reader away from the antagonisms and oppression of real life into a world of the impossible, into a world of Utopian dreams. Our literature, which stands with

> both feet firmly planted on a materialist basis, cannot be hostile to romanticism, but it must be a romanticism of a new type, revolutionary romanticism. We say that socialist realism is the basic method of Soviet literature and literary criticism, and this presupposes that revolutionary romanticism should enter into literary creation as a component part, for the whole life of our Party, the whole life of the working class and its struggle consist in a combination of the most stern and sober practical work with a supreme spirit of heroic deeds and magnificent future prospects ... Soviet literature should be able to portray our heroes; it should be able to glimpse our tomorrow. This will be no Utopian dream, for our tomorrow is already being prepared for today by dint of conscious, planned work."[28]

Zhdanov's speech set the tone for the entire Congress and was not questioned at all. It was seen authoritatively to embody the Party line and clearly reflected Stalin's uncompromising attitude as to the propagandist and political functions of art.[29]

So much, then, for the actual promulgation of the doctrine and its ideological tenets. The Congress had made it clear that, as laid down in the statutes of the new Union of Soviet Writers, the artistic method of Socialist Realism was to be mandatory for all members. But what of the doctrine's theoretical origins and the esthetic demands which it made upon Soviet writers after 1934?

Prime justification for total subordination of literature to the Party's requirements was found by the theoreticians of Socialist Realism in Lenin's now well-known article "Party Organization and Party Literature," published in 1905 and quoted at the beginning of this essay. In it Lenin had stated that anyone writing in Social-Democrat journals should express the general line of the Party. This "party literature," as he called it, must become inseparably linked with the working-class movement and must serve as an indispensable weapon in the proletariat's revolutionary struggle against bourgeois slavery. Though in referring to "literature," Lenin did not primarily mean fiction, after the 1934 Congress his article was seen as advocating the basic element of Socialist Realism, known as *partiinost'*, which was to become the most important factor in Soviet regimentation of art. Literally "party-ness," *partiinost'* (Party-mindedness or Party spirit) means complete submission to the Party line and acceptance of all its policies. Literature cannot exist independently of the society in which it is produced; closely identified with the Party, the writer has civic responsibilities which it is his duty to fulfill, and his work should serve as the vehicle for that fulfillment.

Two further major esthetic concepts are also fundamental to the doctrine. Firstly, *narodnost'* (literally "people-ness"; national character or national traits) means that writers should reflect the life of the ordinary people (the Russian word *narod* has connotations similar to those of the German *Volk*), should demonstrate a sense of devotion to them, and should evince feelings of patriotism for Soviet Russia. In addition, to make it accessible to the common people, literature must be written in simple, comprehensible language free of the "formalistic" and stylistic experimentation often found in work of the 1920s. (As Ronald Hingley reminds us, *narodnost'* also requires in the writer a degree—extreme in the late Stalin period—of political and national chauvinism, whereby foreign characters are generally portrayed as selfish villains but their Soviet counterparts as strong, positive heroes filled with conviction.[30]) Closely allied to *narodnost'* is the principle of *klassovost'* (literally "class-ness"; class character or class nature), which requires the writer to reflect in his work the class ideology of the masses and the objective reality of Soviet society. Thus, since Soviet society is regarded as "classless," all art produced in it and deriving from the people is not only class art but also combines *klassovost'* and *narodnost'*. Furthermore, since Soviet society stands united behind the Communist Party, the *klassovost'* and *narodnost'* of Soviet art are expressed in *partiinost'*, the central tenet of Socialist Realism.[31]

The greatest problem raised for Soviet writers by Zhdanov's formula was that it required them to use the realist techniques of the nineteenth-century Russian classics (especially Tolstoy, Turgenev and Chekhov) in artistic and social circumstances quite unsuited to them. It was Gorky who had devised the slogan "Learn from the classics!" Disturbed by what he saw as a widespread decline in literary standards, particularly in language and style, he wished to keep Soviet literature in the mainstream of the nineteenth-century realist tradition and to have it focus on ordinary members of the proletariat. But the doctrine made a clear distinction between "socialist" realism and what was described as the "critical" realism of the classical authors. While the latter, it was said, had employed realism to negate the Tsarist society in which they lived but had suggested nothing to improve it, the Soviet writer must use the same method optimistically to affirm the new Socialist order.[32] It was his duty not only to describe that order "realistically in its revolutionary development," as Zhdanov had put it, but also to assist the Party in the task of social transformation by helping to "eradicate the vestiges of capitalism ... in people's minds."[33] The word "socialist" therefore reflected this new overtly activist and frankly educative attitude, according to which it was the writer's duty to expose and castigate the "survivals of capitalism" in Soviet society which only delayed the advent of the Communist millennium. Not only, then, did the doctrine of Socialist Realism prescribe strict parameters for the Soviet artist to follow; it also stipulated the prime criterion by which the Soviet critic should evaluate a work of art: how far did it contribute in the educative sense to the consolidation of socialism?

The key word here is educative, because the duty of Soviet writers to serve as educators (or in other words, as didactic political propagandists) led many of them down a difficult path: the search for a hero whom their readers would desire to emulate. However uninspiring many of them may have found Socialist Realism as a doctrine, they were required by it to produce inspiring heroes—heroes whom its pre-Revolutionary predecessor, critical realism, was said to have been unable to produce. These positive emblematic heroes should embody the ordinary Soviet citizen's potential to change the imperfect present into a perfect future, and as such should stand resplendent as "guardians of the Purpose, guides and mentors of the spiritually elevated life of the new Soviet man."[34]

In his detailed study of the positive hero in Russian literature, Rufus Mathewson has explained how many Soviet writers and critics of the 1920s and 1930s based their positive hero types on Tsarist literary models produced by the nineteenth-century utilitarian esthetic.[35] In their critical writings, the "great revolutionary democrats" (Zhdanov's phrase)[36] Belinsky, Dobrolyubov, Chernyshevsky and Saltykov-Shchedrin, had shown their dissatisfaction with conditions in Imperial Russia and had expressed their desire for a new type of socialist, rational man, the "positive hero" who would be able to change the Tsarist status quo. While Belinsky had emphasized the importance for literature of forward-looking optimism, of the notion of art as an instrument of educational and social service, and of generalized typicality of subject matter,[37] Chernyshevsky had stressed the need for exemplary men who would dedicate themselves unswervingly to the socialist cause. His *roman à thèse What is to be Done? (Chto delat'?,* 1863) has as its central character the iron-willed and rigorous Rakhmetov, the epitome of duty and social service who dreams of changing the world. (No wonder that the novel made such a profound impression on Lenin!) Incorruptible, self-assured and devoid of doubt, Rakhmetov is a socialist superman, "the flower of the best people . . . the salt of the salt of the earth."[38] Everything in him and about him is resolutely subordinated to the task of working for the benefit of others. Like the ideal Socialist Realist hero whom he was to engender, this irreproachable and monolithic precursor of the dedicated Bolshevik "leather men in leather jackets" is the embodiment of ascetic self-denial, renouncing enjoyment, affection and even love for the good of the cause. Those leather men— the positive heroes of Socialist Realist fiction—are exemplified with varying degrees of success in the prose works included in this anthology.

III

> "The time has come when the heroic is required."
>
> **Maxim Gorky**[39]

If Chernyshevsky is regarded *ex post facto* as the founding father of Socialist Realism—a status only finally accorded him in the late Stalin period—Maxim Gorky is acclaimed as the method's pioneer *par excellence.* Though he had made his reputation well before the Revolution, he was seen as the last great representative of the Russian classical realist tradition. Moreover, he was thought of as possessing impeccable "proletarian" credentials which endeared him to the regime. In short, he was the ideal choice, and his sixtieth birthday, in 1928, witnessed the start of a Party drive to "communize" him. His play *Enemies* (*Vragi,* 1906) and his revolutionary novel *Mother* (*Mat',* 1907) are regarded as the earliest examples of Socialist Realism. The fact that both works were written long before the doctrine was promulgated is considered unimportant. Pavel Vlasov, the fanatically purposeful and rigidly dogmatic hero of *Mother,* is the direct descendant of Rakhmetov and stands as the earliest representation of the Bolshevik hero. His didactic political evangelism reflects Gorky's own blatant partisanship and makes him the first schematic and inspirational embodiment of Party virtue.

As we have seen, Socialist Realism was not only vague in its formulation but also contradictory in the demands that it made upon writers, and so ideological statements made by literary functionaries during the years 1932 to 1934 tended to define it by citing works considered to exemplify the doctrine rather than by clarifying its intrinsic features. So it is that in addition to Gorky's writings, a number of Soviet works which also appeared before the formulation of the doctrine are now retrospectively held as models of Socialist Realism. These include: Mayakovsky's post-revolutionary poems, Vsevolod Ivanov's *Partisan Tales* (*Partizany,* 1921), Furmanov's *Chapaev* (1923), Serafimovich's *The Iron Flood* (*Zheleznyi potok,* 1924), Gladkov's *Cement* (*Tsement,* 1922–24), Fadeev's *The Rout* (*Razgrom,* 1925–26), Parts I and II of Sholokhov's *The Quiet Don* (*Tikhii Don,* 1928–33) and Part I of his

Virgin Soil Upturned (*Podnyataya tselina,* 1932), the productions of Trenev's play *Lyubov Yarovaya* at the Maly Theater and of Vsevolod Ivanov's *Armored Train 14–69 (Bronepoezd 14–69)* at the Moscow Arts Theater (1927), and Eisenstein's film *Battleship Potemkin* (*Bronenosets Potemkin,* 1925). To these canonical practitioners are added, among writers who appeared in the 1930s, Nikolai Ostrovsky, author of *How the Steel Was Tempered* (*Kak zakalyalas' stal',* 1930–34), Anton Makarenko, the chronicler of juvenile reform schools in his *Pedagogical Poem* (*Pedagogicheskaya poema,* 1934) (also known as *The Road to Life*), and in its sequel *A Book for Parents* (*Kniga dlya roditelei,* 1938), and Alexander Tvardovsky, well-known for his narrative poems about peasant life of which *The Land of Muravia* (*Strana Muravia,* 1936) is the most important. Also recognized as exemplifying the doctrine in their work are, in drama, the producers Nemirovich-Danchenko and Stanislavsky; in film, the director Pudovkin; and in music the composers Prokofiev and Shostakovich. The fact that all the literary works mentioned above were published (or, in the case of Ostrovsky, begun) before 1934, serves to underline Geoffrey Hosking's important remark that though Socialist Realism may have been imposed by politicians, it was actually created by the writers themselves. What the Party did, in effect, was to assemble from the models available to it at the time a "synthetic prototype" which suited its ideological purpose, and then set about imposing it on the literary community.[40]

When the Bolsheviks came to power, the pre-1917 revolutionary type exemplified in Chernyshevsky's and Gorky's works was obliged to devote himself body and soul to the Party's will. This obligation necessitated a fundamental shift in his center of personal gravity, from that of a committed revolutionary, attempting to alter the imperfect Tsarist social order, to that of a Party-led activist who promotes the Soviet status quo. The latter role is far less inspiring than its predecessor, giving rise to the kind of personality which is "manipulated from above, and in turn manipulates those beneath him."[41] This qualitative change in the type explains why the most attractive positive heroes in Soviet literature belong to periods either before Soviet power was consolidated, as during the Civil War, or when it was threatened, as in World War II. The unstable social matrix of wartime enabled genuine popular *(narodnyi)* leaders to emerge, instead of remaining faceless members of a totally politicized social hierarchy. During the 1920s the Civil War was an enormously popular theme in Soviet literature, and in exploring it, writers paid special attention to individual heroic leaders in contrast to the later emphasis placed on the collective.

The most famous early post-revolutionary tribute to individual heroism is Furmanov's *Chapaev* (1923), often described by Soviet critics as the first significant contribution to proletarian prose fiction. Originally conceived as a memoir, the work has been officially accorded the status of a novel because of its ideological importance. Furmanov was praised by critics for revealing the "class essence" of the Civil War and for emphasizing the organizing and leading role of the Party during the struggle. At the same time, he was congratulated for having presented in his Red commander Chapaev "a firm and consistent person of integrity"[42]—the typical proletarian hero.

Chapaev is really a diary written by Furmanov (disguised as Commissar Klychkov in the text), and because it presents momentous historical events witnessed at first hand, is a typical example of "factography"[43] in early Soviet literature. The determined and rational Party Commissar, armed with his conviction that "politics are the mainspring of the Civil War," resolves systematically to "break" the elemental Chapaev, that "wild horse of the steppes," and to direct his unique energies away from anarchy to more considered and socially useful things. At the same time, though, he must preserve the heroic Chapaev myth that so inspires the ordinary fighting men, for like the *bogatyr'* hero of the ancient Russian *bylina* (oral folk epic), Chapaev embodies the popular dream of ultimate triumph.[44] Klychkov's gradual but steady progress towards his goal, coupled with his own achievement of maturity after six months of war, reveals behavior patterns that are fundamental to the standard positive hero: conscious and resolute self-discipline, "awareness of the consequences of every private act,"[45] and an ability to subordinate personal emotions and needs to the Party's political requirements. For all his admiration of Chapaev's qualities, Klychkov never loses sight of the fact that men like the peasant guerrilla leader are not truly part of the proletarian ethos, and that as the masses become politically mature, the need for such outstanding but maverick heroes will pass. Despite its frankly propagandist elements, *Chapaev* is an enthusiastic and ingenuous work, for its propaganda stems not from any sense of duty in the diarist author but from his sincere and deeply-felt political convictions, and its disarming simplicity stands as Furmanov's "expression of an uncomplicated and completely absorbing experience."[46]

If Furmanov pays tribute to individual heroism during the Civil War, Serafimovich's classic Socialist Realist novel *The Iron Flood* (or *The Iron Torrent,* 1924) glorifies the victory of the mass in that mortal struggle. Though less successful than *Chapaev,* the work won official praise because it portrayed with panoramic sweep the emergence of social awareness in the spontaneous movement of thousands of Red partisans and their families retreating from the Whites through the Northern Caucasus. Soviet critics approved of Serafimovich's treatment since it showed the Party's iron will as a force capable of uniting the masses in their heroic struggle. Though Kozhukh, their class-conscious and ruthless peasant leader, is individualized to a degree, the novel's real hero is the mass of the people *(narod),* and it is the behavior of that mass which preoccupies the author. For all the work's abundant repetitive and declamatory passages—Gorky, for one, complained of its artistic shortcomings—*The Iron Flood* is a compelling testimony to Serafimovich's profound faith in the Bolshevik cause, and like *Chapaev* brought its author critical praise for its "clear understanding of the class essence of the Civil War."[47]

While the dramatic context of war makes *Chapaev* and *The Iron Flood* what they are, Gladkov's industrial novel *Cement* (1922-24) is set in the transitional period between the Civil War and the years of peaceful reconstruction which followed it. Though less exciting than its predecessors, it reflects a time in the Soviet Union that, for economic and social reasons, was equally crucial. Acclaimed by Soviet critics as the "first Soviet novel of the working class," it achieved enormous popularity and unlike most of its fellow Socialist Realist works, won its author a measure of recognition abroad.

Like Nikolai Lyashko's novel *The Blast Furnace* (*Domennaya pech',* 1924), *Cement* explores the topical theme of the restoration of factories abandoned during the Civil War. Accordingly, its heroes are not soldiers but ordinary working men and women, and its villains not Whites or Cossacks but obstructive and self-seeking bureaucrats. Its author's central concerns are those of peace-time, too—the problems of factory construction, production and administration—and the realities of industrial life lend the novel an authentic documentary flavor. Like many works of the 1920s, it demonstrates that constructive labor is a prime weapon in the battle to restore normal collective life. Leading the proletarian troops in that battle is the recently demobilized Gleb Chumalov, purposeful, selfless and immensely strong-willed, the first in a long succession of steadfast New Heroes who personify the proletarian "spirit of mortal combat."[48] In Gleb's dealings with his estranged wife, Dasha,[49] and in his forgiveness for the Tsarist engineer Kleist, we find perhaps the best illustration of the positive hero's conscious subordination of private emotions to public duty. If any work of the 1920s expresses unequivocal faith in the Communist cause and fully satisfies the prescriptions of Socialist Realism *avant la lettre,* it is *Cement.* In it confidence triumphs over skepticism, labor conquers idleness, and the forces of socialist good rout those of anti-Bolshevik evil.

Though it is glimpsed only as the prelude to Gladkov's story, the Civil War was still the dominant theme in Soviet literature for much of the 1920s, and Fadeev's short novel *The Rout* (also known as *The Nineteen*, 1925–26), marked a talented return to it. This time, though, the setting was not western Russia as had been the case in *Chapaev* and *The Iron Flood,* but the exotic and remote Pacific Maritime Region in the Far East, north of Vladivostok. Artistically far superior to its predecessors in the canon, *The Rout* has always enjoyed great prestige as an outstanding work of Socialist Realism.

In the theoretical sense, the novel was important because it was seen as presenting for the first time the so-called "harmonious man" who was destined to become the ideal hero of proletarian literature. According to the influential critic Vladimir Ermilov who was responsible for the term, the harmonious man would present a balance between psyche and ideology, instinct and consciousness, the conscious and subconscious.[50] Since the ideas which he acquired consciously would eventually penetrate his subconscious to become instinctive, Ermilov maintained, the harmonious man would manifest his ideology spontaneously, by an unconditioned reflex. The physically frail but authoritative and indomitable Jewish partisan leader, Levinson, was regarded as the prototype of just such a man.[51] (Apparently aware, though, that Levinson still lacked some of the ideal leader's qualities, Fadeev later confessed that the heroic shepherd Metelitsa was meant to embody them and serve as a complement to his commander.)

Other critics praised the novel for its clear and "logically motivated" portrayal of psychological experience and for its refusal to treat the human psyche as mysterious or irrational. Since (unlike Furmanov) Fadeev had focused not on the heroism of guerrilla warfare but on the soldiers' ordinary, everyday life, and since he had not idealized any of the characters, the novel was considered devoid of exaggeration and therefore pervaded by a genuinely heroic and romantic spirit. In addition, it was said, Fadeev had made clear the organizing role played by the Bolsheviks during the Red partisans' campaign. Though the work ended, it was true, with defeat for the guerrillas, Fadeev had succeeded in showing Levinson able to overcome his momentary weakness, and had expressed in his closing paragraph complete confidence in the ultimate triumph of the Bolshevik cause.[52]

With Gorky's exhortation to learn from the classics in mind, critics praised Fadeev for having produced the first truly "Tolstoyan" work in

Soviet literature. He had mastered Tolstoy's technique, they said, employing it not simply in his psychological analysis of character but even in his sentence structure, yet at the same time had managed to avoid the ideology expressed by the master in his "critical" realist novels.

Though Levinson presides over no political agitation in his detachment (in fact, political matters are hardly mentioned at all), with his activist's credo—"To see everything as it is in order to be able to change what exists and to bring nearer what is coming into being and must eventually be"—he expresses the Bolshevik promise of social change leading to a shining future. By his courageous and assured example he wins the trust of his ragged men who follow him without question, and he molds them into a disciplined unit which is ready to suffer and die for the cause. Rejecting sentimentality and irresolution in true positive hero fashion, he allows them to see nothing of his hesitations and doubts, convinced that to lead them successfully he must hide his own weaknesses. As Boris Thomson suggests, however, for all the intriguing contradictions in Levinson's character, Fadeev's portrayal of him has a distinctly disturbing side. Written during Stalin's rise to power, the novel's "embryonic mystique of the leader"[53] is uncannily prophetic of Soviet Russia under the Great Teacher in the 1930s and 1940s.

While *The Rout* is undoubtedly artistically superior to the other exemplars of Socialist Realism included in this collection, first place in the ideological sense among the canonical "works of faith" must go to Ostrovsky's partly autobiographical novel *How the Steel Was Tempered* (also known as *The Making of a Hero,* 1930–34). Though completed before the 1934 Congress, this long and pedestrian work seems to have entirely satisfied official requirements and set the standards for much of the writing that followed Zhdanov's report. Officially ranked now beside Chernyshevsky's *What is to be Done?* and Gorky's *Mother* (by which it was strongly influenced), the novel is regarded as the foremost work in the Socialist Realist tradition. In its hero, Pavel Korchagin, who through the relentless exercise of his will dedicates himself unswervingly to the Party and its ideology, the image of the functional, politicalized Soviet animal finds its apotheosis. This monolithic, intolerant and narrow man who ruthlessly allows nothing to interfere with his obsessive ideal of Communist service, and who ascetically denies himself any personal life, is a paragon of stoicism and devotion, and as such stands first among the "canonized champions of the Vita Nuova."[54]

Like Leonid Leonov's novel *The Road to the Ocean* (*Doroga na Okean,* 1935), (which, though it possesses Socialist Realist traits, was compared unfavourably to Ostrovsky's work by critics), *How the Steel Was Tempered* is steeped in inspiring socialist "uplift," the *sine qua non* of Soviet writing in the 1930s. Through Korchagin's spectacular and agonizing fight against suffering, in which his superhuman stamina flows from an indomitable faith in the cause, Ostrovsky affirms the triumph not only of the human spirit over adversity but also, more importantly, of ideological commitment over political indifference.

Pavel Korchagin was the Party's perfect positive hero, the "Sir Galahad of Socialist Realism,"[55] the purest and noblest knight in the company of the elect at the doctrine's Round Table. Though his image influenced writing later in the 1930s, the best works (among them Yury German's *Our Friends* [*Nashi znakomye*, 1936], Yury Krymov's *The Tanker "Derbent"* [*Tanker 'Derbent'*, 1938], and Veniamin Kaverin's *Two Captains* [*Dva kapitana*, 1939], generally failed to reproduce its fervent crusading flavor. This most popular of Soviet novels—over 40 million copies have been sold—has had an immense influence upon Soviet youth, particularly in the 1930s when Korchagin became a cult figure whose life of will-power and dedication to the Party exemplified that desired by thousands of young Communists. As Hosking reminds us,[56] the story of his life is analogous to the emblematic Puritan biography, and the novel's essentially religious overtones may largely explain its amazing popularity at times of crisis in Soviet history—as during the Leningrad siege in World War II, when starving people queued to buy the novel. If the time is right, as Gorky knew very well, the heroic in fiction can inspire heroism in its readers.

IV

> "Create works of high attainment, of high ideological and artistic content.
>
> Actively help to remould the mentality of people in the spirit of socialism
>
> Be in the front ranks of those who are fighting for a classless socialist society"
>
> **Andrei Zhdanov**[57]

From 1934 until the Nazi invasion in 1941, Soviet literature lived in the sinister shadow of totalitarian Party control which was steadily enveloping the whole of Russian life. That control and the tyranny of

Stalin which enforced it were intensified by mass arrests, imprisonments and executions, and were epitomized by the purge and "wrecker" show trials between 1935 and 1938. In the literary community, however, the Party maintained control covertly for the most part, chiefly through the Communist fraction in the Union of Writers. The official artistic credo of Socialist Realism was proclaimed supreme and exercised a stranglehold on the writer's creativity.

The outbreak of war in June 1941 produced an enormous change, bringing writers a sense of relief and freedom, and breaking what Boris Pasternak at the end of *Doctor Zhivago* calls "the spell of the dead letter." As a wave of patriotism swept the country, the technicalities of Socialist Realism were largely forgotten and writers were encouraged to produce propaganda in support of the war effort. But the freedom which they had welcomed proved all too brief, and in 1943, when the decisive battle for Stalingrad was won, the Party began to tighten its grip on the arts. By the end of the war in Europe it was moving towards absolute control once more. The years from 1946 until Stalin's death in 1953, the period of "Zhdanovism," were to prove the most sterile Soviet literature has ever seen.

Hopes that the wartime freedom enjoyed by writers might last were abruptly dashed on August 14, 1946, when the Party's Central Committee issued a decree which laid down the direction that post-war literature was to take. Sometimes described as the "Zhdanov bombshell," the decree took the form of an attack on two Leningrad journals, *The Star (Zvezda)* and *Leningrad,* which were accused of having published works that were "ideologically harmful." Their editors, it was said, had forgotten the fundamental Leninist tenet that Soviet journals cannot be apolitical:

> The Soviet system cannot tolerate the education of youth in a spirit of indifference to Soviet politics, to ideology, with a couldn't-care-less attitude. The strength of Soviet literature, the most advanced literature in the world, consists in the fact that it is a literature in which there are not and cannot be interests other than the interests of the people, the interests of the state. The task of Soviet literature is to help the state to educate youth correctly, to answer its requirements, to bring up the new generation to be strong, believing in its cause, not fearing obstacles, ready to overcome all obstacles.[58]

Lacking political direction, the decree continued, the two journals had published works "permeated with longing, pessimism and disillusionment." In addition, they had idolized contemporary bourgeois culture in the West and had denigrated Soviet life and people.

Disciplinary action followed. *Leningrad* was suppressed, while the editor of *The Star* was replaced by a member of the Central Committee who would correct the journal's ideological mistakes. Moreover, *The Star* was ordered to ban from its pages the two authors most responsible for its political sins, the satirist Mikhail Zoshchenko and the poetess Anna Akhmatova, together with "others like them."

A week later Zhdanov—whom some at the time even saw as Stalin's heir apparent—gave a report in Leningrad on the two journals, which clarified the decree and stipulated the new Party line in the arts. He then went on to denounce Zoshchenko and Akhmatova in vicious terms. Accusing Zoshchenko of ridiculing the Soviet people, he declared that his portrayal of Russian life was not only vulgar and ugly but also anti-Soviet. Describing Akhmatova as "half-nun, half-whore," he claimed that her work was pervaded by loneliness and helplessness, moods which were alien to Soviet literature and could poison the minds of the young. Both authors had disarmed the Soviet people in their struggle to build Communism, had demoralized Soviet youth, and had undermined the principles of Socialist Realism.[59] Emphasizing the need for *partiinost'* in literature (just as he had at the 1934 Congress), Zhdanov called on writers to portray the "new, fine qualities of Soviet people, to show our people not only in its today, but to look forward to its tomorrow, to help light up with a searchlight the road ahead."[60]

The decree on literature was followed within a month by two more which were equally rigid in the ideological sense and related to the theater and cinema. Bolstered by Zhdanov's report which had clearly been inspired by the Kremlin, all three decrees were designed not so much to limit the artist's freedom as to order him precisely what to produce. Declaring itself the supreme arbiter in artistic matters generally, the Party now publicly identified itself with literature and demanded that all writers observe the principle of *partiinost'* in their work. Strict adherence not only to the spirit but also to the letter of Socialist Realism was required. "Both the Party and artistic literature in our country have one and the same purpose," Fadeev was to say in 1949.[61] After cohabiting for so long, Soviet literature and politics were wed.

The effect upon literature of this unashamed interference by the Party was finally to emasculate it. Stereotyped and rigid patterns replaced the imaginative treatments seen in several works during the war years, and language became bureaucratically formal and stilted. As Tolstoy's beloved hero *truth* was consigned to oblivion, gross falsification became rampant. Soviet life and people were idealized, their bourgeois counterparts condemned, unattractive features of Soviet society glossed over (the so-called "varnishing of reality"), and in accordance with the "No Conflict" theory, struggle and friction kept to a minimum. Any remotely realistic portrayal of Soviet life ran the risk of being denounced as a slander on Soviet reality. The primitive and colorless works which resulted became known derogatively as those of the *Babayevshchina* (a synonym for the rose-tinted portrayal of Soviet life), named after Semyon Babayevsky, a Stalin Prize winner and author of the Socialist Realist novels *The Cavalier of the Golden Star* (*Kavaler zolotoi zvezdy,* 1949) and its sequel *The Light Over the Land* (*Svet nad zemley,* 1951).[62] "Socialist classicism," as Andrei Sinyavsky remarks in his famous essay "On Socialist Realism" *("Chto takoe sotsialisticheskii realizm"),* is a more appropriate description than Socialist Realism for this deeply conservative and "imperial" writing.[63] (Something of an exception was Boris Polevoy's bestseller *The Story of a Real Man* (*Povest' o nastoyashchem cheloveke,* 1946), which in its portrayal of superhuman will power and endurance recalls *How the Steel Was Tempered.* It is the true story of how the Soviet World War II fighter pilot Alexander Maresyev, who lost both legs in a crash, triumphed over his disability and returned to the air force.)

For their part, as Ernest Simmons shows, critics maintained that only authors with the Marxist-Leninist-Stalinist world-view could portray Soviet life correctly, and that only work written from this viewpoint could be considered real art. The Marxist interpretation of Socialist Realism, he adds, "ended in the closed and vicious circle of declaring that only the reality of socialism is real and that therefore everything hostile to socialism is unreal."[64] Needless to say, critics concentrated almost entirely on a work's ideological content and paid scant attention to its literary quality. Not that the latter was very often apparent, for naively simplistic, transparently propagandist and exaggeratedly optimistic writing of the kind foreshadowed by Ostrovsky's novel over a decade before was now the order of the day.[65]

The years since Stalin's death in 1953 have brought increased freedom for Soviet writers. Despite their alternating thaws and freezes, they have witnessed much-reduced enforcement of the doctrine of Socialist Realism and accordingly have made for considerable latitude in the way its principles have been applied.[66] No longer does the formula utterly suffocate imaginative writing as it did during the sterile post-war years, even though it is still officially proclaimed the supreme artistic method. Blatant optimism is no longer obligatory, the glorification of all things Russian has diminished, and the positive hero—at least in the form that the 1930s and 1940s knew him—has virtually disappeared. But as Mathewson reminds us, his disappearance from a doctrine of which he was the cornerstone has not destroyed the ideological argument that produced him in the first place.⁶⁷ Far from it. Soviet criticism continues to require of writers literature which affirms the radiant present and promises a still brighter future as the result of Party guidance. Party leaders, too, continue to assert the need for propagandist and optimistic writing. Speaking at the Third Writers' Congress in 1959, for example, Krushchev declared that the Party is "behind those writers ... who take positive phenomena as their basis ... setting men's hearts alight, urging them forward and pointing the path to a new world." He went on to say that in their positive heroes such writers "epitomize all the best characteristics and qualities of man and contrast them with negative images, demonstrating the struggle of the new against the old, and the inevitable victory of the new."⁶⁸ Thus allegiance to the Party and adherence to the principle of *partiinost'* are still required of writers. In his Central Committee Report of March 1971, Brezhnev made it clear that despite the effects of de-Stalinization, the change had been "simply one of politicians, not of their relationship with the artists."⁶⁹

With the exception, therefore, of Boris Pasternak, Alexander Solzhenitsyn, Yuri Kazakov, Yuri Nagibin, Vladimir Tendryakov, Vasily Shukshin, Valentin Rasputin, Vasily Belov and a few others, most Soviet prose writing during the post-Stalin thaw years has remained broadly in line with the principal tenets of Socialist Realism. At the same time, however, as Hosking explains,⁷⁰ some writers have attempted to revive the artistic expression of those tenets by restoring such themes as youthfulness, public service and self-sacrifice to a fiction which had become intolerably schematic and arid during the late Stalin period.

An illustration of those themes is provided by Sholokhov's well-known novella *The Fate of a Man* (*Sud'ba cheloveka,* 1956–57) (also known as *The Destiny of a Man*), which curiously seems to have awaited publication for a decade after it was written in 1946. Like several works which appeared in the late 1950s, after Krushchev's famous "secret speech" at the Twentieth Party Congress in 1956 had triggered further liberalization, it stresses the importance of the personal and emotional in life as against the rigorous suppression of them in writing during the late Stalin years. This simply written and moving work traces the life story of its hero, Andrei Sokolov, revealing in the apparently ordinary Russian the physical and emotional stamina that enabled him to withstand the extraordinary suffering of war and forced labor under the Nazis. His humanity and goodness have survived intact, and they are traits, Sholokhov implies, characteristic of the average Russian who has the fortitude to endure whatever destiny may bring him. Sokolov, then, embodies sterling qualities typical of the *narod,* qualities from which the entire Soviet land draws its strength. Though beside his predecessors in Gladkov and Ostrovsky, Sokolov is unspectacular and even self-effacing, he possesses the essential moral features of the positive hero type: unflinching stoicism, steadfast patriotism, immense resourcefulness, iron will power, and, however overwhelming the odds, indomitable faith in the Communist cause.

***

This necessarily brief survey has concentrated on the development of Socialist Realism during the 1930s and on its final ossification after the Zhdanov "freeze" of 1946. Needless to say, its simplifications and omissions are many. For example, the declared origins of Socialist Realism in nineteenth-century radical utilitarianism as well as the literary and critical tendencies of the 1920s which preceded the doctrine's formulation have only been sketched. In addition, the way in which critics derived the basic principles of Socialist Realism not only from Gorky and other writers but also from Marx, Engels, Lenin and, later, Stalin, has not been investigated. Moreover, for reasons of space, no attempt has been made to examine works which, though considered exemplars of the doctrine, openly defy its fundamental canons. Foremost among these, of course, is Sholokhov's famous Cossack novel *The Quiet Don,* which asserts the primacy of its hero's personal life over his political experiences.[71]

As we have seen, the promulgation of the doctrine of Socialist Realism in 1932 was the key element in the regime's administrative moves to end the literary friction of the late 1920s by grouping all Soviet writers into a single body, the new Union, which could more easily be made to follow Party dictates and to reflect Party policy. Literature was to be transformed into a convenient and effective instrument for the realisation of Marxist doctrine. Originating as a set of demands put forward by the Party, Socialist Realism is therefore a "collection of political prescriptions rather than a literary phenomenon."[72] For all the forests of paper and seas of ink which have been exhausted since 1932 in attempts to define, reflect and promote the doctrine, it remains essentially a Stalinist device to enlist literature and art in the service of the Communist state. Official Soviet literature, then, has become ideology, and ideology has become literature. Political, not literary, considerations are paramount. As Marc Slonim remarks, "Had the theoreticians of Communist esthetics said that a 'good' work of art is one that supports Communism, and a 'bad' work one that either does not do it or does it half-heartedly, they would have avoided many further troubles."[73] The restrictions imposed by the Socialist Realist straitjacket upon the creative artist's freedom and upon the welfare of imaginative writing are plain, and both Russian literature and her writers bear witness to the untold political violence done them since 1932. Though it is true that the inflexible application of the doctrine characteristic of the late Stalin period has gone and that Socialist Realism has been modified over the years in accordance with shifts in Party policy, its central canons remain sacrosanct in official eyes, and observance of them is still notionally *de rigueur* for Soviet writers.[74]

In conclusion, let us remember that however much we in the West may disapprove of the politicalization of art, many Soviet writers have felt a profound commitment to both the Communist Party and its policies, and have considered it their duty to express that commitment in their work. "The act of artistic creation," as Simmons says, "becomes an act of faith in the system that controls it."[75] Artistically unsophisticated though the result may be, it is very often deeply sincere, and we should not be so ready to disparage it. In the unique political and social situation that obtained in Russia shortly after the Revolution, the positive hero in proletarian writing embodied the convictions, sincerity and devotion of his creator. His moral qualities and practical abilities that were so desperately needed at that difficult time are perhaps best summed up in the words of Vyacheslav Polonsky, a leading Soviet editor and critic of the 1920s:

> He runs the lathe, he carries a rifle, he directs the government, he does big deeds and engages in a work that may remain unnoticed. He builds plants and collectives, railways and blast furnaces. He destroys illiteracy, eradicates religion, banishes the dirt of ages, and uproots the advocates of private property. He loves work. He hates phrases. He is a soldier of the revolution . . . He identifies himself with society. His aim is to understand the world in order to remould it. His personal responses are secondary. Social interests dominate over the egotistic. Indeed, his social and individual interests coincide. His life is broad and embraces a universe . . . [76]

Since the early 1920s—a decade before the doctrine of Socialist Realism was formulated—the positive hero has satisfied the spiritual hunger of generations of countless Soviet readers who find in his stereotyped but heroic image both inspiration and the promise of a better world.

Notes

1. Marc Slonim, *Soviet Russian Literature: Writers and Problems, 1917–1977* (2nd ed.), New York and London, Oxford University Press, 1977, p. 169. See particularly the general survey of the years 1928 to 1934 in chapters 16 and 17.
2. V. I. Lenin, "Party Organisation and Party Literature", (*Novaya zhizn'*, No. 12, 1905), in C. Vaughan James, *Soviet Socialist Realism, Origins and Theory,* London, Macmillan, 1973, p. 104. This is a detailed study of the origins of Socialist Realism. See especially chapter 4.
3. See Robert A. Maguire, *Red Virgin Soil: Soviet Literature in the 1920s,* Princeton, 1968, for a comprehensive treatment of writing associated with the journal in the 1920s.
4. Vaughan James, p. 129.
5. Max Hayward, "Soviet Literature 1917–1962," in Patricia Blake and Max Hayward (eds.), *Dissonant Voices in Soviet Literature,* London, Allen and Unwin, 1964, p. xv. An excellent study of Lunacharsky's activities is Sheila Fitzpatrick, *The Commissariat of Enlightenment: Soviet Organisation of Education and the Arts under Lunacharsky, October 1917–1921,* Cambridge University Press, 1970.
6. Ernest J. Simmons, "Soviet Literature and Controls," in E. J. Simmons (ed.), *Through the Glass of Soviet Literature,* New York and London, Columbia University Press, 1961, p. 8.
7. See Vaughan James, Appendix IV (pp. 116–19), for the full text of the Resolution in English translation.
8. Gleb Struve, *Soviet Russian Literature, 1917–1950,* Norman, University of Oklahoma Press, 1951, p. 83. For a *résumé* of the 1925 Resolution, see pp. 83–85. (2nd ed, 1971).
9. Maguire, p. 169.
10. For details of RAPP's domination, see, for example, Edward J. Brown, *The Proletarian Episode in Russian Literature, 1928–1932,* New York, Columbia University Press, 1953.
11. Max Hayward, "Literature in the Soviet Period (1917–1975)," in Robert Auty and Dimitri Obolensky (eds.), *Companion to Russian Studies* (3 vols.), Cambridge University Press, 1976–80, Vol. 2, 1977, p. 195.
12. See Edward J. Brown, "The Year of Acquiescence," in Max Hayward and Leopold Labedz (eds.), *Literature and Revolution in Soviet Russia, 1917–1962,* London, Oxford University Press, 1963, pp. 44–61.
13. See Vaughan James, Appendix V (p. 120), for the full text of the decree in English translation.
14. Herman Ermolaev, *Soviet Literary Theories 1917–1934: The Genesis of Socialist Realism,* New York, Octagon Books, 1977, p. 108. For details of the dissolution of RAPP, see pp. 119–38.
15. Vaughan James, p. 120.
16. For details of the Writers' Union, see, for example, Ronald Hingley, *Russian Writers and Soviet Society, 1917–1978,* London, Methuen, 1979, pp. 195–7; and Boris Thomson, *The Premature Revolution, 1917–1946,* London, Weidenfeld and Nicolson, 1972, pp. 228–29.
17. Struve, p. 238.
18. See Vaughan James, p. 35.
19. Ibid., p. 121.

20. Ermolaev, p. 144.
21. *The Soviet Writers' Congress, 1934*, London, Lawrence and Wishart, 1977, p. 15. (See pp. 15–24 for an English translation of Zhdanov's address.)
22. Ibid.
23. Ibid., p. 20.
24. Ibid.
25. Ibid., p. 21. (The phrase "engineer of the human soul" was in fact first used by Zhdanov but attributed by him to Stalin. [Vaughan James, p. 126]). I have made minor changes in the published translation. For further details of Zhdanov's speech, see Struve, pp. 244–45.
26. Ibid.
27. Ibid.
28. Ibid., pp. 21–22.
29. For an interesting discussion of the Congress, see Rufus Mathewson, "The First Writers' Congress: A Second Look," in Hayward and Labedz (1963), pp. 62–73.
30. Hingley, p. 199.
31. See Vaughan James, p. 11.
32. Hayward, *Dissonant Voices*, pp. xxii–xxiii.
33. Vaughan James, p. 81.
34. Geoffrey Hosking, *Beyond Socialist Realism*, London, Paul Elek, 1980, p. 11. Chapter 1 (pp. 1–28) offers an illuminating survey of the Socialist Realist tradition.
35. Rufus W. Mathewson, *The Positive Hero in Russian Literature*, (2nd ed), Stanford, Stanford University Press, 1975.
36. Ibid., p. 21.
37. See ibid., pp. 42–5.
38. Quoted in Mathewson, p. 76.
39. Ibid., p. 165.
40. Hosking, p. 6.
41. Mathewson, pp. 251–52.
42. Ermolaev, p. 170.
43. For a discussion of Furmanov's narrative technique, see Richard Freeborn, *The Russian Revolutionary Novel: Turgenev to Pasternak*, Cambridge University Press, 1982, pp. 115–122.
44. For a survey of inspirational virtuous heroes in early Russian literature, see Hosking, pp. 13–14; and Mathewson, chapter 2.
45. Mathewson, p. 185.
46. Helen Muchnic, "Literature in the NEP Period," in Hayward and Labedz (1963), p. 35.
47. Struve, p. 144. See also the more detailed examination of the novel in Freeborn, pp. 105–10.
48. Mathewson, p. 205.
49. See Vera S. Dunham, *In Stalin's Time: Middleclass Values in Soviet Fiction*, Cambridge University Press, 1976, pp. 63–65.
50. See Ermolaev, pp. 61–62.
51. For references to Levinson and other distinguished Jewish heroes in Soviet literature, see Bernard J. Choseed, "Jews in Soviet Literature," in Ernest J. Simmons, *Through the Glass of Soviet Literature* (1961), pp. 110–58; and Hingley, pp. 116–17.
52. The ending of *The Rout* illustrates what Mathewson (p. 198) calls "the characteristic moment of the Soviet novel." Found to varying degrees in each of the works included in this anthology, it appears as a "verbal coda, presented most often in the form of a flat

declaration of faith or belief." As Mathewson shows (pp. 197–99), such a finale is particularly pronounced in *The Rout*. It is also marked in *Cement*. For a discussion of *The Rout*, see Freeborn, pp. 149–55.

53. Thomson, p. 95.
54. Dunham, p. 61. See also the brief survey of the novel in Freeborn, pp. 200–1.
55. Ernest J. Simmons, "The Organization Writer (1934–46)," in Hayward and Labedz (1963), p. 85.
56. Hosking, p. 15.
57. *Soviet Writers' Congress,* (1977), p. 24.
58. Walter N. Vickery, "Zhdanovism (1946–53)," in Hayward and Labedz (1963), pp. 101–2.
59. Hayward, *Dissonant Voices,* p. xxvii.
60. Vickery, p. 104.
61. Simmons, *Through the Glass of Soviet Literature,* p. 19.
62. See Struve, p. 363.
63. Abram Terts (Andrei Sinyavsky), *Fantasticheskii mir Abrama Tertsa,* New York, Inter-Language Literary Associates, 1967, p. 434. This most stimulating essay can be found in English translation in Abram Terts, *On Socialist Realism,* New York, Pantheon Books, 1960.
64. Simmons, p. 13.
65. For details of writing in the late Stalin period, see, for example: Harold Swayze, *Political Control of Literature in the USSR, 1946–59,* Cambridge, Mass., Harvard University Press, 1962; Walter N. Vickery, *The Cult of Optimism: Political and Ideological Problems of Recent Soviet Literature,* Bloomington, Indiana University Press, 1963; Vickery's essay "Zhdanovism (1946–53)," referred to above; and Slonim, chapter 27, "The Aftermath of War."
66. Among studies of post-1953 Soviet literature are: Deming Brown, *Soviet Russian Literature since Stalin,* Cambridge and New York, Cambridge University Press, 1978; George Gibian, *Interval of Freedom: Soviet Literature during the Thaw, 1954–57,* Minneapolis, University of Minnesota Press, 1968; Gibian's essay "Soviet Literature during the Thaw," in Hayward and Labedz (1963), pp. 125–49; Max Hayward's essay "Conflict and Change in Soviet Literature," in Hayward and Labedz (1963), pp. 211–28; Max Hayward and Edward L. Crowley (eds.), *Soviet Literature in the Sixties,* London, Methuen, 1965; Hosking; and Max Hayward, "The decline of Socialist Realism," *Survey,* Vol. 18, No. 1 (1972), pp. 73–97.
67. Mathewson, p. 256.
68. Vaughan James, p. 92.
69. Ibid., p. 98.
70. Hosking, p. 28.
71. See Hingley, p. 201.
72. Ermolaev, p. 159.
73. Slonim, pp. 164–65.
74. See Hingley, pp. 202–4
75. Simmons, p. 20.
76. Quoted in Mathewson, p. 220.

Dmitri Furmanov
CHAPAEV

Furmanov and Chapaev, Ufa (1919).

Dmitri Furmanov (1891–1926)

The third of seven children, Dmitri Andreevich Furmanov was born of peasant stock in 1891 in Sereda (now the town of Furmanov), in Kostroma Province, twenty miles north of Ivanovo-Voznesensk, where his father kept a tavern. In 1897 the family moved to Ivanovo-Voznesensk, a textile town known as "the Russian Manchester," where two years later the boy began school. In the autumn of 1905, he moved to the town's commercial academy where he spent the next three years. In 1909 he entered the non-classical secondary school in Kineshma, northeast of Ivanovo-Voznesensk on the Volga, and then in 1912 left school to begin his studies at the University of Moscow.

Following the outbreak of the First World War, in November 1914 Furmanov left university to become a male nurse. After travelling to Rostov-on-Don and Tiflis, he served on both the Caucasus and Turkish fronts before being transferred in 1915 to Kiev on the southwestern front.

In October 1916 he returned to Ivanovo-Voznesensk and began work as a teacher on courses for workers there. He spent much of 1917 speaking in villages throughout the Ivanovo area. After the October Revolution he initially sympathized with the Socialist Revolutionary (SR) Party and then with the Anarchists, but in July 1918 he joined the Bolsheviks and became a member of the Party's provincial executive committee, vigorously engaging in varied political work in Ivanovo-Voznesensk and the surrounding region.

In early 1919 Furmanov left Ivanovo for Samara and the eastern front with the Ivanovo workers' detachment, to join the Fourth Army. In March 1919 he met Chapaev for the first time, and later that month was appointed Political Commissar in the newly-formed 25th (Chapaev) infantry division, being responsible for political, educational and cultural work among the men. In early August 1919, less than a month before Chapaev's death, he was transferred to the Turkestan front where he assumed overall responsibility for political work. 1920 found him first in Tashkent, with Frunze, and then in Verny (now Alma-Ata) in Kazakhstan, before he was transferred to the Ninth Army in the Kuban.

There he was wounded and awarded the Order of the Red Banner for distinguished conduct. 1921 brought still more moves—to Tiflis and Krasnodar, Rostov-on-Don and Ivanovo-Voznesensk—before he returned to Moscow where he engaged in political and editorial work. In late 1923 he joined the "October" group of writers, and was appointed political editor in the State Publishing House. In March of the following year, already prominent as a literary administrator, he became Secretary of the Moscow Association of Proletarian Writers.

By the mid-1920s, however, Furmanov's health was beginning to fail, and both 1924 and 1925 saw visits to the Crimea for treatment. By early 1926 his condition had deteriorated and in March of that year he contracted meningitis. He lost consciousness and died two days later, aged only 34. In grand military style, a squadron of Red cavalry accompanied his coffin to its resting-place in the Novodevichy Cemetery in Moscow.

***

The corpus of Furmanov's fiction is not large because so much of his short career was taken up by diverse political, military and educational work, and by journalistic writing directly connected with it. His first published piece was a poem entitled "In Memory of D. D. Efremov," which appeared in the Ivanovo-Voznesensk paper *The Ivanovo News-Sheet (Ivanovskii listok)* in 1912. This was followed, in 1916, by a series of sketches from the front, published in the paper *The Russian Word (Russkoe Slovo).* From 1917 onwards he regularly contributed both articles and poems to the Ivanovo paper *The Workers' City (Rabochii gorod),* and from 1920 onwards his reviews and sketches began to appear in many newspapers and journals in places as varied as Moscow, Tashkent, Krasnodar, Tiflis and the North Caucasus.

Furmanov began work on *Chapaev,* the novel which was to bring him fame, early in 1922, and writing rapidly, finished it by January 1923. It appeared in book form that March, published in both Moscow and Petrograd, and went into a second edition later in the year. So immediately popular did the novel become that there were five more separate editions of it before his death. A famous film version of the work was made in 1934. 1923 also saw the publication of Furmanov's story *Red Landing,* which he had finished in late 1921 and which describes the successful Red Army operation against Wrangel's White forces in the Kuban during the Civil War. Like *Chapaev,* Furmanov's second novel, *The Revolt,* which he began in late 1923, was a semi-documentary treatment of the Civil War in a remote part of Central Asia—this time in Turkestan. Completed in 1924, it was published in book form early in 1925. The same year saw the appearance of his collection of sketches and tales *The Path of Struggle,* as well as the shorter volume of stories entitled *Shtark.* Later that year he began work on a long and ambitious novel, *The Writers,* which was to reflect the complex ideological struggle current in Soviet literary circles at the time but which, sadly, was to remain unfinished when he died. 1926, the year of Furmanov's death, brought the publication of several items, among them the cycle of sketches entitled *Seashores,* and the tales contained in his collections *Unforgettable Days* and *The Blind Poet.*

Furmanov, Political Commissar of the Chapaev Division (1919).

CHAPAEV

1. *The Workers' Detachment*[1]

There was such a terrible crush at the station that the platform was dark with people and the Red Army cordon could barely hold back the excited crowd. At midnight the workers' detachment which Frunze[2] had mustered was due to leave for the struggle against Kolchak.[3] From all the factories and mills in Ivanovo-Voznesensk[4] the people had gathered to see off their fathers and brothers, their sons and comrades. ...

These new "soldiers" looked funny somehow—they seemed so awkward and raw. Many of them were wearing their greatcoats for the first time, and the garments sat badly on them, bulging everywhere like dough rising in a kneading trough. But what did it matter? It didn't stop them from being brave young fellows all the same! Just look at that one over there! He had pulled his belt so tight he could hardly breathe, but he was as dashing and jaunty as could be, his heels ringing on the platform as he strode to and fro. Or that one over there, trying to look like an old fire-eater with his nonchalant, sprightly air, his hand resting carelessly on the hilt of his awkwardly-belted sabre as he argued importantly with his neighbor; while a third, with a revolver at his left hip, a pair of hand grenades at his right, and a cartridge-belt coiled around him like a snake, was rushing back and forth along the platform, eager to show off to both relatives and friends in this formidable outfit.

The great dark crowd of workers gazed at their soldiers with unashamed delight and loving pride. They were talking about them.

"They'll learn all right, mate, they'll learn! When they get to the front they'll soon find out what it's all about!"

"You're right there! Being at the front's no picnic!"

Those watching began to stir, and laughing, craned their necks in an attempt to see better.

The crowd was fairly humming with talk.

"We'll drag the devil himself out of hell if we have to!" someone said. "Everybody was moaning 'There's no boots, no greatcoats and nothing to shoot with', but now just look over there!" he went on, pointing towards the carriages to show it was the Red Army men he meant. "We've kitted out nearly a thousand of 'em!"

"How many, d'you say?"

"Well, it must be about a thousand, and there's more getting ready to leave soon. We've collected everything for them too. You can find anything, mate, if you have to—this is no time for hanging about. Things are really bad."

"Yes, they are," someone echoed hoarsely in a low bass voice.

"Yes, they're bad all right, that's for sure! Old Kolchak's pushing for all he's worth, and now there's trouble in the Urals too!"

Then a weaver called Marfa stood on tiptoe, and looking over the heads of the crowd, said:

"That must be them coming, over there!"

Those standing near her stood on tiptoe too, and craning their necks, looked in the same direction. There were three people walking towards them, closely surrounded by the crowd. The tall, thin figure of Lopar, a worker, was especially noticeable, his long black hair and shining eyes clearly visible.

Beside him was Yelena Kunitsyna, a weaver of twenty-two whom everyone loved for the simple, sensible way she talked, her clear mind, and her fine, strong voice which the workers had so often heard at meetings. A quiet, inner joy was shining on her pale, serious face.

Next to Yelena was Fyodor Klychkov. He was not a weaver, and indeed not a worker at all, but a former student. It was only a short time ago that he had come back to Ivanovo-Voznesensk from Moscow, settled in and soon begun to feel at home, running around giving lessons and living on what happened to come his way. During the Revolution he had quickly discovered he was a good organizer, and at meetings would speak with enthusiasm and fervor, though not always very sensibly. The workers knew him well and liked him, looking on him as one of their own.

At the sight of Lopar, Kunitsyna and Klychkov, the crowd on the platform surged forward and a loud whisper ran through it:

"They'll start making speeches now..."

"The train'll be leaving soon..."

"Yes, they'll pull out at twelve..."

"Just you wait and see, they've timed it for midnight exactly!"

Then Klychkov got up on the box to speak. His wretched greatcoat was old and shabby, a relic from the war. His ungloved hands were freezing and he kept thrusting them into his pockets or into the front of his coat, then pulling them out again and blowing on his stiff, red fists. Today he was paler than usual—he had not slept much for the last two nights, and badly at that, and had spent the days rushing about, with the result that he felt worn out. His voice, usually so ringing and clear, was rather hoarse, and it sounded muffled and hollow, as though coming from deep down in a cavern.

Klychkov was to speak first—it was his job to bid farewell to the Ivanovo workers on the detachment's behalf. It was very cold and the crowd was half-frozen, so he would have to hurry. The speeches would have to be short!

Fyodor looked at the crowd and saw there was no end to the dark mass of people—the edge of it was somewhere out beyond the square, dimly lit by its gas lamps. It seemed to him that beyond the thousands of people standing before him, huddled together and stretching away into the darkness, there were many more, and beyond them still more, and so it went on, without end. And at that moment, feeling a sharp stab of pain, he suddenly realized how near and dear this dark crowd was to him, and how hard it would be to part with them.

"Will I ever see them again?" he wondered. "And shall we all come home again one day? Will I ever come back and speak to them as I've so often done these past few years?"

Filled with sorrowful thoughts, not having had enough time to work out his speech and not really knowing what he was going to say, Klychkov shouted in an unusually loud voice—louder, somehow, than he had ever shouted before:

"Comrade workers! There are only a few minutes left now! Very soon the last bell will ring and we shall be leaving. On behalf of the men of this Red Army detachment, I say to you: Farewell! Remember us, we who are your comrades, remember where we have gone and why! And be ready to follow us at the first call! Keep in touch with us, and let the soldiers have what money you can. Food's not easy to come by at the front, comrades, and life's hard there—much harder than here. So don't forget that! And don't forget, either, that many of us are leaving our families fatherless and unprovided for, leaving our children to go hungry—so don't forsake them. It'll be very hard for us sitting in the trenches, suffering on the marches and in battle ... But it'll be a hundred times harder for us to bear those torments if on top of everything else we hear our families are perishing, abandoned and forgotten by all ... Now just one more word before we leave: work! You must work as hard as you can! You're weavers, so you all know that the more cloth you make here in Ivanovo, the warmer we'll be in the snow-covered steppes around Orenburg[5] and Uralsk,[6] as well as everywhere else your cloth goes to. So work as hard as you can, and always remember that victory doesn't only depend on our bayonets, but on your labor too!

Shall we ever see each other again? Well, let's all believe we will! But even if we don't, it's no use feeling sorry about it, for the Revolution doesn't count individual sacrifices. So farewell, dear comrades! On behalf of the men of the Red detachment, farewell!"

As a wild blizzard howls over the snowbound steppe, so the crowd responded with a deep, sobbing roar:

"Farewell, comrades! And good luck! We'll not forget you!"

Then, as the crowd quietened down, the command rang out:

"Detachment! To your places!"

There was a sudden flurry of hats, caps and helmets, followed by the smack of people kissing each other farewell. Above the crowd, ebbing and flowing, drifted the hum of hurried partings, grave words of advice, sorrowful entreaties and vain attempts at consolation.

A mother's shaking head lay on a gloomy Red Army man's shoulder, her gray face wet with tears. She was sobbing loudly and moaning, she and her son, two halves of one being, while the boy was distant and grave, resolute and lost in silent thought.

The detachment had got into the carriages now. The crowd pressed closer, and from the windows of the train it looked like a continuous, formless mass that kept turning this way then that, growling restlessly like an enormous wild beast—a great shaggy bear with a thousand eyes and a thousand paws, its giant body supple and lithe.

The third bell rang . . .

Whistles trilled like nightingales and the engine hooted like an owl, then with a hoarse snort it began to belch smoke and pant breathlessly. The wheels screeched on the frozen rails and crunched as they began to turn, then the carriages creaked and began to roll away . . .

Now the Red Army men were shouting from the carriage windows, and the swaying, black crowd cried out in reply, running after the moving train and shouting as they went. Then the carriages were lost in the gloom, and all that could be heard was something rumbling and clanking far away in the distance as it made its way deeper and deeper into the black darkness. . . .

Downcast and dejected, the weavers left the station, and talking sorrowfully among themselves, made their various ways home through the cold January night.

***

It took the detachment a long time to travel from Ivanovo-Voznesensk to Samara[7]—a good two weeks. In those days, though, even that was extremely quick. The men did not find the journey very tiring—the unfamiliar surroundings helped to keep their spirits up, and the constantly changing impressions invigorated them, so their mood remained extremely buoyant. The striking novelty of everything they saw around them dispelled the gray monotony of the journey and the boredom of waiting for hours in the sidings of remote stations.

Whenever the troop train stopped, there was lively work for it to do. The entire journey was punctuated by noisy meetings, impromptu lectures and group discussions held by those who were interested. This detachment of Bolshevik weavers—well-disciplined, sensible fellows that they were—created a profound impression on the people they met throughout their journey. In those days, railway stations both large and small, little towns, villages and hamlets were all plagued by countless bands of guerrillas and outlaws. No one was in control of them and no one kept track of them. They were made up of every kind of detachment and semi-detachment, all sorts of "local formations"—wild, dubious folk who roamed the length and breadth of boundless Russia without rhyme or reason. And all this vast horde was living at the expense of the local population, refusing to pay for what it used, taking the law into its own hands and wreaking general havoc. The way still lay clear for such riotous lawlessness, for there was no one to check it: in remote districts lost in the depths of the country Soviet power had not yet been consolidated into a powerful force to be reckoned with.

Quite what went on in those troubled days deep in the impenetrable forests of godforsaken provinces no one will ever know. Suffering filled the gray lakes of people's eyes with sorrow as the riotous bands trampled the young shoots of Soviet life and then in drunken frenzy raced wildly on.

There were people in Russia at the time who did not realize that the new government was only just beginning to bring in strong measures to curb these wild marauders, and so in the meantime the peasants in remote rural areas poured out all their accumulated sorrow and bitter anger upon the Bolsheviks, blaming them for their misfortune.

Then suddenly, in this detachment of a thousand Red weavers, both the peasants in the countryside and the inhabitants of small towns saw—to put it bluntly—fine, good people who listened attentively to what they had to say, calmly answered all their questions, explained everything in simple, sensible terms, never ransacked their granaries or tore the cellar doors off their hinges, and if they did take anything, then they paid for it. The peasants were amazed, for this was something quite new, something totally unfamiliar and extremely welcome. Occasionally, when the troop train was held up for days at a time at some remote wayside halt, the local people would appear from their villages and hamlets and gather round to "listen to the wise soldier folk," as they put it.

The work of political agitation was carried on in an admirable fashion, and it served to prepare the ground for the gigantic task which the men from Ivanovo-Voznesensk would perform during the years of the Civil War that were to follow. And where were those men not to be found: along the Chinese border and in the Siberian *taiga*,[8] across the Orenburg steppes and on the Polish frontier, and even in the Sivash strait at Perekop.[9] And where did they not soak the battlefield with their blood? That was why people held them so dear, that was why they were tracked down so relentlessly by the enemy, why they were so loved and hated at the same time. And that is why the memory of them is like a song that echoes forever over the boundless plains of Soviet Russia.

Now these men were travelling to the front in freezing goods trucks amid the hard January frost. They were working, studying and above all thinking and thinking, because they knew they must be ready for anything. They knew one must be able to wage war not only with the bayonet but also with the word, as well as with a clear head, detailed knowledge and the ability to understand everything instantly and explain it to others correctly. In the trucks there was a continuous hubbub as books were read aloud and unlettered men struggled to study, while noisy arguments filled the air like a flock of raucous jackdaws. Then all of a sudden a song would burst forth in the clear, frosty air, a song that was ringing and gay, soaring into the sky like a bird on the wing.

How they sang, those weavers! Their long years of underground struggle had not been for nothing! That was why later on, at the front, there was no regiment in the division that so cherished these songs of struggle or sang them the way the Ivanovo-Voznesensk men did—with such depth of feeling, simplicity and love. Those songs fired the imagination of the other regiments, filling them with enthusiasm and pride. Oh, what a song can do to a man's heart!

***

The closer they came to Samara, the cheaper the bread was at the stations. And not only bread either, but also food in general. Back in hungry Ivanovo-Voznesensk, where not a single pound of bread had been issued for months at a time, the weavers had grown used to looking on a small crust as an enormous treasure. But now they saw there was plenty of bread, and suddenly realized the problem lay not in the lack of it, but in something else. They began to complain bitterly of the general disorder in the country and of the fact that the links between the grain-producing areas and the industrial centers were so weak. Then, as if taking vengeance on this abundance of bread for the long years of hunger, they hurried to make up for all the pounds of it they had never eaten.

As soon as they reached Samara and stopped in a remote siding littered with the skeletons of derelict trucks and piles of rusty rails, the men all spilled out on to the tracks, and crowding together, began to kick up a tremendous fuss, urging their commanders to find out what was going to happen to them as quickly as possible. Where were they to be sent and when? And what for? Would they be setting off straightaway, or would they be kept in the city for a couple of days first?

Only Frunze could provide the answers to these questions, as he was already in command of the Fourth Army. Though he had left Ivanovo-Voznesensk a few days before the detachment and was now in Uralsk, he had left a note for Fyodor at the Revolutionary Military Council's office in Samara. In it he said that Klychkov, Lopar, Bochkin and Andreev were to set off immediately to join him in Uralsk, while the detachment was to follow. With sincere, warm words Frunze went on to greet his fellow-townsmen, and having briefly explained the situation obtaining at the time, pointed out what an enormously difficult task faced them all. Fyodor read the note out to the detachment, and the men listened with delight to the cheering words of their beloved commander.

"Long live Frunze! Hurrah! Hurrah! Hurrah!"

Hats, caps and helmets were tossed in the air and flew around in confusion like a flock of frightened crows.

The friendly tone of Frunze's note threw Fyodor into a fever of excitement, and waving it above his head in a rather ludicrous fashion, he shouted in ingenuous delight:

"Comrades! Comrades! Here it is, this little note! It was written by the Army Commander *himself!* Can't you just feel it was written by a man who is our complete equal in every way? From his comradely manner and his simple tone, can't you tell that with us there's really only one step from ordinary soldier to commander-in-chief? And not even one step either, comrades, for the two go together to make one whole. The two men are one: the commander and the Red Army soldier! That's where the strength of our army lies—in this inner unity, this solidarity and cohesion—that's where our strength lies! So hurrah for our army! And hurrah for our victory!"

Once again the men tossed their hats high in the air with delight and cried "Hurrah!" Their pride and joy, and above all their readiness to fight surged out far and wide, as pebbles are torn up from the sea bed during a violent storm and flung onto the shore.

***

Now events began to follow one another like fleet-footed hares. The detachment received its mustering orders, and its commander was summoned to Army Headquarters and told to ensure that the troops were ready to march.

The four men named in Frunze's note received a reminder from the Revolutionary Council:

"Leave for Uralsk immediately!"

They began to bustle about, hurrying to get ready, and barely had time to say good-bye to the men in the detachment. But it didn't matter, for they believed they would all see each other again in Uralsk soon.

Two troikas pulled away from the Revolutionary Council's headquarters. In the first sat Fyodor and Andreev, and in the second Bochkin and Lopar.

The horses leapt forward and the drivers' whistling rent the air as their whips uncoiled like snakes and cracked. Then, like birds on the wing, the sleighs disappeared into the powdery snow of the blizzard.

2. The Steppe

The mornings are frosty and cold out in the steppe. Both drivers were wrapped up warmly in their shaggy sheepskins, their heads hidden from the dozing passengers behind them by their high, wool collars.

"So you were in Chapaev's[10] detachment yourself, were you, Grisha?" Fyodor asked the young fellow who was driving.

"Yes, it was with him I lost my leg," said Grisha, pointing down to where his other leg should have been. "We kept chasing back and forth all over the steppe the whole summer—the Cossacks were after us and we were trying to fool them. Those Czechs[11] are really stupid, but you can't trick the Cossacks—they grew up round here, so what can you expect? It's only natural."

"Well, and is he young?" asked Fyodor, continuing the conversation.

"Oh yes, he's still young all right—can't be thirty yet . . ."

"And does he come from round here? Is he a Cossack?"

"What d'you mean, a Cossack? How could he be? There's a village not far from Pugachov[12] called Vyazovka, and that's where he's supposed to have lived, but other folk say he used to live in Balakovo[13] first, then came here. So who knows?"

"But what's he like?" asked Fyodor eagerly, and it was clear from his excited face that the conversation had fired his imagination and that he did not want to miss a single word.

"Well, how can I put it? He's a hero, that's all!" answered Grisha, as though thinking aloud. "You might be sitting in a cart, let's say, and all of a sudden the fellows would see him a long way off. 'Chapaev's coming! Chapaev's coming!' they'd shout. You might set eyes on him ten times in a single day, but you'd still want to see him some more—that's the kind of fellow he is, mate! And we'd all climb down off the cart and just stare at him, as if he was some miracle or something. And he'd go walking by, smoothing his whiskers first this way then that—he's very fond of those whiskers of his, and he's always smoothing them down . . .

'Having a rest, are you, lads?' he'd say.

'Yes, Comrade Chapaev, we are . . . ' we'd answer.

'All right then, carry on,' he'd say, and off he'd go. He didn't have to say anything else. He'd spoken to you, that was the main thing, and it made you pleased as Punch. So that's the special kind of man he is!"

"So he's a hero, you say . . . But is he really a hero?" asked Fyodor, probing for more information.

"No doubt about that," said Grisha, jerking his head in a meaningful way. "Just look how he hurried to the Ivashchenkovo[14] factory, for instance. My, how he wanted to save those workers! But he couldn't quite manage it, didn't get there in time . . . He was only a bit late, it's true, but what a lot of workers' blood was shed there all the same, oh my!"

Grisha waved his hand in a quiet gesture and hung his head . . .

Filled with sadness, neither of them spoke for at least a minute. Then Grisha said in a softer voice:

"Some folk say one thing, some say another, but however you look at it, there must have been at least two thousand killed there. The bodies were just laid out in rows between the factory buildings—the whole yard was full of them—mothers and children, and even old women too . . . I'm telling you—they'd shot the lot, no matter who. That's what they'd done, the swine!"

Fyodor could hear Grisha gnashing his teeth in anger as he jerked at the reins.

"Did you see it yourself?" Fyodor asked.

"'Course I did! It was so bad you can hardly bear to talk about it! There was almost nothing left of them—just blood and bits of flesh in the dirt ... The bastards had mowed them down with their machine-guns, no matter who they were!"

"Well, and what did Chapaev do?"

"What could he do? He went crazy with anger, his eyes flashing and his body shaking like a horse that's just been galloping. Then he whipped out his sabre and slashed at a rock with all his might. 'There's going to be a lot of blood shed for all the blood that's been spilt here!' he said. 'We're never going to forget this as long as we live, and we'll have our revenge all right!'"

"And did he get his revenge?"

"He did, and how!" replied Grisha quickly. "He went racing all over the steppe as if he'd gone crazy, and told us not to take a single Cossack prisoner. 'Kill 'em all, the bastards,' he said, 'I'll never forget what happened at the Ivashchenkovo factory!'"

They were silent again for a while. Then Fyodor went on putting questions to Grisha who was only too willing to answer.

"Well, Grisha, and what kind of men did he have with him—his soldiers, I mean—where did they all come from?"

"Why, folk from round these parts, of course—who else could they be? There were fellows like me—laborers off the farms, and poor peasants as well. Then there were some barge haulers too—they'd joined up even before we did ..."

"So was it a regiment you had, then, or what?"

"Yes, we had a regiment when we were in Pugachov, but later on it was mostly just called a detachment. Chapaev himself didn't like to call it a regiment. 'It's a detachment,' he'd say, 'that's right, that sounds more like it ... '"

They drove into Ivanteevka,[15] a large, sprawling village whose wide streets were covered with silvery snow that had been pressed smooth by many wheels. Grisha whipped up the horses, and showing off a little, went racing along at a brisk trot. They drove up to the building that housed the local Soviet, which was situated as usual in the main square where the village administration had formerly been. They clambered out of the sleigh, and treading uncertainly on their numbed feet, took off their sheepskins that were thick with hoar-frost and snow. Then they gathered up their baskets and bundles (pitiful possessions they were too—less than twenty pounds apiece!), and climbed the steps to the Soviet.

The big office was just like any other—uninviting and dull-looking, untidy and dirty.

"Hello, comrades," said Lopar, who had been delayed outside for some reason and was the last to come in.

"Hello," several voices mumbled in reply.

"We'd like to see the chairman . . ."

"He's in there," they answered, pointing to the door of a small room on one side, behind a partition.

Throughout the journey it was Lopar who acted as spokesman for the four travellers. It was he who conducted what negotiations were necessary, he who arranged for fresh horses, found out where they could get something to eat, spend the night and so on.

Fyodor's imagination had been fired by all that Grisha had said, and before him, tormenting, exciting and gladdening him at the same time, stood the legendary figure of Chapaev, ataman of the steppes.

"There's no doubt he's a folk hero," Fyodor thought to himself, "a hero who belongs to the same category of outlaws and freemen as Yemelyan Pugachov,[16] Stenka Razin[17] and Yermak Timofeevich.[18] In their day they accomplished brave deeds, it's true, but Chapaev's living at a quite different time, and his deeds aren't like theirs either. From what Grisha says one might think that the main traits of Chapaev's character are courage and daring. He's really more of a *hero* than a fighter, more a passionate lover of adventure than a conscious revolutionary. The characteristics that are evidently prominent in him and developed to an extreme degree are restlessness and a constant thirst for new impressions. But what an outstanding personality he seems against this historical background of peasant rebellion, and what a picturesque and colorful figure he is!"

An hour and a half later they were driving out of Ivanteevka, and they dozed all the way to Tavolozhka.[19] Arriving there, they made no halt, and after ordering fresh horses, set off straightaway for Pugachov.

As they were leaving Tavolozhka, the peasant drivers kept looking askance at the thick, black clouds drifting like smoke across the dark sky. The wind was fitful and very cold. Blowing from no fixed direction but gusting from all sides at once, as though attacking an invisible enemy, it lunged at him like a watchdog on its chain, sinking its teeth into him and tearing frenziedly at his flesh, but each time being flung off with a gigantic kick. Once more it hurled itself upon him, and again it sprang back infuriated and howling with a convulsive, angry wail. Shaggy snow flurries streaked over the ground, spinning, then racing away. The roads became choked with powdery snow as the twilight of the blizzard descended and swiftly thickened. The wind blew more and more fiercely from every quarter, the sky grew still darker, and the snowflakes whirled higher and higher into the air, spinning in a maelstrom of needle-sharp slivers of ice and swirling snow that drove right into the travellers' faces.

Like moles sheltering deep in their burrows, the passengers sat buried in their sheepskins, while the drivers peered out warily into the gloom. The head wind took their breath away and the biting frost seared their faces. On and on they drove, and the further they went the more wildly the blizzard whirled across the steppe. It was as if the steppe itself were intoxicated by this storm that was so threateningly awesome yet so riotously gay.

It was still about a dozen versts to Pugachov. On the way they met caravans of swaying camels and, here and there, a few lonely horsemen. Many of them probably never reached their homes that night— they either froze to death in the blizzard or were buried in the snow, to be dug out next morning and somehow brought back to life.

A lot of people had been driven into the railway station at Pugachov by the blizzard. When the travellers reached the village and clambered out of their sledges looking like enormous bundles of snow, they were not content simply with sending Lopar on alone as scout, but set out themselves, one to see the station authorities and another to find the local commandant, while the good-natured Bochkin was sent off along the snow-covered tracks to look for a train that might be bound for Uralsk.

After a long search, they finally found a wretched little goods truck in which, as luck would have it, a group of political workers was about to leave for Uralsk. After some explanation, the four travellers climbed in with what few belongings they had. But they had to overcome many more difficulties before they reached Uralsk. Near Yershov[20] the track was covered with snow, so they had to climb down and clear the drifts away. Then the train crawled on again with sickening slowness. They had only got a short distance beyond Yershov when something went wrong with the engine. There was a great deal of fuss, and they had to get off and suffer another long, annoying delay. Next there was trouble with the axle-boxes, which meant yet another stop and still more fuss while running repairs were made, with one new anxiety coming on top of another. As a result it took them two whole days to reach Uralsk, which is really not much more than a stone's throw away from Pugachov!

3. Uralsk

When the four travellers finally reached Uralsk, they telephoned the local commandant from the station. He sent two sledges for them, and climbing in with their few possessions, the friends drove to the Central Hotel. It was terribly cold there, and the rooms were dirty, damp and bare, with nothing to sit or lie down on and nowhere to put their belongings. Somehow, though, they managed to arrange things for themselves, and after having a look round, eventually took a small room, all four of them moving in together as they did not want to be separated.

After draining two samovars of tea one after the other because they were so cold, they found themselves with time on their hands, so set off to wander around the town. On arriving at the station earlier, they had learned that Frunze had left that morning so as to be closer to the front and direct the offensive that had recently been launched. At the time the nearest Cossack positions were no more than twenty versts from Uralsk and it was imperative to drive the enemy back as quickly as possible. These first engagements, incidentally, were not particularly successful for the Red forces and they did not succeed in pushing the Cossacks back until much later, when a more extensive and careful plan had been devised to mount a general offensive from several sectors at the same time—not only from Uralsk, but also from the direction of Alexandrov-Gai.[21] The aim was to attack the large Cossack village of Slomikhinskaya,[22] and having taken it, to cut the high road running from Uralsk through Lbishchensk[23] to Guryev[24]—the road along which the Red forces advancing from the north were to drive the retreating Cossacks.

But of all this later, for everything has its proper place and time, and we shall have occasion to return to the arduous road that leads from Uralsk to Guryev.

***

Fyodor was keeping an accurate diary. Whatever the situation in which he found himself, he always managed to make a note of the most important facts. If he could not write something down in his notebook, then he did so on sheets of paper—perhaps resting on a fence for a few moments while on the march—but he would always be sure to write it all down.

In his diary he usually recorded things which never got into the papers at all, or if they did, were given the most feeble write-up imaginable. Quite why he wrote all this down, he was not really sure—he simply felt a kind of inner need to do so, a need of which he was only dimly aware.

The four friends walked all over the town, back and forth in every direction. Their surroundings were not only new; they were so unusual that they were simply amazing. Wherever they looked they saw soldiers' greatcoats, bayonets and rifles, field guns and military vehicles—the town was a real armed camp. Columns of Red Army men were continually marching through the streets, soldiers could be seen hurrying about on their own, cavalrymen would go galloping by, artillery went rolling slowly past, and caravans of heavily-laden camels swayed majestically by on their way to the forward positions. At that time, though, there was still no conscious, iron discipline in this steppe army, and there were no cadres of politically conscious Bolsheviks in the regiments capable of swiftly transforming them or of giving them proper cohesion and tone. All that would come later, but at the beginning of 1919 it was almost exclusively peasant regiments that were fighting around Uralsk—and they fought magnificently and heroically too—regiments in which there were either no Communists at all or only very few, and half of those were simply masquerading as Bolsheviks.

A few days later, when the Ivanovo-Voznesensk weavers' detachment reached Uralsk and took up positions guarding the town, they came under surreptitious fire from around street corners. This shooting was done by Red Army men belonging to the so-called "free" peasant regiments, whose roisterous behavior was now being curbed by the weavers. But after a very short time, as soon as the peasants saw what the weavers were capable of in battle and how bravely and staunchly they fought, their animosity towards them quickly disappeared, and altogether different and very friendly relations were established between the two forces.

***

There were very few Communists left in Uralsk itself. Some had been killed in action or taken prisoner by the Cossacks, others had been intimidated and forced to flee, and only a handful had remained in the ranks. So most of the political propaganda work in the town was conducted by Bolsheviks who had come from elsewhere.

Tired out by walking to and fro, the friends went back to their cold little box of a room. But just then an orderly arrived from headquarters to tell them that Frunze had returned. In a flash the four were on their feet and hurried away.

They went into Frunze's office. The meeting was extremely friendly, completely without ceremony and sincerely comradely in tone. They all felt that before them was the same unpretentious, approachable comrade whom they had always liked so much. Frunze explained what the situation was at the front and what they could expect, and told them what measures it would be most expedient to take in the immediate future.

Fyodor glanced sideways at Frunze from time to time and was amazed. Where had the man got such a clear understanding of military matters from, and how was it that he had such an unerring grasp of things and never seemed to be at a loss on any question whatsoever? He understood everything with complete ease, took each factor into account and foresaw all eventualities—what a man! And was it really so long ago that he had been no more than a muff of a civilian? Even in those days, though, when Frunze had not been a commander for very long, certain characteristic qualities had manifested themselves clearly in him: the quickness, clarity and depth of his understanding, the ability to make a timely, thorough analysis of a situation and take every detail into account, a confident approach to the solution of problems, and a belief, a colossal belief, in success, a belief, moreover, that was not empty but was well-founded on the facts of the situation.

The five men all sat together, chatting about their native Ivanovo-Voznesensk, their mutual friends and their recent work together, and it was after midnight when they finally broke up. The next morning Frunze left hurriedly for Samara, promising to send them their assignments from there, but saying that in the meantime they should stay in Uralsk and work in the local Party Committee. This casual political work was to keep all four of them busy for a whole week, until they were assigned positions in the army.

***

One evening, after dinner, when they were all together, a telegram arrived to say that Lopar and Bochkin were to leave for Brigade Headquarters the very next day!

It was all over, and the time had come for them to part!

The next morning Bochkin and Lopar climbed into their sleigh, and kissing their friends good-bye, drove away. Then a second telegram arrived. This said that Andreev was to stay in Uralsk and work as commissar in the division, but that Klychkov was to go to Alexandrov-Gai and organize political work in the army group which was being drawn up there and which Chapaev had been appointed to command.

When Fyodor read these words, his heart missed a beat and he could hardly believe it at first. He read the telegram a second, then a third time, but there was no doubt about it.

Chapaev ...

Coursing furiously through his veins, the blood suddenly began to pound in his temples, and for a while he could not speak for sheer excitement.

"A hero like Chapaev!" he thought. "I'll be shoulder to shoulder with him! How amazing it is the way things have turned out! It's really unbelievable! There I was, dreaming about Chapaev as if he were some figure of legend, and all of a sudden it turns out we're going to be together, side by side, just as Andreev and I have been. Perhaps we'll get on well together and even become good friends? Damn it all, it's fascinating the way things have turned out!"

From that moment on Fyodor was possessed by a single thought and filled with a single desire—to see Chapaev just as quickly as possible. No matter what he began to talk about, his conversation would always come back to the subject of Chapaev. From the telegram he gathered Chapaev was not in Alexandrov-Gai at the moment and was only about to go there, but that made no difference, no difference at all ... Fyodor still had to hurry to Alexandrov-Gai straightaway! He did not even wait till the next morning, but was ready to leave Uralsk in three hours. Andreev and he said good-bye to each other, their words of parting simple but full of sincere feeling. Then, leaving his friend behind, Fyodor drove away.

4. Alexandrov-Gai

Fyodor had been assured that the train would get him to Algai (short for Alexandrov-Gai) practically the next day. But then it turned out he would have to change in Yershov, Urbakh and Krasny Kut.[25] Three changes was no laughing matter! Anyone who made a journey by train in 1919 will tell you that to make three changes was a most difficult and wearisome business. Working things out roughly, Fyodor calculated that the journey would take him about a week and a half, so after thinking it over, he changed his mind, got off the train at Dergachi,[26] and set off for Alexandrov-Gai on post-horses—a distance of a hundred and fifty versts as the crow flies.

Once again it was open steppe with its blue horizon and boundless expanse of snow. But here and there the snow had melted and knolls of bare earth showed up black against the whiteness. When there was no strong wind blowing and the sun shone, it was quite warm. That meant spring would soon come dancing gaily in. Out here in the steppe the villages were few—it might be twenty-five or thirty versts from one to the next, and each of them lived its own withdrawn life. Each was like a small republic—it felt completely independent, and being quite convinced that it had no need of anyone or anything from the outside world, had a tendency to be totally self-sufficient. These villages between Uralsk and Algai played an enormously important part in the history of the Civil War in the Ural steppes. Among them were Osinov-Gai, Orlov-Gai and Kurilovo.[27] Not only did they contribute individual volunteers to the Red Army, but also provided entire regiments. It is true, too, that a good many kulaks left these villages to join the Whites, but there is no doubt that the Reds always enjoyed the numerical advantage. When, for example, the Cossacks broke into Kurilovo in 1918, and acting on information supplied by the village kulaks, began to hunt down workers belonging to the local Soviet, the entire mass of villagers rose in revolt, and arming themselves with whatever came to hand, killed most of the Cossacks and drove the rest out of the village. There and then the workers decided to form their own regiment—the Kurilovo regiment it was called. It was in much the same way that the other local regiments were formed too: the Domashkin, Pugachov, Stenka Razin, Novouzensk, Malouzensk and Krasny Kut regiments. Originally they had been formed to protect their native villages, and both commanders and soldiers (there were no commissars to begin with) came from the same place. It goes without saying, therefore, that they were an incredibly close-knit group. The men had known each other for many years, they were often old friends, and many were even related. In the Kurilovo Regiment, for example, there was a father and his five sons. There were also instances, of course, when formerly close friends suddenly separated, one fleeing with the Whites and the other staying behind to become a Red Army soldier in his village regiment. There were even more striking cases, too, when members of the same family broke up, some going over to the Whites and some joining the Reds.

All these local regiments were soon forced by the course of events to leave their native areas and push deep into the Ural steppes. From there they marched against Kolchak and then came back to the steppes again, before being transferred to the Polish front to fight the White Poles.

Among other regiments the most meritorious and heroic was the Moslem Regiment, which comprised men of fourteen nationalities. The majority of them, though, were Kirghiz, a people who till then had been ruthlessly exploited by wealthy, bloodsucking Cossacks for whom they felt an indomitable, bitter hatred.

These volunteer regiments performed truly heroic exploits. Often without cartridges or shells, insufficiently equipped and poorly armed, badly clothed and practically barefoot, they would stubbornly hold their ground and fight with immense courage, time after time defeating the Ural Cossacks who had risen against the Soviet government. In the military sense they were invariably first-class soldiers to a man, though politically they were rather slow to mature and found it hard to understand both the causes and scale of the enormous social struggle that was unfolding at the time. Lax discipline, together with their own peculiar notion of what "freedom" meant, stubborn resistance to the principle of appointment by election, and a poor understanding of instructions and directives issuing from Headquarters—these were the features which for a long time distinguished such spirited and wholly peasant volunteer regiments from those of central Russia to the north.

Alexandrov-Gai was not very different from the other "Gai's" such as Orlov-Gai and Osinov-Gai, or probably from any other steppe village, for they were all rather alike. It was large and straggling, its streets muddy in the center and virtually impassable on the outskirts. In those days, though, Alexandrov-Gai was an extremely busy place, for it housed Brigade Headquarters, the army's Political Department, various command sections and several military units. There was brisk traffic passing in all directions and contact was maintained both with the fighting units and the command posts controlling operations. There was a constant stream of vehicles with people arriving and leaving all the time and cavalrymen forever hurrying off somewhere, while military baggage went crawling by loaded on peasant carts or swaying on the backs of haughty camels. Vehicles were constantly being loaded and unloaded, goods being hauled up and carried away—in fact, Alexandrov-Gai seethed with life in a way it had probably never done before nor ever has since.

***

Around the beginning of March the Red forward positions were near Port Arthur,[28] a practically devastated hamlet situated on the road leading to the large Cossack village of Slomikhinskaya, itself only a few dozen versts from Alexandrov-Gai. By passing through Slomikhinskaya it was possible to come out on to the high road running from Uralsk through Lbishchensk and Sakharnaya[29] to Guryev. The Red Army, then based in Uralsk, was scheduled to launch a general offensive in the very near future, and by means of combined action to drive the enemy back as far as possible from Uralsk, then to destroy the White Cossack Army entirely. From Alexandrov-Gai an attack was to be made on the village of Slomikhinskaya, and after that the offensive was to be developed through the Chizha swamps,[30] before coming out on to the Uralsk-Guryev highroad. This maneuver was designed to cut off the retreat of the Cossack units withdrawing from the Uralsk area under pressure from Red forces. The day when the offensive would be launched was drawing near, and the Algai brigade was now making its preparations with feverish haste.

As soon as Fyodor arrived in the village, he went to the Political Section. To begin with he decided to make himself thoroughly acquainted with the actual state of political work in the brigade by looking through the various documents and reports available. Next, he decided to call small conferences and meetings of the Party cells, cultural commissions, economic control councils, military committee boards and so on. This would enable him to find out a great deal of information in a very short time.

After that he intended to visit the various military units so as to see for himself what state the political work was in on the ground. Finally, he wanted to take part personally as a rank-and-file soldier in the fighting to come, and so earn for himself the reputation of a courageous, fine comrade. This last factor would be crucial for the success or failure of all his political work in the future.

During the next few days, right up until the start of the offensive, Fyodor doggedly did his best to accomplish the tasks he had set himself, but it was only with great difficulty that he managed to gain a reasonably detailed impression of the state of political activity in the brigade as a whole.

The work was not going well, though, and things could not continue like that for very long. He was waiting impatiently for Chapaev to arrive, for only this, he believed, could cut the Gordian knot and clarify the confused situation that existed at the moment.

***

The day after next the offensive was due to begin. But why had Chapaev not arrived yet? Fyodor sent an inquiry to headquarters but received no reply. Tomorrow the last units were to move up to Kazachya Talovka[31] and Port Arthur so as to be in position for the start of the offensive.

The final meeting had been called at headquarters and the detailed plan of attack was discussed for the last time. It was to be mounted from three different directions at once and relied for its success not so much on surprise as on good organization and Red superiority in equipment—machine-guns for the most part.

For the whole of that day and throughout the evening too, one baggage train after another left Alexandrov-Gai for Kazachya Talovka, and the village became almost deserted. The next morning the last few units would leave too, and then Algai would be left unprotected and desolate.

5. Chapaev

Early in the morning—it was only about five or six o'clock—someone knocked loudly on Fyodor's door. He opened it to find a stranger standing there.

"Hello!" said the man. "I'm Chapaev!"

Fyodor's drowsiness was gone in a flash, just as if someone had struck him a sudden blow, and an instant later he was wide awake. He quickly looked Chapaev in the face then stretched out his hand rather hastily, doing his best to remain calm.

"My name's Klychkov," he said. "Have you been here long?"

"No, I've just come from the station . . . My lads are still down there . . . I've sent some horses for them, though."

Fyodor scanned Chapaev with a swift, searching gaze, impatient both to discover and understand everything about him just as quickly as he could. So it is that on a dark night at the front a probing searchlight sweeps keenly to and fro, thrusting into every nook and cranny as it tries to drive the darkness away and lay bare the bashful nakedness of the earth.

"Chapaev is an ordinary-looking man," Fyodor wrote in his diary later, "of medium height, lean and not very strong-looking, with slender, almost feminine hands. His sparse, dark brown hair clings to his forehead in thin strands. His nose is short, narrow and sensitive-looking, his eyebrows are thin and straight, and his lips are thin too, while his teeth are shining white. He is clean-shaven except for a magnificent sergeant-major mustache. His quick eyes are light blue, almost green in color, and they are intelligent and unblinking. His complexion is fresh and clear, without any wrinkles or blemishes, and his face is not at all shiny. He was wearing a khaki service tunic, dark blue trousers and deerskin top-boots, and was carrying a cap decorated with a red band. The tunic had shoulder-straps and there was a revolver at his hip. His silver sabre and green jacket were lying on my trunk where he had flung them down . . . " That was how Fyodor described Chapaev in his diary that evening.

Everybody knows that the first thing anyone feels like after a long journey is a good drink of tea, but Chapaev did not want any. He remained on his feet while he was talking, and sent one of his orderlies off to find the brigade commander and tell him to go to headquarters where he himself would soon follow. Shortly afterwards the fellows who had accompanied Chapaev to Alexandrov-Gai came bursting into the room in a noisy crowd, and tossed their belongings into every corner. They flung their caps and gloves on the windowsills, tables and chairs, threw down their revolvers, and unhooking grenades from their belts, carelessly pushed them in among all the weathered gloves and caps. They had stern-looking, sunburnt faces, their voices were deep and gruff, and their movements awkward and clumsy, while their speech was uncouth and slipshod but at the same time forceful and convincing. Some of them had such a strange way of speaking that one might have thought they were quarrelling all the time. They would ask something in an abrupt, harsh manner, and the others would answer in the same curt tone, almost as if they were angry. And they kept flinging things around the room the whole time . . . After a short while the entire building was resounding with their noisy conversation.

Just a couple of minutes after they had appeared, Fyodor saw one of the newcomers sprawl on his unmade bed, prop his feet up against the wall, and lighting a cigarette, start flicking the ash off to one side, doing his level best to make it fall on Fyodor's small suitcase that was standing close by. Another put his full weight on the frail little dressing-table, which gave a creak, then cracked and slumped to one side. A third smashed a pane out of the window with his revolver butt, while another put his stinking, dirty sheepskin over the loaf of bread on the table so that when they came to eat it later, it smelled absolutely vile.

Chapaev, though, was different from the others. He seemed to have absorbed a little culture, at least, and did not look quite as boorish or behave quite as crudely as the rest. He was like a fiery steed of the steppes that is being held firmly in check on a tight rein. The way his companions behaved towards him was rather different too. Among themselves, they behaved completely without constraint. They would blurt out whatever came into their heads, one giving another a wallop with his cup or spoon, kicking him with his boot or perhaps even splashing him with hot tea from his glass. But as soon as Chapaev joined them, they never took any such liberties with him. It was not because they were afraid of him or felt inferior to him in any way, but because they regarded him with a peculiar kind of respect. It was as if they said to themselves: "Though he's one of us all right, he's still in a special class by himself, and it's not for any old Tom, Dick and Harry to try and be his equal."

This feeling made itself apparent the whole time, and however free and easy their behavior was, however much noise they made and however lustily they swore, as soon as Chapaev came on to the scene, the situation changed in a flash. That was their way of showing how much they respected and loved him.

"I'm leaving in two hours," said Chapaev, "so see the horses are ready! And send some mounted men ahead too!"

Then he issued further orders:

"The commissar here will be going as well, so send a mounted escort of three men. The rest of you will follow us to Talovka. And don't be sparing with the horses either—make sure you get there by evening!"

Long before he met Chapaev, Fyodor had made up his mind to establish a special, careful relationship with him. To begin with he would avoid discussion about purely military matters so as not to reveal his complete ignorance of such things. Instead, he would engage Chapaev in political conversations in which he, Fyodor, would undoubtedly have the upper hand. He would try to draw Chapaev out, encouraging him to speak frankly, getting him to give his opinion on every kind of issue, and even leading him to reveal personal idiosyncrasies and intimate details about himself. For his part, Fyodor would talk more about general education and learning, and here Chapaev would listen rather than speak. And then ... then Fyodor would show himself to be a brave soldier—it was absolutely essential that he do this and as quickly as possible too, otherwise everything would be lost not only as far as Chapaev was concerned, but also probably as far as all the men were concerned too, for without bravery as a soldier no amount of politics or education would be worth a thing! Then, when this work of preparation was done and Chapaev had opened up a little, so enabling Fyodor to understand him better, Fyodor could attempt to become close friends with him. But for the time being he must proceed very cautiously! He must ensure, too, that his attentiveness and courtesy towards Chapaev were not seen as attempts to curry favor with the "hero." (Chapaev, of course, knew perfectly well that his fame resounded far and wide, and that many people would be flattered to be able to call themselves his friends.) Only later, when Chapaev had become Fyodor's "intellectual captive," so to speak, when he had begun to listen to him of his own accord and perhaps to learn something from him—only then would Fyodor be able to meet him halfway in everything. But he must not put on any airs—no, not for anything in the world! Instead, from the very start, he must make simplicity, warmth and a certain degree of coarseness the basis of their relationship so that Chapaev would not think of him as a lily-livered intellectual of the kind that was always regarded at the front with suspicion and undisguised contempt.

All these preparations of Fyodor's were by no means insignificant, because they enabled him in the most rapid and reliable way to feel more at home in the new working environment in which he now found himself, and helped him to become an organic part of it. He did not know yet exactly how far this process of "growing together" would go, but he realized full well that Chapaev and his men—all this semi-partisan mass and its highly unusual activities—were an extremely complex phenomenon which one could not afford to approach without having one's eyes completely open. Though it possessed many positive qualities, it also displayed features which one had to treat with great caution and watch with unremitting vigilance.

Just what kind of a man was Chapaev? How did Fyodor see him, and why had he decided to establish this particular, subtle relationship with him? Was it really necessary to do so?

While still working in the rear, Fyodor had of course heard and read a great deal about the "popular heroes" who suddenly made a spectacular name for themselves on one front or another during the Civil War. When he had looked more closely at them, he had seen that the majority came from the peasantry and very few from the urban proletariat. Working-class heroes were always of a different kind. Raised as he had been in a large industrial center and accustomed as he was to the well-organized and extensive political activity of the weavers, Fyodor had always looked rather askance at the semi-anarchistic, partisan activities of popular heroes like Chapaev. But this did not prevent him from following them with the closest attention or from being delighted by their heroic exploits. He always felt rather wary of them, though, and did so on this occasion too.

"Chapaev is a hero," Fyodor reasoned, "and he embodies all the irrepressible anger and spontaneous protest that have built up in the peasantry over many long years. But God alone knows how such characteristics may develop and what they may turn into! There have been instances (and they have not been few either!) when a fine commander like Chapaev has suddenly gone and bumped off his commissar! And the man wasn't some useless windbag or coward either, but an outstanding, brave revolutionary! Or then again the commander might go over to the Whites altogether, taking his band of partisans with him . . . "

It was because of Fyodor's suspicious attitude towards this uncontrolled guerrilla element that he had decided to establish a relationship with his new milieu in the most careful fashion, and to do so in such a way that he himself would not be swallowed up by his new environment, but on the contrary would exert an ideological influence upon everything in it. He had to start at the top—with Chapaev, the leader, and so it was towards him that Fyodor directed all his efforts and on him that he concentrated all his attention.

"Is everything ready?" Chapaev asked. "Let's go, then!" and he got up quickly from his chair.

Everyone made way for him and he went out of the room first, just as he had come into it.

Outside, near the porch, a crowd of Red Army men had gathered—they had heard about Chapaev's arrival. Many of them had fought with him as long ago as 1918, several knew him personally, and of course every single one of them had heard of him. They stood craning their necks, their eyes shining with wonder and delight and their eager smiles stretching almost up to their ears.

"Long live Chapaev!" yelled someone at the front of the crowd almost before the commander had reached the bottom of the steps.

"Hurrah! Hurrah!"

Now Red Army men were running up from all directions, and as they were soon joined by villagers, the crowd quickly grew.

"Comrades!" said Chapaev.

There was instant silence.

"I've not got time to talk to you now because I'm on my way to the front. But tomorrow we'll be seeing each other up there because we've got a tasty little dish ready for the Cossacks and we're going to give them a treat . . . So we'll be able to have a talk later on, but for now—good-bye!"

Once again the hurrahs rolled out over the crowd. Then Chapaev got into his sleigh and one of his orderlies squeezed in beside him. A mounted escort of three men was waiting to accompany them and a spirited black stallion had been led up for Fyodor to ride.

"Let's go!" cried Chapaev.

The horses lunged forward and shouting louder still, the crowd parted to let the escort and sleigh pass. Away they rode between two lines of cheering Red Army men right to the outskirts of Algai.

The desolate, snow-covered expanse of steppe was monotonous and dreary. During the recent warm spell the steppe mounds had lost their blanket of snow and the bare ground had begun to show through in places, but the fresh blizzards had covered them once more and the new snow crunched in the frost. The horses trotted gaily along with the mounted escort following three or four yards behind the sleigh, no more and no less, always at the same distance, as though they were chained there. Fyodor, though, rode a little to one side and now and then would fall back until the others were a whole verst ahead, then he would put his horse into a full gallop! How good it was to race over the steppe on a horse that was so light on its feet and so eager to gallop!

"Tomorrow," he thought as he rode along at an easy trot, "will see the beginning of my career as a soldier, the start of real life for me ... But how long will it last, I wonder? Who knows what fate holds in store for me? Who can say when the day of victory will come? And when *will* it come, that victory of ours? Day after day will go racing by, while we are on the march or in battle, surrounded all the while by anxiety and danger ... Will we, frail wisps of down that we are, really survive? Which of us will return to our native places and which will remain here, lying in the dark ravines or on the snowy wastes of the steppe?"

About two and a half hours went by in this way. Then Chapaev apparently got tired of sitting still, so he stopped the sleigh and putting one of the escorts in his place, took the man's horse himself. He came riding up to Fyodor.

"So we're to be together now, Comrade Commissar, are we?" he asked.

"Yes," replied Fyodor, and immediately noticed how firmly Chapaev sat on his horse, almost as though he were welded to the saddle.

"Been fighting long, then?" Chapaev asked.

Fyodor felt as though Chapaev were grinning and he detected a note of sarcasm in his voice.

"No, I'm only just beginning ..."

"So you've been in the rear up till now, have you?" asked Chapaev again, and once more his tone seemed mocking.

(One should realize that for soldiers like Chapaev, a man serving in the rear was the most unworthy and contemptible of creatures. Fyodor had suspected this earlier, but during the last few weeks he had become fully convinced of it, having talked on many occasions with commanders and rank-and-file soldiers alike.)

"In the rear, d'you say? I was working in Ivanovo-Voznesensk..." said Fyodor, trying to sound nonchalant.

"Is that on the far side of Moscow?"

"Yes, about three hundred versts," replied Fyodor.

"Well, and what's it like there? How are things going?" asked Chapaev.

Fyodor was glad at the change of subject, and snatching eagerly at this last question, explained to Chapaev what a hungry, difficult life the weavers in Ivanovo-Voznesensk had.

"So life's hard for them, eh?" said Chapaev earnestly. "And it's all because they've not got enough food. If they had enough to eat—why, then everything would be quite different... And all the while this lot are stuffing themselves, the sons of bitches, without giving a damn about..."

"Who are stuffing themselves?" asked Fyodor, not understanding what Chapaev meant.

"The Cossacks... they don't give a damn about anything!"

"Yes, but they're not all like that!"

"Yes they are, the whole lot of 'em!" cried Chapaev. "You don't know them yet, but I'm telling you they're all the same! And it's no good trying to persuade me they're not, either!"

Then Chapaev began to mumble irritably as he rode along.

"But they can't all be like that," Fyodor protested. "Maybe some of them are, but there are others who are on our side. Why, just a minute," he added excitedly, remembering something, "what about our mounted scouts in the brigade here—aren't they all Cossacks?"

"In the brigade?" asked Chapaev, becoming a little thoughtful.

"Yes, yes—right here, in our brigade!"

"But they must be from the town... they could hardly be from round these parts," replied Chapaev, reluctantly giving in to Fyodor's arguments.

"I don't know whether they're from the town or not, but they're certainly in our brigade all right... And anyway, it's just not possible, Comrade Chapaev, that all the Cossacks, every single one of them, are against us. It just can't be like that!"

"Why not? When you've been with us a little while, then . . ."

"No, however long I stay, it'll make no difference—I'll never believe it!" Fyodor's voice was steady and stern now.

"Well, there might be the odd one or two, but there's no point talking about them," said Chapaev, beginning to back down a little. "Of course, there's one here and there, but they don't amount to many really, hardly any at all . . ."

"No, it's not just individuals . . . You're wrong there. People are writing from Turkestan to say Cossack regiments have set up Soviet government over a whole region, and the same thing's happening in the Ukraine and down on the Don as well . . . So doesn't all that count either?"

"Well, you can keep on hoping if you like, but they'll show you soon enough, the bastards!"

"But why should I hope? I'm not hoping for anything," Fyodor explained. "There's a lot of truth in what you say. It's true the Cossacks are like a flock of filthy carrion-crows, it's quite true. Who can possibly argue against that? That's why the Tsarist government took such good care of them. But just you look at the young Cossacks—now they're nothing like the old ones. And it's mostly the young ones who come over to our side. Of course, it's much harder for the old graybeards to accept the Soviet regime . . . at least, it's hard for the time being, till they've understood things properly. After all, they think terrible things about us and believe everything they hear. They say we're turning churches into cowsheds, that we've got all our women in common, that we're forcing everyone to live together and making them all eat and drink at the same table . . . So how on earth can a Cossack reconcile himself to that when for generations he's been used to the Church, to having plenty of everything on his wealthy farm, to hiring peasants to work for him and to enjoying a free life out in the steppe?"

"They're all expl—-oiters," declared Chapaev, getting the word out only with difficulty, "that's what they are!"

"Precisely," said Fyodor, suppressing a smile. "It's exploitation that lies at the root of all the trouble. When everything's said and done, the rich Cossacks don't only exploit the non-Cossack peasants and Kirghiz folk around them—they don't even balk at exploiting their fellow Cossacks either. And that's where discord sets in. But it's only the old folk, even when they've suffered as well, who have reconciled themselves to the situation, because they reckon that's how God meant things to be. The young people look at the situation in a much simpler, bolder way, though—that's why it's mostly young folk who come over to us. You can't alter the old ones—the only way to change them is with a gun!"

"It's our command centers—that's what's wrong..." said Chapaev, dropping another vague but intriguing phrase.

"What command centers?" asked Fyodor.

"Why, they've gone and shoved in all kinds of swine there," Chapaev muttered as though to himself but loudly enough for Fyodor to hear.

Chapaev had now got on to the thing that annoyed him most of all—the question of headquarters and their staffs, generals, orders and the disciplinary action taken for failing to execute them—a question that in those days used to infuriate many men, and not only those like Chapaev.

"But you can't manage without generals," Fyodor said quietly in a reassuring tone. "How could you fight a war if you had no generals?"

"We'd manage without 'em all right!" answered Chapaev, gripping the reins tightly.

"But we couldn't, Comrade Chapaev! You can't get very far with nothing but daring—you need knowledge as well. But what knowledge have we got? And who can provide it apart from the generals? After all, they've studied that kind of thing, so it's their job to teach us. The day will come when we'll have our own teachers, but for the time being we haven't got any. Have we? Of course we haven't! And because we haven't, we'll just have to learn from others!"

"Learn? That's a good one! And what the hell can they teach us? Just tell me that!" retorted Chapaev heatedly. "D'you think they can tell us what to do? Not on your life! I was at that Academy of theirs myself and I hung around there for two months like a fish out of water, then I thought to hell with it and came back here again. There's just nothing for people like me to do there. One of them, Pechkin he was called, some professor or other—bald as a coot he was—says to me at the exam: 'D'you know the River Rhine?' he says. Well, I'd been all through the German war, so how on earth couldn't I know it? But I thought to myself, why the hell should I answer him? 'No,' I says, 'I don't. But d'you know the River Solyanka?' Well, he just stared at me in amazement, because he'd not been expecting that. Then he says 'No, I don't,' he says. 'But why?' 'Then there's no point asking questions!' I says. 'I was wounded on the Solyanka, and I crossed it back and forth five times, so what the hell do I care about that Rhine of yours,' I says, 'what the devil's it got to do with me? But down on the Solyanka I know every single hummock because we were fighting the Cossacks there!'"

Fyodor burst out laughing and looked at Chapaev in astonishment. "What childish ideas this popular hero has!" he thought. "To each his own, it seems—some can acquire knowledge, while others find it quite impossible. This fellow spent two months at the Academy but didn't get anything out of it at all, didn't understand a damn thing. He's got brains all right, though—it's just that he's very green and needs a lot of polishing."

"You weren't at the Academy very long," said Fyodor. "You can't possibly learn everything in two months. It's hard going . . ."

"Might just as well not have been there at all," answered Chapaev, waving his hand in a dismissive gesture. "You can't teach me anything—I know all there is to know!"

"What d'you mean, can't teach you anything?" retorted Fyodor. "A person can always learn something new."

"Yes, but not there!" Chapaev countered excitedly. "I know there's things to learn and what's more I'll learn them too! Now I'm going to tell you something . . . What did you say your name was?"

"Klychkov."

"Well I'll tell you, Comrade Klychkov, that I'm very nearly illiterate. I only learned to write four years ago and I'm thirty-five now, you know! I've lived all my life in ignorance, you might say. Well, never mind—we'll talk about that some other time. Now that must be Talovka we can see, over there . . ."

Chapaev spurred on his horse and Fyodor did likewise. Ten minutes later they were riding into Kazachya Talovka.

6. The Battle of Slomikhinskaya

Kazachya Talovka was a tiny village that had been almost completely burnt to the ground. Only three dingy adobe huts had been left standing and smoke-blackened, naked chimneys were sticking up awkwardly on every side. The hut where Chapaev's party had stopped was crammed with Red Army men, some sitting and others lying on the floor. They had all crowded in here to wait for the order to march.

The fog hanging over the steppe had made the twilight deeper still and it was quite dark in the hut, but the soldiers had found the end of a church candle somewhere and had stuck it on a saucer. A map lay spread out on the table and everybody had crowded round it, discussing details of the next morning's attack. Chapaev sat in the middle of a bench leaning on the table with a pair of compasses in one hand and a sharpened pencil in the other. Regimental, battalion and company commanders as well as rank-and-file soldiers pressed close around him in a dense ring. Some were resting their elbows on the table and others were bending over it, but all were watching intently as Chapaev measured off various distances on the map, his shining compasses striding over the paper like a long-legged little crane. Fyodor and Popov, one of Chapaev's orderlies, were sitting beside him on the bench. This was not really a proper conference—Chapaev was simply taking the opportunity to acquaint his commanders with the tasks facing them and to warn them of the difficulties ahead.

They were all listening in silence, some of them making a note of his orders and the advice he offered. The solemn stillness was broken only by Chapaev's authoritative voice and by the whistling and snoring of the sleeping men close by.

Soon the rest of Chapaev's party arrived from Alexandrov-Gai and came piling into the hut which was now terribly crowded.

Chapaev went on with his instructions:

"If we don't do it right away, we might as well not do it at all! It must be done all at once! We've got to jump on the enemy so fast he won't have a chance of getting away! Send everyone off from here in two hours' time, d'you understand? We've got to be at Port Arthur before sunrise. We must do everything while it's still dark, before it gets properly light, d'you understand?"

Those around him nodded and answered softly:

"Yes, we understand. Of course it's all got to be done in the dark. The dark's what we need . . ."

"You've all got your orders," Chapaev went on, "and I've put down the times and places for you—where to make a halt and when to move off again. You've got to believe, lads, that everything's going to turn out right—that's the most important thing. And if you don't believe we're going to win, you'd better not attack at all. I've put down the times and places for you, but that's not enough to win—you've got to finish the job yourselves. And the most important thing of all is to be careful—nobody must know we're going into the attack—not for anything. If they find out, it'll all be ruined. So if you happen to bump into a Cossack or Kirghiz or even a peasant on the way—it doesn't matter who it is—then hold on to him and don't let him go. We'll sort him out later!"

The business part of the discussion drew to a close.

The men sang and joked till midnight, then curled up wherever they could in the hut and fell asleep.

The attack had been planned in such a way that they should be approaching Slomikhinskaya just as it was beginning to get light. They were to attack in regimental strength from three directions at the same time. The regiment now in Talovka was to advance in the center and attack the village itself, while the other two were to skirt it and swinging round in a semi-circle, strike from the flanks.

It had been arranged that the regiment now in Talovka would leave in carts in about an hour and a half's time. For the moment, though, all was still quiet, and there were no signs of the coming battle.

Fyodor could not sleep. He too had tried to make himself comfortable on the floor of the hut, with his head resting on a cold Cossack saddle, but no, he could not get to sleep! Either he wasn't used to sleeping on saddles or it was the irrepressible sense of unease that filled him on this, the night before his first battle.

But how little it mattered to the others! They had been in action dozens of times before—shell-shocked again and again, their bones broken, their heads punctured and their bodies riddled with bullets—what was it to them? For them there was nothing unusual about this particular night at all. It was the night before a battle—but so what? They had snored their way through many such nights—and this one was no different from any other.

Feeling he would never fall asleep, Fyodor made his way out of the hut. Wouldn't he feel better, he wondered, in the bracing, frosty air outside? The night was quiet and dark—a real steppe night, and high in the sky the stars shone green. The wind was light and free, the kind of wind that only blows over the steppe.

No matter how many times afterwards Fyodor had to spend the night waiting for a battle the next day, all these nights resembled one another in their gloomy grandeur and somber gravity. On a night like this, stepping over the sleeping soldiers as he passed along the waiting skirmish lines, his head would be filled with thoughts of the struggle to come, the suffering it would bring, and those nameless men who had already sacrificed themselves and whose worm-eaten corpses were now rotting on the battlefields of the Civil War.

"Here they lie," he would think, "these soldiers who are exhausted by their endless marches, and tomorrow, at the first glimmer of dawn, they will go into action once more. And many of them will never rise from the battlefield again, but motionless and silent, will remain lying out on the desolate steppe ... Each of them, so small and lonely now, will be left behind to be pecked by the carrion-crows, and after coming to the front in such an unspectacular way, they will leave the ranks without so much as a trace. Each one of them will have given all he possessed, and leaving nothing behind him, silently, with no beating of drums, recognized by nobody and honored by none, he will fall imperceptibly out of the ranks, like a tiny little cog that is lost from an enormous, fire-spitting monster of steel ..."

Fyodor went back into the hut, lay down—and fell fast asleep.

***

It was still completely dark when they saddled their horses and trotted out of Talovka towards Port Arthur. They were all shivering and kept giving enormous yawns because they had not had enough sleep and were nervous about what awaited them. It is cold and raw out in the steppe before dawn, and the chill seems to send sharp, icy needles through one's greatcoat and shirt.

They rode on without talking, and not until they had almost reached Port Arthur and the first bursts of shrapnel began to flash in the murky sky, did Chapaev turn to Fyodor and say:

"It's started..."

"Yes..."

They fell silent again and did not say another word until they reached the hamlet itself. Then they spurred on their horses, and as they began to gallop, their hearts kept lurching and missing a beat with that inexplicable, strange excitement that always fills a man as he approaches the battlefield, no matter whether he is cowardly or daring, timid or bold. No one is calm, and it is only boastful nonsense to say there are people who are completely calm under fire or in battle, because there is nobody like that in the whole human race. It is possible to grow used to appearing calm and to behaving with dignity, managing to control oneself and not giving way to the effect of one's surroundings—that is an altogether different matter. But no one is really calm either in battle or just before a battle—no one, and no one can possibly be so either.

Both Chapaev, the battle-hardened soldier, and Fyodor, the raw novice, were now overwhelmed by this amazing feeling. It was not terror at what lay ahead or the fear of death, but a tautening of all their inner strings to the very highest pitch, an extreme acuteness of thought and awareness, and an incomprehensible, astonishing sense of haste. Fyodor was about to ask Chapaev something, wanting to find out what he was thinking and probe his state of mind, but seeing the serious, almost angry expression on his face, he remained silent. They rode into Port Arthur. The baggage carts had already arrived and their peasant drivers were sitting huddled amid the charred ruins of the burnt-out village, pouring hot tea from their kettles and eating breakfast with great appetite. Chapaev sprang from his horse and climbing on to a high wall made of pressed dung, looked out through his field glasses towards where the shells were bursting. The gloom of early dawn had melted away now and it was quite light. After halting for a few minutes, they remounted and galloped on.

Ahead of them, both moving up to the front and returning from it, lines of carts were steadily crawling along. The first were loaded with ammunition or were empty, on their way to pick up the wounded, while those coming back were invariably carrying one and the same terrible burden—human bodies covered with blood.

Away to the right, across the Uzen River, were several Kirghiz villages, from which the Cossacks had now been driven by the Reds' fire. On the far side of the river two Red Army scouts could be seen walking about, peering into all the gullies and looking behind the heaps of dried dung to see if any wounded comrades were lying there. Nearer and nearer, louder and louder roared the Red battery, and the shells began to fall closer and closer, their bursts growing more and more visible. Now the Red skirmish lines were showing up dark in the distance.

Fyodor and Chapaev walked side by side, leading their horses by the bridle.

It was now about half a verst to the first skirmish line, and when they reached it, Chapaev and Fyodor separated and rode off along opposite flanks. To the right the hamlet of Ovchinnikov came into view.

They were approaching Slomikhinskaya now, and the village was only one and a half or two versts away. They were advancing across a wide, flat plain that could easily be shelled from the village, but the Cossack guns there were silent. What could it mean? The ominous stillness was far more terrible than any shelling. Were the enemy not cunningly preparing something or perhaps getting a trap ready? The only brush with them so far had been on the other bank of the Uzen, but on this side everything was quiet.

Chapaev was galloping to and fro at top speed, busy maintaining contact between the various regiments, giving orders about the supply of shells and enquiring about the baggage carts.

Fyodor rode from one end of the skirmish line to the other, then returning to the right flank, dismounted and walked along beside the men in the line, leading his horse by the bridle. The Red battery had concentrated its fire now, but the village was still just as silent as before. While it remained so, Fyodor walked calmly along in the line, cracking jokes, making rather a pose of his coolness and pretending to be quite familiar with such things. He practically made himself out to be an old veteran begrimed by the smoke of powder.

Letting the Reds approach to within about five hundred yards, the Cossacks suddenly opened fire with their artillery, and then from the windmills on the outskirts of the village machine-guns began to lash the skirmish lines. Fyodor immediately lost his head, though he did not show that something seemed to have turned over deep inside him and gone terribly cold, as if all of a sudden his hot innards had been flooded with a stream of ice-cold peppermint drops. For a few more moments he walked on in the line as before, but then he began to drift away from the others and lagged behind until he was at the rear, sheltering behind his horse.

Suddenly the line dropped to the ground, then sprang up again and lunged forward in a rush before dropping down once more, the men hurriedly digging shallow little holes in the snow to hide their heads in. Still sheltering behind his horse, Fyodor made a couple of rushes too, but then leapt into the saddle and went galloping off. But where to? He did not really know. He had no desire to escape from the battle, but only to get away from this particular place and to go somewhere else where the bullets might not be whining so furiously and where the danger might not be so terribly near. Off he went, galloping along the skirmish line, though he was no longer in front of it but behind it now, racing towards its extreme left flank. The expression on his face was most business-like and serious, and anyone seeing him would never have thought he was galloping away in fright. Instead, you would have been absolutely convinced that he was carrying an extremely important message or racing to a difficult spot on very urgent business.

Then, as though solving the problem of where he should gallop to, a young Red Army cavalryman came racing up from the left flank and muttered in a breathless whisper:

"Where's the machine-guns here? Where's the machine-guns?"

"What machine-guns?" asked Fyodor.

"We've got to have some machine-guns—the Cossacks are charging on the left flank!"

Fyodor immediately realized that this brave warrior was in the same state as he was, but glancing towards where the man was pointing, he saw a black mass of Cossack cavalry sweeping over the snow not far away. An icy chill flooded his chest and his hair stood on end.

"I'll send some from the baggage train right away!" he cried, and whipping up his horse, galloped off to the rear.

When he reached the baggage carts, he did not know what to say. The drivers kept looking at him askance and exchanged knowing smiles—they evidently suspected why this young fellow had suddenly come to join them.

Fyodor realized he had given the game away, and he was tormented by shame. He could not really start laughing or talking with the drivers, nor could he ride away either—after all, where could he go to now? So he hung around like a lost soul by the baggage carts for about an hour and a half. He asked the men for a light, enquired about axle-grease and fodder, tinned goods and bread. He asked them about their native villages too—were they close by or far away? But nothing came of it. His questions seemed empty and stupid, and they meant nothing to anyone. The drivers seemed reluctant to talk to him and moved away in a rather insulting, offhand fashion. Like venomous worms ulcerating and riddling his heart, the minutes crawled agonizingly by, as if taking vengeance on him for his cowardice and disgrace.

The thunder of the guns echoed over the steppe, roaring like a colossal wild beast that has been brought to bay and is bellowing in mortal anguish. Amid all this howling and shrieking, the skirmish lines advanced more briskly, encouraged now by the sound of their own artillery.

In his black cap with its red band, Chapaev galloped from one end of the line to the other, his dark felt cloak flapping in the wind like a pair of devil's wings. All the men could see his lean figure firmly fixed in the Cossack saddle suddenly appear first here then there, before disappearing just as quickly once more. He issued orders as he flew by, gave whatever information was essential, and asked vital questions. And knowing Chapaev so well, the commanders answered him swiftly and briefly, without a single unnecessary word or a moment's delay.

The skirmish lines rushed forward at a headlong run, but at the same moment the Cossack machine-guns opened fire, and as they did so, the men fell face down on the ground, and burrowing into the snow, lay there as though dead, waiting for the next command.

Chapaev was galloping back and forth behind the lines, shouting orders in brief, authoritative phrases and snatching up the replies as he passed.

Then he suddenly wheeled his horse and went racing towards the battery commander:

"Shell the windmills!" he cried.

Then, quickly turning his horse again, he galloped back to the lines. Now the Red guns began to speak more rapidly, their salvoes louder and angrier than before, but the Cossack village responded, hurrying to halt the enemy who were still dashing forward in short rushes. Then the windmills suddenly began to howl too and seemed to be rent asunder with a sharp crackling sound as all the machine-guns in them barked at the same time. Both sides now intensified their fire. But the

Red Army men were drawing closer and closer every moment, their shells falling and bursting with ever-increasing accuracy, and one's heart stood still at the thought that death was so near at hand, that the Cossacks were so close, that they must be utterly destroyed and that the Reds had to burst into the village on top of the enemy.

Suddenly Chapaev went galloping off to the left flank where danger threatened, for the Cossacks were charging there in mass formation. Their galloping horses could already be seen not far away. Chapaev raced up to the battalion commander.

"Don't move!" he cried. "Keep everyone in line! Fire in volleys!"

"Yes, sir!"

Then he galloped off down the lines of soldiers who were hugging the ground.

"Don't panic, lads, don't panic! Keep down! Let them get close—and wait for the order to fire! Stay where you are! Wait for the order to fire!"

How badly the men needed authoritative words during those last fateful moments! They heard Chapaev's voice and they could see he was with them—and immediately they became more calm. Now they felt confident that everything would be all right.

As soon as the mass of charging Cossacks had galloped within range, a volley of shots rang out, followed by another, and then the angry chatter of machine-gun fire lashed out to meet them.

"Rat-a-tat! Rat-a-tat! Rat-a-tat!" the Red machine-guns chattered on and on.

"Cra-ack! Cra-ack! Cra-ack!" echoed the abrupt, regular volleys.

The charging horsemen began to get out of step, then became confused and hesitated for a moment.

"Crack! Crack!" came the sharp volleys once more. Another few seconds, and the mass of riders had stopped moving. A few more moments, and the horses turned back in the direction from which they had come. Now the Cossacks were galloping back with the Red guns chattering after them.

The attack had been beaten off, and already the skirmish lines were on the outskirts of the village. Quicker and quicker came the rushes, and now men were running past the first few mills, pushing deeper and deeper into the village.

Then suddenly a great cry went up:

"Hurrah, comrades! Hurrah!"

The Cossack machine-guns could be heard no more, for the gunners had been hacked to pieces where they lay.

The Red Army entered the village of Slomikhinskaya.

Feeling embarrassed and wretched, Fyodor rode out of his shameful hiding place.

"Our men must be in the village by now," he thought. How ashamed he was to admit to himself that in his first battle he had been lacking in courage, that he had taken fright like a miserable cur and had failed to come up to his hopes and expectations. Where were all the courage, bravery and heroism he had thought about when he was far away from the skirmish lines, shells and bullets?

Feeling a little calmer now, but still just as embarrassed and ashamed as ever, he rode into the village. He kept trying to reassure himself with the thought that the same thing probably happened to all novices the first time they went into action, that he would be able to prove himself later on, and that in his second or third battle he would behave quite differently.

He was not mistaken either, for only a year later he was awarded the Order of the Red Banner for his part in one of the Red Army's most glorious operations. This first battle at Slomikhinskaya was an exremely important and salutary lesson for him, and what happened to him there never occurred again during all the years of the Civil War, even though he found himself in infinitely more complicated and difficult situations than the one at Slomikhinskaya. He managed to develop in himself the qualities he desired: outward calm, self-control, courage, and the ability to size up a situation and quickly decide what to do. These qualities did not emerge straightaway, though, because first of all he had to travel the road which evidently no one can avoid—the road that leads from manifest confusion and cowardice to the state of mind generally considered worthy in battle.

***

Unnoticed by anyone, Fyodor rode up to headquarters which had been established in the enormous house of a merchant called Karpov. Chapaev and all his men were already there.

Turning to Chapaev, Fyodor asked:

"Have you got word to the army?"

"We're just going to do that now. There's good news from Uralsk—they've advanced there too, and now they're clearing the road to Lbishchensk."

"That's good," Fyodor replied.

The order was given for all the men to be summoned to the village square in two hours' time. They were to be told that "Chapaev himself" would address them—that was how he ordered it to be announced: "Chapaev himself is going to speak!"

This was the first time Fyodor had heard Chapaev speak. He had become unaccustomed to such demagogue orators a long time ago. If Chapaev had been addressing an audience of workers, he would have been quite unsuitable and ineffective, and those listening would probably have laughed a good deal at his technique. But here things were altogether different and the effect he created was quite the opposite—his speech proved a tremendous success! Without any introduction or explanation, he began with the matter for which he had called the men together—the question of looting (of which there had been cases since the Reds had taken the village). But as he went on, he began to drag in a huge mass of the most unnecessary trivia—everything that happened to occur to him and that he could possibly tack on somehow to the matter in hand. His words had not the slightest pretension to elegance and no semblance whatsoever of proportion, unity or a single dominant idea, for he simply said whatever came into his head. And yet, despite its countless shortcomings, his speech made an enormous impression, and what was more, the impression was not a superficial one that would soon be forgotten—no, quite the contrary. Instead, it produced an indisputably profound and extremely far-reaching effect. What Chapaev said was steeped through and through in sincerity, vitality, innocence and a rather ingenuous, almost childlike truthfulness. As you listened to him, you realized that this incoherent speech with its countless chance details was not simply idle rubbish, not just an empty pose. Instead, it was an impassioned, candid profession of faith uttered by a noble man, the war cry of a great soldier who felt outraged and was now making his protest. It was a striking and convincing appeal, and if you like, it was an order at the same time, for in the name of truth Chapaev knew not only how to appeal but also how to command!

"I order you," he said, "never to loot again! Only scoundrels do that! D'you understand?"

The crowd of thousands responded joyously to this order with deafening cries of approval that came from the depths of their hearts. Their delight was indescribable.

"I'm your commander," Chapaev went on, "but I'm only your commander when you're in the ranks. At any other time I'm just your comrade. You can come to see me at midnight or in the early hours if you like. You can even wake me up if you have to. I'm always with you, and I'll always talk to you and tell you what you should do. If I'm having a bite to eat, then sit down and join me. That's the kind of commander I am!"

Fyodor began to feel rather embarrassed at this unashamed, childish boasting, but Chapaev only paused for a moment and then, quite unperturbed, cried:

"I'm used to this kind of life, comrades! I never went to any of those academies—I never graduated from them—but I've still raised fourteen regiments, and what's more I was the commander of all of them. And I saw to it that order was kept everywhere. There was never any looting, and what's more nobody ever dragged the priest's cassock out of the church either. 'What are you?' I'd say, 'a priest or something? D'you want to wear that thing, you son of a bitch? No? Then what the hell did you steal it for?'"

Chapaev turned threateningly this way then that and even looked behind him, his glance swift and penetrating, as if he were trying to see the thief he was talking about amid the vast gray mass of soldiers.

"Everybody knows priests lie," he declared with conviction. "They live by cheating—after all, what kind of priests would they be if they didn't cheat? They tell you not to eat meat during Lent, but they'll stuff themselves with roast goose till they nearly burst. Don't take what doesn't belong to you, they say, but they themselves steal all the time—so that's why we're sick and tired of them. What I'm saying's true enough, but all the same, you should leave other people's faith alone—when all's said and done, it doesn't do you any harm, does it? Aren't I right, comrades?"

Chapaev was in a winning situation and he knew it. That was why he had asked his crafty question precisely at that moment. Already roused to fever pitch by his speech, the peasant Red Army men burst into a torrent of wild shouts, as if at last giving vent to feelings suppressed during their long silence. And that was exactly what Chapaev had been waiting for. The sympathies of his audience were now completely on his side, and no matter what he went on to say, the success of his speech was assured.

All around him excited faces shone with delight and eyes glowed bright in rapture. With brief words and chuckles, merry glances and nods, the soldiers expressed their sympathy, agreement and satisfaction. Chapaev now held the collective soul of this vast mass of men in the palm of his hand, for he had made them feel and think exactly as he did.

He ended his speech to a storm of frenzied clapping and hurrahs that took a long time to die away. . . .

Chapaev's stay—very short though it was—with a group of anarchists, his own peasant origins, and his daring temperament—undisciplined and lacking in self-control—all explained his anarchist way of thinking and inclined him to employ guerrilla tactics as a commander.

***

Twilight fell and with it came black fog. Fyodor fell asleep, but it was not long before Chapaev woke him—to sign an order. Fyodor signed it and fell asleep again. Then Chapaev woke him once more. The amazing man sat up all night till morning, without a wink of sleep. Fyodor would wake up and see him sitting there alone, working by the feeble light of a little purple lamp. There he sat, hunched over the map with the same favorite pair of compasses that he had used at Alexandrov-Gai in his hand. He kept measuring and measuring, then would write something down before measuring and writing once more. All night long, till the cocks began to crow at dawn, he sat checking distances on the map amid the lusty snoring of his commanders who were sleeping nearby. Standing at the door with his rifle clutched in both hands, a sentry dozed, and from time to time would bump his gray forehead against the dark edge of his fixed bayonet.

***

They stayed four days in Slomikhinskaya, before Frunze informed them by direct wire that the brigade was being transferred to the Orenburg front. But the situation soon caused this decision to be changed, and the brigade was moved not to Orenburg but to the Buzuluk[32] area instead. At the same time Frunze summoned Chapaev and Klychkov to Samara for detailed discussions.

They were ready to leave in less than five minutes. Both were well aware they would never come to Slomikhinskaya again.

Their spirited horses could hardly stand still in their eagerness to be off—after all, the very best steeds had been chosen for Chapaev!

The troika pulled away...

Shouts of farewell echoed amid the flying snow. One man gave a whoop and another cracked his whip, while a third tossed his cap high in the air. Then, enveloped in the gray sadness of parting, the village was lost amid the snowdrifts...

Steppe, o steppe! The sunset flaming like sheets of red calico in the sky and the snowdrifts as white and soft as down!

The steppe wind is like a maiden's sigh, blowing in cool, fragrant gusts over the white wastes of snow, before being lost in the clear blue sky of early March!

***

From Slomikhinskaya they headed towards Alexandrov-Gai again, back along the same road they had travelled with the regiments only a few days before. On and on they drove, sunk in silence. The steppe is like a cradle to the traveller, for it lulls him into a sweet slumber.

Here was Kazachya Talovka again. Was it so very long ago that they had prepared for battle here, measuring the map with compasses and racking their brains for a way to smash the Cossacks?

So it went on, all the way back to Alexandrov-Gai, with Fyodor absorbed in memories of what he had recently experienced and trying to account for the things he had done.

They did not stay in Alexandrov-Gai for very long. After a bite to eat and a short rest, they set off once more, and using teams of relay-horses now, raced across the steppe all the way to Samara.

7. On the Road

Chapaev was one of those people with whom it is easy to become good friends, but the friendship could fall to pieces just as quickly as it was established. Oh, he would fly into a rage, and ranting and raving, say the most offensive things, swearing and cursing and seeing no further than his nose in his blind fury. But a minute later it would all be over and he would regret it. Then he would start to recall what he had said and take stock of what he had done, trying to sift what was important from what was unimportant, what was serious from what was wild ranting. Then, after he had worked everything out, he would be prepared to back down. But he would not always do so, nor would he do it with everyone either. He would only make concessions if he actually wanted to, and then only to those whom he respected and had time for. On such occasions one had to draw him out and encourage him to be frank. He would respond readily, and occasionally would open up so much that his whole soul would become visible.

He was a noisy man who was fond of shouting, and sometimes seemed so stern that anyone who did not know him felt afraid to approach him—after all, Chapaev might lash him with his tongue or even—who knows?—hit him with his fist if he got angry enough!

That was quite possible too—possible, that is to say, with a stranger who was timid into the bargain. The more afraid of him a man was, the more furiously Chapaev would rant and rave, for he could not bear timid people. A stranger might think he was a real brute, but if you looked a little more closely at him, you would discover a most unpretentious, likable comrade, whose heart was sympathetic to all the stirrings of another's soul and would always quiver sensitively in response to them. And when you had finished talking to him about something, whether you agreed with him or not you always knew the question was settled once and for all. With Chapaev, no issues were ever left open—instead everything was always cut and dried. He said what he thought, and then that was that.

Chapaev always carried his head high and with pride—after all, it was not for nothing that the fame of his exploits resounded far and wide over the steppe. But this glory had gradually clouded his vision, as it were, for it painted him as an invincible hero in his own eyes, and the intoxication of vanity had turned his head.

It was the men closest to Chapaev, though, who caused the greatest sensation about his exploits, both to his face and in his absence. It was they who were always the first to spread stories about him, both true and false, they who painted everything he did in such vivid colors, they who sang his praises in ecstatic terms and told of his unique invincibility. When people lied skillfully to Chapaev or even flattered him openly, he would listen with relish, smacking his lips like a cat over a bowl of cream, often egging them on or even embroidering the story himself. On the other hand, though, he would immediately dismiss a silly toady who could not even lie convincingly, and he would give orders that the man was not to be allowed near him again.

There was another amazing thing about Chapaev, too, and that was his childlike faith in rumors, for he believed in all manner of them, both serious and trivial, as well as in the most arrant nonsense.

He believed, for example, that in Samara they issued ten pounds of shag on ration cards, whereas the men at the front never got a single ounce.

He believed that at army headquarters there was a continuous drunken orgy going on round the clock, that all the commanders there were White Guard experts, and that they were betraying the Reds to the enemy every minute of the day.

He believed that shells, boots, bread, rifles, reinforcements—whatever it might be—all arrived at the front late because of the evil machinations of certain individuals, and not because of the general shortage of such things, the disruption of communications, the damage done to bridges, and so on and so forth.

He believed that typhus was carried by birds, so the more birds there were about, the more typhus there was. He also believed that sugar grew in loaves and by the score, and that if you didn't flog your horse, it would go to the dogs.

Just what did Chapaev not believe in his immense simplicity and purity of heart?

But there was one thing he would never believe: that the enemy was powerful or that it was impossible to defeat him and put him to flight.

"No enemy can stand up to me!" he would declare proudly. "Chapaev doesn't know how to retreat! He's never retreated in his life! So you can tell everyone that: I don't know how to retreat! Tomorrow morning we'll launch an attack along the whole front! Say I ordered it! And if anyone dares to go against it, then bring him here to me! I'll soon teach him how to keep his arse pointing in the right direction!"

In his own sphere and in his own way Chapaev was a tremendous expert and a highly skilled soldier. He had an excellent knowledge of his division, both its rank-and-file men and their commanders, but he knew much less about its political composition and indeed showed almost no interest in such things at all. He was splendidly acquainted, though, with the area in which military operations were being conducted, for he knew it either from memory, having lived there in his youth, or from questioning the local people, or because he had studied it on the map with others who were familiar with it. His memory was extremely retentive and would cling to each and every fact, refusing to let go of it until it was no longer needed. He knew the local people well, too, especially the broad mass of peasants, though he was much less interested in the townsfolk. He knew what kind of peasants lived in this region and what could be expected of them, knew what they could be relied upon to do and what their weaknesses were. In addition, he knew everything anyone needed to know about items such as bread, footwear, clothing, sugar, cartridges, shells and tobacco—he knew about them all, and it was impossible to catch him out in any way.

On the other hand, though, when it came to matters such as political questions and especially issues that lay outside the concerns of his division, he knew nothing about them and did not wish to learn anything either. Moreover, there was a great deal that he simply did not believe at all.

He considered the international labor movement, for example, a pure fabrication. He refused to believe in it and could not possibly imagine it could exist in so organized a form.

He knew not the slightest thing about the Communist Party program either, and though he had been a Party member for a whole year now, he had never read the program and had not the slightest understanding of a single issue contained in it.

Finally, one should always bear in mind Chapaev's attitude towards the "staffs," as he called all the bodies from which he received instructions and orders, as well as ammunition, clothing and reinforcements—everything, in fact, that he was supposed to be supplied with. To the very end of his life he remained virtually incorrigible on this issue. He was firmly convinced that the "staffs" were almost exclusively composed of Tsarist generals who had ensconced themselves in the rear, that they were "selling the Red Army out right and left," that the "people" under the leadership of men such as himself were not to be fooled, and that if they went against the orders of headquarters, they did not as a rule lose out but actually gained as a result. Mistrust of headquarters was something innate in Chapaev, and so bitter was his hatred for Tsarist officers in general that it was very rare indeed for him to allow some wretched little officer or other from elsewhere to join his division. There were, though, a few officers (but they amounted to no more than a handful), who had proved themselves in battle, and these he would remember and respect, though he always remained rather wary of them.

Fyodor discovered all these traits of Chapaev's character quite quickly, and having done so, became even more convinced that first of all he must win his respect, and only then try to change his ideas, restrain him and lead him down the road of *conscious* struggle—not instinctive, blind struggle, however sensational and glorious, however colorful and heroic that might be.

But how could he win Chapaev's respect? The answer was that he must take him prisoner in the intellectual sense, arousing in him a desire for education and learning, for knowledge and wider horizons—for things not only confined to the military sphere.

For the moment, though, Chapaev was like an eagle with a blindfold over its eyes. His heart pounded vigorously and the blood coursed hot in his veins, while his impulses were both passionate and spectacular and his will was indomitable. But he could not yet make out his life's road properly or imagine it clearly ahead of him . . .

So Fyodor took it on himself to enlighten him, if only a little, and to help lead him out on to the true road. Even if he did not succeed and nothing came of it—well, never mind, there was no harm in trying, and anyway it wouldn't make things any worse.

But if he succeeded—oho! How badly the Revolution needed men like Chapaev!

***

No sooner had they left Alexandrov-Gai than memories of Slomikhinskaya, its recent battle and all the events of the last few days began to recede in their minds. Their place was taken by something new—the tremendous but as yet unknown task for which they were now hurrying to Samara. They had still not realized the full extent of the agonizing danger looming on the Kolchak front, and they had not yet heard of the seriousness of recent Red defeats near Ufa.[33] But even so, it was clear they had not been summoned so urgently to Samara for nothing. Something big was evidently being planned, and the role they were to play in it was clearly not to be unimportant.

In all the villages and hamlets they passed through on the journey, Chapaev was known to everyone, and in each place he would be greeted with the same honor and joy. Sometimes his arrival was a really festive affair, with the whole village turning out to see him. All the men would enter into conversation with him and the women would ooh and ah and whisper among themselves, while dozens of little boys would race after his sleigh as he drove away, shouting as they ran. Here and there Chapaev would make one of his "speeches," and both their effect and success were always assured. It was not what he actually said that mattered, but the fact that it was Chapaev himself speaking. His name had magical power, and it made everyone feel that behind what he said—which in itself might be of little significance and rather lacking in content—there lay tremendously important deeds.

During one stage of their journey, Fyodor and Chapaev talked about personal matters—where each of them came from, what they had done in the past and the kind of surroundings they had grown up in. In a word, they talked about many things. When Fyodor had finished giving his own short biography, Chapaev began to talk about himself, and so as not to forget what he had said, Fyodor jotted it all down from memory at the next hamlet they came to.

Chapaev's Biography

"D'you know who I am?" Chapaev asked me today, and his eyes twinkled mysteriously. "My mother was the governor of Kazan's daughter and my father was a gypsy actor.

I know it's hard to believe, but it's quite true, and it was all just like I've said. That gypsy persuaded my mother to run away with him, then when she got pregnant, off he went and left her to fend for herself. Well, what could the poor girl do? She tried this and that, but in the end she had no choice but to go back to her mother—she was a widow by then because my grandfather, the governor, had died, you see ... Anyway, she went back to her mother but died in childbirth, when I was born. So I was left like a puppy that nobody wanted. Where could they get rid of a little thing like me, they wondered. Then someone had an idea. They called in the janitor because he had a brother who lived out in the country. And then they just gave me to the brother, as if I was some kind of toy. So I lived out in the country and grew up with all the other village children. The man had a big enough family as it was, even without me—a whole pack of kids, he had. We used to shout and fight so much it was enough to frighten the life out of you. I can hardly remember anything at all about when I was little, but I don't suppose there was much to remember anyway—in the country it's much the same for everyone, I guess.

When I was nine they sent me out to work, and I spent the next few years knocking about as a hired hand. First of all, they set me to look after a herd of pigs, and I practised a bit on them—they won't give a young lad cows straightaway, you see. Then when I'd done all right with the pigs, they made me a proper herdsman. After that a gang of carpenters took me on and started teaching me their trade. So I worked at that for a while, going around with them from one job to another, then I left them and went to work in a merchant's shop. I learned how to sell things and tried to cheat, but nothing came of it—swindling people just wasn't in my line at all. Merchants live by cheating, you see, and if they don't cheat they starve. It was then I saw through the whole business, and as soon as I did, nothing on earth could make me cheat—I just wouldn't do it, so I left the shop. And if I've got it in for merchants now, then it's all because I know just what they're like, the devils! On that point I'd make a better socialist than Lenin himself, because I've seen merchants at work and I know for sure that everything ought to be taken away from the bastards—they should be stripped completely clean, the swine!

So I thought to hell with shopkeeping, and asked myself: 'What am I going to do now, orphan that I am?' (I was nearly seventeen by then, you see.) Well, I thought and thought, and finally made up my mind to go tramping along the Volga. I'd have a look at all the towns, see the different kinds of people and find out for myself how they lived. So I went and bought myself a barrel organ. I had a girlfriend at the time—Nastya, she was called. 'Nastya,' I says, 'let's go down the Volga. I'll play the organ and sing, you can do a bit of dancing, and that way we can have a good look at the Volga and see all the different towns together, you and me!' So off we went. When winter caught up with us, we'd stay a while in one place and work as hired hands if we got too hungry. But as soon as the April sun began to shine on the fresh green leaves and old Mother Volga started pushing her ice down towards the Caspian Sea, we'd forget we were hungry and set off again, walking on and on, following the river bank all the way. The barrel organ would be playing and the larks singing high above, I'd be singing and Nastya was there beside me ... Oh, I'll never forget you, Nastya, never! How beautiful you were in those days of spring!"

Suddenly Chapaev hung his head and his gay voice became quiet and sad:

"There's a lot of sunshine in April but the trouble is it makes the frozen ground very damp ... I couldn't protect her, that little darling of mine, from the dampness, and she began to wilt like a leaf that's dying ... Soon I only had my barrel organ left for company—I buried my little dancer on the river bank at Volsk ... [34]Then I sold the barrel organ to a gypsy and was left all alone in the world ... But you know, life always seems to take care of people like me—and sure enough, after a while it did. It was getting time for me to serve in the Tsar's army by then. When my call-up came, off I went, and while I was still serving, the German war started. Ever since then I've been in the army, without a break. So that's what my life's been like ..."

"Weren't you married?" I asked him. "I seem to remember you saying something about children ..."

"Oh, yes, but that was before the war. I was married, it's true, but not for long. As soon as the war started, they called me back to my unit right away. Then one day I came home on leave, and heard people saying nasty things about my wife. Well, I just didn't know what to believe, so I says to her: 'Tell me,' I says, 'just how it all happened, in simple, clear words.'

'There's nothing to tell, Vasya,' she says, 'it's just spiteful gossip, that's all.'

Well, spiteful gossip or not, I happened to find out she really had been carrying on in a disgraceful fashion. 'Well, then,' I says, 'you shameless hussy, I did love you once, but now you can clear out, you bitch, because I never want to set eyes on you again as long as I live. And I'm going to keep the kids, what's more!' My, was I sore about it! After all, I'd not seen her for two years, and as for other women—why, I hadn't even so much as touched one. I never used to do things like that. I'd been waiting till I got home again and I'd kept myself just for her. Well who on earth wouldn't have been sore about it? You get back home, and just look at what your wife's been up to in the meantime!

Well, off I went again, back to the front, and I felt so bad about things I started poking my nose into the hottest fire. What difference will it make if I get killed, I thought, my life's ruined now anyway. Well, I was awarded all four St. George crosses, got promoted to NCO, then to sergeant-major, and still no bullet seemed to want to get me. I was wounded several times but I managed to stay alive all the same. There was only one problem, though: I knew how to fight all right but I couldn't read or write. It was really sickening—I'd feel ashamed and jealous because the lads would be reading and writing all around me while I didn't know a damned thing. Then one day, I remember, the ensign called me an ignorant devil and it made me so angry I gave him a real mouthful in reply. After that they ripped off all my stripes and I was an ordinary private again. On the other hand, though, I started to read and write and did it all properly. All this time the war had been dragging on, but then the Revolution came and they whisked me off to Saratov to serve in the garrison there.

Well, I'd think to myself, what the hell's going on? All around me I'd hear a lot of clever talk, with everyone saying why the people had risen in revolt, and I seemed to be the only one who didn't know. So I thought I'd join a party. I asked one sensible fellow to help me, and he arranged for me to join the Cadets,[35] but it wasn't long before I left them and joined the SR's[36]—I could see those lads really meant business. Well, I stayed with them for a while and went to some of their meetings, then I heard about the anarchists. That's it, I thought to myself, they're the ones who've got it right! They'll see to it that folk get everything they need straightaway, and what's more nobody'll be forced to do anything they don't want to—everyone'll be able to do just what he likes. Now just at that time Kerensky[37] was forming a volunteer detachment of Serbs, and I was made commander of it. But it was me who went and ruined everything for them—I turned the whole detachment against Kerensky, I did! So they demoted me again and sent me off to Pugachov where they put me in charge of a company. But you know what those times were like, don't you? In Pugachov we had our own council of people's commissars, and the chairman was—well, to put it bluntly, he was a first-rate fellow. Now for some reason he took a liking to me, you could tell, and he was a chap after my own heart, what's more. When I listened to him talk, it made me want to live in a sensible way myself. Well, this council chairman started teaching me and I began to look at everything quite differently. Then I gave up all that anarchy business and joined the Bolsheviks. I started to read other books as well—I'm a great one for reading now, you know. During the war, as soon as I could read and write, I'd lie there in the trenches and read all the time. I learned about Ataman Churkin[38] and Stenka Razin, about Yemelyan Pugachov and Yermak Timofeich. Next I got hold of a book on Hannibal and one on that Italian fellow Garibaldi too, then I read about Napoleon himself. You see, what I like best of all is when a man knows how to fight and doesn't spare himself if it's necessary. So I know all about those people. And I've read other things as well. I heard there were some good stories by Turgenev, but I couldn't get hold of any, though I can remember everything I've read by Gogol. Oh, if only I could have a bit more education, then my head would start to work in a completely different way. As it is, though, I'm just an ignorant man! I always was ignorant, and I still am!'

Chapaev told me about his life right up to the October Revolution, Fyodor wrote. As for his biography after that, though, what information there is does not seem reliable—that period of his life was much too colorful to be documented accurately. During those years he would race about the steppe like a whirlwind, turning up in one village one day and being seen more than a hundred versts away the next. The Cossacks would tremble at the mere mention of his name and did their level best to avoid joining battle with him, so bewitched were they by his daring raids and his continual triumphs.

***

It took Chapaev and Fyodor four days to reach Samara. They passed through a great many villages on the way, but wherever Chapaev's name was heard, it always produced the same effect.

Arriving in Samara, they reported to Frunze. The latter explained the situation at the front, stressing how necessary it was to act decisively in the present circumstances and saying what kind of commanders were needed at this time. Then, when Chapaev had left the room for a few minutes on official business, Frunze said to Fyodor:

"Now, Comrade Klychkov, this is a serious matter. I'm thinking of appointing Chapaev commander of a division. What do you think? I don't know him very well, but there are lots of rumors about him—you know the kind of reputation he's got. So what's he really like? You've worked with him, if only for a short time."

Fyodor told Frunze exactly what he thought, saying he had a high opinion of Chapaev but qualifying it by pointing out his political immaturity.

"That's just what I think too," said Frunze. "There's no doubt that he's an exceptional person. He's capable of doing an enormous amount of good, but there's still a lot of the partisan in him. Do what you can with him, though, and don't worry about his hot temper either—even the hot-tempered ones can be tamed with time!"

Chapaev came back again, and after making a few preliminary remarks, Frunze informed him of his new appointment, saying he must leave for Uralsk immediately and await further orders there, as the general plan for the coming offensive was not yet clear. Fyodor and Chapaev then said good-bye to Frunze and two hours later they were already leaving Samara. Before their departure Chapaev had asked permission to stop at Vyazovka, his native village, on the way to Uralsk. Frunze had agreed and so they headed there first.

"Have you got relatives in Vyazovka?" asked Fyodor.

"Yes, all the family live there. The old folk, my father and mother—foster ones, that is. Then there's two boys and a girl—they're living with a widow. She's got two kids of her own, you see, so they all live together."

"Is she a good friend of yours?"

"Yes, very good, very good indeed," replied Chapaev with a roguish smile. "A friend of mine died and left her to me in his will..."

***

When they reached Vyazovka they were received in triumph. The chairman of the village Soviet immediately called a meeting in the famous guest's honor, and during it Chapaev made one of his "speeches." That evening in the village hall named after him, the local amateurs put on a play. The acting was dreadfully bad, but on the other hand the enthusiasm shown by the cast was simply colossal, and they were all terribly eager to win Chapaev's approval. Fyodor and he spent the night in the village and the next morning they pressed on to Uralsk.

As time went on, Fyodor became more and more convinced that Chapaev, this flint-like guerrilla hero, could be taken in hand just like a child and be molded like wax into many new shapes. But the task had to be approached very cautiously, for one had to take into account what he would accept and what he would not accept straightaway. The main sphere in which he could most easily be led was that of learning. Here he would willingly follow and even come forward eagerly to meet vigorous, new ideas. But this was the only area in which it was possible to influence him. In all other things he was intractable, rigid and occasionally downright obstinate. The circumstances of his life had dealt harshly with him, but now he realized that there were new directions and a new explanation for everything, and he had begun to reflect on these things. Slowly but surely he was making his way towards the hallowed but hitherto closed gates of wider experience, and just as surely those gates were opening up before him to reveal the road that led towards a new life.

8. Against Kolchak

Chapaev and Fyodor spent ten days in Uralsk, waiting for further orders. The boredom was intolerable, as they had nothing whatsoever to do. They spent their time hanging about the headquarters of the Uralsk Division which was stationed in the town, and maintaining contact with the brigade of their own division, which had not yet been transferred from Slomikhinskaya to the Buzuluk area.

Chapaev became extremely irritable, as was always the case when he had nothing to do. Whenever he was obliged to stop and wait somewhere for a couple of days, he became almost unrecognizable. When he was in such a mood as this, he would find fault with absolutely everyone, cursing them for the merest trifle and even threatening them with disciplinary action.

His tremendous energy and vitality constantly sought an outlet, and when they could not be usefully applied, they would burst forth to no good purpose, and burst forth they certainly did in Uralsk.

At that time the Uralsk Division was holding a front near Lbishchensk and military operations were proceeding neither well nor badly—there had been no major defeats but no significant victories either. Then all of a sudden there was a disaster: a very large number of men were killed in a battle that did not go as had been expected, and the front beyond Lbishchensk began to give way. The Novouzensk and Moslem Regiments were thrown into confusion and the Kurilovo men had to be sent hurriedly to their assistance. It was a real catastrophe, and worst of all it had happened quite unexpectedly, coming like a bolt from the blue.

The reinforcements failed to restore the front, though, and Uralsk was soon surrounded by the enemy, but as we shall see, it would succeed in holding out for many months.

"Here's a telegram," said Chapaev one day, showing it to Fyodor. "Where's it from?"

"Headquarters, with orders to set out tomorrow for Buzuluk. We're not going to Orenburg now."

***

At the time the situation on the roads and railways leading to Samara was unimaginable. Trains were continually either racing or crawling towards Kinel[39] from Orenburg and Ufa, as well as from other places, some of them carrying troops and others provisions and shells. There were armored trains too. In the opposite direction went trains that were empty, hospital trains and still more troop trains, one after the other. Baggage transports kept coming in from Uralsk, too, and marching along with them came soldiers from that sector of the front.

A hasty regrouping was now taking place. Enormous masses of men were being transferred from one sector to another and new forces being brought up, while demoralized troops who were temporarily unfit for action were being withdrawn to the rear. Kolchak had already taken Ufa and was now approaching the Volga, so the situation was becoming critical. Samara was threatened, and with it other large towns on the river too. The position made a withdrawal by the Reds across the Volga a distinct possibility—something that would be a severe blow to the whole of western Russia. Very reluctant to make this withdrawal, the Red command took up the defence with great vigor, resolving to hold out whatever the cost, to wrest the initiative from the enemy and drive him back from the heartland of the new Soviet state. In the Buzuluk area a powerful force was being prepared, for it was from there that the first blows were to be struck. Chapaev's division, the Twenty-Fifth, was entrusted with an important task—to make a frontal attack on Kolchak and, flanked by other divisions, to drive him back from the Volga, the recapture of Ufa being the immediate objective.

In addition to the units moving up from Slomikhinskaya, another brigade which was grouped in the Krotovka district not far from Samara also formed part of the Twenty-Fifth Division, and in this brigade was the Ivanovo-Voznesensk Regiment.

***

Kolchak was advancing along a very extended front towards Perm,[40] Kazan[41] and Samara, and moving in these three directions was a White army of almost a hundred and fifty thousand men. The opposing forces were almost equal to them, the Red Army numbering only slightly fewer. By advancing through Perm to Vyatka,[42] Kolchak was aiming to join forces with the British, and via Samara, with Denikin.[43] Within this fateful, ever-narrowing ring he was hurrying to strangle and then destroy Soviet Russia.

Yes! All these dangers were very much more imminent and serious than many realized at the time. Vyatka and Kazan, Samara and Saratov were already being bespattered by the first showers of spray from the vast White Guard wave. For Kolchak the most important and vital route lay through Samara, for it would bring him closest of all to the heart of Soviet Russia. Not for nothing had his railway carriages been marked with the words "Ufa—Moscow".

His forward patrols had already begun to appear near Buzuluk, and in the last few days he had taken Buguruslan[44] too. The atmosphere was becoming more and more tense as the enemy drew closer, and the general situation was growing increasingly serious.

But the Red Army was ready for battle, its men filled with energy and determination. Its regiments, brigades and divisions were bristling with bayonets, and it was only awaiting the signal. And when that signal came, the entire Red front would hurl itself upon Kolchak, breast against breast, and in mortal combat try its strength against the enemy...

April 28th—that was the unforgettable day which marked the beginning of this most crucial operation. It was on that day that the Red Army launched its offensive against Kolchak.

9. Before Battle

The Red command had no intention whatsoever of evacuating Buzuluk. Instead, everything was put on a war footing and preparations were made for the imminent encounter with the enemy. The local Party group, the Executive Committee and the trade unions rallied round the division which was stationed there, and devoted all their energies to helping the Red Army. The stern slogan "All for the front!" was resolutely implemented here—probably in just the same way that it was being put into effect in scores of other besieged towns too.

Buzuluk was threatened now and enemy patrols kept appearing only a few dozen versts away. Soviet and Party workers were fleeing to the town from every direction, but chiefly from Buguruslan. These people were the ones whom Kolchak's patrols had failed to capture, or whom White sympathizers in the villages had not had time to betray. Many of them immediately enlisted as rank-and-file soldiers in the Red Army, then advanced with the victorious regiments back to their villages to take up their old work once more. Others never left the ranks at all but marched away with their fellow-soldiers into the unknown, remaining ordinary Red Army men just as their comrades were.

In this tense atmosphere, filled with the smell of powder and blood, could be sensed the approach of a whole new phase in the fighting, an important day that would mark the beginning of a great new era. The last few orders were being given and all possible forces being mustered as everything was concentrated on one single goal. Spluttering motorcycles raced through the streets of the small town that was usually so sleepy and quiet, official cars went whirling past, mounted men galloped to and fro, and columns of soldiers went marching by with measured, heavy tread.

Divisional headquarters was located on the corner where the town's two main streets met, and in this building activity never ceased either day or night. All the hurried, tense life of those last few days was concentrated and reflected here.

Chapaev and Fyodor, now inseparable colleagues and close friends, seldom went to their billets, for most of their time was spent at headquarters. Instructions and orders were continually arriving from the command center, various enquiries and reports also kept coming in from their own units, and endless discussions were held on the telephone. The most heated and lengthy exchanges were, of course, those concerning the shortages of every kind, but at the time there were almost as many shortages as requirements. For this reason, discussions with the units and with headquarters were usually conducted in raised voices and were full of assurances and entreaties as well as threats to "resort to the most severe measures." Chapaev thought it was enough simply to put pressure on the "various economic councils" as he called them, for everything that was required to appear in abundance instantly. If he saw a couple of dozen carts or four or five kegs of axle-grease somewhere, or found out that a hundred meters of cloth, a few sheepskins, boots or caps were stored in some depot, he would fly into a rage and demand that the whole lot be turned over to the army. He interpreted the slogan "All for the front!" in much too literal a way, and believed that with these few bits and pieces one could feed and clothe the entire Red Army, a force numbering many millions of men. He would often talk about economic ruin and the inevitable shortages it brought, but he seemed unable to picture it in a concrete way and could draw no conclusions at all from what he himself said. As a rule Fyodor would be able to talk him out of the thoughtless claims he made, and it must be said that he generally managed to do so without much difficulty. It was usually enough to bring forward a couple of serious arguments, and Chapaev would quietly agree with them.

Quietly, though, only quietly! As for expecting him to take back what he had said or openly admit he had been wrong—no, that was something Chapaev would never do! Moreover, in order to influence him, the various arguments had to be presented in a forceful and convincing way—he could not bear people who beat about the bush, and as a rule he did not take what they said into account, no matter what their actual merits might be.

Chapaev was a man who loved a firm, decisive word, but much more than that he loved a firm, decisive deed!

It would seem that in those days just such a commander as he was needed and was indispensable even—a man born of the peasant masses and embodying all the qualities peculiar to them. But once those masses had come of age, the need for such a commander would disappear. Even in those early days a man like Chapaev would not have been effective as a leader for the Ivanovo-Voznesensk Regiment, for example. His primitive speeches would have had no success at all with the weavers, for they valued calm consciousness far more highly than dashing recklessness. They would have talked with him as an equal, without gazing at him in rapture or beaming with happiness all the time. This was why Chapaev liked least of all to visit the weavers' regiment, for they were men sparing with their triumphant welcomes and slow to feel delight.

***

By the time the general offensive against Kolchak was launched, a full thaw had set in. The ice on the rivers had begun to crack and break up, and the bare ground was beginning to show both on the hills and in the valleys, while streams and brooks in spate had washed out the roads. It became impossible not only for the artillery to move over the thin ice and through the mud, but for the cavalry too, and in some places not even a man could make his way forward on foot. Spring was coming masterfully into her own.

Such conditions made troop movement very difficult indeed, and this partly explains the initial slow progress of the Red forces. But only partly, because there were other reasons too. As a result of their first clashes with the Reds, though, the Kolchak forward troops came to a halt as though in hesitation. Then blow after blow began to rain down on them from different directions. The defection to the Red Army of the Taras Shevchenko Regiment threw the Whites into confusion in that sector and immediately gave the Red units fighting there fresh heart. Without allowing the enemy time to collect himself, the Red forces began to press forward more and more urgently. The enemy front was badly shaken now and the initiative passed to the Red Army. The men sensed that a turning point had come, and the change in the situation was clear not only to the perceptive eye. Hopes soared and strength was renewed, for the developing offensive seemed to promise victory.

11. On the March to Belebei[45]

The Chapaev Division was advancing rapidly—so rapidly, in fact, that the other divisions were falling behind and beginning to disrupt the general plan for a combined offensive. Having advanced so far ahead of the others and making frontal attacks as it did so, the Chapaev Division was driving the enemy before it rather than destroying his forces or taking them prisoner. Exhausted by many long marches, the men displayed amazing powers of endurance. They were modest in their demands and ready to fight at any time, whatever their condition and whatever the circumstances. There were instances when they were almost dropping with exhaustion after a march of many versts, and suddenly the enemy would launch an attack. The men's fatigue would disappear in a flash, and after containing the attack, they would first go on to the offensive and then pursue the retreating enemy. But there were times, too, when they were so utterly exhausted by continual marching and fighting that at the very first halt, they would throw themselves down on the ground and sleep like the dead, often without enough guards around them, for they would all fall asleep straightaway—commanders, men and sentries alike.

On and on they went, advancing victoriously from one village to the next, sometimes following narrow paths over the hills or fording the rivers, because the enemy were blowing up the bridges as they retreated. In the dew of morning and the mist of evening they marched, amid constant rain and mud, eating only one day in three, poorly clothed and ill shod, footsore and sick, many of them wounded but steadfastly refusing to leave the ranks. They were irresistible and invincible, enduring every hardship without complaint. They were resolute and proud in defence, courageous and terrible in attack, relentless and dogged in pursuit. They fought like heroes, died like knights of old, and if taken prisoner, perished like martyrs under torture! With such dependable forces as these it was impossible not to triumph—all that was required was the ability to command them. And Chapaev possessed that gift of command to the highest degree—the ability to command just such a body of men, in the precise condition it was in and at the time in question. This mass of men was heroic, but it was raw. The times were dramatic ones, and in the heat of the battle much was forgiven or justified by the exceptional nature of the situation. This human mass was in a state of exaltation, as it were, and its condition cannot adequately be described in words. That condition, I believe, was unique, for it had come about as the result of a whole series of varied events, both large and small, which occurred before or during the Civil War.

There were men like Chapaev only in those days too—at other times there will be no Chapaevs, nor can there be any either. Chapaev was a product of that particular mass, at that specific time, when it was in that precise state. This was why he was able to command the division so successfully. How right he was—though he did not realize it—when he called the famous 25th Division *his* division, the Chapaev Division!

In it were focused and reflected, as in a mirror, the main characteristics of the semi-partisan troops of that time—boundless daring, immense tenacity and powers of endurance, together with inevitable harshness and cruelty. The men considered Chapaev the embodiment of heroism, though as we have seen, there had been nothing exceptionally heroic about what he had done so far. What Chapaev himself did was done by many others as well, but no one actually knew what these others did, whereas everyone knew what Chapaev did—knew it in detail, with various legendary embellishments and even fantastic fabrications. In 1918 Chapaev had simply been an excellent soldier, but by 1919 he was also renowned as an *organizer* and *hero*. He was an organizer only in a particular, relative sense, though, for he could not bear what he called "staffs," relegating to that category all the army departments which did not actually fight with the bayonet—be it the commissariat, the commandant's office, the communications section or what have you. In his eyes it was only the soldier with a rifle who fought and conquered. Another reason why he disliked "staffs" was that he understood little about them and could never organize them properly. Whenever he appeared at headquarters he spent more time giving the people there a roasting than explaining things to them and helping them.

Chapaev was only an organizer in the sense that by the force of his personality—for he possessed such great authority and was so loved by all—he managed to unite and fuse his division into a single whole, filling it with a spirit of heroism and a passionate desire to triumph, while at the same time developing and consolidating heroic traditions among his men. And these traditions—that of never retreating, for example—were held as sacred by the division. In maintaining such traditions, the men of the Razin, Pugachov or Domashkin Regiments would endure the most incredible hardship, withstand an enemy attack and fight under impossible conditions, then transform the situation into a victory. But they would never retreat. For the Stenka Razin Regiment to retreat would have been to disgrace its valiant and heroic name forever!

How magnificent all this was, but at the same time how misguided, harmful and dangerous!

Chapaev was in his element only when he was in action, but as soon as there was a lull in the fighting, he would become restless, grow irritable and bored, and fall prey to gloomy thoughts. But to go racing from one end of the front to the other—that was what he liked best of all! There were times when there was no pressing need for him to do this, but then he would think up a pretext and go tearing off to some place fifty, sixty or even a hundred versts away. He would arrive at a brigade, then the one next to it down the front would hear he was there and call him on the telephone: "Come at once! There's something very urgent!" And away Chapaev would go, galloping for all he was worth. Usually there would be nothing urgent at all—it was just that his commander friends wanted to sit and have a chat with their leader. It was precisely they, Chapaev's comrades-in-arms, who broadcast his heroic deeds and proclaimed his glory. Without them—and the same is true of anyone else in his position—he would never have achieved such renown. Glorious deeds are never enough in themselves to bring resounding fame. What is needed in addition are heralds, blindly loyal followers who believe in your greatness, are inspired and dazzled by it, and find joy in singing your praises.

They, Chapaev's men, considered themselves fortunate simply to be his comrades-in-arms, for the rays of glory that illumined him fell upon them too. In the Stenka Razin Regiment, for example, there were two heroes who had lost both legs in battle. They would crawl along on their stumps, and one of them occasionally managed to get about somehow by using crutches. But neither of them wanted to leave his famous regiment, and they would be overjoyed when Chapaev said a few words to them whenever he arrived. They were not a burden on the regiment either, for both served as machine-gunners in battle.

Our heroic days will pass and people will not believe things like this, thinking they are merely legends, but they really are true . . .

When one pauses to consider whether Chapaev possessed any special, "superhuman" qualities which gave him the everlasting hero's reputation he enjoys, one sees that the qualities he did possess were ordinary in the extreme. There were even many highly desirable human qualities that he did not have at all, while those he did possess were notable only for their distinctive freshness and clarity. But he knew how to make excellent use of what qualities he had. Born as he was of this raw, semi-partisan peasant mass, he managed to galvanize it to the highest degree and infuse it with the spirit it both desired and demanded—and then at the center of it all he placed himself!

Chapaev's fame stemmed not so much from his heroic deeds as from the men around him. This is not to detract in the least from the colossal role he played as a personality in the Civil War, but one should bear in mind that the name of any hero is always surrounded by legend rather than by historically concrete fact. People will ask, though: why was it precisely around Chapaev that these legends grew up? Why was it precisely his name that enjoyed such tremendous popularity?

The answer is that, to a much greater extent than many other commanders of the time, he embodied the characteristics of the raw mass of his men, and the way he behaved suited them down to the ground. He possessed all the qualities of this heroic mass, but in particular those which it especially honored and prized: personal courage and daring, great bravery and resolution. Often these qualities were no more pronounced in him than in others, and sometimes even less, but he himself was so good at presenting his exploits, and the people close to him were so adept at doing so, that as a result his deeds were invariably surrounded by an aura of the miraculous. There were many commanders who were braver and cleverer than he was, many who were more talented and more politically aware, but their names have long been forgotten, whereas Chapaev's name lives on in the popular consciousness and will continue to do so for many years to come. He was, after all, the native son of this peasant environment, and moreover combined to a remarkable degree the characteristics that were to be found among the comrades-in-arms around him.

***

There is no need to describe one military operation after another, no need to go into detail about the merits and demerits of the various orders issued by headquarters, or to chronicle our victories and defeats. That is the concern of those who will write specifically military accounts of this time. In our sketch we make no attempt whatsoever to give a complete account of events in their proper sequence, or to observe strict accuracy of dates, places and names. Instead, we confine ourselves to a portrayal of the way of life that was born of those times and was characteristic of them.

12. Forward

The Chapaev Division was to bypass Belebei from the north, while other forces had been assigned the task of taking the town itself. During the Civil War the destruction of enemy manpower was not always the prime objective. More often than not the aim was to capture territory and particularly to take important, well-known towns. This tendency, though, did not stem solely from military considerations. It occurred for political reasons too, as every large town was at the same time the political center of an extensive region around it, and its occupation by Red or White forces was by no means unimportant for the political morale of that region. In so far as politics were a prime factor in events during the Civil War, each side strove to capture significant points as quickly as possible.

Belebei was not a particularly important town, but it did possess some significance as a place where forces could be consolidated. The brigade on the right flank of the Chapaev Division reached the outskirts of the town just when the decisive battle to capture it was taking place, and having taken part in that battle, the brigade entered the town along with the neighboring division.

The Red regiments then took up position to the north, along the Usen River, and began to wait. The Red forces were on one side of the river and the Whites on the other, and the situation remained unchanged for several days. The men rested, got their strength back and prepared for the next attack. But Chapaev swore and cursed continually, making no secret of his annoyance, for he considered the halt almost criminal.

"What are we resting for?" he would cry. "What kind of fool has a rest at the front? And who needs a rest anyway? Perhaps it's the staffs who need it!" he said mockingly, hinting at possible treachery at headquarters and at a deliberate attempt to slow down the victorious advance of the Red forces.

Outbursts such as this were frequent, and all the way to Ufa Chapaev was dissatisfied with the way the operation was going, despite the fact that his division kept gaining one victory after another. He always felt that he was not given enough scope by headquarters, that the initiative was being taken from him, and that his opinion was not being considered.

But it was useless to try and argue with him, for he would never change his mind about "staffs" and went on mistrusting them to the very end of his life.

The closer the Red Army got to Ufa, the more desperately the enemy resisted. They held on to every convenient position, particularly in the hills, concentrating handfuls of shock troops and making numerous counterattacks. They were careful not to lose their transports either, moving them away in good time and guarding them with large detachments of men.

With every passing day it grew increasingly difficult for the Red forces to advance. Widespread espionage was discovered: Kolchak had agents working for him and was helped not only by kulaks but often by Tatar peasants as well, many of whom had been deceived by stories that the Bolsheviks were only fighting in order to take their Allah away from them and destroy their mosques. There were even occasions when Red regiments were fired on from windows as they entered Tatar settlements, and the shooting was done not by rich villagers but by the poorest of the poor.

***

The Red regiments were now advancing on Chishma.[46] It was clear that the enemy would not surrender such an important point cheaply, for it was the junction of two railway lines—Samara-Zlatoust and Volga-Bugulma. As much as a dozen versts outside the town the enemy trenches began. They were neatly finished, deep and even, with splendid dugouts, secret passages leading down into the valley, and paths running away over the hillside. Entire groves of trees had been cut down and areas cleared for cavalry ambushes, while the fields were covered with thick entanglements of barbed wire. The Reds had encountered nothing like it either at Buguruslan or at Belebei, and had not seen such carefully prepared trenches for a long time now. It was clear that the enemy had made thorough preparations.

But the Whites had lost the initiative back at Buguruslan and could not possibly regain it now, however hard they tried. In the Kolchak army the process of disintegration that was eventually to prove fatal to it was spreading and accelerating. No measures whatsoever—neither concessions nor reprisals—could check this historically inevitable process now. But apart from the general reasons for disintegration, which sooner or later manifested themselves to varying degrees in all the White armies, there were in Kolchak's case special factors which greatly accelerated the process. In the first place, Kolchak mobilized the local population without due care, striving more for quantity of men rather than quality; and secondly, in his attempt to consolidate and unite this enormous mass of mobilized troops with little more than a handful of officers loyal to him, he was inevitably obliged to give these officers a free hand in carrying out reprisals against their men. As a result, all the old forms of military abuse in the treatment of soldiers were revived in the Kolchak army, probably to a greater extent than in any other White force. The ill-assorted nature of the troops and the brutality of their officers were the two main factors which so rapidly accelerated the process of disintegration within the Kolchak army.

It became clear, though, that Kolchak's position was even more serious and still more tragic than had at first been thought, for it emerged that he could not depend unreservedly on his officers either. At any moment, it seemed, they might sell out to the Reds. There was an instance when ten or so Red Cavalrymen ran straight into an enemy skirmish line of a hundred and twenty soldiers and two officers, together with a machine-gun. Nothing would have been easier than to take the Red cavalrymen prisoner or shoot them off their horses in a flash. But what happened was this: the White officers shouted to their men "Hold your fire!", then ran out to meet the cavalrymen, declaring they wanted to go over to the Reds and take all their men with them.

In a word, there was no doubt whatsoever that the Kolchak army was disintegrating, and the Red forces did everything they could to accelerate this process. Propaganda literature was transported to the enemy's rear by the cartload, while millions of open letters, appeals and leaflets of all kinds were distributed by the local population, dropped from aircraft and scattered by Red agitators. The latter penetrated deep into enemy territory, making their way far behind the White front line, and carried on their heroic work there quite openly and fearlessly.

And yet, despite all this, the fighting was so fierce at times that it seemed to give the lie to any assumption that the White Army had begun to disintegrate. It was the most staunch enemy regiments that fought in these bitter encounters, and though there were only a few of them by comparison with the general mass of the White Army, they were superbly equipped and fought magnificently.

At the approaches to Chishma the fighting was so fierce that in some Red companies only thirty or forty men survived. The Red troops fought desperately, filled with a terrible, frenzied inspiration! Armed only with hand grenades, they would hurl themselves at the enemy's armored trains until the track was carpeted with their dead, then run after the iron monsters, shouting "Hurrah!" and pelting them with their deadly missiles. When armored cars appeared, the Red skirmish lines flung themselves flat on the ground and lay there without raising their heads. An armored car cannot fire down at anyone on the ground, so the men were not killed. The vehicle would force its way through their lines and circle about in the rear, firing away to no effect, then as it drove off, the men would leap up and run after it, showering it with grenades just as they did the armored trains. Their heroism bordered on insanity, and many were the Red soldiers mown down by machine-gun fire from the White armored trains and cars at Chishma.

Chishma was regarded as the key to Ufa, and now the road forward lay open. There was every reason to believe that the enemy would withdraw across the Belaya River and put up the stiffest resistance on the far bank.

The Red forces pressed on faster still in urgent pursuit of Kolchak's retreating army.

"Now Ufa's as good as captured," said Chapaev, "if only the right flank doesn't let us down!" (He meant the regiments operating on his right flank.)

But there were no serious delays. Chishma was the last point which Kolchak's regiments had been hoping to hold this side of Ufa, and after they had lost it, their mood seemed to undergo a profound and irrevocable change. From now on there was only an orderly retreat, and the Whites made no more serious attempts on this side of the Belaya River to achieve the breakthrough they were still hoping for, just as the Reds had hoped for the same thing at Buzuluk and Buguruslan.

13. Ufa

The enemy retreated across the Belaya River, blowing up all the bridges as they went, and soon the high far bank was bristling with field and machine-guns, as well as with the bayonets of entire divisions and corps. Large White forces were now concentrated there, for Kolchak had no wish to lose the Ufa sector, and from his advantageous position high on the right bank of the river he had complete command of the Red divisions now advancing from various directions.

The Chapaev Division took up a position directly facing Ufa. Its right flank lay by the enormous high bridge that spanned the river and led straight into the city, while its left curved away as far as Krasny Yar, a small village about twenty-five versts downstream.

The enormous iron bridge was still intact, but no one believed the enemy had left it untouched. They were sure to have mined it, so it could not be used to cross the river. For the time being, then, there was absolutely no means of crossing the Belaya, and it was not until later that some Red Army men discovered a few boats, while others dragged beams and planks down to the water and tied them together to make flimsy little rafts.

Two days before the attack was to be launched, Frunze, Chapaev and Fyodor arrived by motorcar and immediately called a meeting of divisional commanders and commissars at Krasny Yar to clarify the disposition of forces, to consider the various possibilities, and once again to estimate the chances of success.

When the commanders met at Krasny Yar, they needed to take into account not only the number of men in the various regiments and the equipment they possessed, but also their fighting qualities, with specific regard to the current exceptional situation. The choice of which regiment should take the city fell on the Ivanovo-Voznesensk weavers, but it was not by chance that this choice was made. In purely military terms they enjoyed one of the leading positions in the division, but as far as the present situation was concerned, it was their strongly developed class consciousness that was of prime importance, since selfless daring alone might prove insufficient for the task.

The meeting drew to a close. The decisive hour was already drawing near. It was decided that Chapaev himself would command the crossing at Krasny Yar, while Fyodor would return to the bridge and direct operations there until the Red forces entered the city.

***

Already the previous evening there had been an extraordinary amount of activity on the river bank at Krasny Yar, but the silence amid which it all went on was extraordinary too. Men kept hurrying to and fro like shadows, and little groups gathered then melted away and were lost in the gloom, only to form and disappear once more. It was the Ivanovo-Voznesensk Regiment getting ready to make the crossing. And so, amid darkness and silence, the whole regiment was ferried across the river. It was already long past midnight now and dawn was approaching.

Just then the Red batteries at Krasny Yar opened fire and began to shell the nearest enemy trenches, several dozen guns all firing at once. The range had been fixed beforehand and the effects of the shelling soon became clear. It was impossible for the Whites to remain in the trenches under such a barrage, and their line soon wavered and they began to retreat in disorder towards the second line of trenches. When Red scouts reported that this was happening, the artillery ceased firing and the men of the Ivanovo-Voznesensk Regiment who had by now come up close to the enemy trenches, went into the attack. They charged, and drove the Whites back as far as the village of Novye Turbasli.[47] The enemy were retreating in panic now, unable to make a stand anywhere as they went, and the Ivanovo-Voznesensk men entered Novye Turbasli hard on their heels. But then they halted to wait for reinforcements to be ferried across the river—it would have been extremely dangerous for a single regiment to press on alone. So for the time being they consolidated their position in the village. Meanwhile the Pugachov Regiment was advancing along the river bank towards the settlement of Alexandrovka.

By this time, though, the enemy who had been forced upstream had recovered themselves a little, and suddenly began to attack the Ivanovo-Voznesensk Regiment. By now it was already about seven or eight o'clock in the morning. While driving the enemy beyond Novye Turbasli, beating off feint attacks and strengthening their position in the village as they did so, the Ivanovo-Voznesensk men had used up almost all their ammunition and were now left virtually empty-handed, with no hope of having any fresh supplies brought up soon.

Yes—there was nothing left to the weavers now but their bayonets. And then, when instead of feint sorties, the enemy launched a genuine all-out attack, the Red lines wavered, and unable to withstand the pressure, began to fall back. Just then several horsemen came galloping up to the skirmish lines and leapt from their saddles. It was Frunze and with him, Trallin, head of the army's Political Department, accompanied by several of their close associates. Frunze grabbed a rifle and ran forward, shouting: "Hurrah! Hurrah! Forward, comrades!" All the men nearby recognized him and the news spread like wildfire down the lines. The Reds were instantly filled with enthusiasm and flung themselves forward in a furious charge. What an absolutely unforgettable moment! Firing very rarely, because they had so little ammunition, they charged the advancing Whites with fixed bayonets, and so great was their heroic enthusiasm that the enemy lines began to waver, then turned and fled.

By this time cartloads of ammunition were being rushed up from the river bank, and as soon as the skirmish lines lay down beyond Novye Turbasli, men crawling on their bellies brought more supplies up to the lines.

The weavers had managed to turn the tide and had recovered their position. Frunze then left them and rode off to the Pugachov Regiment, which was continuing to advance along the river bank. Then the Stenka Razin Regiment and several battalions from the Domashkin Regiment began to come up as well, and took up positions along the main road. At noon the order was given for a general attack. The Pugachov Regiment was to continue advancing along the river bank, the Stenka Razin and battalions of the Domashkin Regiment were to press on in the center, while the Ivanovo-Voznesensk Regiment was to push forward from the extreme left flank. By that time the weavers had taken the village of Starye Turbasli as well, and had halted there to rest.

***

While he was at the river crossing, Chapaev had talked on the telephone every ten minutes or so with the various regimental commanders. Communications had been extremely well organized, and without this, the operation would have been much less successful. At all times Chapaev knew exactly what the situation was on the other side of the river, and when, for example, the men there grew anxious about the shortage of cartridges or shells, he already knew what it was they needed and sent it across by the very next boat. He was continually enquiring about the morale of the various regiments, asking about the enemy's movements, the strength of his resistance, the approximate amount of artillery he had, whether there were many officers among his troops, and what the general composition of his forces was—in a word he was interested in every detail and took everything into account. At all times he held in his hands the threads controlling the entire operation, and the brief words of advice he gave over the telephone, the instructions he sent by his orderlies—all showed how clearly he saw the situation at any given moment. For a while he was troubled by enemy aircraft, but he was not so much dismayed as angry. The Red pilots had no fuel so they could not take off to engage the enemy. There was no point in Chapaev's ranting and raving, for his aircraft remained grounded just the same, and so all the work on the river bank had to be carried out while the enemy planes dropped bombs and strafed the ground with machine-gun fire. But nothing could be done about it. Soon the Reds' artillery fire forced the enemy aircraft to climb higher, but they still did not go away entirely and their bombing and strafing did a good deal of damage. It was during one of these raids that Chapaev was wounded—a bullet hit him in the head, lodging in the bone. While it was being removed, the instruments slipped half a dozen times in the surgeon's hands as he worked, but Chapaev just sat there and did not say a word, enduring the pain without making a single sound. Then the wound was dressed and he was taken away to Avdon, a hamlet about twenty versts from Ufa. That was towards evening on the eighth, and the general attack was scheduled for the morning of the ninth.

***

The tireless work carried out on the river bank, the exceptional performance of the artillerymen, the vigorous ferrying of troops across the river, and the excellent communications—all attested to the splendid coordination and concerted effort with which the whole operation had been carried out. It was not a case of any single individual's merit, but of a manifestation of the collective's will to achieve victory, and this was apparent both in the issuing of every order and in its execution, as well as in every individual step taken by commanders, commissars and rank-and-file soldiers alike.

The Red units continued to advance without a halt, and by the evening of the ninth they were already on the outskirts of Ufa itself.

***

Everyone was filled with feverish impatience as the hours dragged by. Then, as soon as it became known that Red forces really were approaching the town, the order was given to cross the river. Small boats appeared from somewhere, little rafts made of beams that had been lashed together were dragged down to the river bank, while some of the men simply threw logs into the water and sitting astride them, paddled off across the river.

The enemy opened fire, but though the fire was rapid, it was disorderly and it soon became clear that the Whites were extremely alarmed and perhaps even starting to panic. Then the Red artillery intensified its own barrage, shelling the enemy trenches on the far side of the river. In ones and twos, and in little groups as well, Red soldiers kept paddling across under enemy fire. When they reached the other bank, they leapt ashore and, falling flat on the ground, hurriedly dug up little mounds of earth to protect their heads. Then, sheltering behind them, they opened fire on the enemy.

The Red skirmish line kept growing larger and larger, stretching out further as it did so. Its fire became more and more persistent, too, while the enemy's resistance grew increasingly ineffective and feeble. The Whites were clearly demoralized now.

"Hurrah!" cried the Reds, and leaping up, rushed forward. They took the first line of enemy trenches, putting some of the Whites to flight and taking others prisoner. Then the Red skirmish line lay down again. And in this way, making one rush after another, they moved further and further away from the river, pushing deeper and deeper into the city.

Now Red troops were entering Ufa from various directions, and on every side they met enormous crowds of workers who gave vent to their feelings with tumultuous cries of joy. There were shouts of welcome for the gallant regiments, bursts of laughter and unrestrained tears of gladness. People came running up to the Red soldiers and seized them by their tunics—these men who were strangers to them yet so near and dear at the same time. They kept slapping them on the back in a friendly way and shaking them vigorously by the hand. These were tremendous scenes that simply defy description!

The streets were lined with workers who stood out in front of the crowd. It was to them that victory had brought the most joy. But clustered on the pavements, visible behind all the workers' grimy shirts and smocks, standing in the side streets, sitting on fences or at the open windows of houses, perched on roofs, in trees and even on telegraph poles—were all the other people of liberated Ufa, and they too were overjoyed to welcome the Red Army. Those who were not pleased, though, had fled with Kolchak. Regiment after regiment, the Red troops marched by, streaming on and on in perfect order, their bayonets flashing proudly and their dusty faces calm in the knowledge of their invincible might. That marble-like expression of majestic calm on their weary faces will never be forgotten!

Without a moment's delay the Reds hurried to the prison. Had one inmate at least been left alive, they wondered? Or had the Whites shot them all, down to the last man?

As they fled before the advancing Red regiments, the White generals had not had time to kill the last few prisoners. Just the last few, though ... Only the dark Ufa nights and Kolchak's White gendarmes can say where our comrades lie, those comrades who were led away each night in sad little groups, led away no one knows where, never to return ...

As soon as the prisoners had been freed, guards were posted everywhere—patrols in the town itself and permanent pickets on the outskirts. There was no looting or violence, and no excesses whatsoever—after all, it was the Red Army that had taken the city, an army forged by discipline and steeped in the awareness of its revolutionary duty.

***

Beyond Ufa it was other divisions that drove Kolchak's forces onwards, while the Twenty-Fifth remained where it was, resting for more than two weeks in the Ufa sector. The time was not wasted, though, for the units set themselves in order after their long and exhausting campaign. The various divisional departments also gradually began to straighten themselves out and deal with all the business that had accumulated during the fighting.

Soon, however, alarming reports began to come in from the Uralsk front, for the Cossacks there were winning one victory after another. They had laid siege to Uralsk, apparently, though so far they had not managed to break into the city. This information came from newspapers, military dispatches and telegrams, as well as from letters, but especially the latter. The Red troops in Ufa heard that wild bands of Cossacks were tearing through their native villages like a blazing whirlwind, destroying their farms and torturing or killing those whose menfolk had left to join the Red Army. The regiments became alarmed and anxious, asking to be sent to the Uralsk steppes where they vowed to fight with redoubled vigor against the Cossacks who had gone on the rampage.

Chapaev and Fyodor talked about this a great deal and realized that the transfer of the division was both advantageous and necessary, provided no exceptional circumstances stood in the way. They discussed it with headquarters many times too, and explained to Frunze the kind of mood that had developed among the men, and how unprofitable it would be to transfer them to any front but the Uralsk one. Then individual refugees began to arrive from the areas in question, and with them came ordinary volunteers who had no wish to serve anywhere but in their "own" Chapaev Division. The mood of the men was beginning to reach fever pitch now. Finally, taking account of the situation, headquarters ordered the division to be transferred to the Uralsk steppes. At this news the men's excitement knew no bounds, and they made ready for the fresh campaign as if they were setting forth on a holiday outing. Chapaev, too, was no less pleased than the rank-and-file soldiers—after all, he was going back to the steppes, back to the places where he had already fought for so long and where everything was so familiar, so much a part of him—not at all like it was here among the Tatar villages around Ufa. Preparations to leave were completed as quickly as possible and the division set off.

14. The Relief of Uralsk

Uralsk remained encircled by the besieging Cossacks until the arrival of the Chapaev Division which liberated it. The heroic defence of the city will always be a brilliant chapter in the history of the Civil War. Cut off from the rest of Russia, the people of Uralsk withstood the Cossack siege with honor. Time and again they beat off enemy attacks with great valor, occasionally made sorties themselves, and harried the Whites on every side. The exhausted garrison, reinforced by a wave of Uralsk workers who had volunteered to join it, never complained of hunger or fatigue. Nor did it ever enter their heads to surrender to the exultant foe. This was a struggle to the death, and they all realized there could be no compromise, for capture by the Cossacks would mean certain torture and death by firing squad. Cartridges and shells were already running low in the city, provisions were almost finished, and the heroic defenders might soon have been forced to fight with nothing more than their bayonets, but even this prospect failed to daunt them, so confident and cheerful, so steadfast and calm was their mood. But when they heard that the Chapaev Division was on its way to relieve them, they became more resolute than ever, beating off the last enemy attacks with even greater heroism.

***

There were no major battles on the way to Uralsk, though not a day went by without isolated skirmishes. The Cossacks had good reason to remember the Chapaev regiments from as long ago as 1918, and so did not display any great desire to encounter them head on, preferring to retreat and make raids against them whenever they could. On the road leading to the big Cossack village of Sobolevskaya,[48] for example, the Cossacks attacked the Ivanovo-Voznesensk Regiment with two armored cars in the center, supported by cavalry on their flanks. But this enemy onslaught was met and countered in such a well-organized, calm way that there were not even any Red casualties.

***

Despite continual skirmishes with the Cossacks, the Red regiments made rapid progress, covering up to fifty versts a day.

In villages both large and small, the Red troops were greeted as liberators. Very often the people would come out to welcome them, helping in whatever way they could and sharing their food with them. Chapaev himself would be given an extraordinary reception—he was the "hero of the day" in the fullest sense of the word.

And so, warmly welcomed all the way, the Red regiments drew closer to their goal. Soon they were at the walls of Uralsk itself. One last battle, and lifting their siege, the Cossacks fled. Then, accompanied by a squadron of cavalry and a band, the leaders of the relieved garrison rode ten versts out of the city to meet the Chapaev Division. The two forces met to the thunder of the "Internationale" and to cries of joy, and the men embraced each other with tears of gladness. There was so much they wanted to tell, and all at once too, but they could not manage it, so overwhelmed were they by their emotion and so deeply moved by what had happened.

***

In Uralsk itself the streets were so crowded with workers and soldiers that it was almost impossible to move. The city's entire population had turned out to welcome the division.

"Hurrah for Chapaev! Hurrah for the hero! Long live the regiments of the Chapaev Division! Long live our Red leader—Chapaev!"

These joyous cries resounded throughout the liberated city, and it was hard for Chapaev and Fyodor driving in their car to get through the enormous crowds that thronged the streets. The people gazed at Chapaev in adoration, and welcoming him with loud cries, tossed their caps high in the air and sang triumphant songs of victory. The whole city was decorated with red flags, and everywhere you looked speakers' stands were being set up and meetings opened. Whenever Chapaev made a speech, the crowd went mad with joy, surging like the sea in a storm, for their delight knew no bounds. The first word he uttered brought dead silence, while the last opened the floodgates for a new wave of frenzied delight. Then, before he had time to get back into the car, he would be seized by dozens of workers' hands and tossed high in the air, and as he was finally driven away, the whole crowd would run after his car as though wanting to catch up with it and express their gratitude by showing their delight once more. The Red Army men were accorded no small honor either. The people of Uralsk did their best to surround them with affection and care, cheering them on parade, organizing countless entertainments for them, ensuring they were well fed and giving them everything they possibly could.

The Cossacks had retreated across the river, but they had to be driven still further back without delay in order to prevent them from regrouping and so as to put more distance between them and the city which was such a powerful magnet for them. As far as Chapaev was concerned, there was no finer reward than fresh victories at the front, and so, as soon as the first raptures of welcome had subsided, he was back racing from one regiment to another again and keeping an eye on the work being carried out to enable the river to be crossed.

A bridge was being built across the river, but there were already two Red regiments on the other side which had crossed on anything they could find. The work on the bridge had to be carried out quickly so that artillery could be ferried across—without field-guns the regiments felt helpless, and already the most alarming reports had begun to come in from commanders on the far side.

Chapaev knew how to make people work, but the measures he resorted to were sometimes brutal in the extreme. The times were such, though, that in certain situations any measures at all could be considered permissible. Even the most severe and awful of these—that of hitting a man across the face—was excusable.

People used to say that in 1918 Chapaev had given a certain high-ranking individual a thrashing with his whip. Another had been sworn at by him over the telephone, while a third had got such a violent endorsement appended to an application he had made that it frightened you out of your wits just to read it. What an original figure Chapaev was! There was a great deal that he still did not understand and much that he had not yet properly digested, but there were also many fine and sensible things to which he aspired quite consciously, and not simply by instinct. In another two or three years he would have entirely lost some of the traits that were already beginning to fade in him, and he would have become familiar with a great deal of what was beginning to interest him, broaden his knowledge and attract him. But none of this was destined to be . . .

15. Finale

The Chapaev Division was now marching on Lbishchensk, which lies over a hundred versts from Uralsk. All around them was steppe, nothing but steppe. In this region the Cossacks felt completely at home, finding sympathy and every kind of assistance wherever they went. The Red regiments, on the other hand, were given a hostile reception. Where a few inhabitants had been left behind in the Cossack villages, the soldiers never heard a good word, to say nothing of being given help, but in the majority of cases the large Cossack settlements were completely deserted by the time the Red units reached them, except perhaps for some feeble old crone who had been forgotten by everyone. The retreating Cossacks would frighten the local population with stories about the Bolshevik "cutthroats," and the villagers would load all their goods and chattels on to carts, leaving only the grain in their barns behind, and that more often than not had either been burned or mixed with sand and mud to make a foul swill. Almost all the wells, too, had been filled with earth or their water poisoned, and not a single bucket was to be found. Everything that could possibly be spoiled had been utterly ruined, to the point of being almost unrecognizable. Any buildings that might have proved useful to the enemy had been damaged, demolished or burnt. All this destruction created the impression that the Cossacks had left never to return. Here, in the neighborhood of Lbishchensk, they fought fiercely as they retreated, doggedly beating off the attacking Reds with great skill.

The Chapaev Division had its headquarters at Uralsk, while the advanced units were several dozen versts ahead. There was a shortage of cartridges and shells, uniforms and bread. The hungry Red Army men were now marching through flat wheat country, and in the Cossack villages they would find great heaps of unthreshed grain, yet they themselves had no bread. They were in very dire straits indeed. Bread sometimes did not reach the front for weeks at a time, and when it finally arrived it would be mildewed and half-rotten, and the men would be literally starving. Oh, what unbearably difficult days those were!

Almost every morning Chapaev and Fyodor would drive off to pay a brief visit to one brigade or another. Out here in the steppe the roads were wide and smooth, and one could travel very fast. When their car broke down—and oh, how often that happened!—they would ride on horseback and cover up to a hundred and fifty versts a day, leaving Uralsk at dawn and returning at nightfall. Chapaev was able to find his way about the steppe with perfect ease, and could always determine the location of villages and hamlets, roads and tracks with great accuracy.

Then came a journey deep into the steppe that was to be the last Chapaev and Fyodor ever made together. Just a few days later Fyodor was recalled to headquarters for even more responsible work, and his place as commissar was taken by Pavel Stepanovich Baturin, whom he had known back in Moscow.

It was in vain that Chapaev kept sending grief-stricken telegrams to headquarters, begging the commander-in-chief not to take Fyodor away from him. It was all of no avail, though, for the question had already been decided.

For Fyodor this parting was as hard as it was for Chapaev. He did not know that it would save him from certain death, and that two weeks later Baturin who had replaced him would die in his stead ...

It was not until later that Fyodor began to ask himself in what way Chapaev was a hero, in what his exploits actually consisted, and generally speaking, whether such things as heroic exploits and heroes really exist. Chapaev and he had been inseparable for so long now, hour after hour and day after day. The times had been extremely eventful, full of continual marches and constant fighting. Fyodor had been aware of every move Chapaev had made and he had understood them all, just as for the most part he had understood the hidden motives for them as well. Then, day by day, he went over in his mind the time between their first meeting in Alexandrov-Gai and their last few hours together in Uralsk. He recalled the battle of Slomikhinskaya, Chapaev's enormous capacity for work, the speed with which he moved from one place to another, and his amazing quickwittedness. He recalled the march on Ufa and the battle for the city, then their return to Uralsk once more. But where precisely were the deeds which could be regarded as heroic? Chapaev's fame resounded far and wide, and it was probably more deserved by him than by anyone else. The Chapaev Division had never suffered defeat, and this was largely due to Chapaev himself. To have fused this division into a single unit, to have made it believe in its invincibility, to have trained it to endure the hardships and privations of army life with patience and even with contempt, to have chosen commanders worthy of it, then tempered them and filled them with his own driving will, to have rallied them around him and concentrated their thoughts on a single aim, a single desire—victory, victory, victory—all these accomplishments were heroism indeed! But it was not the kind of heroism that popular legend associated with the name of Chapaev. According to that legend, he was forever galloping up and down the front and, brandishing his sabre, would rout the enemy in person, flinging himself into the fiercest fighting and deciding its outcome. What really happened, though, was nothing of the sort. Chapaev was a fine, perceptive organizer excellently suited to the times, circumstances and environment with which he was concerned, which had given birth to him, and which had raised him to pride of place! If the times had been slightly different and the people around him had not been what they were, no one would ever have heard of Vasily Ivanovich Chapaev, the popular hero! His fame was carried over the steppe and like wisps of down was swept beyond it by hundreds of thousands of Red Army men who themselves had heard of his exploits from others, believed what they had heard, then went into raptures over it, embellishing it with inventions of their own and carrying it further still. But if one were to question these singers of Chapaev's praises, it would become clear that the majority of them had no firsthand knowledge of his exploits, had never met him in person, and did not even know a single authentic fact about him.

But that is precisely how legends about heroes come into being, and it is how the legends about Chapaev were created too.

His name will go down as a brilliant star in the history of the Civil War—and deservedly so, too, for such men as he were extremely rare.

We have now come to the drama which brings this sketch of ours to a close.

Looking back on the past six months, Fyodor hardly recognized himself, so greatly had he developed, so much more inwardly strong had he become, and so tempered had he been by the ordeals he had known. Now he was able confidently and simply to resolve all kinds of problems which before his experience at the front had seemed immensely difficult. Only now did he feel the powerful effect that the months of fighting had had upon him, and only now was he aware of the educational significance of life at the front.

Baturin arrived and put up with Fyodor at his quarters.

The next morning Fyodor bid his friends farewell and kissed them in parting. Then they all went their separate ways—Fyodor to Samara, and Chapaev and Baturin to the front to inspect the various brigades and regiments.

***

The Red forces were still advancing successfully. One brigade, reinforced by a second from another division, was marching down the highroad that led along the Ural River. A third brigade was advancing towards the Bukhara side,[49] as the area beyond the Ural is called. But Chapaev, who always grasped everything so quickly and adapted himself so readily to any change in the situation, realized that here, out in the steppes, it was impossible for the Reds to fight the Cossacks in the way they had recently fought the peasants forcibly mobilized into the Kolchak army. The Cossacks were not to be alarmed or frightened by any loss of territory. All this open expanse of steppe was Cossack country, and they could gallop back and forth over it at will, for wherever they went they were sure of a welcome from its Cossack population. They would live in your rear, infinitely treacherous and elusive, a constant source of very real danger. The Reds' aim now, Chapaev realized, should not be to drive the Cossacks back, to wait until disintegration set in amongst them, or to capture their villages one by one. Though all these things were important, none was paramount. What mattered most was to destroy the Cossacks' manpower, to smash their regiments once and for all. This, then, was the task that Chapaev set himself—the destruction of enemy manpower. The deeper the Red regiments advanced into the steppe, the harder this task would become, for they would run short of supplies, and hunger, thirst and exhaustion would gradually take their toll, while their distance from Headquarters would increasingly make itself felt.

It would be hard for the Cossacks too, but much harder still for the Red forces. This meant that they had to hurry, that they must be prepared for anything—ready to sacrifice both equipment and men, and to give up a great deal now so as not to lose even more later by allowing themselves to be drawn deep into the steppe. And so Chapaev was searching for ways that would lead to his desired goal. Accordingly, forces were concentrated, and Lbishchensk, the second Ural capital, was taken by a frontal attack. Losses? Yes, there were losses, but the results were even more important. Half a dozen more such blows, and the entire campaign would be over.

After capturing Lbishchensk, the Red troops took Goryachensky,[50] but then at Mergenevsky[51] they encountered fierce resistance and had to halt. The retreating Cossacks saw their own position perfectly clearly, and realized what awaited them in the barren sands along the lower reaches of the river. They had to repel the Red forces somewhere here, before it was too late and everything was lost, so they strengthened the defences of their large villages to the utmost. But the Red regiments next made a frontal attack on Mergenevsky, and despite its heavy defences, managed to take it. Many Cossacks were killed, but the Red losses were even heavier, and the victory cost them dearly.

The Red forces were already preparing to march on—through Kalmykov[52] south to Guryev on the Caspian Sea. But then a tragedy occurred that will never, ever be forgotten.

***

Divisional Headquarters were now at Lbishchensk. From there Chapaev and Baturin continued to visit the various brigades by car almost every day. The cold weather of autumn was approaching, and fresh, bracing days were followed by brief twilight, then by silent black nights. The position of the retreating Cossacks was becoming more and more desperate, for ahead of them lay only desolate steppe, endless feather-grass and hunger in territory that was alien to them. If they were to make a stand, it must be now—later on would be too late. So they decided to make a last, desperate effort: they would outwit their vigilant and triumphant enemy and strike him a blow straight in the heart. They decided to make a deep raid from beyond Sakharnaya, through the Kushum valley[53] and past the Chizha swamps—past the very places where back in the spring the Chapaev Division had defeated them at Slomikhinskaya—and, having penetrated undetected to the Reds' rear, with a sudden blow destroy everything they had concentrated in Lbishchensk. At the time there were not only considerable numbers of men and various administrative sections in the town, but also all kinds of military supplies—cartridges, shells and uniforms which had just been delivered—the latter because the division was about to be fitted out with fresh kit since entire companies and even battalions had gone down with typhus due to the privations and filth of the long march. (In fact, during this arduous march from Uralsk to Guryev, many more men fell victim to typhus than were killed in battle.)

The Cossacks thought that once the Reds' Divisional Headquarters had been destroyed and communications cut, the regiments which had advanced a hundred versts downriver would be left empty-handed, and seeing the utter pointlessness of further resistance, would readily surrender. The hitherto invincible Chapaev Division would be smashed, they thought, and its destruction would liberate the Ural steppes from the Red invader.

The Cossacks placed very great hopes on this operation, and for that reason their most experienced military leaders were put in command of it. Dark clouds were gathering over Lbishchensk, but the town lived on, unaware that such a terrible catastrophe was so imminent . . .

That day Chapaev was unusually gloomy. Early in the morning he went racing off in the car to the front, but did not stay there long and returned to Lbishchensk at noon. The Red advance had begun to lose momentum. Typhus was mowing down the men in countless numbers, and the transports could not bring up all the necessary supplies in time. The brigades were doing their absolute utmost, straining themselves to the point of exhaustion, but the situation was too much even for their selfless heroism. So Chapaev was in a very gloomy mood.

***

It was already long past midnight, and the first faint hint of dawn was already flickering in the sky, but the village of Lbishchensk was still peacefully asleep. The advanced Cossack patrols rode silently up to the outskirts of the village and removed the sentries. Behind them came others, and the groups of men closed up and flowed together. Then, when enough of them had gathered, they rode forward in a great, dark mass.

The first warning shots fired by the remaining Red sentries rang out, but it was too late, for the Cossacks had already spread out through the streets of the village. Disorderly, blind firing broke out, with no one knowing where to fire or at whom. The Red Army men leapt up, and wearing nothing but their underclothes, began to rush about in all directions. It was clear they were totally disorganized and unprepared. Separate, small groups of men clustered together haphazardly, while those who had managed to seize rifles tried to hold on to any remotely convenient place where they could take cover, and opened fire into the streets. Then they stopped and ran down towards the river—the general direction taken by the retreating Reds was towards the bank of the Ural. On the outskirts of the village the Cossacks were galloping after the fleeing men, cutting them down with their sabres or capturing them and driving them off. They met with almost no resistance whatsoever. Nevertheless, the enemy were unable to penetrate to the very center of the village. At one place several dozen men had crowded round Chapaev, and forming a skirmish line, they lay down on the ground. Chapaev, too, had come running out only in his underclothes, a rifle in his right hand and a revolver in his left. It was fairly light by this time, and everything could be seen quite clearly. There were two or three minutes of agonizing suspense, then the men in the skirmish line saw a mass of Cossack cavalry galloping towards them. They fired one volley, followed by a second and a third. Then a machine-gun that had been hurriedly dragged up to the line began to chatter and the Cossacks fell back.

But the various small groups of Red soldiers were cut off from one another and there was no communication between them, so the success of one was cancelled out by the failure of those not far away. None of the men knew what was happening around them or what they should do. Realizing they could not achieve rapid success by continuing to make frontal attacks, some of the Cossacks dismounted and began to make their way through the backyards and gardens so as to work round to the defenders' rear.

But where was Chapaev?

The Reds had not been able to hold out in the trenches for very long, because the Cossacks had penetrated those positions too as they moved forward. The only way of retreat now was towards the steep bank of the river. Here the bank rose high above the water, and to climb the ridge towards it was tantamount to making oneself a sitting target, but there was nothing else the Reds could do. Cossack machine-guns had already been set up along the bank, and they were firing down at the water and killing the men who were trying to escape by swimming across to the Bukhara side. Chapaev had already been hit in the arm, and when he wiped his face with his sleeve, he left streaks of blood on his forehead and cheek.

Step by step they retreated towards the steep river bank. There was almost no hope of escape—very few of them were managing to make it across the swift-flowing Ural. But they were determined to save Chapaev.

Four of the men standing closest to him slowly helped Chapaev down the sandy slope towards the water, carefully supporting his bleeding arm as they did so. Then Chapaev and three others flung themselves into the river and began to swim across. Two of them were killed the moment they touched the water. The two others swam on and had almost reached the far bank when a cruel bullet struck Chapaev in the head. By the time his companion had crawled out of the water into the reeds and looked round, there was no one behind him any more. Chapaev had been swept away by the turbulent Ural...

The Red brigades were holding positions at Sakharnaya and Cossack villages higher up the river when the terrible news reached them: Headquarters had been destroyed and together with it the entire Divisional Command and the Political Department; communications had been cut and the supply depot captured, which meant there would be no more cartridges and shells, no more uniforms, boots or bread... The position was desperately serious! The Red troops were exhausted by all the fighting and were weak with hunger, but what was more appalling still was that whole companies were dying of typhus. Cut off and surrounded by Cossacks, with their commanders nearly all dead—what could they do?

To continue the advance would have been senseless, so it was decided to retreat immediately, evacuating their positions unobtrusively in an attempt to deceive the enemy, extremely vigilant though he was.

They marched for almost two days and nights without a halt. There was no time to rest, for every minute was precious. On the second night they reached Lbishchensk. The Cossacks had left the place the day before and had marched off upriver towards Uralsk.

It was night again when the Red forces reached the little village of Yanaisky.[54] Their fatigue knew no bounds and they could barely keep on their feet. The men slumped to the ground and slept like the dead. Even the sentries could not stay awake, and they too soon fell asleep. The Red camp was like a vast kingdom of the dead. And now, in the night, the Cossacks made ready to strike another sudden blow. They crept up until they were almost on top of the enemy, then waited for the first flickering hint of dawn. All was ready and death was hovering over the Red units!

No sooner had the thick September darkness begun to turn gray than a thunderous roar broke from the Cossack lines: "Hurrah! Hurrah! Hurrah!" Then they opened fire in volleys and from somewhere in their rear the White artillery began to boom.

Sound asleep though they had been, the Red Army men sprang up and immediately seized their rifles. But there was no organized resistance, no sense of order, for the first Cossack bullets had killed many of the commanders. As a result, the Reds were thrown into confusion. The disorder was increasing, and at any moment, it seemed, there would be mad, disastrous panic. Nikolai Khrebtov, commander of the division's artillery—he who had done such splendid work at Krasny Yar—went running up to the guns, but not a single gunner was in his place. Some had run off to hide among the wagons, while others were lying face down on the ground, trying to escape the enemy's fire. With a masterful cry Khrebtov got the men to their feet and fired one shell, followed by a second and a third, then the battery began a fierce and devastating barrage. This was enough to prevent panic among the Red troops, for as soon as the men heard and saw their own batteries firing, they roused themselves and took heart, and new commanders quickly appeared in place of those who had been killed. Then a dogged and extremely bloody battle began, the likes of which not even the veteran commanders of the Chapaev Division had ever seen . . .

The Cossacks were driven back several versts. Many Red soldiers perished in the fighting at Yanaisky, but even more Cossacks were left dead on the battlefield. In places they lay in rows where an entire skirmish line had been mown down by the implacable fire of the Red machine-guns.

There were no more battles like that at Yanaisky. It was not long before reinforcements were brought up, and then the Cossacks were driven back through the same villages where only a few days before the Red regiments had passed, hurriedly retreating before their pursuers. Then the Red forces launched another offensive, and advanced as far south as Guryev and the shores of the Caspian Sea.

Through Lbishchensk they marched, too, and pausing to stand motionless over the communal graves of their comrades, sang funeral hymns and swore to fight on to victory. And as they stood, they remembered those who with selfless courage had given their lives on the banks and in the waves of the turbulent Ural.

Moscow, January 20, 1923

Notes

1. With the exception of chapter 1, most of *Chapaev* is set east and southeast of Saratov on the middle Volga, in the remote steppe country around the Ural River where it flows south from Uralsk to Guryev and the Caspian Sea.

2. Mikhail Vasilievich Frunze (1885–1925), military theorist and Red Army commander on the eastern front during the Civil War. Leader of important strike in Ivanovo-Voznesensk in 1905.

3. Alexander Vasilievich Kolchak (1874–1920), Russian admiral. After the 1917 Revolution took an active part in the fighting against the Bolsheviks in Siberia. From November 1918 to January 1920 he was "Supreme Ruler of Russia". Captured by the Bolsheviks, he was shot at Irkutsk in February 1920.

4. Large industrial city, textile center and important railway junction, approximately 175 miles northeast of Moscow. In the late 1800s and early 1900s, well-known for its large and frequent workers' strikes. Named Ivanovo since 1932.

5. Town (and surrounding province) on River Ural approximately 250 miles southeast of Kuybyshev. Named Chkalov between 1938 and 1957.

6. Town on River Ural in extreme north-west of Kazakhstan, approximately 150 miles south of Kuybyshev.

7. Important port and railway junction on the Volga River approximately 550 miles southeast of Moscow. Renamed Kuybyshev in 1935.

8. Geographical name given to coniferous forest in the north of Russia and Siberia.

9. Isthmus joining the Crimean peninsula to the mainland. In November 1920 during the Civil War Red troops forced the Sivash strait nearby and broke through the White defences to liberate the Crimea.

10. Vasily Ivanovich Chapaev (1887–1919), hero of the Civil War. From 1918 commander of Red Army detachment, brigade and finally 25th Infantry Division. Played an important part in the defeat of White forces under Kolchak east of the Volga in summer, 1919.

11. A reference to the Czechoslovak Legion which fought alongside White forces east of the Volga and in Siberia during the Civil War.

12. District town on the Bolshoi Irgiz River northeast of Saratov. Named Nikolaevsk until 1918. Renamed in honor of E. I. Pugachov (see note 16).

13. Town on the Volga northeast of Saratov.

14. Town southwest of Kuybyshev. Renamed Chapaevsk in 1929.

15. Village southwest of Kuybyshev, on the road to Pugachov.

16. (1740 or 1742–75), Don Cossack and leader of peasant rebellion 1773–5, during which he displayed outstanding ability as military commander. Betrayed and executed in Moscow.

17. (c. 1630–71), Don Cossack, Ataman and leader of peasant revolt 1670–71, in which he demonstrated great skill both as strategist and as military commander. Betrayed and executed in Moscow.

18. (?-1585), famous Cossack Ataman. In late 1581 began conquest of Siberia. Killed in battle with Tatars.

19. (Bolshaya Tavolozhka), village northeast of Pugachov.

20. Town approximately 150 miles west of Uralsk.

21. Town approximately 150 miles southeast of Saratov.

22. Location obscure.

23. Small port on the Ural River south of Uralsk. Renamed Chapaev in 1939—Chapaev was killed in action near Lbishchensk—and now home of the Chapaev museum.

24. Town on the Ural River in western Kazakhstan, close to where it joins the Caspian Sea.

25. Towns between Saratov and Uralsk.

26. Town west of Uralsk.

27. Villages southeast of Saratov.

28. Village southeast of Alexandrov-Gai.

29. Small town south of Mergenevo on southern Ural River, approximately 100 miles south of Uralsk.

30. West of Uralsk.

31. (Kaztalovka), village south of Alexandrov-Gai.

32. Town approximately 125 miles north of Uralsk.

33. Large town on Belaya River approximately 250 miles northeast of Kuybyshev. Now capital of Bashkir Republic.

34. Town on west bank of Volga approximately 75 miles north of Saratov.

35. Constitutional Democratic Party, principal liberal and monarchist party in Russia between 1905 and 1917.

36. Socialist Revolutionary Party, left-wing democratic party in Russia between 1901 and 1923. Played central role in Provisional Government after February 1917 Revolution.

37. Alexander Kerensky (1881–1970), Russian politician, lawyer and leading SR after 1910. Minister of Justice, then of War, and finally Prime Minister in Provisional Government after February Revolution. Supreme Commander of Russian armed forces from late August 1917. After October Revolution emigrated to USA.

38. Highly obscure. Possibly a mythical rather than a historical figure.

39. Town and important railway junction just east of Kuybyshev.

40. Large town in western Siberia, approximately 700 miles east of Moscow.

41. City on Volga approximately 450 miles east of Moscow.

42. Large town about 500 miles northeast of Moscow. Renamed Kirov in 1934.

43. Anton Ivanovich Denikin (1872–1947), Commander of the Volunteer Army in South Russia from April 1918.

44. Town approximately 200 miles north of Uralsk.

45. Town approximately 90 miles southwest of Ufa.

46. (Chishmy), town southwest of Ufa.

47. Location obscure.

48. Location obscure.

49. Properly speaking, the desert region around the ancient town of Bukhara in western Uzbekistan, southeast of the Aral Sea.

50. Location obscure.

51. (Mergenevo), town on southern Ural River, approximately 90 miles south of Uralsk.

52. (Kalmykovo), town on southern Ural River, approximately 150 miles south of Uralsk.

53. River valley west of Lbishchensk, Mergenevsky and Sakharnaya.

54. Location obscure.

Alexander Serafimovich (1913).

Alexander Serafimovich
THE IRON FLOOD

Serafimovich and Ostrovsky's widow with Guards officers near Oryol on the western front (1943). Boris Pasternak is in the second row, far left.

Alexander Serafimovich (1863–1949)

A genuine Don Cossack, Alexander Serafimovich Popov (Serafimovich was his usual pseudonym) was born in 1863 in the village of Nizhne-Kurmoyarskaya near Tsimlyansk, about 100 miles east of Rostov-on-Don in what was then the Don Military Region. When he was three, his family left for Poland where the father, a Cossack captain, served with Cossack regiments stationed there. In 1874, when Serafimovich's father was appointed adjutant to the district ataman, the family returned to the Don. They settled in the small town of Ust-Medveditskaya (renamed Serafimovich in 1933), about 175 miles north of Rostov, where the boy entered the classical *gimnaziya.*

When their father died in 1876, the family fell on hard times and the young Serafimovich had to help support them by giving lessons. But the boy's mother managed to secure a military scholarship for him, and in 1883 he enrolled in the mathematics and physics department at the University of St. Petersburg. Here he came into contact with progressive student circles, read Marx, and met Alexander Ulyanov, Lenin's older brother. He then joined a revolutionary student group, and from 1885 his activities brought him under secret police surveillance. In 1887, his final year at university, he was arrested for writing a proclamation about the attempted assassination of Tsar Alexander III in March of that year—an attempt for which Ulyanov and four others were hanged. After four months in prison, Serafimovich was exiled for three years to the town of Mezen in Archangel Province in the far north of Russia. There he met many political exiles, among them the well-known revolutionary and organizer of weavers' strikes, Pyotr Moiseenko, who was to be the writer's friend for many years.

When his term of exile ended in 1890, Serafimovich returned to Ust-Medveditskaya but remained under police surveillance. On regaining his right of free movement in 1892, he went first to Novocherkassk and then to Rostov-on-Don, where for the next few years he made a living by giving lessons and contributing feuilletons, articles and sketches to provincial newspapers. In addition, from 1901 until early

1902 he served as assistant chief clerk in the Don provincial administration in Novocherkassk.

In 1902 Serafimovich moved to Moscow, where he devoted himself wholly to journalistic and literary work. He was invited by the writer Leonid Andreev to join the Moscow paper *The Messenger (Kur'er)*, and then became a member of the *Sreda* ("Wednesday") literary circle, meeting in it such prominent literary figures as Maxim Gorky, Ivan Bunin, Alexander Kuprin and Vikenty Veresaev. In 1903 he joined Gorky's cooperative publishing enterprise *Znanie* ("Knowledge"), which had been established in St. Petersburg in 1898.

The 1905 Revolution saw Serafimovich closely associated with participants in the armed rising in the Presnya district of Moscow, an experience later reflected in his writing. The years before World War I brought not only varied journalistic and literary work, but also much travelling, notably to the Don and, in 1910, to Finland. In 1915, after the outbreak of war, Serafimovich went to Galicia, where together with Lenin's sister, Maria Ulyanova, he served as a medical orderly at the front and also worked as a correspondent for the newspaper *The Russian Gazette (Russkie vedomosti)*.

Serafimovich's reputation was only firmly established after 1917, when he became one of the first writers to support the Bolsheviks. His loyalty to them was rewarded by expulsion from both the "Wednesday" circle and the Writers' Publishing House in Moscow, measures indicative of the anti-Bolshevik mood prevalent among Russian writers shortly after the Revolution. Soon after October 1917 Serafimovich assumed responsibility for the artistic section of *Izvestiya*, and then in March 1918 became a correspondent for both *Pravda* and *Izvestiya*, visiting several fronts during the Civil War. In May of that year he joined the Communist Party.

After the Civil War Serafimovich played an important part in Soviet cultural life, both as an administrator and public speaker, and gave valuable help to several younger writers, among them Furmanov, Ostrovsky and Gladkov. At the same time he engaged in editorial work, notably as a board member of the journal *Creative Work (Tvorchestvo)* and as chief editor of *October (Oktyabr')*. In addition, he travelled throughout the USSR, speaking in factories and workers' clubs in the far north, the Urals and Siberia. 1931 in particular witnessed a memorable journey over the southern steppes, during which he visited Sholokhov at Veshenskaya on the upper Don. Despite failing health, Serafimovich remained extremely active almost to the end of his long life. During World War II, for example, the octogenarian writer visited the front and wrote articles and sketches about the fighting.

One of the first Soviet authors to be awarded a Stalin Prize and the holder of many distinctions, among them Orders of the Red Banner and of Lenin, Serafimovich is now regarded as a founding father of Soviet literature and a veteran proletarian writer. After a protracted illness he died on his eighty-sixth birthday in January 1949 in Moscow.

***

Serafimovich's first published work was the short tale *On an Ice-Floe*. A story of hunters on the White Sea, it was begun in 1887 during his exile and serialized in the newspaper *The Russian Gazette* in February and March 1889. This was followed by *The Snow Desert* (1889) and *On Rafts* (1890), also written in exile, and then by *The Switchman* (1891), a railway story based on the author's experiences while staying near Tsaritsyn (later Stalingrad and now Volgograd) after leaving the north.

In 1901 Serafimovich's first collection of tales was published in St. Petersburg and won him praise from such prominent writers of the older generation as Gleb Uspensky and Vladimir Korolenko. 1902 witnessed the publication of *In the Health Resort,* a tale set in Yalta where the writer had received treatment for tuberculosis. The following year saw the appearance of two southern sea stories, the fishing tale *Into the Storm* and the shorter piece *On the Shore,* which is set in Kerch on the Sea of Azov. In 1903 the "Knowledge" enterprise started to publish Serafimovich's collected works in four volumes (the last appearing in 1910), and at the same time his stories began to figure in "Knowledge" miscellanies—his tale *On the Way,* for example, was included in the enterprise's first miscellany, issued in 1904.

The events of 1905 and Serafimovich's involvement in the Moscow rising found a reflection in several tales, notably *In Presnya* (1906), *The Bombs* (1906), and *How They Were Hanged* (1908). Echoes of the 1905 Revolution were also to be detected in the stories *In the Middle of the Night* (1906), with its portrayal of a workers' mass meeting in the Crimea, *The Glow of a Fire* (1907), describing the burning of church estates, and *At the Precipice* (1907), which mirrors the punitive measures taken by the authorities after the unrest of 1905. These works were followed by a series of tales on various subjects, among them *Forest Life* (1908), set in Archangel Province and based on the author's experiences in exile, *Sands* (1908), a story of peasant greed and murder which was highly praised by Leo Tolstoy, and *Chibis* (1908), a sad tale about a homeless family of farm laborers roaming the author's native Don country.

Serafimovich's first novel was *A Town in the Steppe,* published in the journal *The Contemporary World (Sovremennyi mir)* in 1912 and issued in book form the following year. Written between 1907 and 1910, it portrays the construction of a new industrial town in the Don steppes and the struggle between capitalists and proletarians that accompanies it. Several tales which followed were devoted to the harsh existence of the poor. Among them are *The Three Friends* (1914), about life on a small farm on the Don, and *Short Summer Night* (1916), which deals with the cruel exploitation of children.

During the First World War in stories such as *The Black Three-Cornered Cap* and *The Thermometer* (1914), Serafimovich wrote of the poverty and suffering of ordinary people both at the front and in the rear. A notable product of his experience as a correspondent during the Civil War was the vivid series of sketches and tales *The Revolution, the Front and the Rear* (1917–20).

Serafimovich's main post-Revolutionary work was *The Iron Flood,* now a Soviet classic and the novel for which he is best remembered. Begun in 1921, it was first published in the Moscow almanac *The Depths (Nedra)* in 1924 and appeared as a separate edition later that year.

The Iron Flood marked the high point of Serafimovich's career and he produced comparatively little of significance in the years that followed. 1926, however, brought the publication of *Two Deaths,* a dramatic short story set during the street fighting that accompanied the October Revolution in Moscow, while 1931 saw the appearance of *Over the Don Steppes,* a series of sketches devoted to the life of the Don Cossacks. The latter pieces were intended to serve as a prelude to Serafimovich's third novel *Collective Farm Fields,* which was left unfinished when he died. In addition, before World War II he embarked on an autobiographical novel and continued work on it until the end of his life, though sadly it too remained unfinished at his death.

***

The Iron Flood describes the march of the Taman Army between late August and mid-September 1918, during the Russian Civil War. Red forces, cut off by the Whites on the Taman peninsula between the Sea of Azov and the Black Sea, fought their way under the leadership of E. I. Kovtyukh and I. I. Matveev through the coastal towns of Gelendzhik and Tuapse, then crossed the main Caucasus range to join up with the Red Army of the Northern Caucasus in the region of Dondukovskaya on the Laba River, northeast of the town of Maikop.

THE IRON FLOOD

1

The orchards and streets, wattle fences and huts of the Cossack village were enveloped in thick clouds of stifling dust, and only the tops of the tapering poplars could be seen above it.

From every side came the sound of barking dogs, neighing horses and clanging metal. There were children crying, men swearing, women shouting, and drunken voices singing to an accordion. It was as though a giant beehive had lost its queen and were humming discordantly in confusion.

A fiery haze enveloped the steppe, spreading as far as the windmills out on the ancient burial mound, and there too could be heard the same ceaseless tumult of a thousand-voiced multitude.

Only the foaming river whose cold mountain water went racing past the village was not smothered by the stifling dust, while away in the distance the clear, dark blue mountains rose immense into the sky.

In the glittering, sultry air, red kites—those brigands of the steppe—drifted constantly to and fro, turning their hooked beaks from side to side and listening in amazement. But they could make nothing of it, for never before had there been such a sight.

Was it a fair? But if so, why were there no tents anywhere, why were there no traders or piles of merchandise?

Or was it a settlers' camp? But why were there ammunition wagons and piles of weapons, two-wheeled army carts and stacked rifles wherever you looked?

Or was it an army? But why were there children crying everywhere, nappies hung out on rifles to dry, and cradles swinging from the barrels of guns? Why were there young mothers suckling their babies, cows munching hay beside artillery horses, girls with sunburnt faces hanging pots of millet and lard over pungent fires of dried dung?

All was confusion and disorder amid the clouds of dust, all was commotion and uproar amid the constant hubbub of countless discordant voices.

In the village itself there were only old women, mothers and children left. Not a single Cossack had remained behind—they had all vanished as though the earth had swallowed them up...

2

Audible above the lowing of cows and the crowing of cocks were the voices of the steppe people, some raucous and hoarse, others ringing and firm:

"Hey, lads, hurry up!"

"Come to the meeting, comrades!"

"Over by the windmills!"

As the sun gradually cooled, the fiery dust began to settle, and the poplars emerged in all their towering grandeur.

Stretching as far as the eye could see, orchards slowly appeared from the haze, huts showed up white in the distance, and the village streets and lanes were filled from end to end with a stream of bullock carts and wagons, horses and cows. Passing through the orchards and spreading beyond them, they stretched as far as the windmills that stood out on the burial mound, their long, webbed fingers pointing in all directions over the steppe.

Around the windmills, amid the growing tumult of voices, a sea of people spread ever wider, their sunburnt faces stretching away into the distance further than the eye could see. There were gray-bearded old men, women with tired faces, and young girls with merry eyes. There were little boys darting to and fro between people's legs, and panting dogs with their tongues hanging out. But all these were lost in the vast, ever-surging mass of soldiers. They wore fearsome-looking, tall fur hats, threadbare peaked caps, and felt mountain bonnets with drooping brims. Some had long, narrow Circassian coats, faded cotton shirts or ragged tunics, while others were naked to the waist with cartridge-belts slung across their sunburnt, muscular bodies. And in a disorderly way a forest of burnished, dark blue bayonets bristled above their heads on every side.

Out on the burial mound near the windmills all the regimental, battalion and company commanders, together with the chiefs of staff, had gathered together. Who were they all? Some were Tsarist officers who had risen through the ranks, while others were barbers and coopers, fishermen and sailors from towns and villages alike. All were leaders of small Red Army units which they had mustered in their own villages and hamlets. There were a few regular officers, too, who had gone over to the Red Army.

Vorobyov, an enormously tall regimental commander with a huge mustache, climbed up to speak, and his loud voice rang out over the crowd:

"Comrades!"

"Go to hell!" came the reply.

"Down with him!"

"What kind of a commander are you?"

"Smash him, smash 'em all to hell!"

Near one of the windmills stood a short, very stocky man with square, tightly-set jaws, who looked as if he were made of lead. From under knitted brows his gray, gimlet eyes glittered as they took in everything around him. The shadow cast by his body was very short and its head seemed to be trampled by those standing around him.

"Where the hell are we going now?" someone cried.

"To Ekaterinodar!"[1]

"But the Cadets[2] are there!"

"There's nowhere else to go!"

The man with the iron jaws watched with his gray eyes that were as sharp as gimlets.

Then an irrepressible cry broke from the crowd:

"They've sold us out!"

The man with the iron jaws clenched them tighter still. Filled with despair, he surveyed the raging human sea to its furthest edge, and saw the dark, shouting mouths, the angry red faces, and eyes full of rage that flashed beneath knitted brows.

He felt particularly grieved: after all, he had fought side by side with these men as a machine-gunner on the Turkish front. There had been seas of blood and countless thousands of dead ... Then, during the last few months, they had fought together against the Cadets, the Cossacks and the White generals. They had fought in Eisk, Temriuk, Taman[3] and the Cossack villages in the Kuban.

Then the man unclenched his jaws and said in a soft but iron-hard voice that could be heard above all the uproar and commotion:

"You know me, comrades—we have shed our blood together, and you yourselves chose me as your commander. But if you carry on like this, we shall all be done for. The Cossacks and Cadets are pressing hard on us from every side, and there's not a moment to lose."

He spoke with a Ukrainian accent which disposed the crowd favorably towards him.

But suddenly a terrible silence fell as all heads turned and all eyes looked in the same direction.

Across the steppe, bending low over the stubble with its body stretched out like a taut thread, a black horse was galloping towards them. Wearing a striped red shirt, its rider lay with his chest and face pressed to the animal's mane and his arms hanging down at its sides. Nearer and nearer came the horse. Now everyone could see how, crazed with fear, it was straining forward with all its might, leaving clouds of dust swirling behind it. Its chest was covered with flecks of white foam and its sweating flanks were thick with lather, while its rider, his head still resting on the mane, swayed to and fro in time to the animal's galloping hoofs.

Then a second dark speck appeared out in the distant steppe, and a murmur ran through the crowd:

"Look! There's another coming!"

"Yes, and he's going hell for leather too!"

Then the first black horse galloped up to them, scattering flecks of white foam and snorting. It came to a sudden halt in front of the crowd and sank down on its hind legs. Then its rider in his striped red shirt slid over the animal's head like a sack of flour and slumping heavily to the ground, lay there with his head twisted awkwardly and his arms outstretched.

Some of the crowd rushed towards him while others ran to the horse whose black flanks were sticky with blood.

"It's Okhrim!" they cried as they reached the corpse, then they carefully put it into a more comfortable position. On the man's chest and shoulder a long, bloody sword wound gaped wide, while on his back there was a black spot of clotted blood. The body was already growing cold.

Then, through the crowd, spreading beyond the windmills and away among the carts, echoing with alarm down the streets and lanes of the village, came the cry:

"The Cossacks have cut Okhrim to bits!"

Then the other horseman came galloping up. His closely-fitting shirt, his face and hands, his bare feet and his trousers were all bespattered with blood. But whose blood was it? His own, or someone else's? With eyes that were round with fear, he leapt from his swaying horse and rushed towards the body lying on the ground, its face already covered by the translucent, wax-like pallor of death and its eyes now thick with crawling flies.

"Okhrim!" he cried.

Then he quickly went down on his hands and knees and put his ear to the man's bloodstained chest. But he got up again straightaway and stood over the body with his head bowed:

"My son . . . " he said, "my son!"

For a while he did not move, then suddenly he cried in a hoarse voice that carried away among the carts to the furthest house in the village:

"Slavyanskaya has risen in revolt and so have Poltavskaya, Petrovskaya and Stiblievskaya[4] too! They've put up a gallows in each village—out in the square, in front of the church—and they're hanging anybody they can lay hands on, one after the other! The Cadets have come into Stiblievskaya, laying about them with sabres, hanging and shooting, driving people into the Kuban river with their horses and drowning them. They've got no mercy for those who aren't Cossacks—even old men and women—they treat them all just the same. They're all Bolsheviks, they say . . . The whole of the Kuban's in flames now. They torture those who are in the army, then hang them on trees. Some of our detachments are trying to fight their way through in various places—some to Ekaterinodar and others to Rostov[5] or the sea—but they're all getting hacked to pieces by Cossack sabres!"

Then the man fell silent, and with his head bowed, stood over his son's body once more.

In the leaden stillness all eyes were upon him.

Then he swayed, and seizing his horse's bridle, remounted. The animal's bloody nostrils still flared with stertorous breathing and its sweating flanks were still heaving after the furious gallop.

"Hey, Pavlo! Where are you going?"

"Stop! Come back!"

But he had already set off at a mad gallop and was fast disappearing into the distance. The long, slanting shadows of the windmills went chasing after him across the wide expanse of steppe.

"He's going to his death! It's senseless!"

"But the rest of his family's back there in Slavyanskaya, and his son's lying here—dead . . . "

The man with the iron jaws unclenched them and moving them heavily, said slowly and deliberately:

"Comrades, now there's nowhere left for us to go, because death lies both in front of us and behind us. Those folk over there," and he nodded towards the Cossack huts that were glowing pink in the setting sun, "might cut our throats this very night, yet we haven't got a single sentry or scout, and not even anyone in command. We must retreat! But where to? First of all we've got to reorganize the army. We must choose commanders, but this time it's got to be for good and they'll have to be given the power of life and death over us. Iron discipline's the only thing that can save us now! We'll fight our way through to the north where our main forces are, then they'll reach out a helping hand to us. Do you agree?"

"Yes, we agree!" the steppe resounded with a united roar that echoed among the carts in the streets and lanes, and rolled away through the orchards right to the outskirts of the village, as far as the river itself.

"Good! Then let's choose a commander straightaway, and after that we'll reorganize our detachments. The baggage train must be separated from the fighting units, then each unit must be given a commander."

"We agree!" again the cry echoed over the boundless, yellow steppe.

Once again the man with the iron jaws unclenched them and said:

"Comrades! We must elect a commander, then he's got to pick his staff. So whom do you choose?"

For a moment there was dead silence, and the steppe, the village and the countless crowd all were still. Then a forest of calloused hands was raised, and to the very edge of the steppe, echoing through the spreading orchards and away beyond the river itself, thundered one name and one name alone:

"Kozh-u-ukh!"

Kozhukh clenched his iron jaws and saluted, and those near him could see the muscles working below his cheekbones. Then he went up to the corpse lying on the ground and took off his dirty straw hat. Following his example, all hats were raised and all heads bared as though a mighty wind had swept the crowd, and the women began to sob. With his head bowed, Kozhukh stood motionless for a moment over the body. Then he said:

"Let us bury our comrade with full honors. Come, lift him up."

An army greatcoat was spread out on the ground and Okhrim was laid upon it. Then they lifted him and carried him away.

The crowd parted to let the body pass, then drew together again and streamed on after the bearers in an endless procession, all heads still bared. Behind each of them and inseparable from him went a long, slanting shadow, and those walking behind trampled it underfoot.

Here were the crosses in the graveyard, some standing crookedly, others lying where they had fallen. Around them lay the deserted steppe, covered with scrub that stretched away into the distance. An owl flew silently by and bats flitted softly to and fro. Now and then marble headstones showed dimly white and gilt inscriptions gleamed through the gathering gloom, revealing the tombs of wealthy Cossacks and merchants—monuments to a once prosperous and inviolable way of life ...

Kozhukh climbed the mound of freshly-shovelled earth, his head still bared:

"Comrades! Our brother is dead and we must honor him, for he has perished for our sake. But comrades, Soviet Russia is not dead—no, for it will live until the end of time! We are caught in a trap here, comrades, and away over there are Soviet Russia and Moscow. But Russia will triumph in the end, for in Russia, comrades, power belongs to the workers and peasants, and that power will set everything to rights. We're being attacked by the Cadets—that is by generals, landowners and all kinds of bloodsucking capitalists—bastards, all of them! But to hell with them—we'll not give in! We'll show them all right! So comrades, let us now throw earth on our brother's coffin and swear over his grave to support Soviet power!"

They began to lower the coffin.

Then someone whispered in Kozhukh's ear:

"How many cartridges shall I give them?"

"A dozen."

"That's not many."

"We're short, you know. We've got to be sparing with every bullet now."

A thin volley rang out, then a second and a third, and each time, for an instant, wooden crosses, dark faces and quickly moving spades were illumined in the gloom.

When silence descended, everyone suddenly realized that night had fallen. All was still, there was a smell of warm dust in the air, and the incessant, drowsy murmur of the river brought back vague memories of things they could not quite recall, while away beyond the river, stretching far into the distance, lay the massive, black bulk of the mountains, their jagged peaks dimly outlined against the dark sky.

3

The little black windows stared into the darkness, and in their silent immobility there was an ominous air of mystery.

From the unshaded tin lamp standing on a stool, a plume of smoke rose quickly towards the ceiling, swaying as it went. The floor was spread with a fantastic carpet covered with countless blue and green patches, winding black lines and curious symbols. It was a huge map of the Caucasus.

Crawling cautiously over it in bare feet were the officers, their army tunics unfastened. Some were smoking and trying not to drop ash on the map, while others were totally absorbed in what they were doing and simply went on moving to and fro all the time. Kozhukh was squatting beside the map deep in thought, gazing past the others with a faraway look in his bright, gimlet eyes. Clouds of blue-gray tobacco smoke filled the room.

Rolling in through the dark windows came the incessant sound of the river, a sound of which no one had been aware during the day but which now seemed full of menace.

But no matter how carefully they studied the map, it made no difference. To the left they were hemmed in by the dark blue sea, and to the right and further inland were scores of hostile Cossack villages, both large and small, while lower down, to the south, their way was barred by impassable ranges of ginger-yellow mountains. In a word, they were trapped.

Their huge camp now lay sprawled on the banks of the same black river that wound its way across the map. In the ravines and marshes, in the forests and on the plains, in villages and hamlets all over the map Cossacks were massing. So far, uprisings in the various villages had been put down somehow, but now the whole Kuban in all its vastness was engulfed by the flames of revolt. Everywhere Soviet power had been swept aside. Its representatives in the villages and hamlets had been hacked to pieces, and gallows now stood all over the land, clustering as thick as crosses in a graveyard. On them Bolsheviks were being hanged—most of them non-Cossacks, but some of them native Cossacks too. All these and others were now swinging in death. So where, then, was there to retreat to? Where could they find safety?

"It's obvious—we've got to force our way through to Tikhoretskaya and from there push on to Svyatoy Krest,[6] then after that we'll be able to get north into Russia."

"I say we must fight our way through to join up with our main forces."

"I think we should occupy Novorossiisk,[7] then wait till reinforcements come from the north."

"What I say is this . . . "

"Excuse me, comrade," interrupted a clean-shaven officer, "it's completely impossible to lead an army in the condition ours is in. It's not an army but a rabble, and it's just got to be reorganized. What's more, all these refugee carts bind us hand and foot, so we must separate them from the troops. Let them go where they like—even back home if they want to—but the army must be completely unhampered and free. I propose we draft an order to say we're staying in this village for two days so as to reorganize."

"What on earth are you talking about?" retorted Kozhukh in a voice that grated like rusty iron. "Every man's got relatives in that baggage train—either a mother or a father, a girlfriend or even his whole family. So d'you really think he'll leave them behind? And if we stay here and wait, we'll all be cut to pieces. No, we've got to keep going! We'll have to reorganize the units on the march. We must get past the town as quickly as we can, without stopping, and follow the coast. We'll get as far as Tuapse then take the highroad over the mountains and join up with our main forces—they'll not have gone far. But if we stay here, death gets closer to us every day."

The iron muscles of his face working, Kozhukh stood up, and surveying the commanders with his piercing steel-gray eyes, said:

"We march tomorrow—at dawn!"

5

Suddenly there was a great clattering and clanking, the clanging of iron, and a series of loud shouts. Ta-ta-ta-ta!

"What's that? What is it? Stop!"

What was that flaring across the sky? Was it a fire or was it just the dawn?

"First company! Quick march!"

Dark flocks of rooks wheeled ceaselessly in the red sky, filling the air with their deafening cries.

Everywhere in the gray light of dawn people were putting collars on horses and fastening shaft-bows. Refugees and men attached to the baggage train kept getting in each other's way, occasionally dropping the shafts and swearing in fury.

The work of harnessing went on at a feverish pace, wheels getting caught together as horses were whipped up. Then, with a great banging and crashing the baggage train set off and raced across the bridge at a furious speed, some of the carts becoming locked together and losing wheels as they went.

Rat-tat-tat-tat! Boom! Boom!

Now the artillerymen were frantically fastening the traces to the limbers.

Things had really begun in earnest now: on the outskirts of the village great clouds of smoke were rising quickly into the sky, and the cattle were bellowing for all they were worth.

Kozhukh was sitting in front of a hut. His sallow face was calm, as if he were at a railway station watching everyone hurrying busily to and fro before the train left, and knowing full well that as soon as it had gone, everything would be quiet once more. Every minute men came galloping up on foam-flecked horses bringing reports for him, while close by stood his adjutant and orderlies, ready to carry out his instructions.

As the sun rose higher, the crackle of rifle and machine-gun fire became intolerably fierce.

But to all the reports Kozhukh kept giving one and the same answer:

"Don't waste your cartridges! Treat them like gold and shoot only when it's absolutely necessary. Let the enemy get close before you open fire, but on no account let him reach the orchards—he mustn't get in there! Take two companies from the first regiment and recapture the windmills, then set up machine-guns by them!"

Men kept running up from every direction with alarming reports, but Kozhukh went on sitting there just as calmly as ever, except that the muscles were working on his sallow cheeks now. A voice inside him seemed to be saying cheerfully: "That's fine, lads, just fine!" Perhaps in only an hour or even much less, the Cossacks would break through and hack them all to pieces! Yes, he knew that might happen, but he could see, too, how obediently and promptly battalion after battalion and company after company were carrying out his orders, how fiercely these men of his now fought who only the day before had been more like an anarchist rabble than real soldiers, not giving a damn either for their commanders or for him, yelling their bawdy songs and doing nothing but drink and play about with women.

But when messengers came racing up from the rear and said breathlessly: "There's fighting at the bridge between the baggage carts and the refugees!" Kozhukh's sallow face turned as yellow as a lemon, and he hurried to where all the trouble was.

At the approach to the bridge there was utter pandemonium. Men were hacking with axes at the wheels of one another's carts and hitting each other with whips and sticks. The air was filled with shouting and roaring, the dirge-like wailing of women, and the screaming of children. The bridge itself was hopelessly blocked by carts, their wheels locked together, and by snorting horses entangled in their traces, with people trapped in all the confusion and children screaming in terror. No one could move either backwards or forwards, while from beyond the orchards came the sound of gunfire—Rat-tat-tat!

"Sto-op! Stop!" roared Kozhukh in a hoarse voice that grated like iron, but there was such an uproar that he could barely hear himself speak. Then he shot the nearest horse in the ear.

The peasants rushed at him angrily with their sticks.

"Ha, you devil's bastard! Kill our horses, would you? Get him!"

Together with his adjutant and two soldiers, Kozhukh retreated towards the river, while the sticks swished through the air above their heads.

"Fetch a machine-gun!" Kozhukh ordered hoarsely.

The adjutant slipped like an eel under the horses' bellies and the carts, and a few moments later a machine-gun came rolling up, accompanied by a platoon of soldiers.

With the agility of a wild cat, Kozhukh sprang to the gun, adjusted the cartridge-belt, and rat-tat-tat!—fired a sweeping burst over the heads of the crowd. The wind of death made the peasants' hair stand on end with its chilling song, and they fell back. But from the orchards came the chatter of enemy fire as before.

Then Kozhukh walked away from the machine-gun, and began to shout and swear foully at the peasants at the top of his voice. That calmed them down straightaway. Next he ordered the carts on the bridge that could not be disentangled from each other to be pushed off into the river. The peasants obeyed him and the bridge was soon cleared. Then a platoon of soldiers with rifles at the ready was posted at the approach to the bridge and the adjutant began to let the carts over it in an orderly line.

Nevertheless, they still went galloping across three abreast, with the cows tethered behind the carts tossing their heads as they ran. The pigs went racing across at full speed too, straining at their tethers and squealing as they went. The planks of the bridge thundered, leaping up and down like the keys of a piano, and the sound of the river was lost amid all the uproar.

Away beyond the river and into the distance rolled the baggage carts, stretching out in an immense line and disappearing in clouds of dust. And as they went, the squares, streets and lanes of the village grew more and more empty.

But the Cossacks had surrounded the village now in a wide semicircle whose ends reached the river, and their guns spat incessant fire. They were moving steadily inwards, drawing ever closer to the village, its orchards and the carts still streaming over the bridge. Kozhukh's men fought fiercely, valiantly defending every inch of ground as they struggled to save their mothers, fathers and children. Using their cartridges sparingly, they fired very rarely, but every shot they fired made orphans of Cossack children and brought tears and sorrow to a Cossack family.

Still the bridge rumbled and still the water roared, but just before dawn the village was finally cleared. When Kozhukh's last squadron had thundered over it, the bridge was set on fire, and as the soldiers disappeared into the distance, volleys of rifle shots and bursts of machine-gun fire crackled thick and fast behind them from the village.

7

On and on marched the soldiers alongside the squeaking carts, swinging their arms as they went.

Four Cossacks who had been taken prisoner in the village were being led along with them and questioned on the way.

Then, at a bend in the road, the column halted and the prisoners began to dig a common grave for themselves . . .

But the endless line of creaking baggage carts moved on and on amid thick clouds of dust, winding its way for verst after verst along the country road towards the mountains that showed dark blue in the distance. The carts were packed with bright red pillows, buckets, spades and rakes. Now and then came the blinding flash of a mirror or a samovar, and amid all the bundles of clothing, blankets and rags could be seen the heads of little children and the ears of cats. Hens clucked in their wicker baskets, cows tethered to the carts plodded on behind, and panting dogs with burrs in their shaggy coats went loping along with lolling tongues, doing their best to keep in the shade. On and on went the creaking carts that were piled high with belongings of every kind, for the peasants had hastily flung into them everything they could lay hands on when they had been forced to flee by the Cossack rebellion.

It was not the first time that these non-Cossack folk had been driven from their homes. In recent months isolated Cossack uprisings against the Soviet authorities had forced them to leave several times, but it had never lasted for more than two or three days, because Red troops had always arrived to restore order and then the peasants had all gone home again.

This time, though, it was all lasting very much longer, and the Cossack revolt was in its second week now. But the peasants had only brought enough grain with them to last a few days. Each morning they kept hoping to hear someone say: "Well, you can go back home now," but things were still going on and on and growing more and more confused. The Cossack revolt was becoming increasingly violent, and news kept coming in from every quarter about gallows being put up in the villages and non-Cossacks being hanged. When would it all end? And what would become of the farms they had abandoned?

The wagons and carts creaked on and on, with children's heads swaying to and fro among the pillows and mirrors flashing in the sun, while in an ill-assorted crowd the soldiers straggled along the road and across the tilled fields beside it that had been stripped bare of their sunflowers, pumpkins and melons as if by a plague of locusts. There were no companies, battalions or regiments any more—everything had become disordered and confused, and the men did exactly as they pleased. Some were singing, others quarrelling, shouting and swearing, while a few had climbed up into the carts and dozed off, their heads swaying sleepily from side to side.

Nobody gave a thought to the danger facing them or to the enemy close by, and no one obeyed the commanders either. Whenever an officer attempted to restore at least a semblance of order in this constantly moving human torrent, he was showered with abuse. Shouldering their rifles upside down and swinging them as if they were clubs, they puffed away at their pipes or yelled bawdy songs, shouting "It's not the bloody old regime now, you know!"

Kozhukh was overwhelmed by this incessant flood of people, and his breast felt as if it were gripped by a taut spring. If the Cossacks attack now, he thought, the entire column will be hacked to pieces. His only hope was that when faced with death, the men would obediently form ranks as they had done the day before, and fight. But might it not be too late?

In this wildly undisciplined, noisy torrent of men there were both soldiers who had been demobilized from the Tsarist army then recruited into the Red Army, and others who had joined the Red forces as volunteers, the majority of them minor craftsmen such as coopers, fitters, tinsmiths, carpenters, cobblers and barbers, together with an especially large number of fishermen. They were all non-Cossack folk who had always lived from hand to mouth, ordinary working people for whom the coming of Soviet power had been like a ray of light that had suddenly illumined their cheerless existence, making them feel that life might not always be quite as intolerable as it had been hitherto. But the overwhelming majority of them were poor peasants who had abandoned their farms almost en masse. Only the wealthy people had stayed behind in the villages, because the officers and rich Cossacks would not harm them.

Striking by contrast in their long, narrow-waisted Circassian coats were the Kuban Cossacks, swaying gracefully on their splendid horses. No, these were not enemies but revolutionary comrades! They were poor Cossacks, most of them soldiers who had fought at the front and in whose hearts the Revolution had kindled an undying spark amid all the fire and carnage of war.

Squadron after squadron of them rode by, wearing shaggy fur caps trimmed with red ribbons and carrying rifles slung over their shoulders. Their black and silver daggers and their long sabres shone in the sun, while their fine horses kept tossing their heads proudly. These men alone were disciplined and orderly amid the chaotic flood of people around them.

They were prepared to fight even their own fathers and brothers. They had abandoned everything—their homes, their cattle and all their household possessions—for their farms had been laid waste. Dexterous and graceful, on they rode, the scarlet bows tied by loving hands on their fur hats blazing in the sunlight, and as they rode they sang songs of the Ukraine in their strong, youthful voices.

Kozhukh watched them affectionately and thought: "That's fine, lads! All our hopes are on you!" But his glance was more affectionate still as it fell on the barefoot, ragged horde of non-Cossack folk tramping along in a disorderly fashion amid clouds of dust, for, after all, he himself belonged to them and they were his own flesh and blood.

Like a long, slanting shadow, his past life stretched out behind him, a shadow that one may forget but never escape. It was the most commonplace steppe shadow, the shadow of a toiling family that was illiterate and hungry, a dark, slanting shadow. His mother had not been very old, but her face was furrowed by deep wrinkles and looked tired and worn, for she had always had many children clinging to her skirts. Kozhukh's father had spent his whole life toiling as a hired laborer on wealthy Cossacks' farms, sweating away and working his fingers to the bone, but however hard he had struggled, the family had always been desperately poor.

From the age of six Kozhukh had been a village shepherd. The steppe and its ravines, sheep and cows, clouds scudding across the sky and their shadows racing over the earth below—this was all the schooling he ever had.

Then, because he was a bright lad who was quick on the uptake, he had been hired by a rich Cossack to work in the village shop, and he had taught himself to read and write on the quiet. Then came military service, the war and the Turkish front. He became a first-class machine-gunner. On one occasion in the mountains he made his way with his machine-gun crew towards the Turkish lines and found himself in a valley in the enemy's rear—the Turkish front lay along a mountain ridge. When the enemy division retreated and started to come down from the ridge towards him, he opened fire with his machine-gun and began to mow them down. The men fell in rows like grass before the scythe, and warm, steaming blood rained down on him. Never before had he imagined that one could stand knee-deep in human blood, but it had been Turkish blood so he had soon forgotten about it.

In recognition of his outstanding bravery, he was sent to the school of ensigns. But what a hard time he had there! He thought his head was going to burst with all the learning! But with bull-like doggedness he mastered his studies, then—failed the examinations. Both his teachers and the other officer cadets laughed at him: just fancy, a peasant wanting to become an officer! Riff-raff like him! A country bumpkin! The stupid brute! Trying to become an officer! Ha-ha-ha!

Glaring sullenly at them from under his brows and clenching his teeth, he felt silent hatred for them all. Then he was classed as unsuitable for the officer school and sent back to his regiment.

Once again it was bursts of shrapnel and countless deaths, blood and groans, once again his machine-guns mowed the enemy down like grass before the scythe, for he had an amazingly unerring eye. Amid all the inhuman strain, with death constantly staring him in the face, it almost never occurred to him to wonder for whose sake these seas of blood were being shed—was it for the Tsar, the fatherland or the Orthodox faith? And even if he did occasionally wonder, the answers he found were very obscure, as though wreathed in mist. But what was immediate and clear in his mind was his desire to become an officer, to make his way up amid all the bloodshed, groans and death, to struggle up just as he had managed to become a shop assistant after being only a shepherd boy. And all the while, clenching his stony jaws as the shells burst furiously around him, he remained just as calm as if he were cutting hay in his field back home, and all the while the enemy fell around him like grass before the scythe.

He was sent to the school for ensigns for the second time because there was such a dearth of officers—there were always too few of them at the front as it was. And anyway, he was virtually carrying out the duties of an officer, sometimes commanding sizeable detachments of men and never suffering a defeat. When all was said and done, as far as the soldiers were concerned he was one of them, he had sprung from the same earth as they had, and he was a peasant just like they were. They followed him without question, this man with calloused hands and stony jaws, followed him through fire and water. In whose name did they do it? For the Tsar, the fatherland or the Orthodox faith? Perhaps it was for one of these. But all those things seemed remote, as though wreathed in bloody mist. Instead, what was immediate and vital was to advance, and to advance at all costs. If they had halted, they would have been shot, so it was safer to follow him, their own peasant commander.

How hard, how agonizingly hard it was for him to study! It was enough to make his head split in two. He found it infinitely more difficult to master decimal fractions than to look death calmly in the face under a hail of machine-gun bullets.

And the officers roared with laughter—the officers who packed the school to overflowing in countless numbers, whether they were needed or not—but mostly the latter. After all, the rear is always a safe place crammed with men trying to avoid the front, men for whom thousands of unnecessary posts had been created. The officers roared with laughter. A peasant, a country bumpkin! The dirty swine! How they mocked him and even failed him for answers that in the end, at the cost of immense effort, he managed to get right.

Again they sent him back to his regiment, sent him back saying he was incapable of following the officers' course . . .

Once again he was surrounded by bursts of gunfire, exploding shells, the soulless chatter of machine-guns and the hellish hurricane of blood and death, but he remained just as calm as if he were back at home—a busy, workmanlike peasant to the core.

As immoveable and stubborn as an ox, he pressed on indomitably, as unshakeable as a rock. Not for nothing was he of Ukrainian stock, with a brow that jutted out low over his piercing, gimlet eyes.

Eventually, because of the efficiency he showed in his deadly work, he was sent to the school for ensigns for the third time.

Once again the officers roared with laughter. That peasant again? And once again they sent him back to his regiment, saying he was unfit to follow the course.

Then Headquarters stepped in and ordered crossly: "Promote him to the rank of ensign—officers are extremely scarce at the front!"

Ha-ha! They were scarce all right because they were all running to the rear!

So it was that Kozhukh was contemptuously promoted to the rank of ensign and returned to his regiment with shoulder-straps gleaming on his uniform. He had made it after all. He felt both pleased and sad, though—pleased because he had achieved his goal and got what he wanted by dint of superhuman effort, but sad because the straps gleaming on his shoulders now separated him from his own kind, from the ordinary peasant soldiers who were close to him. Those straps distanced him from these men yet did not bring him any closer to the officers, and so he found himself surrounded by a void.

The officers did not say the word "peasant" to his face, but in camp and in the mess, in their tents and in all the places where two or three men with shoulder-straps gathered, he felt surrounded by a void. Though they never said anything, their eyes and gestures silently said it all: "Peasant, pig, country bumpkin!"

He felt hatred for them—a calm and stony but deeply concealed hatred. He hated and despised them, and concealed his feeling of alienation from the ordinary soldiers beneath his cool fearlessness amid the countless deaths that surrounded him.

Then all of a sudden everything reeled with a tremendous shock. The mountains of Armenia, the Turkish divisions, the Russian soldiers, the bewildered generals with their dismayed faces, the guns that had suddenly fallen silent, and the March snows on the high summits—all were profoundly shaken. It was as if the expanse of earth and sky had been rent asunder and something unprecedentedly vast had appeared in its place—something unparalleled that had nevertheless always been there, always alive far down in the depths of one's being, something that had no name but that once it had appeared was very simple and clear and quite inevitable.

Then new people came, ordinary people with the lean, sallow faces of factory workers, and they began to tear the great rent even wider, opening it more and more. From it came flooding age-old oppression and hatred, and with them age-old but now rebellious servitude.

Then, for the first time, Kozhukh regretted the shining shoulder-straps that he had struggled so hard to win, for he now found himself ranked with the enemies of the workers, enemies of the peasants and soldiers.

When the rolling thunder of the October Revolution finally reached him, he tore off his shoulder-straps with disgust and flung them away. Then, caught up in the tumultuous flood of soldiers heading for home, he hid in the dark corner of a jolting goods truck that was crammed to bursting, and did his best to keep out of sight. The drunken men around him were yelling songs and tracking down officers who were in hiding. If he had been discovered, he would never have survived.

Arriving home, he found that everything had gone to pieces. All the old order, the old social fabric, had fallen apart, while the new was still vague and uncertain. Cossacks were embracing non-Cossacks and at the same time hunting down officers and killing them.

Like tiny seeds of yeast falling into dough, workmen from their factories and sailors from their scuttled ships came flocking to the jubilant peasant regions, and the Kuban rose in revolt like leavened bread. In villages both large and small Soviet power was proclaimed.

Though Kozhukh was not familiar with new words such as "class," "class struggle" and "class attitudes," he grasped their meaning when working men used them, sensing by intuition what they meant. And the thing that had once filled him with stony hatred—the officers—now seemed a mere trifle in comparison with his awareness of the immeasurable class struggle, and with his realization that the officers were simply the pitiful lackeys of the landowners and bourgeoisie.

But the epaulettes he had won seemed to burn his shoulders with shame, for even though the rank-and-file men knew he was one of their own, they still looked at him askance.

Then, just as resolutely, with the same Ukrainian doggedness with which he had won them, he resolved to obliterate the traces of those shoulder-straps with red-hot iron, to cleanse them with his own blood, his own life, and so serve—no, immeasurably more than serve—the countless poor with whom he was indissolubly one, flesh of their flesh.

It was when the new government began to equalize land owned by peasants and Cossacks that the Kuban rose in revolt and Soviet authority was swept aside.

So it was that Kozhukh was now riding amid the creaking of carts, the tumult of thousands of voices, the snorting of horses and the endless clouds of dust.

8

The last halting-place at the foot of the mountains presented a picture of unbelievable confusion. Everything was in uproar, with people shouting, swearing and weeping as various military units and odd groups of soldiers came up, while beyond the camp the sound of gunfire could be heard. And from time to time the thunder of artillery echoed in the distance.

Kozhukh was here too with his column of soldiers and string of refugees. Other detachments kept coming up to join them, streaming in from every direction, all of them hard-pressed and harassed by the enemy. On this last remaining piece of ground tens of thousands of doomed people were crowded together. They all knew that neither

Cadets nor Cossacks would show them any mercy, and that all of them, young and old alike, would be cut down by sabres, riddled by machine-gun fire, hanged from trees or flung into deep ravines before being buried alive.

With enormous difficulty the men belonging to Kozhukh's column were managing both to hold the attacking Cossacks back and to restrain the general panic, but they all knew they could not do so for long.

The commanders were continually conferring with each other, but absolutely nothing came of it, and no one knew what would happen next.

Then Kozhukh said:

"Our only way of escape is to cross the mountains, then make a forced march along the coast by a roundabout route to join up with our army. So I'm leaving now!"

Half an hour later Kozhukh's column set off and no one dared to stop it. As soon as it did so, tens of thousands of soldiers and refugees, carts and animals, raced after it in panic, jostling one another and blocking the road, trying to pass each other and forcing those who were in the way off into the ditches.

Then, like an endless snake, the great column began to crawl up into the mountains.

9

They marched all day and right through the night, then just before dawn, without unharnessing the horses, they stopped, the column stretching for many miles along the highroad. Above the pass, looking as though they were very near, big stars were twinkling. The sound of rushing water came incessantly from the surrounding ravines, and on every side it was so dark that it seemed as if there were no mountains or forests at all. Only the sonorous munching of the horses could be heard. Then, almost before their very eyes, the stars began to fade, distant wooded ridges slowly appeared, and milk-white mist began to fill the long ravines. Then the column roused itself and crawled on once more, stretching for mile after mile along the highroad.

Rising beyond the distant peaks, the sun flooded the world with blinding light, casting long blue shadows over the mountain slopes. The head of the column reached the summit of the pass, and as it did so, everyone cried out in astonishment, for the ridge suddenly fell sheer away into an immense abyss, and like a faint smudge, the town showed dimly white far, far below. And beyond the town, startling in its unexpectedness, the sea rose like a boundless, dark blue wall, a wall of such unparalleled immensity that its deep, rich blueness was reflected in everyone's eyes.

Up over the ridge came streaming more and more ranks of gaily marching men, and as they did so, all were struck by the dense blue wall that seemed to rise to the sky and was reflected in their eyes. Then they all began to swing their arms in excitement as they marched off with long strides down the winding, white highroad.

After them, moving downhill now, came the string of baggage carts, the horses tossing their heads as the collars slid down over their ears, the cows lumbering along at a jog-trot, and little boys racing by astride sticks, shrieking as they went. Men ran quickly along beside the carts, trying to prevent them from gathering speed as they rolled downhill, and so all together, continually twisting to and fro on the winding road, the baggage train and its refugees went hurrying down towards whatever fate had in store for them. And as they went, the mountain ridge rose behind them, gradually blotting out half the sky.

With its head down, the endless, snake-like column skirted the town, and passing between the cement works[8] and the bay, stretched far away into the distance in a thin line. On one side, pressing close to the shore, towered barren, rocky mountains, while on the other, so beautiful that it made the heart miss a beat to see it, lay the soft blue expanse of the sea.

There was not a wisp of smoke or a single white sail to be seen upon it—nothing, save the delicate line of surf endlessly tracing its lace-like pattern on the pebbles of the beach. And in the fathomless silence echoed the age-old song of the sea, a song that only the human heart can hear.

But then a gloomy voice said:

"It makes no difference now—there's no escape for us! We've got the sea on this side, mountains on that, and Cossacks behind us, and even if we wanted to take another road we couldn't, because there isn't one! So the only thing we can do is march on!"

The head of the column now stretched far into the distance along the narrow shore, then disappeared round an outcrop on the coast, its endless, snake-like body skirting the town and its tail still winding down the mountainside as it followed the looping white road.

Here were the cement works and the highroad along the coast, and down the highroad hurried horses and cows, people and dogs, as the snake's tail slowly moved along.

The baggage train was gradually crawling away now, the wheels of the last few carts already raising clouds of dust in the distance as the creaking of their iron axles became almost inaudible. The town and its bay were left behind, and glowing red in the setting sun, the dust slowly settled.

And just then a detachment of Cossacks entered the town from the opposite direction.

10

The weary night dragged by, and without interrupting its tumultuous progress for a single moment, the dark human torrent streamed on.

Already the stars were beginning to turn pale as though in exhaustion and the desolate, sun-scorched mountains were appearing in the gloom of early dawn.

The sky was growing lighter and lighter, and as it did so, the ever-changing sea gradually appeared in all its boundlessness, first a smoky white or soft lilac color, then tinged by the pale blue sky that was reflected in it.

Then the mountain ridges were illumined by the rising sun and countless swaying bayonets caught the light.

Covering the rocky ravines and coming down to the highroad itself were vineyards with white summer cottages and empty villas among them. Occasionally there would be people in rough straw hats standing by them with picks and spades, steadily watching the endless ranks of soldiers marching by with their countless bristling bayonets.

Who were all these men and where did they come from, they wondered. And where were they marching to, swinging their arms so wearily? Their faces were as yellow as tanned hide, their clothes were ragged and covered with dust, and they had dark rings round their eyes. The carts creaked, the horses' weary hoofs beat hollowly on the ground, and there were little children peeping out of the carts.

Then the onlookers' spades began to turn the earth once more. After all, what did it matter to them? But when they grew tired and paused to straighten their backs again, they could see the column marching on and on, patiently following the winding road along the coast, the men's countless bayonets swaying into the distance.

Already the sun had risen high above the mountain crests, flooding the earth with burning light, and the brilliance of the sea made the men's eyes ache. For one hour, then another, then for five hours more, the column marched on and on. Men began to sway and horses kept coming to a halt.

"This Kozhukh must be out of his mind!"

"He'll be the death of us!"

"What's he driving us like this for? There's the sea to our right and mountains to our left, so who can harm us? But if we go on like this we'll all drop dead with exhaustion, Cossacks or no Cossacks! We've already left five horses behind that can't go any further, and people are starting to collapse at the roadside now!"

When the sun was almost at its zenith, they halted for fifteen minutes to water the horses. Streaming with sweat, the people slaked their thirst too, then on they went once more down the scorching highroad, dragging their leaden limbs along in the burning air. Close by them, the sea glittered with unbearably dazzling light. On and on they went, and a muffled but clear murmuring of discontent began to unsettle the ranks. Several battalion and company commanders told Kozhukh they would detach their units from the column, let them rest for a while, then go on independently.

Kozhukh's face darkened but he made no reply, and the column marched on and on.

When night fell they halted, and camp fires began to glow in the darkness for dozens of versts along the highroad. The stunted, wiry scrub had to be cut for kindling as there were no trees in this desolate region. Garden fences belonging to summer villas were broken up, window frames pulled away, and furniture dragged outside, then chopped up and burnt. Over the fires hung pots with thin gruel cooking in them.

One would have thought that in their immense exhaustion all the people would have sunk to the ground and slept like logs. But illumined by the red camp fires, the darkness shimmered with flickering light and was strangely full of life. There was talking, laughter and the sound of an accordion. The soldiers played the fool, trying to push one another into the nearest camp fire, or went off to the baggage train to flirt with the girls. There was buckwheat porridge cooking in the pots hanging over the smaller fires, while the flames of the bigger ones licked at the sooty, black cauldrons of entire companies. Scattered here and there, field kitchens sent clouds of smoke up into the sky.

The vast camp looked for all the world as though it would stay where it was for some considerable time.

17

Night finally came into its own. Now there were no fires to be seen and no voices to be heard, no sound save that of horses grazing. Soon they fell silent too, and some of them lay down on the ground. Before long it would be dawn.

Below the silent, dark mountains the endless, sleeping camp stretched away into the distance.

But in one place and one place alone the darkness failed to cast its irresistible spell of drowsiness: through the trees of a sleeping garden a light was shining, and there one man and one alone remained vigilant for all the rest.

In the enormous, oak-panelled dining room of a villa, its walls hung with valuable paintings that had been pierced and torn by bayonets, there burned a wax candle that was stuck to the table. Its dim light revealed saddles heaped in the corners of the room, rifles stacked in pyramids, and soldiers sleeping in strange postures on the expensive curtains that had been torn down from the windows and spread on the floor. The air in the room was heavy with the smell of sweat of both horses and men.

Positioned in the doorway, a machine-gun peered out into the darkness, its narrow muzzle gleaming like a small, dark eye.

Bending over the magnificent, carved oak table which stretched almost the entire length of the room, Kozhukh stood with his little eyes—those eyes that no one could avoid—fixed on a map spread out before him. The candle-end flickered, dripping wax onto the table, and live shadows went flitting over the walls and floor and across the faces of the men in the room.

Over the mountain ranges that looked like shaggy centipedes and over the dark blue sea bent Kozhukh's adjutant, he too peering at the map.

Nearby an orderly stood ready with his cartridge pouch on his belt, his rifle slung over his shoulder and his sabre at his side. His whole body was flickering in the dancing shadows.

Then for a moment the candle guttered and all the shadows suddenly became still.

"From this ravine here," said the adjutant, pointing at a mountain range, "they can still attack us."

"But they can't break through this way—the mountains are too high for them to reach us from the other side."

The candle dripped hot wax onto the adjutant's hand.

"If only we can get to this turning here, they'll not be able to reach us any more, but we'll have to make a forced march to do it."

"But there's no food left!"

"That doesn't make any difference. Staying here won't bring us any either, so the only chance of escape we've got is to keep moving. Have all the commanders been sent for?"

"Yes, sir, they'll be here in a moment," said the orderly with a movement that set the shadows flickering on his face and neck.

Only outside the huge windows was there stillness, where the black night lay motionless.

Rat-tat-tat-tat ... Shots echoed in the dark ravines somewhere in the distance, and once again the night was filled with menace.

Suddenly heavy footsteps resounded outside, and passing across the verandah to enter the dining room itself, they seemed to bear that menace with them. Even the dim light of the flickering candle showed how thickly covered with dust were the commanders that came in, and because of their immense fatigue, the incessant marching and the heat, their faces all looked angular and drawn.

"What's going on out there?" asked Kozhukh.

"It's all right, sir—we've driven them off," came the reply.

Kozhukh's face seemed to have turned to stone, and as he frowned, his heavy brows jutted out low over his eyes. Then everyone realized that it was not the Cossack attack that was worrying him.

They all crowded round the table, some chewing crusts of bread or smoking, others not really paying attention but gazing wearily at the map lying spread out in the dim light of the candle.

Then Kozhukh said through clenched teeth:

"You're not obeying my orders!"

Immediately flickering shadows began to dance over the tired faces and grimy necks around the table, and the room was filled with raucous voices that were more accustomed to shouting commands in the open air:

"But you've pushed the men too far!"

"My unit's worn out! You'll never get them back on their feet again now!"

"When we halted, my men just dropped down on the ground and fell asleep where they lay! They were too tired even to light any fires!"

"It's just unthinkable to go on marching for so long! If you carry on like this you'll destroy the army in no time at all!"

"No, it's no good!"

But not a muscle moved on Kozhukh's face, and beneath his low brows his small eyes did not so much look at the men as listen and wait. Outside the huge windows that had been flung wide open stood the motionless darkness, and beyond it lay the night itself, full of weariness and unease. No more shots came from the ravine, but the darkness that filled it seemed blacker still because of the silence.

Then Kozhukh said slowly:

"Who's in command? You or me?"

Once again the shadows began to flicker, and as they did so, they seemed to change not only the men's expressions but their faces too.

Then hoarse, excessively loud voices filled the room once more:

"We commanders also have a responsibility towards our men, and it's no less than yours!"

"Even under the Tsar officers were consulted in critical situations, and we've had a Revolution!"

Kozhukh heard what they were saying, but narrowing his small eyes as before, listened to the darkness outside the windows—and waited.

Then he said, forcing the words out through clenched teeth:

"You ought to know, comrade commanders, what kind of position we're in. Both the town behind us and its harbor are occupied by Cossacks. About twenty thousand sick and wounded Red soldiers were left behind there, and every one of them has been butchered by order of the Cossack officers. The same thing will happen to us too. The Cossacks are pressing hard on our rearguard at this very moment. To our right we've got the sea, and to our left the mountains, but in between there's a gap which is where we are just now. The Cossacks are keeping up with us on the other side of the mountains, attacking us through the ravines so that we've got to fight them off all the time. They'll go on attacking us too, until we get to where the mountains turn away from the sea—the range is high and wide there, and the enemy won't be able to reach us any more. So we've got to follow the coast as far as Tuapse which is about three hundred versts away. From there a highroad runs inland over the mountains, and by taking it we can cross back into the Kuban where our main forces are and where our only chance of escape lies. So we've got to make a forced march. We've only enough food left for five days, and after that we'll just have to starve. We've got to march on and on, run for our lives without even stopping to eat, drink or sleep, just run as fast as we possibly can, because that is our only chance of escape! And if we find our way is blocked, we've got to smash through!"

Then he fell silent, not looking at anyone around him.

The crowded room was filled with silence and the fading shadows cast by the guttering candle. The same silence hung in the vastness of night outside the dark windows and over the immensity of the invisible, soundless sea.

Then Kozhukh lowered his eyes and said through clenched teeth:

"Find yourselves another leader—I resign!"

"Comrade Kozhukh," said a brigade commander, "we all realize what enormous obstacles lie in our path. Behind us is destruction but if we delay now, then death awaits us here too. So we must move on with all possible speed. Only you have the resourcefulness and energy to lead the army to safety, and that, I hope, is the opinion of all my comrades too!"

"Right! Correct! Stay in command!" echoed the other commanders quickly.

"How on earth can you resign?" said the cavalry squadron commander, confidently pushing his fur cap so far back on his head that it nearly fell off. "After all, you were chosen by the people!"

Kozhukh shot him an uncompromising glance from under his low brows.

"All right, comrades," he said. "But I'm going to make one absolute condition for you all to sign. From now on, if any man disobeys an order, however slightly, he must be shot. You will all sign to that effect."

"Comrade Ivanko," he went on, "put that down in writing and let the commanders sign it—capital punishment without trial for the slightest disobedience to orders or for any disagreement whatsoever."

The adjutant took a scrap of paper from his pocket, and making room for himself on the table beside the candle, began to write.

"Now, comrades," said Kozhukh, "return to your positions and inform your companies of this decision. It means iron discipline and no mercy for anyone!"

Dawn was already breaking over the sea.

The commanders felt as if a great weight had suddenly been lifted from their shoulders. Now everything was definite, simple and clear. Laughing and joking with one another, they came up to the table to sign the death warrant.

Kozhukh, his level brows still hanging low over his eyes, was issuing brief orders, as if what was happening at the table bore no relation at all to the immense task that he had been called upon to fulfill.

"Comrade commanders," he said, "every unit must be ready to leave within the hour, and you must march with all possible speed. Only halt to let the men drink and to water the horses. In the mouth of every ravine you must post a line of riflemen and a machine-gun. Don't let your units get separated from each other, and ensure with the utmost strictness that the local inhabitants are not harmed in any way. Report the condition of your units to me as often as you can by mounted messengers!"

Then the adjutant folded up the map and Kozhukh and he went out of the villa.

In the vast, now deserted room, its floor littered with cigarette-ends and bespattered with spittle, the forgotten candle-end flickered and glowed red. The air was oppressively heavy now that everyone had gone, and the wood under the candle was beginning to char and crack, sending a wisp of smoke up into the air. All the rifles and saddles that had been in the room were gone now.

Through the great, wide-open doors of the villa lay the sea, now wreathed in the thin, bluish haze of daybreak.

Echoing again and again back and forth along the coast and among the mountains that sloped down to the shore, the drums rolled to wake the sleeping men. Somewhere far away in the distance bugles sounded, calling like a flock of strange brass swans, and the sound echoed in the ravines and along the coast, then faded and died out over the boundless sea. Above the splendid now empty villa an enormous pall of smoke was rising—the candle-end left burning on the table had made the most of its opportunity.

20

The sky was barely light, but already, crawling along the highroad, the head of the column stretched far away into the distance.

To the right lay the same blue expanse of sea, while to the left towered the densely-wooded mountains with their rocky summits.

Over the barren crests came floating the fiery heat of morning, and soon the same clouds of dust hung over the highroad as before. Thousands of flies incessantly pestered both people and animals, familiar flies from the Kuban steppes that had accompanied the column from the very start, remaining with it through the night and rising with it again at dawn.

Twisting to and fro like a great white snake, the dust-shrouded highroad crept deep into the forest. There all was cool shadow and stillness, and rocks could be seen among the trees. Only a few paces away from the road the undergrowth was impassable, for everything was entangled with wild creepers and vines. Mountain shrubs bristled with huge spines and the hooked thorns of strange bushes clutched at the men's clothing. These forests were the home of wild cats and bears, goats and deer, as well as of the lynx that at night utters its loathsome, cat-like cry. For hundreds of versts around there was no sign of a single living soul and there was not a trace of Cossacks either.

The men tightened their belts still more, for the rations distributed when the column halted were becoming smaller and smaller.

On and on crawled the carts, the wounded holding on to them and dragging themselves along, the children's little heads swaying to and fro, and the emaciated artillery horses straining at the traces of the one and only field-gun.

Then, curving in a playful loop, the highroad began to wind its way down towards the sea. Stretching across the infinite blue expanse of water lay a shimmering ribbon of sunlight, a ribbon so dazzlingly bright that it hurt the eyes to look at it.

Translucent, barely perceptible ripples came moving elusively across the water from afar, and endlessly washed the pebbles on the beach.

The vast column crawled on and on along the highroad without a moment's rest, while young men and girls, children and walking wounded ran down to the beach, and tearing off their ragged clothes, plunged headlong into the blue water. Splashing gaily, they sent up clouds of glittering spray that sparkled and flashed with rainbow colors, and their bursts of sunfilled, joyous laughter, their shrieks and cries suddenly brought the coast—hitherto so deserted—gaily alive.

Like a giant beast with kindly wrinkles on its wise-looking face, the great sea grew quiet, affectionately licking the animated shore and the brown bodies that frisked amid showers of spray and bursts of merry laughter.

But the column went crawling on and on.

Those in the sea leapt from the water, snatched up their foul-smelling clothes, and seizing their rifles, ran to catch up with their comrades, droplets of water flashing like iridescent pearls on their sun-burnt skin. Reaching the column marching along the road, they quickly pulled on their sweat-soaked rags again amid cheerful whooping, roars of laughter and bawdy jokes.

Then others came running eagerly down to the sea, tearing off their clothes as they ran, and flung themselves into all the hubbub and glittering spray, while the great beast quietly licked their bodies too with the same translucent, quivering ripples that endlessly lapped the shore.

The column went crawling on and on.

Then, in a wide valley where the mountains drew back on either side, they came unexpectedly upon a village inhabited by Russians. A sparkling little river wound its way down the valley, and peasant huts and cattle could be seen in the fields. One side of the valley was yellow with stubble, so wheat was evidently grown here. The people were originally from Poltava[9] and spoke the same dialect as many of the soldiers.

They shared their wheat and millet with the men as far as they could, and asked them where they were going and why. They had heard that the Tsar had been deposed and that the Bolsheviks were now in power, but they did not know how things stood in the country as a whole. The soldiers told them everything they knew, and then, even though they felt sorry about doing it to their own people, they took all the hens, ducks and geese in the village, despite the women's loud wailing and lamentation.

Without stopping, the column crawled on past the village and away down the highroad.

21

Bending low in the saddle with his fur hat pushed far back on his head, a Kuban horseman came galloping along the road towards the moving column of refugees, shouting:

"Where's the chief?"

The rider's face was streaming with sweat and his horse's wet flanks were heaving.

Shining white, enormous clouds were gathering above the forested mountains and hanging over the road.

"Looks like there's going to be a storm," someone said.

Further on, round a bend in the road, the head of the column had come to a standstill, and now the ranks of infantry behind it were halting too, closing up and becoming confused. Pulling hard on the reins, the drivers of the baggage carts almost ran into the back of the vehicles in front when they tried to stop, and as the process went on, the entire column soon came to a standstill.

"What's wrong? It's too early for a halt yet!"

The rider's sweat-soaked face, his breathless horse and the unexpected halt sent alarm spreading down the column like wildfire. Then, suddenly lending ominous meaning to what had happened, from somewhere far ahead came the faint crackle of gunfire. Though it soon died away, the sound left a clear impression in the silence that had suddenly descended upon the column, and it was an impression that could not be forgotten.

Then Kozhukh drove quickly by in his light cart, hurrying towards the head of the column. A few moments later several horsemen came galloping up from the opposite direction, and cursing violently, blocked the road.

"Get back!" they shouted. "Or we'll shoot! There's going to be a battle soon and you'll be in the way! It's orders—Kozhukh's told us to shoot anyone who disobeys!"

Suddenly alarm gripped them all, and old men and women, young girls and children alike began to howl and wail:

"But where can we go? What are you holding us back for? We belong with you! If we're going to die, then let us all die together!"

But the mounted men were implacable.

"Kozhukh says there's got to be five versts between you and the soldiers. Otherwise you'll get in the way and they won't be able to fight properly!"

"But aren't they our own people? My Ivan's there!"

"And my Nikita!"

"And my Opanas too!"

"You'll go away, and we'll be left behind! You'll leave us!"

As far as the eye could see, there were carts jammed together now. The wounded and those who were on foot were milling about in a vast crowd, and the air was filled with the wailing of women. Blocking the highroad for dozens of versts, the entire baggage train had come to a complete standstill. Overjoyed, the flies settled in dense swarms on the horses' flanks and backs, and covered the children by the score. Maddened by them, the horses tossed their heads in despair and tried to kick them off their bellies with their hoofs. Through the trees the dark blue sea was visible, but no one looked at it, for all eyes were on the small section of road where the horsemen barred the way, while beyond them were the soldiers, their own menfolk who were so near and dear to them all. There they were, just sitting at the roadside or rolling makeshift cigarettes from blades of grass and smoking them.

Then they all stirred, got slowly to their feet and marched away. The empty stretch of road grew longer and longer, and as the dust settled silently upon it, it seemed to signal both menace and misfortune.

But the mounted men were as implacable as ever. An hour passed, then another, and the highroad ahead remained deathly white and empty. Their eyes swollen with weeping, the women wailed and sobbed inconsolably. Through the trees the sea still showed blue, and from above the forested mountains the clouds gazed down on the water.

Then suddenly, nobody knew where from, came a sustained, heavy burst of artillery fire, followed by a second and a third. The volleys roared and the thundering echo went rolling away through the mountains and ravines. Then a machine-gun began its impassive but deadly staccato song.

At that, anyone who had a whip in his hand began to lash the nearest horse in desperation. The animals lunged forward, but swearing furiously, the mounted men too began lashing the horses of the baggage train facing them, flogging them about the eyes, ears and muzzle with all their might. Flaring their bloody nostrils, tossing their heads and snorting, the beasts threshed wildly in the shafts, rearing and kicking with fear-crazed eyes. Meanwhile, the drivers of other carts came rushing up from behind, shouting at the tops of their voices and lashing the horses for all they were worth. Shrieking as though their throats were being cut, the children beat the animals too, hitting them across the belly and legs with sticks and doing their best to hurt them. The women screamed and pulled at the reins with all their might, while the wounded dug the horses in the flank with their crutches.

Terrified, the animals lunged forward in frenzy, overturning and trampling all before them. Snapping bits of their harness and scattering the horsemen, they bolted off down the highroad, their necks outstretched and their ears pressed flat. Then the peasants leapt back into their carts and raced away, while the wounded who had been hanging on to them set off running alongside, and falling down, were dragged along before losing their grip and rolling away into the ditch.

Not until they had caught up with the soldiers did the carts slow down and continue at a normal speed.

Nobody knew what had happened. Some said there had been Cossacks ahead, but how could that be? They had been cut off from the column by the high mountains long ago. Others said it was Circassians, Kalmyks, Georgians or simply people with an unknown name, countless hordes of them. All this made the carts press on even harder to join up with the fighting units again, and there was no way of forcing them back apart from shooting all the refugees down to the last man.

Here and there men in the column broke into song. Straggling on and on down the highroad they went, leaving it occasionally to scramble up the hillside, tearing their already tattered clothing on spikes and thorns as they searched for small, wild apples. Then, pulling wry faces and wincing as they ate, they would stuff themselves with the unbearably sour fruit. Sometimes they would gather acorns under the oak trees and chew them, bitter saliva streaming from their mouths as they did so.

Occasionally, when the mountains receded, they would see a small, yellow field of unripe maize with a hamlet perched on the hillside not far away. Immediately the field would be overrun with scores of people as though by a swarm of locusts. The men would break off the heads of maize and return to the road, crushing them between their palms as they walked on. Then, picking out the unripe grains and putting them in their mouths, they would chew them greedily for a very long time.

The women gathered maize as well and chewed it for a long time too, but they did not swallow it as the men did. Instead, using their warm tongues they pushed the porridge which they had softened with their saliva into the mouths of their small children.

Then from ahead came the sound of shots again and with it the chatter of a machine-gun, but nobody took any notice any more, for they were all used to it by now. After a short time the sound died away.

The string of refugee carts was now firmly attached to the rearmost infantry units, and all together, without a moment's rest, they streamed on and on down the highroad, enveloped in endless clouds of dust.

22

Then all of a sudden, for the first time, their way was barred by the enemy, and a new enemy at that.

But why? And what did he want?

Kozhukh realized that his position was impossible. To his left were the mountains and to his right the sea, while between them lay the narrow highroad. Further on, ahead of the column, a railway-type bridge of steel girders spanned a turbulent mountain stream, and there was no way whatsoever of avoiding it. In front of the bridge the enemy had positioned both machine-guns and artillery, with the result that any army could have been brought to a standstill here. Oh, thought Kozhukh, if only he could deploy all his forces! But that was only possible out in the broad expanse of the steppe.

His troops were stretched out along the highroad and he looked at them. They were ragged and barefoot, half of them only had two or three cartridges each, and the rest had rifles but no ammunition. He himself possessed one field-gun and sixteen shells for it, that was all. But he clenched his teeth and looked at his men as though they had three hundred cartridges apiece and as if his batteries were drawn up in stern array with their ammunition wagons full of shells, while all around them he imagined his native steppe in which the whole column can usually be deployed down to the last man.

Then, with his eyes and face shining with joy at what he seemed to see, he said:

"Comrades! We've fought the Cossacks and we've fought the Cadets too! And we know why we did it—it was because they wanted to destroy the Revolution! Well, we've escaped from the Cossacks—the mountains have shielded us from them and we've had a bit of a breathing-space—but now a new enemy stands in our way. Who are they? They are Georgian Mensheviks, but Mensheviks and Cadets are all the same, for both of them side with the bourgeois and dream of destroying Soviet power!"

Then, playing his last card, he addressed the cavalrymen:

"Comrades, it's your task to take the bridge with a mounted attack!"

Every cavalryman realized that their commander was setting them an impossible, insane task—to gallop in single file (the bridge was too narrow for them to ride abreast) under machine-gun fire. It meant that half of them would litter the bridge with their bodies, while the others, unable to leap over their fallen comrades, would be mown down as they turned and raced back.

But they looked so striking in their long Circassian coats, and their silver-mounted weapons that had belonged to their fathers and grandfathers before them shone so brightly, while their high Caucasian fur caps and flat lambskin hats looked so splendidly warlike and handsome! Their fine horses bred on the Kuban steppes tossed their heads, pulling at the reins in such a spirited way, and everyone was gazing at them with such open admiration that they all cried together:

"We'll do it, Comrade Kozhukh!"

Then the solitary, hidden field-gun began to fire shell after shell at the place beyond the bridge where the enemy machine-guns were concealed, filling the rocky slopes and ravines with a monstrously swelling echo, while the cavalrymen, silently adjusting their fur caps, came racing round a bend in the road without either shots or cries. With necks outstretched and ears laid flat in terror, flaring their bloody nostrils, their horses galloped up to the bridge and then across it.

Crouching under the incessant hail of shrapnel and deafened by the thunder of gunfire that was enormously multiplied by the mountain echo, the Georgian machine-gunners had not expected such foolhardy impertinence on the enemy's part. But they quickly recovered from their surprise and set their guns chattering away. One horse fell, then a second and a third, but the other riders had already reached the middle of the bridge, and a moment later they were across it. Just then Kozhukh's sixteenth and last shell burst and the Georgians took to their heels.

"Hur-rah!" yelled the cavalrymen as they slashed about them with their sabres.

The enemy units positioned a short distance beyond the bridge fired back, then raced off down the highroad to disappear round a bend.

The Georgians who had been defending the bridge and were now cut off from the rest of their forces, fled down to the beach. But their officers had managed to reach the waiting boats before them and were already quickly making for the steamers anchored out in the bay. Soon dense clouds of smoke started to belch from their funnels, and a few minutes later the ships began to move away out into the open sea.

Standing up to their necks in the water, the Georgians stretched out their arms towards the disappearing steamers. They shouted and cursed, they begged for mercy for their children's sake, but it was of no avail, for Kozhukh's sabres were already cleaving their heads and necks, and stains of blood were spreading wide in the sea.

Now the steamers were no more than black specks on the dark blue horizon and they soon disappeared altogether, while on the beach no one was left alive to implore or curse them any more.

23

The highroad ran through a narrow gorge between steep walls of rock that were festooned with the hanging roots of trees laid bare by the rain. The continual bends in the road made it impossible for any part of the column to see what was ahead or behind it. But they could not avoid the gorge or turn back, so the incessant human stream flowed on and on down the rocky corridor, its walls hiding the sea from view.

Then, after a final bend, the gorge opened out, and through its wide mouth dark blue mountains could be seen in the distance. Dense forest came down to a massif that directly faced the mouth of the gorge. The flat mountain top was all rock, and it rose sheer to a height of about thirty feet. That was where the enemy trenches were, and sixteen field-guns were trained avidly on the highroad where it came out of the gorge. When the column attempted to pass out of the rocky gateway, the enemy batteries and machine-guns opened fire, forcing the soldiers to retreat hurriedly behind the rocks. It was clear to Kozhukh that not even a bird could have flown out of the gorge alive. But there was not enough room to deploy all his men. There was only one way out of the gorge—along the highroad—and that meant certain death. He looked down at the little town that showed white far below, and then at the open expanse of the bay dotted with its black Georgian steamers. He had to think of a way out of the situation, but what could it be? Getting down on all fours, he began to crawl over the map that lay spread out on the dusty road, carefully studying every twist and turn, each track and path upon it.

Just then a battalion commander came up.

"Comrade Kozhukh," he said, "we've been down to the coast and it's absolutely impossible to get round that way—the shore's very rocky with steep cliffs rising straight from the sea."

"Is the water deep?"

"Yes, it's waist-deep near the cliffs, but in other places it comes up to your neck or even covers your head."

"But what does that matter?" asked a soldier who had been listening. "There's plenty of rocks that have rolled down off the cliffs into the sea, so we can get past by jumping from one to the next."

Everyone was offering Kozhukh information and making suggestions, some of them strikingly unexpected and clever, and gradually the general situation became clear.

Kozhukh called a meeting of the company commanders. His jaws were set firm, and under his heavy brows his gimlet eyes had a resolute look in them.

"Comrades," he said, "this is what we must do. All three cavalry squadrons will make their way around the town. It'll not be easy—they'll have to follow paths through the forest and down rocky ravines, and in the dark what's more—but it's got to be done, whatever the cost! Then they must attack the town from the rear and break into it!"

He fell silent, staring into the darkness that was descending upon the gorge, then suddenly added:

"All the enemy must be destroyed!"

Setting their fur caps at a rakish angle, the cavalrymen answered: "It shall be done, Comrade Kozhukh!" and leapt into their saddles.

Then Kozhukh went on:

"The infantry regiment . . . Comrade Khromov, take your men down the cliffs to the sea and make your way over the rocks to the harbor. At first light you must attack without firing a shot, and seize the steamers lying at anchor."

Again, after a brief silence, he said:

"All the enemy must be destroyed!"

"Very good, Comrade Kozhukh!"

"Now get two regiments ready for a frontal attack," Kozhukh ordered.

One after another the distant peaks still tinged with the scarlet glow of sunset began to fade, and the deep blue of evening slowly spread all around.

"I shall lead the attack," said Kozhukh.

Then he climbed up on to a rocky ledge. Below him stretched ranks of barefoot, ragged men, indistinct in the fading light, their crowded bayonets bristling.

All eyes were upon him, for it was he who had to solve the question of life or death on which they all depended. It was his duty to find a way out of what everyone could clearly see was a hopeless situation.

Inspired by the thousands of questioning eyes looking up at him, and sensing that the decision whether the men should live or die lay with him and him alone, Kozhukh said:

"Comrades! We have no choice! Either we lay down our lives here or we suffer death down to the very last man at the hands of the Cossacks! The odds facing us are almost insuperable. We've got no cartridges for our rifles and no shells for our field-gun, so we shall have to fight with our bare hands, and there's sixteen enemy guns pointing at us from up there. But if we all attack together, as one . . . " he stopped for a moment, his stern face looking as if it had suddenly turned to stone, then cried in a strange, wild voice that filled those listening with an instantaneous chill:

"If we all attack as one, then the road to safety will lie open before us!"

What he said was perfectly well known already, right down to the last man, but when he spoke in that strange voice, everyone was struck by the unexpected novelty of his words, and the men shouted in reply:

"All as one! We'll either get through or die!"

Now nothing more could be seen in the gathering darkness—neither the rocky sides of the gorge, the forest on the massif, nor the massif itself. The last horses of the cavalry squadron had already melted away into the gloom. The line of soldiers making their way down the ravine towards the sea, holding on to each other's tattered clothing in the darkness and sending loose pebbles rattling away beneath their feet as they went, was out of sight. The last ranks of the two infantry regiments had already disappeared into the thick forest, over which rose the great massif, its sheer, blank face a symbol of death itself. The baggage train had fallen silent too amid the vast stillness of night. There were no camp fires to be seen, no talking or laughter to be heard, and even the children lay quiet and still, their little faces gaunt with hunger.

27

The heat was becoming more and more intense, and an invisible, dead fog hung heavily over the town. Its streets and squares, its embankment and harbor, its yards and the highroad itself were littered with corpses. They lay in motionless heaps in various positions. Some had their heads twisted at a terrible angle and others had no head at all, while here and there brains lay splattered over the roadway, quivering like meat jelly. As though in a slaughter-house, dark streams of clotting blood ran along by the walls of houses and went trickling under the gates.

On the steamers too—down in the crew's quarters and the cabins, on the decks and in the holds, in the coal-bunkers and the engine rooms—the dead lay everywhere, young men with delicate Georgian features and small, dark mustaches.

They hung motionless over the parapet along the embankment, too, and if you looked down into the clear, blue water, you could see still more of them lying peacefully on the greenish, slimy stones that covered the sea bed, with shoals of gray fish moving slowly above them.

Only in the center of the town were a few still left alive, and the crackle of rifle fire and the chatter of a machine-gun came from where a company of Georgians was still holding out around the cathedral, dying heroically as it did so. But after a short while silence fell there too.

The dead remained lying where they were as the living filled the little town to overflowing, crowding its streets and houses, its yards and jetties, while outside the town, along the highroad, the mountainsides and ravines were thronged with horses, carts and people. There were exclamations, laughter and general hubbub.

Through these streets filled with both the living and the dead rode Kozhukh.

"Victory, comrades, victory!" he cried.

And as though the streets were not littered with corpses and the ground not stained with fresh blood, the joyous answer came rolling tempestuously back to him:

"Hur-rah!"

The cry echoed in the distant blue mountains, then faded and died far out beyond the harbor, the ships and the bay, away over the boundless expanse of dark blue sea.

29

In the ocean of velvet-black darkness camp fires flickered with a reddish glow, lighting up the corner of a cart, a horse's muzzle, and faces and bodies that looked as flat as if they had been cut out of cardboard. The night was alive with exclamations, voices and laughter. Snatches of song rang out nearby and died away in the distance, somebody began strumming a balalaika, and then as if vying with it, someone else struck up on an accordion. The camp fires stretched away as far as the eye could see.

But the night was filled with something else too, something nobody wanted to think about ... They were all aware of the heavy stench of putrefaction drifting down from the top of the massif, for that was where the corpses were most numerous.

"So we made our way through the forest," someone was saying, "and got to that rock, but then we thought we were done for, because we couldn't climb the cliff-face and we couldn't retreat either. When the sun came up, we reckoned we'd all be shot."

"A hell of a mess!" said someone else with a laugh.

"We were sure the bastards up there were only pretending to be asleep and we thought they'd open fire on us any minute. From that cliff-top a dozen men with rifles could have wiped out both our regiments as easily as swatting flies. Well, we started going up all the same, climbing on each other's heads and shoulders ... "

"But where was the chief?"

"He was right there, climbing with us! But when we were nearly at the top, with only about fifteen feet to go, the cliff-face suddenly became sheer, just like a wall. We couldn't do a thing—it was impossible to go up any further or come down again, so we all lost heart and went quiet. Then the chief snatched a rifle from one of us, jammed the bayonet into a crack in the rock, and climbed up by standing on the rifle. Then we all did the same, and that's how we got right to the top."

"We lost a whole platoon," put in another, "they were drowned in the sea. We were moving along, jumping like hares from one rock to the next in the dark, but they slipped and fell into the water one after another and all got drowned."

Yet however animated the conversation and however cheerful the camp fires, the surrounding darkness was still filled with what everyone was trying to forget, and the heavy stench of putrefaction came drifting over them just as persistently as before.

Suddenly an old woman pointed into the darkness and said:

"What's that?"

Everyone looked in the direction she indicated. In the darkness where the invisible massif stood, flickering torches could be seen moving to and fro at different levels.

Then a familiar young voice said:

"It's only our men and some of the local folk clearing the bodies away. They've been at it all day."

Everyone was silent. Nobody else spoke.

30

Once again the sun was shining, once again the sea was a brilliant blue, and the outlines of the mountains were smoky-gray in the distance. Both they and the sea seemed to be slowly descending as the road wound its way higher and higher towards the sky.

The little town far below was now only a white smudge that was gradually disappearing from view. The dark blue bay was framed by its long breakwaters, so slender and straight that they looked as if they had been drawn with a pencil, and the abandoned Georgian steamers were no more than black specks out on the water. What a pity Kozhukh's army couldn't have brought them along too!

All the same, though, they had managed to seize a great deal of booty and they now had three hundred thousand cartridges and six thousand shells. Straining at their well-greased, black traces, the splendid Georgian horses were pulling sixteen captured field-guns, while the enemy carts were laden with a great quantity of military supplies—field telephones, barbed wire, medicines and tents. There were ambulance carts too—enough and to spare. But two things were still lacking—bread and hay.

The hungry horses plodded patiently on, tossing their heads wearily. The soldiers tightened their belts, but they were all in good spirits, for they had two or three hundred cartridges apiece now. They marched cheerfully on, enveloped by swirling clouds of hot, white dust, amid the swarms of persistent flies that had become inseparable from the column.

The bullock-carts and wagons creaked endlessly on, while the children's little heads swayed to and fro among the red pillows.

Its countless links moving on and on, the endless human chain crawled up into the mountains once more, climbing past precipices and clefts towards the barren summits, and crawling on like a giant snake towards the pass. From there it would descend into the steppe, where there was both food and forage, and where their own people were waiting.

Towards evening, above the endless creaking of the carts could be heard:

"Mummy! I'm hungry! Give me some food! I'm hungry!"

Their faces gaunt and dark, the barefoot mothers craned their necks like birds and stared with red eyes at the winding highroad as it climbed higher and higher, then they hurried on beside the carts in silence, for there was nothing they could say to their little ones.

Higher and higher they climbed, and as they did so, the trees gradually thinned and finally disappeared altogether. The column was now surrounded by a desolate wilderness of barren rocks, deep clefts and vast, towering cliffs that seemed about to hurtle down upon them. Every sound—the thudding of horses' hoofs and the creaking of wheels—echoed on all sides, becoming strangely magnified and drowning the sound of human voices with its reverberations. From time to time the column had to make its way round the bodies of horses lying in the road.

Then all of a sudden the intense heat began to abate and a cool wind blew off the mountain peaks, while the sky quickly turned gray. Darkness fell almost immediately and then torrents of water began to stream out of the black sky. It was not simply rain but a roaring flood that swept people off their feet and filled the darkness with a furious maelstrom. The water came pouring both from above and below, and in the deluge the column lost all sense of cohesion and direction. Carts became separated and began to lag behind, and as though they were plunged into a raging void, the people no longer saw or knew what was happening around them.

Suddenly a man was swept away ... And now someone else was screaming ... But how could a human cry possibly be heard above the uproar of the storm? All around them the water seethed, as the black sky raged and the wind roared, and it was as though the mountains themselves were hurtling down on to the column. And now it seemed as if the entire baggage train with its horses and carts were being swept away.

One pair of horses, knocked off their feet by the whirling torrent, plunged over a precipice, dragging a cart full of children with them, but those behind went struggling on, believing the vehicle was still in front of them.

In other carts little children buried themselves among the sodden pillows and clothing, crying out for their mothers and fathers, but their desperate screams were drowned by the furious roaring of water. Invisible in the darkness, rocks came hurtling down from the crags above, while the wind howled with a thousand frenzied voices and the rain poured down in endless torrents.

All was engulfed by the vastness of night. Then suddenly, drowning the hellish uproar of the storm, the mountainside itself seemed to crack asunder, and from its innermost depths came rolling such an enormous, thunderous roar that it was too vast even for the immensity of night to contain it. The sound seemed to explode into fragments that went on bursting as they rolled away in every direction, growing louder and filling the invisible precipices and ravines with a booming echo as they did so. The people were deafened by the noise, while the children lay motionless in the carts as though they had been struck dead.

Amid the streaming torrents of water, the lightning constantly flashing in the dark blue sky, and the incessant peals of thunder, the baggage train came to a halt, while the soldiers, ammunition wagons, field-guns, carts and refugees all seemed utterly exhausted. Everything remained where it was, surrendering itself to the furious torrents, the roaring thunder, the wind and the deathly pale light that kept streaking the sky with its intolerable brilliance. The horses stood knee-deep in swirling water now, and there seemed no end to the horror of this tempestuous night.

But when morning finally came, the sun shone brightly once more. The air was limpid as though it had been washed clean, and the light blue mountains were vaporous and airy. Only the people were dark, their faces pinched and their eyes sunken. Summoning up the last ounce of their strength, they helped the horses pull the carts as the road climbed uphill. The animals were all skin and bone now, their ribs showing so clearly through their rain-washed hide that you could count them with ease.

Reports were brought to Kozhukh:

"Three carts have been swept over a precipice together with all the people in them. A wagon has been smashed by a boulder falling down the mountainside, and two men have been struck by lightning. Two more from the third company are missing, presumed dead, and there are dozens of dead horses lying along the highroad."

Kozhukh looked at the road that had been washed clean by the storm, then at the rocks towering sternly above them, and said:

"There'll be no halt for sleep! The march has got to go on without stopping—we must continue day and night!"

"But the horses can't do it, Comrade Kozhukh—there's not a single handful of hay left! At least when we were marching through the forest we could feed them on leaves, but now there's nothing around us but bare rock!"

Kozhukh was silent for a moment.

"We must go on without a moment's rest! If we stop, all the horses will die. Write out the order!"

The mountain air was so miraculously pure that to breathe it was sheer joy, but these tens of thousands of people had no thought for that. Staring down at their feet, they tramped silently along beside the field-guns and carts, keeping to the sides of the road. The dismounted cavalrymen trudged on too, leading their reluctant horses by the bridle.

All around them barren, wild crags towered into the sky, while the narrow, rocky clefts among them were filled with shadow. The bottomless abysses below them threatened destruction and death, while mists drifted through the deserted gorges.

The dark ravines were filled with the incessant creaking of carts, the squeaking of wheels, the thudding of hoofs and a continuous rumbling and clanking, and all this noise, echoing a thousand times on every side, gradually swelled to become an unremitting roar. The people trudged on in silence, but if anyone had uttered a cry it would have been lost without trace in this vast, creaking roar that could be heard for miles around.

Whenever one of the horses came to a halt, all those in the cart were filled with wild terror. Then in savage frenzy they would seize hold of the wheels, and putting their shoulders to the cart and lashing the horse furiously with their whips, they would yell in crazed, frantic voices. But all their desperate shouting, all their frenzied efforts, were swallowed up by the endless, echoing creaking of countless wheels that reverberated a hundred times around them.

The exhausted horse would take another step or two, then stagger and collapse on the ground, breaking its shaft-beam as it fell, and no one could make it get up again. It would lie there with its rigid legs stretched out, its teeth bared, and the light of day dimming in its bloodshot eyes.

Then, snatching the children from the cart, the mother would beat the older ones in a frenzy to make them walk, and take the younger ones in her arms or lift them onto her shoulders. But if there were many of them, too many ... then she would leave one or two of the very smallest behind in the abandoned cart and walk on with dry eyes, without looking back. And behind her, not looking back either, came countless others, trudging on and on just as before, moving carts overtaking the abandoned one, living horses skirting the dead one, rescued children passing by the deserted ones, and echoing a thousandfold, the incessant squeaking of countless wheels steadily swallowed up what had just occurred.

Far away down the highroad, at the head of the column, walked the dismounted cavalrymen, leading their staggering horses by the bridle. The animals could barely walk now, and their ears drooped like those of a beaten dog.

It was becoming very hot, and the countless flies that had disappeared completely during the storm—all clinging in sheltered places under the carts—now filled the air again in dense swarms.

Then suddenly someone said:

"It's the pass!"

After another bend, the highroad began to go downhill, twisting to and fro as it went.

31

"How many of them are there?" asked Kozhukh.

"Five."

"All in a row?"

"Yes..."

His face streaming with sweat, the mounted Kuban scout did not finish what he was saying because his horse was jerking its head violently, making it hard for him to control it. Its flanks covered with foam, the animal was desperately trying to shake off the countless flies swarming round it, tossing its head and pulling the reins from the man's hands.

Kozhukh was sitting in his cart with his adjutant and driver, their faces a dull red color with the heat that made them look as if they had just come out of a steam bath. Apart from the scout there was no one else nearby.

"How far are they from the highroad?"

The scout pointed to the left with his whip. "About ten or fifteen versts, beyond that copse."

"And is there a side road that goes past them?"

"Yes."

"No Cossacks about?"

"No, none at all. Our lads have ridden about twenty versts ahead, and there's no sign of them."

The muscles were working on Kozhukh's face which had become sallow and calm once more.

"Halt the vanguard," he said, "turn the column onto the side road, and make all the regiments, refugees and carts file past the five you speak of!"

Bending slightly over the pommel of his saddle and anxious not to seem insubordinate, the scout said cautiously:

"But it'll mean a big detour, sir ... people are dropping dead with the heat as it is and they're starving too!"

Kozhukh's small eyes gazed into the far distance that was shimmering in the heat, and as he gazed they seemed to turn gray. The people had not eaten for three days now, their faces were gaunt with hunger and there was a famished glitter in their eyes. The mountains were behind them now but they still had to press on with all possible speed so as to escape the barren foothills and reach the villages below, where they could find food for both themselves and their horses. They had to hurry, too, so as not to give the Cossacks time to strengthen their position ahead. They could not afford to lose a single minute, let alone the time it would take to make a detour of ten or fifteen versts.

Kozhukh glanced at the scout's youthful face that was dark with hunger and the heat, then his eyes flashed like steel and he said through clenched teeth:

"Turn the army into the side road and let them all march past what's there!"

"Very good, sir!"

The scout rode off into the swirling clouds of stifling dust. It was impossible to make anything out in it, but one could hear the disorderly ranks trudging on and on in exhaustion, the thudding of hoofs and the creaking of carts. Faces burnt black by the sun and streaming with sweat gleamed dully in the murk.

No one spoke, no one laughed. The great column simply went on and on, bearing its oppressive, fiery silence with it, and in that silence were the same weary footsteps, the same pounding hoofs and the same squeaking wheels as before.

All-enveloping, the stifling, whitish dust filled the air, and invisible in it were soldiers, horsemen, and creaking carts. But perhaps it was not heat or dust that hung in the air, but an all-pervading, profound sense of despair. There was no hope left and no thought of anything, save the inexorable end. These people were now exhausted and starving, barefoot and ragged, but the sun went on blazing mercilessly down on them. And all the while, eagerly awaiting them somewhere ahead, were fully-armed, well-fed and firmly entrenched Cossacks led by their rapacious generals.

Bumping into horses and men as he went, the Kuban scout rode up to the head of the column, and bending forward in the saddle, spoke to the commander of the leading detachment. The latter frowned, then with a glance at the blurred ranks of marching men appearing then vanishing amid the clouds of dust behind him, he stopped and shouted hoarsely:

"Regiment! Halt!"

Immediately, the stifling dust muffled his words as if they had been wrapped in cotton wool, but they seemed, nevertheless, to be heard by those for whom they were intended, and fading away into the distance, the command was repeated in various voices:

"Battalion! Halt! Company! Halt!"

Then suddenly the strange order rang out:

"Left turn!"

And as the column began to move again, each unit was astonished to hear:

"Left turn! Left! Left!"

In amazement at first and then in eager gladness, they turned quickly down the side road. It was stony so there was no dust on it. One could see the infantry units hurriedly turning off onto it, followed by the cavalry, and then, swaying ponderously, by the creaking baggage carts. In dense, black swarms the flies turned off too, and gradually, the highroad with its slowly settling clouds of dust and its oppressive silence was left behind, while the stony track came alive with exclamations and laughter.

"Hey, look!" someone shouted. "There's the chief!"

As they passed, all turned their heads to look at Kozhukh. Yes, there he was, just the same as always—short and stocky, in his battered straw hat with its drooping brim. He stood there watching them, and they could all see his hairy chest through his sweat-soaked, ragged tunic with its open neck. His trousers were in tatters and his feet in their torn shoes were covered with blisters.

"Hey, lads! Our chief looks just like a bandit! If you came across him in the forest, you'd run a mile!"

They all looked lovingly at him and laughed.

But Kozhukh was watching the noisy crowd as it went straggling by, and his observant little eyes that never missed a thing shone dark blue in his iron-gray face.

"Yes," he thought, "they're nothing but a rabble, a miserable rabble! If the Cossacks attacked now, we'd all be done for! They're just a rabble!"

Then all of a sudden someone asked "What's that? What is it?" and the question ran through the crowd.

Dead silence suddenly descended upon the column, and only the tramping of feet could be heard. All heads turned and all eyes stared in the same direction—to where a line of telegraph poles stretched away into the distance like slender pencils hanging on a thread, growing smaller and smaller until they disappeared in the shimmering heat. On the four nearest poles the naked bodies of four men were hanging motionless, the air around them dark with countless flies. Their heads were hanging down on their chests, as if they were pressing their youthful chins on the nooses around their necks. Their teeth were bared and their empty eye-sockets that had been pecked clean by ravens were deep black, while from their bellies, they too pecked open, hung slimy green entrails. On their flanks the skin was gashed and dark where they had been flogged with ramrods. As the head of the column drew near, the ravens flew off the bodies to settle on the tops of the telegraph poles, and cocking their heads on one side, looked down on the crowd.

Four bodies ... But there was a fifth too—the naked corpse of a girl, her breasts cut off and her flesh already burnt black by the fiery sun.

"Regiment! Halt!"

Nailed to the first pole was a sheet of white paper.

"Battalion! Halt!"

"Company! Halt!"

The command was passed down the whole column, the cries dying away in the distance.

The five bodies were sunk in profound silence, and from them came drifting the sickly-sweet smell of putrefaction.

Kozhukh took off his battered straw hat, and everyone else who had anything on his head did likewise.

"Give me that, comrade," said Kozhukh.

The adjutant tore off the sheet of paper fixed beside the first corpse and handed it to him. Kozhukh set his jaws firm, then said through clenched teeth:

"Comrades," he said, flourishing the paper which flashed white in the sun, "this is what General Pokrovsky[10] has sent you. He writes: 'Any person found guilty of having the slightest contact with the Bolsheviks will suffer execution in the way these five traitors from the Maikop[11] works did.'" Then, after a short pause, Kozhukh added: "These are your brothers and ... this is your sister."

Once again he clenched his teeth, unable to say any more. But there was nothing more to be said.

Thousands of shining eyes stared unblinkingly at him, as one single heart—a heart that was immeasurably vast—began to beat throughout the column.

Drops of black blood kept dripping from the empty eye-sockets of the corpses, and the stench of putrefaction floated in the air.

The high-pitched buzzing of the flies and the vibrant, fiery heat gave way to stillness. There was only the deep silence of the grave and the sickly-sweet smell of putrefaction. And the drops of black blood kept dripping.

"Attent-ion! Quick march!"

Then the pounding of heavy feet suddenly echoed in the stillness, filling the burning air with the sound of a measured, even tread, as though one man and one alone, a man of inconceivably vast height and weight, were marching relentlessly along, and as though one giant heart were beating with superhuman power.

On they went, and without noticing it, all quickened their step, unaware that they were marching with more and more of a swing. The sun glared down as before, its heat insanely pitiless.

"That's fine, lads, just fine!" thought Kozhukh to himself as he watched them from under heavy brows, his eyes the color of blue steel. "At this rate we'll do seventy versts a day!"

Then he got down from the cart, and summoning up all his strength so as not to lag behind, marched along with the column, and was soon lost in the endless stream of swiftly moving men.

Standing solitary and bare against the sky, the telegraph poles receded into the distance. The head of the column turned right, back onto the deserted highroad, and as it did so, it was enveloped once again by the inevitable clouds of stifling dust in which nothing was visible. Only the rhythmical pounding of heavy feet, boundless in its immensity, could be heard amid the swirling clouds of dust rolling on down the highroad.

Meanwhile, one unit after another came up to the telegraph poles and halted before them, and the silence of the grave descended upon them too. The commanders read out the General's message from the piece of paper as thousands of unblinking eyes stared at the sight, and then a single heart, a heart that was unprecedentedly vast, began to beat.

The five bodies hung just as motionless as before, their blackened flesh torn and rotting under the nooses and their bones turning white in the sun.

On the tops of the poles sat the ravens, cocking their heads on one side and looking down on the column with flashing eyes, while the air was filled with the heavy, nauseatingly sweet smell of roasted flesh.

Then on they marched with measured tread, their feet pounding faster and faster, and unaware that they were doing so they too gradually formed up into close ranks. On they went, their heads still bared, oblivious now of themselves and no longer seeing either the line of telegraph poles stretching away into the distance or the terribly short, dark midday shadows that they cast. Instead, their glittering eyes were narrowed against the brilliant light and their gaze was fixed on the fiery distance shimmering in the heat.

Quicker and quicker they marched, with ever more swinging stride, their serried ranks turning to the right and streaming back onto the highroad, where the clouds of dust swallowed them up and rolled along with them as before.

Thousands, tens of thousands, passed by the five corpses. There were no longer any platoons or companies, any battalions or regiments, but instead simply one indescribably vast, single mass of men. On they marched with countless steps, gazing ahead with equally countless eyes, a boundless multitude of hearts beating as one.

And all of them to a man had their eyes fixed on the fiery distance.

Behind the column as it moved away all was deserted, and the heavy stench of putrefaction filled the air.

32

Where the highroad left the mountains, the Cossacks were eagerly awaiting the column. They had received information that the horde streaming towards them was carrying incalculable treasure which it had looted on the way—gold, precious stones, clothing, gramophones and a huge quantity of arms and ammunition—but that the people were ragged and barefoot, evidently because of their vagrant kind of life. And the Cossacks, from their generals down to the last rank-and-file soldier, were smacking their lips with impatience, for all this wealth was slowly but surely moving towards them of its own accord.

General Denikin[12] had entrusted General Pokrovsky with the task of forming military units in Ekaterinodar so as to surround the horde as it came down from the mountains and destroy it to a man. Pokrovsky had therefore raised an excellently equipped corps and was now blocking the road along the Belaya River, so called because of the white foam it carries down from the mountains. One Cossack cavalry squadron had already been sent out to meet the horde.

Far away in the distance enormous clouds of white dust began to swirl in the sky.

"Aha!" cried the Cossacks. "There they are!" and set off at a gallop towards them, the wind whistling in their ears.

But only a few minutes later something wholly unexpected, something quite monstrous happened. The cavalry charged and collided with the enemy, but then Cossacks suddenly began to fall headlong from their horses, their fur caps cloven in two, their necks slashed clean through, or both horse and rider bayoneted in a flash. The survivors hurriedly turned their horses and galloped away, bending so low in the saddle that they were hardly visible, but then all of a sudden they began to be picked off by bullets that came whining after them. The confounded, barefoot horde continued to advance, pursuing the enemy for two, three, then five and even ten versts, and if any Cossacks escaped alive it was only because the horses of those chasing them were exhausted.

Not until they reached their own forward positions in the trenches did the remaining Cossacks finally manage to shake off their pursuers.

Kozhukh did not want to deploy all his forces during the daytime. He realized that the enemy enjoyed a considerable advantage in numbers and he had no wish to reveal the size of his own forces, so he waited for darkness to fall. Then, at dead of night, there was a repetition of what had taken place during the day, for not ordinary men but furious devils seemed to fall upon the Cossacks with all their might.

Finally, unable to hold out any longer, the enemy fled, though even then the darkness did not save them, for they still fell in rows before Kozhukh's bayonets and swords.

When the sun rose above the mountain slopes, its long, slanting rays revealed the bodies of many black-mustached Cossacks strewn over the boundless steppe. There were no prisoners and no wounded, for all lay motionless in death.

33

Night had enveloped the vast expanse of steppe, and with it the foothills, the mountains that had loomed dark blue all day on the horizon, and the village on the enemy side of the river. Not a single light shone in the village and no sound came from it, so it was almost as if it did not exist. Even the dogs were quiet, frightened by the guns that had thundered all day. Only the river could be heard.

Ever since morning, from beyond the river that was now invisible in the darkness and from beyond the enemy trenches that showed gray in the gloom, the Cossack guns had thundered with shattering sound. Again and again they had fired, not sparing their shells, and countless puffs of white smoke had kept bursting over the steppe, the orchards and ravines. Kozhukh's response to them had been sporadic, reluctant and weary.

To the Cossacks the position now seemed clear: the enemy were exhausted and feeble, and no longer returned shot for shot. In the late afternoon the ragamuffins had launched an attack across the river, but they had got such a drubbing from the Cossack guns that their ranks had been thrown into confusion and they had been forced to take cover wherever they could. It was a pity night had fallen, otherwise they would really have been routed. But never mind—there was always the next morning to look forward to!

The river roared on and on, filling the darkness with sound. Kozhukh felt pleased and his sharp little eyes glinted like gray steel. He was pleased because in his hands the army was now an obedient, pliant tool. Just before nightfall, he had sent several units forward with orders to make a half-hearted attack then take cover. Now, as he checked the positions of his men in the velvet-black darkness, he found they were all at their posts on the edge of the fifty-foot cliff that dropped sheer to the water. At the foot of the cliff the river roared on and on.

Each soldier lay there in the darkness, feeling for the edge of the cliff and trying to estimate the drop to the water. All the men in these units now lying silently on the ground had studied their positions thoroughly in advance, so they were not simply waiting like sheep for their commanders to tell them where to go and what to do.

Rain had been falling in the mountains, and during the day the river had been covered in furious white foam, but now it was roaring like thunder. The soldiers realized the water must be five or six feet deep by now—some of them had already managed to measure it—and they knew they would have to swim in places. But that was nothing—it could be done easily enough. Before night had fallen, lying in gullies and hollows and among the bushes and long grass as the Cossack shells burst continually above them, each group of men had chosen the particular section of the enemy trench on the far bank that it would attack.

To the left two bridges spanned the river, one a railway bridge made of iron and the other a road bridge built of wood. Neither of them was visible now in the darkness, but the Cossacks had an artillery battery trained on them and had positioned a machine-gun beside them too.

In the darkness that was filled with the incessant roaring of the river, two of Kozhukh's regiments—one of cavalry and the other of infantry—stood motionless facing the bridges.

The Cossacks sat in their trenches listening to the sound of rushing water and keeping their rifles at the ready, though they knew perfectly well the ragamuffins would not try to cross the river at night. After all, they'd had a good enough thrashing during the day. The Cossacks sat and waited, and the night wore slowly on.

Kozhukh's soldiers lay like badgers on the cliff edge, looking over it in the dark, listening to the sound of rushing water just as the Cossacks were, and waiting. And then the thing they were all waiting for—something, it seemed, that would never begin—finally came: slowly and reluctantly, like only the merest hint of it, the dawn began to break.

Suddenly something almost imperceptible went flitting along the left bank of the river, as though an electric current had run through the men or a little flock of swallows had flown silently by in the gloom.

Then, as if they were falling out of a giant sack, soldiers began to scramble down the fifty-foot cliff, bringing crumbling clay, pebbles and sand with them as they came. The river roared on.

Thousands of bodies splashed into the water, but the thousands of splashes were drowned by the thundering of the river. The river roared on, its sound a continuous monotone.

In the gray light of dawn a forest of bayonets suddenly rose up before the astonished Cossacks' eyes, and the air was filled with shouting, curses and groans. These were no longer human beings but a seething, bloody mass of wild beasts. The Cossacks struck the enemy down in dozens, but they themselves fell by the score. Once again this devilish horde, come from God knows where, had fallen upon them with all its might! Were these really the same Bolsheviks whom they had chased all over the Kuban? No, these people were different. Not for nothing were they blackened by the sun, not for nothing were they half-naked and dressed only in rags.

As soon as wild uproar broke out along the entire right bank of the river, Kozhukh's artillery and machine-guns began to bombard the village, firing over the heads of their own men, while the cavalry regiment took both bridges with a furious charge. Behind them, running for all they were worth, came the infantry. The Cossack battery and machine-guns were seized, and Kozhukh's squadrons poured into the village. Suddenly they saw something white come rushing out of a hut and, leaping on an unsaddled horse, disappear with amazing speed into the murk of early dawn.

Now ashen-faced men wearing golden shoulder-straps were being led out of the village priest's house—some of the Cossacks' headquarters staff had been captured. In the yard near the priest's stable their heads were split open with sabres, and their blood soaked the horse-dung that littered the ground.

Near one hut, which had broken glass scattered around it, a small group of railwaymen had gathered.

"General Pokrovsky was spending the night here," they said. "You only just missed him! As soon as he heard you coming, he knocked the window out, frame and all, and wearing nothing but his nightshirt, jumped on an unsaddled horse and galloped away."

The Cossacks had taken to their heels. Seven hundred of them lay dead in heaps in the trenches and more were stretched out in a long line across the steppe. They were all dead. Once again, those who were still alive and fleeing were filled—despite their desperate efforts to save themselves and despite their abject fear—with irrepressible amazement at this mysterious, Satanic force that had overwhelmed them.

Rising over the distant horizon of the steppe, the sun dazzled the fleeing Cossacks with its long, slanting rays.

36

For the fourth day in succession now the guns were roaring when scouts reported to Kozhukh that a new general with artillery, cavalry and infantry had joined the enemy from Maikop. A council was held and it was decided to break through that night and move on.

Kozhukh issued the following orders: first, to cease fire gradually towards evening so as to reassure the enemy that all was well; second, to sight the guns carefully on the enemy trenches, fix the sighting, and stop firing completely for the night; third, to bring up the regiments under cover of darkness and take them as close as possible to the heights where the Cossack trenches were, being careful not to alarm the enemy, and then to lie low there; fourth, to complete all movements of the various units by 1:30 a.m., and then at 1:45 to open volley fire of ten shells each from all the sighted guns; and fifth, after the last shell at 2:00 a.m., to make a general infantry attack on the Cossack trenches. The cavalry regiment was to remain in reserve so as to support the infantry units and pursue the enemy afterwards.

The soldiers lay in long lines pressed close to the hard earth, with the thick, heavy darkness bearing down on them. Thousands of eyes as sharp as those of wild beasts peered into the darkness, but in the Cossack trenches all was quiet and still. Only the roaring of the river could be heard.

The men had no watches, but in each of them the tense spring of anticipation wound tighter and tighter. The night was oppressive and still, and for each of them the two hours after midnight dragged by. Time was slowly passing amid the incessant roaring of the river.

And though this was precisely what they were all waiting for, it still came as an unexpected surprise when the darkness was suddenly rent asunder to reveal fiery-crimson clouds of smoke shining in the night. Thirty guns began to speak with a full-throated roar, firing continuously, and hitherto invisible in the darkness, the Cossack trenches were suddenly illumined by an intermittently flashing necklace of dazzling shell-bursts, their echoing thunder revealing the sinuous line along which men were now dying.

Then, just as suddenly as it had been rent asunder, the darkness closed in again, smothering with instant silence both the flickering, crimson clouds and the inhuman roar of the guns. Above the enemy trenches there rose a line of dark figures that looked like a long stockade in the gloom, and then a new roar, a live roar like that of wild beasts, echoed along them. The Cossacks came staggering out of their trenches, extremely reluctant to have anything to do with this devilish horde, but once again it was too late, for their dugouts were already beginning to overflow with corpses.

Yes, they were a diabolical horde indeed, for they pursued the fleeing Cossacks for fifteen versts, covering them in only an hour and a half.

General Pokrovsky gathered together the remnants of his Cossack squadrons and his officer and infantry battalions, then led them, bewildered and enfeebled, off towards Ekaterinodar, so leaving the way clear for the "ragamuffins", as he had so contemptuously called them.

37

Straining every nerve, their feet thudding hollowly on the ground, the smoke-blackened, ragged ranks marched on with swinging step in close formation, their knitted brows covered with dust. And beneath their brows gleamed the tiny dots of their sharp pupils, forever fixed on the shimmering horizon of the deserted steppe.

Rumbling heavily, the field-guns hurried along too, the horses tossing their heads impatiently amid the clouds of dust, and the gunners keeping their eyes firmly fixed on the dark blue line of the distant horizon.

Amid incessant uproar the baggage carts dragged endlessly on. Solitary mothers trudged along beside other people's carts, their bare feet raising clouds of dust. In their sun-blackened faces eyes that were full of unshed tears shone with a dry glitter. They, too, gazed fixedly at the distant, dark blue line where steppe met sky.

Caught up in the general haste, the wounded tramped on too. One man went hobbling along with his foot wrapped in grimy rags, another, his shoulders hoisted high in the air, swung his crutches out wide as he went, while a third, utterly exhausted, clung to the edge of a cart with bony hands. But all of them alike had their eyes riveted on the dark blue distance.

Tens of thousands of inflamed eyes stared intently ahead, for somewhere out there in the steppe lay the end of all their fatigue and torment, somewhere out there lay happiness.

The sun—their own Kuban sun—was scorching hot.

And all this—the endless creaking of carts amid swirling clouds of dust, the hollow pounding of horses' hoofs, the heavy tread of countless feet and the constant swarms of flies—all this streamed on for mile after mile in a vast torrent, heading towards the alluringly mysterious, dark blue line of the horizon. At any moment the distant steppe would open to reveal what they were all waiting for, their hearts would be filled with joy, and they would cry: "Our people!"

But however far they marched, however many villages, hamlets and farms they passed, it was always the same—the dark blue distance kept receding further and further, remaining just as inaccessible and mysterious as before. And however far they went, they were always told the same thing:

"Yes, they were here, but now they've gone. They were here the day before yesterday, but then they suddenly left in a great hurry."

Yes, they had been here all right: here were a few horse-tethers they had left behind, and there was some hay scattered about. There was horse dung everywhere, too, but now all was deserted.

Here the artillery had obviously made a halt—there were the gray ashes of burnt-out camp fires and the deep ruts made by the wheels of field-guns outside the village as they had turned back onto the high-road.

The old Lombardy poplars at the side of the road had deep, white gashes in their trunks where the bark had been torn by the axles of passing carts.

Everything, everything spoke of their recent presence here, but still the dark blue line of the horizon kept receding, always unattainable.

Kozhukh, his body emaciated and his face burnt black by the sun, rode grimly on in his cart, and like everyone else kept his narrowed eyes riveted day and night on the distant horizon. But for him, too, it remained incomprehensibly and mysteriously deserted. His jaws were tightly clenched.

So village after village, farm after farm went by, and day after day passed too, filled with growing exhaustion.

During the night-halts messengers would bring reports to Kozhukh, but again it was always the same thing—the Cossack units ahead were falling back without firing a shot and letting the column pass. In fact, not a single attack was made on the column, either during the day or at night. Then, without touching the rearguard, the Cossacks would close ranks again after it had passed.

Then Kozhukh issued orders:

"Send mounted messengers to all baggage carts and units, telling them not to lag behind. They are not to halt, but must keep going on and on. No more than three hours are to be allowed for rest during the night!"

Once again the baggage carts creaked onwards, their exhausted horses straining at the traces, and the field-guns rumbled on with ponderous haste. Amid the fiery dust of midday, under the star-strewn night sky and in the half-light of early dawn, the incessant rumbling went on and on across the Kuban steppes.

Once again tens of thousands of eyes were fixed day and night on the distant line of the horizon, probing the expanse of steppe that was hard and yellow after the harvest.

Then suddenly, down all the baggage train, through the units and among the women and children flew the news:

"They're blowing up the bridges! They're retreating and blowing up the bridges behind them!"

And it was true, for wherever the head of the column came to a river or stream, a marshy place or ravine, they found splintered piles and smashed planks sticking up like jagged black teeth. The road was cut and the men were filled with despair.

Frowning, Kozhukh issued orders:

"Repair the bridges and ford the rivers! Make up a special team of all those who can use an axe, and send them ahead on horseback with the vanguard. Take logs, planks and beams from the local people and carry them to the head of the column!"

The axes began their work, and white chips flew through the air, flashing in the sunlight. Then, over the hastily-built, swaying plank bridges, the thousands streamed on with their endless line of baggage carts and field-guns, the horses looking askance at the water and snorting in fear as they went.

On and on poured the human torrent, and as before all eyes were fixed on the same unattainable line that separated steppe and sky.

Then Kozhukh called a meeting of his commanders and with the muscles on his face working, said quietly:

"Comrades, our own people are running away from us as fast as they can... They're retreating and blowing up the bridges behind them. We can't go on like this for much longer—our horses are dropping dead by the dozen, men are leaving the ranks and getting left behind, and the enemy will soon cut them to pieces. For the time being we've taught the Cossacks a lesson—they're afraid of us and let us pass, and the generals keep all their units out of our way. All the same, though, we're trapped in a ring of steel, and if things go on like this for long, we'll be done for, because we've not got many cartridges left and there are very few shells. So we must get ourselves out of this situation!"

Then, uttering the words through clenched teeth, he went on:

"We've got to break through! But if we use a cavalry squadron, the Cossacks will cut them to pieces because our horses are in very poor condition and won't stand a gallop. No—we must do something else! We've got to break through and let our people know we're here!"

Then he said:

"Who will volunteer?"

A young man got to his feet.

"Comrade Selivanov," said Kozhukh, "take two men with you and set off in an armored car—and go like hell! You've got to get through, whatever the cost! And when you do, tell them where we are. What the devil are they running away from us for? Do they want us all to be killed, or what?"

An hour later, as the sun was setting, the armored car stood outside the hut where Kozhukh's headquarters were. It carried two machine-guns, one at the front and one at the rear. Wearing a greasy army tunic and smoking a cigarette as he worked, the driver was busy carrying out a final check on his vehicle. Selivanov and the two soldiers had carefree-looking young faces, but their eyes were filled with profound strain.

The car gave a snort, pulled out and raced away, raising clouds of dust as it went hurtling into the distance. It grew steadily smaller until it was no more than a speck, then disappeared.

But the endless crowds, baggage carts and lines of horses streamed grimly on, knowing nothing of the armored car and its mission. On and on they went, never stopping for a moment, peering both in hope and despair into the dark blue distance.

38

Cossack mounted patrols, scouts and units all let the furiously racing car pass by, taking it for one of their own. After all, what enemy would dare to venture so deep into Cossack territory?

In the late afternoon the white belltower of a large village church appeared in the distance, then orchards and poplars came quickly into view, and white huts rushed towards the car.

Suddenly one of the soldiers turned to his companion with a strange expression on his face and cried:

"It's our people! Our people! Over there!"

"Hur-rah!"

A large mounted patrol was riding towards them, scarlet stars flaring like poppies on their caps. But at the same time, from behind the wattle fences, orchards and huts came the crackle of rifle fire.

Selivanov's heart missed a beat. "It's our own people," he thought, "and they're firing at us!" Desperately waving his cap, he shouted in a high-pitched, broken voice:

"Friends! Friends!"

Then, seizing hold of the driver's shoulder, he cried:

"Stop! Stop! Put on the brakes!"

But the firing went on. Snatching their carbines from their shoulders, the patrol were galloping towards them now, shooting from the saddle and keeping their horses off the road so as to give their comrades firing from the orchards a clear view of the car.

"They'll kill us!" said the driver with stiff lips, and flinging himself away from the wheel, brought the car to a standstill.

The patrol came racing up at a full gallop, and ten black muzzles were trained point-blank on the car. Some of the cavalrymen, their faces distorted with fear, leapt from the saddle, swearing savagely and shouting:

"Get away from the machine-guns! Hands up! Now get out of the car!"

Others sprang from their horses and with deathly pale faces cried:

"Cut 'em to bits! What the hell are you waiting for? They're bloody officers, damn them!"

Unsheathed sabres flashed razor-sharp in the light.

"They'll kill us!"

Selivanov, the two soldiers and the driver immediately jumped out of the car, and as soon as they were surrounded by excited horses' heads, raised sabres and rifles, the tension relaxed, because all four were now away from the machine-guns, the sight of which had so infuriated the cavalrymen.

Then, in their turn, Selivanov and his men let fly with choice swearwords:

"You're crazy! We're your own people! Are your eyes in your backsides or something? You never asked to see our papers! You might've killed us and then it would've been too late! To hell with you!"

The cavalrymen had cooled down a little now.

"But who are you?" they asked.

"Who are we?! You should ask first and shoot later, not the other way round! Now take us to headquarters!"

"But how were we to know?" said the cavalrymen apologetically, mounting their horses once more. "Only last week an armored car came racing up just like you did and opened fire. There was a hell of a panic!"

The four men got back into the car and two cavalrymen climbed in beside them, while the rest cautiously surrounded the vehicle with carbines in their hands.

They drove on into the village and stopped at headquarters which was located in the big house of the priest.

Then they burst in to see the commander of the Red detachment.

Beside himself with happiness and excited by all his recent experiences, Selivanov began to tell of the campaign and the battles with the Georgians and Cossacks, and in his eagerness to tell everything, kept skipping from one event to another.

Then he suddenly stopped short. Resting his long mustache and bristly chin on his palm, the commander sat hunched up without interrupting him, a hostile look in the eyes which he kept firmly fixed on the soldier's face.

Feeling the blood rush to his face and neck, Selivanov stopped in mid-sentence and said in a hoarse voice:

"Here are our papers," and pushed them towards the commander.

But without even looking at them, the commander passed them on to his adjutant, who began to examine them reluctantly as though everything were already decided and they would make no difference. Then, still not taking his eyes off Selivanov, the commander said distinctly: "We have very different information ... in fact, precise reports to the effect that the entire army which marched off the Taman peninsula came to grief on the Black Sea coast and were all slaughtered to a man."

"Forgive me ... but do our documents prove nothing to you?" asked Selivanov. "Is this really the way to treat us? We force our way through to our own people after an inhuman struggle, at the cost of incredible effort, and then ... "

"Nikita," said the commander quietly, getting to his feet, "find the order."

The adjutant rummaged in his briefcase, and taking out a sheet of paper, handed it to the commander, who laid it on the table. Then, standing erect, he began to read it out loud:

COMMANDER'S ORDER NO. 73

> A radio-telegram sent by General Pokrovsky to General Denikin has been intercepted. It reports that an innumerable horde of ragamuffins is advancing from Tuapse and the sea. This wild rabble consists of Russian prisoners who have returned from Germany, as well as sailors. They are extremely well-armed, have a great many field-guns and supplies, and are carrying a large quantity of valuables which they have looted. This armed horde defeats and sweeps aside everything in its path: the best Cossack and officer units, Cadets, and Mensheviks and Bolsheviks alike.

The tall commander looked hard at Selivanov and said again, but with more emphasis now: "And Bolsheviks!"

Then he went on reading:

> In view of this I order you to continue to retreat without making any halts and to blow up the bridges behind you; to destroy all means of crossing the rivers; and to take the boats over to our side of the rivers and burn them. The unit commanders are responsible for ensuring that the retreat is carried out in good order.

Once again the commander looked intently at Selivanov, then without giving him time to speak, said:

"Now look here, comrade. I don't wish to suspect you of anything, but you must try to understand our position: we've never met before, and you can see for yourself what this report says. We just don't have the right ... after all, we're responsible for thousands of people, and we'd be criminals if we ... "

"But they're all waiting for you back there!" cried Selivanov in despair.

"Yes, I know, I know—don't worry! Look here—let's go and have a bite to eat, shall we? You must be hungry and I expect your lads could... "

After the meal it was agreed that Selivanov would drive back in the car accompanied by a cavalry escort who would verify what he had told the commander.

The vehicle drove back more slowly than it had come, the now familiar villages and farms receding into the distance behind it. Selivanov sat between two cavalrymen, their expressions strained as they held their revolvers ready, while all around the car—in front, behind and at each side—more riders rhythmically rose and fell in their wide saddles, first all together then each of them separately as they galloped on, their horses' hoofs flashing in the fading light.

"If we run into any Cossacks," thought Selivanov, "we're done for!"

40

The Caucasian sun was hot even though it was autumn by now, but the distant steppe was dark blue and translucent, and wisps of delicate gossamer sparkled in the grass. Poplars with thinning leaves stood pensive and still, and the orchards were faintly tinged with yellow. The belltower on the church gleamed white in the sun.

Beyond the orchards, away out in the steppe, was a vast human sea, a sea just as boundless in its immensity as it had been when the march began. But there was something different about it now. The same refugees were there with their countless carts, but why did their faces shine with such irrepressible confidence?

The same barefoot, ragged soldiers were there too, but why were they now silently standing to attention in endless ranks as straight as a taut thread? Why did their gaunt faces look as if they had been forged from blackened iron, and why did the dark lines of their bayonets seem as well-proportioned and orderly as martial music itself?

And why, facing them, did the ranks of well-dressed, well-shod men stand in slovenly, loose formation, their bayonets all pointing at different angles, and why were both bewilderment and expectation imprinted on their faces?

In the midst of this human sea was an empty green space with a cart showing up darkly on it.

They were all waiting, and as they did so, silent music seemed to float solemnly over the boundless crowd, rising into the dark blue sky and spreading far and wide over the steppe that was flooded with hot, golden light.

Then a small group of men appeared, and as they drew near, those standing in orderly ranks with faces dark as iron recognized their commanders, all of them to a man just as blackened and wasted as they themselves were. And those who stood facing them recognized their commanders too, for these were well-dressed and had healthy, weather-beaten faces just like their own.

Among the first group walked Kozhukh, short and stocky as always, his body sun-blackened and wasted to the bone. His clothes were as ragged as those of a tramp and his battered, gaping boots showed his dark toes. On his head, its torn brim drooping, was the tattered remains of what had once been his straw hat.

The group of men came up and gathered round the cart. Then Kozhukh climbed up into it, and pulling the straw hat from his head, cast a long, slow glance out over the iron ranks of his own men, over the countless carts stretching away across the steppe and the vast, wretched multitude of refugees who had lost their horses during the march, then he turned to look at the ranks of the main forces.

Each and every one of them was gazing at him. Then he said:

"Comrades! We have walked five hundred versts, barefoot, hungry and cold. The Cossacks pursued us like wild beasts. At times we had no bread, no fodder and no supplies of any kind. Our people died, fell over cliffs and were shot down by enemy bullets. But we had no cartridges, so we had to fight with our bare hands ... "

And though they knew it all, for they had experienced it themselves or knew it from the scores of stories they had heard, Kozhukh's words were still full of shining novelty.

Then he went on:

"We left our children dead in the ravines ... "

At his words the great human sea stirred and began to ripple from shore to shore:

"Our children! Oh, our children!"

Kozhukh looked gravely at them and paused, then went on:

"And how many of our people lie slain by bullets out on the steppe, in the mountains and in the forests, how many of them will lie there now till the end of time?"

Then all heads were bared, and spreading to the furthest edges of the crowd, a deep silence fell, and in the stillness the low sobbing of the women sounded like a funeral chant or the soft rustling of graveside flowers.

Kozhukh stood for a while with his head bowed, then he looked up again, and surveying the countless thousands before him, asked in the silence:

"And for whose sake did those thousands, those tens of thousands suffer such torment? For whose sake?"

Again he looked at the crowd, then said:

"For the sake of one thing and one alone: for the sake of the Soviet government, because it belongs to the workers and peasants who have nothing else but that!"

Then a great sigh broke from countless breasts, for the emotion was more than anyone could bear. Solitary tears began to trickle down the iron faces of Kozhukh's soldiers, crept slowly down the weather-beaten cheeks of the main forces, glistened on the faces of the old men and even shone in the eyes of young girls in the crowd.

"For the workers and peasants!" came the cry.

It was as if their eyes had been opened wide for the first time in their lives, as if an immense, mysterious secret had suddenly been revealed to them.

Then a great swell rose and swept the crowd like a wave thundering over the sea in a storm:

"Hurrah! That government belongs to us! It is our very own! Long live Soviet power!"

Scores of mothers cried aloud too. With their unshed tears and broken hearts, they would never forget those rapacious, barren ravines—no, never! But even those terrible places and the still more terrible memory of them had slowly been transmuted into quiet sorrow, and it too now found a place in the solemn music floating silently above the boundless human sea that covered the steppe.

Those who stood well-dressed and well-fed before the iron ranks of wasted, tattered men, felt like orphans in the face of this triumph that they themselves had not known, and unashamed of the tears welling up in their eyes, they broke ranks and surged forward in a sweeping avalanche towards the carts where the ragged Kozhukh was standing. And their cry rolled out and away across the steppe, spreading as far as the horizon itself:

"Chief! Chief! Lead us wherever you like! We will give our lives for you if we have to!"

Then thousands of hands stretched out to him, and pulling him down off the cart, lifted him above their heads and shoulders and carried him away. And the steppe shook for miles around, resounding with countless voices:

"Hurr—-ah! Hurra—-a—-ah! Hurrah for Kozhukh, our chief!"

They carried him past his own men standing in their orderly ranks, carried him past the place where the field-guns stood and the cavalry squadrons waited, and as he passed, the horsemen turned in their saddles and with faces shining with delight and mouths wide with joy, they cried out in welcome.

They carried him past the refugees and past the carts, and the mothers held up their children to him.

Then they brought him back and carefully set him down on the cart again. He opened his mouth to speak and everyone gasped as if they had never looked closely at him before:

"Look! His eyes are blue!"

It was true—his eyes really were blue after all, a gentle, light blue that was lit with the loving smile of a child.

Then they cried:

"Hurr-a . . . ah for our chief! Long live Kozhukh! We'll follow him to the ends of the earth! We'll struggle for the Soviet government! We'll fight the landowners, generals and officers!"

Kozhukh looked at them all affectionately with his light blue eyes, and as he did so, his mind and heart were seared by the fiery thought:

"I've got no father or mother, no wife and no brothers, I've got no family, no relatives at all . . . All I have is these people whom I've saved from death and led to safety. Yes, I've led them, I myself have done it! But there are millions more like them, all with a noose around their necks, and I shall go on fighting for them. These people are my father and mother, my wife and children, and I have saved these thousands, these tens of thousands, from death, saved them from a terrible death. . . "

The unspoken words were branded on his heart in letters of fire, while his lips were saying: "Comrades!"

Though unable to express themselves, all these people still felt that cut off as they were from the north by limitless steppes, impassable mountains and great, dense forests, they too were helping to create—albeit to a much lesser degree—the thing that was being created on a world scale far away to the north, in the heart of Russia. And they felt that half-naked, barefoot and starving though they were, they were creating it here, all by themselves, without any assistance whatsoever. They did not know how to express this feeling, but they were aware of it just the same. All of them were filled with a steadily growing sense of boundless happiness at being indissolubly linked with that vastness which so far they only dimly knew but which bore the name of Soviet Russia.

***

Innumerable camp fires gleamed in the darkness, while above them shone equally innumerable stars.

Illumined by the flames, the smoke rose gently into the sky, while each as ragged as the next, soldiers and old men, women and children sat wearily around the fires.

Just as the traces of smoke gradually melted away in the star-strewn sky, so the jubilation felt by this vast sea of people slowly faded and died, giving way to fatigue. In the soft darkness, lit only by the light of the fires, it was as though a gentle smile were slowly fading as sleep quietly descended upon them all.

The camp fires gradually went out and silence fell. In the stillness the night was blue—a deep, dark blue.

1924

Notes

1. Chief town in Kuban region of Northern Caucasus. Renamed Krasnodar in 1920.
2. Soldiers drawn from pro-monarchy Cadet Corps, *1924* élite military school for training officers in Tsarist army.
3. Towns on eastern coast of the Sea of Azov.
4. Villages east of Temriuk, near the Sea of Azov.
5. Rostov-on-Don, northeast of the Sea of Azov.
6. Towns northeast of Ekaterinodar (now Krasnodar).
7. Large port on Black Sea, southwest of Ekaterinodar.
8. This detail suggests that the town meant is Novorossiisk, well-known for its cement factories.
9. Town in the eastern Ukraine.
10. V. L. Pokrovsky (1889–1923), White commander of Kuban Cavalry Division in 1918, notorious for his wholesale hanging of people without trial.
11. Town northeast of Tuapse, on the Belaya River.
12. Anton Ivanovich Denikin (1872–1947), Commander of the Russian Volunteer Army from April, 1918.

Fyodor Gladkov
CEMENT

Fyodor Gladkov (1923).

Fyodor Gladkov (1883–1958)

Fyodor Vasilyevich Gladkov was born in 1883 into an Old Believer family of peasant stock in the village of Chernavka in Saratov Province. The boy's parents were desperately poor, and during his early childhood they would travel south during the summer to find work in fisheries on the Caspian Sea and in factories of the North Caucasus. In 1895 the family moved south to Ekaterinodar (now Krasnodar) in the Kuban, where Gladkov worked in a chemist's shop before becoming an apprentice typesetter at a printer's. At the age of fourteen he entered the third class of the local school, and after finishing his studies there took an additional pedagogical course before qualifying as a primary school teacher. In 1902 he moved to the Sretensk district of eastern Siberia, east of Lake Baikal, where he began work as a teacher.

In 1904 Gladkov began to conduct propaganda work for the Socialist Revolutionary (SR) Party in Chita, east of Irkutsk, but in the following year left Siberia for Tiflis, where he entered the teachers' institute. The spring of 1906 found him engaged in propaganda work again, this time for the Bolsheviks, in the town of Eisk on the northeastern coast of the Sea of Azov, where he helped organize strikes by stevedores. It was here that in the same year he joined the Social Democratic (SD) Party. But later that year the danger of arrest forced him to return to eastern Siberia, where he took a teaching job in Sretensk. In November 1906 he was arrested for his part in organizing a Bolshevik group in Sretensk, and was sent to Irkutsk prison. The following year he was sentenced to exile in the village of Manzurka near Verkholensk in Irkutsk Province, where he spent the next four years. It was during this time that tragedy struck, for his parents were savagely murdered by a band of wandering criminals. After serving his term of exile, Gladkov moved south again, to Novorossiisk on the Black Sea coast, where he worked as a clerk before finding a teaching post.

At the outbreak of World War I Gladkov was appointed head of a primary school in Pavlovskaya, a large Cossack village in the northern Kuban, where he remained until the spring of 1918. He was then sent back to Novorossiisk to carry out a reorganization of schools in the area, but when in August 1918 the town was captured by the Whites, he was forced to take refuge in the workers' settlement of a local cement factory. Living illegally there, he engaged in propaganda activity among both working people and soldiers. After the Whites had been driven from Novorossiisk in the spring of 1920, Gladkov became responsible for adult education in the town. In the autumn of that year he served as a volunteer with the Red Army during the campaign against Wrangel in the Kuban, before joining the Political Section of the 14th Brigade of the Ninth Army. The same year, 1920, saw him become a member of the Communist Party. That winter he was appointed editor of the newspaper *The Red Black Sea* (*Krasnoe Chernomor'ye*)—which he edited from October 1920 until the following May—and became head of the regional department of Popular Education.

In 1921, with the help of Maxim Gorky, he moved to Moscow, where he first worked as a director of a factory school, then as a secretary of the journal *New World* (*Novy mir*). He joined the proletarian literary group "The Smithy," and in 1923 became a professional writer, engaging in varied administrative and cultural work at the same time. From 1932 to 1940, for example, he served on the editorial board of *New World*.

Shortly after the Nazis attacked the Soviet Union in 1941, Gladkov became a special correspondent for *Izvestiya* and left for Sverdlovsk in the Urals, where he wrote articles, sketches and tales about industrial plants in the rear working to supply the front. At the end of the war, in 1945, he was appointed director of the highly prestigious Gorky Literary Institute in Moscow, a post which he held until 1948.

A member of the presidium of the Union of Writers and a Deputy to the Supreme Soviet, Gladkov was a prominent literary administrator and well-known public figure. Among his many distinctions were two Orders of Lenin and the Order of the Red Banner. Unfortunately, his last years were dogged by illness and failing strength. He died in December 1958; and was buried in the Novodevichy Cemetery in Moscow.

***

Gladkov's first published work was the tale *Towards the Light*, which appeared in the Kuban newspaper *The Provincial Gazette* (*Oblastnye vedomosti*) in 1900. Clearly imitative in theme of the nineteenth-century poet Nekrasov, it tells of a young girl who becomes a village teacher and dedicates herself to the service of the common people. This first piece was followed by two stories about down-and-outs, *After*

Work and *Maksiutka*, which appeared in the same paper in 1900 and 1901 respectively.

After moving to Siberia in 1902, Gladkov published several sketches and tales in newspapers in Chita, among them *Before Hard Labor* (1903), *They Went Off to War* (1904), and *The Inspection* (1905). The year 1905 also saw the appearance of one of his finest early stories, *Three in One Hut*, which reflected his meeting with three women convicts serving sentences in Siberia. It was followed by *The Outcasts*, a series of sketches about the life of political exiles, begun in 1908 while Gladkov was in exile in Manzurka. His next major piece was the tale *The Abyss*, a picture of life in a Russian village during the First World War. Initially entitled *The Only Son*, it was first published in Gorky's prestigious journal *Annals* in 1917. It was followed by the tales *Spring Shoots* (1921) and *The Fiery Steed* (1922), both of which reflect the author's experiences during the Civil War in the Kuban.

In the winter of 1922 Gladkov began work on *Cement*, the novel which was to assure his literary reputation. Completed two years later, it was serialized in the Moscow journal *Red Virgin Soil* (*Krasnaya nov'*) in 1925, and appeared in book form the following year. Hailed as the first Soviet novel of the working class, it was to enjoy tremendous success not only in the USSR but also, in translation, abroad. Officially recommended for public and school libraries, it sold over two million copies by 1937 and is still widely read today.

1926 saw the completion of Gladkov's well-known long story *The Old Secret Prison*, which was serialized the following year in the Moscow journal *Novy mir*. Begun before the Revolution and thematically linked with earlier works such as *The Outcasts*, it is set in the notorious Irkutsk prison where political prisoners were often held before sentence. Also published in 1927 was the satirical tale *The Cephalopodous Man*, which together with the stories *The Immaculate Devil* (1928) and *The Inspired Goose* (1929) was later included by Gladkov in his *Little Trilogy* of 1933.

Soon after the publication of *Cement* Gladkov began work on his second novel, *Power*, a detailed and lengthy treatment of the successes of construction and industrialization during the first Five-Year Plan. The first two parts of the novel appeared in *Novy mir* in 1932 and the last three in 1937 and 1938.

1941 brought the publication of the deeply lyrical and poetic forest story, *The Birch Grove*, one of the author's favorite works, while 1943 saw the appearance of a collection of tales entitled *The Scorched Soul*. The following year Gladkov published a further volume of stories entitled *The Vow,* which took its title from a tale dedicated to the patriotic heroism of Soviet industrial workers during the war.

Gladkov spent the last few years of his life working on a lengthy autobiographical tetralogy, *Story of My Childhood* (1949), *The Outlaws* (1950), *Evil Days* (1954), and *Restless Youth.* The first two sections of the ambitious work brought him Stalin Prizes in 1950 and 1951 respectively, but unfortunately the final part remained unfinished at his death.

CEMENT

CHAPTER I

THE DESERTED FACTORY

1. On the Threshold of Home

Everything was just as it had been on that morning in early March three years ago. Beyond the buildings and roofs of the factory the sea flashed in the brilliant light, while the air between the mountains and the water glowed like rich, fiery wine. The light blue chimneys, the reinforced concrete walls, the little houses in the workers' settlement, and the mountain ridges in the distance were the color of molten copper in the sun.[1]

Nothing had changed during those three years. The hazy mountains with their rocky cliffs and ravines, their outcrops and scree, were just as they had been in Gleb's childhood. Far away in the distance he could see the familiar quarries up on the slopes, the gravity roadways running down among bushes and rocks, and the bridges and hoists in the narrow ravines. The factory below him was just the same too, a whole city of circular roofs, towers and domes, while stretching over the hillside above it, the workers' settlement was the same too, with its stunted acacias and its little square gardens in front of each porch.

If you went through the gap in the concrete wall that divided the settlement from the factory—there used to be a gate in the wall but now there was only a gap—in the second block of dwellings you would find Gleb's house.

Any moment now his wife Dasha and little daughter Nurka would catch sight of him, and filled with gladness, come running out and fall into his arms. Dasha was not expecting him, and moreover, he had no idea of what she might have suffered during the three years he had been away. In the whole of Russia no road, no path had been left unstained by human blood. Had death only walked down the street here, passing the workers' dwellings by, or had its fiery whirlwind struck Gleb's home too and swept it away?

On a patch of waste ground beyond the wall a few grubby children were playing, while big-bellied, sly-eyed goats wandered here and there, nibbling at the acacias.

Catching sight of Gleb, several cockerels jerked their red combs in surprise and cried angrily:

"Who-o is this?"

Yet all the while in his heart Gleb could hear the deserted quarries, the factory chimneys and the workers' settlement resounding with a deep, subterranean roar ...

From the mountainside he could see the cableway running down among the factory buildings to the wharves and the sea, its concrete supports resembling triumphal arches shaped like a gigantic letter H. Between them stretched the steel cables with their little trucks hanging motionless in mid-air, while beneath them, looking like rust-colored muslin at this distance, was the iron safety-net. Far below, at the end of the wharf, rose the spread wings of the electric cranes, their tracery of girders outlined against the sea.

Splendid! It meant machines and work once more—free work that had been won in a desperate struggle, at the cost of fire and blood.

The goats seemed to be shouting and laughing with the children. The acrid smell of pigsties hung in the air, and wherever Gleb looked there were rank weeds, while the paths running among them were littered with hen-droppings.

What did it all mean? Goats, pigs and hens here? In the old days this kind of thing had been strictly forbidden by the factory management.

Here was the same old wooden fence round the little yard that was just fifteen feet square, and here too was the same outside lavatory that looked like a tiny hut and opened on to the street. But the fence was rather dilapidated now—time and the northeasterly winds had both taken their toll—and its blue-gray paint was peeling.

Any moment now Dasha would come running out with a cry of joy... But how would she greet him, risen again as he was from fire and death? Perhaps she had given him up for dead, or perhaps she had been waiting day in and day out for him ever since the moment he had left her in the night, left her alone with Nurka in their little house.

Gleb threw his kitbag down on the ground and hung his greatcoat on the fence. Then he stood still for a moment, and flinging his arms wide in an attempt to calm himself, wiped the sweat off his face with the sleeve of his army tunic.

He was just about to climb the steps to the porch when the door of the house swung wide open.

A woman with dark eyebrows and a sunburnt face, wearing a man's shirt and a red kerchief, was standing in the shadowy doorway, staring at him in amazement. When she saw the smile on his face, a look of both alarm and joy flashed in her eyes at the same time.

He could see the slightly rounded, girlish cheeks, the familiar, quivering chin, the turned-up nose, the way she cocked her head on one side when gazing intently at something, and the obstinate-looking eyebrows that he remembered so well. It was Dasha all right. But everything else about her—though quite what it was he couldn't say—seemed unfamiliar and strange, and he felt he had never seen it before.

"Dasha!" he cried. "My wife! My darling! Well!"

Breathless with emotion, he rushed towards her.

But she remained standing on the top step of the porch, as though rooted to the spot, and merely brushed him aside in bewilderment as if he were some kind of apparition. Then she blushed deeply and murmured:

"Is it you, Gleb? Oh, my darling!"

But deep in her dark eyes there flickered unaccountable fear.

When he took her in his arms and pressed his lips to hers, she immediately went weak, so weak and still that he thought she was going to faint.

"Well then . . . so you're alive and well, my love!"

But she could not tear herself away from him and went prattling on and on like a little child:

"Oh, Gleb! I didn't even know . . . Where on earth have you come from? And so . . . unexpectedly too!"

She laughed and buried her face in his chest, while he kept pressing her against him, feeling her heart pounding and her body trembling with an irrepressible quivering.

They kept tearing themselves away from one another and gazing rapturously into each other's eyes, then laughing and embracing wildly once more.

Then Gleb lifted her in his arms as if she were a child and started to carry her into the house just as he used to when they were first married. But Dasha broke free and with a knowing smile straightened her clothes.

"My, how impatient you are!" she exclaimed.

Running a comb through her hair and breathing heavily, she backed away from him towards the gate, then suddenly seemed to remember something and cried anxiously:

"Oh, Gleb, I'm late! I must hurry!"

Then more seriously but still with a trace of emotion, she added:

"Call at the Factory Committee office and sign on for your food ration. I haven't got any time at all now ... Oh, Gleb! Oh, comrade! I just can't believe it! You seem quite different—new somehow ... you're familiar and strange at the same time."

"Dasha! What *is* all this? I don't understand ... "

But she was already standing by the gate, smiling at him.

"I have my meals in town now, in the Food Commissariat canteen, and I get my bread ration at the Party Committee office. So you'd better call in at the Factory Committee yourself and register for your bread card. I'll be away for two days—I've got to make an urgent trip out into the country. Have a rest after your journey while I'm gone. I must go now—the cart will be waiting. I really can't ... "

"But just a minute, Dasha. What on earth *is* all this? I've hardly shown my face and suddenly you're off!"

Rushing towards her, he swept her into his arms, but with gentle firmness she freed herself once more.

"But tell me, Dasha, what does it all mean?"

"I'm working in the Women's Section now, Gleb."

"What d'you mean, in the Women's Section? And what about Nurka? Where's she?"

"In the Children's Home ... Now go and rest. I've not got a minute now. We can talk later. You know what it's like—Party discipline and so on ... "

Then away she went with quick steps, her red kerchief teasing him until she reached the wall and seeming to beckon gaily to him as it went.

Then, at the gap in the wall, she glanced back, and with a flash of her white teeth gave him a wave.

Gleb ran to the low fence and shouted:

"Dasha! What about Nurka? She must be big by now! I'll go and see her. Which Children's Home is she in?"

"No, no, don't! We'll go together! Just you have a rest!"

He stood on the porch, watching despondently as she walked away. He simply could not understand what was happening.

He had spent three years amid the tumult of civil war, three fiery years caught up in the whirlwind of awesome events. But how had *she* spent those years, he wondered.

Here he was, back in the house from which he had once fled into the empty night. Here was the factory again, where as a teenager he had always been covered in oil and ash. But the house was empty now and Dasha had not welcomed him as he had imagined she would.

Gleb sat down on the top step of the porch and suddenly felt very tired. It was not because he had walked nearly three miles from the station, but because of what had happened during the past three years and this strange reunion with Dasha.

But why was there such an unusual silence all around him? Why was the air filled with a chirring sound, and why could the scratching of hens be heard all over the workers' settlement?

There were no real factory buildings left any more. Instead they resembled great crumbling blocks of ice, while their dead chimneys looked like cylinders of chill blue glass. There was no longer any soot on their tops either, because the mountain winds had blown it all away, and on one of the chimneys the lightning conductor was gone completely. Had it been wrenched away during a storm, or had it been torn off by human hands? Who could say?

In the old days there never used to be the smell of manure near the factory, but now acrid, mouldy cow dung lay among the wild grass that had crept down from the mountainside.

Over there, in the building at the foot of the slope, was the engineering shop. At this time of day the countless panes in its twenty-foot windows used to blaze with dazzling light, but now only black emptiness yawned beyond the smashed frames.

The town over on the other side of the bay looked different too—it had turned gray and seemed covered with mildew and dust, so that it merged with the hillside. It no longer looked like a town, but more like an abandoned quarry.

Here was the door Dasha had left open, a door leading into an empty house. And down below, in the valley, lay the forgotten, lifeless factory . . .

A rooster came up to the fence, and cocking its head on one side, looked at Gleb with a spiteful, cold eye.

"Who-o's this?" it cried.

3. The Machines

There were two ways from the workers' settlement to the Factory Committee offices. One was along the road that led past the factory buildings, and the other was by a meandering path that ran over the waste tips on the hillside, passing through disused quarries and among clumps of bushes.

From the path up on the hillside the whole factory was visible, complete with its mass of complicated viaducts and towers, its great buildings of concrete and stone that in one place were light and airy like gigantic bubbles, and in another rectangular and austere in the ponderous simplicity of their architecture. Linked one to the next, they climbed above each other or simply rose at various heights from the mountainside, soaring into the sky like giant monoliths. Down in the gorges, perched beside the ruined gravity roadways that were overgrown with bushes and littered with boulders, scattered at the foot of crags or on the waste-tips themselves were lonely little houses built of stone that had been roughly hewn from the light blue rock. The terraced quarries fell away into the ravines to disappear from sight amid the trees of a luxuriant young forest far below, while away in the distance, sweeping from one headland to the next and shimmering in the morning light, lay the sea. Stretching out like taut bow-strings on the far side of the bay were two long breakwaters, each with a lighthouse at its far end, and one could see immense arcs of foam sweeping in towards the factory and wharves then breaking in snow-white surf upon the shore.

Everything still looked just the same as it had three years ago, but then both factory and mountains had quivered incessantly as though filled with a mighty subterranean fire, and the buildings and wharves had been alive too, throbbing with the thunder of unseen machinery and humming with the whine of generators.

Gleb walked along the hillside path, gazing down at the factory and listening to the gloomy silence that was broken only by the murmuring of mountain streams, and he began to feel as if he too were now covered in heavy dust.

Was this really the factory he had known since his childhood, the factory where he had walked the paths every day on his way to and from work? And was this he, Gleb Chumalov from the engineering shop, a true blue-collar worker, now making his way down the overgrown track with a look of sad bewilderment on his face?

In the old days he used to be unshaven—he had sported a turned-up mustache—and because his face had never been free of metal dust and soot it had always looked swarthy. But now he was clean-shaven, and his cheeks and nose were blue-gray and peeling, chapped by the steppe wind. He no longer smelt of oil and ash either, and his back was no longer bent with toil. Now he was simply a Red Army man who wore a green helmet with a scarlet star on his head and the Order of the Red Banner on his chest.

On he went, gazing down at the factory, the chimneys and the quarries, stopping occasionally to think and growing angry as he did so.

"What the hell have they done to us, the bastards? Shooting's too good for the swine! This isn't a factory, it's more like a tomb!"

He made his way down towards the deserted factory yard that was stained black with coal dust and overgrown with rank grass. In the old days great heaps of anthracite had towered into the sky here, their pitch-black crystals flashing like diamonds in the light. The yard was dominated by a steep rock face with yellow and brown strata showing in it. Now the rock itself was crumbling, its fragments obliterating the last vestiges of human toil below. Around the edges of the yard railway lines ran in a semi-circle, while straight ahead, beyond the parapet, the blue factory chimney soared three hundred feet into the sky, rising like an obelisk from the abyss, and beyond it lay the enormous building of the power station.

The factory was like a dead planet now. Icy northeasterlies had shattered its windowpanes, mountain streams had laid the iron ribs of its concrete bare, and rain had turned the heaps of cement dust on the ledges of its buildings into solid rock.

Klepka the watchman came by. He was wearing a long, unbelted smock made of sacking that reached to his knees. His battered shoes looked as if they were made of cement too, and enclosed in them were his bare feet.

"Hey, there, you old devil!" cried Gleb. "What are you doing here, walking around like a bloody ghost? Some guard you are! Why did you let me get past, you old fool?"

Answering in an indifferent tone, Klepka gave his customary warning:

"Unauthorized persons are strictly forbidden here!"

"Oh, you silly old devil! I guess you've gone and lost all your keys too, wandering about over this scrap heap!"

"Keys are no use here any more—all the padlocks have been stolen. So go where you like! There's goats in the factory and rats too, but there's no people any more ... They've all gone."

"You're nothing but an old rat yourself! Hiding away in your hole and wandering about doing nothing!"

Klepka shot him a hostile glance and moved his toothless gums silently.

"Just because you've got a pointed helmet on ... " he said. "It's like the horn of the devil himself! But you're wasting your time—there's nobody left here to push around any more!"

Then off he went, shuffling along in his battered shoes.

Running from the yard down into the main factory building was a high viaduct on stone supports. Holes for machine-guns had been smashed in its concrete sides—the factory had been a White Guard stronghold, and the Whites had turned it into quarters for prisoners-of-war and even used part of it for stables. Those same prisoners' quarters had also served as horrible torture chambers during the foreign intervention.

The interior of the factory was festooned with scores of cobwebs that were heavy with dust, and from the twilit canopies high up in the roof drifted the musty odor of old cement. Here was the gigantic bulk of the furnace, its great door now wrenched away. Swirling with dust, the air roared like a waterfall in the shaft as it was sucked swiftly down.

In the old days a cast-iron door had sealed the awesome mouth of the furnace like a great plug, and the chimney would draw the fiery dross up from the rotary kilns with a mighty roar. Lit by brilliant flames, the red-hot kilns would slowly turn their monstrous bulk, while men went scurrying to and fro like ants beneath them. But now torn lengths of thick iron piping lay tangled everywhere in great loops and spirals.

"Oh, the bastards!" thought Gleb. "What have they done? What have they done, the swine?"

Passing down a series of long tunnels, he finally came to the engine-room. It was filled with the clear light of day and resembled an austere temple, its floor laid with different-colored tiles that made it look like a giant chessboard. Here, like great black idols adorned with copper and brass, stood the diesels. Immovable and firm they stood, in long, orderly rows, each in its allotted place and ready for work. Just a touch, it seemed, and they would spring to life once more, their polished metal flashing in the light. As he looked at them, Gleb could almost feel the waves of hot air rolling towards him. The great fly-wheels seemed to be frozen motionless too. Here in the engine-room, just as in the old days, everything was still spick and span, and each part of the machines testified to someone's loving care. Just as before, too, the tiled floor shone with wax polish, and there was not a speck of dust on the windows. The panes—and there were dozens of them—flashed with blue and amber light. It was clear that a human being remained doggedly alive in here, and thanks to him the machines were still alive too, filled with tense expectation.

Then, wearing a dark blue workman's shirt and cap, the human being himself appeared from the gangway between the diesels, wiping his hands on a scrap of waste as he came. The whole of him was immensely powerful-looking, uncompromising and stern, the whites of his eyes and his teeth gleaming in the light. It was Brynza.

"Ha, ha, Gleb, my old friend!" he cried. "Is it really you? My, and what a fine soldier you are too! Well, that's good! You've certainly cheered me up all right!"

Brynza had almost been born here—his father used to be a mechanic too—and he had grown up among the machines, so the engine-room was his whole life. Gleb and he had spent their childhood together and had begun work at the factory at the same time.

"Well then, so this is our soldier, is it? Come on now, let's have a good look at you! You've got that helmet pulled right down, so all I can see is your nose and that star!"

Gleb flung his arms round him.

"Brynza, old fellow! Are you still here? Ah, God damn you! You've got everything so spick and span anybody would think these engines of yours were running quite normally!"

Brynza grasped Gleb by the arm and led him into the narrow gangway between the diesels.

"Just look at these beauties, my friend!" he said. "They're just like a bunch of young girls, all neat and tidy. But you only have to shout: 'Brynza! Start 'em up!' and all these creatures will set to work again, thundering out their iron music. Engines need discipline, you know, just like that army of yours does!"

"Well now, Brynza, haven't you got a few goats as well, eh? And aren't you doing a bit of pilfering on the side?"

The mechanic burst out laughing, his voice ringing with gay malice.

"Ho-ho, those goatherds know me all right! And as for those pilferers, I'll break their bloody necks! The thieving bastards! I keep a rifle here just in case! Can you see it?" He waved a fistful of waste towards a gun standing in the corner. "They're just like thieves, the swine! They come in here hunting for bits of copper and brass ... "

Gleb patted the shining engines affectionately and kept glancing at Brynza with a look of both surprise and hope in his eyes.

"Well, old friend, you've got things so well organized here I just don't feel like going away! But what a state the factory's in! And what a state the people are in too! So why the hell are you hanging around here, when the place is like an empty shell and all the workers are bone idle and on the fiddle?"

Brynza's face grew dark, and it seemed to Gleb that he had suddenly become hostile and withdrawn. Filled with agitation, the mechanic strode up and down beside the nearest diesel, then said gravely:

"The factory's got to be started again, Gleb, it mustn't die! Otherwise, what the hell did we have a revolution for? Why are we here now? And what's that medal on your chest for?"

Then he added in a quiet, sad voice, as though complaining of something:

"You don't know how machines live, you've no idea ... You'd go crazy if you could see and feel what I do!"

Long ago, when the diesels had fallen silent and the workers had left the factory in droves for revolution and civil war, and for the hunger and suffering they brought, Brynza had stayed behind, alone amid the stillness of the engine-room. He lived just as his shining machines did, and he was just as solitary as they were. He had remained true to them to the very end.

"The factory's got to be started again, Gleb! Machines are machines, my friend, and they can't lie idle! They're at work even when they're standing still. Oh, if only you could understand that! But even if you don't, you've got to do all you can to get things moving again! And you know you can always rely on me!"

Gleb gazed at the lustrous flanks of the diesels and then at Brynza, listening to the profound silence in the vast emptiness around them. He felt powerless, sensing there were no words he could say to his friend, for he himself was filled with profound dismay and appalled by the vast graveyard of machinery that surrounded them. He felt alien here, for everything around him seemed unfamiliar and terrible, as though boundless havoc had been wreaked long, long ago. What could he say to Brynza? After all, he himself did not have a warm place to call his own now, for even his wife had forsaken him at the very moment when all should be forgotten and when nothing should matter but one's beloved ... Surely Dasha could have put off her trip for his sake, couldn't she?

4. Comrades

The narrow, twilit corridor down in the semi-basement of the factory management building was crowded with workmen. Surrounded by clouds of tobacco smoke and begrimed with the dust of roads and quarries, the men all looked alike, as indistinguishable as shadows at nightfall.

Everyone was shouting and swearing about things like the communal canteen, rations and kerosene, clothing-cards and goats.

The door of the Factory Committee office was open, and that room too was packed with jostling, grimy men and filled with smoke. They did not recognize Gleb as he pushed his way through the crowd, and merely glanced in a rather unfriendly way at his helmet with its star and at the Order of the Red Banner on his chest. Then they did not give him another thought.

Gleb made his way into the room and stood at the back of the crowd by the wall. At the table sat the hunchbacked old mechanic Loshak, his face just as dark and rusty-looking as it had been three years ago. Bulky and impassive, he sat there for all the world like a deaf man.

Then he suddenly gave a cough and pressing his fists on the table, got slowly to his feet. For a long time he gazed with heavy eyes at everyone in the room, then coughed again and said:

"Listen, friends, this is how the Soviet government fixes things: it took grain from the peasants to make war on the bourgeois, then it took factories like ours away from the bourgeois—and now there's no work! They took all kinds of trash away from the bourgeois and said to us: 'Share it out among yourselves in your workers' cooperatives so nothing gets wasted. Do just what you like with it!' But what I say is this: let's get the factory started again, then things'll soon be different!"

He sat down again, looking just as massive and gloomy as before.

Gleb eventually made his way through the crowd to the table and greeted the members of the Factory Committee.

"Hello, comrades! It's good to see you again! I've come back to where I used to work!"

The swarthy little consumptive, Gromada—he, too, a mechanic—gave a cry of surprise, then threw up his arms and rushed towards Gleb.

"Loshak, old fellow, can't you see who it is? It's Chumalov! Our Gleb! We all thought he was dead but here he is, as large as life! Just look at him!"

But Loshak looked at Gleb just as indifferently as he looked at all the other workmen who crowded into the Factory Committee office every day from morning till night.

"I can see him," he said. "Well, Gleb, you couldn't have turned up at a better time—the machine shop has gone to the dogs and all they do there now is make things like cigarette lighters on the side! It's a hell of a place!"

Then, with an effort, he stretched a long, heavy hand from behind the table and slowly held it out towards Gleb.

Men from various sections of the factory crowded round them, staring at Gleb in amazement as though he were risen from the dead. Then, exchanging glances and muttering to each other, they too shook him by the hand.

"Right you are, Comrade Chumalov! We've got a job for you, just you wait and see! We've taken matters into our own hands, you might say. Look at the state everything's in! We've got rid of the bosses all right, but just you watch what's going on round here! They're all at it! One strips brass off the machines and another pinches rivets, while somebody else cuts off the driving belts. Oh yes, we're the bosses now all right, make no mistake!"

Gleb was looking at the workmen and nodding happily.

"Ah! Coopers and smiths, electricians and mechanics—you're all here, comrades!" he thought.

Gromada elbowed his way through the crowd with a chair and obligingly put it down beside Gleb.

"Make way, comrades! Make room for Comrade Chumalov! After all, he's our soldier back from the Red Army! And since he's also a worker in our magnificent factory, we must show him off as best we can. If Comrade Chumalov hadn't had such a bad time of it, and landed up in the Red Army after being with the Greens,[2] and so on and so forth, there'd probably be a good many of us who wouldn't have taken the step of joining the Communist Party. So you see, comrades, that's how much Chumalov means to us!"

Vying with each other to be heard, many of the men began shouting:

"So you came through alive after all, old friend, did you? It's good you made it! Well then, just you enjoy yourself for a while! How are you going to spend your time now, comrade? Don't worry about tobacco, though—we'll take care of that for you!"

But Gromada was already waving his big bony hands at the crowd and saying in his chesty voice:

"Comrades, as members of the working class we all fought to gain control of the means of production, but it's disgraceful, comrades, that we're so inclined to defeatism! We've triumphed on every front and eliminated all opposition, so are we really incapable of proper economic labor now?"

Gleb was silent. He gazed at the gaunt faces around him, then at the hunchbacked Loshak and the sickly Gromada—the man was so small, yet his surname was so big[3] and the words he used were so big too—and once again he was painfully aware that here as well he had failed to find the sincere gladness and warmth he had dreamed of all the way home. Everyone seemed pleased enough at his return, but their exclamations and smiles were curiously distant and cold. It was as if all these men had burnt themselves out and were now destined to remain exactly as they were for the rest of their lives. Even in Gromada's noisy outbursts there was something absurdly labored and forced, as though he were trying to show more excitement than was really necessary. Strangely enough, Gleb felt that all these people had something in common with Brynza and Dasha too. Or was it simply that he had been upset by his strange reunion with her?

"Yes, friends," he said, "it isn't a factory you've got here any more, but a scrap heap. What the hell have you been doing all this time? There we were, fighting and getting ourselves killed, but what were you doing? Couldn't you think of any better way of passing the time than keeping goats and making cigarette lighters on the side?"

At the back of the crowd someone gave a hoarse laugh.

"If we'd spent our time loafing round the factory, damn you, we'd all have died like flies! So to hell with the bloody factory!"

The man's laughter and his simple words overwhelmed Gleb, for they rang with the commonplace everyday truth that can crush the most inveterate dreamer. Was this not why the impassioned Gromada's enthusiasm seemed so ridiculously irrelevant amid all these coarse, hungry men? But the speaker's malicious laughter and the contempt he showed not only for his factory and his workman's duty, but also for himself infuriated Gleb. Trying hard to control his anger, he looked at the crowd and his face grew dark with rage.

"Well, and what if you *had* died? You should've given your lives to keep the factory going, instead of turning into a pack of thieves and stealing your own property!"

"Ho, ho! We've heard all that lots of times before from dozens of liars, without you giving it to us all over again!"

With a nonchalant gesture Loshak brushed away a fly that was trying to settle on his forehead, then said in a loud, deep voice:

"So you've come back to the factory, Chumalov, have you? Well, that's good! We'll find work for you all right—we're going to set things straight round here!"

Gromada was looking at Gleb with eyes that burned with emotion and he kept trying to say big words that were beyond him.

Gleb took off his helmet and putting it down on the table, smiled with embarrassment, but his eyes were still full of anger.

"Yes, I've come home, and even my wife's got no time for me now. These days you can hardly recognize the woman you live with, because everything's gone to hell! Loshak, put my name down for a food card, would you, and for meals in the canteen and a bread ration too!"

At this there was a stir among the men and they began to laugh.

"Ho-ho! He's a great talker all right, but his belly's empty just like ours are! You should've mentioned that to begin with, Chumalov! You've come back to join us, old friend, so just you wait and see what life's like round here. Ha! His belly's empty just like ours are!"

In his usual impassioned way Gromada tried to convince the men otherwise:

"When everything's said and done, comrades, Chumalov belongs to us, he's a workman just like we are! And you all know he's been in action and so on!"

"But what's that to us? His belly's empty just the same!"

Gleb stood up and surveyed the grimy crowd, and in his almost expressionless calm there was both menace and despair.

"Comrades! What are you trying to prove to me? My belly's got nothing to do with it! After all, a belly's a belly, damn it! But you've got to have a head on your shoulders too! You've lost yours, though, and instead of behaving like real workers you've turned into a gang of profiteers. But you won't put one over me without a fight, so carry on—shout your heads off and make fun of my belly if you like—you won't offend me! After all, I haven't eaten you out of house and home yet, have I? But I'm ashamed to see you so demoralized—it's worse than treachery! But d'you think I'm going to loaf around like you do? Oh no! I'll fight tooth and nail! Did you think I'd given up the ghost? Well I hadn't—I fought and what's more I'll go on fighting! The Party and the army ordered me to return to my factory and fight for socialism just like I did at the front!"

The men narrowed their eyes in confusion and shuffled their feet.

"You get things going again, Gleb! That's what I say! Isn't that right? Or I'll be damned! Right?" cried Gromada, running round the table in a fever of excitement.

Outside the window, leaning heavily on his stick as he made his way down the concrete path, went a stooping but dignified old man with a silver beard and the look of a gentleman. Gleb saw that it was Engineer Kleist. Once again, just as in the days when the Whites controlled the town, their paths had crossed. How good it would be to run out of the Factory Committee office right now and confront the old man face to face! He would probably be scared to death . . .

CHAPTER II

THE RED KERCHIEF

1. The Cold Hearth

Gleb was never at home at all during the day. The deserted house with its dusty windows and unwashed floors seemed airless and strange now. The walls seemed to press in on him and it felt too cramped to move. Then in the evenings the walls seemed to draw in closer still and the air became noticeably heavier.

He would wander round and round the factory then climb up to the quarries that were overgrown with bushes and weeds, and grow tired to the point of exhaustion.

He would come home again at night, but Dasha would not be there to welcome him as she once did.

In the old days it used to be comfortable and cozy in the small living room, with muslin curtains hanging at the windows and flowers standing in vases on the windowsill as bright and gay as little colored lights. The painted floor used to shine with a mirror-like luster, the white bed would be soft and deep, and the fragrant tablecloth would beckon invitingly to him. The samovar would be boiling away and the teacups tinkling too. It was here that his wife Dasha used to be, singing and laughing, playing with little Nurka and chattering about the morrow.

But all these things were painful now because they belonged to the past, and it made Gleb wretched to see his home looking so neglected, its walls stained with mold.

One night Dasha came in after midnight as usual.

The sooty flame in the paraffin lamp burned with a dim light, while the dusty lampshade on its blackened cord hung like a frosty flower in the air.

Gleb lay on the bed, watching Dasha through half-closed eyes.

No, it was not the same Dasha, the wife he once knew, for that Dasha was dead. This was a different one, a woman with a sunburnt face and a stubborn-looking chin, whose fiery red kerchief made her head look bigger than it really was.

She was undressing by the table, chewing a crust of bread as she did so and not looking at him. Her face was tired and grave.

Returning from her official trip out into the country, she had hurried home only to find Gleb not there—he was out inspecting the gravity roadways. But that evening when he came in she had bustled about in an eager way, and after boiling the kettle to make some tea, had poured a few white saccharine tablets into a dish, then with a knowing look had pushed a little pat of butter towards him. All these things were for him, she'd said—she'd got them at the District Committee. As they drank their tea, she had told him at length about her work in the Women's Section, then had asked him how he had spent the last three years and which fronts he had fought on.

After that they had talked about Nurka. She was a fine little girl, Dasha said, and she was perfectly happy living in the Children's Home. In fact, she didn't enjoy life now unless there were other children around her. Dasha had brought her home once on a public holiday, but the child had spent the whole day longing to go back. It was true there were still many shortages: the food in the children's homes was very poor, milk was in short supply, there was never any sugar, and as for meat, the children hadn't the faintest idea what it even looked like. What was more, the staff were unreliable, and you had to keep a constant eye on every single one of them. But all these things would come right in time and everything would settle down in the end. What about Gleb, though? What was he going to do?

But he had not been listening properly to what she was saying, and kept giving irrelevant answers to her questions. He had watched her, trying to understand her and fathom what kind of person she now was, wanting to arouse in her the quiet submissiveness he remembered so well. He had put his arms around her, then held her close and had been filled with desire. She had held him too, but had kissed him in a guarded way with a look of alarm and fear in her big, grave eyes, and when, overwhelmed by furious passion, he had flung himself upon her, she had said in a sober, rather cross voice:

"Hey now, just you wait! Stop it!"

And her cold words had been just as hurtful to him as a slap in the face. Then, sounding rather offended, she had reproached him:

"You can't even see I've become a different person, can you, Gleb? Don't you realize I'm a comrade of yours now? I've learned something fine and new, and I'm not just a woman any more. Try to understand that. After you'd gone I discovered I was a real person and learned to value myself. It was very hard, and it cost me dear, but now no one will destroy the pride I have in myself—no one, not even you, Gleb ... "

Filled with anger, he had interrupted her rudely:

"Right now it's the woman in you I want, not the person! Are you my wife or aren't you? Yes or no? Have I the right to you or have I become a fool? What the hell do I need all your arguments for anyway?"

But she had pushed him away, saying firmly with a frown:

"How can you love me, Gleb, if you don't understand me? I can't do it like this, I don't want to live in the simple way we did before, and just to give in to you, like any other woman, it isn't in my nature."

Then she had moved away from him, seeming suddenly inaccessible and remote.

With every day that passed she had become increasingly distant from him, withdrawing into herself more and more, and he could tell she was suffering. He was suffering too, though, feeling angry and hurt at the same time. He had come to the conclusion that there was someone standing in his way, that Dasha had found someone else during the past three years, and that she did not wish to share her love between Gleb and the other, his rival. How else was her stubbornness to be explained? It was inconceivable that during the past three years she had never yearned for a man, inconceivable that having found Gleb again, she would not give herself to him with all her heart. After all, he could see she was excited and barely able to control herself, and he had felt her heart pounding under his hand.

Yet here she was, home again but even more distant now than she had been in the early days after his return. How long, damn it, would all this business last, he wondered.

"Tell me, Dasha, what on earth am I to make of it?" he asked. "I've been three years in the army, and I haven't had a moment to think of myself. Now I'm back again I feel terrible. I can't sleep at night because I'm wanting you. I've been back a week now, and you've only spent three nights at home. After all, you know, we've not seen each other for three years!"

Dasha heaved a sigh and said with a tender smile:

"Yes, three years, Gleb."

"I don't understand a damn thing! I just can't make it out to save my life! But d'you remember the night we parted? D'you remember how you looked after me when I was lying up there in the loft? And how you cried when I left? I never forgot those tears of yours, Dasha, not even for a single day. So what's happened, then?"

"Oh, Gleb, so much has changed!"

"Well, that's just what I'm talking about!"

"You see, Gleb, in the old days I was just a little fool. I feel ashamed when I remember what I used to be like . . . "

"I see. So it turns out, Dasha, that I've come back home for nothing, doesn't it? Are you saying to hell with the past?"

She shot him an intent glance, then turned thoughtfully towards the dark window.

"What do you want, Gleb? What have you been thinking all these years? I was left all by myself, completely at the mercy of fate, and I've had to fight to stay alive. I learned how to keep warm even in an unheated room in winter—there's a fuel crisis, you know—and I got used to eating in the canteen." Then she smiled and added jokingly: "I'm a free Soviet citizen now, you see!"

Gleb sat down on the bed, and his eyes—eyes that had seen so much bloodshed and death—flared with alarm.

"But what about Nurka? Have you gone and chucked your daughter out as well, now you're a free woman?"

"That's just downright stupid, Gleb!"

Untying her kerchief, she threw it on the table, and as her hair spilled free, its chestnut curls fell down over her eyes, making her look like a little boy. But she seemed to be gazing down on Gleb with a look of wise condescension, a faint smile playing on her face.

In the darkness outside the window a solitary night bird was calling in the ravine, sobbing like a little child, while inside hungry rats scurried to and fro under the floor.

"Well, all right, then, Dasha. But what if I go to the Children's Home tomorrow and bring Nurka back here? What will you say to that?"

"You can if you like, Gleb—you're her father, after all—but I can't look after her—I haven't time. If you want to take care of her, though, then stay with her—I'll be very glad!"

"But it's you who's her mother! Since when have you turned into some kind of cuckoo, leaving the child God knows where while you go rushing around without giving a damn?"

"I'm a Party member now, Gleb, and don't you forget it!"

He got up from the bed and walked over to the door. Once again he began to feel cramped in the room—the walls seemed to be closing in on him and the floor was swaying beneath his feet.

Dasha took a blanket and pillow off the bed and fetching herself a sheet from the chest of drawers, laid them on the floor. Then she quickly got Gleb's bed ready too.

He had to make up his mind. Did Dasha still love him as before, or had her love died, and together with it had she herself now become a thing of the past?

Whom had she caressed and warmed with her body these past three years, he wondered. Can a vigorous, healthy woman really be like a barren flower?

"So, citizeness," he said, "that's how things stand, is it? We parted with tears, and now we're together again, we haven't got a single word to say to each other!"

"But why do you say that, Gleb? I want to talk to you so much, and I've got so many good things to tell you, but you just reduce everything to ..."

But he was not listening to her, and muttered:

"For three years I thought to myself: my wife's back there waiting for me, waiting for me and ... But when I get home I find I might just as well be a widower, because it's as if I weren't really married at all. Of course, there *was* a man, only it wasn't me!"

Amazed, Dasha rounded on him, her eyes flashing with anger.

"And didn't you have other women while you were away? Go on, tell the truth! After all, I still don't know whether you've come back healthy or riddled with disease!"

She said this through clenched teeth in an offhand way, but there was conviction in her tone. She could see through Gleb and he felt embarrassed.

"Well, all sorts of things happen at the front ... Anyway, you can't compare men and women like that, you know. What's allowed for a man isn't always possible for a woman."

Dasha undressed but did not lie down. Instead, half-naked but quite unashamed, she sat leaning against the wall. With a knowing look in her eyes, she scanned Gleb's face, then clenching her teeth, replied:

"A fine state of affairs that is! So a woman's position's different, is it? Just look what a lousy deal she's got, being a slave who's not allowed to have a will of her own and playing second fiddle all the time! What kind of Communism was it you learned, Comrade Gleb?"

He hardly recognized her now, for from her emanated an unprecedented, new power. Her directness and daring dismayed him. Would she really ever have spoken to him in such a forthright way in the old days? Then she used to think exactly as he did, devoting herself to him unreservedly. Where, then, could she have learned such bold self-assurance?

He went up to her and looked her sternly in the face.

"So it's true, then, is it? Yes?"

Outside the window everything was oppressively quiet, and the starlit stillness was broken only by the chirping of crickets and the ringing of bells far away in the distance.

Out there, beyond the factory, lay the sea, wrapped now in a phosphorescent haze with its surf murmuring and sighing in the darkness.

"I've not asked you anything about the women you had at the front, Gleb, so what have my lovers got to do with you?"

"Just remember this then, Dasha! I'll find out sooner or later, and I'll get to the bottom of all your secret carryings on! So just you wait!"

She moved away from the wall, her eyes flashing.

"Take care, Gleb! I can be just as fierce as you can!"

Where on earth had she got this boldness from, he wondered. Where had she learned to fling up her head so proudly and to parry harsh words with an angry glance?

It was not by fighting in war, not by carrying a food-sack on her back, and not by doing a woman's daily chores that she had learned this. No—her character had been awakened and forged by the collective spirit of the workers, then tempered in the years of fire and blood, amid both the severest hardship and a newfound freedom that was beyond almost any woman's strength.

Gleb felt that he was no longer standing on firm ground and that he was beginning to look foolish in her eyes. Infuriated by his sense of impotence, he seized her by the arms, gripping them so hard that the joints creaked. But Dasha gave no indication that it hurt her.

"Take your hands off me, Gleb! D'you hear? Go away!"

But he lifted her in his arms and flung her down on the bed. They began to struggle, she twisting to and fro as she tried to break free, her half-naked body writhing with the effort. Suddenly, with a dexterous kick, she threw him to the floor and leapt to her feet. Then, pale and breathless, she pulled down her nightdress and said contemptuously:

"I won't let you treat me like this, Gleb! Don't you know me properly yet? Well, start learning now—it's high time you did! So this is the kind of Bolshevik you are! You might be a good soldier, but you haven't got any brains!"

Subdued now, he was sitting on the floor, grinding his teeth.

"Put the light out, Gleb, and lie down. Calm yourself a little—you can't think straight just at the moment. It makes no difference—we won't reach any solutions tonight anyway."

"I just can't understand it, Dasha! There's such a fire in my soul!"

"Lie down and be quiet, Gleb. I'm absolutely worn out, and tomorrow I've got to go out into the country again on another trip. There are thieves all over the district and people are being attacked everywhere...."

She went over to the table and put out the lamp. Gleb could hear her lying down and covering herself with the blanket, then she was quiet. Suddenly he was filled with both suffering and shame. He felt like rushing over to her and beating her, then tearing her to pieces and weeping—weeping and imploring her to caress him. They lay silent for a long time and neither of them moved. Gleb waited, hoping she would get up and come to him, then tenderly, without a word, nestle against him. But she just lay there without moving and he could not even hear her breathing.

"Dasha, darling! Don't torment me like this! Why are you so cold towards me?"

She reached out and taking his hand, pressed it to her breast.

"Dear Gleb, get a grip on yourself, and calm down! Let's try to understand each other a little better. Just wait, darling! It's not easy for me either, you know, but there are things we must think about. I've longed for no one but you these past three years!"

Outside the window the sky was strewn with glittering stars, and from far away in the mountains came the sound of distant thunder. But it was only the northeasterly wind soughing in the trees that filled the dark ravines.

2. The Children's Home

The next morning Gleb sensed through his drowsiness that sunlight was filling the room. The air between the window and the door was fragrant with the smell of spring. Dasha was standing by the table, wrapping the fiery red kerchief round her head.

She glanced at him and smiled.

"Gleb, I've managed to draw up a report for the Women's Section about the day nurseries we want for the children. I've worked out the estimates, but there's no money. We're so dreadfully poor, you know! We ought to squeeze a few things out of the bourgeois ... But you've not seen Nurka yet, have you? Well, we can go to the Children's Home together if you like—it's not far!"

"Now, Dasha, come here!" he said.

She came towards him, a knowing look in her eyes that shone in the morning light.

"Well? What is it?"

"Give me your hand ... That's right," he said. They were both silent for a moment, smiling and waiting to see what the other would say. "God knows if I understand you—you seem just like you used to be, and yet you're different somehow. But then again, perhaps I'm not the person I once was either. All right, let's try and understand each other. After all, everything's different these days—even the sun shines at a different angle!"

"Yes, Gleb, perhaps even the sun's different now too. Everything's changed, it's true, and you've changed too. You seem either younger or older—I'm not sure which ... And inside me everything's turned upside down. You're angry with me, but it's you who's to blame, you know. You weren't a bit interested to hear how I've spent these past three years and what I've been through. If only you knew me a little better and could sense what I feel, then you wouldn't treat me so coarsely. Oh, you are a silly thing!"

And with a laugh she ran out on to the porch.

"Come on then, get ready! I'm waiting for you!"

All the way to the Children's Home Dasha walked in front of him, following the path which wound its way among conifers and dogwood. She kept disappearing from sight then coming into view again, her red kerchief blazing in the light.

The "Krupskaya"[4] Children's Home was a tall building that stood in a ravine, surrounded by clumps of fruit trees. Its walls were of undressed stone laid in a crude but sturdy fashion and firmly cemented. The wide-open windows were as big as the doors, and from the dark interior of the building came a discordant, bird-like hubbub. A massive, curving staircase led up to the first floor, with decorative cement vases set on pedestals along it. Up on the verandah dozens of little children's heads could be seen, shining like melons ripening in the sun, but even from a distance their faces looked deathly pale and gaunt. What were they? Boys or girls? It was impossible to say, for they were all dressed in long, gray smocks. The nurses were outside with them enjoying the sunshine, they too dressed in gray with little white caps on their heads.

Away to the right, stretching beyond the buildings of the home and rising far above them, lay the sea, its deep blue waves flecked with myriads of dazzling sparks. Seeming no bigger than a waterboatman at this distance, a harbor launch was pulling away from the jetty, leaving a triangular wake behind it. Both the town and the mountains beyond it looked very distinct and near.

There they were, mountains and sea, factory and town, lying amid the vast expanse of distance that stretched away to the horizon and embraced the whole of Russia ... And all this boundless immensity resounded like music in the people's hearts, filling them with a song of magnificent toil. Did their hands not tremble in anticipation of the strenuous labor to come? Did their hearts not pound with the blood coursing through them? This was workers' Russia, this was what they were, this was the new world of which mankind had dreamed for centuries!

Dasha was standing by the stairs and smiling at him.

"How good the air is, Gleb! It smells just like the sea! Spring's here at last! Come on—Nurka lives up on the first floor!"

She set off up the stairs, a few steps in front of him as before. On she went, walking as if she were simply on her way home, for she seemed perfectly at ease here.

From up on the verandah Gleb could see more under-nourished little children wandering about like animals among the bare bushes and trees. Huddled in small groups, they scratched in the earth, greedily burrowing for food and looking round furtively like thieves all the time. They went on and on digging, stopping occasionally to tear their booty from each other's grasp, while further away, over by the fence, more children still were swarming over a heap of manure.

Filled with amazement, Gleb nodded towards them and looked hard at Dasha.

"They'll all starve to death, you know, Dasha! You people ought to be shot for this!"

She raised her eyebrows in surprise then looked down, and her chin quivered in a smile.

"Oh, that!" she said. "Scratching in the earth, you mean? That's not so bad—there's far worse things than that! If there'd been nobody to look after them, all the children would have died like flies long ago. We've opened homes for them but there's nothing for them to eat, and what's more, given half the chance, the staff would practically bite their heads off! Some of our people are good, though—the ones we've trained, that is!"

"And Nurka, is she like this too? Does she scratch around in the dirt like these starving little devils?"

"But how's Nurka any different from the rest? She's had a bad time too. If it weren't for our women, all the children would've been eaten alive by lice months ago."

While Dasha and Gleb had been coming down the mountain path, the children had been out on the verandah, but by the time the couple reached the first floor, both children and nurses had disappeared. They had probably gone running off to tell everyone that visitors had come.

The big room upstairs was full of sunlight and the air was hot and heavy. The campbeds stood in two long rows, covered with pink and white blankets that were patched and torn. Nurses kept coming in and out through the doors. The walls were hung with pictures—work the children had done in their collective activity groups.

The nurses paused respectfully as they passed.

"Hello, Comrade Chumalova! The matron's just coming."

Dasha felt she was in charge here.

"Nurka, I'm here! Nurka!" she called.

A little girl in a loose smock—she was very small, the smallest of them all—was already running towards them, laughing and shrieking as she came. The other children began to laugh too and came racing after her.

"Auntie Dasha's come! Auntie Dasha's come!"

Nurka! Here she was, the little rascal! Gleb found it almost impossible to recognize her. She was like a stranger now, and yet there was something familiar about her at the same time.

She came rushing up to Dasha and hid her face in her skirt.

"Mummy! My mummy!"

Dasha was laughing too now. She lifted Nurka in her arms and whirling her round, kissed her tenderly.

"Nurka! My little one!"

This was the old Dasha again, thought Gleb, the one who used to welcome him with Nurka when he came home from work. Here were the familiar gentleness and kindness, the eyes moist with tears, and the melodious voice with a nervous tremor in it that he knew so well.

"Look! Here's your daddy, Nurka! Here he is! D'you remember him?"

Nurka stared at Gleb with a faintly hostile look in her little blue eyes, and frowned.

Gleb laughed, and stretching out his hand, felt a lump rise in his throat.

"Come on, Nurka, give me a kiss! My, how you've grown! You're nearly as big as mummy now!"

But the little girl shrank back and looked intently at her mother once more.

"It's daddy, Nurka!"

"No, it's not daddy! It's a Red Army soldier!"

"But I *am* your daddy, and I'm a soldier too!" said Gleb.

"No, it's not daddy!"

Dasha's eyes were full of tears now, but she was smiling all the same.

"Well, all right then, just this once I'm not your daddy, but you're still my daughter, so let's be friends, shall we? I'll bring some sugar for you next time—even if I have to dig it out of the mountain, I'll bring you some. But why's mummy better than me? You live here all the time and she's somewhere else."

"But mummy *is* here. She's here in the daytime and she's here when it's nighttime too. But daddy's not here, and I don't know where he is. He's away fighting the bourgeois somewhere."

"Aha! You've got that off beautifully!" said Gleb. "Come on then, let me give you a kiss!"

The other children stared inquisitively at him, laughing and eagerly waiting for Dasha to take notice of them too. Vying with each other for attention, the little girls with their close-cropped hair kept holding out bunches of curly violets to her, each of them wanting to give her their flowers first.

"Auntie Dasha! Auntie Dasha!"

Far away somewhere, in one of the rooms, someone was drumming on a piano, and a chorus of children's discordant voices sang with all their might:

> "Arise, ye children of the future,
> Freedom's youth of all the world..."

Laughing, Dasha patted the children on their little heads, and it was clear that they were accustomed to her affection, expecting it just as they did their regular ration of food.

"Well, children, what have you had to eat today? Whose tummy's full and whose is still empty? Come on, tell me now!"

They all shouted their replies, scratching their heads and bellies as they did so. One dirty little boy with bulging eyes kept hawking and swallowing, then scratched his chest and coughed. Gleb went up to him and lifted his shirt, but the boy yelled in fright and ran off into a corner behind the beds so that only his face with its prominent eyes was visible.

"Ah-ha!" cried Gleb. "There's a ferocious fellow for you—he's got himself behind the barricades straightaway!"

Everyone burst out laughing. The sunlight came dancing in through the open windows that were as wide as the doors.

Holding Nurka by the hand, Dasha walked on in front. Gleb was hurt, for here too he felt like a stranger, as Dasha's clear voice rang out among the children. Both here and at home he was lonely and childless now.

Yes, life's difficulties had to be overcome here as well...

They visited every floor of the home, looking first at the dining room where children were sitting at tables laid with crockery, then at the kitchens with their clouds of steam and smell of food. Next they dropped in at the recreation room, its walls covered with children's paintings among the patches of mildew. Here, clustered round a short-haired young woman with a brown birthmark that covered the whole of one cheek, the children were singing discordantly:

"Arise, ye children of the future,
Builders of a brighter world ..."

Domakha and Lizaveta, both of them neighbors of Dasha and Gleb, were working in the home as well. In them, too, Gleb detected something new, something he had never seen before. Domakha was in the kitchen, helping with the cooking. With her sleeves rolled up and her face covered in perspiration, she was bustling about just as if she were at home. She greeted Dasha with a kiss.

They found Lizaveta in the storeroom with the housekeeper. Both of them were tall, handsome-looking women, neatly dressed like nurses. They were weighing out provisions, checking them and making a note of them.

Lizaveta greeted Dasha in her usual rather cool way, but there was a smile shining in her eyes. She only gave Gleb a glance, though, and after that took no more notice of him.

Then once again there were women walking everywhere, some in white caps and some without, but all of them smiling respectfully and even ingratiatingly at Dasha. But they looked suspiciously and askance at Gleb. Who was this man, they wondered. Perhaps he was one of those tiresome inspectors who had to be watched very carefully so as to discover their weaknesses.

Gleb kept taking hold of Nurka's hand and saying:

"Come on, Nurka, give me your hand! You let mummy hold your hand, so why won't you let me?"

But warily the child kept her hands out of the way. Then, when all of a sudden he lifted her in his arms and gave her a kiss, she became submissive and quiet, and for the first time she looked him in the face, her gaze thoughtful and intent.

"Your Nurka's a lovely little girl!"

It was the matron speaking, a small, quick mouse of a woman, devious-looking and sly with a face that was all flashing gold teeth and freckles.

Dasha looked past her, and her expression became stern and cold once more.

"What's so special about Nurka?" she asked. "They're all the same here. They're all lovely children."

"But of course, of course!" replied the matron. "We do all we can for the workers' children! Nowadays they must have all our attention. After all, the Soviet government takes great care of . . . "

Gleb clenched his teeth with anger.

"She's lying," he thought to himself, "we ought to find out what kind of a woman she is!"

And then the matron began to make one complaint after another.

But to these, too, Dasha replied sternly and coolly in a way that Gleb had never heard before:

"Please don't grumble, Comrade Matron! Tell me what's wrong, but don't grumble! Grumbling doesn't get us anywhere!"

"Yes, of course, Comrade Chumalova, of course! It's so pleasant and easy working with you!"

Dasha looked in every nook and cranny in the home, searching high and low and asking many questions. Then, unable to restrain herself any longer, she went into the staff's quarters.

"So this is how things are!" she cried. "Why on earth have you got armchairs and sofas in these back rooms of yours? And ornaments, pictures and flowers too! Didn't I say you mustn't deprive the children of anything? This is disgraceful! Is it really so bad for them to walk on carpets and sit on sofas sometimes? This just isn't good enough!"

"Yes, Comrade Chumalova, you're right, of course. But in my experience of bringing up children . . . Besides, it's harmful and makes them lazy . . . spreads all kinds of dirt and increases the risk of infection."

Sparks flashed in the matron's eyes, but without looking at her, Dasha went on speaking in the same hard voice, angry red blotches showing now on her cheeks:

"I don't give a damn for your experience! Our children used to live like pigs, but what they need now is as much light and air as possible, and good furniture and pictures too! We've got to give them everything we can! We must furnish the clubroom and decorate it. The children should be given the chance to eat and play and enjoy themselves. We adults need nothing, but they must have everything. Come what may— even if it kills us—we've got to give them all we possibly can! And to make sure the staff don't get lazy, they should sleep in dirty back rooms! Don't try to fool me, Comrade Matron! I know a bit more than you do even with all that experience of yours!"

The freckled, quick little woman flashed her gold teeth and laughed with delight, but sharp needles still glinted in her eyes.

"Why, who on earth could doubt it, Comrade Chumalova? You're an exceptional woman, so perceptive and quick. With your guidance everything will go well, everything will be splendid!"

As Gleb and she were leaving, Dasha kissed Nurka once more, and as she did so the other children clung to her with their discordant cries.

Once again Nurka looked long and thoughtfully at Gleb.

"D'you want to come home, Nurka?" he asked. "You can play there like you used to, you know. And mummy and daddy ... "

"Mummy's here! Here she is! But daddy's not here ... That's my bed, over there! We've just had a drink of milk and now we're going to do some marching in time to music!"

Then, for the first time, she put her arms timidly round Gleb, and her little eyes—eyes that were so like her mother's—glowed with the light of a silent question. All the way back from the Children's Home to the main road, Dasha said nothing, her face shining with a tenderness that was slow to fade. But when they reached the road, she said regretfully:

"Well, I'm off to the District Committee now. There's a lot of work to do so I'll not be back till late. There just aren't enough hours in the day for us in the Women's Section. It's not the children we've got to educate, oh no! It's those damned women of ours! If you don't watch them like a hawk, they'll steal everything down to the last crumb before you can say Jack Robinson. Ugh! There are enemies everywhere you look. Oh, and what a lot of them there are too! Like that matron with the gold teeth, for example. You might expect it from people like her, though, but when it comes to our own folk, Gleb, our very own! They're no better than slaves! Well now, what d'you think about squeezing the bourgeois a bit?"

But Gleb could not bear it, for she seemed so unfamiliar and alien now ...

Gloomily, almost with hostility, he muttered:

"We'll think about it—it's not an easy thing to decide. Anyway, what will the provincial committee say about it?"

Dasha smiled distrustfully at him and her chin quivered. Then, with a silent question in her eyes, she shot him a searching glance, but he went on gazing gloomily into the distance.

CHAPTER III

THE DISTRICT COMMITTEE

1. Comrade Zhuk Speaks Out

The Palace of Labor was a large brick building two stories high which stood on the embankment near the long jetty running out on its dark piles into the bay. On each side of the building a damaged concrete wall curved away like a torn ribbon and separated the embankment from the railway line. Through holes and gaps in the wall the rusty rails could be seen branching out as they ran away around the bay. The tracks were lined with grain warehouses as far as the station itself, while far away in the distance, towering like an ancient temple on the mountainside, was the huge grain elevator, its turrets now covered with moss.

The gray wharves with their giant mooring rings lay silent and still, the railway tracks gleamed dully here and there amid the debris of smashed trucks, carts went rumbling along the road by the wall, and the deserted breakwaters enfolded the bay with their curving arms of stone. Far away in the distance, indistinct in the spring haze, the harbor shimmered with myriad iridescent colors, and the white sails of fishing boats bobbed like gulls on the water. Dolphins were leaping and diving out in the bay, their powerful backs gleaming in the light, and shoals of gray mullet flashed silver in the sun.

Desolate wharves and hungry sea ... In what waters and to what shores were Soviet Russia's captured ships now sailing?

Near the Palace of Labor, in front of the entrance with its high pyramid of steps, there had once been a flower garden surrounded by chestnut trees. But now all the flowers were gone, the fence was broken, and the trees had been cut down for firewood. On the red flag that fluttered high above the roof, the brilliant white letters RSFSR kept flickering then vanishing in the wind like fresh camomile flowers.

Gleb entered the corridor. Straight ahead of him, in the conference hall, he could see banners and flags, while running from left to right was a second corridor that was dark and dusty. On the left was the Trade Union Council office and on the right the District Committee's quarters.

The air in the corridor was thick with stale tobacco smoke and the walls were grimy, covered with patches where the plaster was peeling. Workmen with hungry-looking faces were wandering back and forth, their expressions both angry and resigned, while busy officials bustled to and fro among them.

From various rooms both near and far came the sound of voices and laughter, accompanied by the rattling of typewriters and the clicking of rifle-bolts—the latter probably coming from the offices of the Cheka.

Gleb turned down the corridor to his right.

Two men were standing by the glass doors of the District Committee office, their heads clearly silhouetted against the frosted panes. One was bald, with a hooked Turkish nose and a short upper lip, and his mouth was half-open in a smile. The other man was snub-nosed, with a low forehead and heavy chin.

"It's a shame and a disgrace, Comrade! Absolutely disgraceful!" the snub-nosed man was saying. "It's bureaucracy that's ruined us, bureaucracy and red tape!"

"You're wrong, Comrade Zhuk! That's not the point, not the point at all! We've got many enemies, so what we need is merciless terror, otherwise the republic will continue to hang between life and death. That's what we've got to think about! I know what you mean, Comrade Zhuk, but the Soviet government must have a strong, well-proven administrative machine, and even if it *is* bureaucratic, it's got to work efficiently."

"You too! You're just like the rest! You're all the same! But what about the working class? Oh, my dear Comrade Seryozha! All this gives me a pain!"

"Only one thing matters now, Comrade Zhuk, and that's work among the people. Work, work, and more work! The people must quickly penetrate the republic's entire administrative machine and get right to the top. That pithy saying of Comrade Lenin's about the cook[5] must become an established fact. This is what matters, so you're wrong!"

"Oh, Seryozha! You might be what they call a devoted Communist, but you're terribly blind! You ought to have a bit more sympathy for the working class. And as for our enemies—I say to hell with them! We've dealt with them before and we'll do so again if we have to!"

Gleb recognized in the snub-nosed man his old friend Zhuk, a lathe-operator from the "Shipsteel" factory. He was apparently still shouting and complaining just as he used to three years before.

Gleb went up and clapped him on the shoulder:

"Hello, old friend! Still ranting and raving, are you? Just like in the old days, eh? When on earth will you stop it? You should be giving orders, but instead all you can do is complain, you snub-nosed devil!"

Zhuk opened his eyes wide in astonishment, then gave a gasp.

"Gleb! You old fire-eater! Well I'll be damned!"

And he rushed forward to embrace him.

"But is it really you, eh? You and me'll show 'em now! We'll put 'em all in their places! But where on earth have you sprung from, Gleb? Seryozha, this is Gleb, my best friend—we've sweated blood and tears together!"

Gleb and Sergei shook hands, joining fingers warily like strangers, and in the other's palm Gleb could feel the softness and timidity of a girl.

Sergei Ivagin had ginger hair that rose in curls around his bald patch, and there was a gentle smile shining in his eyes. But you couldn't quite make him out, because his smile seemed both mocking and shy.

"I've seen you before, Comrade Chumalov—I saw you earlier when you came to register. There was a question asked about you in the District Committee, so you've arrived just at the right time. Go through into the Secretary's office, would you? There's a meeting going on at the moment, but the Secretary left instructions to send for you immediately. Go on in—his name's Zhidky."

"No, you take him in yourself, Seryozha," said Zhuk, "it's your job! And I'll come with you and watch them trying to grab him with their bare hands!"

"But I'm busy just now, Comrade Zhuk—the Agitation and Propaganda Committee's meeting at the moment, then there's a session of the Education Department, and after that I've got to speak at ... "

"Oh, Seryozha! You might be an educated man but you're so humble and timid you're worse than a monk!"

The three men went into the room. Sitting at a table beside the window wearing a dark blue smock was Polya Mekhova, head of the Women's Section. Showing under the edge of her red kerchief, her fair curls shone in the sun. Her top lip was covered with soft down, like a boy's, and her eyebrows glowed with tiny sparks in the light. Her big eyes with their long lashes rested on Gleb for a moment as he came in, and her eyebrows quivered in a smile.

Dasha was there too, standing to one side near the table and speaking in an emphatic, clear way. She only glanced at Gleb as he came in. There was a crowd of women round her and still more lined the walls, all of them listening to her report about the day nurseries proposed for the town.

Suddenly Zhuk burst out laughing and grabbed Gleb by the sleeve.

"This is a very dangerous place, Gleb, my friend—it's the women's front! They'll scratch our eyes out and peck us to death! So watch out!"

Sergei gave a shy smile.

Dasha tossed her head in annoyance, and folding her arms, fell silent, waiting for the men to leave.

Comrade Mekhova brushed them aside and pretending to be cross, said with a smile:

"Move along now, comrades, and don't disturb us! Please go on now, Dasha."

Then, as Dasha began speaking again, Polya interrupted her and said:

"Comrade Chumalov, would you call in to see me on your way back, please? There's something I want to talk to you about."

Gleb put his hand to his helmet in a salute and answered smartly:

"Yes, ma'am!"

Then Dasha went on with her report.

2. A Concrete Proposal

As soon as Gleb opened the door into Zhidky's room, he was enveloped by clouds of greenish tobacco smoke and overwhelmed by a wave of stuffy heat. But the sun was shining amid all the smoke, and specks of dust glittered like sparks in the air.

The clean-shaven Zhidky sat with a leather jacket thrown over his shoulders. Opposite him, leaning back in his chair with a pipe in his mouth was Chibis, President of the Cheka. He was clean-shaven too. Zhidky had an Asiatic-looking nose with flared nostrils and deep, vertical creases in his cheeks.

Sitting on the window-sill with his feet up against the sash was a thin young man with a swarthy face, wearing a black shirt. It was Lukhava, Chairman of the local Trade Union Council. Propping his chin on his knees, he was listening silently to the others.

Gleb raised his hand to his helmet in a salute, but Zhidky paid no attention to him. After all, so many Party members came to see him that there simply wasn't time to welcome them all.

"Well, all right, then," he said, "we've got our logging areas decided, and we've asked the district Forestry Department to help as well. We've got stockpiles of timber too. But what then?"

He punctuated every sentence with a tap of his pencil on the table.

"Well? What then? The main problem, after all, is the actual supply of wood. All the timber's up over the pass and down along the coast. But our wood supply's already failing, so we must find a reliable and quick way of moving fuel before winter sets in. To hell with makeshift temporary methods—we've got to take the bull by the horns and do the job on a grand scale! What we need is a tremendous effort, and all our energies must be directed towards it. The Forestry Department hasn't carried out the tasks that were assigned to it—there's all kinds of riffraff got themselves fixed up there, a bunch of profiteering bastards who ought to be shot! What's more, the men in the logging areas will be rising in revolt soon because they're starving. Apart from that, we've simply got to have firewood, or our children will start dying like flies. We're in a very tight corner, my friends! There's a meeting of the Economic Council in a week's time, so we must be ready by then. Now, Lukhava, what have you got to say?"

Chibis was not looking at anyone, and it was impossible to tell whether he was deep in thought or simply resting, thoroughly bored by the whole business. Lukhava, though, was hugging his knees to his chest and looking at Zhidky with a self-confident grin.

"There aren't any tight corners, Zhidky—there's no such thing! There are only problems to be solved. You've panicked, my friend!"

Zhidky flared his nostrils and it looked as if he were laughing.

"We'll have to use the mechanical power of the factory," said Lukhava.

Then Sergei Ivagin raised his hand, asking for the floor.

"In connection with the proposal made by Comrade Lukhava, I would like to draw your attention to Comrade Chumalov's presence here. Our discussion of this issue might be assisted if Comrade Chumalov were to give us his opinion on it as a skilled workman at the factory. But now I must go to . . . "

With a wave of his hand Zhidky cut him short.

"Stop! Stop! Old Seryozha's declaiming in his usual sentimental fashion and blushing all over his bald patch!"

"I must go to a meeting of the Agitation and Propaganda Committee, after that to the Education Department board, and then . . . " said Sergei falteringly.

Zhidky invited Gleb to come up to the table.

"Well, Comrade Chumalov, do join us please! I'm afraid you'll have to stand, though—there aren't any chairs left."

Gleb went up to the table and stood to attention.

"I've been demobilized as a skilled worker," he said, "and I'm now at the disposal of the District Committee."

Without taking his eyes off Gleb's face, Zhidky held out his hand.

"Comrade Chumalov, you've been appointed secretary of your factory group. It's totally disorganized at the moment and full of speculators and profiteers. They've all gone crazy, keeping goats and making things like cigarette lighters on the side. What's more, they're stripping the factory bare. But then you probably know all about that already. So it's up to you to get the place in working order—military fashion!"

"We'll do our best, Comrade Zhidky! But every kind of discipline requires a firm basis on which to operate."

"That's true. And now it's your job to create that basis."

Still resting his chin on his knees and chewing a cigarette in one corner of his mouth, Lukhava was watching Gleb through narrowed eyes that glowed like embers. In response to Gleb's words he said casually to Zhidky:

"Send this comrade to the Organization and Instruction Department. We can't waste time with trivial details like this!"

Gleb looked him straight in the eye but said nothing.

Chibis shot Gleb a glance through his half-closed eyelids.

"So you're a skilled worker, and a military commissar too... But why did you leave the army when the factory's been out of action for years now?"

Gleb smiled and examined Chibis's face carefully.

"Out of action, did you say? It's much worse than that! It's like a bloody farmyard, a filthy scrap heap! Let's talk frankly, shall we, comrades? You're wanting to grab the men by the scruff of the neck and get rid of their goats. And you're asking for strong organization as well, aren't you? But where's your basis for that? If you make a clear announcement that the factory is to be started up again, then everything will go smoothly, but unless you do that, all you'll have will be a bunch of swineherds, not workmen!"

Lukhava gave a contemptuous snort and said:

"Heroes with the Order of the Red Banner should have something else besides bravery: they need a proper understanding of the facts of the situation!"

Chibis was leaning back in his chair with a distant, chill expression on his face, and through the film of dust on it one still could not tell whether he was following the discussion or merely resting, utterly bored by the whole business.

The creases on Zhidky's cheeks quivered as he smiled.

"Right! Let's continue our discussion of the fuel problem, shall we?"

After Lukhava's words—words that were just as provocative as his mocking smile—Gleb could hardly control his anger. Then Zhidky suddenly let fly at Gleb:

"Comrade Chumalov, we haven't got a single stick of firewood left and we're practically starving! The kids in the Children's Homes are famished and the workers are completely disorganized. So how on earth can you talk about restarting the factory at a time like this? It's sheer nonsense! It's not the factory that matters! What about the transport of wood from the logging areas? How can the factory be used for that?"

"Without fuel, electricity or machinery you can't do a thing, and that's for sure," replied Gleb.

"Then tell us how we can solve the problem in a practical way."

Gleb was silent for a moment, gazing thoughtfully out of the window.

"I think there's only one way to do it," he said. "We've got to extend the gravity roadway up as far as the pass. We'll start a program of voluntary Sunday work in all the trade unions—that'll take about two weeks. Then once the trucks are working, you can load them with as much wood as you like."

Zhuk clutched at Gleb and grinned with joy.

"Here you are, sitting around like a bunch of half-wits, messing about and wasting time, and then, just look! In his workman's way, by instinct, he ... "

But nobody was listening to Zhuk, and the whole of him—so familiar and commonplace now—was lost to view, just as if he were not there at all. He was always present for everyone to see, but no one ever noticed him, and his words barely reached their ears.

Zhidky was pencilling straight and crooked lines on the sheet of paper in front of him, then dividing them up into shorter ones, and because his face seemed so bored and calm, it began to look haggard and old.

"Lukhava, you wanted to say something about this, didn't you?"

Getting up quickly from the window-sill, Lukhava walked past Gleb then went back to the window again.

"I was thinking along the same lines as Comrade Chumalov, but he has put it far better than I can. I propose we accept his suggestion without reservation and ask him to make a report to the Economic Council."

Zhidky suddenly stood up and flung his pencil down on the table. It bounced off and fell at Gleb's feet.

"This is just Utopian, Comrade Chumalov! Stop going on about the factory all the time! The place is nothing but a stone tomb! It's not the factory that matters, it's firewood! There's no factory any more, only an empty quarry! As far as we're concerned, the factory's a thing of the past and the future, so for the time being let's just talk about the present—and the supply of wood!"

"I don't know what you mean by Utopian, Comrade Zhidky, but if you won't say the word 'factory,' the men will say it for you. What do you mean—the factory's a thing of the past and the future? Have you ever been to it? Do you know how the workers live? Do you know why they're stripping the place bare? Why the wind and rain are eating away at the concrete and iron? And why there's such wholesale destruction going on so that the place is turning into a giant scrap heap? The men don't want to go on living face to face with such failure, and they don't like to see all the trash that's lying around and going to waste either. But here you are, telling them the factory's not a factory any more but an empty quarry! What the hell are they supposed to do after that? They're quite right to strip the machines—as far as they can tell, everything's finished anyway! And now you're pushing them in that direction yourself! So why on earth should they spend their time looking after the factory? And what have you ever said or done to make them into class-conscious proletarians instead of profiteers?"

Zhidky was listening to Gleb with keen interest, flaring his nostrils mockingly.

"You're obsessed with the factory, Comrade Chumalov," he said. "What the hell do we want that place for when we've got robbery and starvation everywhere and all our organizations are swarming with conspirators and traitors? What on earth do we need your workshops and cement for now? For making communal graves? You're campaigning for control of the means of production, while all the time the peasants are advancing on the town like a Tartar horde!"

"Comrade Zhidky," replied Gleb, "I understand all that just as well as you do, but it's impossible to undertake this task without any concrete aim at all and simply expect to accomplish it on the backs of naked, starving men. To hell with all your petty tinkering! What we must fight for now is the restoration of the economy. The guns have fallen silent, and people are returning home and beginning to go about their normal business. The discussion about trade unions and the New Economic Policy[6] is now in full swing, so the question of the factory must be looked at very seriously indeed. We've got to consider which angle we should approach it from, and organize preparatory work accordingly. We've already ended up by having a Kronstadt.[7] And then what about Makhno's campaign?[8] And the Cossack counter-revolution too? The Whites are just waiting for an opportunity to catch us off our guard, fools that we are!"

Chibis got up and went towards the door, but then he stopped and said meaningfully:

"Our Special Department's in a bad state. If we can talk about starting the factory again, why can't we discuss the question of the poor condition the soldiers' barracks are in?"

Then he opened the door and went out in his usual leisurely fashion.

Zhidky watched him go, his eyes lit by a knowing smile.

"Don't let's argue, Comrade Chumalov," he said. "The main problem is the inspiration and organization of the masses. You're quite right there!"

He shook Gleb's hand hard.

"Oh, and by the way, Comrade Chumalov, try and train Zhuk to be a bit quieter while you're at it, will you? He's as fierce as a starving rat!"

Gleb took Zhuk by the arm and led him towards the door.

"Gleb, old friend!" said Zhuk, "you and I are going to move mountains together and work with all our might! That's a fact!"

Then Zhidky called to Gleb in a friendly way:

"Comrade Chumalov! It wouldn't do any harm to have a straight talk with Badin, Chairman of the Executive Committee."

In the doorway Lukhava squeezed Gleb's elbow.

"I've heard about you from Dasha," he said. "We'll discuss your plan and use it as the basis for our work. It's facts we need, not words, then we can get something done. The future may be in our heads all right, but it'll only become a reality if we use our hands."

The two men looked hard at each other for a moment then went their separate ways.

Dasha and Lukhava . . . Could this be the third person in the drama, Gleb wondered. Was it really possible? No—that would be ridiculous. . .

CHAPTER IV

THE "COMINTERN" WORKERS' CLUB

1. The CPR Group

The "Comintern" Workers' Club was housed in the former factory director's mansion, a solidly-built structure of undressed stone in three colors—light blue, yellow and green. The massive, two-storied building rose from the ridges of the mountainside that were now overgrown with clumps of conifers and ivy. It was puritanical and severe-looking in its basic design, rather like a church, but richly and in places extravagantly decorated with ornate verandahs and balconies, accompanied by additional buildings in its courtyards—these too just as solidly and neatly built—and surrounded by flower beds and lawns. Inside there were countless rooms, complicated, twilit corridors, and staircases decorated with oak pilasters topped by stained glass lamps. The walls were decorated with damask paper, set with tasteful panels and hung with paintings by the best old masters, while heavy furniture and huge mirrors filled the rooms.

On the hillside in front of the house and surrounded by an iron fence set in a stone base was an orchard, its paths now overgrown with weeds and its trees badly damaged by goats. Away to both left and right, beyond the ridge, the giant, light blue chimneys of the factory soared into the sky, while on the mountainside high above were the derelict gravity roadways and empty quarries.

In the old days a mysterious old man used to live here, a man whom the workers only ever saw from a distance and whose voice they never heard. It was amazing how this imposing, venerable director could have lived without fear amid the utter emptiness of his thirty-roomed mansion, suffering no nightmares and feeling no horror at the poverty and filth, the stench and squalor of the workers' hovels not far away.

Then came war, revolution and the great catastrophe ... Abandoning his ruined factory, the director fled, helpless and pitiful in his fear. The engineers, technicians and chemists went with him. Only one man was left behind—the chief designer of the factory, Engineer Kleist—and he had shut himself away in his study in the main administration building that stood on the other side of the road facing the mansion which had been his last creation.

Then, one fine spring day when the mountains and sea glowed with fiery light and the brilliantly clear air seemed to stab the eyes with sunlit needles, the factory workers had assembled in the machine shop. There, amid all the jostling, shouting and clouds of smoke, the mechanic Gromada had made a proposal:

"Let's take the splendid mansion where that blood sucker of a director used to live and turn it into a workers' club, and let's call it the 'Comintern' Club!"

So it was that the ground floor of the building was turned into a club and offices for the Party and Young Communist League, while the upper floor was set aside for a library and for the Cheka.

And there—where once profound silence had reigned and the workmen had been strictly forbidden to walk on the concrete garden paths—in the evenings, when the mansion's great plate-glass windows blazed like fire in the setting sun, the club musicians would make their brass trumpets howl and their drums thunder.

All the books were brought from the houses of the engineers who had fled and they were placed on the shelves in the club library. The volumes had shining gilt spines but they were incomprehensible and alien to the men, for only Gothic titles glittered on their covers. But the workers went on living in their hovels and communal dwellings, while the engineers' houses stood empty, their great rooms eerie and still. The workers spent their time making things like cigarette lighters in the machine shop during the day, and looking for their goats on the hillside in the evening, while their womenfolk walked inland to the Cossack villages, where they bought and sold food as petty speculators.

One evening Gleb opened a special meeting of the Party group in the "Comintern" Club. The room was spacious, its walls set with long panels of Karelian birch, while its handmade furniture was inlaid with veneer too. Both furniture and walls shone like gold in the evening sun. Rough benches were brought in from the hall, and Gleb sat down at the table where he could see everyone. The faces around him all looked alike. Details of them seemed different, but they all had something in common which made them merge into one. Why had he never noticed it before? And why was it precisely now that these faces so disturbed him? Then all of a sudden he realized what it was: hunger.

Many of the men had never met Gleb before, but they greeted him in a casual fashion as though he had never been away at all. The last time some of them had seen him was at sunset on that evening when officers had dragged him from the ranks of workmen standing outside the factory gates and then beaten him up together with three of his comrades. Some of the men shook Gleb firmly by the hand and wrinkled up their faces in a forced smile, then not knowing what to say, laughed and uttered a few broken phrases:

"Well? How are you, old friend? And how are things, eh?"

Then, without glancing at him again, they went back to their places. But as they sat down, they looked at him once more, and this time their faces shone with an affectionate, irrepressible smile.

Then Gromada came into the room, laughing and shouting in his chesty voice:

"But that's a completely different matter, Comrade Chumalov, really and truly it is! Now we'll get a move on all right! We Communists might have gone astray for a while over things like cigarette lighters and goats, but don't you allow any arguing now! Speak plainly and have done with it!"

Filled with delight, he turned to the men and said:

"Here you are, you damned idlers! Here's a fellow who's been through death and so on! And I'll tell you something else too. I might be speaking out of turn, but I'll state plainly here and now that it was he, Comrade Chumalov, who made me what I am, and it was through him that I joined the Communist Party!"

Everyone listened to Gromada and laughed, for it was unusual for him to speak like this. Gleb smiled at him too from under his brows as one might smile at an impulsive little boy. Surrounded by clouds of tobacco smoke, the workmen kept coughing.

Loshak was sitting in the far corner of the room. Smaller than the others but noticeable all the same, he sat there in silence, a gloomy, silent question in his eyes.

The women, though, were chattering and laughing. Dasha, their leader, was standing by the wall, and every time she went up to them, they all huddled closer together, whispering and choking with laughter.

Everyone was waiting. Any moment now Lukhava would come in and give his report on the struggle against disorganization and the fuel crisis. It was not Lukhava who finally came in, though, but the barefoot and dishevelled figure of Savchuk, once a cooper at the factory. Corpulent and flabby, he sat down on the floor near the door, hugging his scratched, bruised knees to his chest. Filled with yearning, his bloodshot eyes burned in his swollen face.

Suddenly Dasha went over to the window and flung open the massive inner and outer frames that were as heavy as doors. Straggling from their dwellings, no longer mindful of the factory with its heat and noise, its smell of machines and dust, groups of workmen were crawling up the mountainside, carrying sacks on their backs and covered now with a different dust—the dust brought by the mountain winds. Along hill paths and steppe tracks they went, making their way inland towards the Cossack villages as in the days of primitive barter long ago, all of them driven by hunger and age-old greed. Working men from the factory, men who had once been woken in the mornings not by the crowing of cocks but by the harsh screeching of whistles, had grown used during the past few years to the charm of hen-houses and pigsties. These men who had once worked amid the din of machines had learned to squabble over their goats and hens, and to argue over the food ration that had been gobbled up by someone else's pig because nobody had kept an eye on it. The electricity supply to both the factory and the workers' dwellings had been cut, and the factory whistles were choked with dust, so now the silence of idleness reigned amid this pastoral idyll, broken only by the clucking of hens and the grunting of pigs, while grasping husbands and greedy wives had sullenly shut themselves up in their private little domestic cages.

But here in the "Comintern" club and the factory offices, the Communists were beginning to rub their eyes, though their unwashed clothes and dirty hands still smelled of hen droppings and acrid dung. They sat close together, side by side, and the blare of the trumpets and the speakers' unaccustomed words evoked a forgotten life from the distant past. Gleb, too, belonged to that past, but it was as if he had been there only the day before, for he still smelled of red-hot iron, warm oil and the sulphurous smoke of cooling slag. Once again those listening heard the familiar words:

"Factory ... production ... Gravity roadways ... workshops ... "

Sergei Ivagin came in, and bending close to Chumalov, whispered something to him. Then Gleb stood up and looked sternly at the assembled Party members.

"Comrade Ivagin has come instead of Lukhava, comrades," he said. "Lukhava has gone to see the stevedores—they've gone on strike apparently because of their poor rations. Now let's open the meeting. And please keep quiet! I've got something to tell you. I've heard—and the radio's announced it too—that foreign countries want to trade with us. They've got their eye on the concessions we're offering and they're fitting out their ships accordingly. I don't think we'll take offense at that—no, certainly not! On the contrary, we'll be very glad! We've learned one or two things ourselves now, so they won't fool us any more!"

Gromada got up. He was very agitated.

"Comrades, we are workmen who belong to a famous factory but we have gone and saddled ourselves with pigs and goats and such like. ... It's disgraceful and shameful, my friends! I propose we liquidate all surpluses in favor of our Children's Home, and as we are members of the working class ... "

There was a burst of general excitement, followed by shouting and the waving of hands.

"Hey, you! You're a sharp one all right! What about those bloody pigs? Weren't you keeping some of them too? They're covered in blood, sweat and tears, those damn pigs of yours!"

"And who's been pinching stuff from the villages and farms?"

"You can't cover up for 'em all! To hell with them! Take a decision, Chumalov, and let the group decide!"

"Hey now, comrades!" cried Gleb. "What are you getting so damned excited for, eh?"

He rang the bell and called the meeting to order.

"Now be quiet, comrades! There's no restrictions been put on pigs or goats yet, so you can play around with them as much as you want. When the time comes, we'll sort them out in real proletarian fashion, just like we sorted out the bourgeois. But for the time being, just carry on, by all means, and do whatever you like with them. Now I propose we elect a chairman."

No sooner had he said these words than all the women began waving their hands and shouting in turn:

"Dasha! Dasha Chumalova!"

The men were shouting too:

"Gromada! Chumalova! Savchuk!"

Then Gromada came running up to the table and raising his arms impatiently, cried:

"Comrades! As far as women are concerned, I've no objections at all. Well, women as creatures enjoying equal rights and so on . . . After all, young people must be leaders too, of course, but let them learn a little first. What we need here is a chairman with a beard to match his experience!"

"So where's Chumalov's beard, then? And where have your whiskers gone, Gromada? Has the cat licked 'em off?"

The women were angry now.

"Dasha Chumalova! Dasha!"

Gleb rang the bell again.

"I'll put it to the vote, comrades! Dasha Chumalova is first on the list, and though she's my wife, I've no objections to a woman chairman. Who is in favor?"

But before he could put Dasha's name to the vote, the women began shouting again:

"We want Dasha! Why don't you give the women a chance, you devils?"

Gleb was the first to raise his hand, and he was quickly followed by the women and Sergei. Then one after another, coughing and wheezing, the men reluctantly put their hands up too.

But without raising his own hand, Savchuk bellowed from the corner where he was sitting:

"Send all the women home! I can't stand them!"

Gleb rang the bell once more and stopped the shouting again:

"I put Gromada's name to the vote. Right! Now it's Loshak's turn. And my name's on the list too. Now please take your places at the table, comrades!"

Dasha, Gromada and Gleb were elected to the praesidium, and from then on Dasha presided over the meeting.

"Comrades," she said, "I ask for silence. Give me the agenda, Comrade Chumalov. I now call upon Comrade Ivagin to make his report. You have just half an hour, comrade."

Sergei laughed in amazement and spread his hands in a gesture of hopelessness.

"But your time limit's much too strict, Comrade Chumalova!"

"Don't speak at great length and keep to the point," she replied.

"She gives herself airs all right!" shouted Savchuk "I told you so—we shouldn't have chosen a woman!"

"Be quiet, Comrade Savchuk! Please keep order! You're not in the street now but at a Party meeting!"

Dasha was right—a few minutes was quite enough. After all, what could you tell a workman in a report? He himself knows best what he needs, and cold, bookish phrases were just as incomprehensible and strange, just as alien and lifeless to them as Sergei himself was to the workmen in both spirit and words.

"Comrades! We find ourselves surrounded by monstrous ruin ... The working class is undergoing enormous ordeals ... This is an unprecedented crisis ... We are witnessing the liquidation of the military front ... All our energies must now be directed to the economic problems facing us ... The Tenth Congress of the Party has projected a turning point in economic policy ... The proletariat is the only force capable of ... The revival of the republic's industrial production is required ... Concessions and world markets are what we need ... We have to be on our guard to defend the land of the proletariat ... We must increase our strength tenfold and maintain ranks of iron ... We have broken the enemy blockade ... The working class and the Communist Party will ... The supply of fuel must ... The mechanical power of the factory is ... "

Sergei spoke for a long time, doing his best to choose simple words, but as though to spite him they did not come easily. He sensed that what he was saying made no impression on these sullen men. They were bored and wearied by it all, and they could hardly wait for him to finish. Dasha had already caught his eye sternly a couple of times now and was frowning with displeasure, and when, covered with perspiration, he finally finished and sat down exhausted on his stool, everyone heaved a sigh of relief.

"Comrades, are there any questions for the speaker? No? Right!"

Everyone looked at Gleb in expectation. He stood up, cleared his throat, and for a few moments looked intently at the faces of the men before him.

Though many of them wore a vacantly submissive, indifferent expression, some shone with anticipation and hope. But it was as if most of the men were sitting there filled with apathy, sitting there simply in order to devote a statutory hour to their Party obligations. Gleb knew them well—they would not believe a single eloquent promise or a single eloquent word. That was how they had just reacted to Ivagin's bookish report—they had simply turned a deaf ear to it all. But one only had to say a few words like "Friends! Tomorrow we're going back to the factory!" for each of them to leap to his feet and shout breathlessly: "Comrade Chumalov, we've been waiting for this for a long time! You can take us there right now! All this ruin's gone on far too long!"

When Gleb looked at Dasha and saw her face, its expression unaffected and kind as it always used to be and her eyes lit by an encouraging smile, he felt that in some ways he was to blame for what had happened and that he was unworthy of her. Yet at the same time he could not suppress a feeling of hostility towards her for all her self-assured composure and the unfamiliar, harsh ringing tone in her voice. It seemed to him that her behavior was all insincerity and pretence. Then, for some unaccountable reason, he put his hand on her shoulder and patted it. Her gentle response told him that she found his affectionate touch pleasing and that she had forgiven him his earlier outbursts. And all his sense of injury, all his arguing with her now seemed so insignificant and degrading that he closed his eyes for a moment in shame. If these people knew what a jealous fool he had been when Dasha and he had been alone together! But she had faith in him now, expecting him to utter meaningful, decisive words, and not for a moment did she doubt that only he, her Gleb, could set the hearts of these comrades alight, these comrades who longed to return to work once more.

"Comrades," said Gleb, "don't let's do a lot of talking. We've spent much too long chattering in idleness as it is these past few years, and now it's time to stop. We've forgotten our revolutionary obligations. The factory's not a factory any longer—it's more like a farmyard—and we're stealing the state's property for our own private purposes. Is that really fair, comrades? Now there's two sides to every person, my friends. One side can go to the devil and the other can grab hold of the devil and smash him in the teeth! Our hands aren't meant for looking after pigs and goats, but for other things. We Bolsheviks are a special kind of men, and just as our hearts are special, so are our hands, and so is the task for our brains too. As Comrade Ivagin has said, there's now a new economic policy in Russia. But what does that new policy mean? It means going all out for economic reconstruction. Now, we are the producers of cement, and cement is a powerful binding material. In fact, cement is just what we ourselves are, comrades—the working class. So now we've got to realize and feel that properly. We've loafed around long enough, wasting our time looking after goats. It's time to start real work now—the production of cement for the building of socialism!"

The workmen were excited by Gleb's last words, and many of them leapt up to speak. Raising his hand, Gleb asked for attention, while Dasha rang the bell and called for order.

"Right, comrades," Gleb went on, "let's get down to business! We'll start with the most important thing—the question of fuel. There's no fuel either for the factory or for the workers' settlement. Now we can get fuel for the factory from the state, but what about the town? And the workers? And what about all the children in the Homes? It's no use relying on compulsory requisitioning of firewood—the peasants just won't bring us any. So we'll just have to find a solution to the problem ourselves. We are the only ones who can solve this question. What we've got to do is build a new gravity roadway up to the pass. What does that mean? It means we have to get the first diesel going, start the turbine and get the lights back on in the workers' houses. We've got stocks of gas and oil that we can draw on by warrant. So the gravity roadway must be our first step. We'll organize voluntary Sunday work through the trade unions, and we'll mobilize the engineers and use their technical expertise. So let all your pigs and goats go to hell! Then in a year's time we'll be laughing at ourselves, lads!"

Savchuk made his way forward through the crowd and breathing heavily, banged the table with his fist:

"I demand that the coopers' shop be started up again straightaway!"

Dasha got to her feet and checked him severely:

"Comrade Savchuk! Come to order please! When on earth will you learn to control yourself?"

"I demand ... There are swineherds in here and folk who make cigarette lighters on the side!"

"Comrade Savchuk, for the last time!"

"Gleb, old friend, give your wife a good smack on the backside! She's not mine, or I'd do it for you! Oh, you bloody goatherds! You devils! You've sold your souls for cigarette lighters. Now you've just mentioned the engineers, Gleb, but what kind of a friend is Engineer Kleist to you? After all, he gave you over to be killed!"

"He's right! That damned specialist! He's hidden himself away like a rat in its hole, and he goes sneaking around like a thief! What's the Cheka doing about him?"

Engineer Kleist . . . That man had once held Gleb's life in his hands but had flung him to the executioners. Kleist . . . Surely Gleb's life was worth as much as his!"

Loshak silently raised his hand.

"Comrade Loshak has the floor," said Dasha.

Everyone turned to look at the hunchbacked mechanic.

"It's just like they say, comrades. If you put the right man on the job, then things will go just fine. True enough, Kleist may be a bastard, but what I want to say is this: all right, he did turn Chumalov over to them, but how did he treat Dasha? After all, who was it who saved her from death? It was him, Kleist! We should remember that."

Dasha suddenly became agitated and interrupted him:

"Comrade Loshak, I'm not the subject of this discussion, so please keep to what's in the report. What have Kleist and I got to do with it? What we're concerned about here is the roadway and the supply of fuel . . . " Her white teeth flashed as she spoke. "After all," she went on, "you said yourself we've got to get things right."

Loshak waved his hand in a gesture of hopelessness and sat down again.

Dasha again, thought Gleb. Again this mystery that so troubled his soul . . .

He was thinking hard now, wrestling with his thoughts.

"Comrades," he said, "let me fight my own battle with Kleist, face to face, but let's leave that question aside for the moment. We've got off the point."

The discussion went on quickly and smoothly until a resolution was adopted. It was decided to begin extending the roadway up to the pass immediately, and on the following day to start going through the factory to clear away the rubbish, carry out minor repairs and begin to put everything in order.

Dasha picked up a sheet of paper and glancing at it, looked at the assembled men:

"Comrades, we must consider the question of the Party Committee very carefully. It's essential for us to send several members of the Party group to work out in the country districts."

Her words were greeted by a tense silence. The men seemed stunned. Then they all began to shout at once, breathless and angry:

"This isn't a posting on official business, it's sheer murder! We aren't beasts to be sent to the slaughter!"

"What's all this? You're wanting to throw us like food to the wolves, are you?"

"But comrades, you're Communists, not a bunch of speculators!" cried Dasha. "I'm a woman and I'm telling you that never, not for a single moment, have I trembled before what fate had in store for me. And you know that well enough!"

"Well go yourself if you feel like it!"

Then Gleb stepped out from behind the table, and walking to the middle of the room, silently looked at them all with a hint of menace in his eyes. Then he said in an offhand tone:

"Send me then, comrades, send both my wife and myself! She said it, she called you speculators. And now I'll say it to you too: you're speculators, not workers! But I've been in far worse hornets' nests than those in the country areas round here. You all know I spent three years at the front."

"You may have been in action, Chumalov, but you're not dead yet! Anyway, lots of men have been in action—who hasn't seen bloodshed these past few years?"

"That's true enough. But why didn't I get killed? Because I made friends with death as an equal. And if you've ever seen death, you'll know very well what kind of teeth it's got—they're sharper than a mincer! I'll show you if you like—I'm not shy!"

Tearing off his army tunic and vest, he flung them to the floor, and his body gradually became covered with goose-flesh from his waist to his neck. On his chest the thick hair shone like gold, and as his naked body quivered, its muscles moved under the skin. All of a sudden he seemed very near and dear to them all.

"Anybody who wants to can come up and feel!" he said.

On his chest, on his left arm below the shoulder, and on his flank were long scars, running like pale, purple threads across the skin.

"D'you want me to take my trousers down as well? All right, then, I will! Oh, don't you want me to? I've got decorations like these down there too! You want other people to go off to work instead of you, do you, while you sleep in your goat pens, eh? All right then! I'm off!"

No one came up to Gleb, but he saw how the men's eyes misted with tears and how they all fell silent. They looked at his naked body then quickly turned away in confusion.

"Comrades!" cried Gromada. "This is disgraceful and shameful! Just how far have our souls rotted? Comrades!"

He was writhing at the table, unable to express the storm of feeling that was raging within him.

Then a bearded workman got up from his seat on a bench and struck himself on the chest with all his might. His head was shaking.

"Put my name down!" he cried. "I'll go! I'm not some filthy swine! It's true I've got three goats and a sow with piglets at home, and I've carried a trader's sack down the country roads too—I can't deny it. But we've been cutting our own throats all this time, my friends!"

Behind him a few more heavy hands were raised. Then Dasha, who was gazing at Gleb with eyes full of emotion, waved her hand and said:

"Comrades, is our Party group really any worse than the others? No, comrades! We've got fine workers in it, and fine Communists too!"

Then she was the first to start clapping.

CHAPTER V

THE HIDDEN EMIGRANT

1. The Secret Room

Though the massive, oak-framed windows were never opened, the dust from the quarries filtered through the hinged ventilation panes and settled like velvet on the windowsills between the inner and outer frames. In the mornings, when the mountains glowed with lilac fire and the sun's rays came slanting in through the windows, specks of dust shone iridescent between the panes of glass. Engineer Kleist, once the technical director of the factory, would stand at the window gazing at these tiny, spinning worlds that glowed with the light of geological epochs long ago, and would listen to the profound silence that filled the room.

Since his study was at the end of a corridor where day brought nothing but somnolent stillness and night only ragged shadows and black emptiness, the room seemed comfortingly inaccessible and remote, like the quarry he could see in the distant ravine that was overgrown with sweetbriar and ivy.

Now that the factory lay abandoned, the workings deserted, and the roadways smashed and rusty, life was reduced to its two essential elements—chaos and peace. Why, then, should Kleist not remain the technical director of a dead factory? After all, such a post did not require anything of him whatsoever.

The main thing was not to open the oak-framed windows in his room, but silently to witness the profound significance of the construction work continually being performed by the spiders that lived between the double panes. Suspended now as he was between past and present, Kleist had become aware of the immense architectural beauty of the spiders' webs that festooned the space between the frames. Long-legged and stooping, his silvery hair en brosse, he would stand at the window for a long time, gazing at the pearly-white gossamer of the webs, at the multitude of delicate planes intersecting and inclining at various angles and at the countless radiating stairways that were all interconnected and drawn powerfully taut.

No one ever came to his study now. After all, who could possibly need him when the factory was as silent as the grave and the cement in the warehouses had petrified into rock-hard blocks long ago? Who could need him, when the steel cables were broken and the trucks lay scattered all over the hillside, buried in debris and overgrown with weeds? Who could need him, when dozens of skilled mechanics wandered idly along the highroad and down the factory paths, through the deserted buildings and across the empty yards, spending their time stealing transmission belts and rivets, brass fittings and hoops?

Down below, in the twilit semi-basement where the Factory Committee offices were, shouting and noise went on day after day, and to Kleist the place sounded like a riotous tavern or a den of thieves. Through his dusty windows he could see men going up and down the concrete steps on the mountainside, their gloomy faces gaunt with hunger and privation. They were all totally preoccupied with what they were doing, as if it were an incomprehensible, terrible game, and none of them had any time for him. Everything had turned out splendidly because of his wise caution and the skillfull way in which he had formulated a simple mathematical problem. From his solitary retreat he looked out at the idle men with a combination of mockery, contempt and hatred. Exhausted now by hunger, it was they who had brought both devastation and that greatest tragedy of all to Russia—the Revolution. It was they who had destroyed his future and set the world ablaze as if it were no more than a scrap of factory waste, and now they were much too busy to remember the vestiges of the past that lived on in this secret room.

The concrete yard and the flight of steps outside his window shimmered so brightly in the brilliant light that it seemed as if the ground itself were burning with fiery incandescence and would burst into flame at any moment. The loose cement and pebbles in the yard rattled and crunched under the workmen's boots as they passed constantly in and out of the Factory Committee offices, going in at one door then coming out of another.

But why was a Factory Committee necessary at all, Kleist wondered, when there had never been one in the past and yet the factory had been famous throughout the world? What work could these men possibly have to do, condemned as they now were to idleness amid the ruins of a once magnificent enterprise? Why was there so much anxious running to and fro if tomorrow were destined to be just the same as yesterday, and if beyond it stretched a succession of identical days that were just as pointless as the infinite series of images in a pair of reflecting mirrors?

At exactly one o'clock each day Yakob, the office messenger, would come silently into Kleist's room carrying a small brass tray. His thin, gray mustache and the close-cropped, gray hair on his pink scalp looked curiously translucent, as though they were made of glass. Stooping a little, he would gravely set a cup of tea down on the table and put a few tiny saccharine tablets wrapped in paper beside it. Then he would step back two paces, and bending down, carefully pick up a few specks from the floor and just as carefully put them in the wastepaper basket under the table. The walls of the room were clean and white, and the oak-framed blueprints hanging on them looked just as severely neat and clear as they had in the old days.

"Is it one o'clock already, Yakob?"

"Yes, Herman Hermanovich, one o'clock exactly."

"Very well. You may go now. And don't let anyone in to see me, mind."

"Very good, sir."

"Just dust the windows, Yakob, but don't open them please."

"Very good, sir."

Kleist stood at the window with his back to Yakob, his short, bristly hair gleaming like silver crystal and his old jacket sticking out from his shoulders and hanging down his back like a little tail.

Somewhere far away, the hitherto empty offices echoed with the sound of isolated voices, while abacuses clicked busily like a flock of clucking hens. There were new people in the building already, people sent by the Economic Council, but just who they were and what they were doing, Kleist neither knew nor cared. He still had his forgotten study that was guarded by Yakob, a study in which only the past existed. As for the present, it was whirling by with its noisy automobiles and trucks, urged on by men who had broken free from their chains and learned to shout and swear in an incoherent fashion—something that in the old days had been strictly forbidden by the factory management.

Kleist gazed at the steep hillside with its covering of juniper bushes and its bands of different-colored strata. Higher up, on the mountain ridge itself, towered the great mansion of undressed stone, its towers and arches uplifted to the sky.

"What have they got over there now, Yakob?" Kleist asked.

"The Workers' Club and the Communist Group office, Herman Hermanovich."

"They've brought an incomprehensible new language with them, too ... Please don't let anyone into this room and on no account open the windows. You may go now."

Then, as if for the first time, Kleist looked at the former director's house (just imagine, the Communist Group was in it now!), and admired its striking, lofty grandeur. He, Kleist, had built that house ...

Away to the left, set amid rocks and greenery beyond the mountain ridge, the factory chimneys rose into the sky. Near them was the cableway and beyond it were the arches and domes of the factory itself. Kleist had built those too. He could not have fled abroad without first destroying the buildings of his own creation. But these things of his own making had stood in his way, almost more indestructible than the mountains around them, almost more inexorable than time itself, and now he was their prisoner.

His study with its polished floor still resembled the businesslike workroom it once used to be. The walls were hung with architectural drawings, the oak desk was covered with blueprints, and the massive carved furniture still retained its look of noble dignity. Time had stood still here and the past hung so heavily in the air that its presence was almost palpable.

2. Enemies

But had an error crept into Kleist's logical constructions, or had life temporarily ceased to obey the laws of human reason? Whichever it was, the closed circle of his isolated world suddenly snapped and began to disintegrate like a ring of rusty wire.

Only an hour before, when Yakob's customary appearance had seemed to affirm the immutability of the passage of time, Kleist's whole conception of life was clearly expressed by a strikingly neat and simple diagram—a circle and a tangent. Safely hidden behind a multitude of walls and surrounded by blessed peace, he would sit at his desk over the old factory blueprints, and preserving the time-honored propriety of his study, would instinctively pencil in his English notebook one and the same figure, a circle and a tangent, a figure that held good in each and every situation.

Then all of a sudden everything was smashed to smithereens. The axiom suddenly proved to be an absurdity, and the tangent was transformed into a flying stone that had shattered the protective shell of his existence. And because it had all happened so simply and quietly, Kleist was filled with mortal terror.

He had gone to the lavatory and spent more time there than usual—because of the poor food nowadays he often suffered from abdominal pain. As he came back, he noticed from a distance that his study door was open. This was something neither Yakob nor he ever allowed.

Immediately after Yakob had brought his tea, Kleist had seen a group of workmen standing outside in the yard, looking first towards the quarries and then up at his window. At the time he had felt something like a slight electric shock deep inside him, but his feeling of alarm was only momentary, and he had quickly forgotten it. But now his study door stood wide open, and this time the electric shock was accompanied by nauseating anxiety.

Maintaining his usual dignified air, Kleist walked towards the study with even stride. But he suddenly stopped in the doorway, unable to grasp what had happened, for the windows were wide open and clouds of dust were swirling over the windowsills and table. The mountainside looked huge in the clear air, its rocky terraces and spring greenery distinct in the brilliant light. Far, far away, clearly visible now on the upper slopes of the quarries, stood a little house with two windows. Clouds of fresh tobacco smoke and wisps of filmy cobweb mingled in the moving air that filled the room.

By the window with a pipe in his mouth stood a clean-shaven man wearing an army tunic and dark blue puttees. He had a prominent, square jaw and there were dark hollows in his cheeks.

"Ah, what a long time it's been!" he said gaily, greeting Kleist in a familiar way. "How do you do! You've got yourself so well barricaded in here it's hard to find you!"

With his cloth helmet the man kept sweeping the cobwebs off the doorposts and window-frames, killing the spiders as they tried frantically to crawl away.

"Well, Comrade Director, it's certainly a fine den you've got here, tucked away at the end of a corridor! And everything's well camouflaged too! You've thought it all out very nicely!"

Walking unsteadily now, Kleist went up to the table. There had been a time when this man, his body beaten and torn, had been condemned to death, and with a face that was like a bloody mask had stared wildly at him. But now, all of a sudden, he was back again, and this time he was so strangely, so terribly calm.

"No, I never open the windows . . . "

"You're quite right not to, Comrade Director—after all, it's a poisonous wind that blows from our direction! It's enough to make anyone panic, so I quite understand!"

"Why didn't Yakob inform me of your visit?"

"We'll send that Yakob of yours off to the coopers' shop to saw some wood! We've got no time for flunkeys like him! Now don't you remember me, Comrade Director?"

"Yes, I remember you . . . But what about it?"

"Well now, how can I put it? Here I am, wandering round the factory and looking in every nook and cranny—inspecting past glory, you might say. But all I can see is desolation and ruin. The roadways are smashed, the cables are broken, and everywhere you look there's chaos and devastation. And all the skilled technicians have hidden themselves away like rats in their holes. But why are there cobwebs everywhere? Why are you and the factory all covered with cobwebs—that's what I'd like to know!"

"Let us suppose I have already asked myself that question and answered it too. Now what is it you want of me?"

"Well now. . . I came across your barricade and I thought to myself, let's have a look at the place! It's a devilish habit of mine, you know, Comrade Director, to be so inquisitive!"

"I never indulge in idle conversation. I neither understand what you are saying, nor do I wish to. Now please be so kind as to leave me in peace."

Gleb stepped towards the table and grinned. Then he took his pipe out of his mouth and looked hard at Kleist. Were spiders reflected in his eyes at that moment, or did terrible apparitions seem to swirl around him? Whichever it was, Kleist's face turned a dusty ashen color.

"Citizen Kleist, do you remember that splendid evening when you singled me out in such an unforgettable way? It was a hell of a thrashing they gave me, and I shed plenty of blood too. They gave it me good and hot, I can tell you! But a thrashing like that—provided it doesn't finish you off altogether—stands you in pretty good stead, so I've come to visit you and have a chat about old times . . . I like meeting up with old friends again, Comrade Director!"

He stuck his pipe back into the corner of his mouth and burst out laughing.

"Now allow me to amuse you with a riddle, Comrade Director. Don't worry, it's only a trivial one, but it's funny all the same. One fine spring day there were four friends. Then the damned Whites caught the poor devils and dragged them to this very room. By that time, though, their faces didn't really look much like faces any longer but more like ragged old boots. Now the question is this: why were those battered devils dragged in here and how did four dead fools turn into one living one? Well? Funny, isn't it? But what are you looking so gloomy for?"

And again he burst out laughing, sounding for all the world like some extraordinarily amusing, cheerful fellow.

"We've not seen each other for quite a while now, Comrade Director. 'I'll go and call on an old friend,' I thought to myself. But you don't seem very pleased to see me! How people change! You used to walk about like a hero, but now you seem to have lost heart. That's not good, Comrade Director, you ought to pull yourself together!"

Outside the open window the workmen's voices sounded unusually loud and close now. Grinning, Gleb looked intently at Kleist, as though waiting for him to say something, but the engineer was as silent and still as a corpse.

"Forgive me for the joke, Comrade Director, but don't worry, there's worse things than that. I've got such a cheerful nature, you see, so what can you do with me! Good-bye!"

And turning on his heel, Gleb went quickly out of the room.

Exhausted by the encounter, Kleist sat there for a long time, his face wearing the fixed expression of a man who is suffering from severe shock. Then Yakob came in again, deferential and grave, and stood in the middle of the room. He was upset and his head was shaking. Kleist brought his feverish gaze to bear on him and asked quietly and sternly:

"Well, Yakob? Won't you tell me how it happened?"

"It's not my fault, Herman Hermanovich . . . Nothing's forbidden or impossible for them—anywhere or in anything. They have the power, Herman Hermanovich, and their power is law."

Kleist found Yakob's presence agreeable—there was something reassuring about his steadfast devotion.

"So it's the Communist Group then, is it, Yakob?"

"Yes, it's Chumalov, the mechanic. He's suddenly come back from the war and now he's the boss. Can anything really stand in their way now? They'll destroy us, Herman Hermanovich!"

"But didn't you even try to stop him, Yakob?"

"No, I didn't, Herman Hermanovich. It's regrettable that he's disturbed your routine . . . "

Kleist was silent for a moment, almost as if he had not heard Yakob's last words. Then in a calm, businesslike way he lit a cigarette and said:

"Do you remember, Yakob? There were four of them. They were shot that same night, weren't they? I felt sure they all died . . . "

"They were beaten, Herman Hermanovich, then tortured to death. . . "

"Yes, Yakob, it was a terrible business and I'll never forget it. But there's one thing that should be borne in mind. At the time I acted quite deliberately and completely on my own account. Was it fear on my part? Or terror? Or even revenge? There was only one compelling factor, and that was time, for it is time that controls events. And in the same deliberate way I did everything I possibly could to save that man's wife."

The cigarette between Kleist's index and middle fingers was quivering all the time.

"Stay with me for a while, Yakob . . . I don't feel very well."

"You ought to go home, Herman Hermanovich, you need a rest. . ."

"Where's home, Yakob? Abroad? Hasn't it occurred to you, old fellow, that you and I might now be spending our last few hours on this earth?"

"Now how can you possibly say that, Herman Hermanovich? Our workmen may rant and rave, but they're peaceful enough really, and they'd never commit murder. So don't worry, Herman Hermanovich."

But his head was shaking as he spoke.

Hardly had Yakob uttered these words than Kleist flung himself back in the chair and his face turned a dusty ashen color once more.

"Do you remember, Yakob? I delivered this man up to his death, but his death has rebounded on me. See me out, Yakob . . . "

Kleist rose and with fear in his eyes, walked out past the messenger. In his fussy, old man's way Yakob picked up the engineer's hat and stick, and with short little steps hurried off after him into the dark corridor.

3. Retribution

Following the pebble-strewn path that had been cut out of the rock and wound its way upwards through clumps of juniper and dogwood, Kleist climbed towards the mountain ridge. The darkness of night came floating up out of the ravine beneath him. Hazily transparent in the gloom, thickets of beech and ash showed up faintly on the hillside and in the valley below, while rising above them like huge dark torches, solitary poplars soared into the sky. At the foot of the hillside were the massive buildings of the factory, while beyond them, gleaming like dull crystal in the fading light, lay the sea.

To Kleist everything seemed distant and strange, and only the giant buildings of reinforced concrete that he himself had built seemed comprehensible and familiar. At this terrible hour, when the lifeless factory lay awesomely silent like a vast graveyard full of rusty machinery, he had wandered alone with his stick down the railway tracks and up the flights of steps, then across the upper and lower yards dominated by their high gantries and gloomy towers.

In these deserted buildings he saw only one thing—the grandiose death of the past. His simple formula had proved correct, and now the wheel of events was rolling inexorably down its allotted track. His strange encounter with Gleb Chumalov had shown him that this track had finally come to an end and that his life was now at an end too. He should have blown up the factory long ago while there was still time, and perished with it. That would have been a splendid counter-blow, in complete accordance with the law of equal and opposite reactions. If they were to meet him on the path now, he was perfectly ready for them. Essentially, what remained to be done was the most unimportant thing of all—for them to take him and shoot him in the head.

To what world did the way of life brought by Chumalov belong? Risen from bloodshed and death the man was fearless and invincible, and his eyes gleamed with ruthless power. He was a man with an unyielding, terrifying face beneath an equally unyielding, terrifying helmet. That helmet served to affirm the menacing reality of the present, and it seemed to Kleist that apart from Chumalov's face and helmet, there was nothing else at all.

It would be better if he were to die here, amid all these buildings that he had created, rather than at home. To destroy him here would be to destroy with him all these monuments to his existence.

Over the distant mountains beyond the town, the red sunset was slowly turning pale as molten metal does when it cools, and the great, jagged ridges stood out dark against the sky like the roofs of an immense factory. Somewhere nearby a pulley squeaked as it was hauled up by weary hands, and it was followed by the clatter of falling iron, while at the railway station far below locomotives shrieked as if in fright.

Gleb was standing on the platform at the top of the steel tower. In the old days coal used to be sent down from here into the powerhouse by a line of small trucks. They would descend by elevator into the dark mouth of the shaft, then travel along rails that ran through a series of tunnels as far as the powerhouse itself. But now the platform was deserted, and in its centre, behind the guard rail, yawned a fathomless, black abyss.

Gripping the iron railing of the parapet so hard that his fingers ached, Gleb gazed out at the trucks hanging motionless on their cables, and at the chimneys soaring to the sky.

There had been a time when this factory had lived a tremendous life of its own. It had been an entire city inhabited by tens of thousands of people, and at night the windows of its workshops had shone with brilliant light, while great lamps had gleamed on every side like countless moons and stars. Away over there, down at the wharves in the bay, ocean-going steamers had devoured millions of tons of fresh cement, while from the factory to the docks and back again, long lines of trucks had swung through the air, passing endlessly to and fro.

But all that was in the past, and now there was only stillness and desolation. The factory entrances and gravity roadways were overgrown with grass, rust covered the machinery like a scab, and the walls of the buildings had been eroded by mountain torrents and scarred by gunfire.

Kleist walked slowly on, stopping frequently to gaze at the many-storied buildings as though they were mausoleums of a bygone age. He looked at them and thought for a while, then on he went once more, only to stop and think again.

Gleb leaned over the railing and peered intently at the shadowy figure of Kleist below. Here was a man he could gladly have strangled at any moment—one that would have been the most joyous moment of his whole life. It was Kleist who in his vindictive spite had turned him over to the group of White officers to be tortured and killed, and Gleb would never forget that day for the rest of his life . . .

The factory workers had all been lined up on the main road in front of the office building. (There were only a few of them left by then, as some had gone into hiding while others had joined the Red Army and left the town, but Gleb and his three friends had failed to get away because they had been caught up in the street fighting.) One of the officers had read out a list of names from a sheet of paper, and as he read, he struck each worker with his riding-crop then handed him over to the other officers. In their turn they beat each man too, using revolver butts as well as whips. Dimly Gleb had heard the anguished cries of the workmen standing in line, and for a single moment through his bloody tears he had glimpsed them running away in all directions with the officers chasing them. Then, when his three friends and he were dragged into Kleist's room covered with blood, the engineer had looked at them for a long time, his face very pale and his lower jaw trembling. The officers had kept asking Kleist something but he made no reply, pretending to be calm despite his profound agitation. He had looked intently at Gleb but said nothing, and in his eyes Gleb had seen both compassion and scorn. Then Kleist had said softly with a catch in his voice:

"Yes, this is the man ... And these too. Yes, yes, they're the ones..."

"Have you anything more to say, Mr. Kleist?"

"What may happen next is beyond my control, gentlemen. It is a matter for your judgment."

Then the four friends had been flung into an empty warehouse and beaten till late in the night. At moments of consciousness Gleb had felt the blows, some of them so remote and slight that they seemed to cause him no pain, but others so severe that they almost tore him apart. But terrible though they were, even these blows seemed strangely remote too, as though he were nailed up inside a barrel and someone were kicking aimlessly at its sides.

Coming to in the darkness, it was a long time before he could make out where he was. Then he had begun to crawl around the warehouse, trying to find a way out, but after bumping into the flabby, cold bodies of his friends, he had lain down feebly beside them for a while. Then, creeping along by the wall, he had found a hole that was blocked up with stones. Under cover of darkness he had climbed through it, and hiding among the bushes as he went, had crawled as far as his home. After that no one had seen him again. He would never forget what had happened—not for the rest of his life ...

He had remembered all this today while he was in Kleist's room, and he remembered it again now as he watched the engineer wandering over the wide square below him.

"Good evening, Comrade Director!" he called.

Kleist suddenly stopped and went rigid, but he soon recovered from his surprise and began to peer not at Gleb but at the dark, smashed windows of the powerhouse.

This man Chumalov was everywhere, he thought. He was not pursuing him but merely standing in his path, terrifying him like a figure in a nightmare. It was simply impossible to escape from him. In the old days this man had been lost amid the mass of dark blue workmen's smocks, possessing no face or voice of his own. Unnoticed like all the rest, he had performed his allotted task, being no more than a minute element in the complex, mighty process of the factory's work. Why was it, then, that he, Kleist, once so powerful and strong, could now no longer resist the coarse might of this man? At what point had the enormous change come about? Was it when he had delivered Chumalov up to be destroyed, or was it that moment earlier today, when he had suddenly encountered the man in his study, a figure risen from the past?

"Come up on to the platform, Comrade Director—the grave looks deeper from up here! You're wandering about just like I do, every day... But what's the point?"

The logic of events possesses only one pattern—an ineluctable beginning and an inexorable end. There is no such thing as chance, for chance is an illusion. Obeying the voice of this man who had suddenly come back into his life, Kleist slowly climbed the steps to the platform, trying to maintain his usual dignity and calm.

"Take care, Comrade Director! One false step and you'll go head over heels to your death! It's one hell of a shaft you've built here!"

In an authoritative, chill tone Kleist answered:

"We built it properly, so it would last for centuries."

"Yes, Comrade Director, you certainly put up an invincible fortress here, but it soon came crashing down, didn't it? All your efforts aren't worth a thing! Where are those indestructible centuries of yours now?"

Puffing away at his pipe, Gleb spoke in a good-natured but rather serious way, while Kleist stood there as if paralyzed, leaning on the parapet. His head was shaking, and to his horror he realized he was quite unable to stop it. And just as absurdly an agonizing smile was playing on his lips.

"A grave, a communal grave ... Oh, to hell with it all!" he thought.

Why was this enormous workman standing here, Kleist wondered. Why was he so awesomely withdrawn and quiet? At any moment he could fling him, Kleist, head over heels into the bottomless abyss from which two taut cables came rising up into the steel tower to disappear over the great wheels of the winding gear.

It was strange, but as he looked at Kleist, Gleb did not feel any pain. Either the pain had burnt itself out during his first encounter with the old man, or it had faded and died a few moments ago, when he had seen him looking so lonely and helpless far below. He was even beginning to feel rather sorry for him somehow.

"So, Comrade Director, you're pretty good at building monuments, aren't you? Well, when you die, there's a grave already prepared for you here. D'you see this shaft? We'll send you down it in a truck and bury you under the tallest factory chimney!"

Kleist suddenly straightened up and tore himself away from the rail. Then, reaching out a hand towards Gleb, he muttered in angry confusion:

"Chumalov ... for God's sake, do what you have to do quickly, only please ... please don't torment me!"

Gleb went up to him and burst out laughing.

"Comrade Director! What on earth are you talking about? Get that nonsense out of your head! After all, I'm not a wild animal, you know! All that's in the past now, and we've learned to take stock of everything we do. It's over and done with, so to hell with it. We're living in different times now. What on earth do you think? Couldn't I knock you down and have my revenge if I wanted to? But I need you alive, not dead!"

Kleist looked at him foolishly and trembled as if he had suddenly caught a chill.

"Why do you ... mock me, Chumalov? I don't understand it, and at a moment like this, such a terrible moment ... "

"But it's a splendid moment, Comrade Director! You're worrying about nothing! But I understand, of course. You expected this living corpse Chumalov to take vengeance for the past. After all, you thought, he's got something to remember ... Yes, I've got something to remember all right—three years at the front, for example. The Revolution's the finest school of all, but when you're fighting, you make mistakes and sometimes even commit crimes, so now and then you feel you're still very much a fool. But it's good you can feel that, because it helps you to control yourself. For the time being, though, I'm sure of one thing at least, Comrade Director. There's an enormous struggle about to begin, and it's going to be a good deal harder than fighting and shedding blood in war. It's no joke, you know, the economic front! Now just look! All these great buildings are the product of your talent, the work of your hands. We've got to bring this graveyard back to life, Comrade Director, and then we've got to set it alight! There's a whole new world opening up before us, a world we've already conquered. The years will go by, and that world will shine with magnificent new machinery and splendid palaces. Then man will no longer be a slave but a king, because free and beloved toil will have become the basis of his life!"

Laughing with excitement now, Gleb took Kleist by the arm.

"I feel like day-dreaming a little, Comrade Director. And that's not such a bad thing either, because dreams give life to our thoughts. So set to work, Herman Hermanovich! The first step is to extend the roadway up to the pass so as to ensure the supply of firewood. Then there's the turbines to be repaired. As for the diesels, though, they're ready to start right away, because Brynza's managed to keep them all in good order. Then there's the factory buildings to be repaired. Soon the quarries will begin to work again, the trucks will start moving and the rotary kilns will turn once more..."

But Kleist muttered in an indistinct, choking voice:

"What's been destroyed, what's died, can never rise again... No!"

"Herman Hermanovich, do we really want to resurrect what's been destroyed? No, far from it! You're quite right, of course—the capitalist world's been smashed now, and it'll never rise again. That's a fact! But you're already living in the new world. You've come to us with great knowledge and experience, and our new society needs those qualities. You no longer belong to yourself, Comrade Director! Your mind and strength already lie in the strong, steady hands of others, and if you join in the process of reconstruction and labor you'll experience a thousand times more joy than when you were serving the capitalist system. You were a hireling then, but now you're a free creator. So set to work, Herman Hermanovich, and everything will be splendid!"

Then in a simple, friendly way Gleb shook Kleist by the shoulders, and as he did so, the old man's hat fell from his head and plunged like a night bird into the darkness far below.

In this last exhausting struggle between life and death, Kleist realized that Chumalov's terrifying hands—hands that were themselves ingrained with death—had pinned him securely to life. Stunned, he could not comprehend the meaning of this stupendous event, and filled with a strange feeling of emptiness, stood on the platform weeping tears of happiness...

CHAPTER VIII

BURNING DAYS

1. Workers' Blood

The days burned with intense heat and were filled with feverish activity, while the nights seemed to pass almost unnoticed. Streaming with sweat, Gleb spent his time running first to the Trade Union Council, then to the Party Committee ("Call a general meeting of the Party immediately!"), next to the Railwaymen's Union ("Comrades, speed up the supply of tank-trucks to the oil refinery!"), after that to the Factory Administration, and finally to the power-house where Brynza was always to be found and where the diesels stood all ready for work.

As usual, Lukhava was never at the Trade Union Council, for he could not bear to sit shut up in his office there. Every day from morning till night he would be rushing from one workshop to another and from one union to the next, and everywhere he went he would enter into all the details of production and share in the workers' lives. He organized special meetings and settled disagreements, cursed those who were idle and inscribed the names of Heroes of Labor on the factory's board of honor. He would go bursting into supply sections, food departments and offices, overturning piles of official papers, issuing orders and making demands, and wherever he went he aroused enthusiasm and caused storms of delight. He was never tired—he did not even seem to know the meaning of the word—and his feverish eyes burned with an undying light. That was how Lukhava won the workers' hearts!

At the factory the electricians had begun repairing the wiring, while in the workers' houses electric light bulbs taken from the stores and put into the empty sockets now shone brightly in the darkness. Filled with gladness, the women and children smiled to see them, and the gray mask of hunger on the workers' faces began to melt away in joyous anticipation.

In the machine shop no one was making cigarette lighters any more. Work of a very different kind was going on there now, and amid incessant hammering and whistling, hissing and clanging, the machines were coming back to life. Across the yard from the powerhouse then back to the workshop again went men in dark blue smocks stained with copper, their paths criss-crossing all the time. Only Loshak and Gromada were not there, for they had tasks enough of their own in the Factory Committee offices. And there, down in the basement in rooms that reeked of cement and cheap tobacco—tobacco strong enough to send the devil himself back to hell, so they said—there were endless crowds of people. Men kept walking in and out of the offices, going in at one door and coming out at another. They were pressing for increased rations, but what few reserves of food were available were already being allocated. The word "roadway" was on everyone's lips, and warrants for the delivery of liquid fuel were expected any day now.

Gleb would run from one workshop to the next, seizing tools and cutting, sawing and drilling as though trying to outdo himself. He often looked in on Brynza, and the mechanic would greet him with a cry:

"Ho-ho, Commander! Things are moving at last! But fuel, Commander, we must have fuel! Just fuel—nothing else! And if we don't get it in the next couple of days, I'll blow myself sky-high together with these diesels of mine!"

Rattling their tools as they worked among the machines were his assistants, all of them looking rather like Brynza himself. He kept winking at them, nodding his head with its peaked cap in their direction and grinning happily.

"D'you see, Chumalov? The lads've started work with a will! All the fooling around and idle talk of the past few years are forgotten now, my friend! This is what the power of machines means, and so long as the machines are alive we can't possibly leave them. When you're longing for a machine, it's worse than longing for your sweetheart!"

Then he shouted again, but so loudly now that his voice filled the workshop:

"It's fuel we need, my friend, fuel! Ten tanks' full! That'll do to start with! Just ten tanks' full!"

Together with Kleist, the technicians and the workmen from the quarries, Gleb strode down the ravine and across the yards that were overgrown with grass. With a grave look in his sunken eyes, Kleist was silently inspecting the roadways. Two technicians, both of them old factory hands, walked two paces behind him out of habit, and with servile alacrity quickly caught up with him each time he nodded his head. The engineer did not look at Chumalov and seemed unaware of his presence, but Gleb knew Kleist had eyes only for him, and whenever the Director talked to the technicians, Gleb knew he was really speaking to him and him alone.

It was decided to repair the main transportation system and extend the roadway from its highest point in the quarries up to the crest of the pass, bringing it to a height of eight hundred metres.

Later, sitting in his office over the plans and estimates with the windows wide open now, Kleist leaned back wearily in his chair and said:

"If you can guarantee, Chumalov, that the estimates will be approved in full and that sufficient labor will be available, we can complete the work within a month."

Gleb burst out laughing.

"Well now, Herman Hermanovich, that's just where you and I can't agree! What d'you mean, a month? The job's got to be done in ten working days at the very most! You'll have five thousand men at your disposal, and materials will be supplied to you by the works management the moment you request them. Not a month, Comrade Director, just ten days!"

Kleist looked hard at Gleb and for the first time he gave a faint smile.

The ruined coopers' shop was still little more than a useless shed. Its glass roof had been smashed by stones and its floor was littered with broken hoops, bits of staves and other debris. The workbenches, transmission belts and circular saws were thick with rust and coated with what looked like hoarfrost—it was white dust from the mountains and roads. Everything in the shop seemed bathed in a misty, white light. Was this not why all the unfinished barrels, all the workbenches and saws looked transparent and blue-gray, the color of ice?

One morning Gleb called in here as he was passing. In the old days heaps of woodshavings used to glow like fiery gold on the floor, while the coopers, all covered in sparkling sawdust, would be bustling about at their benches. Gleb did not go any further into the shop because he did not like the feeling of emptiness and desolation in it. But the day would come when this place too would be restored to life. The shavings would glow again with fiery light, clouds of sawdust would fill the air, and the saws would remember the songs of their youth once more.

He was just about to turn away when he suddenly noticed Savchuk. With his back to Gleb, the cooper was sitting at his old bench, examining it to see whether it was still sound and hitting it with his fist, while the wood creaked and groaned like a decrepit old man.

"Ha, ha! You old devil! So you've not forgotten me, eh? D'you feel that?"

Then he went over to the saws and patted their ice-colored discs with his big hand. They rang softly in response to his touch, heaving long, distant sighs as though they were fast asleep.

"Well now, my beauties! Let's see what kind of songs you'll be singing next! Just you wait! There'll be men to look after you again soon, and the coopers'll make barrels with you just like they did before. Not barrels for women to pickle cabbage in, though, but barrels full of cement that'll go to all corners of the earth! Come on now, my lonely ones, don't cry!"

Gleb went quietly out of the workshop then burst out laughing, and as he walked away, looked back affectionately at the door.

That afternoon, as the mountains shimmered in the hot sun and the factory lay silent under its pall of dust, a locomotive belching clouds of smoke appeared, pushing a long line of dirty oil trucks in front of it. Shouting and waving with delight, the workmen came running out of the factory gates to meet it.

CHAPTER IX

THE GRAVITY ROADWAY

1. The Masses

Gleb was aware not of each individual but of the whole avalanche of people both in front of him and behind him. Streaming with sweat, he tore the cement shale loose with his miner's pick. The crowds of workmen doing the same covered the entire mountainside like a colossal swarm of ants, stretching from the factory buildings up to the rocky terraces and spreading away as far as the pylons that carried the power cables.

Fluffy white clouds drifted over the sea, and on the green hillsides the first spring flowers fluttered like countless gay butterflies. Among the rocks and in the ravines, shining bushes gleamed in an opal haze. Both to right and left, the towering mountains sloped away, while in the far distance lay the boundless sky-blue sea. And between the mountains and the sea was an immensity of limpid air.

Leaning on his heavy stick, Kleist personally directed the work of all these men, and the sedate technicians and brisk foremen were constantly at his side, always ready to obey. Stooping and grave, he would calmly issue his quiet instructions. Kleist was now a devoted specialist of the Soviet Republic, and the worker Chumalov had become his friend. Was this not a victory?

Preoccupied, Kleist stopped not far from Gleb to survey the work in progress on the mountainside, and Gleb saw a glimmer of excitement and pride in his eyes. Pushing his helmet to the back of his head and wiping the sweat from his face, he smiled gaily and said:

"Well, Herman Hermanovich, what do you think of it, eh? Do you remember, you said this work would take a month, didn't you? But just look what people can do if they're filled with enthusiasm. They've only been at it three days, and the job's nearly finished!"

Kleist smiled, and maintaining his usual air of dignity, said drily:

"Yes, it's true—with a surge of energy like this one can work wonders. But it's not an economic use of effort, Chumalov, because it's unsystematic and there's no organized division of labor in it. Enthusiasm's like a cloudburst—it doesn't last very long and it can do a great deal of damage."

"But when things are in ruins, Herman Hermanovich, that's the only way to start. Then once we've laid a firm foundation and put everything in order, we'll begin learning the process of production in a systematic way. Anyway, enthusiasm's like a fire, not a cloudburst, Herman Hermanovich—it's a fire in the soul, and in our souls it'll never go out!"

Leaning on his stick, Kleist went on up the hill towards the electricity pylons that were glowing in the sun. Then he stopped and thought for a moment.

"Yes, perhaps this really is a fresh start. Perhaps a new life is beginning after all, a life that will be happier than anyone has ever known before ... "

The air was filled with an almost unbearable smell of scorched grass and hot rock, and the dust made one's eyes and mouth burning hot.

Echoing in the shimmering heat, bells seemed to be ringing far up in the mountains.

It was good, very good. Everything was immeasurably vast and the sun itself seemed to be alive like a human being. Its brilliant light sent the blood coursing through the body, setting it ablaze with longing and filling it with faith in the future.

The clear lines of the rails went sweeping away over their sleepers and plunged into the abyss, plummeting down to where the quarries were, while in the other direction they came rising up into the webbed jaws of the transmission gear. In an hour's time the iron cables would pull taut, hanging like incandescent threads in the sunlit air, and the trucks would start to sing like brass trumpets as they ran up and down, up and down ...

Lukhava was standing on a rocky outcrop between the pylons. Wearing an unbelted black smock that left his chest bare, he was giving orders, waving his arms as he did so.

Dasha went by, carrying an iron spade over her shoulder, and behind her came a crowd of women, all carrying spades too. They were on their way up to the power station to repair the tracks there.

"There she goes," thought Gleb, "my little Dasha, the leader! What a fine wife she used to be ... "

He caught her in his arms as she passed and pressed her close. She gave a laugh, and playfully pulling Gleb's helmet off his head, tossed it to one side. Then she broke away from him and ran on, still laughing as she went. He was about to set off after her but then thought better of it and simply followed her with his eyes. Watching her, he stood still for a moment, then slowly climbed down the rocky terrace and picked up his helmet.

At the head of the construction team, Savchuk was fixing the rails to the sleepers with spikes, brandishing his hammer with the fury of a man intoxicated by his work.

Shouldering his pick again, Gleb began to climb the mountainside towards where the men working on the roadway were cutting down bushes and extending the line up among the rocks. They were preparing the ground for the second track at the same time.

"Go on, Savchuk, give it all you've got! The harder you go at it, the sooner the saws will start singing again in that coopers' shop of yours!"

"But we're giving it all we've got already, you old devil! We'll lay the track right down to those beauties of ours, those saws, just you wait and see!"

The last rails were being fastened to the sleepers now, and looking like giant snakes, the cables ran over the pulleys and went swooping down into the crowds of people far below.

Leaning on their rifles, a detachment of Red Army men were keeping watch up on the pass. Around and above them were thick clumps of green bushes and dwarf conifers.

Exhausted by the work, Sergei Ivagin stepped out of the ranks, his legs trembling with fatigue. He walked over to Polya Mekhova and sank down on the rocks beside her.

"Well then, my dear intellectual!" she said. "Isn't it true that the roots of Communist labor aren't always sweet?" And she stroked his hair affectionately as he gave a bashful, guilty smile. The sweat was streaming down his face and dripping off his nose and chin.

"Polya," he said, "I feel tremendously excited! Days like this are extremely rare in life! How vast everything seems, and what grand proportions and boundless strength it all has! Seeing this makes you walk tall and feel invincible. Let's sit here for a while, shall we, and dream ..."

2. A Struggle to the Death

Because of all the noise made by the work, no one heard the Cossacks' shots to begin with. But the Red Army men up on the pass were already running to and fro, taking cover behind the rocks, racing over the crest of the ridge and firing as they ran. Lukhava was waving his arms and shouting at the top of his voice:

"Keep calm, comrades! Everybody stay where they are! Carry on working! And don't panic!"

But thousands of people were already fleeing off the hillside, streaming not only downwards but also to left and right, many of them falling over before getting up and racing on once more. Here and there someone tried to halt the running crowds, waving his arms and threatening them with his pick or spade.

Then Gleb scrambled up on a rock and cried:

"Comrade Communists, come over here, to me!"

The leading detachment of the Construction Workers' Union came rushing towards him, and after them ran others.

"Stop! Stop!"

But people kept streaming on and on down the mountainside, scattering to left and right among the bushes and rocks.

"The swines! They couldn't stand their ground!"

"They've run off like rats into their holes! Oh, what a miserable lot!"

"It takes all sorts! Some people face up to danger while others turn tail and run!"

Gleb was issuing orders now in a cheerful, lively fashion:

"Savchuk! Dasha! Run down and reassure them! Try to establish order again!"

Holding hands so as to prevent each other from falling, Savchuk, Dasha and a few others set off down the hillside at a run.

Meanwhile, Gleb was still summoning the workers by waving his arms and shouting:

"Comrades! Over here to me! Get your rifles and let's go up to the power station!" Then off he went, climbing quickly up over the sleepers towards the pylons. Behind him surged a whole detachment of men.

The electricians and mechanics went on working in silence, but alarm was already flickering in their eyes.

Lukhava and Sergei were giving out rifles and cartridges now, and as each man took his gun, he could not suppress a smile of joy. They were all equally aware of the importance and seriousness of the moment, and inserting their cartridge-clips with grave faces, walked silently away. But Mitka, a quarry worker and accordion player with a close-cropped, grayish-blue head, came rushing up and yelled:

"Come on now, lads, let me through! Don't push me out of the way! I know where I belong all right! I've been waiting for this a very long time!" Stretching out his hands long before it was his turn, he reached eagerly for the rifle and grew angry when he was pushed to one side.

A few minutes later the whole detachment fanned out and ran off up the hillside towards the pass.

Polya Mekhova was scrambling up over the rocks next to Gleb. He could feel her soft shoulder nudging him and hear her rapid breathing close beside him.

"So you've come as well, Comrade Mekhova," he said, "and you're hard on my heels too! What for?"

"Why shouldn't I come?" she asked. "How is it you can go and not me?"

"It's different for me, and anyway you'll get all tangled up in your skirt!"

Polya was annoyed and gave a scornful snort.

Here and there in front of them both soldiers and workmen were running to and fro, then stopping and kneeling to fire. Far, far away, either beyond the mountains or out at sea, sirens seemed to be wailing.

"But that's the sound of bullets, Gleb!" said Polya. "It's so long since I heard them!"

Gleb climbed on with his rifle at the ready, while beside him went Polya, also carrying a gun. Her long curls glowed in the sunlight.

Gleb's commands were crisp and clear. The detachment was to attack the Cossacks in the rear on the left flank and drive them out of the small wood where they were hiding, then push them on to the bare hillside and bring them under the fire of the soldiers who would destroy them. Gleb himself would direct the attack from the mountain top.

"Can you hear, Gleb?" asked Polya. "They're very close now—they're firing from the summit! They were counting on creating panic, then destroying the roadway!"

But Gleb did not reply. He was scrambling up the steep slope, often stopping to look back at the roadway as he went. Polya kept close beside him.

Far below, the dense crowd of people stirred, and leaving it both in groups and singly, more men still began to climb the hillside, moving up over the sleepers in a long line.

The summit of the mountain shone like an immense green cupola. On it an iron tripod—an old geodesic sign—showed up clearly, its coating of red rust burning in the sun.

Polya and Gleb crawled up on the sharp crest of the mountain. From here they could see out over the wide sweep of the hillside with its trees and copses, its hollows and knolls. Far away in the distance were other ridges that were higher still and hung dark blue in the haze, while above them shimmered isolated peaks capped with pink snow.

Polya and Gleb lay down on a heap of pebbles beside the tripod. The air was full of the odor of scorched grass and the sulphurous smell of hot rock.

"I can't see a thing, Gleb! Where are they!"

Polya got to her knees and leaned forward, moving closer to the tripod. Suddenly there came a sound like the twang of a taut string, and grabbing Polya by the skirt, Gleb quickly pulled her down again. As he did so, the fastener at her waist gave way with a soft tearing sound and snapped. Polya burst out laughing and sat down beside him once more.

"You've torn the hook, you clumsy thing!" she said. "What am I going to do now?"

But she found a pin somewhere and managed to fasten the skirt again.

Running down the mountainside to the right of the crest was a high rocky wall that looked like the remains of an ancient fortress, overgrown with clumps of wild cherry and sweetbriar. Moving among the rocks and taking cover in the bushes as he went, was a bareheaded, swarthy Cossack, creeping stealthily along with his rifle at the ready. He kept crouching down and leaning against the wall, first disappearing from sight then coming into view once more.

"I'm going to shoot him, Gleb!" whispered Polya, "I can't bear the waiting!" The gun was shaking in her hands and her eyes were burning like fire.

"Lie down, I tell you! Or I'll throw you over the edge!" said Gleb, glaring at her threateningly.

Then he set off at a run down the slope towards the Cossack and disappeared from sight. After a few moments Polya caught a glimpse of him again, bent low and running among the ruins of the wall.

Suddenly the Cossack stopped, and jerking up his head with a start, shouldered his rifle.

Polya's heart was pounding so hard it was cramping her breathing, and she seemed to hear shots echoing in the forest far away at the foot of the mountain. Had Gleb managed to take cover, she wondered, or had the Cossack seen him? She wanted to leap up and run towards them, but no, there wasn't time ... Quickly taking aim, she pulled the trigger, and though she did not hear the shot, she felt the rifle kick against her shoulder and a wave of air buffeting her ears. Then she leaped to her feet and raced towards the wall where Gleb was. The rocks burst into splinters of flying stone and dust around her as she ran, scorching her forehead and cheeks.

Near the cliff edge, threshing about in the bushes and snarling, Gleb and the Cossack were locked in a desperate struggle. Suddenly Gleb's rifle clattered at Polya's feet.

His eyes crazed with fury and his face smeared with spittle and sweat, the Cossack was gasping for breath, writhing and grunting in Gleb's arms and trying to drag him down the slope towards the cliff edge.

Then, just as Polya was aiming her rifle butt at the Cossack's head, Gleb seized the man's neck with one hand and grasping his arm at the wrist with the other, suddenly broke it. The Cossack ground his teeth and howled with pain, but Gleb only tightened his hold on the man's neck even more. Polya could see that in another moment they would both plunge into the abyss, so with all her might she struck the Cossack in the ribs with her rifle butt. Bellowing with pain, he went limp and his knees gave way.

"That's it! I'm done for!" he gasped.

Then Gleb's hand slipped from around the man's neck and caught his other arm in an iron grip. The Cossack looked at him like a wild beast that is cornered, his breathing heavy and raucous, and his nose and mouth streaming with bloody slime. Then, jerking his head from side to side, he gulped back the spittle and blood that filled his mouth and bellowed:

"Let me go! I'm finished! I give in!"

Polya seized Gleb by the shoulder and pulled him back.

"Get away from here this minute, Gleb!" she said. "Can't you see we're a sitting target?"

Gleb glanced at her with eyes that were full of incomprehension, then let go of the Cossack's arm. He was gasping for breath too, choking and pulling at the shreds of his torn shirt. Then he put his hand to his holster, but his revolver was not there.

Exhausted by the struggle, the Cossack glanced round and shuddered, then baring his teeth in a bloody grin, sprang towards the cliff-edge.

"Oh, you filthy bastards, you swine!" he shouted. "Tried to catch a Cossack, did you? Well try and catch him now!"

Then he gave a cry and taking a running jump, plunged headlong into the abyss.

Gleb ran to the cliff edge and saw the Cossack's body turning somersaults far below, thudding against rocky outcrops and spinning over and over in the air before hitting the rocks again and bouncing to and fro.

Polya pulled him back from the edge.

The enemy were running out of the wood now and scattering in all directions, firing and stumbling, then falling and rolling over as they came. Shots rang out and a cloud of dust rose over the mountain top where the Red Army men were hidden. Polya was lying on her belly and firing too. The rifle kicked painfully against her shoulder, but filled with wild delight she kept snapping the bolt, taking aim, and firing again and again at the little figures running in the distance.

3. The First Truck

The wheels in the powerhouse were humming like strings, their iron spokes beating like huge dark wings at various inclinations and angles, while the steel cables wound and unwound on the great drums like giant threads of gossamer. Headed by Lukhava and Kleist, a crowd of electricians, Young Communists and workers gazed at the electric flight of the wheels and listened to the music of this machinery that had risen from the dead.

An avalanche of people half a mile long came streaming down the valley, seething with excitement. From the very top of the transmission line right down to the bottom where the pyramid-like, rocky terraces rose into the sky, the crowd was divided into two separate torrents, and between them the four taut cables hummed their endless melody.

From the bottom of the ravine, clinging to one of the steel cables, a square, truncated tortoise was crawling slowly upwards.

Carrying their rifles, the detachment of workers was coming down the terraces from the pass in a disorderly crowd, while the Red Army men were taking up their positions on the ridge once more. At the head of the detachment walked Gleb and Polya, and behind them the body of a dead comrade was being carried down on crossed rifles.

The detachment reached the powerhouse and stacked their rifles. The workmen's faces were covered with dirt. They laid the corpse, its head no more than a mass of bloody flesh, on the concrete platform, and jostling each other, the people pushed towards them.

Silently and gravely, their faces filled with suffering and pain, the workmen stood shoulder to shoulder, gazing down at the dead comrade lying at their feet. Though the corpse was almost unrecognizable, they could see it was Mitka the accordion player. Here too, among the crowd, were girls of the Young Communist League, busy now dressing the wounds of their comrades.

Choking with emotion, a young voice said:

"Oh, you made a mistake, Mitka, old friend! But it can't be helped! Such a cheerful fellow you were too!"

Then more people came up and standing motionless beside the corpse, sighed with pain.

Kleist went up to Gleb and silently shook his head. Then Dasha walked by, looking at Gleb with moist eyes that shone with surprise and joy.

This was it, this was the most important thing of all—the masses. The masses, toil and the winged flight of wheels ... That night the factory's lamps would burn again, shining like great electric moons, while the lifeless bulbs in the workers' houses would suddenly glow once more, patterning the darkness with their tangled threads of light.

Very soon, away over there, dark clouds of smoke would swirl from the factory chimneys, and the little trucks would begin to run down to the wharves and back again, climbing up to the high terraces to devour the shale in the quarries before descending once more.

Lukhava was standing near the winding gear, waving his arms and shouting something to those down below.

Suddenly the great wheel shuddered and came to a halt.

Gleb came running down the steps towards the engine, where covered with the silvery dust of decay, a big flat truck stood level with the concrete platform.

Then he ran back up the steps and shouted to the crowd:

"Comrades, lift the body and lay it on the truck! Let's carry him down with honor! Let him pass through the crowd! That way everybody can see him and pay their last respects."

Carefully and silently, the workmen lifted the dead man and laid him on the truck. Then someone said in an affectionate but mournful voice:

"Comrades! Brothers! Take his pick and his rifle ... and lay them beside him!"

Gleb stepped out on to the platform and standing between the light blue pylons, raised his arm in a sweeping gesture:

"Let her go now! All together!"

To the sound of many voices, the truck sailed away, rolling smoothly over the rails and swooping down the hillside like a bird.

Then, cupping his hands, Gleb shouted as if through a loudhailer:

"Comrades, this man is a sacrifice to conflict and toil! But we should not mourn or weep for him. No—instead we should be filled with the joy of new triumphs, for soon the factory will resound with the clamor of machinery and the roaring of furnaces. We are all beginning the great task of building socialism. Yes—much blood has been shed and there has been great suffering. Many obstacles have lain in our path and many more lie ahead. But this arduous path leads to happiness and the final victory over the world of violence. We are building a new life with our own hands. Bearing the name of Lenin on our lips and filled with faith in the boundless happiness to come, we shall increase our efforts tenfold to conquer the future!"

The truck carrying the body of the dead man, that gay accordion player, rolled down the hillside into the crowd, and baring their heads, all greeted the strange hearse in silence. Then, with sorrowful, grave faces they silently watched it pass.

CHAPTER X

STRATA OF THE SOUL

1. Quiet Moments

Dasha and Gleb came out of the factory canteen on to the main road and turned off down a path that ran among bushes entangled with wild vines and ivy.

The sun was already setting, its light fading beyond the distant mountain ridges. The sky was a deep blue, but above the dying sun it was still fiery red. The mountains looked very near, their slopes falling away from their crests like congealed torrents of once molten iron and bronze, while to the right, running along the steep ridge, the gravity roadway was sharply etched on the hillside like a freshly-ploughed, yellow furrow.

Floating up from the bottom of the ravines and drifting through the crater-like gullies came the purple shadows of evening. But the fiery patches and streaks on the mountain slopes still glowed hot and the rocks themselves still seemed to ring in the heat. On the overgrown path among the bushes hung with blue-gray gossamer, the twilit air of evening was full of the heady smell of spring earth and swelling buds.

"Look, Dasha," said Gleb, "let's walk up the hill and sit down for a while, shall we? I don't feel like going home just yet."

"All right then. I'm tired but I'm not keen to go back either. Besides, it's such a beautiful evening . . . "

All of a sudden Gleb felt deeply moved. Then Dasha took his hand and walked silently beside him. He sensed she was troubled and guessed she was wrestling with herself. She wanted to say something to him, something of her very own that was heartfelt and deeply significant, but she could not bring herself to do so. Yet she had agreed very readily to go up the mountain. So what could it mean?

Past the little houses and gardens they went, neither of them saying a word. Then, still just as preoccupied, they climbed the rocky terraces that led up towards the reservoir. With his arm round Dasha's shoulders, Gleb pressed her close, and she took pleasure in his nearness. The reservoir lay high above the workers' settlement, and from up here the water ran down through a conduit and was distributed to the factory laboratories and workshops.

Skirting the piles of rock that littered the terraces, they passed a gallery whose entrance was closed with a padlocked, rusty door. Then they climbed a flight of steps leading to a wide concrete platform. It was level and flat, and echoed sonorously under their feet.

Below them, at the foot of the mountain, the red roofs of the workers' dwellings ran down towards the factory chimneys, and beyond them were the buildings and towers of the factory itself, while lower still was the purple bay with its edging of surf along the shore. Out beyond the breakwaters lay the sea, boundless in its calm immensity as it rose above the factory chimneys and distant mountain ridges.

From the factory to the settlement workmen were walking both singly and in groups, while across the brown hillside in the distance a little girl was running along the narrow white path, waving her arms as she went.

Far below, in the depths under the concrete platform, the water was splashing, and something immense and alive seemed to be sighing in the expanse around them. And it was as though these sighs were echoing both in the forest and above it, floating up from the twilit valley.

Everything was infinitely airy and vast. The mountains no longer looked like ridges and gullies of stone and rock, but like great stormclouds. The rippling, immeasurable expanse of sea was no longer the sea but an azure abyss, while Dasha and Gleb, up here on the outcrop overlooking the factory, felt as if they were on a fragment of some planet that was hurtling into infinity.

Gleb laid his head on Dasha's knee, and looking up at her face with the down shining on its cheeks, gazed into her large, intent eyes that were filled with both disquiet and love.

"Sitting here under the open sky, I feel like a different person, Dasha," he said. "Here I am, lying with my head on your knee . . . When was the last time I did this? And I don't feel I've ever experienced anything like it either. All I know is that your love was greater and deeper than mine, and that I'm unworthy of you. I've not suffered a hundredth part of what you've been through. So tell me about your suffering, then perhaps I'll come to know myself better too . . . "

All of a sudden a flash of lightning lit the sky and lights began to twinkle everywhere like stars both big and small. Then Gleb was overwhelmed by a wave of delight, and in his excitement raised himself on one elbow.

"Dasha, darling, look! How fine it is to struggle and build one's destiny! It all belongs to us, you know, it's ours! Our strength and our toil! It's like drawing a deep breath, a great, deep breath before striking the first blow and then hitting out with all your might!"

Dasha laid her hands on his chest. She too felt deeply moved, and Gleb could feel her heart pounding.

"Yes, darling, it's good to struggle for one's destiny, though it may mean pain or even death . . . That's a terrible risk, and not everyone can face it. But I managed to because my love for you was stronger than my fear. Then I realized something else too, and I became fond of it—perhaps even fonder than I am of you . . . "

"Tell me, Dasha . . . Whatever it is, tell me. I've learned how to listen now and how to control myself too."

2. The Birth of Strength

On that purple evening Dasha told Gleb about how she had found the strength to endure suffering and how she had discovered the road to happiness . . .

For a few days, recovering from his beating, Gleb had lain amid spiders and mice in their attic, then one night he had gone off into the mountains where the Greens were encamped in the forests and ravines.

Dasha knew he might be leaving her forever, and in despair she kept clutching at him as if he were already dead. She lay sobbing softly on his breast and for a long time would not let him go. Then, when he had finally disappeared into the darkness, she did not light the lamp but lay tossing and turning with Nurka in her arms till dawn glowed at the window. From then on her days and nights were as terrifying as a nightmare.

She awoke from this semi-conscious state just as suddenly as she had plunged into it.

With a noisy stamping of feet and coarse shouting, a group of officers and soldiers armed with revolvers and rifles forced their way into the house and surrounded her. Then several of them asked together:

"Where's your husband?"

Now for the first time Dasha began to shake, because for the first time she was rooted to the spot with terror. Nurka was wriggling and howling in her arms, but she was deaf to the child's cries.

"Tell us where your husband is! We know he was here, so don't try to look all innocent!"

"How should I know where he is? You should know better than me—after all, it was you who took him away!"

But she did not cry. All that happened was that her face turned a bluish color and her eyes took on a transparent look, shining like little pieces of clear glass.

One of the officers—he was so young that he looked scarcely more than a boy, though his face was malicious and cruel enough—kept sitting down then getting up again, smoking incessantly and not taking his eyes off her for a moment. Then suddenly he shouted:

"Come on now, don't lie! You know where he is all right! You know perfectly well! You'll not get away from me!" And he struck the table with his fist.

"You'll be arrested immediately and we'll shoot you in your husband's place! So talk, instead of trying to fool us!"

But she went on standing there, vacant-looking and motionless, then barely moving her lips, said: "But how on earth do I know where he is? Please yourself—kill me if you like! But you can see I'm alone. So what are you tormenting me for?"

The officer was silent for a moment and looked hard at her again. Whether he saw the torment in her eyes or sensed a reproach in Nurka's cries, no one could say, but he suddenly got up from his chair and barked:

"Search the house thoroughly! Look everywhere!"

He made Dasha sit between two bearded soldiers, and until dawn the others rummaged through the whole house, searching every nook and cranny.

"He got away just in time, the swine!"

The next morning, dishevelled and sweating after their fruitless search, the soldiers took Dasha and Nurka to a villa behind the factory. And there, sitting silently in a cellar amid a crowd of unkempt strangers agonized by the knowledge that they were spending their last few hours on earth, she remained until midday. Many of these people spoke to her, but later she could not remember a word of what they had said.

At noon she was brought out of the cellar. The same officer as before looked at her in his malevolent way, then narrowing his eyes, said:

"Well now, young woman, where's your husband, then? Don't lie, because we shan't let you out of here till you tell us! If he's safe, what the hell are you worrying about? Don't be so pig-headed! There's just no point, damn it!"

But Dasha, weak now with exhaustion and anguish, mumbled:

"How do I know where he is? It's you who ought to tell me what you've done with him!"

Behind her someone muttered in disgust:

"Oh, to hell with it, Colonel, let her go! Can't you see she's practically out of her mind with fear?"

But the colonel, tapping his cigarette-case with a cigarette, suddenly said with a smile:

"I'll have you shot for being so stubborn! We do these things very quickly, you know! You'll not be able to play the fool right to the end!"

"All right then, shoot me! Go on! Go on!"

For the first time she burst into tears and began to sob hysterically.

"It was you who beat him up! You! So now beat me up too! Me and Nurka! Me and Nurka! Both of us at the same time!"

She came to outside in the brilliant sunshine and found herself walking down the dazzlingly bright main road. In front of her was the factory, and further away, over on the hillside, lay the workers' settlement, while in the distance she could see the red roof of her now empty house.

And so she began to live alone. She made friends with Motya Savchuk and would spend whole days with her.

Often she would sit on her little porch listening to the streams murmuring down in the ravine, and think of Gleb. Where was he now, she wondered. Was he still alive? And would he come back to her one day?

Then, one afternoon when the mountains were shimmering in the heat, she was sitting on the porch mending some old clothes while Nurka played with a kitten in the little cement yard. The cicadas were singing, and far away beyond the factory, gulls flashed white as they soared high over the sea.

Then a soldier with a big mustache came walking past the low fence. How many men like him walked by in those days! But this one came up to the fence and leaned on a post.

"Dasha!" he whispered, "sit still and don't be afraid! I've brought you news of Gleb. Pick this bit of paper up as quick as you can ... there! Wait for me this evening!"

Then off he went. All she had noticed was that his eyebrows and mustache hung down like scraps of dark tow.

She was about to rush down the steps to the fence, but the soldier glanced back at her and frowned, the scraps of tow hanging down low over his eyes. She realized she must wait till he had gone, walking off down the hill with his swinging gait. But all the same she said affectionately to Nurka:

"Come here, Nurka, come to mummy! Be quick, be quick! Go and pick up that bit of paper over there and bring it to me! That's right! Now come to mummy with it! Quickly now!"

Nurka went tottering over to the fence, grasped the piece of paper in her little hand, and feeling very pleased with herself, ran back to her mother.

"Here, mummy! Here!"

Glancing round, Dasha unfolded the piece of paper and read (could anyone but Gleb have written like this?):

"Darling, I'm alive and well! Take care of yourself and of little Nurka too. Burn this as soon as you've read it. Efim will tell you all you need to know."

It was from Gleb, her dearest, darling Gleb! If he was alive and well and safe, there was no need for him to worry about her, for she was filled with gladness at the news.

That night Efim came to visit her. He smelled of the mountains and forests, but it seemed to Dasha that it was not really the forests he smelled of but Gleb. She sat beside him at the window in the dark room with stars shooting in the sky, and trembled with love for Gleb. Holding his revolver all the time, Efim came straight to the point, his voice hoarse with cheap tobacco:

"You've got to help us, Dasha! I'll tell you rightaway: Gleb's making his way through the White lines to the Red Army. Don't worry about him—he'll make it all right. It's not him we're worried about . . . "

Dasha was shaking, and mumbling thickly, said:

"But tell me, Comrade Efim, mightn't he . . . ? What if he falls into a trap and gets killed? He's all by himself, and surrounded by men who are as savage as wild beasts!"

"It's not him we're worried about, I'm telling you. Gleb says you must take care of yourself and help us. Everything's so uncertain these days, but I'll always be around. Now you're going to be our Green lady, so listen carefully. You'll be helping all our Green comrades, so that means you'll be helping Gleb too. For the time being our people will take the place of a husband for you. So remember now: you must organize all the Green wives into a strong band and get yourself a job in the food section of the factory co-operative. We'll arrange that for you right away."

"But what about . . . what about my daughter? What about Nurka?"

"Give her to some good woman to be looked after. When all's said and done, the child won't fly away like a bird! Now if there's anything else you want to say, then say it!"

Dasha was shaking and it was only with the greatest difficulty that she managed to force out the words:

"But Comrade Efim, perhaps Gleb's all by himself right now . . . all by himself among savage men, with death lying in wait for him at every moment. If he's chosen this path, though, I must follow him down it . . ."

Efim smiled in the darkness and patted her knee affectionately.

"You're a fine girl—I knew it! I'll tell you before you start it'll be pretty dangerous, but you'll not be by yourself, because you've got us with you. And we're strong too!"

Then he disappeared into the night just as mysteriously as he had come.

Dasha asked Motya to look after Nurka in return for part of her food ration, and Motya gladly took the little girl in. She was a kind woman and a good friend, and she looked after the child like a mother.

Then Dasha started work in the co-operative bakehouse. From time to time workmen from the quarries would come in, and showing her slips of paper, would take supplies of bread for "the men on the building sites up in the mountains," as they put it.

Every day she would drop in to see the "Green wives," as they were called. Half of them were engaged in petty speculation. Some cursed their husbands who had fled, spent their time carrying on with other men, and soon forgot their own menfolk altogether, while the rest made a living by washing linen for the White officers. Dasha formed them into a group and gave them work to do, such as going up into the mountains to take clothes, boots and information to the Greens.

She became particularly friendly with three of the women. The youngest was Fimka, a girl with the delicate features of a young lady of noble birth. Her brother Petro was with the Greens. The eldest of the three was Domakha, a big-boned, red-haired woman with three small children who seemed to be perpetually crying. The third, Lizaveta, was a childless young woman with a big bosom and a florid complexion. Fimka was affectionate and submissive, never refusing either any man who wanted her or any woman who needed some of her rations. Domakha, on the other hand, was peevish and resentful towards everyone because of the hardships she had endured, while Lizaveta was unapproachable, taciturn and aloof. These were the women whom Dasha had formed into a group, and they were the only people with whom she spent her free time.

Occasionally Efim would come to see them at dead of night, and tapping them on the knee with his revolver, would say:

"You know, comrades, one thing's for certain: you've got to keep quiet and forget everything you've ever heard. You've even got to bite your tongue off if needs be. Your tongue's your own worst enemy—it's like a silly tail that wags when it shouldn't. So if you ever get found out and they nab you, then bite your tongue off and spit it out! So just remember this: your tongue won't move any mountains but it can wipe out a whole fortress!"

So it was that Efim became their first teacher and friend.

Dasha lived in this way for about a year, and during that time it was as if she were born anew. Her old domestic life already seemed offensively humiliating and trivial, and she knew she would never return to it. But her work with the other women and her link with the Greens filled her with new thoughts and armed her with experience.

Then, one fresh, sunny morning when she was standing behind the counter in the bakehouse, a group of officers armed with rifles pushed the crowd aside and burst in. Terrified, the people scattered in all directions. Dasha was put in a truck in which she was surrounded by officers, then driven quickly away to a villa—the one where she had once been locked up with Nurka. There she was flung into the same cellar as before. Once again there were dozens of people sitting and lying around her, and once again they were all strangers, exhausted and half-crazed in expectation of death.

Dasha had thought a great deal about how she should behave in such circumstances, and about how she must not show any weakness. She could endure anything—torture and perhaps even death—but if they used Nurka as a threat, then she could never bring herself to sacrifice her, never tear the child out of her heart.

In the gloom of the mildewed cellar she caught sight of a pair of eyebrows and a mustache that looked like scraps of dark tow. But Efim made no sign that he recognized her, and she realized she must not give the slightest hint that she knew him either. Not far away, sitting in a huddle of people, Fimka was sobbing, and beside her sat her little brother Petro, his boyish cheeks still covered with down. He was stroking Fimka's shoulder and hair, and whispering something. His face looked dark, like that of someone who has been fatally poisoned.

And now, for the first time in her life, Dasha came to know the full horror of human suffering.

They dragged Efim away first then came back for her. The same young colonel as before glanced at her and recognized her straightaway.

"Aha, so you've come back to visit us again, have you? Well, this time you won't get away! Now then, tell me how you fed the Greens! Why did you lie before when you said you didn't know where your husband was?"

Dasha pretended she knew nothing at all.

"How do I know where my husband is? It was you who beat him up, and now you're trying to involve me with the Greens!"

"We'll see if you're telling the truth right now," he said. "Take her to the kitchen and feed her well!"

She was dragged away to another, smaller cellar. Here the air was heavy with the stench of rotting corpses and the floor was covered with filthy slime. There was a naked man lying on the floor, covered with blood. Panting and snarling, two burly Cossacks were thrashing him with ramrods.

Suddenly a whip lashed Dasha's back, searing her flesh like fire.

"One! Two! Take that, you swine!" cried the Cossacks. "Let this bitch have a look at you, you handsome fellow!"

Dasha felt faint and almost collapsed, but somehow she managed to get a grip on herself and moaned:

"What are you tormenting me for? What for?"

"Let's make it a bit hotter for the bastard!"

Again they thrashed Efim as he lay there flat on his back, tossing his head from side to side but making no sound. All of a sudden, Dasha sensed the boundless strength and torment hidden by his silence. Only now did she realize what endurance meant, and saw she must regard her own silence as a sacred duty. Here lay Efim all mutilated by his tormentors, but his suffering was as nothing beside the great secret which safeguarded the vital business of the revolution and ennobled him as one of its mighty warriors.

"Now then, talk, you bloody bitch! Tell us what tricks you got up to with this bastard! If you tell us, we'll leave him alone and you can go free."

"I don't know a thing! As far as I'm concerned ... What are you insulting me for, you beasts?"

Once again her back was seared with intolerable, fiery pain. Her heart felt as if it were filled with boiling blood, and she cried out in a piercing voice:

"But what have I done to you? What are you beating me for?"

"Talk! Or else you'll get the same as him! So choose!"

Then she realized these people knew nothing about her—they had no definite information. They had simply arrested her, either on suspicion or because of rumor. Neither Lizaveta nor Domakha were here. But what about Fimka? Well she was here for a different reason—because of her brother. They'd probably caught him in her room—after all, he often used to go and visit her at night.

"I've nothing to tell you! What can I say? I keep to myself and don't interfere with anybody!"

"Give that bastard another ration! That's it! Right! Hit him! Harder! Let the swine have a good taste and make him grunt!"

Efim was already racked with convulsions as he lay in the filth on the floor, but the Cossacks went on wearily thrashing him, their ramrods sending fragments of bloody flesh flying through the air.

All of a sudden, Fimka's little brother, Petro, was flung to the floor beside Dasha. Filled with terror, he leapt to his feet, slipped and fell down again, then sprang up and ran away once more, his bare feet pattering in the bloody mire that covered the floor. Brandishing their ramrods, the Cossacks chased after him. Petro gave a terrible scream and began to batter himself against the wall with all his might.

With crazed eyes Dasha watched her comrades being tortured, and mute with horror, could not look away. She gazed and gazed at them, and saw nothing but blood.

She eventually came to in the bright room where she had been questioned earlier and where the colonel was now sitting with two officers, screwing up his eyes because of the smoke from his cigarette.

"Well, young woman, how did you like our kitchen, eh? Now let's have a chat, shall we?"

"I don't know a thing! There's no point tormenting me any more!"

"So don't you know that young fellow in there and that girl, then?"

"Yes, I know Fimka, and I know Petro too—I've known them ever since they were small . . . "

The two officers whispered something in the colonel's ear. He frowned at first then his cheek began to twitch.

"Give her to us, Colonel," they said, and leering at Dasha, came towards her.

She flung herself into a corner of the room and put out her hands to shield herself.

"No! No! I'd rather die! Kill me right now instead!"

The colonel raised his hand and smiled.

"All right then. Nothing will happen if you tell the truth, so come over here and talk."

"I don't know a thing, I don't know anything at all! Aren't you ashamed?"

The colonel leaned back in his chair and narrowed his eyes maliciously.

Then the two officers seized her under the arms and dragged her off to another room . . .

Till midnight she lay in the cellar, barely alive, her breasts and legs bare. She remained lying on the floor just as they had flung her down. Fimka crawled over to her, rested her head on Dasha's breast for a moment and gave a moan, then crawled away again. Twice Dasha seemed to see Nurka before her. The little girl was stamping her feet and squealing with happiness, but Dasha reached towards her, crying out with fear and revulsion:

"No, Nurka, don't! Oh, don't, don't!"

Then she forgot her, as though the child had been no more than an image in a lifeless dream.

After midnight—she remembered that, too, as if it were only a dream—she came to once more, this time because of the rattling of a truck. She found herself sitting on its wooden floor with several people lying silently beside her. She recognized Fimka, Petro and Efim. All around them stood Cossacks with rifles.

Later only one thing would remain clear in her memory: the sight of the glittering, multi-colored stars which seemed so near—no more than a stone's throw away.

She knew she was going to her death. She knew that in a moment the truck would stop and they would all be flung out on the ground. Then they would be led on to the sand and down towards the sea, and there her chest would be riddled with bullets. She knew all this, and at the thought of it her heart seemed to melt away like a block of ice, but she felt no fear. It was as if none of it were really happening, as if it were only a tedious dream of the kind one does not believe, knowing all its images will soon fade and die. Then once again she seemed to see Nurka. This time the child was running towards her, stretching out her little arms and giving a single, short cry: "Oh!"

The comrades lying on the floor of the truck—Efim, Fimka and Petro—were jolting about like corpses, but Dasha felt no pity for them now, because in her breast instead of a heart there was only a block of ice.

When the truck finally came to a halt, she was pushed out on to the ground. Fimka stood close beside her, shivering with cold, clutching at Dasha's dress and pressing up against her like a child. Efim lay like a corpse at their feet. But Petro, badly disfigured by the flogging, kept tossing his head from side to side and stamping his feet. His face was dark with congealed blood and he kept groaning and spitting all the time.

Urgently and sternly, as if it were not she but someone else speaking, Dasha whispered in Fimka's ear:

"Keep quiet, keep quiet! You must keep quiet! Be blind and dumb! Keep quiet!"

Then it seemed to Dasha as though dozens of people had suddenly fallen on her and pushed her to one side.

It was four Cossacks who were urging Fimka and Petro forward with their rifles.

When they were only a short distance away, Fimka suddenly cried out and began to flutter like a frightened bird. She waved her arms and tried to run back to Dasha.

"Dasha, dear Dasha! What are they doing to me?" she cried.

The Cossacks swore at her and pushed her on. She began to struggle and with a scream fell down on the sand, but they seized her by the arms and lifted her up once more. Silently she took a few more steps, then stopped again and cried anxiously:

"Oh! What have I done? I've gone and left my shawl in the truck!"

But they seized her by the arms again and dragged her off into the darkness.

Out there, out on the curving sweep of sand where the sea stretched away like dark ploughland into the gloom, Dasha could only make out dim shadows that seemed to be dancing drunkenly on the spot.

Again Fimka's shrill cry rent the air:

"I don't want to! No, don't blindfold me! I'm so young! I want to see my death with my own eyes!"

And right up to the volley she kept shouting:

"I want to see it with my own eyes! I want . . . "

When the shots rang out, it seemed to Dasha that Fimka's cries went on drifting over the sea for a long time.

Then a menacing shadow came up to her.

"For the last time, tell us who's working with the Greens! I give you my word you'll be allowed home immediately if you do. Or else . . . out there—can you see? Well the same thing will happen to you!"

But just as before Dasha answered vacantly:

"I don't know a thing, not a thing! I don't know anything at all!"

"All right! Take this fellow next!"

They dragged Efim away, and this time instead of a volley Dasha only heard a single shot.

Once again the officer's menacing shadow came up to her.

"I'll give you thirty seconds!"

"Go on then, shoot! Shoot! Just don't torment me, that's all!"

She felt that any moment now she would fall down on the ground and start struggling in the way Fimka had.

Then they seized her and flung her into the air, and as she fell, she struck her head against a piece of iron.

Once again the truck was rattling along, and once again, very near, no more than a stone's throw away, it seemed—the stars shimmered like droplets of gold, while above the mountains the misty sky glowed like fire.

Then they took her back into the room where she had been questioned, and without looking at her, the same colonel said in a distinct but offhand tone:

"Engineer Kleist has made himself responsible for you. We don't trust you, but we do trust him, so you can go now. But just remember this: if we ever catch you again, you'll never leave here alive. And bear this in mind too: nothing happened to you here, and you didn't see anything either. If you ever breathe a word about this place, the same will happen to you as happened to those swine just now. Now get out—quick march!"

After this, Dasha did not say anything to a soul, but learned to choose her words carefully and speak little. From now on she only spent the night at home. Her little house became stained with mold, and cobwebs and dust gathered in its corners. The flowers on the windowsill withered and faded, Dasha's face grew pale, and her eyes turned very clear and cold. She spent many hours with Motya, that kindly housewife and good friend. She grew close to Savchuk and Gromada too, and would sit with the hunchbacked Loshak for hours on end. All three men were quietly preparing for the arrival of the Red Army, and so she told them about her secret work. Formerly they had slept at night and watched the mountains during the day, but now they suffered from insomnia when it was dark and pretended not to see anything when it was light.

With a silent question burning in their eyes, soldiers would call on Dasha. Just to look at them, anyone would have thought they had come to play the fool a little and have a bit of fun with a young widow. They would call a couple of times then disappear, and new ones would come in their place. But as to where the others had gone, Dasha's clear eyes said not a word.

Now British ships were lying at anchor out in the bay, taking aboard countless numbers of aristocratic and wealthy people who had fled from the north.

From somewhere far beyond the mountains the earth shook with a muffled, subterranean rumbling, and at night the immense thunder seemed to bring stars falling from the sky, cascading like fire in the darkness.

Then, one hot spring morning when it was impossible to distinguish either the blue sea from the equally blue sky, or the fragrant air from the scent of blossoming trees, Dasha made her way into the town. Through piles of stinking refuse she walked, passing among the corpses of horses and men and witnessing the horror of panic and death on every side. With her red kerchief blazing on her head, she was looking for

Communists. On she went, all alone, while the people of the town, still dazed by what had happened, dared not venture out of their houses. On she went, both her kerchief and her eyes shining with happiness and pride.

Then, catching sight of a group of mounted Red Army men with scarlet armbands that glowed like magnificent poppies in the light, she walked towards them. She looked at the soldiers and laughed, and they laughed too, waving and calling to her:

"Hurrah for the red kerchief! Hurrah for our woman comrade!"

***

Overwhelmed by all that Dasha had said, Gleb lay motionless with his head on her knee, and for a long time could not speak. Here she was, his own dear wife, sitting beside him, her voice and face just the same as always and her heart beating just as in the old days. But it wasn't the Dasha of three years ago, for she had gone forever.

Then a wave of inexpressible love for her swept painfully over him, and he embraced her with trembling arms. Choking as he fought back the tears, he groaned with both impotent fury and deep fondness.

"Dasha, darling! If only I'd been here! And if only I'd known! My heart's breaking, Dasha! Why have you told me all this? And what can I do with myself? Right now I feel as if I've been wounded! How can I possibly bear it all? I and you and those officers . . . Oh, Dasha! Death came between us, but you're still alive! You followed your own road and found your own way of fighting. As for me, though, I'm going out of my mind! Oh, help me to understand, Dasha!"

"Gleb, what a good man you are! And how dear you are to me!"

Till night fell they sat together as they had not sat since the early days of their marriage.

CHAPTER XV

SCUM

2. A Difficult Transition

Before the Economic Council met, Gleb arranged for a report on the need for partial resumption of work at the factory to be included in the agenda. The warehouses were empty, the report said, but there were enough staves in stock to make a hundred thousand barrels. Moreover, the cement mill could be started straightaway, and cement shale could be calcined in one of the furnaces immediately—the rock lay ready in stockpiles of thousands of cubic feet up in the quarries. All that was needed was to set the second line of the gravity roadway in motion. The first line would be used to transport wood.

Gleb presented the report, with Kleist acting in his capacity as technical expert. Lukhava and Zhidky spoke briefly but emphatically in favor of accepting the report, and made the following proposal:

"To begin preparatory work immediately for the resumption of production."

Then Lukhava introduced the following motion: "To send Comrade Chumalov to the Bureau of Industry in Moscow in order to secure the prompt implementation of decisions taken by the Economic Council and to obtain increased supplies for the factory immediately."

When the meeting ended, Gleb went up to Kleist, and taking him by the arm, said with a laugh:

"I'll go all right, as sure as twice two makes four! Oh, I'll stir things up at that Bureau, make no mistake! Come on, Herman Hermanovich, let's be off! This is no ordinary technical director, comrades—he's worth his weight in gold! He's an amazing specialist of the Soviet Socialist Republic! We'll show you, so watch out!"

The following day Gleb left for the Bureau of Industry, promising to be back in a week.

At the factory work was now in hand to repair the railway tracks, buildings and machinery at various parts of the site. From early in the morning till late in the afternoon, the sultry air—already filled with the chirring of cicadas and heavy with dust—resounded with the clanging of metal, the whining of lathes and the rattling of trucks, while all day long the windowpanes of the powerhouse hummed like a vibrating string.

The roadway being used to transport wood was in continuous operation now, and day in, day out the trucks went rattling up and down the mountainside and the cables sang like flutes as they wound and unwound on their drums. Down on the wharves railway wagons rumbled to and fro, steam locomotives whistled discordantly, and heavy sleepers fell into the empty trucks with a bang that echoed like a volley of pistol shots across the harbor.

Out on the sparkling waters of the bay a few ships rode sadly at anchor as though in bewildered anticipation of something.

Dasha was often away from home, either working at the Women's Section, attending various meetings or travelling out of town on official business. Each week Lizaveta would assemble the local women in the club hall where they would argue noisily till midnight, and drifting out through the open windows, the wild uproar would disturb the pensive stillness of evening that filled the woods and ravines. As they dispersed in the darkness and made their various ways home, the women went on shouting just as they once had when quarrelling over chickens, eggs and other domestic trifles.

Each morning and evening, when she called at the Children's Home to visit Nurka, Dasha could see that the little girl was melting away like a candle. The skin on her face had become as wrinkled and yellow as an old woman's, and she would gaze at her mother with eyes so full of sadness that it seemed to Dasha they had witnessed something inexpressibly tragic.

Nurka talked much less these days, too, and her expression was pensive and sad, while whenever Dasha said good-bye to her, she seemed almost indifferent.

For the first time that year, Dasha felt intolerable anguish, but she kept it hidden deep in her heart and so no one knew of it...

Nurka, her one and only dearest Nurka, was melting away like a candle, and no one could say why. What was the good of doctors if they couldn't explain what was happening and if they were powerless to cure the illness that was destroying the child? But it wasn't really a question of doctors—Dasha knew better than all the doctors on earth why Nurka was fading away like a star at dawn.

A little one does not only need its mother's milk, for it is nourished too by her affection and tenderness. It withers and fades if she does not breathe upon its head, if she does not warm it with her closeness and surround its slumber with her presence and spirit.

Only she, Dasha, was to blame, and she would never forget it. And yet, the source of that blame did not really lie within her. It lay instead in the force of circumstance, that force in whose power she now found herself, that force which had denied death its due and had awoken her to life through struggle and suffering.

But one thing and one thing alone remained and was always there: little Nurka was fading away like a dying ember. For the moment she was still there, but soon she would not be there any more. Once she used to kick her little legs as she lay at Dasha's breast, then she had begun to crawl and walk and prattle, growing steadily bigger all the time. Later, when for the first time in her life Dasha had known the horror of imminent death, her suffering was unbearable, for she could not bring herself to forget Nurka and sacrifice her. The mother in her had been about to betray the revolutionary, and it was only the torment suffered by her comrades and the terrible yet beautiful death of Fimka that had finally devastated her soul and extinguished the persistent image of her daughter. Then, not simply with her mind but with her entire being she had realized that there was another, more powerful kind of love than a mother's love for her child, and she had learned that one only becomes aware of that love in the last few moments before death.

Now, as she looked at Nurka again, looked at her old woman's face with its sunken eyes that were filled with sadness at the approach of death, once again, as before, she could not bring herself to surrender her. Yes, Nurka was her life's sacrifice, and the knowledge served as a deadly reproach. One morning she had the following conversation with her:

"Nurka, do you feel any pain, little one?"

Nurka shook her head—no, she didn't.

"What do you want? Tell me."

"I don't want anything."

"Would you like to see daddy, perhaps?"

"I want some grapes, mummy."

"It's still too early, darling, the grapes aren't ripe yet."

"I want to stay with you, so you'll never go away and always be near. And I want some grapes, you and some grapes . . . "

She was sitting on Dasha's knee, all warm and close, an inseparable part of her.

Later, as Dasha was putting her to bed, Nurka gazed at her for a long time, deep in thought, then murmured longingly:

"Mummy! Mummy!"

"What is it, darling?"

"Stay here, mummy! Don't go away!"

When Dasha left the Children's Home, she did not turn on to the main road as she usually did. Instead, she walked off into the bushes and flung herself down on the grass in a lonely place where the sunlight dappled the greenery around her and there was a rich smell of earth. Weeping bitterly, she lay there for a long time, her fingers tearing at the leaf-mold beneath her.

4. Obstruction

After Gleb's departure the work of repairing the factory went on with feverish haste. The windows and glass roofs still had many broken panes in them, and dark holes fringed with rusty shreds of steel still gaped in the reinforced concrete walls. But the twilit depths of the factory, where electric lamps shone like stars, echoed with the incessant ringing of hammers, the whining of drills and the clanging of metal.

Two hundred men were working there—the total labor force available. The repair of the rotary furnace required special care as its steel plating had to be reriveted and its fireproof lining relaid. They also had to make new metal castings for the crushing machine, the hoists, the mill and the intricate driving gear. The reservoir tanks for liquid cement were badly damaged and new rotary mixers had to be made, while the entire piping system with its complicated cylindrical sieves and interconnected wooden and metal components had to be replaced. But there was least work of all to be done in the powerhouse, where Brynza was. He was still very much alive, so the diesels were alive too.

Covered in light blue dust, workmen went bustling to and fro all day long, climbing round the kilns, running along the overhead gantries and the network of scaffolding, parapets and stairways, incessantly riveting, cutting and sawing, constantly entangled in lengths of cable, shouting with excitement and choking with the heat and dust—all of them to a man filled with the ecstatic frenzy of toil.

Work on the second roadway, though, was continuing more quietly and calmly. The track was being relaid in various places, while the viaducts were being repaired and the rails cleared of rubble.

As before, the factory was still desolate and covered with dust, but already one could sense its living breath and feel the new vibration of its machinery. Down in the engine-room the diesels were already throbbing day and night without pause.

Every day, looking stern and grave, Kleist would make an inspection of the factory. He was dressed all in white, and for the first time a restrained but joyous smile flickered on his face. Just as in the old days technicians and foremen were in constant attendance on him, and just as briefly as before, he would issue orders to them, nodding his head as he spoke. But with the workmen he was as taciturn and curt as always, and would pass them by, indifferent and aloof.

Gleb had only meant to go for a week but he was away a whole month. As early as the second week of his absence the repair work began to be interrupted, and towards the end it came to a complete standstill. The factory management was no longer either carrying out the plan that had been approved or fulfilling requests for materials, and it soon became impossible to get any sense at all out of the Economic Council. They always gave the same old answer—the problem lay with the Bureau of Industry or the Cement Trust or the State Planning Commission . . .

In the factory management offices the spruce, neat specialists were frank with Kleist:

"Why don't you forget all this nonsense, Herman Hermanovich? The factory can't possibly be started up again. Don't you understand? Anyway, what on earth do we need the place for? It's simply ridiculous! But let's suppose we do get it going again and the warehouses are stocked with cement. What then? Where's the market for it? There isn't one! In the old days our cement went chiefly to foreign buyers, but what about now? Construction projects? But nothing's being built and nothing can be either, because there's no productive capacity and no capital. They've kicked up a hell of a fuss trying to get the factory started again—you've got to give them credit for that!—but they just haven't the experience, the competence or the capacity for constructive work. How can they have, when private enterprise and capital are completely lacking? They'll not get very far with that nationalization program of theirs either, so whether we like it or not, we'll just have to turn to the foreigners."

Smoking quietly, Kleist listened gravely to what the specialists had to say, then said briefly but weightily:

"I have not come here to discuss questions of political economy and the general financial condition of Russia. My task is rather more modest. It is to request from the factory management that the plan of production be fulfilled in the immediate future. At the moment the repair work has come to a halt and for that the management is responsible."

The specialists looked down at their hands and concealed their mocking smiles beneath a veneer of amiable courtesy.

"But the management has got nothing to do with it, Herman Hermanovich—it receives all its instructions from the Economic Council. So please apply directly to them."

These men were newcomers, sent from the Council, but beneath the pretence of loyalty to the new regime they still cherished the past. Kleist cherished it too, but for him it was remote and dead now, reduced to ashes by the conflagration of the present, and only its smoldering embers were left. Kleist realized there was no longer any common ground between these people and himself. He saw how their faces fell at his unexpected reply and how their mockery and distrust were masked by smiles. This queer old man was either too clever by half, they thought, or he'd been terrified out of his mind by the Bolsheviks. . . .

Kleist went next to the Economic Council, where he was received just as deferentially as if he belonged there. All the officials smiled at him exactly as they had in the management offices—enigmatically but meaningfully, their gold teeth flashing and their eyes full of scorn.

Just as coolly and gravely as before, Kleist explained the reason for his visit, and just as before he received the same politely official replies, made through a haze of veiled mockery:

"Yes, Herman Hermanovich, the delivery of materials in accordance with your estimates has been halted and the figures will probably have to be revised. You see, we cannot go against our instructions from the Bureau of Industry and the Cement Trust. For the time being the appropriate conditions simply do not exist ... The chairman of the Economic Council is an experienced and careful man (as they said this, a mocking smile danced in their eyes), and he takes a very firm line. He's not at all fond of jokes ... Everything's been done much too quickly. Anyway, what will the Cement Trust say? There are reasons to suppose that in the Bureau of Industry and particularly in the Cement Trust itself, all this venture with the factory will not meet with general approval. So we're waiting for authoritative instructions."

Now Kleist walked alone without his technicians and foremen, wandering through the factory buildings and down the railway tracks. For hours on end he inspected the deserted construction sites and yards, the dismantled machinery and the debris left by interrupted work, and as he went he tapped gloomily with his stick at the piles of discarded materials and wreckage. During these silent walks he only ever met one man—the watchman Klepka, his eyebrows and beard still flecked with cement.

Gleb returned from his journey all dishevelled and dirty, but his eyes were shining as if they had been rinsed clean. He did not go home first but hurried straight to the factory. He spent only a very short time there, though, and then, pale with fury, strode quickly up to the roadway. Everywhere he looked he saw nothing but desolation and ruin, just as in the first few days after his return from the army. Then, choking with rage, he went racing off to the factory management offices.

Deafened by his oaths, the spruce, neat specialists were rooted to the spot in astonishment and dismay. Those who were on their way somewhere stopped dead in their tracks and those who were sitting at their desks got hurriedly to their feet, while others who were busy writing did not even dare look up. Even before he had crossed the threshold, Gleb began to deafen them all with his cries, giving it to them straight from the shoulder:

"Tell me what bastards have played this dirty trick? I'll smash their faces in for this treachery! Where's the director? I'll send all you swine off to the Cheka right now for counter-revolution and sabotage! You reckoned that because I wasn't here you could get up to your old tricks again, didn't you? You thought that with me out of the way your nasty little schemes would go unnoticed! You sons of bitches, I'll string you all up!"

He ran from one room to the next, apparently looking for somebody yet finding no one, knocking over chairs, sweeping papers off desks and colliding with people who stood in his way. Like pretty little dolls the typists cowered in fright at their desks, hiding their hair-dos behind the keyboards of their typewriters.

Speechless with fright, the men remained standing or sitting where they were, and when Gleb left them and ran on, they exchanged fearful glances and raised their hands to their mouths in alarm.

When his fit of rage had subsided a little, Gleb flung his greatcoat and kitbag down in one of the rooms and went storming into the director's office. Müller had short, silvery-gray hair that covered his skull like stubble, a close-cropped gray mustache and gold pince-nez. He received Gleb with the same combination of astonishment and dismay as his colleagues had done, but did his best to keep calm at the same time. He stood up and held out his hand across the desk.

"What were you making such a racket for out there, Comrade Chumalov? You curse loud enough to break the windows!"

Gleb did not sit down and did not even seem to notice Müller's outstretched hand either. Standing beside the desk, he asked menacingly:

"Who gave the order to stop work at the factory?"

Müller spread his hands in a gesture of submissive helplessness.

"Come on, don't play the fool with me, Müller! Just tell me straight: what bastard was it who ruined all the work when it was in full swing?"

Müller flinched, his pince-nez flashing, and his face suddenly looked very tired and gray.

"First of all, Comrade Chumalov, I must ask you to be rather more careful about what you say. The factory management has got nothing to do with it. The reason we stopped work was that the Economic Council found it impossible to continue repairs because the necessary resources were lacking and the sanction of higher economic bodies was not forthcoming."

"Show me the Council's order! And all the correspondence too—right now! You bastards have come to an agreement with that bunch of crooks in the Council, haven't you? You thought you'd cheat me behind my back, didn't you? You thought they'd give me a good dressing-down at the Bureau of Industry, and then you reckoned on striking while the iron was hot and pulling a fast one! Well just carry on with your little game, you swine, and I'll get a noose put round your necks as quick as greased lightning, make no mistake!"

"Comrade Chumalov, what grounds have you got for making such serious accusations against us? I protest categorically! You say the most offensive things without even thinking about them. We're not little children, you know! We can't exceed our instructions! Anyway, we've no longer got anything to do with this project—all the stores have been put under seal by the Economic Council and all the documents removed from the files by the Council's representative. So if you're going to make a fuss, be so kind as to do it at the Council, not here!"

Gleb rounded on Müller and banged the table with his fist.

"Don't talk such nonsense! I know all about your dirty little schemes, and you'll soon find out how bastards like you get put up against a wall! You all thought I was a fool and tried to take me for a ride, but I'm going to smash your heads in for this! And just remember something else too: the men are going to start work again first thing in the morning! The repairs have got to be finished in two months' time and by the autumn the factory will be working at full capacity again. Is that clear?"

Müller shrugged his shoulders and with an embarrassed smile tried to say something in reply, but only choked on his dry tongue.

Out on the square in front of the Factory Committee offices bored workmen were huddled in small groups, some sitting in the shade of the wall and others waiting by the office doors. They were all smoking, chatting and laughing noisily. The consumptive Gromada was standing in the doorway on the top step of the porch, swinging his bony fists to and fro and shouting hoarsely in excitement.

"So you see, comrades, that's how things stand at the moment, but as members of the working class we're obliged to act in a politically conscious way, and so on. Both as a group and at our meeting we passed a resolution, and since the Trade Union Council and the Building Workers' Union are our own organizations, we shall defend our interests in every way and hand the matter over to the Revolutionary Tribunal. And then we'll pin a charge on all these sons of bitches!"

The men were growing agitated now and began shouting and clapping.

Then Savchuk in a ragged shirt pushed his way through the crowd, and waving his arms, shouted like one possessed:

"They must be smashed, the bastards! What are you all waiting for? I can't stand it!"

All of a sudden Gleb came running down the wide concrete steps and was quickly surrounded by a dense mass of sweating, dusty faces. Almost immediately confusion and uproar broke out in the crowd.

"Here's Chumalov! Here he is! Oh, you old rogue, you son of a bitch! Ho-ho! He'll sort them out all right, the old fire-eater! My goodness! You certainly went off and left us at a bad time, Gleb!"

But amid these joyful cries very different, gloomy voices could be heard too:

"What's gone wrong then, Chumalov? And what the hell does it all mean? If this is how we're going to work, we might as well give up now!"

"Is it some kind of joke or what? We know whose dirty tricks these are!"

"Ha! Those profiteering bastards are still fast asleep and dreaming of the good old days under the Tsar!"

"They're waiting for their old bosses to come back, the filthy swine!"

"But why the hell should we worry about them? Just put 'em up against a wall, and that'll be that!"

A strong odor of cheap tobacco and sweat came drifting from the crowd, and because of the men's hot breath it was stifling in the tremendous crush. Gleb pushed his way through the crowd and went up the steps towards Gromada.

"Comrades," he shouted, "tomorrow morning work at the factory will start again at full speed, and when the whistle blows, everyone will go back to his old job. We'll soon get to the bottom of all these intrigues, then we'll be able to call somebody to account. I'm going to the Economic Council, comrades, and I shall demand merciless punishment for these counter-revolutionaries. At the Bureau of Industry I obtained approval for all the orders requesting materials. Fuel supplies have been sent back here with me and men are being sent for more rivets too. First of all, though, we've got to get the crusher going, and after that the mill."

Immediately the men rushed to Gleb and slapping him joyfully on the back and deafening him with their cries, seized him by the arms. Then somebody caught him by the legs, someone else grasped him round the waist, and suddenly a multitude of strong hands flung him into the air.

"Hold on tight, lads! Let old Chumalov have it now! Hup! Higher! Hup!"

"Stop it, you devils! Stop!" cried Gleb, laughing as his arms and legs flailed in the air above the workers' heads. But he was clearly enjoying every minute of it and considered the men's noisy delight not only perfectly natural but also quite unavoidable.

When they finally put him down, he stood surrounded by his tired comrades, then suddenly found himself face to face with Savchuk.

"Gleb! You old devil! Get the coopers' shop going again and at full speed too! I can't stand it! I'll smash them all!"

Gleb was winking at one of the workmen and jokingly showing his fist to another.

"Gromada!" he shouted. "Where's Gromada? Send him over here, lads! Come on, Gromada, let's go!"

Gleb did not go straight to the Economic Council, though, but got out of the cart at the door of the Executive Committee offices.

Seizing Gromada under the arms, he dragged him up the stairs to the first floor. Gromada was wheezing and gasping for breath, and his eyes bulged with the effort.

As soon as the dishevelled old man sitting outside the chairman's office saw Gleb coming, he moved aside and opened the door.

Badin, Chairman of the Executive Committee, was not alone—Shramm, Chibis and Dasha were with him.

Dasha glanced at Gleb, and as her eyes opened wide in astonishment they were filled with both anxiety and joy. It was not joy that Gleb saw in her eyes, though, but something quite different, something that he had never seen before and that was as profound as a heavy sigh. Why did her eyes look so dark? They were very round and dry, burning hot as though she had a fever. Once again her soul was like a deep well, and like the water at the bottom of a well she seemed inaccessible and remote.

He made no attempt to go up to her and she remained sitting to one side without looking at him any more. She was just like a stranger.

"Comrade Badin!" said Gleb.

"Aha, Chumalov! At last! Where on earth have you been all this time, damn you? Well come along then, give us your report, please! My goodness, look how sunburnt your face is! They must have given you a good roasting up there!"

And he gave Gleb a friendly smile.

But Gleb remained standing beside Gromada, and in a gloomy tone, without pausing for breath, began to speak:

"Comrade Badin! Gromada, a member of the Factory Committee, and I have hurried here to find out on whose orders and for what reasons work at the factory has been halted. Everything there is in a state of total disintegration and chaos, and a disgrace like this simply cannot be overlooked. I want to know what bastards have been spreading counter-revolution and sabotage here. The workmen are very restless now, and it's clear that deliberate bad management like this does more harm than a raid by our enemies."

Standing by the table facing Badin, Gleb was beside himself with rage, and his cheek twitched involuntarily.

"Comrade Chairman of the Executive," he went on, "I'm telling you straight out that it's impossible to carry on like this! The question is extremely serious and poses a direct threat to our whole economic program here. You were quite right when you called it economic counter-revolution, and we've got to put a stop to it! Whoever's responsible should be stood up against a wall, and we've got to kick up a fuss in every institution concerned. We've messed about long enough with all this White Guard crowd and now the time has come to give them a good thrashing! I must inform you, Comrade Badin, that both the resolutions adopted by the Economic Committee and our requests for supplies have been approved in full. Tomorrow work will begin again at the factory, and the Factory Committee will take the seals off the stores and make an inventory of all the stock. And I'll tell you something else, too, Comrade Badin: we demand categorically that a new management team for the factory be set up. If this isn't done, we'll take it all the way to Moscow!"

Then, pulling a bundle of papers from his tunic, Gleb flung them down on the table.

"There's all the documents for you! We've had the Bureau of Industry rammed down our throats for long enough, so now it's your turn to see what it's like!"

As he left the office, Gleb bumped into Dasha in the corridor—she must have been waiting for him. Though she stood calmly in front of him, there was a look of agony in her eyes. Then she said quietly but with a catch in her voice:

"You're back, Gleb, but you're too late ... Little Nurka's dead. She's buried now, and you weren't back in time ... She's gone, but you weren't here ... She's not here any more, my love!"

At first Gleb felt as though someone had dealt him a terrible blow in the chest, then everything went quiet and still, as if he had suddenly gone deaf. Then he turned very cold inside and his legs went weak as though he had just fallen from a great height. For a long time, unable to take his eyes off Dasha's face, he could not say a word.

"What? But that's impossible! Nurka? But it just isn't true! How on earth can it be?"

Dasha stood leaning against the wall and Gleb could see she was quietly weeping, choking back the tears that were streaming down her cheeks on to her trembling chin then falling on her breast. But she made no attempt to wipe them away and seemed to be smiling in helplessness and resignation. Close by, also leaning against the wall, stood Gromada, seized with a sudden fit of hoarse coughing.

CHAPTER XVII

A THRUST INTO THE FUTURE

1. "We Shall Go On!"

The reopening of the factory was scheduled for the fourth anniversary of the October Revolution. It was decided to hold a ceremonial session of the town Soviet in the "Comintern" Club so as to combine the anniversary with the celebration of this first great victory on the labor front.

Gleb divided his time between the factory and the management offices. He went rushing from one building to the other, and from one workshop to the next, surrounded by piles of equipment and clouds of dust, and simply could not resist snatching up tools and hurling himself into any task that presented itself. The repair of the furnaces and the crusher was almost finished now. The gravity roadway was already in operation, and several times a day the great wheels in the powerhouse would gaily swing their spokes at various inclinations and angles, while the heavy rollers rumbled along the tracks with a thunderous booming that sounded like the pounding of distant sledgehammers. Only the overhead cableway running down to the wharves was still silent as before, its trucks hanging motionless in the air and the safety net beneath them glowing dull red with rust. But the clock on the factory tower with its white face that was six feet across—the clock that had not worked for three years now—had begun to move its great hands once more, and at night, illumined by arc-lights, showed the time so clearly that it could be seen more than half a mile away.

In the coopers' shop, too, preparations for work were under way. The benches were being repaired, the rubbish and dirt cleared away, and truckloads of staves brought in from the stores. Covered in sweat and dust, Savchuk was shouting and swearing for all he was worth (coopers are always good at cursing anyway), and together with his comrades was continually knee-deep in bundles of hoops and staves and piles of rotten shavings.

Every day Gleb called in at the engine-room where he would immediately become almost a different person. The light in here was a deep blue, the color of the sky, and the windowpanes and tiles shone bright and clean. The nickel and brass fittings on the black diesels gleamed in the light, and the whole room was filled with the soft, melodious murmuring of cylinders, levers and pistons. This austere yet gentle music soothed Gleb's soul with a quietly masterful resonance that seemed to echo deep in his heart. For a long time he would gaze from behind the brass safety-barrier at the giant fly-wheels that seemed so light in their spinning flight, gaze at the broad, red-brown driving belts that streamed and quivered like live things as they sped over the drums, and as he gazed he would lose all sense of identity. Here, close to the wheels that were so elusive in their whirling movement, the silence was disturbing, and as the waves of hot, moist air flowed over his arms and face, his soul was filled with profound emotion. Fascinated, he was lost in contemplation of this winged, iron flight, and stood there devoid of all thought, oblivious of time and space.

Usually it was Brynza who roused him from his reverie. Taking Gleb by the arm, he would silently lead him over to the great glass window, where amid the haze of distant peaks the boundless expanse of sea and sky shone a light, fathomless blue.

But this was no longer the Brynza whom Gleb had met last spring. True, he wore the same greasy old cap that looked like a flat pancake pulled down over his nose, true, he had the same jutting, grimy cheekbones and chin, and the same brown mustache. But his eyes were unblinking and cold now, gleaming like the nickel and brass fittings on his diesels. He did not shout or lose his temper any more either, but listened carefully to the whispering and murmuring of his engines.

The conversation between them would often go like this:

"Well, Commander?"

"Well, my friend?"

"What's next, then?"

"We shall go on, Brynza!"

"And we shan't break our necks in the process?"

"What d'you mean? Have you gone crazy or something? We'll have to get you into the Party, old fellow, and make you see a bit further than these diesels of yours!"

"Now be off with you, Commander! Get out of here! What do I want with the Party if all that exists for me is my engines? The Party's one thing but these engines of mine are another. I don't know much about the Party but I do know plenty about engines, and if these engines are alive, they've just got to work. Anyway, I've no time for people who talk too much!"

Brynza suddenly stopped short, then stooping a little, plunged into the twilit gangway between the diesels and without looking back, disappeared from sight.

One day, while Gleb was inspecting the repair work going on inside the various buildings that echoed with the continual crashing of metal and the shouts of workmen, he ran into Kleist. The strange look in the engineer's eyes had surprised him more than once already, for they burned with immense fatigue and troubled enquiry. Kleist took Gleb gently by the arm and they went silently out on to the viaduct, then shoulder to shoulder they walked up to the platform high on the tower where they had stood on that memorable evening not long ago. To their right, far below, the diesels were murmuring, and the dynamos hidden in the factory's depths sang like bass strings. Up on the roofs workmen crawled to and fro, looking so small at this distance that they seemed no bigger than dolls. Sheet-iron clanged discordantly, reminding one of the harsh calling of jackdaws, and from time to time hammers resounded, echoing like the roll of distant drums. The windows of the factory buildings were no longer gaping black holes fringed with splintered woodwork and broken glass. Now they were richly iridescent, and, reflecting the azure sky, flashed like fiery mirrors in the brilliant light.

The autumn air was limpid and vibrant, still glowing with the sunlight of summer, while above the sparkling waters of the bay sea-gulls soared like wisps of white cloud. And everywhere—in the air, underfoot and in the rocks themselves—there was a muffled, subterranean rumbling that sounded like the boom of distant breakers. Somewhere nearby, a drill was shrieking as it bored its way through a rusty pulley.

"Well, Herman Hermanovich?" said Gleb. "It turns out that if a fool has the guts to say 'I'm strong,' then he can't be such a fool after all! We Communists don't dream so badly when all's said and done! On the anniversary of the October Revolution you and I are going to start all this enormous place moving again. You deserve to be congratulated as director of the factory! This evening your nomination for Party membership has been approved and a telegram has been sent to the district center."

Kleist smiled through the spasms flickering over his face, and maintaining his usual dignity, shook Gleb's hand hard.

"Gleb Ivanovich," he said, " I beg you to forget the grave crime I committed against both you and your friends. The awareness that I am responsible for the torture and death of others gives me no peace . . . and I feel as though I cannot bear this horror any more."

He looked at Gleb with eyes full of hope and could not stop his hands trembling.

Gleb's face suddenly went thin and drawn, and as it did so it took on a harsh, terrible look. But it only lasted a moment.

"Herman Hermanovich," he said, "what's past is over and done with. In those days people were at each other's throats all the time. But you must remember something else too: if you hadn't saved my wife, there'd be nothing left of her today. And now you're one of our workers, a man with a splendid mind and hands of gold. If it hadn't been for you, we couldn't have done a damn thing. Just look what we've managed to achieve with your guidance!"

"My dear Gleb Ivanovich, I'll devote all my knowledge and experience, all the rest of my days to our country! There's no other life for me now and no other task than to struggle for our future!"

Then, for the first time, Gleb saw Kleist's eyes fill with tears. He shook the old man's hand and laughed.

"Well then, Herman Hermanovich, let's be friends, shall we?"

"Yes, let's be friends, Gleb Ivanovich!"

Then, leaning on his stick, Kleist walked away with firm step.

2. Hearth and Home

Dasha did not sleep at home any more now. She had moved to Polya Mekhova's room in the House of Soviets after receiving a note from Polya saying she was ill and asking Dasha to come and stay with her for a while.

That evening Dasha had set off to town with a bundle under her arm, walking with the same quick step as when she went about the business of the Women's Section. She had only come home again for her bedding.

"Well, Gleb," she had said, "you'll have to look after yourself for a while now . . ."

Filled with astonishment, Gleb had quickly got up from his stool.

"Yet another surprise! You might at least tell me where you're off to now! Are you going on official business or what?"

"When you're in town, drop in to see Polya. She's asked me to go and stay with her for a while—she's feeling very bad."

"And how long will you be looking after her for?"

"I don't know, Gleb. Well, I must be off now! Anyway, don't expect me back soon, because I'm not sure how things'll work out. Perhaps it's better for both of us like this . . . "

Embarrassed, they fell silent, and unspoken words lay hidden beneath their trembling smiles.

"Well, I'm off," she said. "Good-bye for now . . . "

"All right, then. Go, if you must . . . "

He saw her as far as the gate, and when they reached it he took her by the hand. She looked up at him, offering him her lips, and he put his arms round her and kissed her. He sensed she was not simply leaving the house in the way she usually went off to work or left on official business. This time she was carrying away with her all their past life together. Perhaps she would never return, and perhaps here, in her last glance, there was both regret for the past and joy at the prospect of the new road ahead. He could no longer say to her in his old masterful way:

"I'll not allow you to leave the house! I'm sick and tired of it all! Are you my wife or just a stray woman I happen to be living with? I don't want to give up my rights. And why do you prefer Polya to me? Really, you know, you take too much on! Your freedom isn't boundless, you know, you've got responsibilities towards your husband as well! It's bad enough that you've sacrificed Nurka! Your past lies like a curse between us! Don't lead me into disgrace! You can find work at the factory too!"

But he had no authority to say such things any more, because Dasha had taken that authority away from him long ago. It was not simply his wife standing before him now, but a human being who was equal to him in strength and who had shouldered all the burden of the past few years. Dasha was not a wife now, but simply a woman who no longer felt any affection for her man. In a moment she would leave and perhaps never return, and in time she would become just as remote from him as all other women were. Well, all right, so be it! Until now they had lived together in the same room, slept separately at first and then in one bed—together. But not for a single moment had Gleb been able to forget the essential thing: the old Dasha was gone, and in her place there was a different, new woman who tomorrow might go away and never, ever return.

The last thread of their conjugal life—little Nurka—had snapped. Their daughter had died, and there had been times when their common sorrow had brought them very close to each other. But then days of great responsibility had followed—at the factory for him and in the Women's Section for her—and whenever they had met in the evening at home they had sensed that their dream of personal happiness was nothing but an illusion.

Then, as they parted that evening, Gleb had wanted to say something meaningful and serious to her, but he had not been able to do it. He had not known what to say, and yet it had to be said—without fail. If he did not say it now, he had realized, he would never say it at all. For her part, Dasha was able to listen to what he had to say, and she was sensitive and quick on the uptake too, but she no longer accepted him for what he was. There was too much of the old husband left in him—an inordinate need for affection, enormous jealousy, and a persistent desire to restrict her to house and home.

"Well, all right then, Dasha ... I really can't understand our life together now—there seems to be some kind of snag in it and I'm completely worn out by it all!"

She looked down at her feet and tried to crush with her heel a smooth little pebble that kept slipping away each time her shoe pressed on it.

"I don't know which of us is worn out the most, Gleb ... But I can never be the person I used to be. And I'm no good just as a woman for someone's bed. There's nothing worthwhile in our life now, so what on earth's the point of going on tormenting ourselves for nothing? Let's have a rest from each other and give ourselves time to think."

"Why don't you just say it straight out, Dasha! You don't love me any more and you've got no time for me now ... Life's much better for you without a husband!"

She shot him a glance from under her lowered brows and blushed deeply.

"Well, and what if it's true, Gleb?"

He realized his words had touched her on the raw.

"Then I'd say it's time to finish it! Nothing will make any difference now!"

"Yes, everything's got so confused and so much has been destroyed ... " she said. "Somehow our love will have to be arranged differently, but just how that can be done, I really don't know. We'll have to think about it, give it a little thought and reach an understanding. But one thing is important: we must respect one another and not impose any ties on each other. At the moment we're still bound to one another by fetters, Gleb. I still love you, darling, but you've got to burn yourself out, then everything'll be all right."

She heaved a sigh and smiling in embarrassment once more, said:

"Well, I'm off now ... "

Gleb turned pale and with a groan pressed his fist to his forehead. His heart was burning with anguish.

Dasha was walking away towards the gap in the wall with her bedding under her arm. Gleb waited. In a moment she would look back and wave to him. But she did not. He just caught a fleeting glimpse of her red kerchief and then it disappeared behind the wall.

For a long time now Dasha had been out every day and had not come home till late in the evening. She had often been away on official business too, and then she had been gone for days at a time. But now all of a sudden everything seemed desolate, everything was oppressive and strange—this house, the street with its little front gardens, and that wall which separated him from Dasha forever. What did he need his empty house for now? Or his front garden and the little yard six feet square? Dasha had spoken to him in an unfamiliar, almost alien tongue. Now she had gone, perhaps never to return. And Nurka was dead. Now there was no Dasha and no Nurka any more. Only he was left. What a hellish life! Like a rock-crusher it smashed everything to smithereens—day to day existence, destiny and even love itself . . .

Gleb walked away from the gate, but instead of going back into the house, turned off down the narrow street towards the factory.

4. Waves

On the high platform next to Gleb stood Zhidky, Secretary of the District Party Committee, Badin, Chairman of the Executive Committee, several members of the Factory Committee, and Kleist. But Gleb felt as if he were completely alone, because the countless heads of the crowd tossed like a choppy sea below him, a mass of people radiant with color like fields of sunflowers stretching away on every side as far as the eye could see.

At the foot of the tower, in a long line running to right and left, red flags burned like a chain of beacon fires. The tower was ablaze with scarlet too, for the banner of the Party Group hung down from the railing with its luxuriant tassels cascading towards the crowd, while on the other side of the platform, where Zhidky and Badin were standing, hung another banner belonging to the Building Workers' Union. Beneath the parapet, falling in a rich torrent of color, hung yet another banner, enormous and crimson, with huge white letters on it that shone like fresh spring flowers and read:

WE HAVE CONQUERED ON THE CIVIL WAR FRONT, AND WE SHALL CONQUER ON THE ECONOMIC FRONT TOO

The vast crowd was stirring and swaying, gay with its flashing red kerchiefs, pale and dark faces, and multicolored hats and caps, with banners flapping on every side like great red wings. They hid part of the crowd from view, but beyond them new columns rippled and eddied in the distance, while on the cliff top itself more people still could be seen. They swayed over the slopes and crest of the mountain, climbing higher and higher, while far away in the distance more banners and flags gleamed scarlet like a vast, bright field of poppies. Down below, an endless stream of people was still pouring out of the ravine. Far away a band was playing a march, while nearby all was immense movement and booming sound.

The autumn day was cool and clear, shining with amber-colored light. Distant things looked near, and the faintly hazy air was bracing. Gleb gazed at the mountains and the sky. High above him droned an invisible aeroplane, and silken threads of gossamer drifted in the azure expanse, shimmering like dusty mother-of-pearl.

He gripped the iron railing, unable to control the shaking in his legs. Where was this countless multitude of people coming from? There were already about twenty thousand gathered here, but still new columns kept marching on and on, without end. There were more of them over there, too, about a quarter of a mile away, streaming through the bushes and rocks on the brown hillside, merging with the general mass and climbing higher and higher up the slopes.

Not far away to the right, beyond the tower, a detachment of Red Army men was standing at ease. Once he had stood just like that too—was it really so very long ago? And now he was back here, a factory worker once more. The factory! What enormous energy had gone into it! And what a struggle it had been! But here it was—a great, handsome giant! Not long ago it had been nothing but a corpse, no better than a colossal scrapheap, a huge rats' nest, an enormous ruin. But now the diesels thundered and the cables hummed, the pulleys sang and the trucks went rattling by once more. Tomorrow the first rotary furnace would begin to roar as it turned on its giant spindle, and out of that awesome, huge chimney over there gray-white clouds of steam and dust would billow into the sky.

Surely it was all worthwhile, that this countless multitude should come here and rejoice in their common victory? What was he, Gleb, amid this boundless sea of people? No, it was not a sea but a living mountain, dead rocks miraculously resurrected into human beings. Ah, what immense power there was here! These were the people who with picks and spades had cut through the mountains to build the roadway. That had been back in the spring, on a sunny, clear day just like this. It was then, too, that the first blood had been shed. But now the town had wood for fuel and everything was ready for the factory to be reopened. How much blood there was flowing in this great army of toil! There was enough of it to last for many years to come! The new roadway was working now, the shipyards would reopen shortly, and the steam mills would soon begin to roar once more. As for later on, surely there were enough mountain streams to make the installation of turbines worthwhile?

Once there had been terrible days and nights of fighting during which Gleb had feared for his life and thought anxiously of Dasha. How long ago it all seemed now, how insignificant and remote! Dasha ... but she was no longer there. She was lost in the crowd and nowhere to be seen. All that was unimportant and almost non-existent now. And it seemed to Gleb that he no longer existed either, for there was only the rapturous crowd around him, and within his heart he could feel thousands of other hearts beating too. The working class, the new republic, the great new life they were all building ... By God, he thought, we may know what suffering means, but we certainly know how to rejoice too!

"Chumalov!"

Kleist was standing beside him, his face grave and pale, and his eyes very dry.

"Herman Hermanovich! My friend!"

Kleist turned and walked away to the other side of the platform, his shoulders shaking with emotion.

The banners and flags were waving and fluttering, the air was filled with singing and shouting, and the planks under Gleb's feet were shaking with the tumult. People were dancing, clapping and singing in chorus. You could see pebbles and shale crumbling away with the vibration and slipping down the rock faces.

Gleb could hardly keep still any longer. He wanted to leap from the high platform into the sea of heads below him, wanted to shout at the top of his voice till he went hoarse with the strain. What would it matter? How could anyone really bear this incomparable spectacle? This was what he had lived for all these months, and now it was right here, all gathered into a single mighty force.

Going up to Badin and Zhidky, he asked in an apparently casual tone:

"Well then, shall we begin?"

"Yes, Chumalov," answered Badin, "it's time to start. I'll speak for fifteen minutes, then you can take over. And give it all you've got! Then as soon as you've finished, give the signal!"

Down below on the main road, the dense columns with their banners were still marching towards them, while from behind them, amid the gray concrete walls of the factory, came the thunderous music of brass bands and the sound of stamping feet and singing.

It was a long time before the crowd settled down, a long time before the clamor of voices faded and died away like ripples spreading on water, but eventually the singing stopped and the bands fell silent.

Then Badin began to speak. He spoke in a cool, clear, formal way.

How can one possibly convey what he said? He said everything that was necessary for a festive occasion such as this. He spoke of the Soviet regime, the New Economic Policy, socialist reconstruction, Comrade Lenin, the Communist Party and the working class. Then he came to the main point which was this:

"And here is one of our victories on the economic front—a colossal, superhuman victory—the reopening of our factory, this giant of the Republic! You all know, comrades, how our struggle began. Last spring we struck the first blows with hammers and picks at these mountain strata. Those first blows brought us the gravity roadway and a supply of fuel. From then on, the men of the Builders' Union never laid their hammers down, and by striking blow after blow they forged the whole complex transport system of this enormous factory. Today, the fourth anniversary of the October Revolution, we celebrate a new victory on the proletarian labor front. During the struggle the working class has brought forth its own organizers and heroes. Can our toiling masses ever forget the name of that fighter, that Red Army soldier who has selflessly devoted his life to the great cause of the Revolution? Can they ever forget the name of Comrade Chumalov? Here, too, on the labor front, he is just the same selfless hero that he was on the battlefield ... "

Suddenly nothing more could be heard, for it was as if the mountains themselves had moved and come crashing down on Gleb. There was an immense roaring and howling, a vast rumbling and booming, as though a great earthquake were beginning. The tower swayed and shook as if it were made not of steel girders but of flimsy wire. Far below and somewhere further away still, the bands blared with thunderous, brassy sound.

Pale and stunned, Gleb was muttering strange words, gasping for breath, waving his arms and laughing uncontrollably.

"Speak, Chumalov! It's your turn now!"

But why speak, when everything was perfectly clear without words? There was no need to say a thing. What did his life matter when it was no more than a tiny drop in this vast ocean of lives? Why speak, when his own voice and tongue were superfluous here? He had no words to say, no life to live apart from this great mass of people.

Afterwards he could not really remember what he had said. His voice sounded indistinct and feeble, he thought, whereas in actual fact his words were amplified by the echo and resounded all over the mountainside.

"It is not greatly to our credit, comrades, when we struggle to build our proletarian economy, for we do it of our own free will, and moreover, it is a struggle that belongs only to us. In this we are all of one mind and spirit. So if I'm a hero, then you're all heroes, and if we don't work with all our might to achieve that heroism, then we deserve to go to hell! But I'll say one thing, comrades: we shall accomplish everything and create everything we need, because the Party and Comrade Lenin have called upon us to do so! And if only we had a few more technical directors like Engineer Kleist here, together with a few other things besides, then we'd work miracles that would astound the world! We staked everything on our own blood, and with that blood we set the whole world ablaze! Now, tempered by fire, we're staking everything on our labor, and our hands and brains are quivering not with exertion but with longing for fresh tasks. We're building socialism, comrades, building our own proletarian culture. So on to victory!"

Then Gleb seized a red flag and flourished it high above the crowd. Immediately the mountains echoed with thunderous noise and the air was caught up in a furious whirlwind as a metallic howl resounded far and wide. The sirens began to wail—one, two, three—all together yet discordantly, loud enough to burst one's eardrums with waves of deafening sound, and it was as though not the sirens but the mountains themselves were resounding, and together with them the crags and the people, the buildings and the chimneys of the factory itself.

1922–1924

Notes

1. *Cement* is set in and around the Black Sea port of Novorossiisk, in the Krasnodar Region of southern Russia. Founded in 1838, the town eventually became famous for its important cement industry, large works being established there in 1882, 1898 and 1912.
2. Colloquial name given during the Russian Civil War to men who hid in the forests so as to avoid service with the White armies.
3. The Russian noun *gromada* means mass or bulk.
4. Named after Lenin's wife, Nadezhda Konstantinovna Krupskaya (1869–1939).
5. A reference to the remark made by Lenin in 1917 that "every cook must be able to run the state."
6. Inaugurated in 1921, the New Economic Policy (or NEP as it came to be known) remained in force until 1928 and involved a partial restoration of a capitalist-type economy in the Soviet Union.
7. Anti-Bolshevik revolt by sailors and Red Army soldiers at the Kronstadt naval base on the Gulf of Finland in March, 1921. It was crushed with great severity by troops loyal to the regime.
8. Nestor Ivanovich Makhno (1889–1934), the leader of an anarchist and peasant anti-Bolshevik movement in the southern Ukraine during the Russian Civil War, from 1918 to 1921.

Alexander Fadeev
THE ROUT

Alexander Fadeev (1921).

Alexander Fadeev (1901–1956)

Alexander Alexandrovich Fadeev (who also used the pseudonym of Bulyga) was born on Christmas Eve, 1901 in the town of Kimry on the Volga east of Tver (now Kalinin). His father was a village teacher and his mother a doctor's assistant. After moving to Vilno (now Vilnius) in Lithuania and then to Ufa, 700 miles east of Moscow, in 1908 the family moved again, this time to the south Ussuri region in the Far East. In the village of Sarovka near Iman, close to the Manchurian border north of Vladivostok, the boy entered the local school. 1912 brought yet another move, to the village of Chuguevka further south in the same region. In the autumn of 1912 Fadeev entered the Commercial Academy in Vladivostok where he was to spend the next six years.

In the summer of 1918 the Japanese occupation of the Pacific Maritime Region began, and in September of that year Fadeev joined the Communist Party and became active in the Bolshevik underground movement in the Vladivostok area. In the spring of 1919, with the Red partisans under pressure from the White Cossacks and Japanese, Fadeev left the academy without taking his final examinations and joined the partisans in the Suchan region east of Vladivostok. After retreating with them deep into the *taiga* in the summer of 1919, he saw action at Khabarovsk and Spassk and was seriously wounded, before joining the Red Army and serving in eastern Siberia.

In the early spring of 1921, Fadeev travelled to Moscow as a delegate to the Tenth All-Russian Party Congress. Later that year he took part in the suppression of the Kronstadt naval rising in Petrograd and was seriously wounded again during the fighting. After spending several months in hospital, he was finally demobilized.

He then entered the Academy of Mines in Moscow, continuing his Party work at the same time. But he was soon obliged to give up his studies again, for in the spring of 1924 he was sent south to Krasnodar in the Kuban, and then in the autumn to Rostov-on-Don, where he engaged in Party and journalistic work, notably for the Rostov paper *The Soviet South (Sovetskii Yug)* and the literary journal *Lava* which he helped establish.

The summer of 1925 saw a visit to Nalchik in the Caucasus where he wrote *The Rout,* and in late 1926 he returned to Moscow where he continued his political activity for the Writers' Association and his editorial work. The years that followed brought much travelling, both at home and abroad. While 1932, for example, saw a visit to Ufa, the following year saw a journey back to the Far East and places connected with his youth. 1937 brought a visit to Spain during the Civil War there.

During the Second World War Fadeev devoted himself to the war effort, visiting the front for *Izvestiya, Pravda* and other papers, and writing reports and sketches about the fighting. In February, 1943 he visited the coal mining town of Krasnodon north of Rostov to gather material for his novel *The Young Guard* (1945). At the end of the war Fadeev resumed his political activities, visiting Britain in 1947, Iceland and Poland in 1949, and Czechoslovakia and Austria in 1951.

Throughout his career Fadeev was a highly influential literary theoretician, administrator and critic whose zeal was rewarded by two Orders of Lenin. He was one of the leaders of the Russian Association of Proletarian Writers (RAPP) active between 1926 and 1932, and he served on the editorial boards of several prestigious journals. In 1934 he was elected to the presidium of the newly-formed Union of Soviet Writers, and from 1946 to 1954 served as General Secretary of that organization. In addition, in 1939 he became a member of the Party's Central Committee and he served as a Deputy to the Supreme Soviet from 1946 until his death. He was also a leading member of the world peace movement, and on several occasions headed Soviet delegations at international peace congresses.

Unfortunately, Fadeev's last years were dogged by a serious kidney disorder, neuritis and alcoholism, and as his capacity for creative work decreased, he fell victim to bouts of depression. In May, 1956 he committed suicide at the early age of 54 and was buried in Moscow. Though the official reason given for his death was alcoholism, he may well have been troubled by his conscience about his role as a powerful functionary during the Stalin years.

***

Fadeev's first published work was the tale *Against the Current* (which appeared in the Moscow journal *The Young Guard (Molodaya gvardiya)* in 1923. (In 1934 he revised the piece, changing its title to *The Birth of the Amgunsky Regiment.*) The story is based on an episode during the transfer of partisan units to regular Red Army forces in the spring of 1920, during the Japanese intervention in the Far East. It was followed by *The Flood* (1924), set in a village in the *taiga,* a tale which reflects the social contrasts brought out by the revolutionary movement in the south Ussuri region between the February and October revolutions of 1917.

Fadeev conceived *The Rout,* his third published piece, in 1921, but did not begin systematic work on it until 1925 while he was in Rostov-on-Don. Initially entitled *The Enemies,* it was completed in 1926, and the following year was issued as a separate edition in Leningrad, though excerpts of it had appeared in several journals from 1925. The novel draws on the author's experiences with the partisans in the south Ussuri region from July to September, 1919, when the detachment with which he was serving was forced to retreat from the Suchan valley deep into the *taiga.* Levinson is based on a real partisan commander, Pevsner, with whom Fadeev served for a year. Now a Soviet classic, the novel was first filmed in 1931 and again in 1958.

Fadeev began writing his second novel, *The Last of the Udege,* while he was working on *The Rout.* Sadly, this first attempt at a broad treatment of the Civil War in the Far East—its title refers to a strange and virtually extinct native tribe in the region—was to remain unfinished. Though four parts of it were published in journals between 1929 and 1940, just six chapters of its fifth and final part appeared between 1940 and 1956. While 1939 saw the appearance of Fadeev's tale *Earthquake* and 1944 that of his war sketches *Leningrad during the Siege,* the following year brought the publication in serial form of his third novel, *The Young Guard,* which appeared in a separate edition in 1946 (bringing Fadeev a State Prize) and in a revised edition in 1951. Based on fact, the novel reflects the heroic exploits of Young Communist underground workers in the small Donbass town of Krasnodon during the German occupation in World War II.

From 1951 until his death Fadeev worked on a fourth novel, *Black Metallurgy,* which was also to remain unfinished as only eight chapters of it were completed. Even more ambitious than *The Last of the Udege,* this last work was intended to show the Soviet people in peacetime, reflecting the triumphs of socialist labor and the process of growing Communist awareness in Soviet society.

In addition to his fiction, Fadeev in his capacity as a leading literary functionary produced a large number of critical and publicistic works. Notable among them are his manifesto piece *The Highway of Proletarian Literature* (1928), the articles and speeches contained in the volume

Literature and Life (1939), and the collection of theoretical and critical articles on literature and art, *After Thirty Years,* which appeared in 1957 shortly after his death.

THE ROUT

1. Morozka

His battered Japanese sabre clattering on the steps as he went, Levinson walked down into the yard. The sweet smell of buckwheat came drifting from the fields as the hot July sun floated overhead in a pink-white haze.

Doing his best to keep a noisy flock of guinea-fowl at bay with his whip, Morozka the orderly was spreading out some oats on a tarpaulin to dry.

"Take this to Shaldiba's detachment," said Levinson, holding out a parcel, "and tell him . . . No, there's no need—it's all written down."

Morozka turned away and flicked his whip in annoyance. He didn't feel like going to Shaldiba's detachment at all. He was sick of these tedious official journeys and these parcels that nobody needed, but most of all he was tired of seeing that strange look in Levinson's eyes. Like wide, deep pools, they took him in from head to foot and detected many things about him of which he himself was unaware.

"Well, what are you waiting for?" asked Levinson crossly.

Morozka went to the stable and led out his horse. The long-maned little stallion twitched its ears suspiciously. It was a strong, shaggy trotter that looked rather like its master—it had the same clear, greenish-brown eyes and bow-legged, stocky build, and the same innocent yet roguish look about it.

"Mishka! Oh, you devil!" growled Morozka affectionately as he tightened the saddle-girth. "Mishka! You goddam son of a bitch!"

Then away he went, riding out of the yard at a trot.

The overgrown country road ran along the river bank. Beyond the river stretched fields of buckwheat and corn flooded with brilliant light, and in the distance the dark blue peaks of the Sikhote-Alin[1] range shimmered in the haze.

Morozka belonged to a family who had been miners for two generations now. His grandfather—a man neither blessed by God nor favored by his fellowmen—had tilled the fields in Suchan,[2] but his father had given up ploughing the earth to mine coal instead.

Morozka had been born in a dark wooden hut near Pit Number Two, just as the hoarse whistle was summoning the morning shift to work.

At the age of twelve he had learned to get up when the factory whistle sounded, to push coal trucks down the track, to swear obscenely and to drink vodka, for there were about as many bars at the Suchan mine as there were headframes above the shafts.

About two hundred yards from the mine the valley narrowed and came to an end, and then the volcanic hills began. From their slopes great fir trees covered with moss looked sternly down on the mining settlement, and on misty mornings thick with hoar-frost the Manchurian deer from the *taiga*[3] would try to drown the factory whistles with their calls. Through the dark blue clefts in the mountain ridges and over the steep passes, day in, day out loaded trucks would go crawling down the colliery tracks towards Kangauz[4] station. Up on the mountain ridges the drums of the winding gear that were black with grease and quivered with the strain constantly wound and unwound their heavy cables. Down at the foot of the mountains where stone buildings huddled incongruously among the fragrant pines, men toiled all day long they knew not why, while little steam locomotives whistled discordantly and the electric hoists hummed on and on.

In that life Morozka had not sought new paths but had been content to follow the well-tried, old ones. When the time came, he had bought himself a pair of flared top-boots made of box-calf and a sateen shirt, and on high days and holidays had started going down to the village in the valley. There, like all the other young miners, he would play the accordion, fight with lads from the village, sing bawdy songs and chase the local girls.

When the time came, he had gone off to the front and been put in the cavalry. There he had learned to look down as all cavalrymen do on the "footslogging rabble" as the infantry was called. He had been wounded six times, shell-shocked twice, and had finally been discharged before the Revolution.

Returning home, he had drunk his head off for a couple of weeks then married a kind-hearted but rather loose woman who was a coaltruck pusher in Pit Number One. Everything Morozka did he did without thinking, for life seemed just as simple and plain to him as a little round melon from the Suchan fields.

Perhaps it was just on impulse, too, that in 1918, taking his wife with him, he had set off to join the Reds and help defend the Soviets.[5]

Be that as it may, from then on there was no going back to the pit for him. The Soviets did not last long and the new authorities had little time for fellows like Morozka.

The orderly came riding into the Sviyagino[6] military sector. Beyond a hill covered with bright green hazelnut trees lay the village of Krilovka[7] where Shaldiba's detachment was quartered.

Suddenly a strange crackling sound crashed and rolled away on the other side of the hill. Then came a second, and a third... It sounded as though a wild beast had broken loose from its chain and was tearing furiously through the thorny scrub.

"D'you hear that? It's gunfire!" muttered Morozka excitedly, drawing himself up in the saddle.

"Forward—gallop!" he cried, his voice agitated and urgent.

Thrusting his toes into the stirrups in his usual way, he unfastened his holster with trembling fingers as Mishka raced through the bushes to the top of the hill.

To the right, moving past Krilovka in perfect straight lines as though they were on parade, ran dozens of identical little figures with yellow and green bands on their caps. To the left, disordered groups of men were racing in panic through the golden-eared barley, firing as they ran. The infuriated Shaldiba—Morozka recognized him by his pointed badger-skin cap and his black horse—was lashing out right and left with his whip but still could not halt his fleeing men. Morozka could even see some of them furtively tearing off their red arm-bands.

"The swine! What the hell are they doing?" he muttered, growing more and more excited because of all the firing.

In the last group of men fleeing in panic was a lean young fellow in a short civilian jacket, his head bandaged in a white kerchief. He was dragging his rifle awkwardly along the ground and limping as he went. The group of men was thinning rapidly all the time, and then the young fellow in the kerchief fell too. He was not killed, though, but tried to get up several times and crawl after the others, stretching out his arm and shouting something Morozka could not hear.

But his companions were running faster now, and without looking back, were leaving him behind.

"The swine! What the hell are they doing?" exclaimed Morozka again, clutching his carbine with clammy fingers.

A few seconds later, leaning forward in the saddle like a bird in flight, he was racing across the field. Buzzing like fiery gadflies, bullets whined angrily over his head, while the ears of barley went hissing by under the horse's flying hoofs.

"It hurts! Oh, it hurts!" groaned the wounded man as Morozka flung him across the saddle. The young fellow's face was pale, clean and immature-looking, even though it was smeared with blood in places.

"Shut up, you whining devil!" hissed Morozka.

A few minutes later, letting go of the reins and supporting his passenger with both arms, he was galloping back round the hill towards the hamlet where Levinson's detachment was quartered.

2. Mechik

To tell the truth, Morozka had not liked the look of the fellow he had saved from the very start.

He did not care much for nice, clean-looking people—in his experience they were all unreliable good-for-nothings who could not be trusted. Besides, right from the outset the wounded boy had shown precious little courage.

"Ninny!" Morozka muttered scornfully through clenched teeth as the unconscious fellow was laid on a bed in one of the village huts. "Just a scratch and he's gone all to pieces!"

"Stop talking nonsense!" cut in Levinson sternly. "Baklanov! Get this lad to the infirmary as soon as it's dark!"

The boy's wounds were dressed. In the side pocket of his jacket they found a little money, a few papers (his name was Pavel Mechik), a bundle of letters and a photograph of a young girl.

Two dozen sullen men, their unshaven faces burnt dark by the sun, took turns in examining the girl's gentle face framed by its fair curls, and then amid general embarrassment the photograph was put back in its place. But the wounded boy was still unconscious, lying on the bed with his arms stretched out lifelessly on the blanket and his lips immobile and bloodless.

Mechik did not feel them carrying him in a jolting cart out of the village in the sultry, dove-gray evening, and only came round when they laid him on a stretcher at the infirmary. His first sensation of the stretcher's smooth, swaying movement merged with the equally vague awareness of the starry sky floating above his head. Then he was enveloped by impenetrable, shaggy darkness, and caught the strong, fresh smell of pine needles and rotting leaves, a smell so pungent that it was almost as if the whole forest had been steeped in alcohol.

Then he was filled with silent gratitude towards the men who were carrying him so gently and with such care. Trying to speak, he began to move his lips, but before he could say a word, he lost consciousness once more.

By the time he came round again it was daylight, and a magnificent lazy sun was shimmering in the spreading branches of a pine tree above his head. He was lying on a camp-bed in the shade. To his right stood a tall, lean, very upright man in a gray hospital smock, while to his left, bending over his bed, was the gentle figure of a woman, her heavy, chestnut-gold plaits hanging down over her shoulder.

The first thing that struck him as he looked at her calm face with its big, misty eyes, her warm, brown hands and her fluffy plaits, was a sense of all-embracing kindness and tenderness.

"Where am I?" Mechik asked softly.

The tall man stretched out a hard, bony hand and felt his pulse.

"That's all right," he said calmly. "Varya, get everything ready for the dressing and call Kharchenko . . ."

It was very painful when the rough gauze was pushed into wounds that had already begun to dry, but all the while Mechik could feel the gentle touch of the woman's hands and so he did not cry out.

"That's fine," said the tall man as he finished the dressing. "There's three good holes but only a scratch on the head. They'll all be healed in a month or my name's not Stashinsky."

Then they washed Mechik, and when it was done he raised himself on his elbow and looked around.

A few people were bustling about near a big log hut not far away. A wisp of bluish smoke rose from its chimney, and on its roof the resin was rising in the hot sun. An enormous woodpecker with a black beak was tapping busily away on a tree trunk at the edge of the forest. Wearing a hospital smock, a little old man with a blond beard stood quietly leaning on a stick and gazing about him in a good-natured way.

Over the old man, over the log hut and over Mechik himself hung the heavy stillness of the *taiga,* its air steeped in the heady smell of resin.

***

About three weeks earlier, on his way out of town with an official authorization hidden in his boot and a revolver in his pocket, Mechik had only had the vaguest idea of what awaited him. Cheerfully whistling a merry little tune as he walked along, he felt the blood coursing vigorously in his veins and longed for swift movement and struggle.

The men stationed out in the hills—he only knew of them from the newspapers—sprang to life before his eyes, wreathed in the smoke of gunpowder and surrounded by heroic exploits. He was filled with curiosity and dreams of bold deeds, as well as with agonizingly sweet memories of the fair-haired girl.

As he came into Krilovka several men leapt from the bushes with their Berdan[8] rifles pointed at him.

"Who are you?" asked a hatchet-faced fellow in a sailor's cap.

"I'm . . . I've been sent from town . . ."

"Where are your papers?"

Mechik had been obliged to take his boot off so as to get his authorization out of it.

Later that day he had begun to enjoy full rights as an equal member of the detachment.

But the men around him proved to be not in the least like those created by his vivid imagination. They were much more lice-ridden and dirty, much coarser and tougher than he had expected. They would steal cartridges from each other, swear obscenely over every trifle, and fight till the blood flowed for a scrap of bacon fat. They scoffed at Mechik for the slightest reason—because of his correct manner of speech and his civilian jacket, because he did not know how to clean his rifle properly, and even because he ate less than a pound of bread at dinner time.

And yet, despite all this, these men were real, live people, not characters from books.

The infirmary stood on a promontory at the confluence of two streams. At the edge of the forest where the woodpecker was tapping away, black Manchurian maples tinged with purple rustled in the breeze, while below, at the foot of the slope, the streams clad in silvery ferns sang their tireless song. There was only a handful of sick and wounded, and only two seriously injured men—a partisan from Suchan called Frolov who had been shot in the stomach, and Mechik himself.

Each morning, when the two men were carried out of the stuffy hut, Pika, the quiet, little old man with the fair beard, would come up to where Mechik lay. Mechik loved to listen to him talk—he liked the old man's soft, sing-song voice and the slow gestures that seemed to rise from his very soul.

But he liked it even more when the nurse came to see him. She washed and sewed for the whole infirmary, and one sensed in her a vast love for her fellow human beings. To Mechik she showed particular tenderness and care, but as his condition gradually improved, he began to see her in a more physical light. She was rather round-shouldered and pale, and her hands were unusually large for a woman, but she walked with a curiously vigorous gait and her voice always seemed full of promise.

Whenever she came and sat down on the bed beside him, Mechik found it hard to lie still, though he would never have confessed as much to the girl with fair curls.

"She's loose, that Varya," said Pika one day. "While her husband Morozka's away with the detachment, she spends her time carrying on with the men back here..."

"But why's she... like that?" Mechik asked, trying to hide his embarrassment.

"God knows! She's just so affectionate she can't say no, that's all!"

From then on Mechik began to watch Varya more closely. It was quite true—she did carry on a lot with the men, and in fact made up to anyone who was not a proper invalid. After all, though, she was the only woman in the infirmary.

One morning, after she had dressed Mechik's wounds, she lingered a moment and began to tidy his bed.

"Sit with me for a while..." he said, blushing.

When she had finished the bed, she sat down beside him.

From under his pillow Mechik took out a small bundle wrapped in newspaper. The fair-haired girl looked up at him from the faded photograph, but she did not seem as attractive as before. Her expression was one of affected gaiety, and though Mechik was afraid to admit it, he now found it rather odd that he had once thought so much of her. Then, without knowing why or even whether it was the right thing to do, he handed the photograph to the nurse.

She examined it closely to begin with, then held it out at arm's length. Then she suddenly gave a cry and dropping the picture, leapt up from the bed and quickly looked round.

"That's a pretty tart!" called a mocking voice from behind a maple tree.

Glancing sideways, Mechik saw a strangely familiar face with an unruly lock of chestnut hair showing under a peaked cap.

Varya quickly recovered herself and burst out laughing.

"Well, you certainly gave me a fright all right!" she said in a singsong, coy voice. "Where on earth did you spring from, you hairy devil?" Then, turning to Mechik, she added: "This is Morozka, my husband. He's always up to mischief!"

"Oh, we've already met... just for a while," said the orderly, emphasizing the last word with a sarcastic grin.

Mechik lay there as though stunned, feeling so ashamed and hurt that he could not speak. Varya had already forgotten about the photograph, and as she talked to Morozka, she trod on it, but Mechik felt too ashamed even to ask her to pick it up.

When they had gone off into the forest, though, he managed to retrieve it himself, clenching his teeth with the pain in his legs as he did so. Then he tore it to shreds.

3. Sixth Sense

Morozka and Varya did not come back from the forest until after midday. They seemed sluggish and tired, and tried not to look at each other.

Riding past Mechik on his way out of the clearing, Morozka glanced at him and gave a sly grin.

Later on, as he was riding along the mountain slopes in the green shade of the ravines, Morozka's thoughts kept returning to Mechik. "Why the hell do people like him join up with us anyway?" he wondered with annoyance. "When we first started, there was nobody, but now we've got going, they're all wanting to join . . ."

So preoccupied was he with these unusually serious thoughts that he did not notice that he had ridden out into the valley. There, amid sweet-smelling couch-grass and wild clover, the scythes were singing their customary song and the country folk were in the middle of another hard day's work. The men had beards as curly as the clover itself, and their long smocks that reached to their knees were soaked with sweat. On and on they walked through the field with measured step, bending their legs a little as they moved, and the fragrant swaths of limp grass fell rustling at their feet as they went.

Then, catching sight of the armed horseman, they paused in their work, and shading their eyes with calloused hands, watched him slowly pass.

Beyond a bend in the river, near the watermelon fields that belonged to the village chairman Khoma Ryabets, Morozka reined in his horse. The fields had a neglected, desolate look, for when the owner is busy with village affairs, his land becomes choked with weeds, his grandfather's hut falls into disrepair, the plump melons barely ripen in the bitter wormwood, and the scarecrow watching over the fields begins to look like a dying bird.

In Ryabets' little garden, Levinson had spread out a tattered map on a small round table in the shade, and was busy questioning a scout who had just returned.

Dressed in a peasant's quilted jacket and wearing bast shoes, the man had made his way far behind the Japanese lines. His round, sunburnt face was still glowing with excitement at all the danger he had managed to avoid.

According to what he said, the Japanese had set up headquarters at Yakovlevka.[9] Two enemy companies had been transferred from Spassk-Primorsk[10] to Sandagou,[11] he went on, but the Sviyagino branch-line was now free of enemy troops, so he had been able to travel by train as far as Shabanovsky Springs,[12] accompanied by two armed men from Shaldiba's detachment.

"But where's Shaldiba retreated to?" asked Levinson.

"To the Korean farms," replied the scout. "His fellows got a sound thrashing at Krilovka," he went on briskly, sniffing as he did so. "Now half his men have gone back to their villages, and Shaldiba himself's all set to winter on a farm and is stuffing himself with *chumiza*.[13] They say he's drinking a lot too—gone right off his head, he has!"

Levinson compared this new information with what he had been told the day before by a bootlegger from Daubikhe[14] called Stirksha, as well as with news sent from town. There was something wrong. He had a peculiar nose for that sort of thing—a kind of sixth sense, like a bat has when it is flying in the dark.

There was something wrong, too, about the cooperative chairman who had left for Spasskoe[15] two weeks earlier and had still not returned, as well as about the handful of Sandagou peasants in the detachment who had suddenly begun to feel homesick and had deserted two days ago. Finally, there was something odd about the lame smuggler Li-Fu who had been heading for Uborka[16] along with the detachment but then had suddenly turned off, no one knew why, and made for the upper reaches of the Fudzin River.[17]

Levinson set about questioning the scout again, studying the map carefully all the time. He was unusually persistent and dogged, like an old wolf of the *taiga* which may have lost a lot of teeth but still masterfully leads the pack with the unsurpassed wisdom it has inherited from its forefathers.

"Well, but didn't you ... smell anything peculiar in the air?" he asked.

The scout stared at him, not understanding what he meant.

"No, I didn't ... " he replied guiltily. "What does he think I am—a dog or something?" he thought to himself, feeling both bewildered and offended.

"All right then, off you go!" said Levinson, giving the whole thing up as a bad job and narrowing his blue eyes mockingly as he watched the scout get up and leave.

Left alone now, he walked about the garden, deep in thought. Pausing by an apple tree, he spent a long time watching a sand-colored beetle with a large head burrowing in the bark, and then in some mysterious way came to the conclusion that unless something were done soon, the detachment would be destroyed by the Japanese before very long.

At the garden gate he bumped into Ryabets and his own lieutenant, Baklanov, a stocky young fellow of about nineteen in a khaki tunic with a Colt in his belt that was never idle for long.

"Listen, my friend," said Levinson, turning to Ryabets, "there's something I must talk to you about ... in confidence."

He took the village chairman by the arm and, leading him aside, asked him to collect during the next two days enough bread to make about ten *poods*[18] of rusks.

"But make sure nobody knows what they're for," he added.

Then, left alone with Baklanov, Levinson ordered him to increase the ration of oats for the horses from the following day:

"Tell the quartermaster to give them a full measure each," he said.

4. Alone

Morozka's arrival had disturbed the peace of mind that Mechik owed to the untroubled way of life in the infirmary.

"Why did he look at me so scornfully?" he wondered when the orderly had ridden off. "It's true he did get me out of a tight corner, but does that give him the right to make fun of me? The main thing is that they're all the same, the whole lot of them ... " He looked at his delicate, thin fingers, then at his legs in their splints under the blanket, and the old sense of injury he had tried to suppress welled up in him once more, filling his heart with pain.

From the moment the hatchet-faced fellow had challenged him so roughly on the road into Krilovka, everyone had treated him not with kind offers of help but with gibes and sneers, and no one had made any effort to understand why he felt hurt. Even in the infirmary, where the stillness of the forest breathed peace and love, people treated him kindly only out of a sense of duty. But the most painful thing of all was to feel so isolated after his blood—his very own blood—had been spilt in that field of barley.

Suddenly all his experiences of the past month overwhelmed him, and with trembling lips he tried to hold back the tears, but they welled up all the same and began to stream thick and fast down his face. Then he covered his head with the blanket, and no longer attempting to restrain himself, wept softly, trying not to shudder or sob in case anyone noticed.

For a long time he wept inconsolably, his thoughts as bitter as his tears. Then after a while he grew calmer and lay motionless, his head still under the blanket. Varya came up to him several times—he recognized her firm gait—but after pausing hesitantly by his bed, she went away again.

When it grew dark, two people came up to where he lay—it was Varya and someone else. Carefully lifting him on the camp-bed, they carried him into the hut. It was hot and damp inside.

Varya stood beside him for a few moments, then cautiously lifting the blanket from his head, asked:

"What's wrong, Pavel, dear? D'you feel bad?"

It was the first time she had called him by his Christian name.

He could not make out her face in the gloom but he was aware of her presence all the same, just as he sensed, too, that they were now alone in the hut.

"Yes, I do feel bad . . . " he replied in a low voice.

"Do your legs hurt?"

"No, it's not that . . ."

Then she quickly bent down, and pressing her large, soft breasts against him, kissed him on the lips.

6. Levinson

Levinson's detachment had been resting for over a month now and during that time it had accumulated a considerable amount of equipment and supplies, among them stud horses, baggage carts and large field-kitchen cauldrons, around which garrulous, ragged deserters from other detachments would huddle. The men had grown very lazy and slept more than they needed to, sometimes even when they were on guard. And yet, despite the disturbing news he had received, Levinson was reluctant to set all this unwieldy mass of men in motion. He was afraid to act too hastily, and moreover fresh information kept first confirming then making light of his misgivings. On more than one occasion, though, he accused himself of being excessively cautious, especially when news came that the Japanese had evacuated Krilovka and his scouts then failed to contact any enemy forces for many miles around.

No one apart from Stashinsky, though, knew of Levinson's hesitation. What was more, no one in the detachment was aware that he was even capable of hesitating at all, as he never confided his thoughts or feelings to anyone, and was always ready with a short, sharp "yes" or "no" in reply to questions. Consequently, everyone believed him a man of an exemplary, special kind. All the partisans, and especially young Baklanov who did his best to emulate his commander in every way, even to the extent of imitating his outward appearance, thought roughly like this: "Of course I've got a lot of faults and many weaknesses too. There's a lot I don't understand and many ways in which I can't control myself. I'm fond of things like sweet melons, bread and milk, and shiny boots to win the hearts of village girls at a dance, but as for Levinson—now he's a different kettle of fish altogether! You couldn't ever suspect *him* of anything like that! He understands everything and always does things the right way. He doesn't chase the girls like Baklanov and he doesn't go stealing melons like Morozka either. He only ever thinks of one thing—the business at hand. So you just can't help trusting and obeying a special man like that . . ."

From the day Levinson had been chosen as commander, nobody had been able to imagine him in any other capacity, and it seemed to them all that the most distinctive thing about him was precisely the fact that he was in command of their detachment. If he had told them how as a child he used to help his father sell secondhand furniture, how his father had dreamed all his life of making a fortune but had played the violin badly and been afraid of mice—they would all have considered it a rather bad joke. But Levinson never spoke of such things. It was not that he was secretive, but that he realized they all regarded him as a "special kind" of man. He knew, too, that he possessed many of the weaknesses common to others, but he believed that one could only be a successful leader if one made others aware of their weaknesses while suppressing and concealing one's own. Equally, he never attempted to make fun of young Baklanov for imitating him. At Baklanov's age he, too, had imitated his superiors, because they had seemed just as exemplary to him as he now did to Baklanov. Later on, he had realized that his teachers were not as he had imagined, but he had felt grateful to them nevertheless. After all, Baklanov not only imitated the way he, Levinson, behaved but also drew on his whole experience of life—how he worked, fought and acted in general. Levinson knew that the mannerisms would disappear with the years, while his personal experience, supplemented by Baklanov's own experience, would be handed down to new Levinsons and Baklanovs, and this process, he felt, was tremendously important and necessary.

At about twelve one rainy night in early August a dispatch rider arrived at the detachment. He had been sent by old Sukhovei-Kovtun, the partisan forces' chief-of-staff. Kovtun wrote that the Japanese had attacked Anuchino[19] where the main partisan forces were concentrated, and that there had been a fierce battle near Izvestkovaya.[20] Hundreds of partisans had been tortured to death, he said, and he himself, suffering from nine bullet wounds, was now hiding out in a winter hunting-shelter and had not got very long to live . . .

News of the defeat had already begun to spread through the valley with ominous speed, but the dispatch rider was the first to bring it to Levinson's detachment. Every man in the relay before him had sensed that this was the most terrible message he had carried since the beginning of the partisans' campaign. The riders' alarm even communicated itself to their horses, and baring their teeth, the shaggy beasts galloped furiously from one village to the next, racing down the sodden country roads, their hoofs flinging up showers of mud as they went.

Levinson received the relay message at about twelve-thirty in the morning, and half an hour later a mounted platoon commanded by the shepherd Metelitsa rode off past Krilovka and quickly fanned out along the remote tracks that climbed the Sikhote-Alin range, carrying the alarming news to detachments in the Sviyagino military sector.

For the next four days Levinson gathered information from the various scattered detachments, and all the while his mind worked in an expectant, groping way, almost as if he were listening for something. But he continued to speak to those around him just as calmly as usual, narrowing his light blue eyes as mockingly as ever. His whole manner was designed to give the impression that he understood perfectly well why all these events had occurred and where they were leading, that there was nothing in the least unusual or alarming about them, and that a long time ago he had worked out a precise, foolproof plan to save the detachment. In actual fact, though, not only had he no such plan at all, but in general he felt extremely bewildered, like a schoolboy who has suddenly been told to solve a problem with a great many unknown factors in it. What was more, he was still waiting for news from town. One of his men, Kanunnikov, had set off for town a week before the alarming relay message had reached them, but he had still not returned.

Kanunnikov finally appeared five days later, tired and hungry, his face covered with stubble.

"There's been a roundup in town and Kreiselman's in prison . . . " he said, mysteriously producing two letters from his sleeve with the adroitness of a card sharper. "The Japanese have landed in Vladimiro-Aleksandrovskoe[21] and in Olga[22] too . . . The whole of Suchan's been routed and things are really in a bad way!"

Levinson glanced at the two envelopes, and putting one of them in his pocket, began to open the other. It confirmed what Kanunnikov had just said. Behind the official language that was full of apparent cheerfulness, the bitter taste of defeat was only too clear.

"Who wrote this?" asked Levinson. "Was it Sedykh?"

Kanunnikov nodded.

"You can see that," Levinson went on, "because he always divides everything up into sections . . . " Then mockingly he made a mark with his fingernail under the words 'Section IV: Urgent tasks.'

The section consisted of five paragraphs, four of which seemed impracticable to Levinson. The fifth ran:

"The most important thing required of the partisan leadership now—and it must be achieved at all costs—is the preservation of small but effective and well-disciplined fighting units, around which later . . ."

"Call Baklanov and the quartermaster," said Levinson quickly.

Without reading any further to find out exactly what would happen to the fighting units later, Levinson put the letter in his map case. Then, in a mechanical way, he fingered the second letter, and glancing at the envelope, realized it was from his wife. "That can wait," he thought, and put it away again.

When the quartermaster and Baklanov appeared, Levinson already knew what he and the men under him must do: they must do absolutely everything to preserve the detachment as a fighting unit.

"We're going to have to pull out of here soon," he said. "Is everything in order? You must be ready at a moment's notice! Is that clear? Baklanov, see to it . . ."

Towards evening Levinson called a meeting of the detachment's platoon commanders.

The reactions to his report were varied. One of the commanders, Dubov, sat through the whole meeting in silence, occasionally tugging at his thick, drooping mustache. It was clear he would support Levinson in whatever he proposed. But particularly strong opposition to Levinson's proposal to leave came from Kubrak, commander of the second platoon. Nobody supported him, though—he was a native of Krilovka, and everyone knew that he was more interested in the fields of his village than in the detachment's affairs.

Then Metelitsa put forward a plan for retreat, and as he spoke it became clear that this passionate man was neither afraid of long distances nor slow on the uptake in military matters.

However, taking advantage of a heated discussion in which everyone thought himself cleverer than the others and refused to listen to them, Levinson substituted his own plan—which was much simpler and safer—for Metelitsa's. But he did it so unobtrusively and skillfully that his new proposal was put to the vote as though it had come from Metelitsa himself, and it was accepted unanimously.

In the letters which Levinson sent in reply—one to town and the other to Stashinsky—he informed them that in a few days' time he would transfer the detachment to the village of Shibishi,[23] near the upper reaches of the Irokhedza River.[24] But he ordered the infirmary staff to stay where they were and await further orders.

It was late at night when he finished work, and by then the paraffin in the lamp was running low. A smell of dampness and mold came drifting in through the open window, and he could hear the cockroaches rustling behind the stove and Ryabets snoring in the next hut. Then he remembered his wife's letter, and after pouring some more paraffin into the lamp, began to read it. There was nothing new in what she wrote, nothing to gladden his heart. Things were just the same—she still could not get a job and had been forced to sell everything she possibly could. She was only managing to survive thanks to the workers' Red Cross, and the children were all suffering from anemia and scurvy. And yet the whole letter was filled with boundless concern for him, her husband. Fingering his beard thoughtfully, Levinson began to write a reply. At first he was reluctant to reawaken the memories connected with that part of his life, but little by little he gave in to his feelings and the expression on his face gradually softened. He covered two sheets of paper in his small, barely legible hand, and what he wrote contained many words of a kind no one would ever have believed were familiar to him.

Then, stretching his arms and legs, he went out into the yard. After standing there for a little while, he led his stallion out of the stable, and saddling it, rode off to check the sentry posts.

Keeping close to the bushes, he made his way quietly towards the cattle pen.

"Who goes there?" challenged the sentry sternly, rattling his rifle bolt.

"Friend..."

"Is that you, Levinson? What the hell are you doing, wandering about at this time of night?"

"Have you seen any patrols?"

"Yes, one of them rode out about a quarter of an hour ago."

"All quiet?"

"Yes—so far ... Got a smoke?"

Levinson poured some of his Manchurian tobacco into the man's hand, and then, fording the river, rode out into the fields.

The pale moon shone down, and the shadowy clumps of bushes, their leaves heavy with dew, rose up out of the gloom. The river flowed loudly over the shallows, the sound of each ripple distinct on the stones in the water. Then, out on a hillock in front of him, the dim silhouettes of four horsemen began to bob up and down against the sky. Levinson turned off into the bushes and stopped. He could hear men's voices not far away. Then he recognized two of them—they were his scouts.

"Now then," he called, "hang on a minute!" and he rode out on to the road. The scouts' horses snorted and shied.

"You certainly gave us a fright!" said the leading rider in a cheery voice that barely concealed a note of alarm. "Whoa! You bastard!"

"Who's that you've got with you?" asked Levinson, riding right up to them.

"It's Osokin's patrol. The Japanese are in Maryanovka ..."

"Maryanovka?" said Levinson with a start. "But where's Osokin and his detachment?"

"In Krilovka," replied one of the scouts. "We had to retreat—the fighting was terrible and we couldn't hold out any longer. Then they sent us here—to get in touch with you. Tomorrow we're setting off for the Korean farms ... " The scout leaned forward heavily in the saddle as though the cruel weight of his own words were crushing him. "Everything's gone to pieces. We've had forty men killed—more than we've lost all summer."

"Are you leaving Krilovka early?" asked Levinson. "If not, I'll come back with you ..."

It was almost daylight by the time he returned to his detachment, his eyes red and his head heavy with lack of sleep.

His conversation with Osokin had finally convinced him that his decision to leave in good time, covering up the detachment's traces as he did so, was the correct one. The sight of Osokin's detachment had served eloquently to confirm this. It had gone completely to pieces, just as an old barrel with rusty hoops and rotten staves falls apart under a heavy blow from the head of an axe. The men no longer obeyed their commander and spent their time wandering aimlessly about the village, many of them drunk. Levinson remembered one man in particular. Gaunt and dishevelled, he sat in the square near the main road staring at the ground with lacklustre eyes, and in blind despair fired bullet after bullet into the whitish gloom of early dawn.

Returning to the detachment, Levinson immediately sent off his two letters, though he did not tell anyone he had made up his mind to evacuate the village that same night.

7. Enemies

In his first letter to Stashinsky, Levinson told him of his anxieties and suggested that the infirmary gradually be wound up so as to avoid unnecessary burdens for the detachment later on. The doctor read the letter several times, and as he did so those around him began to feel anxious and gloomy. It was as if from the small, gray envelope in Stashinsky's thin hands Levinson's anxiety came creeping out towards them all, banishing the peace and quiet that had settled in the most secret corners of each man's soul.

All of a sudden the fine weather came to an end. The sun shone for a while and then it rained, while the wind soughed dolefully in the dark Manchurian maples, always the first trees to sense the breath of approaching autumn. The wounded who had been staying in the infirmary were already leaving to return to their native villages. Wrapping their wretched belongings in a bundle and smiling sadly, they shook all their friends by the hand. After checking their dressings for the last time, Varya kissed them good-bye, then away they went, their new bast shoes sinking into the moss as they disappeared from sight in the mysterious, dank depths of the forest.

Now only Frolov and Mechik were left. Wearing a new leather shirt that Varya had made for him, Mechik was lying on his camp-bed, propped up with a pillow. His head was no longer bandaged, his hair had grown and fell in thick, yellowish curls around his face, while the scar on his temple made him look older and more serious.

"You'll soon be well again, then you'll be leaving too," said Varya sadly.

"But where shall I go?" Mechik asked uncertainly, and was suddenly taken aback at his own question. It was the first time it had occurred to him, and it gave rise to obscure but familiar feelings which brought him no joy. He pulled a wry face and said bitterly: "I've got nowhere to go!"

"What d'you mean?" asked Varya in astonishment. "You'll be able to join Levinson's detachment! Can you ride? It's a cavalry unit, you see... But it doesn't matter if you can't—you'll soon learn!"

She sat down on the bed beside him and took hold of his hand. But he did not look at her. The thought that sooner or later, come what may, he would have to leave, seemed strangely out of place, and it was as bitter as gall.

"Don't be afraid," said Varya, as if she knew what he was thinking. "You're so young and handsome, but you're so shy too ... So shy," she said again tenderly, and throwing a swift glance around her, kissed him on the forehead. There was something almost maternal in the touch of her lips. "Things are different in Shaldiba's detachment, but you'll be all right with Levinson ... " she whispered, not finishing the sentence. "Shaldiba's men are mostly peasants from the countryside, but nearly all ours are miners. They're friendly fellows and easy enough to get on with ... You'll come and see me as often as you can, won't you?"

"But what about Morozka?"

"Oh, don't worry about him—he's used to it by now. Anyway, he carries on too ... But never you mind, don't lose heart. The main thing is to come and see me whenever you can. And don't give in to anybody either—just you stick up for yourself! There's no need to be afraid of our lads—they just seem fierce, that's all ... There isn't really anything frightening about them—it's just the way they look. You've got to show your own teeth, that's all ..."

"And d'you ever show yours?" Mechik asked.

"I'm a woman, so I don't really need to—love's how I do things. But for a man there's no other way ... " After thinking for a moment, she added: "I'm just afraid you won't be able to manage it, though." Then, bending towards him again, she whispered: "Perhaps that's why I love you ... I don't know ..."

"It's true—I'm not brave at all," thought Mechik, propping his chin on his hands and staring up at the sky. "But am I really incapable of managing it? I've got to do it somehow, though ... after all, others do ... And when all's said and done, what have I got to be depressed about?" he wondered, beginning to feel he had no reason at all to be despondent. "I've got to put myself on an equal footing with them right-away and not give in to anybody ... or to myself for that matter—she's quite right about that! The men are different here, so I've got to change too. And what's more, I'll do it!" he said to himself with a firmness he had never known before, feeling what was almost a son's gratitude towards Varya for what she had said and the kindness she had shown him. "Everything will change then, and I'll be a completely different person."

A few days later a second letter from Levinson arrived at the infirmary, brought by Morozka.

"Well? Are we going to have to run for it?" Stashinsky asked him as he tore open the envelope. "Call in at the hut later for the answer, will you?" he added.

Varya stood in front of Morozka, fingering her apron and for the first time feeling rather uncomfortable at seeing her husband again.

"Why have you been away so long?" she asked eventually in an apparently indifferent tone.

"Missed me a lot, have you?" he said mockingly, sensing her remoteness from him and feeling bewildered by it. "Well never mind, you'll be able to make up for it in a minute when we go into the forest..."

"That's all you ever think about," she replied drily, not looking at him and thinking of Mechik instead.

"Shall we go, then?" he asked guardedly, without moving from where he stood.

Varya dropped her apron, and tossing back her plaits, set off along the path into the forest with an affectedly casual gait, resisting the temptation to look back at Mechik. She knew he would never understand that she was merely fulfilling a tiresome duty.

Morozka and she walked on in this way for quite a while, keeping a distance from each other and not saying a word. Finally, unable to bear the suspense any longer, Varya stopped and turned to him in expectation. He came nearer but still did not take hold of her.

"You're playing a crafty game, you whore!" he said suddenly in a hoarse voice. "Gone and fallen for someone, have you?"

"What's that got to do with you?" she asked, looking up and staring him boldly in the face.

Morozka was well aware that Varya carried on with other men while he was away, just as she had before they were married. But his attitude to it had always been one of total indifference. As a matter of fact, he had never really known true family life and had never felt like a married man, but now the thought that someone like Mechik could be his wife's lover was very hurtful to him.

"So who is it you've fallen for, then? I'd like to know," he asked with exaggerated politeness. "Is it that mother's little darling over there?"

"And what if it is?"

"Oh well, he's all all right, I suppose ... nice and clean," agreed Morozka. "You'd better make some hankies for him to wipe his snotty nose on!"

"I will if I have to, and what's more I'll even wipe his nose for him! D'you hear? I'll wipe it for him myself!" she said, thrusting her face right up to his.

"Well, all right, do as you please!" Morozka replied. "Perhaps you'll be a grand lady one day!" Then he turned sharply on his heel and strode back down the path towards the hut, knocking the heads off the forest flowers with his whip as he went.

"Listen, wait a minute!" she cried, suddenly filled with pity for him. "Vanya!"

"I don't want the gentry's leftovers," he said harshly, "but they're welcome to try mine!"

Seeing Morozka returning so soon from the forest, Mechik realized that Varya and he had not hit it off together, and guessed that it was he, Mechik, who was to blame. An unaccountable sense of guilt together with a strange feeling of gladness stirred within him, and he was afraid to look Morozka in the face.

With every step Morozka took towards him, Mechik's sense of guilt increased and his gladness diminished, and he stared at the orderly with timid eyes, unable to look away. Reaching his horse, Morozka seized it by the bridle, and Mechik was suddenly overwhelmed by the bitterly hostile look in his hate-filled eyes. In that brief moment Mechik felt so painfully humiliated, so intolerably vile, that he tried to say something to Morozka, but though his lips moved, he could not utter a sound. There were no words he could say.

"Sitting around here in the rear," sneered Morozka, "and in a new leather shirt, what's more!" Then he uttered a long string of foul oaths.

"What are you swearing for?" asked Mechik, flaring up angrily. "I've had my legs smashed—and it wasn't in the rear either!" he said, trembling with bitterness and hurt pride. "We all know about front-line soldiers like you," he added, blushing, "and what's more I'd tell you so too, if I weren't indebted to you . . ."

"Aha-a! That's got you, hasn't it?" yelled Morozka. "Forgotten how I pulled you out of a tight corner, have you? Dragging people like you around with us is a damn nuisance!" he shouted. "You're nothing but a pain in the neck!"

Hearing all the noise, Stashinsky and Kharchenko came rushing out of the hut.

"What are you shouting for?" asked Stashinsky.

Varya and Pika appeared too, running from different directions out of the forest and both shouting at the same time. Then Morozka leapt into the saddle and began to lash his horse with his whip—something he only did when he was extremely angry. Mishka reared and lunged forward as though he had been scalded.

"Morozka, wait! You've got a letter to take!" shouted Stashinsky in dismay, but Morozka was no longer there. From the depths of the forest came the sound of furiously galloping hoofs which gradually died away in the distance.

8. The First Move

During the night the platoon commander Dubov was suddenly woken by a violent dig in the ribs.

"What's the matter? What is it?" he asked with a start, then sat up. No sooner had he opened his sleepy eyes to look at the dim little night-light than he heard the sound of a distant shot. A few moments later there was a second.

"Get up, quick!" shouted Morozka. "There's firing on the other side of the river!"

Isolated shots were ringing out one after another now, coming almost at regular intervals.

"Wake the lads!" ordered Dubov. "Run as fast as you can to all the huts! And hurry!"

A few moments later, fully dressed and armed, he ran out into the yard. It was cold and still, and the sky was already growing light. Along the hazy paths of the Milky Way stars seemed to be racing in confusion. Then from the dark opening of the hayloft the dishevelled figures of partisans scrambled out one after another, swearing and cursing as they came. Buckling on their cartridge belts, they led out their horses, and as they did so hens flew off their perches with a furious squawking that made the animals rear and neigh.

"To arms!"

"Turn out! Mount your horses!" Dubov ordered. "Dmitry! Semyon! Run to all the huts and wake the men! At the double!"

A rocket flew up from the village square in front of headquarters and hissed smoking across the sky. A sleepy old woman put her head out of a window then quickly disappeared again.

Eventually, accompanied by the frenzied barking of dogs, the platoon tore off to headquarters, filling the frightened streets with the furious clatter of horses' hoofs and the ringing of steel.

Dubov was amazed when he saw the whole detachment already assembled in the village square. The baggage train stretched away down the main road, all ready to leave, and many of the men had dismounted and were sitting near their horses, smoking and waiting. Dubov scanned the crowd, searching for the small figure of Levinson, and finally caught sight of him standing near a pile of logs under a flare and talking quietly to Metelitsa.

From five of his men who had just come back across the river, Dubov learned that there were no enemy forces there at all, and that the men had simply been firing into the air on Levinson's orders. It was then that Dubov realized Levinson had simply wanted to test the detachment's readiness for action.

When the detachment had formed up and the roll call was taken, it was discovered that many men were still missing, most of them from Kubrak's platoon. Kubrak himself had been to say good-bye to his relatives the day before and was still not sober. What was more, the whole detachment could see he was drunk. Only Levinson seemed not to notice. If he had, he would have been forced to relieve Kubrak of his command, and there was no one to take his place.

Levinson rode past the ranks of men and then, returning to the center, raised his hand. It hung stern and chill in the air, and amid the sudden silence the mysterious sounds of night could clearly be heard.

"Comrades ... " he began, and his voice, quiet but distinct, was as audible to every man as the beating of his own heart. "We're leaving here ... The Japanese forces—though there's no need to exaggerate them—are nevertheless large enough to make it advisable for us to lie low for the time being. That doesn't mean we'll be completely out of danger, though. No—we're always in danger, and every partisan knows it. But are we true to our name of partisans? Not today we aren't, not by any means! We've got about as much discipline as a bunch of schoolgirls! What if the Japanese had really attacked just now? They'd have wrung our necks like chickens! Shame on you!" Levinson suddenly bent forward, and his last few words lashed out like an uncoiled spring, so that every man felt like a chicken which has been seized in the dark and is having its neck wrung by merciless, iron fingers.

Then Levinson stood up in his stirrups and with a flick of his whip, shouted: "Atten—-tion! From the right in threes ... quick march!"

The riders' curbs all jingled in unison and their saddles creaked loudly in the stillness, then swaying in the gloom like a great fish in a deep pool, the dense ranks began to move away, away towards the timeless spurs of the Sikhote-Alin range. And beyond the mountains the equally timeless dawn was breaking, heralding the new day.

9. Mechik in the Detachment

Until the last day of Mechik's stay in the infirmary, his strange relationship with Varya continued. It resembled a game in which each knew what the woman wanted and the man feared, but in which neither of them could bring themselves to take a decisive step.

During her long-suffering and difficult life, in which there had been so many men that she could not tell them apart now by the color of their eyes or hair, or even by their names, Varya had never felt able to call any of them "My dearest, my darling!" Mechik was the first to whom she could say—and did say—these words. It seemed to her that he and he alone—so handsome, modest and gentle—could satisfy her longing for motherhood, and she felt she had fallen in love with him for this very reason.

Though Mechik desired what she desired with all the imagination and ardor of his scarcely matured youth, he persistently avoided being alone with her. He was shy because he had not yet known a woman, and he felt he would be unable to manage things as other people did, but instead would make a shameful mess of it.

He left the infirmary together with Pika, and they said farewell to everyone rather awkwardly, as though they hardly knew them. But Varya caught up with them on the forest path.

"Let's at least say good-bye properly," she said, her face flushed with running as well as with embarrassment. Then she furtively slipped into Mechik's hand an embroidered tobacco-pouch of the kind young girls at the mine used to make for their sweethearts.

Both her embarrassment and the gift were so uncharacteristic of her that Mechik felt very moved, but because Pika was there he only touched her cheek with his lips in response. As they parted, Varya looked at him with misty eyes and her lips began to quiver.

"Come and see me, mind!" she called when they had already disappeared among the trees, then hearing no reply, she sank down on the grass and burst into tears.

The mouth of the Irokhedza River was now occupied by both Japanese troops and forces under Kolchak.[25] Pika was afraid, and Mechik could not persuade him to skirt the village and pass down the valley, so they were obliged to scramble up unfamiliar goat tracks that led over the hills. On the second night they had to climb down a series of steep, rocky cliffs to the river and nearly killed themselves in the process, as Mechik was still rather unsteady on his feet. It was almost morning when they reached a Korean peasant's hut, where they hungrily gulped down a bowl of unsalted *chumiza*.

Then they made their way across scattered farms where no one knew a thing about the Japanese. When they asked whether Levinson's detachment had passed that way, the peasants simply pointed upriver and then asked for news in their turn.

Mechik and Pika reached Shibishi towards evening. The little village lay at the foot of a wooded hill, glowing in the warm light of the setting sun. Near a small, dilapidated chapel that was overgrown with lichen, a noisy group of men with wide, red cap-bands were playing skittles. A short little fellow in big top-boots with a long ginger beard—it made him look like a gnome from a children's fairy tale—had just thrown his sticks disgracefully wide of the mark, and now all the men were laughing at him. The little man smiled shyly, but it was clear he was not in the least put out and was enjoying himself immensely.

"There he is, that's Levinson," said Pika.

"Where?"

"Over there—the one with the ginger hair ... " Pika replied, and leaving the bewildered Mechik where he was, went shuffling over to the little man with amazing speed.

Mechik remained standing to one side, not sure whether to go up to the men or wait until he was called.

"That's the wounded fellow Morozka brought in," someone said, recognizing him. Hearing them talking about him, Mechik went nearer.

The little man who had just played skittles so badly turned out to have large, piercing eyes that seemed to probe deep into Mechik, and turning him inside out, hold him motionless for a few moments, as though weighing up everything about him.

"I've come to join your detachment," Mechik began, blushing because he had forgotten to turn down his rolled-up sleeves. "I used to be with Shaldiba ... till I was wounded," he added, trying to lend weight to his words.

"Have you ridden a horse before?" asked Levinson.

"No," Mechik confessed.

"A pity," said Levinson. "Baklanov, give him Zyuchikha," and he narrowed his eyes craftily. "She's harmless enough ... But take care of her—your platoon commander will tell you how to manage her ... Now which platoon shall we put him in?"

"Kubrak's, I think—he's short of men," said Baklanov.

"All right," agreed Levinson. "Off you go now ..."

Zyuchikha was a bleary-eyed, doleful-looking mare with a dirty white coat, hollow back and pot belly—a docile peasant's horse that had ploughed many an acre in her life. And what was more, she was in foal.

"Is this for me?" asked Mechik in a weak voice.

"She's not much to look at, it's true," said Kubrak, "and her hoofs are a bit weak too, but you can still ride her, though . . ."

"Haven't you any other horses?" Mechik asked, suddenly filled with impotent fury both at Zyuchikha and the prospect of having to ride her. With trembling lips, Mechik gazed above the horse's head into the distance, making no attempt to listen to what Kubrak was saying about how to look after her. He felt as if this appalling mare with her disgraceful hoofs had been given to him quite deliberately, so as to humiliate him right from the start. Recently he had begun to examine everything he did from the standpoint of the new life he was about to embark on, but now he felt there could be no question of starting any kind of new life with such a loathsome animal as this. No one would be able to see he had become a completely changed man who was now strong and sure of himself. Instead, everyone would think he was just the same ridiculous Mechik as before, a fool who could not even be trusted with a good horse.

Away he went, feeling annoyed with himself and resentful towards all the partisans, but especially towards Levinson. "What do I care?" he thought, pouting sulkily. "It makes no difference . . . I'm still not going to look after that horse! She can die for all I care! Let's see what Levinson says then—I don't give a damn!"

In the days that followed Mechik really did neglect the mare, taking her out only for exercise and occasionally to the watering place. After a short time Zyuchikha became covered with mange, was perpetually hungry and thirsty, and rarely enjoyed anyone's attention, while Mechik won general dislike as an "idler and swank."

From then on the busy life of the detachment passed him by. He was no longer able to perceive the mainsprings of its mechanism and did not sense the necessity of everything that took place in it. Amid this feeling of alienation, all his dreams of a bold, new life soon evaporated, though he did learn how to stand up for himself without being afraid, ceased to bother about his clothes, and grew very sunburnt, so becoming—outwardly at least—indistinguishable from his fellows.

10. The Beginning of the Rout

Having withdrawn to a remote area, Levinson almost lost touch with the other partisan detachments, but the scraps of information which he occasionally managed to glean produced a painful picture of collapse. The disquieting wind that blew from the Ulakhe[26] valley brought with it the smell of smoke and blood.

By way of winding paths through the *taiga* that had remained untrodden for many years now, Levinson made contact with the railway line. There he was told that a special train carrying enemy uniforms and arms was scheduled to pass shortly, and the railwaymen promised to inform him of the exact day and time. Realizing the detachment's whereabouts would be discovered sooner or later, and knowing it would be impossible to winter in the *taiga* without warm clothing or ammunition, Levinson decided to make the first move. The blaster Goncharenko quickly set his mines, and in the misty night, slipping unobserved through enemy territory, Dubov's platoon suddenly appeared on the railway line.

Goncharenko's mine uncoupled the goods trucks from the rest of the train without damaging the passenger carriages. With a thunderous explosion that sent clouds of smoke billowing into the air, lengths of broken rail flew overhead and crashed shuddering down the embankment.

While mounted enemy patrols scoured the neighborhood for the partisans, Dubov bided his time with his heavily-laden horses in the Sviyagino forests, then slipped away through the mountain gorges under cover of darkness. A few days later he reached Shibishi without having lost a single man. The same day Levinson divided up all the supplies, issuing his men with greatcoats, cartridges, sabres and rusks, and only keeping back what the pack horses could carry.

The whole of the Ulakhe valley as far as the Ussuri River [37] was now in enemy hands. New forces were assembling near the mouth of the Irokhedza, and Japanese patrols were on the prowl everywhere, stumbling upon Levinson's scouts again and again. Towards the end of August the Japanese began to move upriver. They advanced slowly, making long halts, and moved carefully from one farm to the next, feeling their way at every step and sending out frequent reinforcements on their flanks. In the iron determination of their advance, slow though it was, could be sensed the progress of a self-confident yet altogether blind force.

Levinson's scouts would return wild-eyed from their patrols, and their reports usually contradicted one another.

"What d'you mean?" Levinson would ask brusquely. "Yesterday you said they were at Solomennaya and this morning they turned up at Monakino.[28] So what on earth are they doing? Going backwards?"

"I d-don't know," stammered the scout. "Perhaps it was the vanguard that was at Solomennaya..."

"But how d'you know it was the main forces you saw at Monakino and not the vanguard?"

"The peasants said so . . ."

"You and your peasants!"

"You'll have to go and have a look for yourself," said Levinson, turning to Baklanov, "otherwise we're all going to be killed like flies here. Take someone with you and set off at first light."

"Who shall I take?" Baklanov asked.

"Anybody you like . . . What about that new man in Kubrak's platoon—Mechik? You can find out what kind of fellow he is."

The scouting mission could not have been more welcome to Mechik. During the short time he had been in the detachment, he had accumulated so many unfulfilled desires that they weighed heavily upon him, their oppressive burden making it impossible for him to break out of the painfully narrow circle in which he found himself. Now he felt he could break out of that circle with a single bold stroke.

Baklanov and he set out before dawn. The forested ridges were just beginning to turn pink and the cocks were crowing for the second time in the village at the foot of the mountain. It was cold, dark and rather frightening. The unusual surroundings, the expectation of danger, and the hope of success gave rise in both men to that elated, martial mood beside which all other feelings seem insignificant.

All the way there they kept running into scouts who lied just as before, and as he listened to them, Baklanov simply shook his head. At a farm three versts from the village of Solomennaya they left their horses and continued on foot. The sun was long past its zenith now, and the luxuriant sheaves of reaped corn cast soft, dark shadows on the quiet fields. When they met a cart on the road Baklanov asked its driver whether there were any Japanese in Solomennaya.

"They say half a dozen of them turned up first thing this morning, but we've not seen anything of them all day."

"That means they really are in Monakino," said Baklanov. "Those half-dozen were scouts."

Greeted by the lazy barking of dogs, they entered the village and saw a horse and cart standing outside an inn. They went inside and drank some milk in Baklanov's favorite fashion—out of a bowl with pieces of bread floating in it. But they had only taken a few steps from the inn when a fat woman came running out of a narrow street, holding up her skirts and almost bumping into them in her haste. When she saw them, she stopped in astonishment, then cried in a shrill voice:

"Oh, my dears, where on earth are you going? There's an enormous crowd of Japs near the school! They're coming this way, so be off with you this minute! They're coming this way, I tell you!"

Before Mechik had time to grasp what she had said, four Japanese soldiers with rifles slung over their shoulders came out of the same street, marching in step. With a shout Baklanov whipped out his revolver and fired almost point-blank at two of them. Mechik saw bloody tatters come flying out of their backs, then both men fell to the ground. But Baklanov's third cartridge jammed and his revolver would not fire any more. One of the remaining Japanese took to his heels, but the other tore the rifle from his shoulder. Just then Mechik fired at him several times in succession, his last few bullets striking the man as he lay writhing in the dust.

"Run!" shouted Baklanov. "To the cart!" A few seconds later they were tearing down the village street amid clouds of dust. Baklanov was standing up in the cart, lashing the horse with the ends of the reins for all he was worth and glancing behind him every moment to see whether they were being pursued. Somewhere in the middle of the village at least half a dozen buglers could be heard sounding the alarm.

"They're here all right ... the whole lot of 'em!" yelled Baklanov, filled with a kind of triumphant fury. "D'you hear those bugles?"

But Mechik could not hear a thing. Hugging the bottom of the cart, he was beside himself with joy at being safe and at the thought that the man he had shot was now writhing in the hot dust, growing weaker and weaker in the last throes of death.

Only a few moments later Baklanov was laughing.

"It worked out pretty well, didn't it? And you put up a good show too, old fellow! If it hadn't been for you, he'd really have riddled us, make no mistake!"

After they had driven about two versts without hearing any sound of pursuit, Baklanov stopped the cart near a solitary elm tree whose branches overhung the road.

"You stay here while I climb up and see what's happening," he said.

Half an hour later he saw about twenty horsemen riding out of Solomennaya at a walking pace. They were already halfway towards him when from his vantage point he caught sight of the infantry. They were marching out of the village in serried ranks, their weapons gleaming amid the clouds of dust.

In their headlong race back to the farm Baklanov and Mechik all but killed the horse. Then they mounted their own horses and a few moments later were galloping back towards Shibishi. With his usual foresight Levinson had not waited for them—it was night before they returned anyway—but had strengthened the pickets, Kubrak's platoon being dismounted for the purpose. Once they were back, Mechik handed his mare over to Baklanov and went off to join his platoon.

Though he was exhausted, he did not feel like going to sleep. A mist was rising from the river and it was cold. He lay on his back on the ground, gazing up at the stars which were barely visible in the dark void beyond the curtain of mist. Only a few moments later, it seemed, he was already sitting up, blinking sleepily and groping for his rifle, and he saw it was completely light. Men were bustling to and fro around him, rolling up their greatcoats, while Kubrak had forced his way through the bushes and was looking at something through his field glasses. All the men kept crawling up to him and asking:

"Where? Where?"

Finding his rifle at last, Mechik scrambled up the bank as well and realized the question referred to the enemy. But seeing no sign of them either, he too asked:

"Where?"

"What are you all crowding round for?" the platoon commander hissed. "Spread out and make a skirmish line!"

While they were crawling into position along the bank, Mechik kept craning his neck and trying to catch a glimpse of the enemy.

Then came the command:

"Plat—-oon!"

Mechik thrust his rifle forward, still unable to see anything, and at the word "Fire!" he fired at random.

"Fire!" cried Kubrak again, and once more Mechik fired.

"Aha! They're running away!" the men around him cried, then they all suddenly began talking loudly and incoherently, their faces excited and gay.

"Enough! Enough!" shouted the platoon commander. "Don't waste your cartridges!"

By questioning those around him, Mechik found out that a Japanese patrol had come riding up. Just then came the booming report of a field gun, filling the valley with an echo in reply. But the shell exploded harmlessly somewhere beyond the village. Then machine-guns began to bark in their furiously breathless way and rifles spoke again and again, but the partisans did not return the fire.

The next time Mechik had to fire, he could actually see the Japanese. They were advancing in lines, running from one bush to the next, and they looked so near that Mechik thought the detachment could not possibly escape from them now even if they wanted to. What he felt was not fear, though, but a sense of agonizing expectation: when on earth would it all end?

The partisans set off at a run, racing in wild disorder at first then straggling along in single file. Mechik ran with the rest without understanding why he was doing so, but feeling despite his confusion that what was happening was not as accidental and senseless as it seemed, and that a whole series of people were directing both his own actions and those of the men around him. When they reached the village and he had collected himself a little—the men were moving at a walking pace now, strung out in a long line—he involuntarily began to look for those who were controlling his destiny. Levinson was walking along in front, swinging his enormous Mauser in such a funny way and looking so small that it was hard to believe he was the chief guiding force in all this operation. But while Mechik was trying to reconcile this conflict, a furious hail of bullets began to whine maliciously around them. The line of men suddenly rushed forward and several of them fell to the ground.

Mechik did not come fully to his senses till the detachment reached the forest and began to make its way along a mountain path that had been ploughed up by the hoofs of horses. It was quiet and dark in the *taiga,* and the sternly majestic Siberian pines sheltered them all with their peaceful, moss-grown branches.

11. Hard Days

After the battle the detachment hid in a remote ravine overgrown with mare's tail and ferns. Soon, however, a shortage of provisions forced Levinson to leave this refuge and go down into the neighboring valley. For several days the detachment moved to and fro among the tributaries of the Ulakhe River, growing more and more exhausted by clashes with the enemy and by forced marches. The number of farms still unoccupied by the Japanese was decreasing rapidly, and every handful of oats or crust of bread could only be secured at the cost of fighting. Time and again wounds that had not yet managed to heal were opened once more, and the partisans grew fiercer and grimmer than ever.

Levinson firmly believed that his men were motivated not only by their instinctive desire for self-preservation but also by another, no less important urge that was hidden from superficial observation and not even acknowledged by most of the partisans themselves. Because of this urge, everything they had to suffer—even death itself—was justified by their ultimate goal, and without that goal none of them would have chosen to risk his life in the Ulakhe *taiga*. But Levinson knew, too, that this profound instinct of theirs lay buried deep under the endlessly trivial but pressing needs of everyday life, under all the anxieties for one's own small yet vital self, because each man needed to eat and sleep, and because the flesh is weak. Overwhelmed by a host of petty cares and conscious of their own weakness, they had passed on, as it were, their greatest burdens to those stronger than themselves, to men such as Levinson, Baklanov and Dubov. They had charged them with the responsibility of devoting more attention to the demands of others than to their own need for food and sleep, and at the same time had entrusted them with the task of reminding others of what was most important too.

Levinson was constantly with his men now—he led them into battle, ate from the same cooking pot as they did, and went without sleep at night because he was checking that they were at their posts. Moreover, he was practically the only man in the detachment who had not forgotten how to laugh. Even when he was talking to the men about the most ordinary matters, in everything he said one could hear: "Look, I'm suffering with you as well—tomorrow I, too, might get killed or die of starvation, but I'm always cheerful and determined, because all this business of dying isn't so important after all!"

And yet, in spite of all this, the invisible ties that bound him closely to his detachment were snapping one by one with every passing day ... And the fewer those ties became, the harder it was for him to persuade the men to obey him. Slowly but surely he was becoming a force that was distant from the detachment.

After a march of many versts over the Udege[29] mountain spur, during which the men lived only on grapes and mushrooms which they steamed over their camp fires, the detachment came out into the Tiger[30] valley and reached a lonely little Korean farm twenty versts from the mouth of the Irokhedza River. Here they were met by an enormous, bareheaded man as hairy as the long goatskin boots he wore, with a rusty Smith and Wesson in his belt. Levinson recognized him: it was Stirksha, the bootlegger from Daubikhe.

"Aha, Levinson!" he cried in greeting. "So you're still alive, eh? That's good! But they're after you round here, you know!"

"Who are?"

"The Japs and Kolchak's men ... Who else?"

"But perhaps they won't find me!"

"Perhaps they will," said Stirksha mysteriously. "They're not fools, you know—they've gone and put a price on your head ... dead or alive!"

"Oho! And are they offering a lot?"

"Five hundred Siberian rubles."

"That's dirt cheap!" said Levinson with a grin.

Early the next morning the detachment was cut off from the mountains by the enemy, and only after a battle lasting two hours in which Levinson lost almost thirty men did he manage to break through into the Irokhedza valley. The Kolchak cavalry were following hard on his heels, so he was forced to leave all his pack horses behind, and it was not until noon that he came out on to the familiar track leading to the infirmary.

It was then that he suddenly felt he could barely stay in the saddle any longer. After the incredible strain of that day his heart was beating very slowly, so slowly that he almost thought it might stop at any moment. He longed to sleep, and lowering his head, immediately seemed to drift away in the saddle, and as he did so, everything around him became insignificant and simple. Suddenly, feeling a kind of inward jolt, he gave a start and looked round. But nobody had noticed that he had been asleep. All the men could see their commander's familiar, slightly bent back in front of them. How could any of them possibly imagine that he was just as tired as they were and that he wanted to sleep just as much as they did? "But ... have I the strength to carry on?" Levinson wondered. He shook his head and suddenly felt a faint but very unpleasant trembling in his knees.

12. Highways and Byways

The detachment was riding up a steep ridge where the grass had been eaten away by mountain goats. The cold, bluish-gray sky stretched away above their heads, and far below dark blue valleys could be dimly seen. Dislodged by the horses' hoofs, large stones kept rolling down into the abyss.

Then the riders were surrounded by the golden leaves and dry grass of the *taiga,* itself enveloped now by the expectant stillness of autumn. The gray-bearded Manchurian deer were casting their coats amid the yellow tracery of spreading branches, cool springs sang in the stillness, and the transparent dew stayed on the ground all day long, it too yellowed by the falling leaves. In the golden fading of the *taiga* one seemed to sense the mighty breath of a huge creature that possessed everlasting life.

Varya, Stashinsky and Kharchenko, who had all been attached to Kubrak's platoon, were riding almost at the rear of the column. At bends in the ridge the whole detachment was visible, stretched out in a long line. In front, bending forward in the saddle, rode Levinson, while just behind him, unconsciously imitating his pose, was Baklanov.

All the time, Varya was aware of Mechik's presence somewhere behind her. Ever since he had left the infirmary he had been constantly in her mind, and she lived only for their next meeting. It was with thoughts of him that her most secret dreams were bound up, dreams which she would never have confessed to a soul but which seemed so alive and real that they were almost palpable. She imagined how he would appear before her at the edge of the forest—fair-haired and handsome, slim and a little shy—then she felt his breath on her cheek and heard his tender, loving words. In short, she imagined her future relationship with him as happy as it could possibly be, and tried not to think about what really might happen and cause her sorrow.

All through the first day's march she was tormented by the desire to see him again and talk to him, but she did not once look behind her, and even when the column halted for dinner she made no attempt to go up to him. "Why should I go running after him like a little girl?" she thought. "If he really loves me as he said he did, then let him come to see me. But if he doesn't, then never mind—I'll stay by myself, and nothing will come of it after all."

Evening was falling and the ravines were growing dark, while the mist was thickening over the springs and drifting slowly down into the valleys. The horses were snorting wearily. But still Mechik did not come near Varya and clearly had no intention of doing so. The more convinced she became that he would not come to her, the more painfully she felt the emptiness of her dreams, and the harder it grew to part with them.

The detachment came down into a gully to camp for the night, and the shadows of men and horses began to flit to and fro in the dank gloom. Suddenly, at the bottom of the gully, a camp fire began to glow, silently snatching from the darkness the shaggy heads of horses and the tired faces of men amid gleaming cartridge belts and rifles.

Stashinsky, Kharchenko and Varya rode off to one side and dismounted.

When they had eaten something, though, and warmed themselves by the fire, all three felt more cheerful, and the alien, cold world around them began to seem familiar and warm.

"Why am I so hard on him?" thought Varya, feeling her usual gentleness and kindness returning as a result of the cheerful fire and the *kasha*[31] she had eaten. "The boy's sitting there feeling lonely just because of my stupidity. After all, I've only got to go up to him and everything will be just the same as before . . ."

So there and then she decided to put everything else out of her mind and go to him, no longer seeing anything degrading or wrong about taking such a step.

All that day Mechik had felt as if he were drifting in a strange, shroud-like mist that separated him from other people, a mist composed of somber thoughts of loneliness and death.

Towards evening the mist had fallen away, but he still did not feel like seeing anybody and was afraid of everyone around him.

It was only with difficulty that Varya found his camp fire, for the whole gully was illumined by them, with the men singing amid their smoke.

"So this is where you've hidden yourself away, is it?" she said, coming out of the bushes with a pounding heart. "Hello!"

Mechik gave a start, and glancing at her with frightened, distant eyes, turned away towards the fire.

"I've come to find out how you are, seeing you've completely forgotten us!" she said in a singsong, excited voice.

But Mechik just shrugged his shoulders and said nothing.

Varya suddenly felt very hurt. After all, it was for his sake that she had come, but all he could do was shrug his shoulders.

"Oh, I shouldn't have done it, I shouldn't," she thought, and all of a sudden something alarming and big seemed to snap inside her.

Then, bending her head low, she walked away with small, quick steps and disappeared into the darkness.

13. Their Burdens

On the fifth day of the march, the detachment came down to the headwaters of the Khanikheza River.[32] They were riding along an old winter track thickly covered with withered couch-grass. Though none of the men had got even so much as a crust left from the provisions which the assistant quartermaster had laid in at the infirmary, they were all in good spirits, feeling sure that shelter and rest were not far away now.

"Halt! Halt!" suddenly shouted the men at the head of the column. The command was passed right down the line, but as the riders in front came to a standstill, those at the rear continued to press forward and the column was soon thrown into confusion.

"Hey! Call Metelitsa!" came another cry, and that too was passed down the column. A few moments later, swooping past like a hawk, the herdsman Metelitsa came racing by, and with an involuntary sense of pride the whole detachment watched him pass, admiring his splendidly instinctive horsemanship which owed nothing whatsoever to any formal style of riding.

"Metelitsa's going out on reconnaissance," said Dubov, "and we're going to spend the night here."

The men ahead were already dismounting.

Levinson had decided to camp for the night in the forest because he was not sure whether the lower reaches of the Khanikheza were free of enemy forces. But he hoped that even if the enemy were there, he would still be able—by using scouts and carefully feeling his way—to get through to the Tudo-Vaku[33] valley where both horses and grain were plentiful.

During the entire journey he had been tormented by an intolerable pain in his side that had grown steadily worse from day to day. He knew by now that this pain, which was due to anemia and fatigue, could only be alleviated by weeks of good food and rest. But since he was well aware that it would be a long time before he could enjoy such things, he did his best to adapt to the situation, assuring himself that it was "just a trifling indisposition," that he had always suffered from it, and that it could not possibly prevent him from fulfilling the task that he considered it his duty to perform.

That night, waking suddenly as he had often done recently, Levinson lit a cigarette and went off to inspect the sentry posts.

After a short while he heard the soft murmuring of the brook. He stood still for a few moments, listening to the sounds of the dark forest, then smiling to himself, walked on more quickly than before, deliberately making the grass rustle under his feet so that he might be heard.

"Who is it? Who's there?" called a shaking voice from the darkness.

Levinson realized it was Mechik and without answering, walked straight towards him. A rifle bolt rattled in the stillness, but then it jammed and squeaked plaintively.

"You should oil it a bit more often," said Levinson drily.

"Oh, it's you!" answered Mechik with sudden relief. "But I do oil it ... I don't know what's wrong with it." He looked at his commander in embarrassment, and forgetting the bolt was still not in place, lowered the rifle.

Mechik had been put on the third sentry shift, which began at midnight. No more than half an hour had passed since the corporal of the guard's unhurried footsteps had died away in the grass as he made his way back to the camp.

In essence, for the whole of that time Mechik had been preoccupied by a single thought to which he had kept returning, no matter what else he was thinking about.

What this thought amounted to was that, one way or another, and as quickly as possible, he should leave the detachment.

His earlier life in town—a life which had once appeared so tedious and dismal—seemed extraordinarily happy and carefree now that he thought he might return to it, and indeed he had come to feel that it was the only kind of life possible for him.

"Well, how are you getting on?" asked Levinson. "Everything quiet?"

"Yes," answered Mechik, looking at him rather timidly.

"Well, don't worry—things'll be better soon," said Levinson. "If we can just get through to the Tudo-Vaku valley, it'll be much easier there ... D'you smoke?"

"No, I don't," replied Mechik.

"But don't you ever feel like a smoke? 'A good smoke's just the thing,' Kanunnikov always used to say. Now that was a good partisan for you. I still don't know whether he made it to town safely or not ..."

"But why did he go?" Mechik asked, and his heart suddenly began to pound as a vague idea occurred to him.

"I sent him there with a message. He was meant to deliver our report too."

"But you can send somebody else, can't you?" said Mechik in an unnatural voice. "Aren't you thinking of sending anyone?"

"Why?" asked Levinson, suddenly on the alert.

"Oh, I was just wondering, that's all ... If you are sending anybody, I can go for you. I know the town well ..."

"No, I'm not thinking of sending anyone else ... " replied Levinson slowly and thoughtfully. "Have you got relatives there or something?"

"No, but I used to work there ... What I mean is, I do have relatives there, but it's not because of that ... No, you can rely on me—when I was working in town I often had to deliver secret packets."

"And who did you work with?"

"The Maximalists,[34] though at the time I didn't think it really mattered who you worked with ..."

"But what about now?" Levinson asked.

"Now I just don't know what's right and what's wrong," replied Mechik quietly, not sure what answer Levinson was really expecting from him. "No, do you know why I mentioned all this?" he blurted out, his voice shaking nervously. "The reason is that it seems to me I'm a lousy partisan, and I think it'd be much better if you sent me away ... No—don't think I'm afraid or hiding anything from you—it's just that I can't seem to do anything properly and I don't understand a thing ... I can't make friends with anyone here, you see, anyone at all, and there's no one I can turn to for help either. But is that really my fault? When I first came here, I approached everybody with an open heart, but I've met nothing but coarseness and mockery, even though I've been in action with everyone else and was seriously wounded into the bargain—as you know ... I realize that if I were stronger, they'd pay attention to me and be more wary of me, because strength's the only thing they understand here ..."

"So that's the kind of fellow you are ... What a mess!" thought Levinson, listening with growing curiosity to what lay behind Mechik's impassioned words.

It seemed to Mechik that the most important thing he had said was how intolerable life was for him in the detachment and how everybody insulted him, and he thought what a good thing it was that he was talking quite openly at last, without beating about the bush.

"Well, I can't do anything for you," said Levinson finally in a stern tone which had a note of kindness and pity in it too. "You've only got yourself to blame. And there's nowhere for you to go either. It would be downright stupid to leave—you'd just get killed, that's all. So you'd better think things over properly first ..."

"What a muddle-headed fellow he is!" thought Levinson afterwards, as he walked quietly back through the dark grass. He was disturbed by the whole conversation with Mechik. He thought the man really was weak-willed, feeble and lazy, and found it very depressing that such wretched good-for-nothings were still being born and living in Russia. "Yes," he thought, quickening his step, "as long as millions of people in our country still exist amid poverty and filth, as long as they still plough with primitive wooden ploughs and believe in a cruel, stupid God, then such weak-willed, lazy people, such useless good-for-nothings, will go on being born in it ..."

He felt deeply disturbed, because these were his most profound and intimate thoughts, and also because the essential meaning of his own life lay in overcoming the hardship and poverty he saw all around him. He knew there would have been no Levinson at all but someone completely different, if he had not been driven by an overwhelming desire to see men become strong and kind, to see them become beautiful and new. But what hope could there possibly be of beautiful, new men when countless millions were still forced to live such wretchedly primitive, such unspeakably poverty-stricken lives?

"But was I myself really like him once?" Levinson wondered, and as his thoughts returned to Mechik, he tried to remember what he had been like as a child and as an adolescent. But he could only recall that period of his life with great difficulty, for too thick and firm, too important in the personal sense, were the strata laid down within him by later years—when he had already become the person whom everyone knew simply as *Levinson,* the man who always marched at the head of his detachment.

The only thing he could remember was an old family photograph of a puny-looking Jewish boy with big, ingenuous eyes, wearing a little black jacket and gazing with unusual intentness at the place in the camera where he had been told a pretty little bird would fly out. But as it happened no bird had flown out at all, and he remembered how he had almost cried with disappointment. How many more disappointments like that had he been obliged to suffer before finally becoming convinced that "life just isn't like that"?

Once he was convinced of it, though, he had realized what endless misery human beings suffer because of all those deceitful stories about pretty little birds—birds which are supposed to fly out from somewhere and which so many people spend all their lives fruitlessly waiting for . . . "To see everything as it is in order to be able to change what exists and to bring nearer what is coming into being and must eventually be"—this was the wisdom, the most simple yet most difficult wisdom of all, that Levinson had finally achieved.

Reaching the camp, he made his way towards his own fire. It was still smoldering faintly, and lying beside it, wrapped in his greatcoat and fast asleep, was Baklanov, looking for all the world like a good-natured, well-fed puppy. "Just look at him!" thought Levinson affectionately, and smiled. After his conversation with Mechik it was particularly pleasant somehow to see Baklanov.

Then, with a grunt, Levinson lay down beside him, and as soon as he closed his eyes he seemed to begin swaying to and fro, and no longer aware of his body, floated away until all of a sudden he plunged headlong into a bottomless black pit.

14. Metelitsa Goes on Reconnaissance

When Levinson sent Metelitsa out on reconnaissance, he ordered him to return at all costs the same night. But the village to which the platoon commander had been sent was in actual fact much further away than Levinson had thought. Metelitsa had left the detachment at about four in the afternoon and had galloped hard, but when twilight fell the rustling grass of the *taiga* was still speeding incessantly past him in the chill light of the dying day. By the time he finally emerged from the forest, it was already quite dark.

He rode to the top of a hillock. To his left, just as before, stretched a dark range of volcanic hills, curving away into the distance like the spine of a huge monster, while not far away he could hear the sound of a river. Further off, stretching across the road, shone the still, yellow lights of a village. Far away to his right the line of volcanic hills curved aside and disappeared in the dark blue gloom.

Hobbling his horse, Metelitsa set off along a path that led beside the river, and half an hour later he found himself close to the village. It was already asleep. There were no lights shining anywhere now, and faintly lit by the stars, the well-thatched roofs were barely visible among the quiet, empty orchards. From the peasants' gardens came the smell of freshly-turned, damp earth.

Metelitsa passed a few more lanes, and skirting the village church, finally reached the painted fence around the priest's orchard. He looked over it into the garden and listened carefully, then hearing nothing suspicious, sprang softly over the fence.

The orchard was full of trees with spreading branches, but most of the leaves had already fallen. Trying to check the pounding of his heart and holding his breath as he went, Metelitsa made his way deeper into the orchard. All of a sudden the bushes came to an end where a path cut through them, and about forty yards away to his left he saw a lighted window. It was open, and there were people sitting inside.

A few moments later he was standing behind an apple tree right by the window, listening carefully and trying to remember everything that was being said.

There were four men in the room, and they were playing cards at a table set far back from the window. To Metelitsa's right sat a little old priest with thin, oily hair and quick, darting eyes. His small hands moved deftly over the table, their doll-like fingers shuffling the cards soundlessly. He kept trying to peer under every card as he dealt it, so that his neighbor, who had his back to the window, glanced swiftly at each card he received then immediately hid it under the table. Facing Metelitsa sat a handsome, rather stout officer, a sluggish-looking but apparently good-natured man with a pipe in his mouth. It was probably because he was plump that Metelitsa took him for the squadron commander. However, for some unaccountable reason he was most interested in the fourth player—a man with a flabby, pale face and eyelashes that never seemed to move. He wore a black Cossack cap and a plain felt cloak which he wrapped closely round him each time he played a card.

Contrary to what Metelitsa had expected to hear, they were talking about the most uninteresting and ordinary things, and most of their conversation concerned the game itself.

After a while, Metelitsa crouched down, and moving sideways, began to creep away from the window. But just as he turned down the path he suddenly came face to face with a man carrying a Cossack greatcoat over his shoulder. Behind him were two others.

"What are you doing here?" the man asked in surprise.

Metelitsa sprang aside and dashed off into the bushes.

"Stop! Hold him! Get him! Over here, men! Hey!" several voices shouted. Then shots cracked out in the darkness.

Metelitsa was racing blindly away now, but there were already voices yelling somewhere ahead of him, and he could hear the angry barking of dogs coming from the street.

"There he is—stop him!" someone shouted, rushing towards him with outstretched arms. Then a bullet screamed past Metelitsa's ear, but he fired back, and the man who had been chasing him stumbled and fell.

"You're wrong—you won't get me!" cried the herdsman triumphantly, not believing until the very last moment that they would catch him.

But all of a sudden someone big and heavy fell on him from behind and pinned him to the ground. He tried to free one arm, but a savage blow on the head stunned him . . .

Then they all began to beat him one after another, and even as he lost consciousness, he could still feel blow after blow raining down on him . . .

***

In the hollow where the detachment was still asleep, it was damp and dark, but beyond the orange-tinted forest across the Khanikheza River the sun was already rising. Its air filled with the smell of autumn leaves, the new day was breaking over the *taiga*.

"The platoon commander's not back yet . . . " thought the sentry, but reluctant to disturb Levinson without good cause, he woke Baklanov instead.

"What? Isn't he back yet?" Baklanov asked, sitting up. "Well, wake Levinson then!"

Though he was still fast asleep, Levinson heard his name, and opening his eyes, quickly sat up. Glancing at the sentry and then at Baklanov, he realized that Metelitsa had not come back and that it was high time they moved on. The next moment he was on his knees, and as he rolled up his greatcoat, answered Baklanov's anxious questions in a rather offhand manner.

"Well, what of it?" he said. "I thought as much ... We're bound to meet him on the way."

But the thought that something might have happened to the platoon commander had taken complete possession of Levinson. He could not possibly imagine Metelitsa even motionless, let alone dead. He liked the man not for any outstanding social qualities, but for his extraordinary physical tenacity, the sheer animal vitality which surged perpetually in him like an inexhaustible spring and in which Levinson himself was rather lacking. Whenever he saw the herdsman's agile figure that was always so ready for action, he would forget his own physical weakness and imagine he could be just as indefatigable as Metelitsa was. He was even secretly rather proud of having such a man under his command.

The thought that Metelitsa might have fallen into the enemy's hands—though Levinson himself was becoming increasingly convinced of it—seemed incredible to the detachment. Each weary man painstakingly tried to drive the idea out of his mind, for if it were true, it would mean nothing but misfortune and suffering. And so they believed it could not possibly be true.

At last Levinson gave the order to set out. They rode for one hour, then two, but the platoon commander did not appear on the path in front of them. Another two hours went by, but there was still no sign of him.

Sunk in stern, brooding silence, the detachment rode on towards the edge of the forest.

15. Death

Metelitsa regained consciousness to find himself in a big, dark shed. He was lying on the bare ground, and the first thing he felt was the cold dampness of the earth penetrating his body. Then he remembered everything that had happened. The blows which had rained down on him were still ringing in his head, his hair was matted with dried blood, and he could feel clots of it on his forehead and cheeks.

The first reasonably clear thought that came into his head was about the possibility of escape. He groped his way round the shed, feeling every crack in the walls and even trying to force the door, but all his efforts were in vain. He was surrounded by cold, lifeless wood, and what chinks it had in it were so hopelessly small that he could not even see through them.

But he went on groping until he finally realized there definitely was no hope of escape. Once he had become convinced of it, though, the question of his own life and death ceased to interest him. Now all his mental and physical energies were concentrated on what was of paramount importance to him: how could he, Metelitsa, who had always been famed for his courage and daring, show those who were going to kill him that he was not afraid of them and moreover felt nothing but contempt for them?

Before he had time to answer this question, footsteps sounded outside the door, the bolt grated, and in the feeble morning light two armed Cossacks came into the shed. Standing upright with his legs planted wide apart, Metelitsa looked at them with narrowed eyes.

"Come along, country boy," said the leading Cossack.

Lowering his head stubbornly, Metelitsa walked out.

A few minutes later he found himself standing in front of the man he had seen the night before—the one in a black fur cap and felt cloak—and soon realized he was in the room he had watched from the priest's garden. The handsome, stout officer whom he had taken for the squadron commander was there too, but now, as he looked at both of them, a series of barely perceptible signs told him the commander was not the stout officer but the man in the cloak.

"What were you doing in the garden yesterday evening?" the man asked quickly, coming up to Metelitsa and staring at him with sharp, unblinking eyes.

Metelitsa stared silently back at him, his mocking gaze fixed on the other's face and his whole manner showing his determination that no matter what questions they asked him and however much they tried to force him to answer, he would say nothing to give them any satisfaction...

When the Cossacks dragged the dying Metelitsa away by the feet, he was still clutching at the grass, clenching his teeth with the pain and trying to lift his head, but it kept falling back and trailing helplessly along the ground ...

Half an hour later the Cossack squadron rode out of the village and galloped away up the same road that Metelitsa had travelled the night before.

***

Feeling just as anxious as the others, Baklanov could finally restrain himself no longer.

"Listen," he said to Levinson, "let me ride on ahead—after all, God knows what we might be up against!"

He spurred on his horse and more quickly than he had expected, came out to the edge of the forest. There, no more than a quarter of a mile away, he saw a squadron of about fifty mounted men riding down a slope. They were moving at a walk in rather loose formation.

Baklanov turned back and signalled to Levinson to stop.

"Are there many of them?" asked Levinson after hearing him out.

"About fifty."

"Kubrak, Dubov—dismount!" ordered Levinson quietly. "Kubrak—you take the right flank, Dubov the left . . ."

Putting Baklanov in command of Metelitsa's platoon and ordering him to remain where he was for the moment, Levinson dismounted and walked on ahead of his men, swinging his Mauser and limping slightly as he went.

Then he ordered the detachment to form a skirmish line in the bushes. The enemy squadron was quite close now, and by their yellow trouser-stripes and cap-bands Levinson could see they were Cossacks. He could even make out the commander in his black cloak too.

Though the enemy were few in number, Levinson was filled with excitement just as he had been in the early days of his military career many years before. In that career he could now distinguish two different phases, and though they were not divided by any definite line, they were still quite distinct from each other because of the feelings they had aroused in him.

During the first phase, when—though he possessed no military training and was unable even to handle a gun—he had been obliged to take command of a large number of men, he had not felt that he was really in control of them but that events were occurring independently both of him and his volition. During this first, short phase of his military career, almost all his strength of mind had been devoted to overcoming and concealing from others the fear for his own life which he could not help feeling in battle.

However, he had grown accustomed to the situation very quickly and had managed to achieve a state of mind in which fear for his own life was no longer an obstacle in being responsible for the lives of others. During this second phase of his career he had acquired the capacity to direct events, and the more clearly he had detected their actual course and the correlation between forces and the men involved in them, the more developed this capacity had become.

The enemy squadron was so near now that the partisans could hear the drumming of the horses' hoofs and the men's restrained conversation, as well as make out several of their faces. Levinson could even see some of their expressions—particularly that of a handsome, stout officer with a pipe in his mouth who had just ridden out in front of the others.

"How my heart's beating!" thought Levinson. "Is it time to fire yet? Is it? No, wait till they get to that birch tree with the torn bark . . ."

"Plat-oo-oon!" he suddenly cried in a high-pitched, long drawn-out voice just as the squadron reached the tree. "Fire!"

At the sound of Levinson's voice, the handsome officer looked up in astonishment, but the next instant his peak-cap flew off his head and his face took on an expression of unbelievable helplessness and terror.

"Fire!" Levinson shouted again, and aiming at the handsome officer, pulled the trigger.

The Cossacks were thrown into confusion. For a few seconds the panic-stricken riders and rearing horses bunched together, the men shouting something that was inaudible amid all the gunfire. Then a lone horseman in a black fur hat and felt cloak broke free from the rest and pranced out in front of the squadron, reining in his horse and brandishing his sabre. But the others paid no attention to him. Several of them were already lashing their horses and galloping away, and a few seconds later the rest of the squadron dashed after them. Then the partisans leapt up from their hiding place and the most daring of them raced off in pursuit, firing as they ran.

"Get the horses!" shouted Levinson.

A few moments later the whole detachment was galloping after them.

Swept along by the avalanche of horses and men, Mechik galloped in the middle of the crowd of riders. Not only did he feel no fear, but he had even lost his usual habit of observing his own thoughts and actions then assessing them from a position of detachment. All he knew was that the enemy were running away, and like the other partisans he was doing his utmost to catch up with them.

Suddenly the shaggy stallion galloping in front of him stumbled and plunged headlong to the ground, and with arms outstretched its familiar-looking rider flew over the animal's head. Then, like the others, Mechik swerved to avoid something big and dark that was writhing on the ground.

No longer seeing the familiar-looking back in front of him, Mechik fixed his eyes on the small wood that was rushing towards him. Just then several men galloping close beside him veered sharply to the left, but not knowing why they had done so, Mechik kept on riding straight ahead until he flew in among the trees, scratching his face on the branches as he did so.

All of a sudden he found himself alone—alone in the soft stillness of the birch wood, amid golden leaves and grass ...

By the time he rode out into the open again, the detachment had gone. About two hundred yards away lay a dead horse, its saddle lying to one side, while next to it, clasping his knees in despair, a man sat motionless. It was Morozka.

Mishka was lying on his side with his teeth bared, his big eyes glassy and staring, and his forelegs with their sharp hoofs bent as if even in death he were ready to gallop away. Morozka was gazing past him with shining, dry eyes.

"Morozka!" Mechik called softly, stopping in front of him, his heart suddenly filled with pity for both the man and his dead horse.

But Morozka did not stir. For a few moments neither of them said a word, neither of them moved. Finally, heaving a sigh, Morozka unclasped his hands, got to his knees, and without looking at Mechik, began to unfasten the saddle. Then with a grunt he slung it over his shoulder and set off towards the wood.

"Let me take it for you!" cried Mechik. "Or you can have my horse if you like and I'll walk!"

Morozka did not look back, though, but only bent lower still under the weight of the saddle.

Anxious now to avoid him, Mechik made a long detour to the left, and after skirting the wood, saw a village down in the valley not far away. In a wide hollow to his right, stretching as far as the ridge that curved away into the gray distance, was a forest.

By the time he rode into the village, most of the detachment had already gone off to their billets, while those who remained were standing in a crowd near a large hut with tall, carved window frames. His face covered with sweat and dust, and his cap askew, Levinson was standing on the porch giving orders. Mechik dismounted near the fence where the detachment's horses were standing.

Night was falling. Somewhere only a stone's throw away drunken voices were singing merrily and someone was playing an accordion.

Mechik looked round the corner and saw Morozka staggering clumsily down the middle of the street with his accordion, holding the instrument at arm's length in front of him and drawing it out for all he was worth. Behind him came a crowd of men who were just as drunk as he was, none of them wearing belts or caps.

"A-ah! My dear old friend!" cried Morozka in drunken but hypocritical rapture as he caught sight of Mechik. "Where are you going? Come and have a drink with us! Oh, to hell with you, then! We'll all die anyway!"

The men crowded round Mechik, thrusting their jovial, drunken faces close to his, putting their arms around him and breathing the smell of stale spirits into his face. Then someone pushed a half-chewed cucumber and a bottle into his hands.

"No, no, I don't drink," said Mechik, trying to move away, "I don't want to ..."

"Drink, damn you!" cried Morozka, almost weeping in his drunken ecstasy. "Oh, Jesus Christ! We'll all die anyway!"

"Only a little then, please—I don't drink, you see," said Mechik, finally giving in.

He took a few gulps from the bottle. Then Morozka, drawing the accordion as wide as it would go, began to sing in a hoarse voice, and all the others joined in.

"Come along with us!" said one of them, taking Mechik by the arm and pressing a bristly cheek up against his face.

And off they went down the street, joking together as they stumbled along, frightening the village dogs with their noise, and cursing themselves, their own kith and kin, and this uncertain, harsh world—cursing them all to the very sky that rose darkening over their heads like a great starless cupola.

16. The Swamp

Varya had not taken part in the attack—she had stayed behind in the forest with the baggage train—and so did not reach the village until all the men had gone off to their quarters. But she noticed the huts had been occupied in a haphazard fashion, at random. All the platoons had got mixed up, nobody knew where anyone else had gone, and no one obeyed their commanders any more—in fact the whole detachment had disintegrated into a series of separate, independent groups.

Only Dubov had managed to billet his platoon in an orderly fashion, using neighboring huts. Some of his men were on guard on the outskirts of the village, while others were helping Levinson lay in supplies. On that day, what had previously been concealed by the general activity of things and by the daily routine in which everyone had so far shared, suddenly emerged quite clearly: it was mainly Dubov's platoon that was keeping the detachment together.

Varya learned from the men that Morozka was alive and had not even been wounded. "So he's all right," she thought. "Well, I'm glad..."

It was night when all of a sudden, far beyond the village where the Khanikheza highroad began and the sentries were posted, three shots rang out—the agreed signal of alarm. Barely had Morozka lifted his tousled head from the hay than the signal came again, then immediately, cutting through the still darkness, a machine-gun began to chatter in reply, howling like a wolf in the night...

It had stopped raining now but the wind had stiffened. There was a shutter banging somewhere, and yellow, wet leaves went whirling by in the gloom. Dubov's orderly ran down the street, knocking at the windows and shouting as he went, and lights began to go on in the huts.

While the platoon was forming up, the firing spread in a semicircle as far as the river itself. Shells began to whine through the air and flaring tongues of flame soared crackling into the sky above the village. Baklanov, his greatcoat tightly belted and a revolver in his hand, came running up and shouted:

"Dismount! Form up in single file! Leave twenty men with the horses!"

A few moments later he cried "Follow me! At the double!" then plunged into the darkness. Close behind him raced the line of men, belting their greatcoats as they ran.

A few moments later they came face to face with the sentries who were running away.

"There's a whole army of them!" the fleeing men shouted, waving their arms in panic.

Just then a salvo crashed from the enemy's field-guns, and the shells burst in the middle of the village, illuminating for an instant a patch of sky, the crooked bell tower of the church and the priest's garden glistening with dew. Then the sky seemed to become even darker still. The shells were bursting one after the other now, at short, regular intervals. Somewhere on the outskirts of the village something was on fire—a haystack or a hut was ablaze.

Baklanov had to hold back the enemy till Levinson had managed to rally the detachment, scattered as it was all over the village. But it was too late. Before Baklanov even had time to lead his platoon to the village common, he saw by the light of the bursting shells the enemy lines running towards them. Judging by where the enemy's fire was coming from, he realized they were trying to encircle the partisans on the left flank, from the direction of the river, and he guessed they would probably break into the village from that side at any moment.

His platoon began to return the enemy's fire and to retreat to the right, running in small groups and zig-zagging through the orchards, gardens and lanes. Suddenly, with a fearful yell the enemy cavalry came racing by from the direction of the highroad, and a dark, roaring avalanche of horses and men poured headlong down the village street.

No longer attempting to hold back the enemy, Baklanov's platoon which had by now lost about ten men, ran off across the still unoccupied area of ground towards the forest. Almost at the edge of a narrow ravine where the last few village huts stood, they came upon Levinson and the rest of the men who had been waiting for them. The detachment's ranks were noticeably thinner now.

"Here they are!" said Levinson with relief. "To your horses—and quickly!"

They mounted and galloped at full speed towards the forest which showed dark down in the hollow. But the enemy had apparently caught sight of them, for machine-guns began to chatter behind them as they fled. Then shells came hurtling down from high above, and with a loud hiss they plunged into the ground at the horses' feet. The animals shied, opening their hot, bloody mouths and whinnying in terror. The riders closed up again, leaving bodies writhing on the ground behind them.

Looking back, Levinson saw an enormous glow over the village—a whole section of it was ablaze now—and in the light, fiery-faced little figures could be seen darting to and fro, some in groups and others singly.

All of a sudden, Stashinsky, who was galloping beside Levinson, toppled from his horse and for a few seconds was dragged along the ground with one foot caught in his stirrup. Then he fell, and his horse galloped on alone, while the whole detachment wheeled to avoid the doctor's body, not wishing to trample it.

"Levinson, look!" cried Baklanov in excitement, and pointed to the right.

The detachment was already at the bottom of the ravine and was rapidly approaching the forest, but from above, silhouetted against the sky, the enemy cavalry was racing to head them off.

"Quick! Quick!" shouted Levinson, spurring on his horse and glancing behind him all the time.

At last they reached the edge of the forest and dismounted. Baklanov with Dubov's platoon once again stayed in the rear to cover the retreat, while the rest hurried in among the trees, leading their horses by the bridle.

In the forest it was quiet and peaceful. Left behind now, the chatter of machine-guns, the crackle of rifle fire and the thunder of field-guns seemed remote and failed to disturb the stillness.

Levinson gave his horse to his orderly, Efimka, and showing Kubrak which way to go, told him to press on ahead, while he himself stood to one side so as to see how many men he had left.

Peering into the gloom, they walked past him, with water splashing under their feet. The ground was very wet and marshy, and now and again the horses would sink in up to their bellies.

Then, limping with both feet now, Levinson walked on, following behind his men. But suddenly the detachment came to a halt.

"What's wrong?" he asked.

A few moments later the answer came back down the column:

"We can't go any further—there's a swamp . . ."

Suppressing the trembling that suddenly filled his legs, Levinson ran on ahead to where Kubrak was. Scarcely had he disappeared among the trees than the whole mass of men came flooding back and began to rush about in every direction, but on all sides, blocking their path, lay a viscous, dark swamp. There was only one way out of here, and that was the way they had already come. But the sound of gunfire at the edge of the forest no longer sounded so remote, and it seemed to be drawing nearer every moment.

Then suddenly Levinson himself appeared in their midst, holding aloft a blazing pinewood torch which illumined his pale, bearded face with its clenched teeth and large, burning eyes that flitted from one man to the next. And in the sudden silence, his shrill, hoarse voice rang out so that all could hear it:

"Listen to my orders! We're going to lay a brushwood road across the swamp—there's no other way out . . . Borisov, take your men and go back and help Baklanov! Tell him to hold on till I give the order to retreat . . . Kubrak! Detail three men to keep in touch with Baklanov . . . Now listen, all of you! Tether your horses! Two squads are to cut down willow bushes! And don't spare your sabres either! All the rest of you will be under Kubrak's orders. You must obey him without question. Now, Kubrak, follow me!" Levinson turned his back on the column and stooping, walked towards the swamp, holding the smoking torch high above his head.

Suddenly the whole mass of men, dejected and subdued, was gripped by a fever of superhumanly rapid and obedient activity. In the twinkling of an eye horses were tethered, axes started to ring and alder trees began crashing down under the blows of sabres. Borisov's platoon raced off into the darkness, their weapons rattling and their feet squelching as they ran, while towards them hurried other men, already carrying the first armfuls of willow branches to begin the work ... Then came the crash of a falling tree, and the huge, spreading mass of leaves fell with a rustling splash into the soft, treacherous swamp. By the light of the blazing pine torch the men saw the dark green, weed-covered surface slowly heaving and rolling like a gigantic serpent.

There, amid water and mud, in the very face of death, the men worked like demons, illumined by the smoky flame of the torch that picked out from the darkness their distorted faces, bent backs and the great tangled heap of branches. Tearing off their greatcoats, they labored on and on, and through the rents in their trousers and shirts could be seen sweating flesh that was scratched and bleeding. They had lost all sense of time and space, all awareness of shame, pain and fatigue. Now and again as they worked, they scooped up with their caps the stagnant water that reeked of frogspawn, and like a pack of wild animals hastily gulped it down ... But the sound of firing was drawing steadily nearer, growing louder and fiercer every moment. Baklanov kept sending back one man after another to ask: "Will it be long? How long will it be?" He had lost almost half his men now, among them Dubov who had bled to death from his countless wounds, and he was slowly retreating, yielding inch by inch. Already the enemy's bullets were whistling thick and fast over the swamp, and several men working there had been hit. Varya was busy dressing their wounds. Frightened by the gunfire, the horses neighed frenziedly and reared in terror. Some of them had broken free from their tethers and raced off into the forest, but falling into the swamp, they could only whinny piteously for help.

Then, hearing the brushwood road was ready at last, the men holding back the enemy took to their heels.

Shouting, waving their torches and weapons, and dragging their reluctant horses behind them, the detachment surged on to the brushwood road almost en masse. The terrified horses refused to obey the men leading them and struggled frantically. Crazed with fear, the animals behind clambered on to those in front, while the brushwood kept cracking and giving way. Almost at the far side, where the swamp met the opposite bank, Mechik's horse fell off the brushwood and had to be dragged out of the water with ropes amid a furious torrent of abuse. Mechik clutched convulsively at the slippery rope which kept jerking with the animal's frenzied struggling, and getting his legs entangled in the muddy branches beneath him, he pulled and pulled at the terrified beast with all his might.

The last to cross the brushwood road were Levinson and Goncharenko.

The blaster managed to lay a charge of dynamite, and just before the enemy reached the crossing place, the brushwood was blown to smithereens.

After a while the men came to and saw that it was morning. Before them lay the *taiga,* decked in sparkling pink rime. Bright patches of light blue sky showed through gaps in the trees above their heads, and they could see that far away in the distance, beyond the forest, the sun was rising. Throwing down the burning torches which for some reason they were still carrying, they looked at their torn, bleeding hands and their exhausted, steaming horses—and marvelled at what they had accomplished that night.

17. The Nineteen

Five versts from the place where the brushwood road had been laid, a bridge carrying the Tudo-Vaku highroad spanned the swamp. The previous evening, fearing that Levinson might not spend the night in the village, the Cossacks had prepared an ambush on the road, about eight versts beyond the bridge.

They had stayed there all night, waiting for the detachment to appear, and had heard the salvoes of artillery fire in the distance. The next morning a messenger came galloping up with orders that they were to remain where they were, since the enemy had broken through the swamp and were now heading towards them. Only ten minutes or so after the messenger had ridden past, Levinson's detachment—knowing nothing of the ambush—came out onto the Tudo-Vaku highroad.

The sun had already risen above the forest and the hoar-frost had melted long ago. The sky spread high above them, transparently blue and cool, and the trees, their golden leaves glistening, bent low over the road. The day promised to be warm, not like an autumn day at all.

But Levinson gazed at all this bright, shining beauty with vacant eyes, and did not take it in. He looked at his exhausted detachment, trailing dejectedly along the road with two-thirds of its men missing, and realized how desperately tired he was and how powerless he was to do anything for these men now. But they and they alone still mattered to him, they alone were still near and dear to him. These faithful men trudging wretchedly along behind him were dearer to him than anything in the world, dearer even than his own life, because not for a single moment could he forget that he was indebted to them. But he felt he was no longer capable of doing anything for them, that he was no longer really their commander, and that it was only they themselves who were still unaware of it, continuing to trail submissively after him like a herd accustomed to following its leader.

He tried to concentrate on something practical and useful, but his thoughts kept wandering and becoming confused. His eyes kept closing too, and vague sensations of his surroundings, fragments of memories, and strange images, all of them contradictory and obscure, swirled soundlessly in his head in an ever-changing, incorporeal swarm ... "Why this long, endless road, these shining, wet leaves and this lifeless sky of which I have no need any more?" he wondered. "What must I do now? Ah yes—I must get through to the Tudo-Vaku valley ... But how tired I am! And how sleepy I feel! What more can these men possibly want of me when I need to sleep so much! He's talking to me about scouts ... Yes, yes, of course ... we must send out scouts, and then ... sleep ... sleep ..."

"What did you say?" Levinson asked suddenly, looking up.

Baklanov was riding beside him.

"I said we ought to send out scouts."

"Yes, yes, we ought ... " answered Levinson. "See to it, then, please ..."

A few moments later someone came riding past at a weary trot, and Levinson saw it was Mechik. It seemed wrong somehow for Mechik to be going on ahead as a scout, but he could not work out exactly why it was wrong, and the next moment he forgot all about it. Then someone else went riding by.

"Morozka!" shouted Baklanov as the second scout rode away. "Make sure you don't lose sight of each other ..."

"Is Morozka still alive?" thought Levinson. "But Dubov's dead ... Poor Dubov!"

Mechik, who had already ridden quite a long way ahead, looked back. Morozka was about a hundred yards behind and the detachment was still visible too in the distance. Then both the detachment and Morozka disappeared round a bend.

The road wound its way along wet slopes thickly covered with oaks and maples still bearing their dark crimson leaves, then it began to climb and Mechik's mare slowed to a walk. Dozing in the saddle, he made no attempt to urge the horse on, and from time to time he came to and gazed in bewilderment at the timeless forest all around him. It had neither beginning nor end, just as there was neither beginning nor end to his drowsy, vacant state.

Suddenly his horse snorted with fright and shied into the bushes. Mechik quickly looked up and in a flash his drowsiness was gone, giving way to indescribable terror. Standing in the road just a few yards in front of him was a group of Cossacks.

"Get down!" said one of them in a hoarse whisper.

Just then another seized Mechik's horse by the bridle, but with a faint cry he suddenly slipped from the saddle and flung himself head-long down the hillside. His arms crashed painfully against a wet tree-trunk and he leapt to his feet, then fell over once more. Speechless with terror, he floundered on all fours for a few moments, then getting to his feet again, raced off down the ravine. They were chasing him—he could hear the bushes crashing behind him and someone gasping with fury and cursing as he ran . . .

Morozka, knowing there was another scout ahead of him, also paid little attention to what was going on around him. He was in that state of extreme fatigue when all thoughts, even the most important of them, completely disappear, and there remains only the urgent desire to rest—to rest at all costs. He did not think of his own life any more, or of Varya either, but only of the time when the promised land would at last open out before him and he could lay down his weary head and rest. That promised land he imagined as a large, peaceful village flooded with sunlight and filled with grazing cows and fine people, a village fragrant with the smell of livestock and hay. He dreamed of how he would tether his horse, have a piece of sweet-smelling rye bread with a bowl of milk, then climb up into a hayloft and fall fast asleep with his warm greatcoat wrapped round his feet and his head tucked deep in the straw . . .

When the Cossacks' yellow capbands suddenly rose up before him and his horse jibbed sharply, his joyous vision of a large, sunlit village merged with the instantaneous realization that unparalleled, vile treachery had just been committed . . .

"He ran away, the filthy bastard!" thought Morozka, suddenly imagining with extraordinary clarity the loathsome, clear eyes of Mechik, and feeling at the same instant agonizing pity both for himself and for the men behind him.

He did not mind that in a moment he would die and therefore cease to suffer, feel and move, but he realized quite clearly he would never see the sunlit village of his dreams. Nor would he ever see the dear, good friends riding behind him again. But they were all so much a part of him, those unsuspecting, exhausted men who had entrusted themselves to him, that he thought of nothing else other than to warn them of the danger threatening them. He snatched his revolver from its holster, and holding it high above his head so that he would be better heard, fired three times into the air, as had been agreed...

At the same instant there was a flash and a roar, and the world seemed to split in two. Morozka and his horse fell into the bushes, the man's head flung back.

When Levinson heard the shots, they seemed so incredible given his present state of mind that at first he could not even grasp what they meant. He only understood their true significance when he heard the volley fired at Morozka, and then the detachment's horses stopped dead in their tracks with their heads raised and their ears pricked up.

Suddenly, with total clarity, Levinson saw the simple, boyish face of Baklanov before him, a face blackened by gunsmoke and coarsened by fatigue. Holding his revolver in one hand and clutching his horse's withers with the other, he stared intently towards where the shots had come from. He was leaning forward a little in anticipation of orders from Levinson, and his ingenuous face with its high cheekbones burned with the all-consuming passion in whose name the detachment's best men had perished.

Levinson gave a start and drew himself up, and as he did so, his body was filled with a pleasurable yet painful quivering. Then he suddenly bared his sabre and leant forward like Baklanov, his eyes shining.

"Shall we break through, eh?" he asked in a hoarse voice, lifting his sabre high above his head so that it flashed in the sun. Seeing it, each partisan gave a start and drew himself up in the stirrups.

Baklanov cast a ferocious look at the sabre, then turning round to face the detachment, shouted something in a harsh, shrill voice, something Levinson did not catch, for at that very moment, carried away by the same inner urge that filled Baklanov and had made him raise his own sabre, he put his horse into a gallop, feeling sure the whole detachment would immediately follow...

When he looked back a few moments later, the men were indeed galloping after him, bent low in the saddle with their chins thrust forward in headlong flight, their eyes burning with the same passionate light he had seen in Baklanov's.

But this was the last coherent impression that Levinson had, because the next instant something deafening and blinding came crashing down on him, crushing him then whirling him away. No longer conscious of what was happening and aware only that he was still alive, he went hurtling into a seething, orange abyss.

***

Mechik did not look behind him, and though he could no longer hear his pursuers, he knew they were still chasing him. When the three shots rang out and the volley crashed, he thought they were firing at him, so he ran faster still. All of a sudden the ravine widened out into a small wooded valley. He kept turning to right and left until he suddenly slipped and rolled down a slope once more. Just then came a new volley, much louder and heavier than the first, followed by a second and a third, thundering on and on without pause. The whole forest echoed and came to life . . .

"Oh, my God, my God!" he cried, shuddering at each new report and running on, summoning up every last ounce of his strength.

But gradually the sound of firing died down, as though it had changed its direction. Then it ceased altogether.

After looking back several times, Mechik realized he was not being pursued any more. Breathless, he sank to the ground behind the nearest bush, his heart pounding furiously. He lay there for several minutes without moving.

Then he suddenly sat up and clutching his head, gave a loud groan. He dug his fingers into his hair and with a mournful howl began to roll about on the ground. "What have I done? Oh, what have I done?" he kept saying, rolling to and fro on his elbows and stomach. With every movement he made he saw more clearly the true meaning of his flight, as well as of the first three shots and of all the firing that had followed. "How could I have done it? I, such a good, honorable man who wished no one any harm? Oh, how could I?"

The more loathsome and vile his behavior seemed, the more noble and pure he felt he had been before committing this shameful act.

He was tormented not so much because dozens of men who had entrusted themselves to him had perished as a result of his action, as because its indelibly filthy, abominable stain gave the lie to all the purity and goodness he felt he possessed.

Mechanically he pulled out his revolver, and filled with horror, stared at it for a long time. But he knew he would never kill himself, knew he was incapable of doing so, because there was nothing he loved more in all the world than himself—his feeble, white hands, his whining voice, his suffering and his actions—even the most despicable of them. Hastily he put the revolver back in his pocket.

He was not groaning or weeping any more now. Covering his face with his hands, he lay quietly on his stomach, and all that he had lived through since leaving town a few months ago began to pass through his mind. The naive dreams of which he now felt so ashamed, the anguish of his early encounters and first wounds, Morozka, the infirmary, old Pika with his wisps of silvery hair, Varya with her big, sad eyes, and finally, the terrible crossing of the swamp, before which all else paled.

"I don't want to go through all that any more," he thought with sudden resolve. "I just can't stand it any longer. I simply can't live such an inhuman, base life any more."

He continued to reproach himself, but could no longer suppress the hope and joy which began to stir in him at the thought that he was now completely free and could go where nobody would ever know what he had done. "I'll go back to town now," he thought, "I've no choice but to do that, anyway . . ."

He took out his revolver again and flung it far away into the bushes. Then he found a small spring, and after washing himself, sat down beside it. But he still could not bring himself to go up on to the road. "What if the Whites are there?" he wondered.

"But what difference does it make if they are?" he suddenly thought.

Then, heaving a deep sigh, he buttoned up his shirt and wandered slowly off in the direction of the Tudo-Vaku highroad.

***

Levinson did not know how long his state of semi-consciousness had lasted. It seemed a very long time, though in actual fact it was no more than a minute. When he came to he was amazed to find himself still in the saddle, though the sabre was no longer in his hand. Close in front of him was the black-maned neck of his galloping horse, one of its ears stained with blood.

It was only then that he became aware of the firing and realized it was directed at them because the bullets were whining thick and fast overhead. But he also realized that the shooting was coming from behind them now and that the most terrible moment was behind them too. Just then two riders drew level with him, and he recognized Goncharenko and Varya. The blaster's cheek was covered with blood. Then Levinson remembered the detachment and looked back, but there was no detachment left any more. Instead, the road was littered with the bodies of horses and men. A few riders, led by Kubrak, were desperately trying to catch up with the rest, while further back were other little groups of men that were growing smaller every moment. Someone on a limping horse had fallen far behind, and was waving one arm and shouting. But he was quickly surrounded by men with yellow cap bands who began beating him with their rifle butts, and he swayed and fell. Levinson winced and turned away.

Just then, Goncharenko, Varya and he reached a bend in the road and the sound of firing grew fainter. Mechanically Levinson reined in his horse a little, and one by one the partisans who were left alive came riding up to him. Goncharenko counted nineteen of them, including Levinson and himself. Then without saying a word, they all galloped downhill for quite a while, their frightened eyes gradually filling with gladness at seeing the narrow, yellow road running silently into the distance ahead of them . . .

Little by little the horses slowed to a trot and then to a walk.

Hanging his head, Levinson was riding a few yards ahead of the others, deep in thought. All of a sudden he reined in his horse and looked round. The eighteen men behind him all stopped too, and it suddenly became very quiet.

"Where's Baklanov?" asked Levinson.

The eighteen men looked at him in silence and dismay.

"Baklanov was killed . . . " said Goncharenko eventually, and stared hard at his big, gnarled hand that was holding the reins.

Sitting hunched in the saddle beside him, Varya suddenly fell forward onto her horse's neck and began to weep, sobbing loudly and hysterically. The animal twitched its ears wearily and drew in its sagging lower lip.

For a few moments more Levinson's eyes stared into the distance above the men's heads. Then his whole body suddenly seemed to shrink and slump, and everyone saw he had grown very frail and looked much older. But he was no longer ashamed of it and no longer tried to hide it. He sat with downcast eyes, slowly blinking his long, wet lashes as the tears rolled down his beard. The men looked away for fear they might break down too.

Then Levinson turned his horse again and rode slowly on. The detachment set off behind him once more.

But again and again, remembering Baklanov was no longer there, Levinson began to weep.

So it was that they rode out of the forest—all nineteen of them.

The trees came to an end quite unexpectedly, and they saw before them a vast expanse of light blue sky and red-brown, harvested fields that were flooded with sunlight and stretched away as far as the eye could see. Near a clump of willows by the deep, blue water of a small river lay a wide threshing-ground, resplendent with its peaked haystacks and golden sheaves of corn. Here a completely different life was in progress, a life that was sonorous, busy and gay. The threshing-machine whirred with a dry, clear sound, sheaves of wheat flew through the air, and excited voices and bursts of girlish laughter could be heard amid the swirling clouds of chaff glittering in the light. Beyond the river, their lower slopes standing deep in curly-yellow woodland, dark blue mountains towered into the sky, and over their jagged peaks translucent, pinkish-white clouds, risen like foam from the salt sea far beyond, came pouring down into the valley, bubbling and frothing like milk fresh from the cow.

With eyes that were still wet with tears, Levinson gazed at the expanse of sky and earth that promised both food and rest, gazed at the unfamiliar people on the threshing-ground whom he would soon have to make just as near and dear to him as the eighteen men riding silently behind him—and he ceased to weep. After all, he had to go on living and doing his duty.

1925–26

Notes

1. A range of mountains approximately 1,200 kms. long in eastern Primorskii krai (Maritime Region) in the extreme southeast of the USSR between the valleys of the Rivers Ussuri and Amur to the west and the Sea of Japan to the east. Over 70% of the Maritime Region is forested. Most of *The Rout* takes place in the area east of the Ussuri River and Lake Khanka, in the Maritime Region, between 44 and 46 North and 133 and 135 East, in the hinterland of Vladivostok and the newer port of Nakhodka.

2. Town in the south of the Maritime Region, east of Vladivostok and north of Nakhodka. It was renamed Partisansk in 1972.

3. Geographical name given to coniferous forest in the north of Russia and Siberia.

4. Town west of Suchan.

5. Russian Workers' and Soldiers' Councils of Deputies (Delegates).

6. Village east of Lake Khanka and northeast of Spassk-Dal'nii.

7. Village. Location obscure.

8. Single-shot rifle of American origin, improved in the 1860s by the Russian engineers Gorlov and Gunius, and used by the Russian army between 1868 and 1891.

9. Village on the Daubikhe River north of Arsenev.

10. (Spassk-Dal'nii), town southeast of Lake Khanka, approximately 250 kms. north of Vladivostok. It was named Spassk until 1930.

11. Village on the Sandagou River, east of Arsenev.

12. Village. Location obscure.

13. A cereal similar to millet.
14. Railway settlement on the Daubikhe River near Arsenev.
15. Village. Location obscure.
16. Village on the Fudzin River, northeast of Arsenev.
17. Eastern tributary of the Ussuri River.
18. Old Russian measure of weight equal to 16.38 kg. or approximately 36 lb. avoirdupois.
19. Town south of Arsenev on the Daubikhe River.
20. Village. Location obscure.
21. Town on the Suchan River north of Nakhodka.
22. Port on the Sea of Japan, northeast of Vladivostok.
23. Village. Location obscure.
24. Eastern tributary of the Ussuri River.
25. Alexander Vasilievich Kolchak (1874–1920), Russian admiral. After the 1917 Revolution he took an active part in the fighting against the Bolsheviks in Siberia. From November 1918 to January 1920 he was "Supreme Ruler of Russia." Captured by the Bolsheviks, he was shot at Irkutsk in February, 1920.
26. Eastern tributary of the Ussuri River.
27. Chief river in the Maritime Region and primary tributary of the Amur River.
28. Village northeast of Suchan.
29. Part of the Sikhote-Alin range.
30. Tributary of the Suchan River in the south of the Maritime Region.
31. Dish of cooked grain or groats.
32. Eastern tributary of the Ussuri River.
33. Eastern tributary of the Ussuri River.
34. Faction of the left SR (Socialist Revolutionary) Party after 1904, close to the Anarchists. They believed in the use of terrorism against the Tsarist regime and advocated a peasant-based socialism. They supported the Bolsheviks until the Treaty of Brest-Litovsk (1918), but later were opposed to them.

Nikolai Ostrovsky in Berezdov in the western Ukraine (1923).

Nikolai Ostrovsky
HOW THE STEEL WAS TEMPERED

Ostrovsky's Communist Party membership card, dated 1924.

NIKOLAI OSTROVSKY (1904–1936)

Nikolai Alexeevich Ostrovsky's brief life was dogged by illness and suffering. The fifth child of poor parents, he was born in 1904 in the village of Viliya near Ostrog in Volhynia Province, south of Rovno in the western Ukraine. His father was a seasonal laborer who had originally worked in a malthouse, while his mother was the daughter of a local forester. He attended the village school until he was nine and after leaving with a certificate of good conduct, spent the spring and summer of 1913 working as a herdsboy. Late the following year the family moved to the railway town of Shepetovka, southeast of Rovno, where in January 1915 Ostrovsky entered elementary school, only to be expelled that spring by his scripture teacher. In September of that year he began work in the kitchens at Shepetovka station, and after being dismissed early in 1917 for falling asleep on duty, found a job in a timber yard. In January 1918 he became first a stoker's mate and then an electrician at the local power station.

When in the spring of 1918 the Germans occupied Shepetovka, the fourteen-year-old Ostrovsky ran errands for the town's underground Bolshevik organization. In July of that year he joined the Komsomol in Shepetovka and in August volunteered for the Red Army, leaving for the front shortly afterwards. Early 1920 found him serving in the famous Kotovsky cavalry brigade, and during the fighting near Odessa later that year he was wounded and contracted typhus. Returning to the ranks, he participated in the First Cavalry Army's historic attack on Berdichev and Zhitomir in early June 1920, and later that month took part in the capture of Novograd-Volynsky. In mid-August he was seriously wounded by shrapnel while in action near Lvov and was sent to hospital in Kiev. That October he was demobilized on medical grounds and the next month returned to Shepetovka.

The summer of 1921 found him back in Kiev, where he worked in the railway workshops, served as secretary of the local Komsomol and studied in his spare time, before taking part that November in the construction of the Boyarka branch line southwest of the city. But continuing illness—rheumatism and typhus—severely undermined his health, and in August 1922 he was sent to Berdyansk, a resort on the Sea of Azov, for treatment. That October, at the age of eighteen, Ostrovsky was officially declared an invalid. His deteriorating condition did not, however, prevent him from continuing doggedly to serve the cause in whatever way he could, and for the rest of his life he showed amazing courage and determination. In 1923 he was appointed both Commissar of the Red Army's Second Training Battalion and Komsomol secretary for Berezdov in the western Ukraine, and in January 1924 he was transferred to Izyaslav, west of Shepetovka, as head of the Komsomol district committee there. In August of that year he joined the Communist Party.

But persistent illness was steadily taking its toll. December 1924 brought a visit to Kharkov for treatment, and he was obliged to spend the whole of 1925 there. In May 1926 he moved to a sanatorium in Yevpatoria in the Crimea, but by December polyarthritis had deprived him of almost all mobility, and he became virtually bedridden. After further treatment in Novorossiisk on the Black Sea coast, in December 1927 he began a correspondence course at the Sverdlov Communist University in Moscow, and despite still more treatment in Sochi, by June 1929 he had successfully completed his studies. August, however, brought complete loss of vision, and after unsuccessful surgery in Moscow he returned in 1930 to Sochi. Undaunted by almost total paralysis and by blindness, he persevered and, by half-writing and half-dictating, began work on his first novel. Amazingly, too, he wrote articles for newspapers and journals, and spoke many times on the radio. The house specially built for him in Sochi became a place of pilgrimage where he would regularly talk with readers and writers, and lead discussion groups for young Party workers.

In April 1932 Ostrovsky was accepted as a member by the Moscow branch of the Association of Proletarian Writers, and in June 1934 he joined the newly-formed Union of Soviet Writers. On October 1st of the following year he was awarded the Order of Lenin. After visiting Moscow for treatment during the early months of 1936, he went back to Sochi in May before returning to the capital once more in October. December of that year, though, brought a sudden deterioration in his condition and he died later that month, aged only thirty-two. The funeral urn containing his ashes was interred in the Novodevichy Cemetery in Moscow.

***

Ostrovsky began writing Part One of his novel *How the Steel Was Tempered,* his only complete literary work, in November 1930 in Sochi. It was finished in late 1931, and early chapters of it appeared in issue four of the Moscow journal *The Young Guard* (*Molodaya gvardiya*) in 1932, before the work was published in book form at the end of the year. After returning to Sochi in June 1932, Ostrovsky embarked on Part Two of the novel and continued work on it throughout 1933. This second part was serialized in *The Young Guard* from January 1934 onwards, and appeared as a separate edition later that year. The novel was to remain a bestseller for a decade, selling over five million copies in dozens of editions at home and being widely translated abroad. In 1935 Ostrovsky wrote a film scenario of the work in collaboration with the director M. B. Zats, while a screen version was eventually made in Kiev in 1958.

In January 1934 Ostrovsky began to plan a second work, *Born of the Storm,* a novel about the Civil War in the Ukraine which was to remain unfinished at his death. In December of that year he was able to dictate the first few chapters, and in the following April excerpts from early sections of the work were published in the Sochi newspaper, *Sochi Truth (Sochinskaya pravda).* The complete chapters of Book One were finally serialized in the journal *The Young Guard* in 1935 and 1936. The first volume of *Born of the Storm* appeared in book form in Moscow on the day of Ostrovsky's funeral, December 26, 1936.

HOW THE STEEL WAS TEMPERED

PART ONE

1

"All those who came to my house before Easter to be tested stand up!"

The speaker, a flabby man in a priest's cassock with a heavy cross around his neck, glared at the class.

His evil little eyes seemed to transfix the six children—four boys and two girls—who rose from their seats and looked at him apprehensively.

"You can sit down," he said, motioning to the girls.

They quickly did so, heaving sighs of relief.

Father Vasily's small eyes were fixed on the four boys.

"Now then, my friends, come over here!" he said.

He rose, and pushing back his chair, walked right up to the boys who were now standing huddled together.

"Which of you young ruffians smokes?" he asked.

"We don't smoke, Father," they all answered timidly.

The priest's face turned crimson with anger.

"So you say you don't smoke, you scoundrels! Who was it then who put tobacco in my dough? You don't smoke, eh? Well we'll soon see about that! Turn out your pockets! Come on, be quick about it! D'you hear me? Turn them out!"

Three of the boys began to empty their pockets out onto the table. The priest examined the seams carefully, looking for traces of tobacco in them, but he could find nothing. Then he turned to the fourth boy, a dark-eyed lad in a thin gray shirt and blue trousers that had been patched at the knees.

"What are you standing there like a statue for?" he asked.

Looking at the priest with eyes full of hatred, the boy replied sullenly: "I haven't got any pockets," and ran his hands down the sides of his trousers to prove it.

"Ah-hah! So you say you've got no pockets, eh? D'you really think I don't know who could play a nasty trick like ruining my dough? And d'you think you'll be allowed to stay on at school this time too? No, my lad, you're going to pay for this! Last time I only let you stay because your mother begged me to keep you, but now you're finished! So get out of the class!" And grasping the boy painfully by the ear, he flung him out into the corridor and slammed the door behind him.

The rest of the class sat silent and cowed. No one could understand why Pavel Korchagin had been thrown out. Only Seryozha Bruzzhak, Pavel's best friend, had seen him sprinkle a handful of tobacco into Father Vasily's Easter cake dough while the six unsatisfactory pupils were waiting in the priest's kitchen.

Sadly Pavel sat down on the bottom step of the school porch, wondering how he could go home and what he would tell his mother— his mother who worked from morning till night at the customs inspector's and always worried so much about him.

He choked back the tears.

"Now what shall I do?" he wondered. "And it's all because of that damned priest! Why on earth did I have to go and put tobacco in his dough? It was Seryozha's idea anyway! 'Come on,' he says, 'Let's play a trick on the nasty old devil!' So we did. Now Seryozha's got away with it but I'll be kicked out for sure!"

Pavel's feud with Father Vasily had begun a long time ago—it went back to the day when he had been caught fighting with Mishka Levchukov and had gone without his dinner as punishment.

He had caught it pretty hot from his mother that time too.

But the next day she had gone to school and begged Father Vasily to take her son back. From then on Pavel had come to loathe the priest with all his being, hating and fearing him at the same time. He could never forgive anybody for doing him an injury, however slight it might be.

After that, Pavel had suffered many a slight at Father Vasily's hands. The priest would often send him out of the class, make him stand in the corner day in, day out for a trifling misdemeanor, and never once tested him on what he had been given to learn, with the result that just before Easter Pavel had been forced to go to be examined. It was there in the priest's kitchen that he had sprinkled tobacco into the dough.

No one had seen him do it, but Father Vasily had guessed who the culprit was all the same.

***

The proprietor of the station buffet, a pale, middle-aged man with colorless, watery eyes, cast a brief glance at Pavel.

"How old is he?" he asked.

"Twelve," the boy's mother replied.

"All right, then, he can stay. He'll get eight rubles a month and his food on the days he works, and he'll do twenty-four hours at a stretch every other day. And there's to be no pilfering, mind!"

"No, of course not, sir!" exclaimed the mother fearfully. "He won't steal . . . I'll vouch for that!"

"Well then, he can start today," answered the proprietor, and turning to the woman behind the counter, said: "Zina, take this boy to the scullery and tell Frosya to set him to work in Grishka's place."

The woman put down the knife which she was using to slice some ham, and nodding to Pavel, led the way across the dining room towards a side door that opened into the scullery. Pavel followed her. Hurrying after him, his mother whispered quickly:

"Now Pavel, my dear, do your best and don't disgrace yourself!" Then, watching her son with sad eyes, she made her way towards the door.

In the scullery work was in full swing. There was a mountain of knives, forks and plates piled high on the table, and several women were drying them with long towels flung over their shoulders.

A dishevelled, red-haired boy slightly older than Pavel was busy seeing to two enormous samovars.

The scullery was thick with steam rising from a large vat full of hot water where the dishes were being washed, and at first Pavel could not make out the faces of the women working near it. So he just stood there, unsure what to do.

Then Zina went up to one of the women, and tapping her on the shoulder, said:

"Here, Frosya, I've brought you a new boy to take Grishka's place, so you'd better tell him what to do."

Then, turning to Pavel, Zina pointed to Frosya and said:

"She's in charge here, so do what she tells you!" And with that she turned and went back into the buffet again.

"All right," Pavel answered softly and looked enquiringly at Frosya who was standing in front of him. Wiping the sweat from her brow, she examined him from head to foot, then rolling up one sleeve which had slipped down over her elbow, said in a surprisingly pleasant, husky voice:

"It's not a very nice job, dearie! This vat here's got to be heated in the mornings and kept hot so there's boiling water all the time. Then you've got to keep plenty of firewood chopped, of course, and there's the samovars to look after as well. Then you'll have to clean the knives and forks when they need it and take out the slops. There's plenty of work to do, my dear, so you'll be kept busy enough," she said, speaking with a Kostroma[1] accent and emphasizing her "a's." Her flushed face with its little turned-up nose and her pleasant way of speaking made Pavel feel a bit more cheerful somehow.

Suddenly the scullery door opened and three waiters came in carrying trays piled high with dirty dishes.

One of them, a broad-shouldered, cross-eyed fellow with a heavy, square jaw, said: "You'd better get a move on in here! The twelve o'clock's due any minute, and you're all dawdling!"

Then, glancing at Pavel, he asked:

"Who's this, then?"

"He's the new boy," answered Frosya.

"Ah, the new boy," he said. "Well now, just you listen to me," he went on, laying a heavy hand on Pavel's shoulder and pushing him over towards the samovars. "You're supposed to keep these boiling all the time, my lad, but look! One's gone out already and the other's barely lit. Now I'll let you off today, but if it happens again, you'll get a thick ear! D'you understand?"

Without saying a word, Pavel set about seeing to the samovars.

So it was that his working life began. Never had he worked so hard as on that first day. He realized that this wasn't home where he could disobey his mother whenever he liked—the cross-eyed waiter had made it quite clear that if he didn't do as he was told, he would suffer for it.

Pushing one of his boots down over the chimney pipe and using it as a bellows, Pavel soon had sparks flying from the enormous potbellied samovars. Then he snatched up the slop buckets and dashed outside to the waste pit. Next he put fresh wood on the fire under the boiler and dried the wet towels on the hot samovars—in other words he did everything he was told.

At seven o'clock the next morning, exhausted after a night without sleep and hours spent running to and fro, he turned the boiling samovars over to the boy who was to relieve him—a fat-faced lad with sly-looking little eyes.

Pavel's first day at work had passed off successfully enough and he strode home with the proud feeling of a man who has honestly earned his rest. Now he too was a worker and no one could call him a scrounger any more.

The morning sun was slowly climbing above the enormous bulk of the saw-mill, and soon the little house where he lived would come into sight. Yes, there it was, just behind the big property that belonged to the Leshchinsky family.

"Mother's probably already up by now, and here I am, just coming home from work," he thought, and quickened his step, whistling softly as he went. "Getting kicked out of school didn't turn out so badly after all! That damned priest wouldn't have given me a moment's peace anyway, so now he can go to hell for all I care!" he said to himself as he neared the house.

His mother was busy with the samovar out in the yard, but catching sight of her son, she asked anxiously:

"Well, how did you get on?"

"Fine," answered Pavel.

She was on the point of warning him about something, but Pavel understood what she meant because through the open window he caught sight of his brother's broad back.

"So Artem's come home, has he?" he asked, feeling rather embarrassed.

"Yes, he came back last night. He's going to stay here now and work down at the railway yards."

Rather hesitantly, Pavel opened the front door and went in. As he did so, the huge figure sitting at the table with his back to the door turned round and Pavel found his brother's stern eyes gazing at him from beneath bushy black brows.

"Ah-hah, so our tobacco lad's come home, has he?" said Artem. "Well, well now, that's good!"

His brother's words of greeting did not bode well for Pavel. "So Artem knows about it already," he thought. "Looks like he's going to give me a good telling-off or even a thrashing as well!"

He had always been rather afraid of his elder brother.

But Artem evidently had no intention of thrashing him. Instead, he sat on a stool with his elbows resting on the table and looked intently at Pavel, his expression one of both amusement and mockery.

"So you've graduated from university, eh, finished all your lessons, and now you're busy carrying out the slops, are you?" he said.

Pavel stared down at the head of a nail that was sticking up from a cracked floorboard. Then Artem got up from the table and went out into the kitchen.

"Doesn't look as if I'm going to get a thrashing after all," thought Pavel with a sigh of relief.

Later on, at tea-time, Artem calmly questioned him about the incident at school.

Pavel told him everything that had happened.

Then, pushing his empty cup away, Artem said:

"Now listen to me, my lad. What's done is done, but from now on you've got to watch your step and not play the fool at work. Just do everything you're told, because if you get kicked out of there too I'll give you the worst hiding you've ever had in your life. So just you remember that! You've given mother enough trouble as it is! Wherever you go, damn it, something or other always goes wrong and you get yourself into hot water! Now, enough's enough! When you've worked at the station buffet for a year or so, I'll try to get them to take you on as an apprentice down at the railway yards, because you'll never get very far if you spend your time messing about with slops! What you've got to do is learn a trade. You're still a bit young just now, but in a year's time I'll see what I can do—they might just take you on. I'm moving back home and I'll be staying here from now on, so mother won't need to go out to work any more. She's slaved long enough for all kinds of swine as it is! But just you watch out, Pavel, you've got to be a man now!"

Then Artem got to his feet and drawing himself up to his full height, put on the jacket that was hanging over his chair and said to his mother:

"I'm going out for an hour or so." Then, stooping in the low doorway, he went out of the house. But as he walked past the window on his way across the yard, he called to Pavel:

"There's a pair of boots and a pen-knife I've brought for you. Mother'll give them to you."

***

The station buffet was open continuously, both day and night.

Five different railway lines met at this junction, so the station was always crowded with people. Only for two or three hours at night, during the interval between two trains, was the place ever quiet. Hundreds of troop trains were continually passing through on their way to and from the front, some bringing the maimed and wounded back and others carrying a constant stream of fresh men in gray overcoats that all looked monotonously alike.

Pavel worked like a slave in the buffet for two years—two years in which he hardly saw a thing except the kitchen and scullery. In the enormous basement kitchen work went on at a feverish pace. More than twenty people were continually busy there, while ten waiters scurried to and fro all day long between the restaurant and the kitchen.

By now Pavel was being paid not eight rubles a month but ten. He had grown taller and broader during those two years, and had been obliged to suffer many hardships in that time. For six months he had slaved away as a kitchen-boy but then had been sent back to the scullery by the all-powerful chef. The man had taken a dislike to this taciturn boy—after all, he might suddenly stick a knife in you if you so much as boxed his ears. Pavel's temper would have cost him his job long ago had it not been for his boundless capacity for work. He could keep at it much longer than anybody else and never seemed to get tired.

When work in the buffet was at its busiest, Pavel would dash to and fro like one possessed, hurtling in and out of the kitchen with loaded trays and taking the flight of four or five steps at a single bound.

At night, when all the bustle in the buffet subsided for a while, the waiters would gather in the storerooms downstairs and engage in wild card games. Pavel would often see large heaps of bank-notes lying on the tables. He was not surprised at these sums, though, for he knew that each waiter received thirty to forty rubles a shift in tips, some of it fifty kopecks or even a ruble at a time. They would get drunk on this money later and spend it all on cards, and because of this Pavel felt hatred for them all.

"Damned swine!" he thought. "There's Artem, a first-class mechanic, but all he ever gets is forty-eight rubles a month, and I only get ten. But they rake in all that in a single day—and for what? Just for carrying trays in and out! Then they go and blow it all on drink and cards!"

To Pavel the waiters were just as alien and loathsome as his employers. "They spend their time prancing around like flunkeys here, the swine, while their stuck-up wives and sons strut about town like the idle rich," he thought angrily.

Working in the buffet, he caught a glimpse of the lowest depths of life—its very dregs that were as dark as the water at the bottom of a well—and the odor of dank mold drifted over this boy who was so eager for unexplored, new things.

Artem did not manage to get his brother taken on as an apprentice at the railway yards—they would not hire anyone under fifteen. But all the same, feeling strongly drawn to the enormous, soot-blackened depot, Pavel looked forward eagerly to the day when he could leave the station buffet for good.

In the meantime he often went down to see Artem at the yards and would check the carriages with him, trying to help as much as he could.

***

But Pavel was to leave his job at the station much sooner than he had expected, and moreover he was to do so in a way he had never anticipated.

One frosty January morning when he had finished his shift and was ready to go home, the boy who was due to relieve him failed to turn up. Pavel went to see the proprietor's wife and said he was leaving, but she refused to let him go. So though he was already very tired, he had to work a second shift, and by evening was so exhausted that he could hardly keep on his feet. But during the night interval he had to fill the vats again and have them boiling by the time the 3 a.m. train arrived.

He turned on the tap but no water came out—the pump was evidently not working properly—so, leaving the tap on, he lay down on the woodpile to wait for the water to come on. But overcome by fatigue, he soon fell fast asleep.

A few minutes later the tap began rumbling and gurgling and water started to run into the vat. Filling it to the brim, it overflowed on to the tiled floor of the scullery which as usual was deserted at this early hour. So the water flowed on unchecked, flooding the entire floor then seeping under the door into the buffet.

Gradually the streams of water crept under the luggage belonging to dozing passengers, but no one noticed them until the water reached a man who was lying on the floor. Suddenly he leapt to his feet with a cry of alarm. Then everyone rushed for their luggage and there was uproar.

But the water still came pouring in.

The waiter Prokhoshka who had been clearing the tables in the second dining room came rushing up when he heard all the commotion. Leaping over the pools of water on the floor, he ran to the kitchen door and with a great effort flung it open. But the water that till now had been held back by the door came bursting into the dining room in a furious torrent.

At this, the shouts grew louder still, and the waiters on duty went rushing into the scullery, where Prokhoshka hurled himself on the still sleeping Pavel.

Blow after blow rained down on the boy's head, stunning him with pain.

Still half-asleep, he did not know what was happening. He was only aware of blinding flashes of light before his eyes and a searing pain shooting through his body.

He was so badly beaten that he could hardly drag himself home.

The next morning, grim-faced and frowning, Artem asked him what had happened.

Pavel told him.

"And who beat you up?" Artem asked in a hollow voice.

"Prokhoshka."

"All right. Now just lie still."

Then Artem put on his sheepskin jacket and without another word went out of the house.

***

"Can I see Prokhor, the waiter?" asked the stranger, speaking to Glasha, one of the dishwashers.

"Yes, he'll be here in a minute, so hang on," she replied.

The workman leaned his huge bulk against the door.

"All right, I'll wait," he said.

A few moments later, Prokhor kicked the door open and came into the scullery carrying an enormous pile of dishes on a tray.

"That's him," said Glasha, pointing towards the waiter.

Artem stepped forward and laying a heavy hand on Prokhor's shoulder, looked him straight in the eye and asked:

"What did you beat up my brother Pavel for?"

Prokhor tried to free his shoulder from Artem's grip, but a terrible blow from the workman's fist sent him crashing to the floor. He struggled to get up, but then a second blow, even more terrible than the first, laid him flat on his back once more.

Frightened out of their wits, the dishwashers scattered.

Then Artem turned and made for the door.

Prokhor was tossing about on the floor, his smashed face covered with blood.

That evening Artem did not come home from the railway yards, and his mother found out that he was being held by the police.

He eventually returned six days later, in the late evening when his mother was already asleep. Coming in to see Pavel who was still sitting up in bed, he asked affectionately:

"Well, lad, are you feeling better now?" Then he sat down beside him. "There's worse things, you know!" And after a moment's silence, he added: "Never mind! You'll be going to work at the power station soon—I've already spoken to them about you. You'll be able to learn a real trade there!"

Grasping Artem's enormous hand in both his own, Pavel squeezed it hard.

2

The shattering news spread through the little town like wildfire: "The Tsar's been overthrown!"

But the townsfolk simply could not believe it.

Then one day when a blizzard was raging, a train came crawling into the station. Two students in greatcoats and armed with rifles, accompanied by a detachment of revolutionary guards wearing red armbands, poured out on to the platform. They arrested the station policemen, an old colonel and the commander of the local garrison, and at that the townsfolk finally believed the news. Then thousands of people came streaming down the snow-covered streets towards the main square.

There they listened avidly to the new words: freedom, equality and brotherhood. Tumultuous days followed, days filled with excitement and jubilation. Then things gradually became more calm, and the Red flag flying over the town hall where the Mensheviks had set up headquarters was the only reminder of the change that had taken place. Everything else remained just as it was before.

Towards the end of winter a regiment of horse guards was billeted in the town. In the mornings squadrons of them would ride down to the station to catch deserters from the Southwestern Front.

The guards were strapping, burly fellows with well-fed faces. Most of their officers were princes or counts, and they had golden shoulder-straps and silver piping on their breeches just as in the days of the Tsar—almost as though there had been no revolution at all.

The year 1917 was passing steadily by, but for Pavel and his friends nothing had changed and the old bosses were still there. It was not until the rains of November set in that something out of the ordinary began to happen. People of a different kind started to appear at the station, more and more of them soldiers from the front, and they bore the strange-sounding name of "Bolsheviks."

Quite where that weighty, resounding name came from, nobody knew.

Now the guardsmen found it increasingly hard to check the flow of deserters from the front, and down at the station the crackle of rifle fire and the smashing of windows could often be heard. The troops were leaving the front in droves now, and if anyone tried to stop them they used their bayonets. By early December they were pouring through the station by the trainload.

Then the guards surrounded the station in force, intending to check the mounting tide of deserters, but they were greeted by bursts of machine-gun fire. The gray-coated troops streaming out of the railway carriages towards them were men totally inured to death.

The soldiers drove the guards back into town, then returned to the station to continue their journey, streaming on and on by the trainload.

***

One morning in the spring of 1918 Pavel was on his way home from the power station where he had been working as a stoker's mate for a year now.

The little town was buzzing with excitement, and he sensed it straightaway. As he walked along he kept meeting more and more people carrying one, two and sometimes even three rifles each. Not knowing what was happening, he hurried home as fast as he could

Running into the house, he had a quick wash, then hearing from his mother that Artem was not back yet, he hurried out again.

After running down a couple of streets he almost collided with a boy who was staggering along carrying a heavy infantry rifle with its bayonet fixed.

"Where did you get that from?" he asked, stopping him.

"The Red partisans were giving them out opposite the school, but there aren't any left now—they've all gone! This is my second one!" he declared proudly.

Pavel was terribly disappointed by what the boy had said.

"Oh damn! I should've gone straight there instead of going home first!" he thought despairingly. "And now I've missed my chance!" Then, suddenly struck by an idea, he spun round and catching up with the boy in a couple of bounds, tore the rifle from his grasp. "You've got one already, so that's enough! This one's for me!" he declared in a tone that seemed to allow no answer.

Infuriated by this act of daylight robbery, the boy flung himself at Pavel, but the latter sprang back and pointing the bayonet at him, cried:

"Keep away or you'll get hurt!" The boy burst into tears of helpless rage and ran off, swearing at Pavel with impotent fury as he went. Feeling very pleased with himself, Pavel raced home. He leapt over the garden fence, and running into the shed, laid his new treasure across the beams under the roof. Then whistling gaily, he went into the house.

* * *

The Germans entered the town just three days after the Red partisan detachment had left. Their arrival was announced by the whistle of an engine down at the station which had been almost deserted for several days now. The news spread through the little town like wildfire:
"The Germans are coming!"

The town began to bustle and seethe like an ant-hill that has suddenly been disturbed, for although the inhabitants had known for a long time that the Germans were on their way, they had somehow not quite believed it. And now all of a sudden these terrible Germans were not simply on their way any more but actually here, right in town.

The Germans came from the station, marching in single file down both sides of the main road and leaving the middle free. They wore dark green uniforms and carried their rifles at the ready, rifles that were tipped with broad, knife-like bayonets. They wore heavy steel helmets and had enormous packs on their backs, and they came marching into the town in an endless stream. But they made their way cautiously along the road, ready to repel an attack at any moment, even though no one had the slightest intention of attacking them.

At their head marched two officers with Mausers in their hands, while in the middle of the road walked the interpreter, a sergeant-major in the Hetman's[2] service, wearing a dark blue Ukrainian coat and a tall fur cap.

The Germans formed up on the square in the center of town, and the drums rolled. A small crowd of the rather bolder townsfolk had gathered.

The Hetman's interpreter in the Ukrainian coat climbed up onto the porch of the chemist's shop and in a loud voice read out an order issued by the German Commandant, Major Korf. It ran thus:

§ 1

All citizens of this town are hereby ordered to surrender any firearms or other weapons in their possession within 24 hours. Anyone found guilty of disobeying this order will be shot.

§ 2

Martial law is declared in the town, and citizens are forbidden to appear on the streets after 8 o'clock in the evening.

Major Korf
Town Commandant

The commandant's staff set up headquarters in the building that had once housed the town's administration and then after the 1917 Revolution had been used by the Soviet of Workers' Deputies. By the entrance stood a sentry who wore not an ordinary steel helmet but a ceremonial one with an enormous imperial eagle on it. In the yard of the same building was a storeroom for the arms that were to be surrendered by the local population.

***

As soon as he heard the commandant's order, Artem hurried home. Meeting Pavel in the yard, he took hold of him by the shoulder and asked him quietly but firmly:

"Did you bring any weapons back from the partisans' store?"

Pavel had been meaning to keep quiet about the rifle, but he could not bring himself to lie to his brother, so told him all about it.

They went to the shed together. Taking the rifle down from its hiding place up on the beams, Artem removed the bayonet and bolt, then grasping it by the barrel, swung it with all his might against one of the posts in the garden fence. The butt was smashed to smithereens. He hurled what was left of the gun far away on to the piece of waste ground beyond the garden, then dropped the bayonet and bolt into the pit under the privy.

When he had finished, he turned to his brother and said: "Now Pavel, you're not a small boy any more, and it's high time you realized you can't fool around with guns! I'm telling you seriously now—don't ever bring anything like that into the house again—it might cost you your life. And don't try playing any tricks on me either, because if you do bring something in and they find it, then it'll be me who gets shot first! They won't touch a youngster like you. These are bad times we're living in, d'you understand?"

Pavel promised not to bring anything dangerous into the house again.

5

It was a foul, dark night, one of those nights when even with their eyes wide open people cannot pierce the gloom, and make their way about blindly, expecting to fall into a ditch at any moment and break their necks.

It was one of those nights, and yet there was a man moving through the village.

Reaching the Korchagins' house, he knocked cautiously at the window. Then, hearing no answer, he knocked again, more loudly and urgently this time.

Inside, Pavel was dreaming that a strange creature quite unlike a human being was aiming a machine-gun at him. He was trying to escape but there was nowhere to go, and now the machine-gun had started its terrible rattling.

Its chattering was even making the window-panes rattle now.

Waking up, he jumped out of bed, and going to the window, tried to make out who it was outside but all he could see was a blurred, dark shape.

He was alone in the house—his mother had gone to stay with her elder daughter whose husband was a mechanic at the sugar refinery, while Artem was away in the next village, earning a living by wielding a sledge-hammer in the blacksmith's forge.

And yet the only person who could be knocking was Artem.

Pavel decided to open the window.

"Who's there?" he called into the darkness.

A figure moved outside the window and a gruff voice replied:

"It's me, Fyodor!"

Then two hands appeared on the window-sill and the head of Fyodor Zhukhrai, a Bolshevik sailor who was a friend of Artem's, rose up until it was level with Pavel's face.

"I've come to stay the night, lad," he whispered. "Is that all right?"

"But of course!" replied Pavel warmly. "You know you're always welcome! Climb in!"

Slowly Fyodor squeezed his great bulk in through the window. Then, closing it behind him, he remained standing there for a few moments listening, and when the moon slipped out from behind a cloud and shone on the road, he scanned it carefully. Then turning to Pavel, he asked:

"We won't wake your mother, will we?"

When Pavel told him that there was no one else in the house, Fyodor began to feel more at ease and spoke more loudly:

"Petlyura's[3] cut-throats are really after me now, lad, make no mistake! That's twice they've made a general search for me, and today they nearly nabbed me! I was just on my way home, you see, going by the back way, of course, and I stopped by the shed to see if the coast was clear. Then I suddenly caught sight of someone standing in the garden—he was hiding behind a tree but his bayonet gave him away. So of course I cast off there and then, and headed for your place. I'll drop anchor here for a few days, lad, if you don't mind. All right? Well, that's good!"

Then, still breathing heavily, he began to pull off his muddy boots.

Pavel was glad Fyodor had come. The power station had not been working for quite a while now, and he had felt bored on his own in the empty house.

They lay down. Pavel fell asleep straightaway, but Fyodor lay awake smoking quietly. Then he got up again and treading softly on his bare feet, went over to the window and gazed out into the street for a long time. Eventually he lay down again and overcome by tiredness, fell asleep, his hand warming the butt of the heavy Colt under his pillow.

***

Fyodor Zhukhrai's unexpected arrival that night and the week spent with him in the house proved extremely significant for Pavel. For the first time in his life he heard much that was exciting and new, and the few days spent in the sailor's company were to be decisive for the young stoker.

For his part, forced into hiding like a rat in a trap, Fyodor made the most of his enforced inactivity by conveying to the eager Pavel all his bitter hatred for the Ukrainian nationalists who were throttling the region.

Fyodor spoke in a language that was colorful, simple and clear. There were no doubts in his mind at all, and he saw plainly where the road ahead lay. Gradually Pavel realized that the tangle of different political parties with fine-sounding names—Socialist Revolutionaries, Social Democrats and Polish Socialists—were all bitter enemies of the working class, and that the only truly revolutionary grouping which steadfastly fought the rich was the Bolshevik Party.

Earlier he had felt hopelessly confused about all this.

And so it was that Fyodor Zhukhrai, this big, strong Baltic sailor weathered by countless sea squalls, a confirmed Bolshevik who had been a member of the Russian Social Democratic Labor Party since

1915, spoke of life's harsh truths to the young stoker, who listened spellbound.

"I used to be just like you, lad, when I was a boy," he said. "Never knew what to do with my energy, and it would always get the better of me. We were very poor, and sometimes just to look at those well-fed, pampered little sons of the gentry all dressed up to the nines would be enough to make me see red. I often used to give them a thrashing but all I ever got out of it was a damn good hiding from my dad! So it's no good—you can't change anything on your own. Now you've got all the makings of a fighter for the workers' cause, Pavel, but you're still young and you don't have much understanding yet of what the class struggle really means. But I'll show you the right road, lad, because I know you'll be all right one day. No, I can't stand the quiet, smug sort! Right now the whole world's on fire! The slaves have risen in revolt and the old life's got to be scuttled once and for all! But to do that we need lads with guts, not silly little sissies who'll go crawling off and hide as soon as the fighting starts! What we need is fellows who'll hit out without mercy and give no quarter!"

Fyodor's fist crashed down on the table.

Then he got up, and frowning, began to pace to and fro, his hands thrust deep in his pockets.

He was depressed by his enforced inactivity and very much regretted having remained behind in the little town when the partisans left. Now, believing that to stay any longer was pointless, he had decided to make his way through the enemy lines to join the Reds.

A group of nine Party members would remain behind in the town to carry on political work.

"They'll manage all right without me," he thought to himself irritably. "I can't sit around here any longer doing nothing! Enough's enough—I've wasted ten months as it is!"

A day or so later Pavel asked him: "What exactly are you, Fyodor?"

Fyodor got up and thrust his hands in his pockets. He did not understand what Pavel meant at first.

"D'you mean you don't know?" he said.

"Well, I think you're a Bolshevik or Communist or something," Pavel replied in a low voice.

At that Fyodor burst out laughing, merrily slapping his broad chest in its tight-fitting, striped jersey.

"Yes, that's true, lad! And after all, you know, Bolshevik and Communist mean one and the same thing!" Then he suddenly became serious. "But now you know that about me, remember you mustn't ever tell anyone, unless of course you want to get me hung, drawn and quartered! D'you understand?"

"Yes, I understand," replied Pavel firmly.

Fyodor used to go out in the evenings and not come back till late at night. He was busy making arrangements with the Party comrades who would stay behind when he left, and he was discussing the work they had to do.

Then one night he did not come back at all, and when Pavel woke the next morning he saw that the sailor's bed was empty.

Filled with a vague sense of foreboding, he dressed quickly and hurried out of the house.

***

After walking about ten yards down the street, Pavel caught sight of two men coming round a corner on the main road. In front, wearing a black cap pulled down low over his eyes, walked a broad-chested, stocky fellow, his unbuttoned jacket revealing a striped jersey under it. He had a big dark blue bruise on one cheek.

Just three paces behind him, his bayonet almost touching the man's back, came a Petlyura soldier in a gray coat with two cartridge pouches at his belt.

From under his shaggy sheepskin hat he was watching the back of the prisoner's head through narrowed eyes. His tobacco-stained, yellow whiskers bristled on either side of his face.

Pavel was rooted to the spot with astonishment—he had recognized the arrested man as Fyodor straightaway.

"So that's why he didn't come back last night!" he thought.

Fyodor was coming nearer and nearer, and Pavel's heart began to pound furiously. His thoughts raced madly one after another, and it was in vain that he tried to stop them and take stock of what was happening. There just wasn't enough time to think, but one thing was clear: Fyodor was done for.

As he watched the two men drawing nearer, Pavel was overwhelmed by the whirlwind of feelings that had seized him.

"What am I to do?" he wondered desperately.

He shot a quick glance behind him. The street leading into town was deserted—there wasn't a soul in sight. In front of him a woman in a short spring coat was hurrying across the road. She wouldn't interfere, he thought. He couldn't see the second street that led away from the crossroads, and only far away in the distance, on the road leading to the station, were a few people visible.

Pavel moved towards the side of the road. Fyodor did not notice him until they were just a few yards apart.

He glanced at the boy out of the corner of his eye and his bushy eyebrows quivered. Then he recognized him, and his surprise made him slacken his pace for a moment, and the soldier's bayonet pricked him in the back.

"Hey, you!" cried the guard in a shrill falsetto. "Get a move on or I'll give you one with this butt!"

Fyodor quickened his step. He was about to say something to Pavel then stopped himself and simply waved his hand as if in greeting.

Afraid of attracting the soldier's attention, Pavel turned away as Fyodor passed him, pretending to be quite indifferent to what was going on.

And then, all of a sudden, it happened: just as the soldier drew level with him, Pavel lunged at him, and seizing his rifle, knocked the barrel downwards with a sharp movement.

The bayonet struck the pavement with a loud, grating sound. The attack caught the soldier completely by surprise and for a moment he was dumbfounded, but the next instant he jerked the rifle towards him with all his might. But by throwing the whole weight of his body on it, Pavel managed to keep hold of it. A shot rang out, and after hitting a paving-stone, the bullet ricocheted with a whine into the gutter.

Hearing the shot, Fyodor sprang aside then spun round. The soldier was trying desperately to tear the rifle from Pavel's grasp. He kept turning the gun round, twisting the boy's arms painfully as he did so, but Pavel still would not let go. Then, infuriated, the soldier knocked Pavel off his feet with a sharp movement, but even this failed to free the rifle, because as he fell to the ground, Pavel dragged the soldier with him.

At that crucial moment no force on earth could have made him let go of the rifle.

In two bounds Fyodor was at his side. Swinging through the air, his iron fist came crashing down on the soldier's head and a moment later he had been wrenched away from the boy lying on the ground. Then, after two more smashing blows in the face, he slumped into the gutter like a heavy sack.

Then the same strong hands that had delivered those blows lifted Pavel up and set him on his feet again . . .

***

The final blow which he received in the back sent Pavel hurtling with outstretched arms against the wall of the dark room to which they had brought him. Then, badly beaten, he groped around and finding something that felt like a plank-bed, sat down. He was exhausted and extremely dispirited.

His arrest had come as a complete surprise. How had the Petlyura men found out about him, he wondered. After all, nobody had seen what had happened. And where was Fyodor?

He had left the sailor at his friend Klimka's place. From there Pavel had gone on to Sergei Bruzzhak's house, while Fyodor had stayed behind to wait for evening so as to slip out of town.

The Petlyura men had got very little out of their search of the Korchagins' house. Artem had taken his suit and accordion away with him to the village where he was working now, and his mother had taken a trunk with her, so though the soldiers searched every nook and cranny, they found almost nothing.

As for the journey to the commandant's office, though, that was something Pavel would never forget. The night was pitch dark and the sky overcast, and he had staggered blindly along in a half-dazed state, urged on by savage kicks aimed at him from behind and each side.

Now he could hear voices in the next room where the commandant's guard was quartered, and a bright strip of light showed under the door. He stood up, and feeling along the wall, groped his way around the room. Facing the plank-bed he found a window that was covered by a stout, ribbed grating, but when he gave it a pull, it would not move. The place had evidently been a storeroom.

After that he made his way towards the door and stood there for a few moments, listening. Then he pressed the handle gently. The door gave a sickening squeak.

"Needs some oil, the bloody thing!" said Pavel, and swore violently under his breath.

Through the narrow chink that opened before him, he caught sight of a pair of calloused feet with gnarled toes sticking out over the edge of a bunk. He gave another gentle push on the handle and the door squeaked again, though quite shamelessly this time. Then a dishevelled, sleepy figure got up from the bunk and, scratching his lice-ridden head with all five fingers of one hand, launched into a long, lazy tirade. When the torrent of foul abuse had finally come to an end, the figure reached for a rifle standing at the head of the bunk and declared coolly:

"Shut that door! And if you look in here again, I'll give you a bloody good..."

Pavel pulled the door to once more, and as he did so, a roar of laughter came from the next room.

He did a great deal of thinking that night. His first attempt to join the great struggle of which Fyodor had spoken had ended in miserable failure. At the very first step he had been caught and shut up like a rat in a trap.

And when, still sitting up on the plank-bed, he drifted off into a restless sleep, the image of his mother arose before him, with her thin, lined face and the dear eyes that he knew so well. And with her image came the thought: "It's a good thing she's away—it makes it easier to bear!"

A dim, gray square of light from the window was beginning to show up on the floor.

The darkness was gradually fading. Dawn was breaking.

6

There were three of them in the storeroom now. A bearded old man in a threadbare caftan was lying on his side on the plank-bed, his thin legs in their wide canvas trousers drawn up under him. He had been arrested because the horse belonging to the Petlyura man billeted with him was missing from his shed. An elderly woman with furtive little eyes and a pointed chin was sitting on the floor. She made a living by selling home-made vodka and had been arrested on a charge of stealing a watch and other valuables. In the corner under the window, his head resting on his crumpled cap, lay Pavel, who by now was in a state of semi-consciousness.

But he could not sleep, and indeed all thoughts of rest had vanished without trace, as the persistent question: "What's going to happen next?" kept turning round and round in his head.

His bruised body ached painfully because the guard had beaten him with bestial fury.

The corners of the room were sunk in darkness. Another night lay ahead, a stifling, restless night filled again with thoughts of the unknown. It was the seventh night of his imprisonment, but to Pavel it seemed as if he had already been there for months. The floor was hard and his body was racked with pain. The day before he had seen Seryozha Bruzzhak through the window—he had stood out on the street for quite a while, looking up longingly at the windows of the building where Pavel was.

"He seems to know I'm here," Pavel had thought.

For the last three days someone had brought sour black bread for him, but the guards would not say who it was. And for two days now the commandant had pestered him with questions. What could it all mean?

During his interrogation Pavel had not given anything away and indeed had denied everything he was accused of. But quite why he had kept silent, he did not really know. He wanted to be strong and brave like all the men he had read about in books, but on the night of his arrest when he was being taken to prison, one of the guards had said as they passed the great dark bulk of the steam mill: "What's the point of dragging him around, sir? A quick bullet in the back and that'll be that!" And Pavel had felt afraid. Yes, the thought of dying at only sixteen was terrible! After all, death would mean the end of everything!

***

Out on the town square in front of the modest little church with its old-fashioned steeple, extraordinary things were happening. On three sides the square was lined with neat rectangles of troops from the regular infantry division, mustered in full battle dress.

Well-equipped and shod from stores that had once belonged to the Tsarist army, its units consisting mainly of wealthier peasants who were fighting the Soviets, the division had been transferred here to defend this extremely important railway junction.

Five different railway lines converged at Shepetovka,[4] and for Petlyura the loss of this junction would have meant the end.

So the Chief Ataman had decided to inspect his troops personally, and now everything was ready for his arrival.

Petlyura was to be welcomed with great ceremony. The blue and yellow Ukrainian flag had even been hoisted, and the new recruits were to take the oath of allegiance to it.

The divisional commander set off in a ramshackle Ford to meet Petlyura down at the station.

When he had gone, the infantry commander summoned Colonel Chernyak, a tall, well-built officer with a dashingly twirled mustache.

"Take someone with you and inspect the commandant's quarters to make sure everything's in order back there. If you find any prisoners, have a look at them and get rid of any riff-raff!"

Chernyak clicked his heels obediently, and taking the first Cossack captain he happened to see, galloped away.

* * *

Colonel Chernyak and the captain cantered up to the commandant's quarters and dismounted. Leaving their horses with an orderly, they went quickly into the guardroom.

"Where's the commandant?" Chernyak barked at the soldier on duty.

"I don't know," the man mumbled, "he's gone off somewhere."

Chernyak looked round the dirty room at the unmade beds with Cossacks of the commandant's guard sprawling on them. The men had not even got up when the two officers came in.

"What kind of pig-sty is this?" roared Chernyak. "And what are you all lounging about like hogs for?"

Then one of the Cossacks came up, and giving a copious belch, muttered:

"What are you shouting for? We've got a loudmouth of our own here as it is!"

"What did you say?" yelled Chernyak, bounding towards him. "D'you know who you're talking to, you ugly swine? I'm Colonel Chernyak! D'you hear, you son of a bitch? On your feet this minute, all of you, or I'll have every man flogged!" The infuriated colonel began to race up and down the guardhouse. "I'll give you one minute to sweep up all this dirt, tidy these beds, and make your filthy mugs look a bit more presentable! You're more like a bunch of thieves off the highroad than Cossacks!"

Seeing that things were taking a bad turn and that they might really be in for a flogging—they all knew what Chernyak was like—the Cossacks began to run about like scalded cats, and in no time at all work in the guardhouse was in full swing.

"We ought to have a look at the prisoners, sir," suggested the captain. "After all, who knows what kind of folk they've got locked up here. If the chief looks in, there could be a hell of a row!"

"Who's got the key?" Chernyak asked the sentry. "Come on, open the door this minute!"

A sergeant jumped up and immediately unlocked the storeroom door.

The captain pushed it open with his foot.

"There's not enough light in here—open it wider!" ordered Chernyak.

Peering into the room, he scrutinized the prisoners' faces.

"What are you in here for?" he snapped at the old man sitting on his plank-bed. Hitching up his trousers, the man half rose, and frightened by the colonel's sudden question, stuttered:

"I don't really know myself! They just locked me up, so here I am! An army horse went missing from my shed, but I didn't have anything to do with it."

"Whose horse was it?" interrupted the captain.

"An army one, of course. The men billeted at my place sold it and drank the money, then they blamed me!"

Chernyak swiftly looked the old man up and down, then with an impatient jerk of his shoulder, cried:

"Pick up your things and get out of here!" Then he turned to the old woman.

"And what are you here for?" he asked.

Swallowing the piece of pie she was chewing, the old woman rattled off a ready answer:

"It's nothing but a crime for me to be in here, mister chief, sir! They drank my vodka, poor widow that I am, then went and locked me up!"

"So you run a liquor business, do you?" Chernyak asked.

"Business? No, of course not!" the woman replied in an injured tone. "The commandant came and took four bottles, then never paid me a penny. That's how it always is: they drink your liquor but won't pay! Now you wouldn't call that doing business, would you?"

"That's enough!" said Chernyak. "Now get the hell out of here!"

Pavel was sitting on the floor, utterly bewildered by what was happening.

Now Chernyak was standing in front of him and examining him with his black eyes.

"Well, and what are you here for?" he asked.

Pavel had a quick answer ready.

"I cut the skirt off a saddle to make some soles," he said.

"What saddle?" asked the colonel, not understanding what the boy meant.

"Well, we've got two Cossacks billeted at our place and I cut a bit off an old saddle to sole my boots with. But the Cossacks hauled me in here for it." Then, filled with mad hope at the chance of regaining his freedom, he added: "If I'd known it wasn't allowed, I wouldn't . . ."

The colonel looked scornfully at him.

"What the hell has the commandant been doing filling the place with people like this?" Then, turning to the door, he shouted at Pavel: "Off you go home, and tell your father to give you the thrashing you deserve! Well go on now, clear out!"

Still unable to believe his ears, Pavel rushed to the door, his heart pounding as if it were fit to burst. Running through the guardroom, he slipped out into the yard behind Chernyak as the colonel made his way outside. A moment later he was through the wicket-gate and out on the street.

***

After jumping over yet another fence, Pavel finally came to a halt. He had no energy to run any further, for the hungry days spent in the airless storeroom had sapped his strength.

Another few moments, and Artem was embracing him so hard that Pavel's bones creaked with the pressure.

"Pavel! My little brother!" Artem cried.

***

And so it was decided: Pavel would leave Shepetovka the next morning. Artem would arrange for Sergei Bruzzhak's father to hide him in the cab of an engine taking a train to Kazatin.[5]

Artem, usually so serious, was beside himself with joy at finding his brother again after all the anxiety about what had happened to him. Now he was filled with boundless happiness.

The brothers walked quickly through the morning mist to the station, and by a roundabout way came up to the wood store.

There the powerful locomotive rolled slowly towards them, surrounded by clouds of hissing steam.

Old Bruzzhak was looking out of his cab.

Pavel bid Artem a hasty farewell, and gripping the iron handrail of the engine, climbed up the steps.

Then, from a distance, came the rumbling of the train as it gathered speed.

8

For over a year now, Pavel Korchagin—a Red Army soldier in Kotovsky's[6] cavalry brigade—had been racing back and forth across his native land, first astride machine-gun carts or gun limbers, then riding on a small gray mare that had lost an ear. During these months he had become much stronger and had grown into a man matured by suffering and privation.

His skin which at first had been chafed by heavy cartridge pouches till it bled, had healed long ago, and a hard callous had formed on his shoulder where his rifle-strap cut into it.

Pavel had seen many terrible things during the course of that year. Together with thousands of other soldiers who were just as ill-clad and ragged as he was, but burning with the inextinguishable flame of struggle for the power of their class, he had tramped the length and breadth of his native land, and only twice had the hurricane of war swept on without him.

The first time was when he had been hit by a bullet in the thigh, and the second was when in the bitter cold of February 1920, he had fallen victim to typhus, tossing to and fro in a sweltering, sweat-soaked fever.

That typhus had taken an even more terrible toll of the ranks of the Twelfth Army than the Polish machine-guns had. By then the Red Army was spread out over a vast area, operating across almost all the northern Ukraine and making it impossible for the Poles to advance any further. No sooner had Pavel recovered from typhus than he rejoined his unit.

His regiment was now holding the station of Frontovka,[7] on the branch line that ran from Kazatin to Uman.[8] Frontovka lay in the forest and consisted of a small station building together with a handful of abandoned, half-demolished cottages around it. Life for ordinary folk in these parts had become impossible, because for the third year running now, bloody fighting kept flaring up then dying down again. How many times had Frontovka changed hands during that time?

And now once again great events were in the offing. While the Twelfth Army, its ranks terribly depleted and rather disorganized now, was falling back towards Kiev under pressure from the White Poles, the new proletarian republic was preparing to strike a crippling blow at the enemy who were intoxicated by their victorious advance.

All the way from the distant Northern Caucasus, the battle-hardened divisions of the First Cavalry Army were being transferred to the Ukraine in a campaign that was to be without parallel in the history of war. The Fourth, Sixth, Eleventh and Fourteenth cavalry divisions came up to the Uman area one after another, grouping in the rear of the Red front and sweeping Makhno's[9] guerrilla bands aside on their way to the crucial battles ahead. In all, there were sixteen and a half thousand men in this force, sixteen and a half thousand horsemen scorched by the fiery steppe sun.

All the attention of the Supreme Red Army Command was focused on preventing this imminent and decisive blow from being anticipated by the enemy, and great care was taken by headquarters to ensure the successful grouping of this vast mass of men.

***

The flames of the camp fire flickered like shreds of ruddy cloth in the fading light, and dark brown rings of smoke went spiralling into the sky, driving away the restless swarms of midges. A short distance away, a group of soldiers lay spread out in a semi-circle around the fire, their faces glowing like burnished copper in the light of the flames.

Water was boiling in the mess-tins lying in the bluish ashes. Suddenly a furtive little tongue of flame crept out from under a burning log and licked at someone's curly head. The man jerked his head away and growled:

"Damn it!"

The men around him burst out laughing.

"The lad's so keen on learning he can't even feel the fire!" boomed a middle-aged man with a close-cropped mustache who had just been checking the barrel of his rifle against the firelight.

"Come on, Korchagin, tell us what you're reading!" said another.

The young Red Army man fingered his singed tuft of hair and smiled.

"It's what you might call a really good book, Comrade Androshchuk! Ever since I got hold of it I haven't been able to put it down!"

Pavel moved his saddle closer to the fire, and settling himself down on it, opened the thick little volume on his knees.

"It's called *The Gadfly*,[10] comrades—I got it from the battalion commissar and it's made a very powerful impression on me. If you'll sit quietly, I'll read a bit of it to you."

"Go on, then, fire away! We're all listening!"

After reading the last few pages to them, Pavel laid the book down on his knees and gazed pensively into the fire.

For a few moments nobody said a word. All were deeply moved by the gadfly's fate.

"A grim story, that!" said Sereda, breaking the silence. "But I suppose there are people like that in the world. There's not many who could stand what he did, but when you're fighting for an idea, you can put up with anything!"

The book had clearly made a profound impression on the soldier and he was visibly moved.

"No, a fellow doesn't mind dying if he's got something to die for," said Androshchuk with conviction, pushing one of the mess-tins closer to the fire with a stick. "That's what gives a man strength. You can die without any regrets if you know you're in the right. That's how heroes are made. I knew a lad once—Poraika was his name. Well, when the Whites got him cornered in Odessa, he blew himself and a whole platoon of them up with a grenade in a flash. They didn't even have time to get at him with their bayonets before he dropped the grenade at his feet and—bang! Blew himself and all those Whites around him to bits! He wasn't much of a lad to look at, you know—not on the surface anyway. Not the kind that gets books written about them, though he'd be well worth writing about! There's a lot of good lads like that among our people!"

The following day, returning from a patrol, Pavel tethered his horse to a tree and went over to speak to Kramer, the unit's political instructor, who had just finished drinking tea.

"Listen, Kramer," he said, "what would you say if I transferred to the First Cavalry Army? There's going to be important things happening there soon—after all, they're not being massed in such numbers just for the hell of it, are they? But we're going to have to hang around here and miss all the fun!"

Kramer looked at Pavel in astonishment.

"What d'you mean, transfer?" he asked. "D'you think the Red Army's like a cinema where you can keep changing seats just when you like? I've never heard anything like it! If we all started running about from one unit to another, a fine state of affairs that would be!"

"But what difference does it make where you fight—here or there?" asked Pavel, interrupting him. "After all, I'm not deserting to the rear, am I?"

But Kramer flatly refused to allow it and went on:

"But what about the question of discipline? You're all right, you know, Pavel, but in some ways you're a bit of an anarchist and you think you can do just what you like. But you're forgetting that the Party and Komsomol depend on iron discipline. And the Party must always come first. Each one of us must be where he's most needed, not where he wants to be!"

When Kramer had calmed down a little, Pavel said quietly but firmly:

"All that's quite true, but I'm transferring to Budyonny's[11] cavalry just the same."

And the following evening Pavel was missing from the group of men around the camp fire.

***

On June 5th, 1920 after a few brief but fierce skirmishes with the enemy, Budyonny's First Cavalry Army broke through the Polish front where the flanks of the Third and Fourth Polish armies met, routed an enemy cavalry brigade under General Savitsky that was blocking its path, and swept on towards Ruzhin.[12]

After learning from prisoners that a Polish army headquarters was located in Zhitomir (in actual fact, the whole front headquarters was there), the commander of the First Cavalry Army decided to take Zhitomir and Berdichev,[13] both of which were important railway junctions and administrative centers. By dawn on the 7th of June, the Fourth Red Cavalry Division was already racing towards Zhitomir.

On the right flank of one of the squadrons in place of a man called Kulyabko who had been killed, rode Pavel Korchagin.

Without reining in their heated horses, the division fanned out as they approached Zhitomir and galloped on towards the town, their unsheathed sabres flashing silver in the light.

The earth groaned under the pounding hoofs, the horses' breath came raucously, and the men stood up in their stirrups as they galloped furiously along.

The ground flashed past under the flying hoofs and the big town with its many parks came racing towards them. Then the first few gardens flew by, and as the cavalry burst into the center of town, an awesome battle cry as terrible as death itself shook the air: "Hurr-a-ah!"

The Poles were so stunned by the onslaught that they offered almost no resistance, and the local garrison was quickly crushed.

Bent low over his horse's neck, Pavel galloped on. Beside him was his comrade, Toptalo, on his thin-legged black, and Pavel saw the spirited cavalryman cut down a Polish legionary with a merciless sabre blow before the man even had time to shoulder his rifle.

The horses' iron hoofs rang out on the cobbled roadway. Then suddenly at a crossroads the two riders came face to face with a machine-gun positioned right in the middle of the street, with three soldiers in light blue uniforms and rectangular Polish caps bending over it. A fourth man, a lieutenant with snake-like coils of gold braid on his collar, levelled his Mauser at the riders as soon as he saw them galloping towards him.

Neither Toptalo nor Pavel had time to rein in their horses so they raced on towards the machine-gun, straight into the jaws of death. The officer fired at Pavel but missed, and singing like a sparrow, the bullet whined past his cheek, then the next moment, knocked off his feet by Pavel's horse, the lieutenant fell flat on his back, striking his head on the cobblestones as he did so.

But just then the machine-gun began to chatter in wild frenzy, and Toptalo and his horse fell to the ground, riddled by a dozen bullets.

Snorting in terror, Pavel's horse reared then lunged with its rider over the bodies on the ground, heading straight for the men by the gun. Then Pavel's sabre flashed through the air and sank deep into the blue rectangle of a Polish cap.

Again the sabre flashed upwards, ready to fall upon a second head, but the galloping horse leapt aside and Pavel was safe.

Like a furious mountain torrent, the Red squadron came pouring over the crossroads, and dozens of sabres flashed through the air.

***

The long, narrow corridors of the prison echoed with joyous cries.

In the cells that were filled to overflowing with gaunt-faced prisoners, there was tremendous excitement. They could hear the sound of fighting outside—but could they really believe that these men who had suddenly burst into the city from God knows where were their friends? Could they really believe that it meant freedom at last?

Now they could hear shots in the prison yard and men were running down the corridors. Then suddenly came the cry, the indescribably longed-for cry: "Comrades, you're free!"

Pavel ran up to a door with a tiny window in it from which dozens of eyes were staring, and brought his rifle-butt down furiously on the lock. Then he hit it again and again!

Already prison guards were being led down the corridors, urged on at the point of revolvers, and the place was filling with unwashed, ragged prisoners who were wild with joy.

Flinging one of the cell doors open, Pavel went running inside.

"Comrades, you're free!" he cried. "We're Budyonny's men—our division's just taken the city!"

Her face wet with tears, a woman rushed towards him, and flinging her arms around his neck as though he were her own dear son, she burst out sobbing.

The liberation of five thousand and seventy-one Bolshevik prisoners and two thousand Red Army political workers whom the White Poles had herded into these stone dungeons to await the firing squad or gallows, was far more precious to the division than any spoils of war, and almost more important than the victory itself. So it was that for over seven thousand revolutionaries the impenetrable darkness of night had suddenly been replaced by the brilliant sunlight of a hot June day.

Down the street escorted by a guard of cavalry, marched a column of Polish prisoners. At the prison gates stood the regimental commissar, writing down an order in his field notebook.

"Cruelty to unarmed prisoners," Pavel heard him say firmly as though he were speaking to himself, "will be punished by death. We are not Whites!"

And as Pavel rode away from the prison gates he recalled the closing words of the order which had been issued by the Revolutionary Military Council and read out to the whole regiment:

"The land of workers and peasants loves its Red Army and is proud of it. And it requires that on that army's banner there be not a single stain."

"Not a single stain," whispered Pavel.

***

The capture of Zhitomir was a severe blow to the Polish rear, and the enemy poured out of Kiev in two streams, fighting desperately to break free of the iron ring that encircled them.

Pavel lost all sense of his own individuality during those furious days, filled as they were with fierce encounters with the enemy. He felt submerged in the general mass of men, and like all his comrades, seemed to have forgotten the word "I," for only "we" was left—*our* regiment, *our* squadron, *our* brigade.

But events were whirling by with the speed of a hurricane, and every day brought something new.

Budyonny's Cavalry Army swept on in a relentless avalanche, striking blow after blow until the entire Polish rear was mangled and smashed. Then, intoxicated by their victory, the Red divisions hurled themselves with passionate fury at Novograd-Volynsky,[14] the town at the very heart of the Polish rear.

As the ocean wave dashes itself against the rocky shore then rolls back only to rush on once more, so the Red cavalry fell back only to press onward again and again with the terrible cry of "Forward! Forward!"

Nothing could save the Poles now—neither their barbed wire entanglements nor the desperate resistance put up by their units garrisoned in the city. Then, on the morning of the 27th of June, Budyonny's cavalry forded the River Sluch in mounted formation and burst into Novograd-Volynsky, driving the Poles out of the city towards the small town of Korets.[15]

It was during this time that Pavel had a most extraordinary encounter. One day he was sent by his brigade commander to the station where an armored train was waiting. Taking the steep railway embankment at a canter, he reined in his horse by the first carriage of the train. With the black muzzles of its guns protruding from its turrets, the gray-painted armored train looked formidable in its impregnability. Several men in greasy overalls were busy beside it, raising the heavy steel plating that protected the wheels.

"Where can I find the train commander?" Pavel asked a Red Army man in a leather jacket who was going past carrying a bucket of water.

"Over there," the soldier replied, pointing towards the locomotive.

Riding up to the engine, Pavel asked:

"Who is the commander?"

A man with a pock-marked face who was all dressed in leather turned to Pavel and said:

"I am the commander."

Pavel took a package out of his pocket.

"Here's an order from the brigade commander," he said. "Please sign on the envelope."

Resting the envelope on his knee, the commander signed his name across it. Over by the middle wheel of the locomotive a man was busy with an oil can. Pavel could only see his broad back and the butt of a revolver sticking out of the pocket of his leather trousers.

"Here you are, then," said the commander, handing the envelope back to Pavel.

Pavel picked up the reins and was about to set off again, when the man with the oil can straightened up and turned round. The next moment Pavel had leapt off his horse as though swept from the saddle by a violent gust of wind.

"Artem!" he cried.

Covered though he was in oil, the mechanic put down his can and seized the young soldier in a bear-like hug. "You young devil! So it's you, is it?"

***

On the 19th of August during a battle in the Lvov[16] area Pavel lost his service cap. He reined in his horse to retrieve it, but the Red squadrons ahead were already cutting their way through the Polish lines. Just then Pavel's comrade, Demidov, came hurtling through the bushes on his way down to the river, and as he flew past, he cried:

"The divisional commander's been killed!"

Pavel gave a start. Letunov, his heroic commander, a comrade of such selfless courage, had perished! Pavel was filled with savage fury.

Then, urging on his already exhausted horse Gnedko with the flat of his sabre, he raced off into the very thick of the fighting.

"Kill the bastards! Cut them down! Smash the Polish gentry! They've killed Letunov, the swine!" And in blind rage he slashed at a figure in a green uniform. Filled with wild fury at the death of their commander, the Red cavalrymen hacked an entire platoon of Polish legionnaires to pieces.

Then away they galloped over the battlefield in pursuit of the enemy, but the Polish artillery was already firing at them and shrapnel rent the air, scattering blood and death on every side.

Suddenly there was a blinding green flash before Pavel's eyes, thunder roared in his ears, and a fragment of red-hot steel seared his skull. Then the earth began to spin in a terrible, incomprehensible way beneath him and slowly turning, lurched to one side.

He was thrown from the saddle as if he were as light as a feather, and hurtling over Gnedko's head, crashed to the ground.

And then instant darkness fell.

9

The octopus has a bulging eye about the size of a cat's head, a dull red eye that is green in the middle and burns with iridescent, pulsating fire. The octopus is a mass of tentacles which squirm and writhe like dozens of tangled snakes, their loathsome scaly skin rustling as they twist to and fro. Now the octopus is moving. The man can see it close in front of him. And now the tentacles are crawling over his body. They are cold and sting like nettles. Then the octopus puts out its sting and sinks it deep into his head, and writhing convulsively like a leech, it begins to suck his blood. The man can feel the blood draining out of his body into the swelling octopus. And with its sting sunk in him, it sucks on and on, and the pain of its sucking is unbearable.

Then, somewhere far, far away, he hears the sound of human voices:

"How's his pulse now?"

And another voice, a woman's this time, answers softly:

"It's a hundred and thirty-eight, and his temperature's thirty-nine point five. He's delirious all the time."

Now the octopus has disappeared, but the pain from its sting still remains. Pavel can feel someone's fingers touching his wrist. He tries to open his eyes, but his eyelids seem so heavy that he hasn't the strength to lift them. And why does he feel so hot? His mother must have heated the stove. Then again he can hear voices somewhere:

"His pulse is a hundred and twenty-two now."

He tries to open his eyes again, but there is a fire burning inside him and he feels as if he is suffocating.

A drink! Oh, how he longs for a drink! He'll get up in a minute and have a good drink. But why can't he get up? He tries to move, but his limbs refuse to obey him and his body feels as if it belongs to someone else. His mother will bring him a drink of water in a minute. He'll say to her: "I want a drink of water." But there's something stirring beside him again. Is it the octopus creeping up once more? Yes, there it is, he can see the red light of its eye . . .

Then, from a long way away, he hears the soft voice again:

"Frosya, bring some water!"

"Whose name is that?" Pavel wonders, but the effort of remembering is too much for him and he is engulfed by darkness once more. Then, after a few moments, he comes drifting out of the gloom and again remembers: "I'm thirsty."

Then he hears voices saying:

"He seems to be coming round."

Then more and more clearly, and closer now, he hears that gentle voice:

"Would you like a drink, comrade?"

"Am I really ill?" he wonders. "Or isn't it me they're talking to? Oh yes—I've got typhus, that's what it is." Then for the third time he tries to lift his eyelids, and finally manages it. The first thing he detects through the narrow chink of his half-open eye is a red ball hanging above his head, but then the ball is blotted out by a dark shape. The shape bends over him and his lips feel the hard edge of a glass, then there is moisture, life-giving moisture. The fire within him dies down and goes out.

Satisfied now, he whispers:

"That's better."

"Can you see me, comrade?"

It was the dark shape standing over him that was speaking, and just before he fell asleep again, he managed to say:

"I can't see you but I can hear you . . ."

"Now who would have thought he'd pull through? But just look how he's clung to life! He's got a remarkably strong constitution. You can feel proud of yourself, Nina Vladimirovna—you've quite literally saved his life!"

And filled with emotion, the woman's voice answered:

"Oh, I'm so glad!"

After thirteen days of delirium, Pavel Korchagin had finally regained consciousness.

His young body had not wanted to die, and slowly he had recovered his strength. It was like being born all over again, for everything seemed miraculous and new. Only his head still felt unbearably heavy in its plaster cast and he was still too weak to move it, but feeling had returned to his body, and he could already clench and unclench his fists.

***

Nina Vladimirovna, a junior doctor at the military hospital, was sitting at the little table in her room leafing through a thick notebook with a lilac cover. It contained brief entries written in her small, slanting hand:

August 26, 1920

Several seriously wounded men were brought in today by hospital train. One of them has a very bad head wound. We put him in the bed over in the corner by the window. He is only seventeen. They gave me an envelope containing the documents found in his pockets, together with his case notes. His name is Pavel Andreevich Korchagin. Among his papers were a dog-eared membership card (No. 967) of the Ukrainian Komsomol, a torn Red Army identity document, and a copy of a regimental order certifying that Korchagin was given an official commendation for the exemplary fulfilment of a reconnaissance mission. There was also a note, apparently written by Korchagin himself, which said:

"In the event of my death, I request my comrades to write to my brother Artem Korchagin, Mechanic, Railway Yards, Shepetovka, Ukraine."

Korchagin has been unconscious ever since he was hit by a shell splinter on August 19th. Tomorrow Anatoly Stepanovich is going to examine him.

August 27

Today we examined Korchagin's wound. It is very deep, the skull is fractured, and the entire right side of the head is paralyzed. There is a hemorrhage in the right eye which is badly swollen.

Anatoly Stepanovich wanted to remove the eye to prevent further inflammation, but I persuaded him not to as long as there is still hope that the swelling may go down. He agreed.

In doing this I was prompted solely by esthetic considerations. The young man may recover, and it would be a pity if he were disfigured by the loss of an eye.

He is delirious all the time and tosses to and fro, and we have to be at his bedside constantly. I spend a great deal of time with him. He is so very young, and I am determined to tear him from Death's clutches if I possibly can.

Yesterday I spent several hours in his ward after my shift was over. He is the most serious case there. I sat beside him listening to his ravings. Sometimes what he says sounds like a story, and I've learnt quite a lot about his life in this way. But at other times he swears dreadfully and uses the most terrible language. For some reason it hurts me to hear him saying such awful things. Anatoly Stepanovich says he won't recover. "I just can't understand how the army can take people like this—they're hardly more than boys!" the old man mutters angrily. "I think it's disgraceful!"

August 30

Korchagin still hasn't regained consciousness. He has been moved to a special ward for hopeless cases. Frosya, the orderly, sits beside him nearly all the time. She knows him, apparently—they used to work together a long time ago. How attentive and kind she is towards him! Now I, too, am beginning to fear that he is a hopeless case.

September 2

It is eleven o'clock at night. This has been a wonderful day for me. My patient, Korchagin, has regained consciousness and so the crisis has passed. I have spent the last two days at the hospital without going home.

Now I cannot express my joy at the knowledge that one more life has been saved. It means one fewer death in our ward. The recovery of a patient is the most rewarding thing of all in this exhausting work of mine. They become attached to me, just like children.

Their affection is genuine and simple, and I grow fond of them too, so that when they leave, I sometimes weep. It may sound rather foolish, but I just can't help it.

September 10

Today I wrote Korchagin's first letter to his family. He says that he's not been seriously wounded and that he'll soon recover and come home again. He has lost a lot of blood, is as white as a sheet, and still very weak.

September 14

Korchagin smiled for the first time today. He has a very nice smile. Usually he is terribly serious for his age. He is making an astonishingly quick recovery. Frosya and he are great friends now, and I often see her at his bedside. She must have told him about me and probably praised me up to the skies, because now he always greets me with a faint smile. Yesterday he asked:

"What are those black marks on your arm, doctor?"

I didn't tell him they were bruises made by his fingers gripping my arm while he was delirious.

September 17

The wound on Korchagin's forehead is healing nicely now. We are amazed at the truly boundless fortitude with which he endures the painful business of changing the dressing.

Usually in such cases the patient groans a lot and is hard to manage. But this one just lies there without saying a word, and when the open wound is painted with iodine he just pulls himself very taut like the string of a violin. Often he loses consciousness, but not once during all this time have we heard him even so much as groan.

We all know now that if he does groan it means he's lost consciousness. Where on earth does he get this amazing endurance from, I wonder?

September 21

Korchagin was wheeled out on to the big balcony for the first time today. How glad he was to see the garden, and how greedily he breathed in the fresh air! His head is still swathed in bandages and only one of his eyes is open. But that shining, moving eye gazed out at the world as if seeing it for the first time.

October 8

Korchagin walked unaided in the garden for the first time today. He kept on asking me when he can leave the hospital. I said it would be soon. I know now why he never used to groan. I asked him what the reason was and he replied:

"Read *The Gadfly,* then you'll understand!"

October 14

> Korchagin was discharged today. He and I said good-bye very warmly. The dressing has been removed from his eye and now only his forehead is bandaged. The eye has gone blind but it looks quite normal. I felt very sad at parting with this fine young comrade, but that's how it always is: once they've recovered, they leave us and we may never see them again. As we were saying good-bye, he said:
> "Pity it wasn't the left eye I lost! How on earth am I going to shoot straight now?"
> He's still thinking about the front!

***

After his discharge from the hospital, Pavel stayed for a while with his friends the Buranovskys in Kiev.

One day he saw an order posted up in the street that had been signed by Zhukhrai, Chairman of the Regional Cheka. His heart leapt with joy. It was only with the greatest difficulty, though, that he managed to gain admission to the sailor's office, because the sentries on the door would not let him in. He kicked up such a fuss that he was nearly arrested, but in the end he had his way.

Fyodor welcomed him most warmly. He had lost an arm—it had been torn off by a shell. The two men began to talk about work straightaway.

"You can help me crush the counter-revolution here in Kiev till you're strong enough for the front again," said Fyodor. "So come and start tomorrow!"

***

Eventually the struggle with the White Poles came to an end. The Red Army had pursued the enemy almost to the walls of Warsaw itself, but having expended all their material and physical reserves, and having left their supply bases far behind, they were unable to take this last stronghold and were obliged to fall back. So it was that the "miracle on the Vistula," as the Poles call the Red Army's withdrawal from Warsaw, occurred, and the Poland of the White gentry survived. The dream of a Polish Soviet Socialist Republic was not yet to be fulfilled.

For the time being, though, the blood-soaked land of Russia needed a respite from war.

Pavel was unable to visit his family as Shepetovka was once more in the hands of the White Poles and had become a temporary frontier town. Peace negotiations were now in progress.

So Pavel went on staying with Fyodor, spending his days and nights in the Cheka carrying out various assignments.

But it was not long before the strain of work started to tell on his still weak condition. He began to get violent headaches which grew more and more frequent, and finally, after two nights without sleep, he collapsed and lost consciousness altogether.

When he felt better, he took the matter up with Fyodor:

"Don't you think I should transfer to some other kind of job, Fyodor?" he said. "I'd very much like to go back to the railway shops and work at my old trade again. They told me at the medical board that I'm unfit for military service, but the work here's worse than being at the front! You see, Fyodor, I'm not much use to you if I can hardly stay on my feet, am I?"

Fyodor looked anxiously at him.

"No," he answered, "you don't look very good at all. It's my fault—I should've let you go much earlier than this, but I've just been too busy to notice."

Not long after this conversation, Pavel presented himself at the District Committee of the Komsomol with a certificate to the effect that he was being placed at the Committee's disposal.

After a short interview with a dark-complexioned girl it was decided that he should become secretary of the Komsomol organization in the railway shops where he was to work.

***

Peace was finally signed with the Poles, and the little town of Shepetovka remained in the Soviet Ukraine. A river thirty-five kilometers away now marked the frontier. Then, one memorable morning in December 1920, Pavel returned to the town where he was born.

He stepped out onto the platform that was powdered with snow, and glancing up at the station sign *Shepetovka I,* turned left and made straight for the railway yards to look for Artem. But his brother was not there. Then, wrapping his army greatcoat more tightly about him, he set off through the woods towards the town.

Maria Yakovlevna turned when she heard the knock at the door, and said:

"Come in!" But when the snow-covered figure came pushing

through the doorway into the house and she saw her dear son's face, she clutched at her heart, speechless with joy.

Then she pressed the whole of her thin little body close against him, and covered his face with kisses as tears of joy streamed down her cheeks.

Holding her in his arms, Pavel gazed down at his mother's face that was exhausted by longing and lined with care, and did not say a word, waiting till she was a little calmer.

Once again the light of joy shone in the eyes of this woman who had known so much unhappiness, and for the next few days she could not talk enough with or gaze enough at the son whom she had never expected to see again. But her joy knew no bounds when just three days later Artem came home too, bursting into the little house late at night with his knapsack over his shoulder.

Both the sons had returned and so the Korchagin family was together once more. After escaping death, the brothers were reunited, having survived all their harrowing ordeals and misfortunes...

"So what are you going to do now?" Maria Yakovlevna asked them.

"It's back to the repair shops for me, mother," Artem replied.

As for Pavel, after spending two weeks at home he returned to Kiev where his work was waiting for him.

PART TWO

2

"Now look here," said Fyodor, pressing his finger on the map that lay spread out on the table. "This is Boyarka[17] station, and the timber's being felled here, six versts away. There's two hundred and ten thousand cubic meters of wood stockpiled there. It took a whole army of men eight months to do that, working their guts out, and what's the result? The railway and town are still without firewood. To haul that timber the six versts to the station would take five thousand carts at least a month, and that's provided they each make two trips a day. The nearest village is fifteen versts away. Now d'you realize what this means? Look, according to the plan, felling was supposed to start here and move towards the station, but those bastards went the other way instead, deep into the forest!"

Fyodor's clenched fist fell heavily on the waxed map.

Each of the thirteen men around the table clearly envisaged the imminent horror of a situation which Fyodor did not need to describe. Winter was close at hand now, and they saw hospitals and schools, official buildings and thousands of townsfolk caught in the icy grip of bitter cold. And they saw the railway stations swarming with people and only one train a week to cope with all the traffic.

There was silence as each of them pondered the situation.

Then Fyodor unclenched his fist.

"There's only one way out, comrades: we've got to build a narrow-gauge line six versts long from the station to the felling area in the space of just three months. And what's more, we've got to do it so that the first section, running as far as the edge of the felling area, is ready in just six weeks' time. I've been working on a plan for the past week now, and in order to do it,"—Fyodor's voice cracked in his dry throat—"we'll need three hundred and fifty workmen and two engineers. There are enough rails and seven locomotives down at Pushcha-Voditsa,[18] but the trouble is there's nowhere in Boyarka for the men to live—apart from the schoolhouse the place is in ruins. So we'll have to send them out there in groups for two weeks at a time—they'll not be able to stand it any longer than that. The Komsomol will rush as many members there as it can. There's the Solomenka section to begin with, and then some people from town. It's going to be a very hard job, but if the youngsters are told it'll save the railway and town, I'm sure they'll do it!"

The official in charge of the railway shook his head in disbelief.

"I'm afraid you won't manage it," he said wearily. "To lay six versts of track out in the wilds under the kind of conditions we've got now—with the autumn rains and then the frosts coming..."

But without even looking at him, Fyodor cut him short:

"You should've paid more attention to the fuel problem in the first place, Andrei Vasilievich! That track's just got to be laid and what's more we'll do it! After all, we're not going to sit around twiddling our thumbs and freeze to death, are we?"

***

The autumn rain lashed the men's faces. Dark gray and heavy with moisture, the clouds drifted low over the earth. Late autumn had stripped the forest bare, and now the old hornbeams stood downcast and sullen, their gnarled trunks covered with brown moss. Pitiless autumn had torn away their luxuriant attire, and now they were sorry-looking and naked.

The buildings of the little station huddled lonely and forlorn deep in the forest. A strip of freshly-dug earth led from the stone platform in the goods yard away into the trees. Workmen were swarming all over it like ants.

The sticky clay squelched unpleasantly underfoot. Crowbars rang dully and spades grated on stone over by the embankment where the men were digging furiously.

But the drizzle fell on and on as if through a fine sieve, and its chill droplets penetrated the men's clothing. The rain threatened to wash away what their labor had accomplished, for lumps of clay kept slipping down the embankment in a thick, viscous mass.

Soaked to the skin, their clothes sodden and cold, the men worked on, and did not leave the site till late in the evening. And with every day that passed, the strip of freshly-dug earth pushed deeper and deeper into the forest.

Not far from the station loomed the grim shell of what had once been a stone building. Everything that could be pilfered, ripped out or blasted loose had been carried off by marauders long ago. What had once been windows and doors were now only gaping holes, and a dark opening yawned where the stove used to be. Like bare ribs, the rafters showed through the smashed roof.

Only the concrete floor in the four large rooms had remained intact, and at night four hundred men slept on it in their mud-caked, sodden clothing. Streams of muddy water ran from their clothes when they wrung them out at the door, and they would heap bitter curses on the rain and marshy earth. Huddling together for warmth, they lay in closely-packed rows on the hard floor that was thinly covered with straw. Their clothing steamed but it did not dry, and the rain seeped in through the sacking over the empty window frames and trickled down onto the floor. It drummed heavily on the remains of the corrugated iron on the roof, and the wind whistled through the big cracks in the door.

In the morning the men would drink tea in the dilapidated hut that served as a kitchen, then go off to work on the embankment. Day in, day out, with sickening monotony, their dinner consisted of plain lentils without any meat, and a pound and a half of bread that was as black as coal.

That was all the food the town could provide.

But the men endured all the hardships of Boyarka with grim determination, and with every day that passed the new embankment stretched a little further into the forest.

But the rain poured on and on without ceasing.

With an effort, Pavel pulled his foot out of the sticky clay, and the sharp sensation of cold told him that the rotten sole of his boot had finally parted company with the uppers. Ever since his arrival at the construction site, his ragged boots had been a constant source of discomfort. They were never dry and the mud that seeped into them would squelch as he walked. Now one sole had gone completely and his bare foot was treading on the icy mire. The broken boot meant that he couldn't go on working. Pulling the remains of the sole out of the mud, he looked at it in despair and broke the promise he had made to himself not to swear. Carrying the remains of the boot, he set off back to the living quarters. There he sat down in the field-kitchen, and unwrapping his muddy footcloth, stretched out his numb foot towards the warm stove.

Odarka, the permanent way man's wife who had been taken on to help the cook, was busy cutting up beetroot at the kitchen table.

"My boot's fallen to bits," said Pavel, explaining his untimely presence in the kitchen.

Odarka examined it with an expert eye.

"No use trying to patch it—there's no point," she said. "But you can't go around like that—you'll ruin your foot for good with the cold. I'll tell you what I'll do: I'll bring you an old galosh we've got lying about at home. You can't walk about like that—the frosts'll be starting any day now and then you'll be done for!" she said sympathetically, and putting down her knife, went out of the kitchen.

She was soon back again with a big galosh and a strip of canvas.

As he wrapped his dry foot in the canvas and put it into the warm boot, Pavel looked at the cook in silent gratitude.

***

About four and a half kilometers from Boyarka station a group of men with spades were digging furiously into a hillside that stood in the way of the new line.

Just then Fyodor Zhukhrai and the Party worker Akim Tokarev appeared down in the cutting, and the men up on the hillside caught sight of them.

"Look! Who's that down there?" cried Trofimov, a slant-eyed mechanic from the railway workshops, nudging Pavel and pointing to the newcomers. The next moment, still carrying his spade, Pavel was racing down the hill. Under the peak of his helmet his eyes smiled in warm greeting, and when he reached Fyodor, the sailor went on shaking his hand much longer than those of the others.

"Hello, Pavel!" he said. "My goodness, I hardly recognized you in that queer rig-out!"

Fyodor inspected the hillside, then drove out in the sledge to where the timber had been felled. When he came back, the men were still digging away with the same dogged persistence. Fyodor looked at the swiftly moving spades and the workmen's backs bent with the effort, then said softly to Akim:

"There's no need for Party meetings or political agitation here. You were right, Akim, when you said these lads were worth their weight in gold. This is where the steel is tempered!"

Fyodor gazed at the men with admiration and stern, yet tender, pride. Filled with a common desire, they were toiling to bring the steel artery of the railway up to the stockpile of timber—that precious source of warmth and life.

The cherished goal of the stockpiled fuel was now in sight, but the advance towards it was agonizingly slow, for every day typhus would tear dozens of badly-needed men from the workers' ranks.

One day, on his way back from work to the station, Pavel began to stagger along like a drunk, his legs ready to give way at any moment. He had felt ill for quite a while now, but today the fever gripped him more fiercely than usual.

The typhoid which had already decimated the workers had finally begun to claim Pavel too. But his sturdy constitution had resisted it, and for the past five days he had found the strength to get up from the straw-covered concrete floor in the morning and go off to work with all the rest.

But now a sharp pain stabbed his chest at every step he took, his teeth were chattering with cold, and his vision was so blurred that the trees seemed to be spinning around him like a strange merry-go-round.

He only just managed to reach the station. Once there he took a few more steps then lost his balance, and felt a dull pain as his head hit the ground. The snow was pleasantly cool on his burning cheek.

They found him a few hours later and carried him back to the living quarters. He was breathing heavily and could not recognize those around him. A doctor's assistant who examined him diagnosed lobar pneumonia and typhoid fever. As for his inflamed joints and the ulcers on his neck, they were trivial compared with the pneumonia and typhoid which in themselves were quite enough to kill him.

Alyosha Kokhansky who came from the same town as Pavel, was entrusted with the task of getting him home to Shepetovka.

It was only with the help of all Pavel's work team that they managed to get the unconscious man and Alyosha into the packed railway carriage. Fearing infection, though, the passengers objected violently and threatened to throw the men off the train en route.

But eventually the train set off.

Alyosha safely delivered the sick Pavel to his people, then came down with typhus himself.

3

Youth emerged victorious and typhus did not destroy Pavel. For the fourth time he crossed the border between life and death, and returned to life once more. It was a whole month, though, before he could get out of bed. Thin and pale, he staggered across the room on his unsteady feet, clinging to the wall for support as he went. With his mother's help he got as far as the window and stood there for a long time gazing out on the road where little pools of melted snow shone in the sunshine. It was the first thaw of early spring.

Just outside the window, a gray-breasted sparrow was busily preening itself on the branch of a cherry tree, glancing furtively at Pavel from time to time with its quick little eyes.

"Well then, so you and I got through the winter together, eh?" said Pavel softly, tapping on the window pane.

His mother looked up with a start.

"Who are you talking to out there?" she asked.

"Nobody. It's only a sparrow ... There now, he's flown away, the little rascal," Pavel answered with a faint smile.

By the time spring had finally come into its own, he began to think about returning to town. He was strong enough to walk now, but there seemed to be something wrong with his body. Then, when he was out walking in the garden one day, a sudden, excruciating pain in his spine knocked him off his feet, and it was only with the greatest difficulty that he managed to get up again and stagger back to the house. The next day he had the doctor give him a thorough examination. Finding a deep hollow in his spine, the doctor asked in surprise:

"How did you get this?"

"Oh, it's from a stone, doctor. In the fighting near Rovno[19] a three-inch gun opened up on the highroad behind us, and a stone hit me in the back ..."

"But how on earth did you manage to walk after it? Hasn't it ever bothered you?"

"No. At the time I couldn't get up for a couple of hours, but then it passed and I got back on my horse. It's never troubled me till now."

Frowning, the doctor examined the hollow carefully.

"Yes, my friend," he said. "It's a very nasty thing indeed. The spine doesn't like being knocked about like that. Let's just hope it won't crop up again. All right, Comrade Korchagin, you can get dressed now."

And the doctor looked at his patient with sympathy and concern.

***

One day Pavel went to see his brother. Artem was married now and living with his wife's people. His wife Styosha was a rather plain young woman from a poor peasant family.

As Pavel walked into the yard, a tiny window opened in the little old cottage and Artem called:

"Come on in, Pavel!"

An old woman with a face as yellow as parchment was busy with an oven fork at the stove. She shot Pavel an unfriendly glance as he went by, and began clattering the iron pans.

Artem was sitting at the table looking rather embarrassed—he knew that neither his mother nor his brother approved of his marriage. They simply could not understand why someone whose family had been proletarian for generations had broken off his friendship with Galya—the stonemason's beautiful daughter and a dressmaker by trade whom he had courted for three years—to go and live with the drab Styosha and be the breadwinner for a family of five. Now, after a day's work down at the railway yards, Artem had to slave away at the plough in an attempt to revive the family's run-down farm.

***

Artem knew that his brother disapproved of his desertion to what Pavel called the "petty bourgeois element," and he watched his brother taking stock of everything around him.

They sat there for a while, exchanging the kind of trivial remarks that are usual at first meeting, then Pavel got up to go. But Artem stopped him.

"Wait a little, Pavel, and have a bite to eat with us—Styosha'll be bringing the milk in a minute. So you're leaving tomorrow, are you? But aren't you still a bit weak?"

Just then Styosha came in. She said hello to Pavel, then asked Artem to come out to the barn and help her carry something. So Pavel was left alone with the old woman who was hardly talkative.

He got up, and without waiting for his brother to come back, went out. As he closed the gate behind him, he caught sight of the old woman watching him suspiciously through the end window of the house.

"What the devil made Artem come out here?" he wondered gloomily. "Now he's going to be tied down for the rest of his life. Styosha will have another baby every year and Artem will be stuck here like a rat in a trap. And who knows? He might even give up his work at the railway yards into the bargain!" So Pavel thought sadly as he strode down the empty streets of the little town. "And there I was, hoping to interest him in political work!"

Pavel was happy at the thought that tomorrow he would be leaving and going back to the town where all his friends were. The big city, with all its vitality and might, its endless stream of bustling humanity, its clattering trams and hooting automobiles, drew him like a magnet. But most of all he longed for the enormous brick factories and soot-blackened workshops, with their machinery and the soft humming of transmission belts. He yearned for the swiftly spinning flight of giant flywheels, for the smell of machine-oil and for all that had become so much a part of his life. Here, though, roaming the streets of this quiet little town, he was filled with a vague feeling of depression, so it was not surprising that the place had become tiresome and alien to him.

He had torn himself away from this once and for all a long time ago, and felt a much greater affinity now for the big city, since that was where strong comradeship and vigorous toil were to be found.

By this time, without noticing it, he had reached a small pine wood, and he stopped for a moment where the road forked. To his right, screened from the wood by a high, spiked fence, stood the gloomy bulk of the old prison, and beyond it lay the white buildings of the hospital.

It was here, on this wide stretch of open ground, that his comrades had been choked to death by the White hangman's noose. Pavel stood for a while in silence on the spot where the gallows had been, then walked over to the edge of the ravine and went down to the little cemetery where his comrades lay in their communal graves.

Someone's loving hands had planted a green hedge around the cemetery and laid wreaths of spruce branches on the line of graves. The pines rose slender and straight on the top of the bluff, and young grass spread a silky green carpet over the slopes of the ravine.

It was quiet and sad here on the outskirts of the little town. There was only the gentle rustling of the trees and the smell of spring rising from the regenerated earth. It was here that his comrades had gone courageously to their deaths, in order that life might be beautiful for those born in poverty, for those whose very birth had meant the beginning of slavery.

Slowly Pavel raised his hand and took off his cap, and his heart was filled with immense sadness.

Man's most precious possession is life itself. It is given to him but once, and he must live it so as not to feel agonizing regret for years wasted in aimlessness, so as never to know burning shame for an ignoble, petty past, and so that when he is dying, he should be able to say: "All my life and all my strength have been devoted to the finest cause in the world—the struggle for the liberation of mankind." And one should make haste to use every moment of life, for after all an illness or accident may suddenly cut it short.

Filled with these thoughts, Pavel turned and walked away from the cemetery.

***

Back at home his mother was sadly preparing for her son's departure, and as he watched her, Pavel could see she was trying to hide her tears.

"Won't you stay after all, Pavel?" she asked. "It's hard for me now, living all alone in my old age. It doesn't matter how many children you have because as soon as they're grown up they go off and leave you. Why do you have to go running back to the city? You can live here just as well. Or has some bob-tailed little miss there gone and taken your fancy? Nobody ever tells your old mother anything, you know. Artem went and got married without saying a word to me, and as for you, you're a lot worse! The only time I ever see you is when you've gone and got yourself crippled!" she said softly as she packed her son's few belongings into a clean bag.

***

Pavel went to the station by himself—he had persuaded his mother to stay at home because he did not want to see her weeping as he left.

The waiting crowd piled furiously into the train. Pavel climbed onto one of the topmost bunks and sat there watching the excited passengers shouting noisily in the gangway down below.

When the train set off, the uproar subsided a little, and as always on these occasions the passengers set about the task of stuffing themselves with food.

It was not long before Pavel fell asleep.

***

Arriving in Kiev, he made at once for Kreshchatik Street in the center of town. Slowly he climbed the steps to the bridge across the river. Everything around him looked just the same, and nothing had changed. He walked over the bridge, sliding his hand along the smooth railing, and was about to go down the steps on the other side when he suddenly stopped—there wasn't a soul on the bridge, and in the boundless heavens the night presented a majestic spectacle to his enchanted eyes. Darkness enfolded the horizon like black velvet, and flickering with a phosphorescent glow, a countless multitude of sparkling stars burned in the night. And down below, where along an invisible line earth merged with sky, the city showered the darkness with millions of lights...

In the Special Department office on the Kreshchatik, the duty officer told Pavel that Fyodor Zhukhrai had left town a long time ago. Pavel was so disappointed by the news that he silently turned and walked away without even asking the man for further details. Then, suddenly overwhelmed by weariness, he sat down on the steps of the building to rest.

After a while the noisy bustle of the street dulled the pain he felt at the news of Fyodor's departure. But where was he to go now, he wondered.

***

The offices of the Party's District Committee were full of activity as usual. The front door opened and closed continually, the corridors were crowded with people, and the muffled clicking of typewriters could be heard behind the door of the Administration Department.

Pavel stood about in the corridor for a while in the hope of seeing a familiar face, but not finding one, went in to see the secretary. The official, wearing a dark blue Russian shirt, was working at a large desk.

"What can I do for you?" he asked, finishing what he was writing.

Pavel told him his story.

"I want you to send me back to the railway workshops, comrade," he said, "so please issue the necessary instructions."

The secretary agreed, then jotted a few words down on a slip of paper.

"Give this to Comrade Tufta," he said, "and he'll arrange everything for you."

* * *

The days passed quickly. They could hardly be called commonplace, for every one of them brought something new, and as he planned his work each morning, Pavel would be annoyed to find that the day was all too short and that some things he had planned always remained undone.

He was now staying with his old friend Okunev, Secretary of the Komsomol District Committee, and was working in the railway shops as an electrical fitter's mate.

In the evenings he would work late in the public library. He had made good friends with all three women librarians, and by using his powers of persuasion he had finally won the longed-for right to browse freely among the open shelves. Resting a ladder against the huge bookcases, he would sit on it for hours on end, leafing through one volume after another in search of interesting material. Most of the books were old, and what modern literature there was modestly occupied one small bookcase. In it were to be found a handful of pamphlets dating from the Civil War, Marx's *Das Kapital,* Jack London's *The Iron Heel,* and a few other items. Looking through the old books on the shelves one day, Pavel discovered the novel *Spartacus.* After reading it in just two nights, he moved it to the small bookcase, putting it beside the numerous works by Maxim Gorky. This process of selecting interesting books that were dear to his heart went on for quite a long time.

4

This is the border—two wooden posts standing facing one another in silent hostility, each representing a world of its own. One of them is planed smooth and polished, painted black and white like a sentry box, and crowned by a single-headed eagle fixed firmly in place with stout nails. Its wings outstretched and its talons gripping the striped pole, the bird of prey glares with malevolent eyes at the metal shield on the opposite post, its curved beak thrust forward. Just six yards away is the other pole, a sturdy, round, rough-hewn oak post sunk deep in the ground. On it is a cast-iron shield bearing a hammer and sickle. Between these two posts and the worlds they represent lies a deep gulf, though they stand only six yards apart on level ground. And no one can cross those six yards without risking his life.

This is the border.

Stretching for thousands of kilometers from the Black Sea in the south to the Arctic Ocean in the far north, stands the motionless line of these silent sentinels of the Soviet Socialist Republic, bearing the great emblem of toil on their iron shields. The post topped by the rapacious bird of prey marks the start of the border between the Soviet Ukraine and bourgeois Poland. It stands ten kilometers away from the remote little Ukrainian town of Berezdov,[20] and opposite it is the Polish settlement of Korets.

The Russian frontier posts run across fields and push through clearings in the forest, plunging unseen into ravines and climbing hillsides to appear again on ridges, and then, reaching the high bank of a river, look out over the snowbound plains of an alien land.

***

The saddles creaked rhythmically as the horses trotted along at an even pace. On the black stallion's muzzle, around its nostrils and on its hair lay frosty rime, and the horse's breath drifted away like white steam in the air. The battalion commander's piebald mare moved gracefully, arching her slender neck and nibbling playfully at the bit as she went. Both riders wore gray army greatcoats belted at the waist and bearing a major's three red squares on the sleeves, the only difference being that Battalion Commander Gavrilov's collar tabs were green, while his companion's were red. Gavrilov was a border guard officer, and it was his battalion that manned the frontier posts on this seventy-kilometer stretch of the border. His companion was a visitor from Berezdov—Battalion Commander Korchagin of the Military Training Organization.

Snow had fallen during the night, and now it lay soft and fluffy, untrodden by either man or beast. The two men rode out of a copse and trotted off across a stretch of open ground. About forty yards to one side stood two border posts.

"Whoa!" cried Gavrilov, and he suddenly reined in his horse. Pavel wheeled his stallion to find out why the commander had stopped. Gavrilov was leaning forward in the saddle, scrutinizing a strange line of tracks that looked as if someone had run a small toothed wheel over the snow. Some cunning little creature had passed by here, putting one foot behind the other and confusing its tracks with complicated twists and turns. It was hard to make out which way the animal had been moving, but it was not this set of tracks that had made the commander halt. Just two yards away lay another set lightly covered by a sprinkling of powdery snow. They were the footprints of a man. Whoever it was had made no attempt to conceal his tracks—they led straight towards the woods and indicated quite clearly that the person had come from the Polish side of the frontier. The commander urged his horse forward, and the footprints led him back to the border guard's path. The tracks showed up distinctly for a dozen paces or so on the Polish side.

"Somebody crossed the border last night," the commander muttered. "The third platoon's been caught napping again—there's no mention of anything in the morning report! The devils!" Gavrilov's graying mustache silvered by rime hung down severely over his top lip.

"You've got to keep your eyes peeled all the time on the border," he said to Pavel as they trotted down the wide road leading from the frontier towards Berezdov. "The slightest mistake can cost you a lot—you just can't afford to be caught napping in a job like ours. It's not so easy to slip across the border in daylight, but at night you've got to keep a sharp look-out all the time. Just judge for yourself, Comrade Korchagin: on my sector the border cuts right through four villages, which makes things very difficult. No matter how close together you post your men, every time there's a wedding or some other celebration, you get all the relatives from one side crossing to the other. And no wonder either—it's only twenty yards or so from one cottage to the next, and the stream's shallow enough for a chicken to wade through! There's a bit of smuggling going on as well. True, a lot of it's on a very minor scale—some old Polish woman might bring a couple of bottles of *zubrovka*[21] across and so on—but on the other hand there's quite a lot of large-scale stuff going on too, with wealthy people running it."

As Pavel listened to what the commander was saying, it seemed to him that life for the border guards must be like one long reconnaissance mission.

"Tell me, Comrade Gavrilov," he said, "is all this business just limited to smuggling, or is there something much more serious going on as well?"

"Yes—that's just the trouble," the commander replied gloomily.

* * *

Berezdov was a remote little town deep in the provinces that had formerly been in the Jewish Pale of settlement. It consisted of two or three hundred small houses scattered about at random and an enormous marketplace with a couple of dozen little shops in the middle of it. The square was always dirty and littered with manure.

A large garden adjoined the small church, and in it stood a big old house that had once belonged to the village priest. A wearisome mustiness had filled its desolate rooms where the priest and his wife had lived, a couple who were just as old and dreary as the house itself and who had grown sick and tired of each other long ago. But as soon as new masters took over the place, the dreariness was swept away, for the house became the headquarters of the Berezdov Communist Party Committee. On the door of a small room to the right of the entrance hall the words "Komsomol District Committee" had been written in chalk. It was here that Pavel spent part of his working day, for as well as being Commissar of the Second Military Training Battalion, he was serving as secretary of the recently-formed Komsomol District Committee.

It was eight months since he had left Kiev, yet it only seemed like yesterday. He pushed a pile of papers aside, and leaning back in his chair, fell to thinking about the past...

The big house was quiet. It was late now and the Party Committee office was deserted. Trofimov, the Committee Secretary, had gone home a short while ago, leaving Pavel alone in the building. The frost had woven a fantastic pattern on the windowpanes, but the room was warm—there was a paraffin lamp alight on the table and the stove was burning well. Pavel sat there recalling the recent past. He remembered how in August the railway workshop Komsomol had sent him as youth organizer with a repair train to Yekaterinoslav.[22] Until late in the autumn he had travelled with the train's crew of a hundred and fifty men from one station to another, repairing the damage done by war and clearing away burnt-out, smashed railway carriages. Though not trained as a fitter and unaccustomed to the heavy work, he had wielded a wrench along with the rest and tightened hundreds more rusty bolts than he had ever done before.

Late that autumn the repair train had finally returned home, and the railway shops were once more the richer by a hundred and fifty pairs of hands . . .

***

Just before the frosts set in, rafts of timber floating downstream had blocked the river. Then the late autumn floods had broken them up and the much-needed wood was lost, swept away by the rushing waters. Once again the railway settlement of Solomenka had sent its men to the rescue, this time to save the precious fuel.

Reluctant to lag behind his comrades, Pavel had concealed from them the fact that he had caught a bad chill, and when a week later the timber had been stacked on shore beside the wharf, the autumn dampness and icy water had woken the old enemy which had been slumbering in his blood—and Pavel had come down with a high fever. For two weeks he was racked by acute rheumatism, and when he left the hospital to return to the repair shops, he could only work by straddling the bench. The foreman would look sadly at him and shake his head. A few days later a medical board had declared him unfit for work. After that he was given his discharge pay and papers certifying his right to a pension, which he indignantly refused to accept.

With a heavy heart Pavel had left the railway workshops. Leaning on a stick, he could only move slowly, for every step caused him excruciating pain. His mother had written to him several times, asking him to visit her, and now he remembered her once more. But her words to him at parting came back to him: "The only time I ever see you is when you've gone and got yourself crippled!"

At the Regional Committee office he was handed two personal documents neatly rolled up—his Party registration and Komsomol certificates—and then, saying good-bye to as few comrades as possible so as not to add to his sorrow, he had set off for his mother's. For two weeks the old woman had steamed and massaged his swollen legs, and a month later he could walk without a stick once more. He was overjoyed, for once again twilight had been replaced by the light of dawn. Shortly afterwards he had travelled by train to the district center, where three days later he was given a document authorizing him to go to the regional registration office to be enlisted as a political worker in a military training unit.

A week later he had arrived in this small, snowbound town as military commissar attached to the Second Battalion. The District Committee of the Komsomol had also entrusted him with the task of rallying the uncoordinated Komsomol groups in the area and setting up a youth organization in the new district. And so it was that Pavel's life had taken a new turn.

***

A mere handful of Bolsheviks—only nineteen altogether—devoted all their energies to the task of consolidating Soviet authority throughout the district. This was a new administrative area, so everything had to be started from scratch. Moreover, the close proximity of the border called for constant vigilance.

Pavel and the small group of activists gathered around him toiled from morning till night arranging re-elections of the local Soviets, organizing cultural activities, tracking down smugglers, fighting bandits, and carrying out Party and Komsomol work among military units stationed in the area.

From saddle to desk and from desk to the square where platoons of young recruits were doing their drill; then to the club, the school and two or three committee meetings—such was the daily routine of the military commissar attached to the Second Battalion. And as often as not his nights were spent on horseback with his Mauser at his side, nights whose stillness would suddenly be broken by the harsh cry "Halt! Who goes there?" and the rattling of a fleeing cart laden with contraband from across the border.

***

This year the anniversary of the October Revolution was to be celebrated along the border with even greater enthusiasm than usual, and Pavel was elected chairman of the committee organizing the festivities. Five thousand peasants from three neighboring villages marched to the frontier in a procession half a kilometer long, carrying crimson banners and accompanied by a brass band with the Military Training Battalion marching at its head. Maintaining extremely strict formation, the column marched along the Soviet side of the frontier parallel to the border posts, making for the villages that had been cut in two by the demarcation line. The Poles had never seen such a spectacle before. At the head of the column rode Gavrilov and Pavel, and behind them the banners rustled in the breeze, the band played and songs rose from the crowd! Dressed in their holiday best, the villagers were in high spirits, the girls laughing merrily, the adults marching along gravely and the old folk proceeding with an air of solemn triumph. The great human river ran away into the distance as far as the eye could see. One of its banks was the frontier, but not a single foot left Soviet soil to step over that forbidden line. Pavel gazed at the torrent of people streaming past him.

The Soviet border guards greeted the column with happy smiles, while the Polish sentries looked on in bewilderment and dismay. Even though the Polish command had been notified of it in advance, this procession so close to the frontier still caused alarm on their side. Mounted patrols moved restlessly to and fro, the guard detail had been increased five-fold, and reserves were hidden in the gullies near the border ready for any emergency. But the procession kept safely to its own side of the frontier, marching gaily along and filling the air with its singing.

Now the head of the column was descending the hillside towards a village that had been cut in two by the border. The Soviet half of the village had prepared to welcome the guests in grand style. The inhabitants had gathered at the little frontier bridge over a small river, and the young men and girls had lined up along both sides of the road. On the Polish side the roofs of cottages and barns were covered with people who were watching what was happening on the opposite bank. There were crowds of peasants, too, standing on the steps of houses and by the garden fences. As the procession began to pass the people lining the road, the band struck up the "Internationale." Then, from a roughly-constructed platform decorated with greenery, stirring speeches were made by both young men and gray-haired veterans alike. Pavel made a speech too, using his native Ukrainian, and his words flew over the border and could be heard on the far side of the river. But there it was decided that what he said should not be allowed to kindle the hearts of those listening, and a mounted patrol of gendarmes began to move quickly through the village, driving the people indoors with their whips and firing into the air to frighten them.

The village streets were soon deserted. Driven off the roofs by the shooting, the young folk disappeared too, while those on the Soviet side looked on and frowned. Then, filled with indignation, an old shepherd climbed up on to the platform with the help of a few village lads, and cried in an agitated voice:

"D'you see that, you young 'uns? They used to beat us like that too, but not any more, because nobody's allowed to whip us peasants now! We've done with the gentry and we've done with their floggings too! The power belongs to us these days, so just make sure you hold on to it, you young 'uns! I'm an old man now and not much good at speech-making, but there's a lot I'd tell you if I could! I'd tell you how we used to break our backs every day of our lives in the Tsar's time, and that's why it hurts so much to see those poor folk over there!" And waving a bony hand towards the far side of the river, he burst into tears in the way that only little children and old men do.

***

Korchagin's battalion was called up to take part in the autumn maneuvers of the territorial forces. Marching in torrential rain, the battalion covered the forty kilometers to the divisional camp in a single day, setting out early in the morning and reaching its destination late at night. Gusev, the Battalion Commander, and Pavel, his Commissar, made the journey on horseback. The eight hundred recruits reached the barracks utterly exhausted and fell asleep straightaway. The headquarters of the territorial division had been late in summoning the battalion, and the maneuvers were due to begin the next morning when the newly-arrived units were to undergo inspection. Drawn up on the parade-ground, the battalion—now in uniform and carrying rifles—presented a totally different picture. Both Gusev and Pavel had devoted a great deal of time and effort to training the men entrusted to them, and were quite confident that they would pass muster.

***

For several days now the weather had been unusually fine for that time of year. The maneuvers were drawing to a close, and on the fifth day the exercises were taking place in the neighborhood of Shepetovka where the maneuvers were scheduled to end. The Berezdov Battalion had been given the task of capturing the railway station from the direction of Klimentovichi village.

Finding himself on home ground, Pavel showed Gusev the best approaches to make. Then, divided into two parts, the battalion made a wide, enveloping movement, and unnoticed by the "enemy," attacked them at the rear and burst into the station building with loud cries of "Hurrah!" According to the decision of the official observers, the operation was declared a brilliant success. The station remained in the hands of the Berezdov contingent, while the battalion that had been defending it withdrew to the woods after being judged to have lost fifty percent of its men.

Gusev was congratulated on the success of his operation, while representatives of the defeated battalion shifted from one foot to the other in embarrassment and did not even try to justify themselves.

"I can't take the credit for it, though," said Gusev. "It was Korchagin who showed us the way—he belongs round these parts."

***

The maneuvers were over. After receiving an excellent report, the battalion went back to Berezdov, while Pavel, who felt completely exhausted now, stayed behind to rest for a couple of days at home. Leaving his horse at Artem's place, he slept for almost two days, then on the third went down to see his brother at the railway yards. Here, in the great soot-blackened engine-shed, he felt completely at home, and greedily drank in the smoke from the burning coal. He felt powerfully drawn to this place—after all, he had known it since childhood and had grown up here, and it had become part of him. Having been away from it for so long, he felt as if he had lost something very precious. It was many months since he had heard the whistle of a locomotive, and just as a sailor feels moved at the sight of the boundless expanse of turquoise sea whenever he returns to it after a long stay ashore, so Pavel, the stoker and fitter, had yearned for his familiar surroundings. And it was a long time before he had been able to come to terms with this feeling. He did not say much to his brother whom he found working at a mobile forge, but he noticed a new furrow on Artem's brow—he had two children to feed now, and life was evidently hard for him. Though he did not complain of anything, Pavel detected the truth all the same.

They worked together for a couple of hours, then said good-bye. At the railway crossing Pavel reined in his horse and looked back at the station for a long time. Then, touching his black stallion with the whip, he galloped off at full speed down the road that ran through the forest.

He reached Berezdov towards noon.

***

One day a few weeks later Pavel was suddenly handed an envelope marked "Urgent." Opening it, he read:

> To the Berezdov District Committee of the Komsomol. Copy to the District Committee of the Party. By a decision of the Regional Committee, Comrade Korchagin is recalled to the Regional Committee for appointment to important Komsomol work.

So it was that Pavel bade farewell to the district where he had worked for the past year.

His comrades shook his hand hard as he left—so hard that it almost hurt—and embraced him like a brother. Then, as his horse turned out of the yard on to the main road, a dozen revolvers fired a volley in a farewell salute.

5

The entry into history of the year one thousand nine hundred and twenty-four was marked by bitter cold. January gripped the snowbound land of Russia, and from the second half of the month howling blizzards and persistent snowstorms raged.

In the southwest of the country the railways were blocked with snow, and men fought against the savage elements.

The steel propellers of snow ploughs bit deep into the drifts in an attempt to clear a path for the trains. Telegraph wires laden with ice gave way in the blizzards and frosts, and of the twelve principal lines in the Soviet Union, only three—the Indo-European and two direct government lines—were still in operation.

In the telegraph office at Shepetovka station three morse code apparatuses continued their tireless chatter that was intelligible only to the trained ear.

The two girl operators were new to the job, and the length of tape that they had tapped out since their first day at work here would not have exceeded twenty kilometers. But their colleague, the old telegraphist working beside them, had passed the two hundred kilometer mark long ago. Unlike the girls, he had no need to read the tape to make out the message, frowning as he tried to decipher difficult words. Instead he simply wrote the words down one after another as the apparatus clicked them out. Now his ear suddenly caught the message:

"To all! To all! To all!"

As he wrote it down, the old telegraphist thought to himself: "Must be another of those official orders about clearing snow." Outside the window the blizzard still raged, the wind hurling snow flurries against the glass. For a moment the old man thought someone was knocking at the window, and turning his head, could not help admire the delicately beautiful pattern which the frost had traced on the panes. No human hand could possibly match that exquisitely intricate etching of leaves and stalks!

Carried away by the spectacle, he stopped listening to the telegraph for a few moments. But when he finally tore his gaze from the window and picked up the tape to read what he had missed, the apparatus had clicked out:

"At 6:50 pm on January 21st . . ."

Quickly writing down the words, then dropping the tape again, he rested his head on his hands to listen.

". . . yesterday in Gorki[23] the death occurred of . . ."

Slowly he wrote the words down. How many messages had he heard in his long life, messages that were both joyous and sad, and how often had he been the first to hear of the happiness or sorrow of others! He had long ceased to reflect on the meaning of clipped, terse phrases, simply hearing the words then mechanically writing them down without thinking what they actually meant.

Now somebody had died and someone else was being informed of it. The old man had forgotten the opening words: "To all! To all! To all!" Then the apparatus clicked out the letters "V-l-a-d-i-m-i-r I-l-y-i-c-h," and he translated the little hammer taps into words. He sat there quietly, feeling rather tired. Somebody called Vladimir Ilyich had died somewhere and someone else would hear the sad news later today then burst out sobbing in grief and despair. But as far as he was concerned, that grief belonged to someone else and he was only a chance observer. The apparatus tapped out a row of dots, a dash, more dots then another dash, and from the familiar sounds he caught the first letter and wrote it down on the telegraph form in front of him. It was the letter "L." After it came the second letter, "E." Beside it he painstakingly wrote an "N," immediately added an "I," then automatically picked up the last letter—"N."

Then the apparatus tapped out a pause, and for a fraction of a second the telegraphist's gaze rested on the word he had written: "LENIN."

The apparatus continued its tapping, but now that the familiar name was registered on the man's consciousness, it came back to him once more. He looked at the last word again—"LENIN." What? he thought. Lenin? Now the entire text of the telegram flashed through his mind. For a few moments more he stared at the telegraph form in front of him, and for the first time in all his thirty-two years' work could not believe what he had written.

Three times he scanned the lines, but the words obstinately refused to change: "The death occurred of Vladimir Ilyich Lenin," they said. Then the old man leapt to his feet and snatching up the spiral of tape, fixed his eyes on it. The two-meter strip of ribbon confirmed what he could not bring himself to believe. Then, turning to his colleagues with a face that was now deathly pale, he cried out in fear:

"Lenin is dead!"

***

The news of the terrible loss slipped out through the now wide-open door of the telegraph office and swept through the station with the speed of a whirlwind. It burst out into the snowstorm, whirling over the tracks and points, and together with the icy blast of the wind swept in through the half-open, iron-bound doors of the railway repair shop.

Inside a locomotive was standing over the first inspection pit, and a repair crew was busy overhauling it. Zakhar Bruzzhak and Artem were straightening the bent bars of the fire grate—Zakhar holding the grate steady on the anvil while Artem hammered it.

Suddenly the figure of a man appeared in the brightly-lit doorway, then was swallowed up by the shadows inside. The blows of the hammer on the iron grate drowned the man's first cry, but when he came running up to the crew working on the engine, Artem paused with his hammer in mid-air.

"Comrades! Lenin is dead!"

The hammer slowly descended, then Artem silently lowered it to the concrete floor.

"What did you say?" he asked, his shaking hand clutching at the sheepskin of the man who had brought the terrible news.

And he, covered with snow and gasping for breath, said again in a dull, broken voice:

"Yes, comrades, it's true! Lenin is dead . . ."

And because the man spoke so quietly, Artem realized that the terrible news was true. And only then did he make out the man's face: it was the secretary of the local Party organization.

The repair crew were climbing out of the inspection pit now and they listened in silence to the news—the death of the man whose name was known to all the world.

Then somewhere outside the gates a locomotive shrieked and all the men gave a start. Its cry was echoed by a second engine away on the far side of the station, and then by a third. Their anguished, mighty chorus was joined by the siren at the power-station, its wail as piercing and shrill as the sound of flying shrapnel. Then all was drowned by the clear, sonorous cry of the splendid high-speed locomotive that was about to leave with a passenger train for Kiev.

People were crowding into the railway shops now, pouring in through all four gates. Then, when the big building was filled to overflowing, the funeral meeting began amid profound silence.

The old Bolshevik Sharabrin, secretary of the Shepetovka District Committee, addressed the gathering:

"Comrades! Lenin, the leader of the world proletariat, is dead! We have suffered an irrevocable loss, for the man who founded the Bolshevik Party and taught it to be implacable towards its enemies is now no more. The death of the leader of our Party and our class serves as an appeal to the best sons of the proletariat to join our ranks . . ."

Then the strains of a funeral march rang out, hundreds of heads were bared, and Artem, who had not wept for fifteen years now, felt a lump rise in his throat as his powerful shoulders began to shake.

The usual sound of conversation in the hall was stilled as scores of men choked with sorrow. Their eyes were filled with alarm, for they were like the crew of a ship in a storm whose tried and trusted helmsman has suddenly been swept overboard.

***

The death of Lenin brought hundreds of thousands of new workers into the Bolshevik Party, and so, though the leader was no more, the Party's ranks were not thrown into confusion. So it is that a tree which has thrust its mighty roots deep into the earth need not perish even if its very crown is cut away.

6

Two years passed. Impartial time steadily counted off the days and months, while the headlong, multicolored pageant of life constantly filled those days with something new, so that they were never alike. The one hundred and sixty million people that made up the great nation of Soviet Russia—the first people in the world to become master of their own vast land and her countless resources—were engaged in the heroic task of resurrecting their national economy from the ravages of war. Steadily the country was gaining new strength, and the gloomy sight of abandoned, lifeless factories had now become a thing of the past.

For Pavel those two years flew by in such ceaseless activity that he barely noticed them. He was not one to take life easily, greet each new day with a lazy yawn, and go to bed on the stroke of ten. Instead, he was eager to live, and urged others to be eager too.

He allowed himself very little time for sleep. Often a light would be burning in his window till late into the night, and inside the room a group of people would be sitting at the table engrossed in a book. Their studies kept them busy. During the past two years they had worked their way through the third volume of *Das Kapital,* and the highly intricate mechanism of capitalist exploitation was now comprehensible to them.

***

When summer came, Pavel's friends left one after another to take the vacation they longed for. Those whose health was rather poor went off to the coast, and Pavel helped them make arrangements, finding them places in sanatoriums and securing financial help for them. Away they went, looking pale and tired, but filled with gladness at the prospect of a holiday. The burden of their work fell on Pavel's shoulders, and he bore it just as patiently as a good horse pulls a heavy cart up a steep hill. They would come back sunburnt and full of energy, and others would leave in their turn. All through the summer one or other of them was missing from the office, but life never once slackened its rapid pace, and for Pavel to miss a day's work was unthinkable.

And so it was that the summer passed.

Pavel did not like the approach of autumn and winter, for they always brought him a great deal of physical distress.

This year he had looked forward especially eagerly to the coming of summer. It was agonizingly painful for him to admit to himself that his strength was waning with every passing year. There were only two ways out of the situation: either to acknowledge that he was no longer capable of carrying out the difficult tasks which his intensive work demanded, and to declare himself an invalid, or to remain at his post for as long as he possibly could. He chose the second course.

One day, at a meeting of the District Committee of the Party, Dr. Bartelik, an old Bolshevik underground worker now in charge of public health in the area, came over and sat down beside him.

"You don't look too good, Korchagin," he said. "How's your health? And have you been up before the medical board? You haven't? Just as I thought! But I reckon you need a check-up, my friend, so come over on Thursday evening and we'll have a look at you."

Pavel did not go, though—he was too busy—but Dr. Bartelik did not forget about him, because a few days later he called for Pavel and took him to the medical board. After a thorough examination in which Bartelik himself took part as a neuropathologist, the following recommendation was made:

> The medical board considers an immediate vacation essential, together with a lengthy course of treatment in the Crimea, to be followed by further prolonged and detailed treatment. Otherwise serious consequences are inevitable.

This statement was preceded by a long list of Pavel's ailments in Latin, from which he understood only that the main problem lay not in his legs but in his central nervous system which had been seriously impaired.

And so, in three weeks' time he was to leave on vacation—the first in his whole life. A place had been reserved for him at a sanatorium in Yevpatoria,[24] and an authorization to that effect already lay in his desk drawer.

During those last few days, though, he pressed on even harder with his work—among other things convening a plenary meeting of the District Komsomol—and without sparing himself, made every effort to tie up the loose ends so that he could leave with complete peace of mind.

***

The "Communar" sanatorium was owned by the Party's Central Committee. Surrounded by rose bushes and sparkling fountains, its white buildings were set amid gardens and entwined with vines. The white coats of staff and the swimsuits of people on vacation were to be seen everywhere. A young woman doctor entered Pavel's name in the records, and then he was shown to a spacious room in the corner section. There he found dazzlingly white bed linen, perfect cleanliness and peace—blessed, undisturbed peace. After a refreshing bath and a change of clothes, he hurried down to the sea.

Stretching as far as the eye could see was the majestically calm, dark blue expanse of water running away to the horizon like a sheet of polished marble. In the far distance the skyline was lost in a bluish haze, and the molten sun was reflected on the sea with patches of ruddy fire. Far away through the morning mist the massive outlines of a mountain range could be seen. Pavel filled his lungs with the invigorating freshness of the air, and could not tear his eyes away from the immense expanse of calm, dark blue water.

A lazy wave came rolling slowly up to his feet and gently licked the golden sand of the beach.

7

Next to the sanatorium was the big garden of the central clinic, and the patients would use it as a short cut on their way back from the beach. Here, in the shade of a spreading plane tree beside a high limestone wall, Pavel loved to sit and rest. Hardly anyone ever came to this quiet place, and from it he could watch the people walking along the garden paths during the daytime, and listen to the music of the band in the evening, yet avoid the annoying crowds in the large resort.

Today, too, he had hidden himself away here. With pleasure he stretched out on his wicker chair, and feeling drowsy after his swim, began to nod off in the hot sunshine. His bath towel and the book he was reading—Furmanov's *The Revolt*[25]—were lying on the chair beside him. His first few days in the sanatorium, though, had brought no relief from his nervous condition, and his headaches had not diminished. The doctors were still trying to diagnose his complex and obscure illness, but Pavel was sick and tired of their examinations, with all the everlasting auscultation and tapping. They wearied him dreadfully, so he did his best to avoid his woman doctor—a nice Party member with the strange name of Yerusalimchik—who found it very hard to track him down and persuade him to see one specialist or another.

"Honestly, doctor, I'm sick to death of the whole business!" he would say. "Half a dozen times a day I've got to tell the same old story and answer all kinds of stupid questions like was my grandmother ever mentally ill or did my great-grandfather suffer from rheumatism? Well how the hell do I know what he suffered from? I never even knew him! Then every doctor tries to persuade me to confess I once had gonorrhea or something even worse, till I swear I feel like hitting them over their bald heads! Just let me have a rest, that's all I want! If they're going to be diagnosing what's wrong with me all the six weeks I'm here, I'll become a danger to society!"

Dr. Yerusalimchik would laugh and joke in reply, but a few minutes later she would take him by the arm, and chattering brightly, lead him off to see the surgeon.

Today, though, there was no examination in the offing, and it was still an hour till lunch time.

***

When Pavel left the sanatorium, the Central Committee appointed him District Komsomol Secretary in one of the industrial areas, and just a week later he was addressing a meeting of the local organization there for the first time.

Late that autumn, though, the District Committee's car in which Pavel was travelling with two other Party workers to a remote part of the region, skidded into a ditch and overturned.

All the car's occupants were injured, and Pavel's right knee was crushed. A few days later he was transferred to the Surgical Institute in Kharkov, where after an examination and a series of X-rays of his swollen knee, the doctors held a consultation and advised an immediate operation.

Pavel gave his consent.

"Tomorrow morning, then," said the stout professor who was in charge, and he stood up to go. The other doctors left the room behind him.

***

In the operating room were several people with gauze masks over their faces.

There were nickel instruments flashing in the light, a narrow operating table and a huge basin beneath it. The professor was still washing his hands as Pavel lay down on the table. Behind him swift preparations were being made for the operation. Pavel looked round. The nurse was setting out lancets and forceps close by, while his ward doctor, Bazhanova, was unwinding the bandage on his leg.

"Don't look, Comrade Korchagin," she said quietly, "it's bad for the nerves."

"For whose nerves, doctor?" Pavel asked with a roguish smile.

A few minutes later a heavy mask was put over his face and he heard the professor say:

"Lie still now—we're going to give you some chloroform. Breathe deeply through your nose and start counting."

"All right," answered a calm voice that was muffled by the mask. "I apologize in advance for any unprintable remarks I may make."

The professor could not help smiling.

Then came the first few drops of chloroform and the suffocating, loathsome smell.

Pavel took a deep breath, and doing his best to speak clearly, began counting. And so it was that the curtain rose on the first act of his tragedy.

***

Artem almost tore the envelope in half as he opened it, and feeling anxious for some reason, unfolded the letter. He scanned the first few lines, then unable to tear his eyes away, glanced quickly at the rest of the page.

Dear Artem, *he read,*

We write to each other very rarely, perhaps just once or twice a year, but is it frequency that matters? You say you and your family have moved from Shepetovka to the Kazatin railway yards. And you tell me you're finding it hard to study in your "old age," but you don't seem to be doing too badly to me! You're wrong to refuse so stubbornly to leave the yards and become chairman of the Town Soviet. After all, you fought for Soviet power, didn't you? Then use it! Take over the Town Soviet tomorrow and set to work!

Now let me tell you a little about myself. There's something wrong with me, and I've been spending far too much time in hospital recently. They've carved me up twice now, and I've lost quite a lot of blood and got rather weak, but nobody's told me yet when it will all end.

I've lost touch with my work and have taken up a new profession—that of invalid! I have to tolerate a good deal of pain, and as a result of it all I've lost movement in my right knee. I've got several scars on various parts of my body, too, and the latest medical discovery is that seven years ago I injured my spine. Now they tell me this injury may cost me dear, but I'm ready to endure anything provided I can return to the ranks eventually.

There's nothing more terrible for me than to fall out of the ranks—it's something I can't even bear to think about. And that's why I'm letting them do whatever they like with me, but there's still no improvement and the clouds seem to be getting thicker and darker all the time. After the first operation I went back to work as soon as I could walk, but it wasn't long before they had me back in hospital again. Now I'm being sent to the "Mainak" sanatorium in Yevpatoria, and I'm due to leave tomorrow. But don't worry, Artem—after all, it'll not be very easy to finish me off! There's still enough life left in me for three! You and I will do some good work yet, my lad! So take care of yourself and don't overdo things, because health repairs cost the Party far too much later on. The years bring us experience and study gives us knowledge, and all that's much too precious to be wasted by lying around in hospital. I shake you by the hand.

Pavel

While Artem was knitting his bushy brows over his brother's letter, Pavel was saying good-bye to Dr. Irina Bazhanova at the hospital.

"So you're leaving for the Crimea tomorrow, are you?" she asked, giving him her hand. "But, Comrade Korchagin, you've not forgotten our conversation about letting my father have a look at you before you go, have you? I've given him a detailed account of your illness and I'd like him to examine you. He could do it this evening."

Pavel agreed straightaway.

That evening Irina showed Pavel into her father's spacious office.

The famous surgeon gave him a thorough examination. His daughter had brought all the X-rays and results of the tests from the clinic. Pavel could not help noticing how pale she suddenly turned when her father made some lengthy remark in Latin. He gazed at the professor's large bald head as he bent over him, trying to read something in his piercing eyes, but the doctor's face was inscrutable.

When Pavel had dressed again, Bazhanov courteously bid him farewell, explaining that he was due at a meeting and entrusting his daughter with the task of telling Pavel the results of his examination.

Not long afterwards Pavel was lying on the couch in Irina's tastefully furnished room and waiting for her to begin. But she did not know how to start or what to say. It was extremely difficult—her father had told her that so far medicine was unable to halt the destructive inflammatory process at work in Pavel's body. "This young man is doomed to lose all movement in his limbs," he had said, "and we are powerless to avert the tragedy."

Dr. Bazhanova did not think it wise either as a physician or as a friend to tell Pavel the whole truth, and so, choosing her words carefully, she only gave him a small part of it.

"I'm sure, Comrade Korchagin, that the mud baths in Yevpatoria will bring a big improvement, and that by the autumn you'll be able to return to work."

But she had forgotten that his sharp eyes had been watching her carefully all the time she was speaking.

"From what you say, or rather from what you don't say, I can see the situation is very serious," he said. "Remember that I asked you always to be perfectly frank with me. There's no need to hide anything—I shan't faint or try to cut my throat. But I very much want to know what's in store for me."

But she avoided giving him a direct answer by making a joke, so Pavel did not find out the truth about his future that night. Then, as they were saying good-bye, she said softly:

"Don't forget that I'm your friend, Comrade Korchagin. After all, who knows what life has in store for you? So if ever you need my advice or help, please write, and I'll do everything I possibly can for you."

Then, looking out of the window, she watched as the tall figure, leaning heavily on a stick, slowly made its way from the door to the waiting horse-cab.

***

Yevpatoria again. The intense heat of the southern sun. Noisy, sunburnt people in gold-embroidered skullcaps. A ten-minute drive by car brought the newcomers to a two-storey, gray limestone building—the "Mainak" sanatorium.

Towards the end of his month's stay, however, Pavel's condition began to deteriorate and the doctors ordered him to remain in bed. For the rest of his time there he was not allowed to get up.

A week before his departure he received a letter from the Ukrainian Central Committee informing him that his leave had been extended for a further two months and that on the advice of the sanatorium doctors any return to work in his present condition was out of the question.

A sum of money was enclosed with the letter.

Pavel accepted this first blow just as years before he had taken Fyodor's punches when the sailor was teaching him to box. Then, too, he had reeled with the shock but had recovered himself straightaway.

Then, one day, quite out of the blue, he received a letter from his mother. She wrote that in a small coastal town not far from Yevpatoria lived an old friend of hers, Albina Kyutsam, whom she had not seen for fifteen years. Now she begged Pavel to pay Albina a visit while he was in the south. As things turned out, this chance letter was to play a highly significant role in Pavel's life.

A week later his sanatorium friends bade him farewell down at the jetty, and the next morning the cab bringing him up from the harbor stopped outside a little house with a small garden. Pavel sent the driver to ask whether this was where the Kyutsams lived.

There were five in the Kyutsam family: Albina, the mother, a plump, middle-aged woman with dark, mournful eyes and traces of faded beauty on her face; her two daughters, Lelya and Taya; Lelya's young son; and old Kyutsam, the head of the household, a disagreeable, fat man who looked rather like a hog.

Kyutsam worked in a cooperative store and the younger daughter Taya did whatever unskilled work she could find, while Lelya, who used to be a typist, had recently separated from her husband, a rowdy drunkard, and now had no job at all. She spent her time at home, looking after her little boy and helping her mother with the housework.

Apart from the two daughters, there was a son called George who was away in Moscow.

The family greeted Pavel very warmly. Only the old man eyed him with suspicion and even hostility.

Pavel patiently told Albina all the family news he could, and at the same time asked about their life.

Lelya was twenty-two. A simple girl with short auburn hair and a broad, open face, she soon grew friendly with Pavel and readily let him into all the family secrets. She told him that the old man ruled the family with a coarsely despotic hand, suppressing the slightest manifestation of initiative or independence on the others' part. Narrow-minded, bigoted and extremely captious, he kept the family in a perpetual state of fear, and by so doing had earned himself the hostility of his children and the hatred of his wife, who had struggled against his tyrannical rule for the past twenty-five years. The daughters always sided with their mother, and the incessant family quarrels were poisoning all their lives. And so the days went by, filled with endless bickering over both major and minor issues.

Pavel did not meet the younger sister, Taya, till late in the evening after his arrival. When she came into the house, he could hear the mother whispering to her about him in the hall. As Taya said hello to Pavel, she gave him her hand and blushed right to the tips of her ears in embarrassment at seeing the young stranger. Pavel kept hold of her strong, calloused fingers for a few moments before letting them go.

Taya was getting on for nineteen. She was not beautiful, but her big, dark brown eyes, her delicate, slanting eyebrows, fine nose and fresh, resolute-looking lips made her attractive enough. Her firm young breasts showed clearly under her striped worker's blouse.

The sisters had two tiny rooms to themselves. In Taya's room there was a narrow iron bed, a chest of drawers decorated with various knick-knacks and topped by a small mirror, and two or three dozen photographs and postcards on the walls. On the windowsill stood two flower pots with a crimson geranium in one and pale pink asters in the other. The muslin curtain at the window was tied back by a pale blue ribbon.

"Taya doesn't usually let members of the opposite sex into her room, but she's evidently making an exception for you," said Lelya to Pavel, teasing her sister.

The following evening the family were sitting drinking tea in the old couple's part of the house. Taya was in her room but she could hear the general conversation. Old Kyutsam was stirring his glass of tea in a preoccupied way and casting occasional malevolent glances over his spectacles at the guest facing him.

"I think the marriage laws nowadays are a disgrace," he was saying. "Married one day, then unmarried again the next if you want! Complete freedom to do just what you like!"

He spluttered and began to cough. Then, having got his breath back, he pointed at Lelya and said:

"Just look at her there—she went and took up with that fancy man of hers and got married without so much as a by your leave, then separated from him in just the same way! And now, if you please, it's me who's got to feed her and that little brat of hers! It's scandalous!"

Mortified, Lelya blushed, and with tear-filled eyes looked away from Pavel.

"So d'you think she ought to live with that parasite instead?" he asked, not taking his angrily flashing eyes off the old man's face.

"She should've taken more care who she was marrying in the first place!" Kyutsam replied.

Then Albina intervened in the argument. Trying hard to suppress her indignation, she said quickly and jerkily:

"Listen, why must you start talking about things like this in front of a guest? Can't you find anything else to say?"

The old man rounded on her in a flash.

"I tell you I know what I'm talking about! Besides, since when has anybody told me what to do?"

That night Pavel lay awake for a long time thinking about the Kyutsams. Brought here quite by chance, he had unwittingly become a participant in the family drama, and now wondered how he could help the mother and daughters release themselves from bondage. His own life was hardly free of difficulties, though, and many problems still remained to be solved, so it was harder than ever to take decisive action.

There was only one way out of the situation: the family had to be broken up and the mother and daughters must leave the old man for good. But that was not so simple to achieve. Pavel was in no position to arrange this revolution, for he was due to leave in only a few days and might never see the family again. Would it not be better just to let things take their course instead of trying to kick up a fuss in this cramped little house? And yet the loathsome image of old Kyutsam gave him no rest. Several schemes suggested themselves to him, but none of them seemed feasible.

The next day was Sunday, and when Pavel came back from a stroll around town he found Taya alone in the house—the others had gone out visiting relatives. He went into her room and feeling rather tired, sat down on a chair.

"Why don't you ever go out and enjoy yourself?" he asked.

"I never feel like it," she replied in a low voice.

Then Pavel remembered the plans he had thought of during the night and decided to put them to her.

Speaking quickly so as to finish what he was saying before the others returned, he came straight to the point:

"Listen, Taya, you and I are good friends, so what's the point of beating about the bush? I'll be leaving soon. It's a pity I've got to know you all just at a bad time, when I'm in rather a mess myself, otherwise things might have turned out differently. If this had happened a year ago, say, we could all have left here together. There's always plenty of work for people like you and Lelya! You've just got to forget the old man—it's useless to expect him to change—and the only way out for you's to leave home. But that's impossible at the moment. I still don't know what's going to happen to me, and that's why I'm rather at a loss, so to speak. So what can we do now? Well, I'm going to insist that they send me back to work. The doctors have written all sorts of nonsense about me, and my comrades are trying to make me go on having treatment for ever, but we'll see about that ... I'll write to my mother and we'll work out how we can put an end to this business here. Anyway, I can't leave you all as you are—that's for sure. But you've got to realize, Taya, that this will mean a big change in your family's life and especially in yours. Do you want that, and have you the strength and will to go through with it?"

Looking up, she replied quietly:

"Yes, I do want it, but as for having enough strength—I'm not sure."

Pavel quite understood her lack of certainty.

"Well, never mind, Taya! So long as you want to do it, we'll manage. But tell me, are you very attached to your family?"

Caught unawares by his question, she hesitated before replying.

"I feel very sorry for mother," she said eventually. "Father's made her life miserable and now George is tormenting her too. I do feel very sorry for her ... even though she's never loved me as much as she loves George ..."

They talked a great deal that day, and then, shortly before the rest of the family came back, Pavel said jokingly:

"I'm surprised the old man hasn't got you married off by now!"

Taya threw up her hands in horror.

"Oh no!" she exclaimed. "I'll never get married! I've seen what Lelya's had to go through, and that's enough for me! No, I shan't get married—not for anything in the world!"

Pavel grinned.

"So your mind's made up for the rest of your life, is it? But what if some splendid young fellow—a really good guy—comes along ... what then?"

"No, I still won't get married! They're all fine while they're courting!"

Pavel laid his hand soothingly on her shoulder.

"All right—you'll get along well enough without a husband, but you mustn't be too hard on the lads, you know! It's a good job you don't suspect me of trying to court you, or there really would be trouble!" and he patted her arm in a friendly fashion.

"Men like you don't marry girls like me. Anyway, what good would I be to you?" she said softly.

***

A few days later Pavel left by train for Kharkov. Taya, Lelya and Albina accompanied by her sister Rosa all came down to the station to see him off. As they said good-bye, Albina made him promise not to forget her daughters and to help them find a way out of their difficult situation. They bade him farewell as though he were one of the family, and there were tears in Taya's eyes as he left. Looking out of the carriage window, Pavel watched as Lelya's white kerchief and Taya's striped blouse grew smaller and smaller until they finally disappeared.

Arriving in Kharkov, Pavel went to the Central Committee as soon as he had rested after the journey. There he waited to see his old friend Akim, and when they were alone together at last, Pavel asked to be sent back to work immediately. But Akim shook his head.

"No, Pavel, that's impossible!" he said. "We have the decision of the Central Committee's Medical Board which says: 'In view of Korchagin's serious condition, he is to be sent to the Neuropathological Institute for treatment and should not be allowed to return to work.'"

But Pavel pleaded his case so passionately that Akim could not resist and finally gave in.

The next day Pavel was already hard at work in the Special Department of the Central Committee Secretariat. He felt that he only had to be busy again for his lost strength to return, but from his first day back he saw he had been wrong. He would sit at his desk for eight hours at a stretch without taking a break for lunch, simply because the physical effort of coming down from the third floor and crossing to the canteen in the next building was too much for him. Very often first his arm then his leg would suddenly go numb, and sometimes his whole body was paralyzed and he would run a temperature. Some days when it was time to leave for work, he found that he was not strong enough to get out of bed, and by the time the attack passed, he realized with despair that he was a whole hour late. Eventually he was given an official reprimand for being late, and he realized that this was the beginning of what he dreaded most—he was beginning to fall out of the ranks.

Twice Akim helped by having him transferred to other duties, but eventually the inevitable happened, and only a month after his return to work, Pavel was confined to his bed once more.

This time Akim was adamant, but to his categorical insistence that Pavel should enter the clinic, the latter replied in a low voice:

"I'm not going anywhere—there's no point! There's only one thing left for me to do—take my pension and retire! But that's something I'll never do! You can't make me give up my work! I'm only twenty-four, and I won't spend the rest of my life as an industrial invalid, wandering from one clinic to another, knowing it can't do me the slightest bit of good! No—you've just got to find me some work that suits my condition. I can work at home or I can even stay somewhere in the office ... But don't ask me to be a penpusher who spends his time signing letters! I've got to have the kind of work that'll give me the satisfaction of knowing I can still be useful!"

Ringing with emotion, Pavel's voice was rising higher and higher.

Akim knew what profound feelings filled this passionate young man. He realized all the tragedy of Pavel's situation, and knew that for a man who had devoted the whole of his short life to the Party, to be torn from the ranks and doomed to a life deep in the rear was terrible. So he resolved to do everything in his power to help him.

"All right, Pavel," he said, "don't worry. We've got a meeting of the Secretariat tomorrow, so I'll put your case to the comrades there. I give you my word I'll do all I can."

Pavel got heavily to his feet and gave Akim his hand.

"Do you really think, Akim, that life can drive me into a corner and squash me flat? So long as my heart beats here," and he pressed Akim's hand to his chest so Akim could clearly feel the dull pounding, "so long as it beats, nobody will be able to tear me away from the Party. The only thing that can force me out of the ranks is death, so remember that, my friend!"

Akim did not reply. He knew this was not simply an empty remark, but the passionate cry of a warrior who has been mortally wounded in battle. He knew, too, that men like Pavel cannot feel or speak in any other way.

Two days later he told Pavel that he was to be given the opportunity of working in the editorial office of a large newspaper, but before he could do so, it was necessary to check whether he was suitable for literary work.

Arriving at the editorial office, Pavel was courteously received, and then the woman assistant editor, an old Party underground worker and a member of the Presidium of the Ukrainian Central Control Commission, asked him a few questions.

"What education have you had, Comrade?"

"Three years of primary school."

"Have you been to any of the Party's political schools?"

"No."

"Well, never mind—you can still be a good journalist without that. Now Comrade Akim has told us all about you. We can give you things you needn't necessarily do here but at home, and generally speaking, we can provide conditions of work that are suitable for you. Nevertheless, work of this kind requires extensive knowledge, particularly in the sphere of language and literature."

All this seemed to herald defeat for Pavel. And indeed, during the half-hour interview it became clear that his knowledge was inadequate. Then, in the trial article which he was asked to write, there were over three dozen stylistic irregularities and a considerable number of spelling mistakes which the woman had underlined in red.

"You have considerable ability, Comrade Korchagin," she said, "and with hard work you may learn to write well one day. But at the moment your grammar is faulty, and from your article it's clear you don't know the Russian language very well. That's not surprising, though, considering you've had no time for study. But unfortunately we can't use you, though as I said before, you have considerable potential. If your article were to be edited without altering the content, it would be splendid, but you see, we haven't enough editors as it is."

Leaning on his stick, Pavel got to his feet, his right eyebrow twitching spasmodically.

"Yes, of course, I see what you mean," he said. "What sort of writer would I make anyway? I used to be quite a good stoker and a reasonable electrician into the bargain. I could ride a horse pretty well too, and I knew how to stir up the young Komsomols, but I wouldn't be any good in your line of business."

Then, saying good-bye, he left the room.

At a turning in the corridor he stumbled and would have fallen over if a woman who was just passing had not caught him in time.

"What's the matter, Comrade?" she asked. "You look quite ill!"

It took Pavel several seconds to recover, but then, gently letting go of her, he continued on his way, leaning heavily on the stick as he went.

From that day forward, he felt that his life had gone into a decline. Work was now out of the question, and more and more often he had to spend the whole day in bed. Then the Central Committee released him from his duties and arranged for him to receive a pension. When the pension finally came, it brought with it a document certifying that he was now an industrial invalid. The Central Committee then gave him money and issued him with papers giving him the right to go wherever he wished.

Letters kept coming from the Kyutsams inviting him to come and see them in the little coastal town. Life there was becoming intolerable, they said, and they wanted his help.

And so one morning Pavel left the quiet Moscow flat where he had been staying with friends. The train carried him swiftly southwards to the sea, bearing him away from the rainy autumn of the north to the warm shores of the southern Crimea. He sat by the window watching the telegraph poles racing by, his brows tightly knit and a resolute gleam in his dark eyes.

8

Down below, the waves lapped against the rocks. A dry wind blowing from distant Turkey fanned Pavel's face. Protected from the open sea by a concrete breakwater, the harbor nestled on the shore in an irregular, curving arc. A range of mountains came to an abrupt end at the coast, falling to the sea in a steep cliff, and high above, tiny white cottages stood perched on the hillsides.

It was quiet here in the old park outside the town, and the yellow leaves of autumn came floating down on to the paths that were overgrown with grass.

The park was deserted. Pavel found a bench on a cliff top overlooking the sea, and sitting down, lifted his face to the gentle autumn sun.

He had come to this quiet place to think things over and decide what to do with his life. It was time to reach some conclusions and take a decision.

With his second visit to the Kyutsams the strife in the family had reached fever pitch. Hearing of the visitor's arrival, the old man had flown into a rage and kicked up an unbelievable fuss. Naturally enough, it fell to Pavel to lead the opposition against him. Then the old man unexpectedly met with a vigorous rebuff from his wife and daughters, and after Pavel's first day there the house split into two hostile camps. The door leading to the parents' half of the building was boarded up and one of the small side rooms was rented to the guest. Pavel paid Kyutsam his rent in advance, and the old man seemed reassured by the fact that now his daughters had cut themselves off from him, they no longer expected him to support them.

Far away in the distance, almost on the horizon, drifted the dark trail of smoke from a steamer. A flock of seagulls swooped low over the water, calling harshly as they went.

Pavel sat with his chin resting on his palms, deep in thought. In his mind's eye the whole of his life went flitting by, from childhood right up to the present. How had he spent those twenty-four years, he wondered—worthily or unworthily? Going over them one at a time in his memory, he examined the past like an impartial judge, and with a profound sense of satisfaction came to the conclusion that he had not lived his life so badly after all. There had been a good many mistakes, it was true, mistakes that he had made because of foolishness and youth, but most of all because of ignorance. The main thing, though, was that he had not missed the impassioned days of fervor, for he had played a part in the bitter struggle to establish Soviet power, and on the crimson banner of revolution there were a few drops of his own life-blood.

Moreover, he had not left the ranks until his strength had failed him. But now, struck down by illness and no longer able to keep his place in the firing line, he had nowhere left to go but field hospitals in the rear. He remembered how as they were galloping into Warsaw, one of his comrades had been struck by a bullet and had fallen to the ground beneath his horse's hoofs. His comrades had hastily dressed the wound, then handing him over to the orderlies, had raced on once more—in pursuit of the enemy. The squadron had not checked its advance because of the loss of one man. So it was in the struggle for a great cause, and so it had to be.

But what was he to do with himself now that he had suffered defeat and there was no longer any hope of returning to the ranks? What was to be done? The unanswered question was like a menacing black abyss that yawned before him.

What was there left to live for now he had lost the thing that was most precious of all to him—the capacity to fight? How was he to justify his existence today and on all the cheerless days to come? How was he to fill his time? Simply by eating, drinking and breathing? To remain a helpless bystander, looking on while his comrades continued to fight their way forward? Be a burden on them? No! Better to put a bullet through his heart and have done with it! He had lived his life well enough, so now he should be able to bring it to a timely end. Who would condemn a warrior for putting himself out of his misery?

He felt the flat butt of the Browning in his pocket, and with a familiar movement his fingers closed over the grip. Then he slowly pulled the gun out of his pocket.

"Whoever would have thought you would come to this?" he said to himself.

The muzzle stared contemptuously back at him. He laid the pistol on his knee and cursed bitterly.

"All this is nothing but cheap heroics, my lad!" he said. "Any fool can shoot himself! It's the easiest way out and the most cowardly too! You can always shoot yourself when things become too hard! But have you really tried to get the better of life? Have you done everything you possibly can to break out of the iron bonds that tie you? Now put that gun away and don't ever breathe a word of this to a soul! Learn how to go on living even when it becomes unbearable! Do something useful with your life instead!"

Then he got up and set off towards the road.

***

Taya was still awake when he got back—she had been worried by his long absence. What could have happened to him, she wondered. And where was he? She remembered the cold, hard look she had seen in his eyes that morning, eyes that were usually so bright and warm. He never talked much about himself, but all the same she sensed he was suffering about something.

As the clock in her mother's room struck two, she heard the garden gate creak, and throwing her jacket over her shoulders, went out to open the front door.

"I was beginning to worry about you," she whispered with relief when he came into the hall.

"Nothing's going to happen to me as long as I'm alive, Taya," he answered softly. "Is Lelya asleep? You know, I don't feel a bit tired. I want to tell you about what happened today. Let's go to your room, shall we, otherwise we'll wake Lelya."

Taya hesitated for a moment. How could she let him come to her room and talk when it was as late as this? And what would her mother think if she found out? But she couldn't say this to him because he'd be offended. What did he want to tell her anyway, she wondered, as she led the way to her room.

"Now this is what I want to say, Taya," Pavel began in a low voice after they had sat down in the dimly-lit room, so close to each other that she could feel his breath on her cheek. "Life sometimes takes such a strange turn that it amazes you. Things haven't been going too well these past few days, and I wasn't really sure how I could go on living. In fact, things have never seemed quite so black as just recently. But today I've taken an important decision, so don't be surprised at what I have to say."

Then he told her about everything he had gone through during the past few months and a great deal of what had been in his mind in the park.

"So that's the position," he said. "Now I'll get down to the most important thing of all. The trouble in this family's only just beginning, so we must get out of here into the fresh air and move as far away from this lousy place as we can.

We've got to make a completely new start, and now that I've taken a hand in the struggle, I'm going to see it through. Our own lives—yours and mine—are far from happy at the moment, so I've decided to put some warmth into them and cheer them up. Do you understand what I mean? Will you be my companion and my wife?"

So far Taya had been listening to him with profound emotion, but his last few words made her start with surprise.

"I'm not asking you for an answer tonight, Taya," he went on. "You must think everything over very carefully first. Perhaps it's hard for you to understand how such things can be put so bluntly without all the usual courting and such like, but nobody really needs that kind of rubbish. I'm giving you my hand, darling—here it is! If you'll put your trust in me, you'll not be disappointed, because there's a great deal I can give you, and vice versa. Now this is what I've decided: our agreement will remain in force till you grow up to be a real human being and a true Bolshevik. And if I can't help you do that, I'm not worth a brass farthing! So we mustn't break our agreement till then. But once you've grown up, you'll be free of all obligations to me. After all, who knows what might happen? I may turn into a complete physical wreck, and in that case, remember, you mustn't consider yourself bound to me in any way."

He was silent for a few moments, then went on in a warm, gentle voice:

"So for the time being I'm offering you my friendship and my love."

He held her hand in his and felt at peace, as though she had already given her consent.

"But you won't leave me, will you?" she asked.

"I can give you my word, Taya. All you have to do is believe that men like me do not betray their friends ... provided they don't betray me," he added somberly.

"I can't give you an answer tonight," she said, "it's all so sudden."

Pavel stood up.

"Go to bed now, Taya," he said, "it'll soon be morning."

And off he went to his own room. He lay down without undressing and was asleep as soon as his head touched the pillow.

The table by the window in Pavel's room was piled high with books brought from the local Party library, heaps of newspapers and several writing-pads filled with notes. Two chairs, a bed and an enormous map of China that was pinned up over the door leading to Taya's room and was dotted with little red and black flags, completed the furnishings. The staff at the local Party Committee office had agreed to supply him with material and had also promised to ask the librarian at the biggest public library in town to send him whatever he needed. So it was not long before big parcels of books began to arrive for him. Lelya was amazed at the way he sat reading and making notes all day long with only short breaks for lunch and tea. In the evenings, which he always spent with the sisters, he would tell them about what he had been reading.

For the first time in eight years Pavel found himself with plenty of time on his hands and no responsibilities whatsoever. And he read with the avid eagerness of the newly-enlightened, sitting over his books for umpteen hours a day. Just how far this would have told on his health if he had continued is hard to say, but a seemingly casual remark from Taya one day changed everything:

"I've moved the chest of drawers away from the door into your room, so if ever you want to talk to me, you can come straight through."

Pavel blushed. She gave a happy smile—their agreement was signed and sealed.

***

Now the old man no longer saw the light shining late at night through a chink in the shuttered window of Pavel's corner room, and Taya's mother noticed a gleam in her daughter's eye, the glow of a happiness that Taya could barely conceal. The faint shadows under her eyes shining with inner fire spoke of sleepless nights, and more and more often the strumming of a guitar and her singing echoed through the little house.

Lelya was the first to discover the reason for the undying light in Taya's eyes, and from that day forward the shadow of estrangement fell between the sisters. Soon the mother found out too, or rather guessed, and she felt troubled—she had never expected it of Pavel.

"Taya's not the wife for him," she said one day to Lelya. "What on earth will come of it all, I wonder?"

Uneasy thoughts began to stir in her mind, but she could not bring herself to say anything to Pavel.

Then young people began to visit him and sometimes there was hardly enough space for them all in his little room. It was the study circle of young workers which the Party Committee had assigned to Pavel in response to his insistent demand for propaganda work. And so it was that his days passed.

Once more he had grasped the helm firmly with both hands, and the ship of life, having veered dangerously off course, was now steering towards a new goal. His dream of returning to the ranks through reading and learning seemed to be coming true at last.

Then all of a sudden one day the ne'er-do-well student George turned up from Moscow, accompanied by his new wife.

His arrival served to widen the rift in the Kyutsam family even more. Without so much as a moment's thought, he immediately sided with his father and in an underhand way began to undermine Pavel's position, doing his level best to drive him out of the house and persuade Taya to break with him.

Two weeks after George's arrival, Lelya got a job in a nearby town and left home, taking her mother and young son with her. At the same time Pavel and Taya moved to a small town on the coast a long way away.

***

Artem did not receive letters from his brother very often, and whenever he found a gray envelope addressed in the familiar, angular hand waiting on his desk in the City Soviet, he felt his usual calm desert him. It was just the same this time too.

> Dear Artem,—he read,—I'm writing to tell you what has been happening to me recently. I don't think I ever write letters like this to anyone apart from you, but you know me well and understand everything I say.
>
> Life continues to deal me one blow after another on the health front. No sooner have I managed to struggle to my feet after one setback, than another, even fiercer than the last, lays me low once more. The most terrible thing about all this is that I'm quite powerless to stop it. First I lost the use of my left arm—that was bad enough, but then my legs failed me. I could only just manage to move about in my room as it was, but now I have trouble even getting from my bed to the table. And what's more, there's probably worse to come. As for what tomorrow may bring—nobody knows.
>
> I don't go out of the house any more now, and I can only see a very small stretch of the sea from my window. Can there be any greater tragedy than for a man to have a treacherous body that refuses to obey him together with the heart of a Bolshevik—a Bolshevik who longs passionately to work and be alongside his comrades in the great army that is advancing along the whole front like an avalanche of steel?
>
> But I still believe that I shall return to the ranks one day, and that in time my bayonet will take its place once more amid the columns leading the assault. This is something I must believe, and indeed, I have no right not to believe it. For ten years the Party and Komsomol taught me the art of struggle, and the words of our leader Lenin apply equally well to me: "There are no fortresses that Bolsheviks cannot take!"
>
> I spend all my time studying now—books, books and more books. I've done a great deal, Artem. I've worked through all the main classics and passed my first-year exams for the correspondence course at the Communist University. In the evenings I take a study group of young Party members—these comrades are my link with the practical work of the Party organization. Then there's my wife Taya's development and education—and of course her love and tender caresses too. She and I are the best of friends. Our household is run very simply—with my pension of thirty-two rubles and her earnings we manage quite well. She's following the same kind of path that I took to join the Party: for a while she worked as a domestic servant, and now she has a job as a dishwasher in a canteen (there's no industry in this little town, you see).
>
> The other day she proudly showed me her first delegate's card issued by the local Women's Section. To her this document isn't simply a little piece of cardboard. Now I can see the birth of a new woman taking place in her, and I'm doing my best

to help that process. The time will come when she'll work in a big factory, and then, as part of a large community she'll finally achieve political maturity. But while we're living here, she's following the only possible course that's open to her.

I shake your hand.

Yours, *Pavel*.

***

Life went on as before, with Taya working and Pavel studying. But before he had time to consolidate what he had done with the study group, another disaster crept up on him unawares: both his legs were completely paralyzed. Now he only had the use of his right hand. When after vain attempts to move he finally realized that he could no longer do so, he bit his lips till the blood came. Taya bravely concealed her despair and the pain she felt at being powerless to help him, but he said to her with an apologetic smile:

"It's time for you and me to go our separate ways, Taya. After all, it wasn't part of our agreement to get into a mess like this. I'm going to think things over good and proper today, my girl!"

But she refused to let him go on, and unable to stop herself from bursting into tears, buried her face against his chest.

When Artem found out about his brother's latest misfortune, he wrote to his mother, and Maria Yakovlevna immediately left her house and went to stay with her son and his wife. Now the three of them began to live together, and Taya and the old lady became the best of friends.

But Pavel carried on with his studies in spite of everything.

One bad winter's evening Taya brought home the news of her first victory—she had been elected a member of the City Soviet. From then on Pavel saw very little of her. After finishing work in the sanatorium kitchen where she washed dishes, she would go straight off to the Women's Section at the Soviet, and not come home till late in the evening, feeling very tired but full of new impressions. The day when she would apply for candidate-membership of the Party was drawing near, and she was preparing for it with great excitement. But then misfortune struck yet another blow, for Pavel's progressive disease was steadily doing its destructive work. All of a sudden an excruciating pain seared his right eye and spread rapidly to the left. And as everything around him became covered by a dark curtain, for the first time in his life he knew the horror of total blindness.

A terrible, new and apparently insurmountable obstacle had arisen in his path and now barred his way. His mother and Taya were filled with despair, but coolly and calmly he came to a decision and said:

"I must wait and see what happens. If it turns out there's really no possibility of advancing any further, if everything I've done to return to the ranks has been swept away by this blindness—then I must put an end to it all."

He then sent letters to his friends, and in their replies they urged him to stand firm and continue the struggle.

It was during these grim days that Taya came home one evening full of excitement and announced joyfully:

"Pavel, I've been elected a candidate-member of the Party!"

As he listened to her account of how the local Party cell had accepted this new comrade into its ranks, Pavel recalled his own first steps in the Party years ago.

"Well, Comrade Korchagina," he said, squeezing her hand, "you and I are a Communist faction now!"

The next day he sent a letter to the secretary of the District Committee, asking him to come and see him. That evening a mud-bespattered car pulled up outside the house, and a few moments later Volmer, a middle-aged Lett with an enormous beard that reached right up to his ears, was shaking Pavel's hand.

He stayed for about two hours, and forgot all about the meeting he was supposed to be attending later that evening. He walked up and down the room, listening to Pavel's impassioned appeal for work, then finally said:

"Stop talking about study groups, Korchagin. First of all you've got to rest, and then we'll see about your eyes—it might still be possible to do something for them. What about going to Moscow for treatment, eh? You think it over . . ."

But Pavel interrupted him:

"But it's people I need, Comrade Volmer, real, live people! I just can't go on living all by myself. And I need them now more than ever before! So please send the young folk to me—those who've had the least experience of life. They're veering far too much to the left out there in the villages, and wanting to set up communes because the collective farms aren't giving them enough scope. After all, if you don't keep an eye on them, those Komsomols often try and dash forward ahead of the main column. I used to be like that myself, so I know!"

Volmer thought for a few moments, then suddenly slapped himself on the forehead as an idea struck him:

"I know what we'll do—we'll send you Lev Bersenev. You couldn't wish for a finer comrade! He's a man after your own heart, so the two of you should get on famously together—just like a couple of high-voltage transformers! He'll rig up a radio for you—he's an expert at that sort of thing. I often sit up till two in the morning at his place, you know, with those headphones of his on."

The following evening Lev Bersenev came to see Pavel, and it was midnight before he left. When he said good-bye to his new friend, he felt as if he had just found a brother whom he had lost many years before.

The next morning men were at work climbing over the roof and fixing a radio antenna in place, while Lev was busy in Pavel's room setting up the receiver, telling him fascinating stories about his experiences as he did so. Pavel could not see him, of course, but from what Taya had told him, Lev was a tall, slim, fair-haired man with bright eyes and quick movements, which was exactly how Pavel had pictured him the moment they first met.

Then, as twilight fell, three little valves began to glow in the room and Lev triumphantly handed Pavel the headphones. The air was filled with an uproar of sound, for the morse code transmitters down in the harbor were twittering away like sparrows, while somewhere not far off the coast a ship's telegraph was emitting an endless stream of dots and dashes. But then, amid all the crackling, the tuning coil picked out and held on to a confident voice that was saying calmly:

"This is Moscow speaking..."

The little radio could pick up about sixty stations in various parts of the world. And so, the life from which Pavel had suddenly been excluded by his blindness came bursting in through the steel membranes of his headphones, and he was able to feel its mighty breath once more.

Seeing the way Pavel's eyes were shining with delight, the weary Bersenev smiled.

***

Everyone in the big house was fast asleep. Taya was murmuring restlessly as she slept. She came home late these days, very tired and shivering with cold, and Pavel and she had little time together. As she became increasingly involved in her work, she had fewer free evenings, and he would remember what Lev Bersenev had said on this score:

"If a Bolshevik has a wife who's his Party comrade, they rarely see one another. But there are two advantages in that: one, they never get tired of each other, and two, there's never any time to quarrel!"

And anyway, how could Pavel object? After all, it was only to be expected. There used to be a time when Taya would devote all her evenings to him, and there had been more warmth and tenderness in their relationship then. But in those days she had only been a friend and wife to him, whereas now she was his pupil and Party comrade.

He realized that the more she matured politically, the less time she would be able to give him, and he accepted this as inevitable.

He was given another study group to lead, and once again the house was filled with the sound of voices in the evenings. The hours he spent with these young people filled him with cheerfulness and vigor.

The remainder of his time was spent listening to the radio, and his mother had great difficulty in tearing him away from the headphones at mealtimes.

The radio gave him what his blindness had taken away—the opportunity to study and acquire knowledge, and his all-consuming desire for learning helped him forget the excruciating pain that racked his body, the fire that seared his eyes, and all the suffering that a bleak, unkind life had brought him.

When the radio broadcast the news from Magnitostroi[26] about the heroic exploits of the young comrades who had succeeded his own generation of Komsomols, Pavel was filled with happiness.

He imagined the blizzards and the cruel Urals frosts that were as savage as wolves. He could hear the wind howling and saw amid the swirling snow a detachment of second-generation Komsomols working at night by the light of arc lamps on the roofs of the huge factory, struggling to save the first sections of the enormous plant from the ravages of ice and snow. Compared to this, the railway construction project in which the first generation of Kiev Komsomols had battled with the elements seemed very small beer indeed! The country had grown since then, and its people had grown too.

Then down on the Dnieper[27] the floodwaters burst their steel barriers and surged on, sweeping away both men and machines as they went. And once again the young Komsomols hurled themselves at the elements, and after a furious two-day struggle without either sleep or rest, brought the raging torrent back under control. In the vanguard of this mighty struggle there now marched a new generation of Komsomols.

9

Eighteen months had passed since Pavel's arrival in Moscow, eighteen months of indescribable torment.

At the clinic Professor Averbakh had told him quite frankly that there was no hope of restoring his sight at the moment. Sometime in the dim and distant future, he said, when the inflammation had subsided, it might be possible to operate on Pavel's pupils. In the meantime, though, he advised an operation to halt the inflammatory process.

The doctors asked Pavel for his consent and he gave it, telling them to do whatever they thought necessary.

Three times he felt Death's black wing brush him as he lay for hour after hour on the operating table with the surgeon's lancets cutting into his neck to remove the parathyroid gland. But he clung tenaciously to life, and after hours of anguished suspense Taya would find him deathly pale but still alive, and as calm and gentle as always.

"Don't worry, darling," he would say, "it's not so easy to finish me off, you know! I'm determined to go on living and kicking up a fuss if only to spite what all these learned doctors say! They're right about everything as far as my health goes, but they're very much mistaken when they try to write me off as totally unfit for work. I'll show them yet!"

Pavel was determined to rejoin the ranks of those building the new life, and he knew now what path he must take to accomplish it.

***

Winter was over, spring had burst in at the open windows, and Pavel, having survived yet another operation, made up his mind that weak though he still was, he would not stay in hospital any longer. To spend so many months surrounded by human suffering, amid the groaning and lamentation of patients who were incurably ill, was infinitely more difficult than enduring his own suffering.

And so, when another operation was proposed, he refused.

"No," he said firmly, "I've had enough. I've shed plenty of blood for the sake of science, and now I need what's left for other things."

The same day he sent a letter to the Central Committee asking for their help in arranging for him to stay in Moscow where his wife was working, since it was now pointless to continue his wanderings in search of treatment. It was the first time he had ever turned to the Party for help, and in response to his letter, the Moscow Soviet found him accommodation. And so it was that Pavel left hospital with the sole desire of never returning there again.

Taya was a full member of the Party now. Extremely assiduous in her work at the factory, despite all the tragedy of her personal life she never fell behind the best shock-workers, and her comrades soon demonstrated their confidence in this quiet woman by electing her a member of the Factory Committee. The pride Pavel took in his wife who was now proving to be a true Bolshevik made his suffering easier to bear.

***

One day Dr. Bazhanova arrived in Moscow on official business and came to see Pavel. They had a long talk. Filled with fervor, he told her of his plans to return to the ranks in the near future.

The doctor noticed a wisp of silvery hair on his temple and said softly:

"I can see you've been through a great deal, but you still haven't lost any of your enthusiasm, and that's what really counts. It's good you've decided to make a start on the work you've been preparing these past five years. But how on earth are you going to manage it?"

Pavel smiled at her reassuringly.

"Tomorrow some friends are bringing me a sort of stencil made of cardboard—I can't write without it because the lines keep running into one another. I tried to think of a way round the problem, then suddenly hit on the answer—the strips cut in the cardboard will stop my pencil running off the straight line, you see. It's quite difficult to write without actually being able to see what you're writing, but it's not impossible—I've tried it, so I know. It took me a long time to get the hang of it, but now that I've learned to write more slowly, forming each letter very carefully, the result's quite good."

And so it was that Pavel started work.

He had conceived the idea of writing a novel about the heroic Kotovsky Division.[28] The title had come to him of its own accord: *Born of the Storm*.

From that day forward his whole life was centered on the writing of the novel, and very slowly, line by line, the pages came into being. Totally entranced by the world of images, he would become oblivious of everything around him, and for the first time in his life came to know the torment of creative work, when unforgettably vivid scenes that were so distinct in his mind could not adequately be transferred to paper and would emerge pale and lifeless, devoid of passion and fire.

He had to commit everything he wrote to memory, word by word, and the slightest interruption would make him lose the thread and slow down his work.

During the course of his writing he sometimes had to recite whole pages from memory and occasionally even entire chapters, and there were occasions when his mother feared that her son was going out of his mind. While he was working, she did not dare disturb him, but as she was picking up the sheets of paper that had slipped to the floor, she would say timidly:

"I wish you'd do something else, Pavel. It just can't be good for you, writing all the time . . ."

But he would only laugh at the old woman's fears and assure her that he hadn't quite "gone off the rails" yet.

***

Three chapters of the book were finished now, and Pavel sent them off to his old comrades from the Kotovsky Division in Odessa for their opinion. It was not long before he received a favorable reply. But on its way back the manuscript was lost in the post, which meant that six months' work was wasted. It was a terrible blow, and Pavel bitterly regretted having sent off the only copy of the manuscript he possessed.

But there was nothing for it except to begin all over again, and six weeks later the first chapter was ready once more.

A family by the name of Alexeev shared the apartment with the Korchagins. The elder son, Alexander, was secretary of one of the district committees of the Komsomol. He had an eighteen-year-old sister, Galya, who had just finished her studies at a factory workshop-school. She was a cheerful, lively girl. Pavel asked his mother to speak to her and find out whether she would help him with his writing by acting as secretary. Galya readily agreed.

From then on Pavel's work progressed much more quickly. Indeed, so much was done in the space of a month that he was amazed. Galya's enthusiastic support and sincere concern were a great help to him. Her pencil would rustle softly over the paper, and whenever a particular passage appealed to her, she would read it back to him, genuinely delighting in his success. She was practically the only person in the apartment who really believed in his work; the others felt that nothing would ever come of it, and that he was simply trying to occupy himself during the long hours of enforced idleness.

Galya would come to see him regularly, and as her pencil rustled along, unforgettable scenes from the past came steadily into being. At moments when Pavel lay lost in thought, overwhelmed by memories, Galya would watch his eyelashes quiver and the expression in his unseeing eyes change as they reflected the swift passage of his ideas. Somehow she found it almost impossible to believe that those eyes of his could not see, for their unblemished pupils were so full of life.

When the day's work was done, she would read out what she had written, and Pavel would listen intently, his brow knitted in a frown.

"What are you frowning for, Comrade Korchagin?" she would ask. "It's good, isn't it?"

"No, Galya, it's bad."

The pages which he did not like he would rewrite himself. Sometimes, hampered by the narrow slit in the stencil, he would lose patience and fling it aside, then, filled with boundless rage at life for having robbed him of his sight, he would snap the pencil and bite his lips till the blood came.

As the work neared completion, forbidden feelings began to burst free more often than usual from the bonds of his ever-vigilant will. Among them were sadness and that long series of simple emotions, both passionate and tender, to which almost everyone but himself had the right. But Pavel knew that if he succumbed to a single one of them, the consequences would be tragic.

***

At last the final chapter was finished, and Galya spent the next few days reading the completed manuscript to him.

The following morning it would be sent off to Leningrad, to the Cultural Department of the Regional Party Committee. If the book were approved there, it would be sent on to the publishers—and then . . .

Pavel's heart beat anxiously at the thought. Then . . . it would mean the beginning of a new life for him, a life won at the cost of years of unremitting, dogged toil.

The fate of his book would decide his own fate. If the manuscript were rejected, it would mean the end of everything for him. But if, on the other hand, it were considered only partially unsatisfactory, and if it were thought that its shortcomings could be remedied by further work, he would immediately launch a new offensive.

His mother took the heavy parcel containing the manuscript to the post office. Then there followed days of anxious waiting. Never in his life had Pavel waited with such agonizing impatience for the post as he did now, living from the morning delivery to the evening one. But there was still no answer from Leningrad.

The continued silence from the publishers was beginning to look ominous. With every day that passed, the presentiment of disaster grew stronger, and Pavel admitted to himself that an outright rejection of the manuscript would destroy him. In that case he could not possibly go on living—there would be nothing left to live for.

At moments such as these he would remember the park overlooking the sea, and time and again he asked himself the question:

"Have you done everything you possibly can to break free from the iron bonds holding you and return to the ranks so as to make your life worthwhile?"

And he would answer:

"Yes, I believe I have!"

At last, when the waiting had become almost unbearable, his mother who had been agonized by the suspense no less than he had, came running into the room and cried:

"News from Leningrad!"

It was a telegram from the Regional Committee—a terse message on a telegraph form saying: "Novel heartily approved. Publication under way. Congratulations on your victory!"

Pavel's heart began to pound with excitement. His long-cherished dream had come true at last! The iron bonds had been burst asunder, and now, armed with a new weapon, he could return to the ranks and to life once more.

1930–1934

Notes

1. Town on the River Volga, north-east of Moscow in European Russia.
2. Title of military commander in the Ukraine.
3. Simon Vasilyevich Petlyura (1879–1926), one of the leaders of anti-Bolshevik nationalist forces in the Ukraine.
4. District town and important railway junction west of Zhitomir in the western Ukraine.
5. Town south-west of Kiev in the western Ukraine.
6. Grigory Ivanovich Kotovsky (1881–1925), Commander of famous cavalry corps in the Civil War.

7. Village. Location obscure.
8. Town south of Kiev in the central Ukraine.
9. Nestor Ivanovich Makhno (1889–1934), leader of an anarchist and peasant anti-Bolshevik movement in the southern Ukraine during the Civil War, from 1918–21.
10. Novel by Ethel Lilian Voinich (1864–1960), Irish-born writer who lived in Russia from 1887 to 1889 before moving to the USA. *The Gadfly* (1897; published in Russian translation as *Ovod* in 1898), deals with the Italian liberation struggle 1830–40 and is her best-known work. It became very popular in Russia and served as the basis for several films, plays and an opera.
11. Semyon Mikhailovich Budyonny (1883–1973), marshal of the Soviet Union, Civil War hero and Commander of the First Cavalry Army, 1919–21.
12. Town near Kazatin, southwest of Kiev.
13. Town south of Zhitomir.
14. Town and railway junction west of Kiev and north-west of Zhitomir.
15. Town west of Novograd-Volynsky in the north-west Ukraine.
16. City in eastern Poland, center of an area now forming part of the western Ukraine.
17. Town south-west of Kiev.
18. Location obscure.
19. Town west of Kiev in the north-west Ukraine.
20. Town between Novograd-Volynsky and Rovno in the north-west Ukraine.
21. Polish sweet grass vodka.
22. Large industrial city on the lower Dnieper, renamed Dnepropetrovsk in 1926.
23. Village outside Moscow where Lenin lived from mid-May 1923 until his death. (Now Gorki Leninskiye.)
24. Coastal resort in the western Crimea.
25. *Myatezh* (1925) by Dmitry Andreevich Furmanov (1891–1926).
26. The large iron and steel plant and its associated industrial complex, built between 1929 and 1934 at Magnitogorsk in the southern Urals, one of the early triumphs of socialist industrial construction.
27. That is, at the large hydro-electric power station, Dneproges, at Zaporozhe on the lower Dnieper, built between 1927 and 1932.
28. Famous cavalry division commanded by Grigory Ivanovich Kotovsky (1881–1925), hero of the Civil War.

Mikhail Sholokhov in the late 1950s.

Mikhail Sholokhov
THE FATE OF A MAN

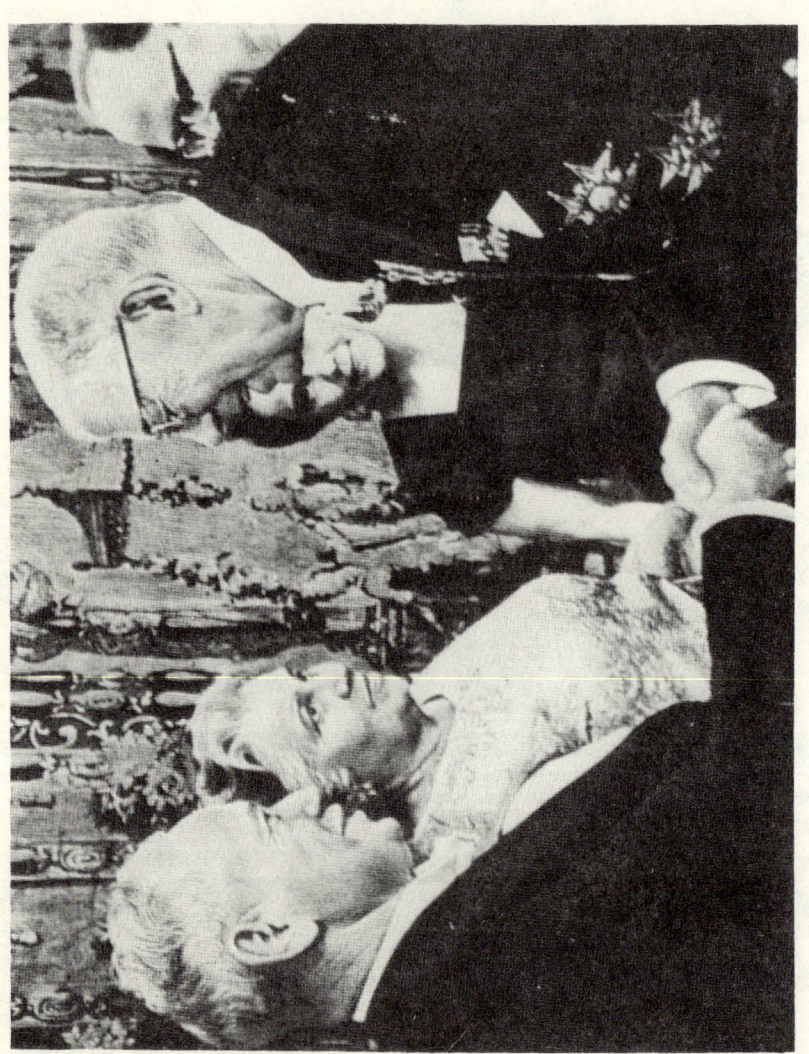

Sholokhov being congratulated by King Gustav VI of Sweden after receiving the Nobel Prize for Literature (Stockholm, 1965).

MIKHAIL SHOLOKHOV (1905–1984)

Mikhail Alexandrovich Sholokhov was born in May 1905 in the village of Kruzhilin near Veshenskaya, about two hundred miles north of Rostov-on-Don, in what was then the Don Cossack Military Region. Contrary to popular belief, neither of his parents was of Cossack stock. His father, Alexander, whose family had moved to the Don from Ryazan Province in the 1800s, was Russian, while his mother, Anastasia, though the widow of a Cossack ataman, belonged to the peasantry. (The boy's parents were not in fact married, and he was not legitimized until 1912.) Though Sholokhov's father had only attended primary school, he was a comparatively well-read and cultured man. He worked first as a salesman for a trading firm and later as the manager of a steam mill. The boy's mother, however, who had worked as a maid for a local landowner after losing her parents very early in life, did not learn to read and write until her only child had begun school.

When Sholokhov was five, the family moved to the neighboring village of Karginskaya, where the local teacher gave the boy lessons, and in the following year he entered primary school there. In the late summer of 1914, however, his father sent him to Moscow for treatment for an eye condition, and in 1915 the boy entered the Shelaputin *gimnaziya* in the capital. But schooling in Moscow proved too expensive, and the boy was soon moved south once more, to a school in Boguchar on the upper Don south-east of Voronezh. When in 1918 the Germans occupied Boguchar, he had to return home to Veshenskaya, where he entered the local school. During the Civil War the Sholokhov family moved several times about the Don region, an experience which gave the boy a detailed knowledge of the area that was to serve him well in his writing. In 1919 the Sholokhovs moved back to Karginskaya and settled there for good. In the following year the fifteen-year-old boy began work as a teacher in an adult literacy organization before serving for a while with grain requisitioning detachments in the region. The latter duties nearly led to his execution when he was captured by anti-Bolshevik bandits, but he was spared because of his youth. In the five years that followed he was to take a variety of jobs, among them those of primary school teacher, stevedore, accounts clerk, stonemason and journalist. In addition, early in 1921 he helped to establish a youth theater in Veshenskaya where he wrote and acted in several plays.

In October 1922 Sholokhov moved to Moscow where he enrolled on an educational course for workers. Twelve months later he joined the "Young Guard," a group of young writers in the city, and began to attend study groups in which literary technique was taught by established poets such as Nikolai Aseev and prose writers such as Viktor Shklovsky. In late 1923 Sholokhov left Moscow for Karginskaya once more, and in the following January married a teacher of well-known Cossack stock, Maria Gromoslavskaya, whom he had met some years before in Bukanovskaya on the Don. A few weeks later, he returned with his wife to the capital and spent the next twelve months working on the editorial boards of various activist papers.

In May 1924 Sholokhov returned to the Don, first to Karginskaya and then, in 1926, to Veshenskaya, which was to remain his home until his death almost sixty years later. It was late the following year that he met the veteran Cossack writer, Alexander Serafimovich, author of *The Iron Flood* (1924), who was to become his mentor and champion.

From the late 1920s Sholokhov became increasingly involved in politics, and in 1930 he played an active part in the collectivization program being effected on the Don. In the same year he left Russia to visit Maxim Gorky, the *doyen* of Soviet letters, in Sorrento (he had first met Gorky near Moscow in 1929 and impressed the older man), but on reaching Berlin was refused an Italian visa and returned to the Don. In 1932 his application to join the Communist Party was accepted. Two years later he was elected to the presidium of the newly-formed Union of Soviet Writers, and it was as a representative of that organization that in 1935 he visited Denmark, Sweden, Britain and France. In 1939, already a Deputy to the Supreme Soviet, he was elected a full member of the highly prestigious USSR Academy of Sciences.

When the Nazis attacked the Soviet Union in 1941, Sholokhov became a war correspondent on the Southwestern Front. In November of that year his family was evacuated from Veshenskaya to western Kazakhstan in order to avoid the ravages of German occupation. In July 1942, during an air raid on Veshenskaya, the writer's elderly mother was killed and many of his manuscripts were destroyed. He spent the next two years as a war correspondent and reported part of the fighting for Stalingrad.

Re-elected to the Supreme Soviet after the war, Sholokhov became involved in political work once more. In 1948 he visited Poland, and in 1951, Bulgaria, while in 1954 he was elected to the Secretariat of the Writers' Union. During the summer of 1957 he and his wife visited Scandinavia, and in September of that year they were invited to stay with Khrushchev at his villa in Yalta. Sholokhov's friendship with Khrushchev became very close, and when Khrushchev visited the USA in 1959, the writer travelled with him. In the same year Sholokhov visited Britain, France, Italy, Denmark, Sweden and Finland. In 1961 he was elected a member of the Central Committee and in the next few years visited Scandinavia, Italy and Britain once more. Prominent among his numerous Soviet distinctions were the Order of the Patriotic War, Hero of Socialist Labor, and three Orders of Lenin, while his foreign awards included honorary doctorates from the universities of Leipzig, East Germany, and St. Andrews, Scotland. 1965 saw Sholokhov accorded the greatest honor of all, when he was awarded the Nobel Prize for Literature.

Sadly, the following year was notable for his vehement public attack on the writers Daniel and Sinyavsky, who were tried for having published their works abroad. At the Writers' Union conference in the spring of 1967, Sholokhov went on to make an outspoken attack on experimentation in literature and on those "liberals" who had protested at the harsh treatment given to Daniel and Sinyavsky.

***

Sholokhov's first published work was an essay entitled *The Trial*, published in the Young Communist League newspaper *Young Pravda* (*Yunosheskaya Pravda*) in Moscow in 1923 under the pseudonym M. Sholokh. This was followed by another essay, *The Three*, which appeared a month later in the same paper. Both pieces reflect his concern at the glaring inequalities of the NEP years in the mid-1920s. His first short story proper, *The Birthmark*, was published in the Communist Youth newspaper *The Young Leninist* (*Molodoi Leninets*) in 1925. Set during the Civil War, the tale displays many features characteristic of Sholokhov's mature work and points to the social disintegration brought by revolution, as father fights son and the Don runs with blood.

The following year, 1926, saw the appearance of Sholokhov's first collection of stories, *Tales from the Don,* published in Moscow with a foreword by the influential Serafimovich. This was followed later that year by a second collection, entitled *The Azure Steppe.* The stories in both volumes offer a vivid and frequently naturalistic picture of events during the Civil War and of the untold suffering which it brought to

Cossack folk on the Don. Violence, hatred and brutality are recurrent motifs, conveyed in a style that is colorful, brisk and racy.

Returning to the Don in 1926, Sholokhov spent the next two years working on the first book of his principal work, *The Quiet Don* (also known in English as *And Quiet Flows the Don*), the novel which was to bring him resounding fame. The history of its publication is complex. In 1927, Serafimovich, who had been impressed by Sholokhov's *Tales from the Don,* persuaded the editorial board of the Moscow journal *October* (*Oktyabr'*), of which he was chief editor, to accept the manuscript of Book I of the novel. The work was serialized in that journal from January to April 1928, and later in the year appeared in a separate edition, published in both Moscow and Leningrad. This first book of the novel covers the years 1912 to 1914 and portrays the age-old Don Cossack way of life before World War I. Book II, which takes the reader through the First World War and Revolution, from 1916 to early 1918, was serialized in *October* between May and October 1928, and in its turn was published in book form the following year. (Shortly after the appearance of Book II, rumors began to circulate in Moscow that Sholokhov had plagiarized an autobiographical manuscript written by a White Cossack officer, Fyodor Kryukov (1870–1920.) Needless to say, Sholokhov angrily protested his innocence, and the local branch of the Writers' Association acquitted him of all accusations made against him, but the controversy about partial or full plagiarism of the text continues to this day.) In 1931 Sholokhov submitted Book III of the novel, which deals with the Cossack rebellion during the Civil War (1918–1919), to Maxim Gorky, and by gaining his approval secured its publication in serial form, chiefly in *October,* between 1929 and 1933. In March 1935, *Izvestiya* published the first chapter of Book IV, which covers the years 1920 to 1922 and shows the final establishment of Bolshevik power on the Don, and by December 1939, all four books of the novel were finished. The following year the first complete edition of the novel was published in Moscow, and in 1941 Sholokhov was awarded a State Prize.

In the autumn of 1930 Sholokhov had begun work on his second major novel, *Virgin Soil Upturned,* the first volume of which examines the effect of forced collectivization on a Cossack village in the Don region. While this first volume was published in late 1932, the major sections of Book II, which deal with an anti-Soviet White Guard plot in the village, were finished only between 1959 and 1960, though the work had been serialized in *Pravda* in preceding years. The complete novel first appeared in book form in 1960 and brought Sholokhov a Lenin Prize that year.

When Hitler attacked the Soviet Union in 1941, Sholokhov turned energetically to the writing of patriotic and anti-Fascist articles, pamphlets and sketches in support of the Russian war effort. Notable among his propaganda works is the novella *The Science of Hatred* (1942), which shows a Russian soldier's loathing for the Fascists. In 1943 Sholokhov also began work on a major novel about the war, *They Fought for their Country*. Only parts of it were ever published, however, chapters appearing very irregularly in serial form between 1943 and 1969, and the work remained unfinished at his death.

December 1956 saw the appearance of the now well-known novella about the Second World War, *The Fate of a Man,* which was serialized in *Pravda* (on 31 December 1956 and 1 January 1957) and brought Sholokhov another Lenin Prize. The work is based closely on the author's experience. Sholokhov met the Andrei Sokolov of the story during a hunting trip in the Don region during the early spring of 1946, but when the chance passer-by found out who Sholokhov was, he hurriedly left, so the author never learned his real name. Deeply moved by the encounter, Sholokhov decided there and then to write a story about it. Though he completed the work in seven days, it was not published until ten years later.

The last two decades of Sholokhov's career saw much publicistic work in the form of articles, essays and sketches, notably those contained in the collections *A Word about our Homeland,* published in 1951 and 1965.

His major works have been adapted for the stage and screen on many occasions. Opera versions of *The Quiet Don* were staged in 1936, of *Virgin Soil Upturned* in 1937, and of *The Fate of a Man* in 1961. The first film version of *The Quiet Don* appeared in 1930, followed by remakes in 1938 and 1948, and then by a new three-part epic version in 1958, made at the Gorky film studios in Moscow. The first film of *Virgin Soil Upturned* in 1940 was followed by a second in 1960–61. A highly successful screen version of *The Fate of a Man* appeared in 1959, produced by Sergei Bondarchuk who also played the leading role of Sokolov.

In his later years, living in seclusion down on his beloved Don, Sholokhov took to drink and acquired the reputation of a fiercely vindictive, anti-intellectual reactionary who made virulent public denunciations of dissident writers on the regime's behalf. Daniel and Sinyavsky, he implied, should have been shot for their misdeeds, Boris Pasternak, he asserted, was a "hermit crab," and Alexander Solzhenitsyn, he declared, was a "Colorado beetle." Mikhail Sholokhov died in February 1984, at the age of 78, and was buried in Veshenskaya on the Don.

THE FATE OF A MAN

Dedicated to Yevgenia Grigorevna Levitskaya, Member of the Communist Party of the Soviet Union since 1903.

The first spring that came to the upper reaches of the Don after the war was unusually swift and vigorous. In late March a warm wind began to blow off the Sea of Azov and after only two days the sands on the left bank of the Don were completely clear of snow. Out in the steppe the snow-filled ravines and gullies were flooded with water, and as the ice covering them broke up, the streams burst their banks and the roads became almost completely impassable.

It was just at this difficult time of year that I had to travel to the village of Bukanovskaya.[1] The distance was not very great—only about sixty kilometers—but it turned out to be rather hard going. My friend and I had set off before dawn. Though our pair of well-fed horses strained at the traces, they could barely pull the heavy cart along. The wheels kept sinking right up to their axles in the mixture of wet sand and snow beneath them, and after only an hour white flecks of foam had appeared on the horses' cruppers and flanks and under the narrow breech-bands, while the fresh morning air was filled with the strong, heady smell of horse sweat and warm harness that had been thickly smeared with dubbin.

Where the going was particularly hard for the horses, we got off the cart and walked beside it. So all in all it took us about six hours to cover the thirty kilometers as far as the ford across the Yelanka River.[2]

Not far from the small village of Mokhovsky[3] the little river that used to dry up completely in places during the summer had burst its banks and flooded the marshy water-meadows with their alder trees for an entire kilometer around. We were going to have to make the crossing in a flimsy-looking, flat-bottomed boat that could not carry more than three people at a time. We stopped and unharnessed the horses. In a collective farm shed on the other side of the river a battered old jeep that had been standing there for most of the winter was waiting for us. With some trepidation the driver and I got into the dilapidated boat, while my friend stayed behind on the bank with our things. No sooner had we cast off than water came spurting up in little fountains through the rotten planks at the bottom of the boat. We plugged them with anything we could lay hands on and kept bailing all the way across. It took us an hour to reach the other side. Then the driver went to fetch the jeep from the village and brought it back to the boat. Picking up an oar, he said:

"As long as this blasted old tub doesn't fall to bits in the water, I'll be back with your friend in a couple of hours, not before."

The village was quite a long way from the river, and near the water's edge reigned the kind of stillness one finds in deserted places only in very early spring or late autumn. A smell of dampness and the sharp, bitter odor of rotting alders came drifting off the water, while from the distant, mist-shrouded steppes near the Khopyor River[4] a gentle breeze brought the barely perceptible but eternally youthful smell of earth that has only just lost its covering of snow.

Not far away, on the sand at the water's edge, lay a length of broken wattle fencing. I went and sat down on it to have a smoke, but putting my hand in the right pocket of my quilted jacket, discovered to my dismay that my pack of "Belomor"[5] cigarettes was completely soaked. While we were crossing the river, a wave had splashed over the side of the boat and covered me in muddy water up to the waist. At the time I hadn't had a moment to worry about my cigarettes because I'd had to drop my oar and bail as fast as I could to stop the boat from sinking. Now, though, very annoyed at my thoughtlessness, I carefully took the sodden packet out of my pocket and squatting down, began to lay out the moist, brown cigarettes one by one on the fence to dry.

It was midday, and the sun was as hot as in May, so I hoped the cigarettes would soon be ready. In fact, it was so hot that I even began to regret having put on my quilted army trousers and jacket for the journey. It was the first really warm day of the year, and it felt good sitting there alone, abandoning myself to the stillness around me. I took off my old army cap with its earflaps to let the breeze dry my hair after the hard work of rowing, and idly watched the full, white clouds drifting across the pale blue sky.

After a while I noticed a man coming out onto the road from behind the last few houses in the village. He was leading a small boy by the hand, who judging by his height must have been about five or six, that's all. They were trudging along towards the ford, but when they reached the jeep, turned in my direction. The tall, rather hunched man came right up to me and said in a deep, chesty voice:

"Hello, my friend!"

"Hello!" I replied, shaking his big, calloused hand.

Then he bent down to the boy and said:

"Say hello, son!"

Looking me straight in the face with eyes that were as clear as the sky, the boy gave a faint smile and then boldly held out a pink little hand. I shook it gently.

Taking the half-empty knapsack off his back and sitting himself down wearily beside me, the father said:

"This little companion of mine's nothing but a nuisance! He wears me out! If you walk fast he breaks into a trot—and then it's impossible to keep up with him!"

He was silent for a while, then asked:

"And what about you, mate? Waiting for your boss, are you?"

I felt rather awkward about telling him I wasn't a driver, so I answered:

"Yes, looks like I'll have to."

"Is he coming over from the other side?"

"Yes."

"D'you know if the boat'll be here soon?"

"In about two hours, I think."

"That's quite a long time. Well then, let's rest for a bit—I'm not in any hurry ... Got your cigarettes wet, have you? Well, mate, wet tobacco's like a doctored horse—it's no good at all! Let's have some of my old shag instead."

Putting his hand into the pocket of his thin khaki trousers, he pulled out a worn tobacco pouch made of dark red silk, and as he unrolled it I glimpsed the words that were embroidered on one corner of it: "To our dear soldier, from a pupil in the 6th class at Lebedyan[6] Secondary School."

We sat there smoking the strong, home-grown tobacco and for a long time neither of us spoke. I was just about to enquire why he was out at a time when the roads were so bad and where he was going to with the boy, when he asked:

"Driving all through the war, then, were you?"

"Yes, nearly all of it."

"At the front?"

"Yes."

"Well, I had a bellyfull there too, mate, and more besides, I can tell you!"

He laid his big, swarthy hands on his knees and sat with his shoulders hunched up. Glancing sideways at him, I suddenly felt sad ... Have you ever seen anyone with eyes that look as if they have been sprinkled with ash and are filled with such unassuaged pain and sadness that it is hard to look into them? Well, that's just what his eyes were like.

He pulled a twisted, dry stick out of the fencing and with it silently traced an intricate pattern on the sand. Then he said:

"Sometimes I just can't sleep at night. I stare into the darkness and think to myself: 'What did life have to go and torment me like this for? Why did it have to punish me so much?' But there's never any answer, either when it's dark or when the sun's shining up there in the sky ... No, there's no answer and there'll never be one either!" Then he suddenly seemed to remember something, and nudging his little son affectionately, said: "Off you go now, laddie, and play down by the water ... There's always something little boys can find to do by a big river. But don't get your feet wet, mind!"

He watched his son go running down to the water's edge and gave a muffled cough. Then he began speaking again, and I listened to him carefully.

"To begin with, I had a very ordinary kind of life, you know. I'm from Voronezh Province[7]—I was born there in 1900. During the Civil War I served in the Red Army, in Kikvidze's division.[8] In the famine of twenty-two I made for the Kuban[9] and worked my guts out for the kulaks,[10] otherwise I wouldn't be here now. But my mother and father and my little sister back home starved to death. So I was left alone, without a single relative in the whole world—no one, not a soul. Well, a year or so later I came back from the Kuban, sold the house and went to live in Voronezh. To begin with I worked in a carpenters' cooperative, then I went into a factory and learned to be a fitter. It wasn't very long before I got married. My wife was an orphan—she'd been brought up in a children's home. Oh, I found myself a fine girl there all right! She was good-tempered, cheerful, always eager to please, and clever too—much cleverer than me. She'd had things hard right from being a kid and perhaps that had made her like she was. To anyone who didn't know her she wasn't all that pretty, I suppose, but I was living with her all the time, so for me there wasn't anyone more beautiful in the whole world, and there never will be either!

Sometimes I'd come home from work feeling tired and bad-tempered as hell. But oh no—she'd never be rude to me in return. Instead she'd be quiet and gentle—couldn't do enough for me—and though we didn't have much, she'd always do her best to make me something nice. I'd look at her and start feeling a bit better, then after a while I'd put my arms round her and say: 'I'm sorry, Irina darling, I was very rude to you—I've had a bad time at work today.' Then everything would be all right again between us and my mind would be at rest. And d'you know, mate, what that does for your work? In the morning I'd get up full of beans and go off to the factory, and anything I laid hands on would go with a swing, just like clockwork! That's what it's like having a clever girl for a wife ...

Well, soon the children started arriving. First we had a little boy, then a year or so later two girls ... That's when I stopped going about with my friends and started taking all my pay home—after all, we had a fair-sized family by then and I just couldn't afford to drink any more. Sometimes on my day off, though, I'd have a glass of beer, but that would be that.

In 'twenty-nine I got interested in vehicles, learnt a bit about engines and started driving a truck. Then I got keen on it and didn't want to go back to the factory any more—driving was a lot more fun. So ten years came and went without my even noticing them—it was just like a dream. But what's ten years anyway? Just you ask any middle-aged man if he's noticed the time slipping by, and he'll say he hasn't noticed a damn thing! The past's like that steppe out there. This morning we were crossing it and everything was as clear as a bell all around, but now we've walked about twenty kilometers there's a haze hanging over it and you can't tell forest from grass or ploughland from meadow ...

All those ten years I worked day and night, earning good money, and we lived just as well as anyone else. The children were a joy to us too: all three of them used to get top marks at school, and Anatoly, the eldest, turned out to be so good at math that he even had his name mentioned in one of the Moscow papers. Where he got such a gift for the subject from I just don't know, mate, but it made me ever so pleased and I felt very proud of him—terribly proud I was!

During those ten years we saved up a bit of money and just before the war started we built ourselves a little house with two rooms, a small porch and a pantry. Then Irina bought a couple of goats. Well, what more did we need? There was milk for the kids to have with their kasha,[11] we had a roof over our heads, clothes for our backs and shoes for our feet, so everything seemed just fine. The only thing was, though, that I'd built the house in a bad place—the plot they'd given me wasn't far from an aircraft factory. If that little house had been somewhere else, then my life might have turned out quite differently ...

And then it came—the war. The next day I got my call-up papers from the local office and the day after that it was 'Report to the station, please!' The whole family came to see me off—Irina, Anatoly and my daughters Nastya and Olya. The kids all took it very well, though the girls couldn't help shedding a tear or two. Anatoly just kept shivering a bit as if he was cold—he was getting on for seventeen by then, you see. But as for Irina ... well, I'd never seen her in such a state all the years we'd been married. In bed the night before, my shirt had been wet through with her tears, and the next morning it was just the same again ... When we got to the station I felt so sorry for her I could hardly bear to look at her: her lips were all swollen with crying, her hair was sticking out from under her kerchief, and her eyes had an empty, dull look in them, like someone who's gone crazy. When the officers gave the order to board the train, she flung herself at me and clasped her arms round my neck, shaking all over just like a tree that's being chopped down ... The kids tried to persuade her to stop and so did I, but it wasn't any good—she just went on and on! The other women were chatting quietly with their husbands and sons, but Irina was clinging to me for all she was worth, shaking all over without saying a word. So I said to her: 'Come on, Irina darling, pull yourself together! You might at least say something to me before I go.' Then she said, sobbing every other word, 'Andrei ... my darling ... we'll never ... see each other ... again ... in this world!'

There I was with my heart nearly breaking with pity for her and she goes and says a thing like that! She should've realized it wasn't easy for me to say good-bye to them all either. After all, I wasn't exactly going off on a picnic myself! Then I got angry with her, pulled her arms from round my neck and gave her a gentle push. Well, it only seemed gentle to me, but I used to be as strong as an ox in those days. She staggered back but then came towards me again with her arms outstretched, so I shouted at her: 'Is this really the way to say good-bye? D'you want to bury me before my time?!' But then I took her in my arms again because I could see she wasn't herself at all ..."

He suddenly stopped short, and in the silence that followed I heard a gurgling, choking sound coming from his throat. His emotion communicated itself to me and I shot him a sidelong glance, but I could not see a single tear in those eyes of his that looked as if they were full of dead ash. He sat there just hanging his head, but his big hands were shaking, his chin was quivering and his firm lips were trembling too ...

"Don't, my friend, you mustn't remember that!" I said softly, but he didn't seem to hear me. Then, making a tremendous effort to master his emotion, he suddenly said in an oddly changed, rather hoarse voice:

"To the end of my life, right to my dying day, I'll never forgive myself for pushing her away like that!"

He fell silent again and this time said nothing for a long while ... Then he coughed and went on:

"I tore myself away from her, then took her face in my hands and kissed her, but her lips were as cold as ice. Then I said good-bye to the kids, ran to the train, and jumped on the step as it was pulling away. It moved off very slowly, taking me past my family again. I looked out and saw my poor little kids all huddled together, waving at me and trying to smile but not quite managing it somehow. Irina had her hands pressed to her breast, her lips were as white as chalk, and she was whispering something, gazing at me without blinking, her whole body straining forward as if she were walking in a strong wind ... And that's how I'll remember her for the rest of my days: her hands pressed to her breast, her lips deathly white, and her eyes wide-open and full of tears ... That's how I usually see her in my dreams too ... What did I push her away for? Even now when I remember that moment it's like a blunt knife twisting in my heart ...

We were sent to a unit near Belaya Tserkov[12] in the Ukraine, and I was given a ZIS-5[13] truck to drive. And that's what I went to the front in. Well, there's no point telling you about the war—you saw it for yourself and you know what things were like to start with. I often used to get letters from home but I didn't send many myself. Now and then I'd just write and say everything was okay, that we were doing a bit of fighting, and though we were retreating, I'd say, it wouldn't be long before we got our strength back and then we'd give the Krauts something to think about all right. Well, what else could you say? Those were bad times and you never felt much like writing ...

I didn't even get a year's fighting done, though... I was wounded twice during the first few months but only slightly both times—first in the arm, then in the leg. The first time it was a bullet from a strafing aircraft, and the second a shell-splinter. Those Germans punched a lot of holes in the sides and top of my truck as well, mate, but I was lucky to begin with. Yes—and my luck held for quite a long time too, but then I finally came a cropper ... In May of 'forty-two I got taken prisoner near Lozovenki.[14] We were in an awkward position: the Germans were attacking hard and it so happened that one of our 122-millimeter howitzer batteries had nearly run out of ammunition. So we loaded my truck up with shells right to the very top—I worked so hard on the job myself that my shirt was sticking to my back with sweat! We had to be as quick as we could, too, because the enemy were closing in on us—we could hear tanks blasting away to our left and gunfire to the right and ahead of us, and things were starting to get a little bit too hot ...

Our company commander said to me: 'Can you get through, Sokolov?' But he needn't have asked. Did he think I was going to sit there twiddling my thumbs while my mates were getting killed? 'What d'you mean, sir?!' I replied. 'I've just got to get through, and that's that!' 'Well, then,' he says, 'get moving! And step on it!'

Well, I stepped on it all right—I've never driven so fast in my life! I knew I wasn't carrying a load of potatoes and that I should be careful with what I'd got aboard, but how the hell could I be careful when the lads were out there fighting empty-handed and the whole road was under artillery fire? Anyway, I'd done about six kilometers and nearly reached the turning off onto the dirt road that led to the gully where the battery was, when what do I see? My God! There was our infantry running back across the open fields to the left and right of the road with shells bursting among them as they went. Well, what could I do? After all, I couldn't turn back, could I? So I gave the truck all she'd got! I'd already turned off down the dirt track and there was only about another kilometer to go to the battery, but I never managed to reach our lads, mate ... A long-range gun must have landed a heavy shell near my truck. I never heard the explosion or anything, but instead something seemed to burst inside my head and I can't remember any more. How I came out of it alive I just don't know, and I've no idea how long I lay there about thirty feet from the ditch at the roadside either. When I came to, I couldn't get up at all—my head was jerking from side to side and I was shaking all over as if I'd got a fever. Everything had gone dark before my eyes, there was something grinding and scraping in my left shoulder, and I ached all over as if somebody had been hitting me, say, for two days running with everything he could lay hands on ... Well, I crawled about on my belly for a long time, then somehow or other I managed to stand up. I still couldn't work out where I was or what had happened to me, though—my memory had gone completely. But I was too frightened to lie down again—I was scared that if I did I'd never get up again and then that would be that. So I just stood there, swaying from side to side like a poplar in a high wind.

When I came to properly and had a good look round, my heart felt as if someone was squeezing it with a pair of pliers: the shells I'd been carrying were scattered about all over the place, my truck was lying upside down not far away all smashed to bits, and as for the fighting, well it was going on behind me by that time ... Yes, behind me!

Well, there's no use pretending—when I realized what had happened, my legs gave way and I fell down just as if I'd been pole-axed, because I could see I was cut off behind the enemy lines or to put it another way, I was already a prisoner of the Fascists. But that's how things go in war ...

Well, I lay there and after a while I heard the rumble of tanks. Four medium German ones went racing past me at top speed towards where

I'd come in the truck ... Now what d'you think I felt like when I saw them? Then a few tractors pulling guns came past, followed by a field kitchen and some infantry. There weren't many of them, you know, not more than a single company, I suppose. I had a quick look at them out of the corner of my eye, then pressed my face flat to the ground again and closed my eyes: it made me sick to see them and my heart sank ...

When I thought they'd all gone past, I looked up again and suddenly saw six submachine gunners walking along about a hundred yards away. As I looked at them they turned off the road and came straight towards me. And none of them said a word. 'Well,' I thought, 'this is it!' I sat up—I didn't want to die lying down, after all—then got to my feet. One of them halted a few paces away and suddenly unslung his gun. It's funny the way a man's made, you know, but at the time I didn't feel any panic or fear. I just looked at him and thought: 'In a minute he's going to give me a short, sharp burst, but where will he aim? At my chest or my head?' As if it mattered a damn what part of me got riddled with his bullets!

He was a young, well-built sort of fellow with dark hair, but his lips were as thin as a knife blade and he kept screwing up his eyes in an evil kind of way. 'A man like that won't think twice about killing me,' I thought to myself. And then sure enough—up went his gun. I looked him straight in the eye and didn't say a word. But one of his mates, a lance-corporal or something who was a bit older—even middle-aged, you might say—shouted something then pushed him to one side and came up to me. Then he muttered something in his own language, bent my right arm at the elbow and felt the muscles, you see. When he'd tested them, he said: 'O-o-oh!' and pointed down the road westwards, to where the sun was setting. 'Off you go, you swine,' he says, 'and work for our Reich!' So it was he who'd turned out to be the boss after all, the son of a bitch!

Well, where didn't they send me in the two years I was a prisoner— I must have seen half of Germany in that time! First I went to Saxony to work in a silicate factory, and then to the Ruhr where I hauled coal down a mine. After that it was to Bavaria where I worked as a laborer and then on to Thuringia. God only knows what German soil I didn't have to tread! The scenery in those parts might all be different, mate, but the way they knocked our lads about was just the same everywhere you went. Those goddamn bastards used to beat us like nobody here would ever beat an animal! They'd punch us, kick us, hit us with rubber truncheons or with any bit of iron they happened to have handy, not to mention with rifle butts and things like that.

They'd beat you just because you were Russian, because you were still alive in God's world, or because you were working for them, the swine. They'd beat you for giving them a dirty look, taking a wrong step, or not turning round the way they wanted you to. They'd beat you just so that one day they could finish you off altogether, so you'd choke on the last few drops of your own blood and give up the ghost with it all. I reckon there weren't enough ovens in the whole of Germany for us prisoners to be shoved into!

Everywhere we went they used to give us exactly the same kind of food: a hundred and fifty grams of ersatz bread made half-and-half with sawdust, and some thin pigswill with swedes in it. Sometimes they'd give us hot water to drink, sometimes they wouldn't. But what's the point of talking about it—judge for yourself: before the war started I weighed about a hundred and ninety pounds, but by the autumn of the following year I didn't weigh much more than a hundred. I was nothing but skin and bone, and sometimes I hardly had the strength to move around either. But you had to keep on working without saying a word, and the kind of work they gave you would've been too much even for a cart-horse.

At the beginning of September they transferred a hundred and forty-two of us Soviet prisoners from a camp near Küstrin[15] to Camp B-14, not far from Dresden. By then there were about two thousand Russians in that camp. We were all put to work in a stone quarry, cutting, chiselling and crushing that damn German rock of theirs by hand. The daily norm was four cubic meters per man, and that was for someone, mark you, who could hardly keep body and soul together as it was. Well, that's when things got really bad: after two months, out of the hundred and forty-two men in our section there were only fifty-seven left. So what d'you think of that? Tough going, eh? We'd hardly had time to bury our mates when a rumor started going round the camp that the Germans had already taken Stalingrad and were pushing on into Siberia. It was just one thing on top of another, and they kept us at it so hard you hardly had time to look up from the ground. Anyone would've thought we were asking to be buried in that foreign German earth of theirs! And every day all the camp guards used to get drunk and bawl out their songs, whooping it up for all they were worth . . .

After a while they put about three hundred of us who were the strongest on a scheme to drain some marshes, then we were sent to the Ruhr to work in the mines. And that was where I stayed till 'forty-four. By that time, though, our lads had knocked some of the stuffing out of Germany, and the Fascists didn't look down on us prisoners quite so much any more. Then one day they lined us all up, the whole daytime shift, and a visiting Oberleutnant said to us through an interpreter: 'Anyone who was a driver before the war or in the army—one pace forward!' Seven of us who'd been drivers stepped forward. Then they gave us some old overalls and sent us under escort to Potsdam. When we got there we were all split up. I was detailed to work in 'Todt'[16]—that was what the Germans called a set-up they had for building roads and defenses.

My job was to drive a German engineer-major about in an Opel Admiral. Oh, now that was a Fascist pig for you! He was a little fellow with a potbelly, as broad as he was tall with a backside on him as big as any woman's. He had three chins hanging down over his collar at the front and three great big rolls of fat on his neck at the back. He must have carried a good hundred pounds of pure fat on him, I reckon.

For about two weeks I drove that major from Potsdam to Berlin and back, and then he was sent to the front to supervise the building of defenses against our troops. By then, though, I just couldn't sleep at night any more—I'd lie awake for hours wondering how I could get back to our lines and home to Russia.

One day we drove to the town of Polotsk,[17] and for the first time in two years I heard the thunder of our artillery. Well, you can just imagine how my heart began to pound, can't you, mate? Even when I'd started taking Irina out it never used to beat like that! The fighting was going on to the east of Polotsk, about eighteen kilometers away. The Germans in the town had got very jumpy and nasty, and my fat major started drinking more and more. During the day we'd drive out of town and he'd give orders about building the defenses, then at night he'd sit there drinking all by himself. After a while his whole body swelled up and there were big bags under his eyes.

'Well,' I thought, 'there's no point waiting any longer, now's my chance! And I'm not going to escape by myself either, because I'm going to take my fat friend along with me—he'll come in very useful over on our side!'

I looked among some ruined buildings, came across an iron bar that weighed four or five pounds, and wrapped a bit of rag round it so that if I had to hit him with it there wouldn't be any blood. After that I found a length of telephone wire lying on the road, and when I'd carefully got everything ready, I hid it all under the front seat. Then, one evening a couple of days before I finally said good-bye to the Germans, I was on my way back after filling up with petrol when I saw a German NCO staggering along the road drunk as a lord and holding on to the wall as he went. So I stopped the car and led him behind a pile of rubble, then pulled off his uniform and took his cap. Then I hid the whole lot under the seat with the rest of the stuff and I was ready.

On the morning of the twenty-ninth of June the major told me to drive him out of town in the direction of Trosnitsa[18]—he was in charge of building some defenses there. So off we went. He was dozing quietly on the back seat while I sat at the wheel with my heart hammering so hard it was nearly jumping out of my mouth. I drove fast to begin with but once we were outside the town I slowed down, then stopped the car, got out and had a look round. There were just two trucks coming slowly towards us, but they were still a long way off. I got the iron bar out and opened the back door wide. My fat friend was leaning right back in the seat and snoring away just as if he was tucked up in bed with his wife beside him. Well, I gave him one with the bar on the left temple, and his head sagged on to his chest. Then just to make sure, I gave him another one, but I didn't want to kill him—I had to get him over to our side alive because he'd be able to tell our lads a thing or two. I took his pistol from its holster and shoved it in my pocket, then pushed a metal bracket I'd picked up down behind the back seat, put the telephone wire round his neck, and tied it to the bracket with a good knot—that was so he wouldn't fall over on his side when I drove fast. Then I quickly got the German uniform and cap on and drove straight for where the ground was rumbling and all the fighting was.

The German front line lay between two pill-boxes. As I drove towards it, a few machine-gunners jumped out of a dugout and I slowed down on purpose so they'd see I had a major in the car with me. They all started shouting and waving as if to say I mustn't go any further, but I pretended not to understand, put my foot down and tore past them at about fifty miles an hour. Before they realized what was happening and had time to open fire on the car, I was already in no man's land, weaving in and out among the shell-holes just like a hare.

By now the Germans were firing at me from behind and then our lads got a bit cross and sprayed me with machine-gun fire from in front. They put four bullets through my windscreen and riddled the radiator... Then not far away I saw a lake with a little wood near it and some of our lads running towards the car, so I drove in among the trees, opened the door, fell out on to the ground and kissed it. I could hardly breathe for joy...

A young fellow with khaki shoulder-straps of a kind I'd never seen before, was the first to come running up, and he said with a grin: 'Aha, you damn Kraut, so you're lost, are you?' Then I tore off the German uniform, flung the cap on the ground and said to him: 'You silly young fool! What kind of a Kraut can I be when I was born and bred in

Voronezh? I've been a prisoner-of-war, don't you see? Now untie that fat pig sitting in the car, get his briefcase and take me to your commanding officer.' I gave him my pistol and then I was passed from one person to another, till by evening I'd got as far as the colonel in command of the division. By that time they'd given me something to eat, taken me to the bathhouse, questioned me and issued me with a new uniform, so when I went into the colonel's dugout I was all clean and tidy and in good shape. The colonel got up from his desk and came towards me, and then in front of all the officers he embraced me and said: 'Thank you, soldier, for the fine present you've brought us from the Germans! Your major and his briefcase have told us more than twenty prisoners could have done. I'm going to recommend you for a decoration!' His words and his kindness moved me deeply, and I couldn't stop my lips from trembling. All I could manage to say was: 'Comrade Colonel, please enlist me in an infantry unit.' But he just laughed, slapped me on the shoulder and said: 'What kind of soldier d'you think you'd make when you can hardly stand on your feet? No, I'm sending you off to hospital right away. They'll see to your scratches and fatten you up a bit, and after that you'll go home to your family for a month's leave. Then when you come back we'll work out where to send you.'

After that the colonel and all the officers who were in the dugout with him shook my hand in a very friendly way, and I came out of there feeling absolutely on top of the world, because in the two years I'd been a prisoner I'd forgotten what it meant to be treated like a human being. Mind you, though, mate, it was still a very long time before I could get out of the habit of pulling my head down whenever I talked to the high-ups, as if I was still scared they might hit me. That was the kind of training they gave you in those Fascist camps . . .

As soon as I got to the hospital I wrote Irina a letter. I told her briefly how I'd been taken prisoner and escaped with the German major. And for the life of me I just don't know why, but I bragged like a child to her! I couldn't even stop myself from telling her the colonel had promised to recommend me for a decoration . . .

For two weeks I did nothing but eat and sleep. They just gave me a bit of food at a time, only at frequent intervals. The doctor said if they'd given me as much as I wanted straightaway, I might have turned up my toes. Anyway, it wasn't long before I got my strength back again. But after two weeks had passed I wasn't interested in food any more because there was still no reply from home, and I must admit, I started feeling a bit miserable. I couldn't even think about food any longer, I wasn't sleeping any more, and all kinds of unpleasant thoughts kept coming into my head ... Then in the third week I got a letter from Voronezh. It wasn't from Irina, though, but from an old neighbor of ours, Ivan Timofeevich, a joiner. Well, I wouldn't wish a letter like that on anyone! He said that as early as June 'forty-two, the Germans had attacked the aircraft factory and my house had suffered a direct hit from a heavy bomb. Irina and the girls had been there at the time ... Well, he said, there was nothing left of them at all, and where the house had been there was only a deep hole now ... To begin with I couldn't finish reading that letter. Everything went dark before my eyes and my heart felt so full of pain I thought it would never be right again. But I lay on my bed for a while and got a bit of strength back, then finished reading the letter. My neighbor went on to say that Anatoly had been away in Voronezh when the bomb had fallen. That evening he'd visited the place where the house had been, looked at the hole, and then he'd gone back to town the same night. But before leaving he'd told my neighbor he was going to volunteer for the front. And that was all.

When the pain in my heart had eased a little, I remembered how desperately Irina had clung to me when we'd parted at the station. So in that woman's heart of hers she'd known all along we'd never see each other again. But at the time I'd just pushed her away ... Once I'd had a family and a home of my own—it had all taken years to get together—but everything had been destroyed in a flash, and now I was alone. 'But isn't this ruined life of mine just a dream?' I wondered. And you know, when I'd been a prisoner I used to talk to Irina and the kids nearly every night—to myself, of course, under my breath—trying to cheer them up, saying I'd be home again soon and telling them not to feel sorry for me. I'm strong, I used to say, I'll get through, and one day we'll all be together again ... But as it turned out, for two whole years I'd been talking to the dead!"

The man fell silent for a moment, then said in a faltering, soft voice: "Let's have a smoke, mate—I feel as if I'm choking."

We lit our cigarettes. Somewhere in the flooded water-meadows a woodpecker was tapping away with a clear, ringing sound. The warm breeze was still stirring the dry leaves on the alders just as gently as before; the clouds were still drifting by high in the blue sky like taut, white sails; but in those moments of sorrowful silence the boundless world preparing for the great fulfillment of spring—that everlasting affirmation of life—seemed altogether different to me.

It was too painful to remain silent for very long, so I asked:
"And what happened then?"

"What happened then?" he echoed reluctantly, "Well, the colonel gave me a month's leave, and a week later I was back in Voronezh. I walked to the place where I'd once lived with my family. But there was just a deep hole full of rust-colored water with weeds all round it as high as your waist ... Everything was as deserted and still as a graveyard. Oh, it was so painful for me, mate! I stood there for a while, my heart full of sorrow, then I went back to the station. I couldn't even bear to stay another hour there, so I set off for my unit again the same day.

But about three months later a flash of joy burst into my life, like a ray of sunlight breaking through the clouds: I got news of Anatoly at long last. He sent me a letter from another front, or so it seemed—he'd got my address from our old neighbor, Ivan Timofeevich. It turned out he'd been to artillery school to begin with—his gift for math had stood him in good stead there. A year later he'd passed with distinction and gone to the front, and now he said he'd been promoted to the rank of captain, was in command of a battery of 'forty-fives,' and had been awarded six orders and medals. In other words, he'd left his old man far behind! And so once again I felt terribly proud of him! Say what you like, but my own son was a captain and in command of a battery. That was no mean feat! And he'd got all those decorations too! No matter that his old man was carting shells and stuff around in a Studebaker truck! His dad's days were gone, but he, already a captain, still had his whole life ahead of him ...

That winter we went on advancing without a break and so we didn't have time to write to each other very often, but one morning towards the end of the war, when we were close to Berlin, I sent Anatoly a note and got a reply the very next day. Then I realized my son and I had come up to the German capital from different directions and were quite close to each other now. I was so excited I could hardly wait for the moment when we'd meet. Well, we met sure enough ... Right on the morning of Victory Day, May the ninth, Anatoly was killed by a German sniper ...

That afternoon the company commander sent for me. When I went into the room I noticed an artillery lieutenant-colonel whom I'd never seen before sitting with him. He stood up as if in the presence of a senior officer. My company commander said to me: 'It's you he's come to see, Sokolov,' then he turned away to the window. An electric shock suddenly seemed to go through me because I sensed something was wrong. Then the lieutenant-colonel came up to me and said quietly: 'Bear up, father! Your son, Captain Sokolov, was killed at his battery this morning. Come with me.'

I swayed but managed to stay on my feet. Even now it still seems like a dream when I remember how the officer and I drove in that big car through those streets strewn with rubble. I can only dimly recall the soldiers drawn up in a line and the coffin draped with red velvet. But I can still see Anatoly just as clearly as I can see you now, mate. I went up to the coffin. It looked like my son lying there and yet it didn't too. I remembered him as just a young lad, always happy and smiling, with narrow shoulders and a sharp little Adam's apple that jutted out on his thin neck. But this was a broad-shouldered, handsome young fellow, lying with his eyes half-closed as if he was gazing past me and away into the distance. Only the corners of his mouth still showed a hint of the smile my son always used to have on his face—the little Anatoly I once knew ... I kissed him and stepped aside. The lieutenant-colonel made a speech. Anatoly's comrades were all weeping, but I couldn't cry—the tears seemed to have dried up in my heart. Perhaps that's why it still hurts so much ...

So it was that I buried my last hope and joy in that alien German soil. The battery fired a volley over my son, bidding their commander farewell as he set out on his long journey, and deep inside me something seemed to snap ... When I got back to my unit I was like a different man. Soon after that I was demobilized. But where was I to go? Back to Voronezh? Not on your life! Then I remembered I had a friend living in Uriupinsk[19] who'd been invalided out of the army back in the winter—he'd once invited me to go and stay with him—so off I went to Uriupinsk.

My friend and his wife had no children and lived in a little house of their own on the outskirts of town. Though he'd been invalided out of the army, my friend worked as a driver at a truck depot, and I managed to get a job there too. I moved in with him and his wife, and they gave me a home. We used to take all kinds of loads to various parts of the town, and in the autumn we switched over to carrying grain. It was then that I got to know my new son, the one that's playing down there on the sand.

After a long run in the truck you'd come back into town, and the first thing you'd do, of course, would be to call at the café for a bite of something and a drop of vodka to help take away your tiredness. Drink's a bad habit, I know, but I must admit it had got a fair old grip on me by that time ... Then one day I noticed a little boy near the café, and the day after I saw him again. What a ragamuffin he was! He was absolutely filthy—all smeared with melon juice and covered with dust, and his hair all untidy, but his little eyes were shining like stars do at night after it's been raining! After a while I got so fond of him that funnily enough, I started missing him and I'd hurry to finish my trip so as to see him near the café. That's where he used to get his food, you see—he just ate whatever people happened to give him.

On the fourth day I came straight back from the state farm with a load of grain and pulled up at the café. There was my little boy sitting on the steps swinging his legs, and judging by the look of him he was absolutely famished. I put my head out of the window and shouted: 'Hey, Vanya! Get in quick, and I'll give you a ride to the elevator, then we'll come back here and have some dinner!' He gave a start, then ran down the steps, scrambled up on the running board and said softly: 'How d'you know I'm called Vanya, uncle?' And he opened his little eyes wide, waiting for me to answer. Well, I just told him I'd seen a lot of things in my time and knew everything.

He came round to the right-hand side of the truck and I opened the door for him. Then I sat him on the seat beside me and off we went. He was a lively little fellow, but for some reason he suddenly went quiet and thoughtful, and kept looking up at me from under those long, curly eyelashes of his and heaving a sigh. Only a little fellow he was, and yet he already knew how to sigh! Now was that the right kind of thing for a kid of his age to be doing? 'Where's your father, then, Vanya?' I asked. 'He was killed at the front,' he whispered. 'And what about your mummy?' 'She was killed by a bomb when we were on the train.' 'Where were you coming from on the train?' 'I don't know, I can't remember ...' 'And haven't you got any family round here at all, then?' 'No, nobody.' 'But where d'you sleep at night?' 'Anywhere I can find.'

I felt hot tears welling up in me and I made up my mind there and then. 'Why should we both suffer separately like this?' I thought, 'I'll take him in as my own son.' And straightaway my heart felt easier and lighter somehow. Then I leaned over towards him and said softly: 'Vanya, d'you know who I am?' And he answered with a sigh, just breathing the word out: 'Who?' And I said to him just as softly as before: 'I'm your father.'

My God, what do you think happened then? He flung his arms round my neck, kissed me on the cheeks, forehead and lips, and started chirping merrily away like a little bird in such a shrill voice that the noise in the cab was deafening: 'Daddy dear! I knew it! I knew you'd find me! I just knew you would, whatever happened! I've been waiting so long for you to find me!' He nestled up against me, his whole body quivering like a blade of grass in the wind. Well, my eyes had gone all misty, I was trembling all over, and my hands were shaking ... How on earth I managed to keep hold of the wheel, I just don't know! But all the same I quickly pulled over to the side of the road and switched off the engine. While my eyes were like that I was afraid to drive any further, just in case I happened to knock someone down. Well, we sat there for about five minutes with him still pressing up against me for all he was worth, trembling from head to foot but not saying a word. Then I put my right arm round him and with my left hand turned the truck round and set off back to where I lived. When all was said and done, what did I need the elevator for after that? How on earth could I think of going there after what had happened?

I stopped the truck at the gate, picked up my new son and carried him up the path. He'd got his little arms right round my neck and just wouldn't let go, pressing his cheek up against my bristly chin as if he was stuck to me with glue. And that's how I carried him into the house. My friend and his wife were both there at the time. In I went and winked at them, first with one eye then with the other and said cheerfully: 'Well, I've found my little Vanya at last! So here we are, good people!' My friends guessed what was up straightaway and started bustling about doing things, but the boy just wouldn't let go of me. In the end, though, I managed somehow to put him down. Then I washed his hands with soap and water and sat him at the table. My friend's wife poured him a bowl of cabbage soup and when she saw how he gulped it down she burst into tears. She just stood there by the stove, crying into her apron. My little Vanya saw she was crying and ran up to her, tugged at her skirt and said: 'What are you crying for, auntie? Daddy found me near the café and so everyone should be glad, but you're crying!' But she— God bless her soul!—only cried all the more, the tears just streaming down her face!

After dinner I took him to the barber's to get his hair cut, and when we got home again I gave him a bath in the washtub and wrapped him in a clean sheet. Then he put his arms round me and fell asleep just like that, with me holding him. So I laid him carefully in bed, drove off to the elevator and unloaded the grain, then took the truck back to the depot. After that I hurried off to do a bit of shopping. I bought him a pair of flannel trousers, a little shirt, some sandals and a straw cap. When I got home again I lay down beside him and for the first time for weeks fell fast asleep. I woke three or four times during the night, though, to find him nestling in the crook of my arm like a little sparrow under the eaves, snoring away softly, and my heart was filled with such joy that words just can't express it! I tried not to move for fear of waking him, but all the same I couldn't resist it, and after a while I got up very quietly, struck a match, and just stood there, feasting my eyes on him . . .

I woke just before dawn and couldn't make out why it felt so stuffy in the room. But it was my little son: he'd slipped out of his sheet and was lying stretched right across my chest with his foot on my neck. He's a bit of a fidget when you're sleeping beside him, but I've got used to him now and I miss him if he's not there. At night I can stroke him while he's asleep or smell the little curls on his forehead, and it takes some of the pain out of my heart—makes it feel a bit softer, you know, because it's turned to stone with sorrow . . .

To begin with he used to ride about with me in the truck but then I realized that wouldn't do. After all, what do I need when I'm on my own? A thick slice of bread and an onion with a pinch of salt will last a soldier all day long. But with him it's different. First you've got to give him some milk, then boil him an egg, and he can't manage for very long at all without hot food. But I had my work to do and it wouldn't wait. So one day I plucked up my courage and left him in the care of my friend's wife. Well, he just cried his eyes out all day long, and in the evening he ran off to the elevator to meet me. I didn't get back till late at night but he was still there waiting for me.

I had a hard time with him to begin with. One day I felt worn out so we went to bed while it was still light. Usually he'd be chirping away like a little sparrow, but this time for some reason he was very quiet. 'What are you thinking about, son?' I asked, but he just stared up at the ceiling. Then he said: 'Dad, what did you do with your leather coat?' Now I'd never had a leather coat in my life! But I had to wriggle out of it somehow. 'I left it behind in Voronezh,' I told him. 'But why were you looking for me for so long?' he asked. So I said: 'Son, I looked for you in Germany, Poland and all over White Russia, and then you finally turned up in Uriupinsk.' 'Is Uriupinsk nearer than Germany?' he asked. 'And is it far from our house to Poland?' And on we went, chatting like that till we fell asleep.

But d'you think, mate, he'd asked about that leather coat just out of the blue? No—there was a reason for it all. It meant at some time or other his real father used to wear a coat like that, and the boy had suddenly remembered it. A kid's memory's like summer lightning, you know: it suddenly flashes out and lights everything up for a moment, then dies away again. And that was how his memory worked, in quick flashes, just like summer lightning.

We might've gone on living together in Uriupinsk for another year or so, but that November I had an accident. I was driving along a muddy road through a village when my truck suddenly went into a skid. There just happened to be a cow in the way and I knocked it down. Well, you know how it is—all the women came out and started making a hell of a fuss, a crowd gathered round, and a few minutes later a traffic policeman showed up. I pleaded with him to go easy on me, but he took my license away just the same. Then the cow got up, stuck its tail in the air and went galloping off down the street. But I still lost my license! So I spent the winter working as a joiner and then got in touch with an old friend who'd been in the army too—he works as a driver in your part of the world, near Kashary[20]—and he invited me to come and stay with him. 'You'll be able to work as a joiner for six months or so,' he said, 'and then you can get a new license in our area.' So now my son and I are making our way to Kashary.

But to tell you the truth, you know, even if I hadn't had that accident with the cow, I'd still have left Uriupinsk because my sadness won't let me stay in one place for very long. When my little Vanya grows up a bit, though, and has to start school, then I'll probably give in and settle down somewhere. But for the time being we're tramping Russia together."

"It must be hard for him to walk," I said.

"Well, he doesn't walk much on his own feet at all, you know, because most of the time he rides on my back. I put him on my shoulders and carry him, and when he feels like stretching his legs, he gets down and runs along at the side of the road, jumping and kicking like a little goat. It's not that, though, mate—we'd manage somehow or other—the trouble is my heart's got a knock in it somewhere, needs a new piston ... Sometimes it goes and gives me such a stab I nearly black out. I'm worried I'll die in my sleep one night and frighten the little lad out of his wits. And that's not the only problem either: nearly every night I dream of the dear ones I've lost. Most of the time it's as if I'm behind barbed wire and they're on the other side, free ... I talk to them, Irina and the kids, but as soon as I try to pull the barbed wire apart, they disappear and seem to melt away before my very eyes ... And there's another amazing thing too: during the daytime I always manage to keep a good grip on myself and you'll never get a complaint or even so much as a sigh out of me, but at night I sometimes wake up and my pillow's wet through with tears ..."

Suddenly, through the trees, came the sound of my friend's voice and the splash of oars.

Then the stranger who seemed such a close friend of mine now, got up and held out his big hand that was as strong and firm as a block of wood.

"Good-bye, mate, and all the best!" he said.

"All the best to you too, and have a good journey to Kashary!"

"Thanks. Hey, son! Let's go down to the boat!"

The boy ran to his father's side, and taking hold of the right-hand edge of his quilted jacket, set off with little steps, doing his best to keep up with the big man who was striding down towards the river.

Two orphaned human beings, two grains of sand flung into unfamiliar places by the unprecedented hurricane of war ... What did the future hold for them? I wanted to believe that this Russian, this man of indomitable will, would endure whatever befell him, and that the boy would grow at his side into a man capable of surmounting any obstacle in his path, capable of enduring anything if his native land called upon him to do so.

It was with great pain and sadness that I watched them go ... And perhaps everything would have turned out all right as we parted had it not been for Vanya. After he had taken a few steps, stumbling along on his short, little legs, he turned and waved to me with his tiny pink hand. All of a sudden a gentle but sharp-clawed paw seemed to grip my heart and I turned quickly away. No, those elderly men whose hair turned gray during the years of war do not only weep in their sleep, for they weep during their waking hours too. What matters is to be able to turn away in time. But the most important thing of all is not to wound a child's heart by letting him see the reluctant tear that burns your cheek—the cheek of a man ...

1956

Notes

1. Situated on the Khopyor River near its confluence with the Don, in western Volgograd province, northwest of Volgograd.
2. (Yelan') small tributary of the Don, in northern Volgograd province.
3. Hamlet on the Yelan' River.
4. Tributary of the Don which it joins at Ust'-Khopyorskaya in western Volgograd province.
5. Popular brand of Russian cigarettes (*Belomor* is an abbreviation for *Belomorsko-Baltiiskii kanal*, the canal in north European Russia which links Lake Onega with the White Sea).
6. Town in Lipetsk province, north of Voronezh.
7. Some 275 miles southeast of Moscow.
8. Named after Vasily Isidorovich Kikvidze (1895–1919), a military hero of the Civil War, Red Army Commander in 1917–1918, then a Divisional Commander in the campaign against the White Cossacks on the Don. He was killed in action.
9. Region in northwest Caucasus.
10. Literally "fist." Pejorative term for wealthy peasant.
11. Dish of cooked grain or groats.
12. Town in Kiev province, south of Kiev.

13. Stands for *Zavod imeni Stalina* (Stalin Factory), where motor vehicles were made.

14. Location obscure. Sholokhov may mean Lozovenka, a village south of Kharkov and west of Izium in the Ukraine.

15. (Kostrzyn) town east of Berlin and north of Frankfurt an der Oder.

16. The "Organisation Todt" was named after Fritz Todt (1891–1942), whom Hitler appointed General-Inspektor für das deutsche Strassenwesen in 1933. He was in charge of the building of the Reichsautobahnen and in 1938 organized the German fortifications in the west (Westwall). The Organisation Todt was formed that year.

17. Town north of Minsk in Belorussia.

18. Village east of Polotsk and west of Vitebsk, in Belorussia.

19. Town on Khopyor River in northwest Volgograd province.

20. Village in northern Rostov province, northeast of Voroshilovgrad.